Pro SharePoint 2007 Development Techniques

■ ■ ■

Margriet Bruggeman and
Nikander Bruggeman

Apress®

Pro SharePoint 2007 Development Techniques

Copyright © 2007 by Margriet Bruggeman and Nikander Bruggeman

ISBN-13 (pbk): 978-1-59059-913-6

ISBN-10 (pbk): 1-59059-913-6

Trademarked names may appear in this book. Rather than use a trademark symbol with every occurrence of a trademarked name, we use the names only in an editorial fashion and to the benefit of the trademark owner, with no intention of infringement of the trademark.

Lead Editor: Jonathan Hassell
Technical Reviewer: Sahil Malik
Editorial Board: Steve Anglin, Ewan Buckingham, Tony Campbell, Gary Cornell, Jonathan Gennick,
    Jason Gilmore, Kevin Goff, Jonathan Hassell, Matthew Moodie, Joseph Ottinger, Jeffrey Pepper,
    Ben Renow-Clarke, Dominic Shakeshaft, Matt Wade, Tom Welsh
Project Manager: Candace English
Copy Editor: Benjamin Berg
Associate Production Director: Kari Brooks-Copony
Production Editor: Kelly Gunther
Compositor: Patrick Cunningham
Proofreader: Paulette McGee
Indexer: Beth Palmer
Artist: April Milne
Cover Designer: Kurt Krames
Manufacturing Director: Tom Debolski

Distributed to the book trade worldwide by Springer-Verlag New York, Inc., 233 Spring Street, 6th Floor, New York, NY 10013. Phone 1-800-SPRINGER, fax 201-348-4505, e-mail orders-ny@springer-sbm.com, or visit http://www.springeronline.com.

For information on translations, please contact Apress directly at 2855 Telegraph Avenue, Suite 600, Berkeley, CA 94705. Phone 510-549-5930, fax 510-549-5939, e-mail info@apress.com, or visit http:// www.apress.com.

The information in this book is distributed on an "as is" basis, without warranty. Although every precaution has been taken in the preparation of this work, neither the author(s) nor Apress shall have any liability to any person or entity with respect to any loss or damage caused or alleged to be caused directly or indirectly by the information contained in this work.

The source code for this book is available to readers at http://www.lcbridge.nl/download.

Contents at a Glance

Contents

About the Authors

MARGRIET BRUGGEMAN began her professional career as a quality assurance engineer. She then became a software developer, architect, consultant, and trainer. Margriet is an independent consultant who specializes in building .NET applications using the latest Microsoft technologies. She has worked for companies such as Interpay, Ericsson, Ford, Corus, Interpolis, and SNS Reaal. Margriet has written numerous articles, coauthored multiple SharePoint books, and was awarded the prestigious Most Valuable Professional (MVP) award from Microsoft for her work on the SharePoint Portal Server platform. Margriet is very fond of animals, and when not busy doing IT-related activities, she can be found near dogs, cats, horses, rabbits, birds, and other fuzzy creatures. Margriet can be reached at info@lcbridge.nl.

NIKANDER BRUGGEMAN started his career building web sites using HTML, CGI, and Perl. Later, when JavaScript 1.0 was released, he built numerous web sites based on LiveWire technology while working for a Netscape-oriented company. Nikander then moved to a company that specializes in Microsoft technology. Currently, Nikander is an independent consultant who specializes in building .NET applications using the latest Microsoft technologies. His current work includes software design, development, consulting, and training, and he has worked for companies such as Universal Music, Arvato-Bertelsmann, Coca-Cola, Shell, Intel, and Sara Lee/DE. He was given the prestigious Most Valuable Professional (MVP) award from Microsoft for his work on the SharePoint Portal Server platform, and has coauthored several SharePoint books as well as written numerous articles. He lives in the heart of Amsterdam, and when not developing software or writing about it, he loves to watch sports and movies. Nikander can be reached at info@lcbridge.nl.

About the Technical Reviewer

SAHIL MALIK (www.winsmarts.com) is a Microsoft MVP and INETA speaker. He has authored numerous books and articles, and can be seen speaking at major conferences around the world. His talks are high-energy, highly charged, and highly rated. He works as a consultant and trainer centered around Microsoft technologies. Sahil also blogs about various technical topics at http://blah.winsmarts.com.

Acknowledgments

Writing a book is time-consuming and a lot of work, and we have seen many acknowledgments in books where the author feels guilty for neglecting his or her partner or family. In our case, we have not lost any time at all, as we wrote this book together, which made working on the book a lot of fun.

We have three cats and a rabbit, and normally we would say it is rather strange to thank an animal because the chances that the animal will read the acknowledgments section of the book are pretty slim. But in this case, we want to make an exception, because one of our cats has taken an unusual interest in this book. She spent many hours accompanying us during writing, sleeping on the test server, and urging us onward by standing guard over our computer room. So here goes: thanks to our cat, Wijfie.

We sure want to thank Jonathan Hassel: if you had not asked us to write a follow-up for the book *Pro SharePoint 2003 Development Techniques*, this book would not exist.

We also want to thank Candace English, Benjamin Berg, Kelly Gunther, and the other people at Apress. It sure was nice working with you guys!

Special thanks go to our technical reviewer, Sahil Malik. You have done an excellent job making this a better book, and we do appreciate it. You are also a very funny guy.

As a final note: we are extremely glad that the book is finished and we are finally able to book our vacation to West Pomerania.

Enjoy the book!

Introduction

We have been working with SharePoint technology since the beta release of SharePoint Portal Server 2001 and have seen the product evolve to SharePoint 2007. The sheer number of new features added to this product line is huge, and we are pleased to note how popular this product has become, since we love working with it.

You should read this book if you want to expand your knowledge about developing solutions for both Windows SharePoint Services 3.0 and Microsoft Office SharePoint Server 2007. A few sections only apply to MOSS 2007, but those have been clearly identified.

Unfortunately, nowadays SharePoint is such a big topic that you cannot cover every available topic and still provide in-depth information, so we had to choose which topics to include.

Since we have started working with Microsoft Office SharePoint Server 2007, we have noticed time and again that all SharePoint developers seem to share a common interest in four topics: building workflows, improving business intelligence, using InfoPath, and creating interactive web environments using Ajax techniques. Therefore, when we decided to write a new book about SharePoint 2007, it was crystal clear to us that we needed to dedicate a considerable portion to these Big Four topics.

That is not all we discuss in this book. With the passage of time, we have seen that new and interesting topics related to SharePoint technologies have arisen, and we have made sure to include a bunch of them. These topics will not be found in the typical SharePoint book you might have lying about, and we hope you will have fun learning about them.

What Does This Book Cover?

This book discusses different contemporary development techniques for doing SharePoint development. Every chapter is independent of the other chapters, so you can read the book from cover to cover or in any other order you see fit according to your personal interest.

Chapter 1, Incorporating ASP.NET 2.0 into Microsoft Office SharePoint Server 2007: This chapter discusses the ins and outs of building ASP.NET 2.0 web parts in a SharePoint 2007 environment, laying the foundation every SharePoint developer needs. You will learn how to use the new Visual Studio 2005 Extensions for Windows SharePoint Services to build web parts fast, as well as the drawbacks of this approach. The chapter also discusses how to configure web parts via properties, how to use resources in web parts, and how you can provide a better user interface by adding web part menu verbs. You will also see how to create editor parts that can be shown in the web part tool pane to enhance a web part's configurability. Then, we will discuss how to deploy a web part within a SharePoint server farm via a SharePoint solution file. The final topic of this chapter discusses how to enhance web part development using the Guidance Automation Toolkit.

Chapter 2, Creating Interactive Web Parts Using ASP.NET Ajax: This is a very complete chapter about doing Ajax development in web parts. Ajax is a framework for communicating client-side with servers in an asynchronous manner; this chapter starts with a discussion of Ajax and the ASP.NET Ajax framework. We dedicate a small portion of this chapter to an overview of all available Ajax frameworks for ASP.NET. After that, we show you how to add service virtualization to a web service to make sure the web service is able to run in a SharePoint context. Then, you will learn the ins and outs of using JavaScript within web parts, and you will see how to use JavaScript in the Content Editor web part, how to use web part tokens, and how to render JavaScript within a web part. We will discuss an advanced JavaScript technique called on-demand loading. We will talk about debugging JavaScript and devote some attention to the impressive debugging capabilities of Visual Studio 2008 (code-named "Orcas"). You will learn how to issue remote calls within a browser from the client side via the XMLHttpRequest object and web service behavior. Then, a discussion is included of available web service message types, including plain text, HTML responses, XML messages, and JSON messages. ASP.NET Ajax–enabling a SharePoint site is a tricky manual task, but in this chapter, we will show you how to do it. Then, you will learn everything you need to know about using ASP.NET Ajax in web parts, with various useful examples including a company contact web part, a performance counter web part, an auto-completion web part, client-side connectable web parts, and creating a web part that uses client callbacks and the People Picker control.

Chapter 3, Enhancing Business Intelligence via SQL Server 2005 Reporting Services: This chapter contains the most extensive information about using SQL Server 2005 Reporting Services in a SharePoint 2007 environment we have seen, including a thorough discussion of the new SharePoint 2007 capabilities offered by SQL Server 2005 Service Pack 2.0. You will learn how to run Reporting Services in native mode and SharePoint integration mode, see how to build a report, explore the available reporting services web parts, and learn how to use Report Center. Then, you will see how to build reports in SharePoint and how to develop a custom reporting services extension.

Chapter 4, Building Human-Oriented Workflows Using Windows Workflow Foundation: Building workflows using Windows WorkFlow Foundation is quite a large topic. Because of this, we have written a large chapter that includes all the information you need to start being prolific in building workflows in a SharePoint environment. The chapter starts with a discussion of the basics of Windows Workflow Foundation, including discussions about activities, components, and workflow styles. Then, the chapter guides you through the creation of a basic workflow using SharePoint Designer 2007. After that, you will see how to build advanced workflows using Visual Studio 2005 Designer, including the creation of initiation forms and custom task forms. After building such a workflow, you will learn how to deploy and debug workflows. Then, we discuss how to use forms to capture and automate your business processes. The final topic of the chapter discusses how to create and use a custom activity in a workflow.

Chapter 5, Building a Domain-Specific Language for Connectable Web Parts: This chapter combines two interesting topics: building connectable web parts and creating a domain-specific language. First, the chapter provides more background on the topic of software factories and the development of domain-specific languages. Then, we go into further detail about the available Microsoft DSL tools that can help you build a domain-specific language. The next part of the chapter discusses everything you need to know about building connectable web parts. The chapter starts with a little history lesson discussing connectable web part techniques that have preceded the SharePoint 2007 web part connection framework. You will learn how to create a connection for web parts implementing a custom interface. You will learn about the available predefined web part connection interfaces, the use of transformers, and the available set of predefined transformers. After that, you will create a custom transformer. The final part of this section shows how to create field, row, table, and parameters connections. The next part of this chapter explains how to use the Web Part Connection Language (WPCL), a freely downloadable domain-specific language that makes creating connectable web parts significantly easier. The final part of this section discusses in detail how we created the WPCL.

Chapter 6, Reusing Presentation Layers via Web Services for Remote Portlets: The Web Services for Remote Portlets (WSRP) protocol is a web services protocol for aggregating content and interactive web applications from remote sources. In this chapter, we will discuss what WSRP is and how this specification can be of help in portal implementations. After that, we will look deeper into the WSRP specification. Also, we explain how to configure a generic WSRP consumer web part in SharePoint and how to build WSRP producers.

Chapter 7, Changing Code Privileges Using Impersonation, Elevation, and Delegation: Code is executed under a given identity. There are several techniques available for you to do this. You can use the LogonUser and RevertToSelf Win32 API calls to access resources that are not controlled by the SharePoint object model, or you can use new techniques offered by the SharePoint 2007 API to access SharePoint resources. These techniques include the use of the SPUserToken object, the RunWithElevatedPrivileges method, and the CodeToRunElevated delegate. All techniques will be discussed extensively. In impersonation scenarios, you will typically need a place to store the user credentials used during impersonation. Passwords need to be stored in a safe place; this chapter shows you how to encrypt sensitive data in an application configuration file and discusses how to use SharePoint Single Sign-on to store user credentials in a safe and encrypted way, although you will need Microsoft Office SharePoint Server 2007 to use the latter technique. In cases when you need to access resources located on other computers on the network, you need to use delegation. This chapter discusses how to set this up. The final topic of this chapter discusses how to impersonate identities using Windows Communication Foundation (WCF).

Chapter 8, Working with InfoPath in a MOSS 2007 Environment: This chapter starts out with a discussion of InfoPath itself. Along the way, you will learn what InfoPath Trust levels are and how to use an InfoPath form as a SharePoint site content type. You will see how to share data connection files in a data connection library, and how to use data coming from a SharePoint list. Then, we will discuss how to update and save an InfoPath form programmatically. You will also learn how to implement InfoPath Submit buttons, providing an alternative way to store the data in InfoPath forms. After that, we will show you how to use one of the exciting new features of SharePoint 2007: Forms Services 2007. The final part of this chapter contains a detailed overview of the use of the BizTalk Windows SharePoint Services adapter in a SharePoint 2007 environment.

Chapter 9, Deep Traversal of SQL Full-Text Extensions: The final chapter of this book discusses an important topic that seldom gets the attention it deserves. This chapter explains how to work with SQL Full-Text Extensions. You will learn how to fire a SQL Full-Text Extensions query via the SharePoint object model, the SharePoint web services API, and the MOSS Query Tool. Then, we will take a close look at the elements of the SQL Full-Text query language. The final part of the chapter discusses common pitfalls and answers common questions that arise when working with SQL Full-Text Extensions.

Who Is This Book For?

This book is targeted toward SharePoint 2007 developers who want to expand their knowledge about the shape of the landscape of SharePoint 2007 by discussing a large range of interesting topics that help provide quality SharePoint solutions. The book will provide information and insight about contemporary development techniques that will help you in your daily activities as a SharePoint developer.

Source Code

The code listings in this book are available on the Apress web site and can be downloaded from our web site at http://www.lcbridge.nl/download.

What Do You Need to Use This Book?

Each chapter discusses the requirements for testing the techniques and examples described in the chapter. In general, you will need to have access to SharePoint 2007 and Visual Studio 2005. Other requirements will be discussed on a per-chapter basis.

Incorporating ASP.NET 2.0 into Microsoft Office SharePoint Server 2007

SharePoint technologies have been around for a couple of years now and have proven to be quite useful for companies around the world that are implementing portal, team collaboration, or enterprise content management (ECM) strategies.

The development model for working with SharePoint technologies has changed considerably in Microsoft Office SharePoint Server 2007, largely influenced by the release of Microsoft .NET Framework 2.0. This chapter covers the integration between the exciting new features of ASP.NET 2.0 and Microsoft Office SharePoint Server 2007.

First, we will discuss how the integration between Microsoft Office SharePoint Server 2007 and .NET Framework 2.0 works. Then, we will look at the benefits offered by the Visual Studio 2005 Extensions for Windows SharePoint Services 3.0. After that, we will create some web parts using these tools and show you how to use a couple of the new ASP.NET 2.0 server controls within web parts along the way. The chapter finishes with a discussion of the Guidance Automation Toolkit, also known as GAT, and how it can be used to enhance the development experience.

Architecture Overview

Before looking at Microsoft Office SharePoint Server 2007, we shall take a quick look at its predecessor. SharePoint Products and Technologies 2003 is more or less integrated with IIS 6.0 and ASP.NET 1.1, using an ISAPI filter that intercepts all IIS page requests. In most cases, requests are forwarded to ASP.NET; in other cases, the ISAPI filter determines that a request should be forwarded by an HTTP handler called SharePointHandler. In the latter case, SharePoint passes page requests to the SafeMode parser, a construct specifically created for SharePoint Products and Technologies 2003. The most important features provided by the SafeMode parser are related to advanced caching scenarios and implementing additional security measures. The biggest problem associated with this architecture is that it is not built on top of ASP.NET technology. As a result, the ASP.NET runtime does not always handle all incoming requests first, and therefore does not have the chance to initialize a request with the ASP.NET context. This, along with the use of the custom SafeMode parser, has caused problems and confused a lot of the SharePoint 2003 developers out there.

ASP.NET 2.0 was released well after SharePoint Products and Technologies 2003. But even so, you can configure SharePoint Products and Technologies 2003 to support ASP.NET 2.0, as we discussed in detail in the first edition of this book (which can be found on Amazon.com at the following location: http://www.amazon.com/Pro-SharePoint-2003-Development-Techniques/dp/1590597613/ref=sr_1_2/102-5827992-1824111?ie=UTF8&s=books&qid=1179750099&sr=8-2).

Microsoft Office SharePoint Server 2007 has been redesigned completely when it comes to integrating with ASP.NET 2.0; it is now built on top of ASP.NET 2.0 and is far more reliant on the features provided by the ASP.NET 2.0 infrastructure.

■**Note** Configuring SharePoint Products and Technologies 2003 to support ASP.NET 2.0 used to be tricky. In Microsoft Office SharePoint Server 2007, integration is available out of the box. Planning and installing Microsoft Office SharePoint Server 2007 remains a complex topic, but it falls outside the scope of this book. The book *Microsoft SharePoint: Building Office 2007 Solutions in C# 2005* by Scot Hillier (Apress, 2007) contains extensive information about this topic, including capacity planning guidelines, deployment architectures, and detailed instructions on how to create a SharePoint 2007 development environment using Virtual Server 2005.

In Microsoft Office SharePoint Server 2007, incoming requests are always handled first by the ASP.NET runtime. The SharePoint ISAPI filter has been removed, and instead the Microsoft Office SharePoint Server 2007 infrastructure relies on ASP.NET 2.0 by defining HTTP modules and HTTP handlers responsible for handling SharePoint-related requests.

■**Note** All HTTP requests are handled by the ASP.NET engine, which ensures that the ASP.NET context is initialized entirely before SharePoint gets a chance to process a request.

In the web.config file of a SharePoint web application, you will notice that the `<httpHandlers>` section contains an HTTP handler called `Microsoft.SharePoint.ApplicationRuntime. SPHttpHandler`. This handler ensures that the SPHttpHandler will eventually handle all requests for all file types (for instance, .aspx, .txt, .doc, or .docx files). You can find the web.config file by following these steps:

1. Open a command prompt and type the following command: **inetmgr**. This opens Internet Information Services (IIS) Manager.

2. Expand the [server name] (local computer) node.

3. Expand the Web Sites node.

4. Right-click the SharePoint web application and choose Properties. This opens the [web application] Properties window.

5. Click the Home Directory tab and copy the value of the Local path text field.

6. Open an instance of Windows Explorer and navigate to the path found in the previous step.

7. Open the web.config file found in this folder in any text editor.

When the ASP.NET engine is finished processing a request, it calls the SharePoint Virtual Path Provider (also known as the WSS File provider or SPVirtualPathProvider). ASP.NET 2.0 introduces the concept of *virtual path providers*, which are pluggable components that integrate with ASP.NET and can be used to parse .aspx pages. The SharePoint Virtual Path Provider is able to retrieve .aspx pages from a SQL Server database with full-text extensions and does not suffer from the limited functionality regarding page parsing found in SharePoint 2003.

Microsoft Office SharePoint Server 2007 supports two types of pages: uncustomized and customized.

Uncustomized pages are page templates that are located on the file system of the web server. Customized pages are modified page templates that are written to a SharePoint content database. One task the SharePoint Virtual Path Provider is responsible for when handling a page request is deciding whether the page is located on the file system or in a content database. The SafeMode parser optionally parses pages that are retrieved from the database.

■Note Microsoft Office 2007 SharePoint Designer can be used to customize pages or undo customizations (also known as reverting back to the original template). In SharePoint Products and Technologies 2003, customized pages were called *unghosted pages*; uncustomized pages were called *ghosted pages*.

After the SharePoint Virtual Path Provider has had the opportunity to handle (but not compile) a page, it returns the result to the ASP.NET engine that compiles the page, which then asks the virtual path provider to fetch the page layout class, which is also compiled. The ASP.NET engine adds SharePoint context data to the web metadata and then retrieves the master page associated to the SharePoint page. The master page is compiled, and a response is returned to the client. Figure 1-1 shows an overview of the page-handling process in Microsoft Office SharePoint Server 2007.

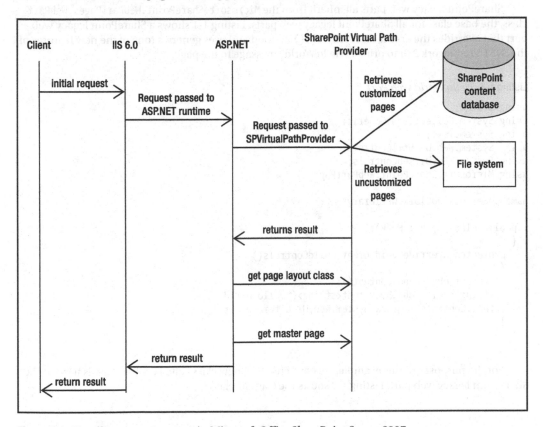

Figure 1-1. *Handling a page request in Microsoft Office SharePoint Server 2007*

Web Parts Overview

After the huge success of web parts in SharePoint technologies, web parts have been incorporated into ASP.NET 2.0. This has had an effect on Microsoft Office SharePoint Server 2007, which supports the use of ASP.NET 2.0 web parts. There is also support for SharePoint legacy web parts, accomplished by rebasing the web part base class, which will be discussed later in this section.

Although support for SharePoint 2003 web parts is still available primarily for legacy reasons, they are not the only reason. The web part connection model in ASP.NET 2.0 is in some ways inferior to the connection model for SharePoint legacy web parts. Because of this, you may want to use SharePoint legacy web parts instead of ASP.NET 2.0 web parts. You might want to use SharePoint legacy web parts when you want to

- Create cross-page connections. Differences in the web part connection model will be discussed in Chapter 5.

- Use web part caching.

- Communicate with web parts outside web part zones.

Other than that, it is strongly recommended that you use ASP.NET 2.0 web parts when creating new web parts.

SharePoint legacy web parts all inherit from the `Microsoft.SharePoint.WebPartPages.WebPart` class, the base class for all SharePoint legacy web parts. Listing 1-1 shows a SharePoint legacy web part that overrides the `CreateChildControls()` method and uses generics (one of the new features of the .NET Framework 2.0) to print a "Hello World" message to the page.

Listing 1-1. *Hello World Web Part*

```
using System;
using System.Collections.Generic;
using System.Text;
using System.Web.UI.HtmlControls;
using System.Web.UI.WebControls;
using Microsoft.SharePoint.WebPartPages;

namespace LoisAndClark.WPLibrary
{
..public class MyWP : WebPart
  {
    protected override void CreateChildControls()
    {
      Content obj = new Content();
      string str1 = obj.MyContent<string>("Hello World!");
      this.Controls.Add(new System.Web.UI.LiteralControl(str1));
    }
  }
}
```

For the purposes of this example, we have created a new class called `Content` that is used in the SharePoint legacy web part. Listing 1-2 shows the `Content` class.

Listing 1-2. *Example Class Using Generics*

```
namespace LoisAndClark.WPLibrary
{
  public class Content
  {
    internal Content() { }

    public string MyContent<MyType>(MyType arg)
    {
      return arg.ToString();
    }
  }
}
```

All ASP.NET 2.0 web parts inherit from the `System.Web.UI.WebControls.WebParts.WebPart` base class. Listing 1-3 shows an ASP.NET 2.0 web part that writes a "Hello World" message to the page that contains the web part.

Listing 1-3. *The Complete Code for a Hello World Web Part*

```
using System;
using System.Runtime.InteropServices;
using System.Web.UI;
using System.Web.UI.WebControls.WebParts;
using System.Xml.Serialization;

using Microsoft.SharePoint;
using Microsoft.SharePoint.WebControls;
using Microsoft.SharePoint.WebPartPages;

namespace LoisAndClark.WPLibrary
{
  [Guid("c22d5295-81a3-4a23-97ed-3a0a3e8caecf")]
  public class WPLibrary : System.Web.UI.WebControls.WebParts.WebPart
  {
    public WPLibrary()
    {
      this.ExportMode = WebPartExportMode.All;
    }

    protected override void Render(HtmlTextWriter writer)
    {
      writer.Write("Hello World!");
    }
  }
}
```

Notice the presence of the GUID class attribute. This attribute explicitly (instead of automatically) assigns a GUID to this class. Including this GUID is necessary; otherwise web part deployment via Visual Studio 2005 extensions for Windows SharePoint Services 3.0 fails. If you right-click a web part library that was created using Visual Studio 2005 extensions for Windows SharePoint Services 3.0 in Visual Studio 2005 and click the SharePoint Solution tab, you will see a solution called Solution ([web part library name]). (Solutions are discussed in detail in the section "Deploying a Web Part," later in this chapter.) This solution contains a separate feature for every web part, as can be seen in Figure 1-2. During deployment, the class GUID of every web part is used as the GUID for a feature containing a web part.

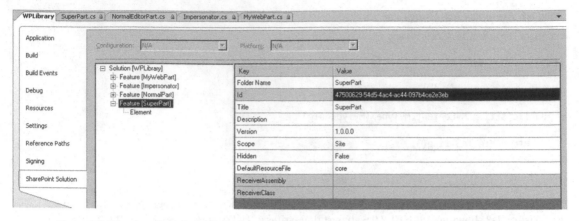

Figure 1-2. *Viewing SharePoint Solution properties*

In order to be able to support both SharePoint legacy web parts and ASP.NET 2.0, the `Microsoft.SharePoint.WebPartPage.WebPart` class is rebased. In SharePoint 2003, this class used to inherit from the `System.Web.UI.Control` class; in Microsoft Office SharePoint Server 2007, the `Microsoft.SharePoint.WebPartPage.WebPart` class inherits from the `System.Web.UI.WebControls.WebParts.WebPart` class. This is shown in Figure 1-3.

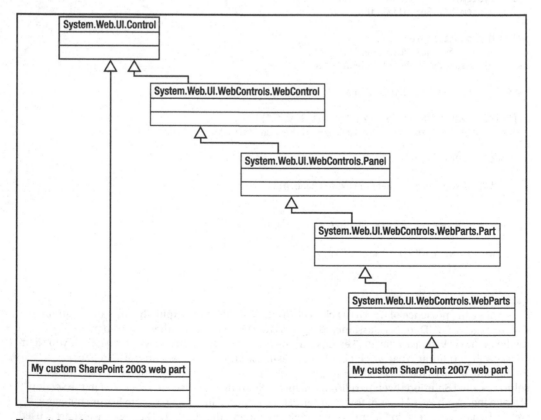

Figure 1-3. *Rebasing the SharePoint web part class*

■**Note** If you have the choice, create ASP.NET 2.0 web parts instead of SharePoint legacy web parts; this is the approach recommended by Microsoft.

HYBRID WEB PARTS

Besides ASP.NET 2.0 and SharePoint 2003 legacy web parts, there is a third flavor of web parts: hybrid web parts. Hybrid web parts, just like SharePoint legacy web parts, inherit from `Microsoft.SharePoint.WebPartPage.WebPart`. Hybrid web parts use ASP.NET 2.0 web part development techniques and capabilities combined with SharePoint capabilities. There are a couple of things you can do to make a web part hybrid:

- Use the `IPersonalizable` interface. This interface is new in .NET 2.0 and defines capabilities for the extraction of personalization state.
- Use the `[Personalizable]` attribute, which enables a particular property on a web part for personalization.
- Omit the use of XML serialization attributes.

There are a couple of drawbacks associated with creating hybrid web parts, things you can do in a normal SharePoint legacy web part but cannot do in hybrid web parts:

- Hybrid web parts cannot return tool parts via the `GetToolParts()` method. Instead, you will need to use controls that inherit from the `EditorPart` class (via the `CreateEditorPart()` method).
- Properties within a hybrid web part that are serializable will not be persisted unless you define a type converter for them.

However, some SharePoint capabilities can be leveraged within hybrid web parts. These capabilities are considered advantages of hybrid web parts:

- You can use the SharePoint 2003 web part caching framework to store items per user or per web part in memory or in SQL Server.
- You can use the SharePoint 2003 web part connection interfaces. You might want to use these interfaces when you want to create web parts that support cross-page connections or client-side communication. Web part connection interfaces are discussed in detail in Chapter 5.
- You can use the asynchronous features of web parts.

Although hybrid web parts are a somewhat esoteric topic and our guess is that you will not see them used often, it is good to know they exist. In Microsoft Office SharePoint Server 2007, we do not recommend that you create hybrid web parts anymore. The reason you might have wanted to create a hybrid web part in the past is for migration purposes; in SharePoint 2003, you could have created a hybrid web part that combined SharePoint capabilities with ASP.NET 2.0 web part development techniques. Such a hybrid web part would operate like a normal ASP.NET 2.0 web part that is easy to migrate to Microsoft Office SharePoint Server 2007.

In the final part of this section, we will take a closer look at the anatomy of the ASP.NET 2.0 web part. The most important parts of an ASP.NET 2.0 web part are as follows:

- OnInit(): This event handler is called immediately before the OnInit() method of the page that hosts the web part. This method can be used to initialize values required within the web part.

- OnLoad(): This event is called immediately before the OnLoad() method of the page that hosts the web part. This method is typically used to interact with the controls that are part of the web part.

- CreateChildControls(): This method can be used to add child controls to a web part and define event handlers for those child controls.

- PreRender(): This is the last event that occurs before the web part output is rendered to the page.

- Render(): This method sends the web part to its HTML writer. This method calls the following methods: RenderBeginTag(), RenderContents(), and RenderEndTag().

- RenderContents(): This method is responsible for adding content to the web part's HTML writer.

- UnLoad(): This event occurs when the instance of the web part is discarded; at that time, the response is already sent back to the client. This is a good place to release any handles to resources that are still left open.

Listing 1-4 shows an ASP.NET 2.0 web part that incorporates the basic anatomy, as described previously.

Listing 1-4. *Example Web Part Incorporating Important Parts of a Web Part Anatomy*

```
using System;
using System.Runtime.InteropServices;
using System.Web.UI;
using System.Web.UI.WebControls;
using System.Web.UI.WebControls.WebParts;
using System.Xml.Serialization;

using Microsoft.SharePoint;
using Microsoft.SharePoint.WebControls;
using Microsoft.SharePoint.WebPartPages;

namespace LoisAndClark.WPLibrary
{
  [Guid("c22d5295-81a3-4a23-97ed-3a0a3e8caecf")]
  public class WPLibrary : System.Web.UI.WebControls.WebParts.WebPart
  {
    public WPLibrary() : base()
    { }

    protected override void OnInit(EventArgs e)
    {
      base.OnInit(e);
    }

    protected override void OnLoad(EventArgs e)
    {
      base.OnLoad(e);
    }
```

```
    protected override void CreateChildControls()
    {
      TextBox txtAddress = new TextBox();
      txtAddress.ID = "txtAddress";
      Controls.Add(txtAddress);

      Button btnSubmit = new Button();
      btnSubmit.ID = "btnSubmit";
      btnSubmit.Click += new EventHandler(btnSubmit_Click);
      Controls.Add(btnSubmit);
    }

    void btnSubmit_Click(object sender, EventArgs e)
    {
      throw new Exception("The method or operation is not implemented.");
    }

    protected override void OnPreRender(EventArgs e)
    {
      base.OnPreRender(e);
    }

    protected override void Render(HtmlTextWriter writer)
    {
      base.Render(writer);
    }

    protected override void RenderContents(HtmlTextWriter writer)
    {
      writer.Write("Hello world!");
    }

    protected override void OnUnload(EventArgs e)
    {
      base.OnUnload(e);
    }
  }
}
```

This concludes our web part overview. Detailed information about creating web parts falls outside the scope of this book. If you want to learn more about creating web parts that support ASP.NET Ajax, please refer to Chapter 2. For detailed information about creating connectable web parts, please refer to Chapter 5.

WSS 3.0 Tools: Visual Studio 2005 Extensions

When you start using Visual Studio 2005 to develop custom SharePoint solutions, one of the first things you should do is download Visual Studio 2005 extensions for Windows SharePoint Services 3.0 (VSeWSS). This is a set of tools for developing custom SharePoint 2007 solutions, supporting Windows SharePoint Services 3.0 (or any product built on top of it). The tools can be downloaded from the following location: http://www.microsoft.com/downloads/details.aspx?familyid= 19f21e5e-b715-4f0c-b959-8c6dcbdc1057&displaylang=en. After the download, double-click on VSeWSS.exe and follow the installation procedure. In the rest of this section, we will assume you have correctly installed Visual Studio 2005 extensions for Windows SharePoint Services 3.0.

Project Templates

If you have installed VSeWSS and then start Visual Studio 2005 again, you will find that a new set of Visual Studio project templates is available when you create a new project. The new project templates are available in the Visual C# ➤ SharePoint section, as shown in Figure 1-4. The following project templates are added by Visual Studio 2005 extensions for Windows SharePoint Services 3.0:

- Team Site Definition
- List Definition
- Empty
- Blank Site Definition
- Web Part

Note Figure 1-4 contains other templates in the SharePoint project types section that are related to workflows. Those templates are not installed by Visual Studio 2005 extensions for Windows SharePoint Services 3.0, and will be discussed in detail in Chapter 4.

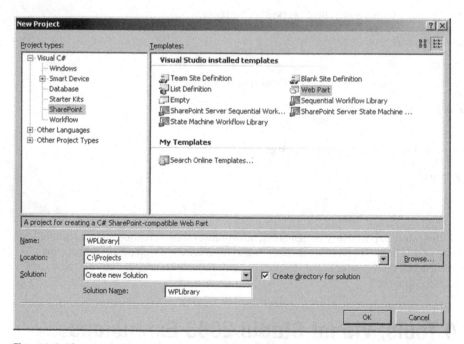

Figure 1-4. *SharePoint Visual Studio project templates*

Visual Studio 2005 extensions for Windows SharePoint Services 3.0 also contains a set of item templates that can be used within SharePoint projects for Visual Studio 2005. The following item templates are added by VSeWSS:

- List Definition
- Content Type

- Web Part
- List Definition from Content Type
- Field Control
- Module

The item templates for Visual Studio are found in the Visual C# Project Items ➤ SharePoint section of the Add New Item – [name of project] window. This is shown in Figure 1-5.

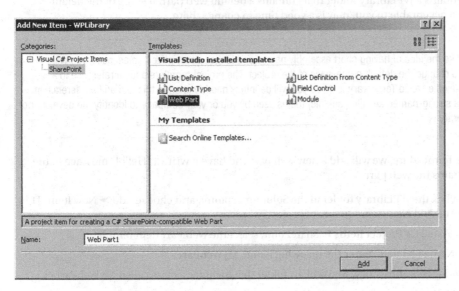

Figure 1-5. *SharePoint Visual Studio item templates*

The following section discusses the Web Part project template as well as the similarly named Web Part item template. Although the other templates are certainly interesting enough to look at, discussing them falls outside the scope of this chapter.

■**Note** It is somewhat confusing that the project template and item template for creating web parts share the same name. In our opinion, it would have been better if the project template had been called Web Part Library.

Web Part Project Template

The Web Part project template for Visual Studio 2005 extensions for Windows SharePoint Services 3.0 makes creating web part libraries easy. In this section, you will learn how to create a web part library, how to create a web part, and how to deploy and debug a web part. The following procedure explains how to create a web part library:

1. Start Visual Studio .NET 2005.
2. Choose File ➤ New ➤ Project. This opens the New Project window.
3. Select Visual C# ➤ SharePoint and choose the following template: Web Part.
4. In the Name text field, enter the following name: **WPLibrary**.

5. In the Location text field, enter the following location: **c:\projects**.

6. Make sure the Create directory for Solution check box is selected.

7. Click OK.

A new web part library based on the Web Part project template is created. It automatically contains references to the Microsoft.SharePoint assembly, it is strong named (see the section "Installing and Using the Web Part Library Template" in this chapter for more information about strong naming), and it contains a WPLibrary folder that contains a default web part. If some of the default settings are not acceptable to you, now is a good time to change them.

Note If you like the idea of having short assembly names and longer, descriptive namespaces, you will probably want to change the default namespace of the project. The project template adds a reference to a strong-named key file called Temporary .snk, so you will definitely need to change this and add a reference in your project to a strong-named key file (.snk file) that is used by you or your company to identify the developer of the web part library.

In the next procedure, we will add a new web part and have it write a "Hello!" message to the page that contains the web part.

1. Right-click the WPLibrary folder in the Solution Explorer, and choose Add ➤ New Item. This opens the Add New Item - [name of project] window.

2. Under Visual C# Project Items ➤ SharePoint, select the Web Part item template.

3. In the Name text field, enter the following name: **MyWebPart**.

4. Click Add. This adds a new MyWebPart folder that includes a class called MyWebPart.cs.

5. Open MyWebPart.cs. This is an ASP.NET 2.0 web part.

6. Add the following code to the body of the MyWebPart.cs class:

```
protected override void RenderContents(HtmlTextWriter writer)
{
  writer.Write("Hello!");
}
```

One of the nice features of the Web Part project template is the ability to package a web part within the project as a SharePoint feature. Features make it easy to deploy and activate web parts (and they can do a lot more than that).

You have fine-grained influence over the settings of a web part feature. The following procedure explains how to configure feature settings:

1. Right-click the WPLibrary project and choose Properties.

2. Click the SharePoint solution tab.

Note More information about the available settings can be found in the MSDN article "Creating a Windows SharePoint Services 3.0 Web Part Using Visual Studio 2005 Extensions" (http://msdn2.microsoft.com/en-us/library/aa973249.aspx) in the section "Customizing the Web Part Solution Package."

At this point, you are almost ready to deploy the web parts in your web part solution. First, you must configure to which SharePoint site the web part solution needs to be deployed. This is explained in the next procedure:

1. Right-click WPLibrary and choose Properties.

2. Click the Debug tab.

3. In the Start Action section, make sure the Start browser with URL radio button is selected.

4. Enter the SharePoint site URL into the Start browser with URL text field.

■**Note** If you fail to specify a correct SharePoint site URL, the following error message appears during deployment: "No SharePoint Site exists at the specified URL."

Deploying a web part has never been easier; all you need to do is press F5 (or Debug ➤ Start Debugging). When you do this, a couple of things happen:

1. The web part solution is compiled.

2. The web part solution is packaged as a feature.

3. If a previous version of the web part feature exists, it is removed.

4. The web part library is added to the Global Assembly Cache (GAC).

5. The web part feature is deployed to the SharePoint site URL you specified earlier.

6. If deployment is successful, the web part feature is activated.

7. The web parts in the web part library are added to the <SafeControls> list in the web.config file of the SharePoint web application that contains the web part.

8. The web part gallery is modified so that the site can use the web parts.

9. Internet Information Services (IIS) is restarted.

10. If debugging is enabled, Visual Studio 2005 automatically tries to attach to the w3wp process hosting the web part.

■**Note** The bin\debug folder of a web part library created using Visual Studio 2005 contains a setup.bat file that can be customized to deploy the web parts created in the web part library. You can find more information about web part deployment in the section "Deploying a Web Part," later in this chapter.

Now, you should go ahead and add the web part to a web part page. The following procedure explains how to do this:

1. Navigate to the SharePoint site URL you specified earlier.

2. Choose Site Actions ➤ Edit Page. This opens the page in Edit Mode.

3. Choose a web part zone and click the Add a Web Part link. This opens the Add Web Parts — Web Page Dialog window.

4. Locate the All Web Parts ➤ Miscellaneous section and select the MyWebPart Web Part check box.

5. Click the Add button.

This adds the MyWebPart web part to the page. If you want to go ahead and debug this web part, follow these steps:

1. Open a command prompt and type **inetmgr**. This opens Internet Information Services (IIS) Manager.

2. Expand the [computer name] (local computer) node.

3. Expand the Web Sites node.

4. Locate the SharePoint web site that contains your web part, right-click it, and choose Properties. This opens the [web site name] Properties window.

5. Click the Home Directory tab.

6. Copy the value of the Local Path text field.

7. Open Windows Explorer and navigate to the local path you copied in the previous step. This opens the root folder of the SharePoint web application that contains your web part.

8. Set a break point to a line of code in the web part.

9. Press F5.

After deployment, Visual Studio 2005 attaches automatically to the process hosting your web part, and break mode is entered automatically. This is shown in Figure 1-6.

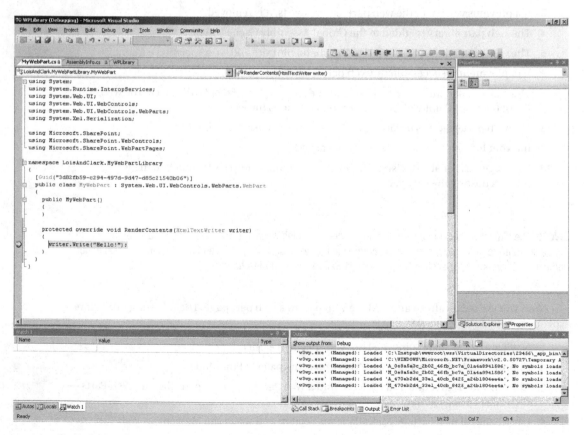

Figure 1-6. *Using the web part template to debug a web part*

DEBUGGING WEB PARTS

Whenever an error occurs in a web part, Microsoft Office SharePoint Server 2007 shows a generic error message. If you want to see a detailed error message, you should open the web.config file of the SharePoint web application that contains the web part, locate the `<SafeMode>` node, and set the `CallStack` attribute to true. If you want to be able to see more than a generic server error message, you should locate the `<customErrors>` element and set the mode attribute to Off.

You do not need to set the `debug` property of the `<compilation>` element to true to be able to debug a web part. This setting tells ASP.NET to generate symbol tables (.pdb files) when compiling pages. Since your web part code is contained in an assembly, you can debug the necessary .pdb files by building a Debug version of the web part library. When the debug symbols are present, you can debug web parts by attaching to the process (an instance of w3wp.exe).

However, if you want to be able to debug web parts by letting Visual Studio 2005 auto-attach to the process, you do need to set the `debug` attribute of the `<compilation>` attribute to true. In that case, you also need to raise the trust level for the SharePoint web application containing your web part to WSS_Medium or greater.

Be careful: setting the `debug` attribute of the `<compilation>` attribute to true has an undesirable side effect. Every time you run the web part library project, a .bak copy of your web application's web.config file is created.

The blog post "Debugging web parts – a full explanation of the requirements," written by Maurice Prather, discusses the previously discussed techniques in detail. The blog post can be found at the following location: `http://www.bluedoglimited.com/SharePointThoughts/ViewPost.aspx?ID=60`.

Whenever you are auto-attaching to a process in Visual Studio 2005, the web server is restarted in order to recycle the w3wp.exe process hosting your web part. This is overkill. Instead, it is much faster if you just restart the application pool that hosts the SharePoint web application containing your web part and then manually attach to the process hosting your web part. You can restart the application pool via iisapp.vbs (located in the [drive letter]:\windows\system32 folder) using the following command:

```
iisapp.vbs /a "[application pool name]" /r
```

You can make attaching to this process even easier by installing the Debugger feature for SharePoint, created by Jonathan Dibble. This feature adds a new menu item to the Site Actions menu of a SharePoint site and is described in detail in the blog post "Debugger 'Feature' for SharePoint" at `http://blogs.msdn.com/sharepoint/archive/2007/04/10/debugger-feature-for-sharepoint.aspx`. The feature can be downloaded from the SharePoint 2007 Features site at CodePlex (`http://www.codeplex.com/features/Release/ProjectReleases.aspx?ReleaseId=2502`). This list of free SharePoint features is maintained by Scot Hillier.

SharePoint Solution Generator

You have seen that Visual Studio 2005 extensions for Windows SharePoint Services 3.0 contains a set of project and item templates. The final part of the Visual Studio 2005 extensions is the SharePoint Solution Generator. This is a stand-alone tool that can be started by choosing Start ➤ All Programs ➤ SharePoint Solution Generator. SharePoint Solution Generator is a convenient tool that allows you to generate either site definitions or list definitions in the form of Visual Studio 2005 projects (.csproj files) based on existing SharePoint sites and lists.

■**Caution** The current version of the tool (version 1.0) breaks if the default IIS web site is not extended with SharePoint functionality. You can extend the default IIS web site via SharePoint Central Administration ➤ Application Management ➤ Create or extend Web Application. If the default IIS web site is not extended with SharePoint functionality, you will get an unhandled exception once you start generating a Site or List definition.

ASP.NET 2.0 Server Controls

In this section, we will show you a couple of the ASP.NET 2.0 server controls used within a SharePoint web part. ASP.NET 2.0 server controls contain great functionality for database access, calendars, text boxes, drop-down lists, and a lot of other common composite web functionality. Controls are essential to the ASP.NET programming model. In ASP.NET 2.0, there are nearly 60 new server controls.

Configuring Web Parts

If you are building a generic web part, you probably will need to be able to configure it on a per-web part basis. You can use web part properties and the Web Part Editor tool pane to configure web parts, as you will see in this section. Such configuration information is stored in the SharePoint content database.

To demonstrate web part configuration via properties, we will create a web part that uploads a local file to a SharePoint document library. File upload in ASP.NET 1.x was possible, although you did have to jump through some hoops to get everything working. For example, you had to add enctype="multipart/form-data" to the page's <form> element. The new ASP.NET 2.0 FileUpload server control makes the process of uploading files to the hosting server as simple as possible.

The FileUpload control displays a text box and a Browse button that allow users to select a file to upload to the server. The user specifies the file to upload by entering the fully qualified path to the file on the local computer (for example, C:\Temp\Test.txt) in the text box of the control. The user can also select the file by clicking the Browse button and then locating it in the Choose File dialog box. You need to hook up an event handler to a Submit button, which calls the SaveAs() method of the FileUpLoad control. Via this method, you can specify the location where the file will be saved. The file will not be uploaded to the server until the user clicks the Submit button.

To build this web part, we need three configurable properties to store the following information:

- Site collection URL
- Site URL
- Name of the document library that is going to hold the uploaded file

If you want to create a configurable property, you first need to add the [Personalizable] attribute to a property to indicate that the property supports personalization. You also need to specify the personalization scope that associates the scope of a web part property to the state a web part page is running in. This determines which configuration data is retrieved from the SharePoint configuration database. You can set the personalization scope to either Shared or User.

Setting the personalization scope of a web part to Shared ensures that the data associated with a page running in Shared mode is retrieved. In this case, the configuration information applies to all users viewing the web part.

You can also set the personalization scope of a web part to User to make sure that the data associated to a page running in User mode is retrieved. Such configuration information indicates that configuration information is retrieved for the currently executing user.

In this example, we are not interested in user-specific data; we are interested in application-specific data. As a result, we will set the personalization scope to Shared. You will also need to set the [WebBrowsable] attribute to true to make it appear in the web part tool pane. In addition, you can use the [WebDisplayName] and [WebDescription] attributes to define a friendly name and description for the web part property. This information is shown in the web part tool pane. The following code fragment shows a web part property containing the URL of a site collection that is personalizable, stores configuration on an application-wide basis, and defines a friendly name and description:

```
private string _strSiteCollectionUrl;
[Personalizable(PersonalizationScope.Shared),
WebBrowsable(true),
WebDisplayName("Site Collection URL"),
WebDescription("Enter the URL of the site collection that contains the
list a document is uploaded to")]
public string SiteCollectionUrl
{
  get { return _strSiteCollectionUrl; }
  set { _strSiteCollectionUrl = value; }
}
```

The web part in this section opens a site collection containing the document library that will hold the uploaded file. Then, it opens the site that contains this document library, and finally, it opens the document library itself. In this example, we are saving uploaded files to the root folder of the document library by using the Add() method of the RootFolder object's Files collection. By passing the input stream of the FileUpload control to the Add() method, you can save a file to a document library. The next code fragment shows how to save a file uploaded via the FileUpload control in a document library, overwriting files that have the same name:

```
using (SPSite objSite = new SPSite(SiteCollectionUrl))
{
  using (SPWeb objWeb = objSite.OpenWeb(SiteUrl))
  {
    SPList objList = objWeb.Lists[ListName];
    if (_objFileUpload.HasFile)
    {
      objList.RootFolder.Files.Add(_objFileUpload.FileName, ➥
      _objFileUpload.PostedFile.InputStream, true);
    }
  }
}
```

The complete code for a configurable web part that uses the FileUpload control to upload a file to a SharePoint document library is shown in Listing 1-5.

Listing 1-5. *The FileUpload Web Part*

```
using System;
using System.Runtime.InteropServices;
using System.Web.UI;
using System.Web.UI.WebControls;
using System.Web.UI.WebControls.WebParts;
using System.Xml.Serialization;

using Microsoft.SharePoint;
using Microsoft.SharePoint.WebControls;
using Microsoft.SharePoint.WebPartPages;
```

```
namespace LoisAndClark.AspNetExample
{
  [Guid("288802c4-4dfe-45b6-bb28-49dda89ec225")]
  public class NormalPart : System.Web.UI.WebControls.WebParts.WebPart
  {
    FileUpload _objFileUpload = new FileUpload();

    protected override void CreateChildControls()
    {
      Controls.Add(_objFileUpload);

      Button btnUpload = new Button();
      btnUpload.Text = "Save File";
      this.Load += new System.EventHandler(btnUpload_Click);
      Controls.Add(btnUpload);
    }

    private void btnUpload_Click(object sender, EventArgs e)
    {
      using (SPSite objSite = new SPSite(SiteCollectionUrl))
      {
        using (SPWeb objWeb = objSite.OpenWeb(SiteUrl))
        {
          SPList objList = objWeb.Lists[ListName];
          if (_objFileUpload.HasFile)
          {
            objList.RootFolder.Files.Add(_objFileUpload.FileName,
            _objFileUpload.PostedFile.InputStream, true);
          }
        }
      }
    }

    private string _strSiteCollectionUrl;
    [Personalizable(PersonalizationScope.Shared), WebBrowsable(true),
    WebDisplayName("Site Collection URL"),
    WebDescription("Enter the URL of the site collection that contains
    the list a document is uploaded to")]
    public string SiteCollectionUrl
    {
      get { return _strSiteCollectionUrl; }
      set { _strSiteCollectionUrl = value; }
    }

    private string _strSiteUrl;
    [Personalizable(PersonalizationScope.Shared),
    WebBrowsable(true), WebDisplayName("Site Collection URL"),
    WebDescription("Enter the URL of the site that contains
    the list a document is uploaded to")]
    public string SiteUrl
    {
      get { return _strSiteUrl; }
      set { _strSiteUrl = value; }
    }

    private string _strListName;
    [Personalizable(PersonalizationScope.Shared),
```

```
    WebBrowsable(true),
    WebDisplayName("List name"), WebDescription("Enter the name of the list that
    will contain the uploaded document")]
    public string ListName
    {
        get { return _strListName; }
        set { _strListName = value; }
    }
  }
}
```

Figure 1-7 shows the FileUpload web part (called NormalPart) in action. First, the web part allows you to choose a local file (test.txt) that you want to upload to a SharePoint document library.

Figure 1-7. *Choosing a local file to upload*

Figure 1-8 shows the end result. The local file test.txt is uploaded to a document library called Shared Documents.

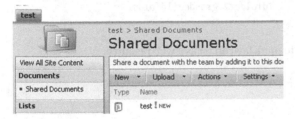

Figure 1-8. *The local file is successfully uploaded to the Shared Documents document library.*

Using Resources in Web Parts

Most web parts use external resources such as images or JavaScript libraries. Such resources can be deployed to the _layouts virtual directory of a SharePoint web application, which is a suitable location because every user has sufficient rights to access it without being able to modify the resources located there. However, since the advent of ASP.NET 2.0, there is another possibility: web resources. In this section, we will use the BulletedList server control to demonstrate the use of web resources.

■Note The images subfolder of the _layouts folder is an excellent place to store custom resources because every user has sufficient rights to read resources in it. The images folder can be found at the following location: [drive letter]:\Program Files\Common Files\Microsoft Shared\web server extensions\12\TEMPLATE\IMAGES\.

The BulletedList control, as the name says, displays a bulleted list of items in an ordered (<ol> HTML element) or unordered (<ul> HTML element) fashion. The BulletedList control has extra features, such as the option to choose bullet style, data binding, and support for custom images. The bullet style lets you choose the style of the element that precedes the item. For example, you can choose to use numbers, squares, or circles. Child items can be rendered as plain text, hyperlinks, or buttons. The web part example in this section shows a bulleted list made with the BulletedList control that uses a custom image.

Web resources allow you to include external resources such as images and JavaScript libraries in assemblies. This allows you to include such resources in the web part assembly, if you want. For reasons of better component design, we have decided to create a new assembly that contains web resources.

Note This is also known as the Common-Closure principle, which requires that the content of an assembly should be closed against the same kinds of code changes. If you want to learn more about component design, we advise you to read the book *Agile Software Development* by Robert C. Martin.

If you want to create web resources, you need to add them to an assembly and mark them as Embedded Resources using Visual Studio 2005 by setting the resource's Build Action property to Embedded Resource. After doing that, you need to add a [WebResource] attribute for each embedded resource in the assembly to enable the resource to be used as a web resource. The constructor for the [WebResource] attribute accepts two parameters: web resource and content type. The web resource consists of three parts:

- *Assembly namespace*: For example, LoisAndClark.WebResources
- *Folder structure*: For example, folder1.childfolder2.grandchildfolder3
- *Resource name*: For example, favicon.gif

The following code fragment shows how to mark favicon.gif as a web resource:

```
[assembly: WebResourceAttribute(
"LoisAndClark.WebResources.gfx.favicon.gif",
"image/gif"
)]
```

You will also need to create a dummy class, which we will call PlaceHolder.cs. This class does not actually need to do anything, but it is used by clients to obtain a reference to the resource assembly when retrieving resource URLs. This will be shown later in this section. Here is the code fragment for the dummy class:

```
public class PlaceHolder
{}
```

In the next procedure, you will learn how to create a new assembly that contains a custom image. The custom image is used by a BulletedList control to display a list in a web part called NormalPart:

1. Open web part library project. If you are not sure how to create a web part library project, please refer back to the section "WSS 3.0 Tools: Visual Studio 2005 Extensions."

2. Choose File ➤ Add ➤ New Project. This opens the Add New Project wizard.

3. In the Project types section, click Visual C#.

4. In the Templates section, choose Class Library.

5. Choose the following name: WebResources.

6. Choose the following location: c:\projects\wplibrary.

7. Click OK.

8. Rename Class1.cs to PlaceHolder.cs.

9. Rename the namespace from WebResources to LoisAndClark.WebResources.

10. Right-click the References folder and choose Add Reference. This opens the Add Reference window.

11. In the .NET tab, locate System.Web and click OK.

12. Right-click the WebResource project and choose Properties. This opens the WebResources page.

13. Click the Application tab and add the following value in the Default namespace textbox: **LoisAndClark.WebResources**.

14. Click the Signing tab and select the Sign the assembly check box.

15. In the Choose a Strong-Name Key file drop-down list, choose <New...>. This opens the Create Strong-Name Key window.

16. In the Key file name text box, add the following value: **WebResourcesKey**.

17. Do not select the Protect my key file with a password check box.

18. Click OK.

19. Right-click the WebResources project and choose Add ➤ New Folder.

20. Enter the following folder name: **gfx**.

21. Right-click the gfx folder and choose Add ➤ Existing Item. This opens the Add Existing Item - WebResources window.

■**Note** In this example, we are using a custom image called favicon.gif. If you do not want to break the code that is discussed later, you should note that casing is important.

---

22. Click favicon.gif. In the Properties window, set the Build Action property to Embedded Resource.

23. In the WebResources project, expand the Properties node and double-click AssemblyInfo.cs.

24. Add the following statement to the top of AssemblyInfo.cs:

```
using System.Web.UI;
```

25. At the bottom of AssemblyInfo.cs, add the following attribute:

```
[assembly: WebResourceAttribute(
"LoisAndClark.WebResources.gfx.favicon.gif",
"image/gif"
)]
```

■**Note** The first part of a WebResource constructor accepts the name of the resource, consisting of the namespace of the assembly, the folder structure, and the name of the resource itself. Remember that casing is important here! The second part of the constructor accepts the type of the resource. In this case, image/gif is used to indicate that the web resource is an image. The most common other option is to include a JavaScript library as a web resource. If you want to add a JavaScript library instead of an image, use text/javascript instead of image/gif.

At this point, you have created a new assembly called WebResources that contains the custom favicon.gif image. Next, we will show you how to build a web part that displays a custom image that is deployed as a web resource in a bulleted list.

Note When resource assemblies are compiled in debug mode, caching is not enabled. When resource assemblies are compiled in release mode, caching is enabled.

You can use the GetWebResourceUrl() method of the Page.ClientScript object to obtain a URL reference to a web resource. The first argument of this method accepts the type of the server resource, which can be obtained by determining the type of the dummy class called PlaceHolder.cs, like so:

```
typeof(LoisAndClark.WebResources.PlaceHolder)
```

The second argument is the name of the server resource, consisting of the namespace, folder structure, and name of the resource. In this example, the fully qualified name of the resource is

```
LoisAndClark.WebResources.gfx.favicon.gif
```

The next code fragment shows the complete code for obtaining a URL reference to a web resource:

```
Page.ClientScript.GetWebResourceUrl( ➡
typeof(LoisAndClark.WebResources.PlaceHolder), strResource);
```

The URL that is retrieved will look like this:

```
/WebResource.axd?d=[Assembly key]&t=[last write time of resource assembly]
```

The next procedure explains how to create the NormalPart web part that displays a bulleted list using a custom image that is available as a web resource:

1. Switch to your web part library. Ours is called WPLibrary.

2. Right-click the References node and choose Add Reference. This opens the Add Reference window.

3. Click the Projects tab. Select WebResources and click OK.

4. Open the web part class file. Ours is called NormalPart.

5. Add the code from Listing 1-6.

Listing 1-6. *Consuming Resources Within a Web Part*

```
using System;
using System.Runtime.InteropServices;
using System.Web.UI;
using System.Web.UI.WebControls;
using System.Web.UI.WebControls.WebParts;
using System.Xml.Serialization;
using Microsoft.SharePoint;
using Microsoft.SharePoint.WebControls;
using Microsoft.SharePoint.WebPartPages;
using Microsoft.SharePoint.Administration;
using Microsoft.SharePoint.Utilities;
using System.Net;
using System.Net.Mail;
```

```
namespace LoisAndClark.AspNetExample
{
  [Guid("288802c4-4dfe-45b6-bb28-49dda89ec225")]
  public class NormalPart : System.Web.UI.WebControls.WebParts.WebPart
  {
    protected override void CreateChildControls()
    {
      string strResource = "LoisAndClark.WebResources.gfx.favicon.gif";
      string strUrl = ➦
      Page.ClientScript.GetWebResourceUrl( ➦
      typeof(LoisAndClark.WebResources.PlaceHolder), strResource);

      BulletedList objBullist = new BulletedList();
      objBullist.BulletStyle = BulletStyle.CustomImage;
      objBullist.BulletImageUrl = strUrl;
      objBullist.Items.Add("One");
      objBullist.Items.Add("Two");
      objBullist.Items.Add("Three");
      objBullist.Items.Add("Four");

      Controls.Add(objBullist);
    }
  }
}
```

Now, you have created all the code you need. The last step you need to perform is to deploy the WebResources assembly to the Global Assembly Cache (GAC) to make sure the web resources are available to the web part. One way to do this is to open [drive letter]:\Windows\Assembly. Drag and drop WebResources.dll into the Global Assembly Cache. The resulting BulletedList control is shown in Figure 1-9.

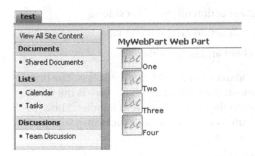

Figure 1-9. *The BulletedList control in a web part*

Web resources are great for packaging resources in assemblies. This allows you to tie specific versions of an assembly to a specific set of resources. However, there are some drawbacks associated to the use of web resources:

- You cannot embed every type of resource in an assembly. For instance, you cannot embed .asmx, .ascx, and web.config files as web resources.

- It is hard, if not impossible, to debug embedded resources.

Alternatively, you could store resources in a separate virtual directory.

Note It is possible to deploy resources using a solution (.wsp) file. Creating solution files is discussed in detail in the section "Deploying a Web Part," later in this chapter. You can use the Location attribute of the <ClassResource> element in the web part manifest file to specify resource files. Do not use the FileName attribute; this attribute is still present but it is only used in SharePoint 2003.

Web Part Menu Verbs

Every web part on a SharePoint page has a web part menu that contains standard options such as the ability to minimize or close the web part. An example of a standard web part menu is shown in Figure 1-10.

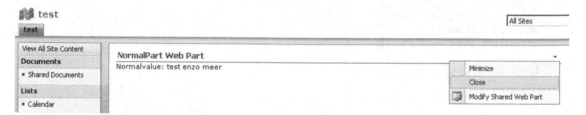

Figure 1-10. *The standard web part menu*

In this section, you will learn how to create custom web part menu verbs that are added to the verbs menu in a web part's header. To start with, it is good to realize that there are three kinds of web part menu verbs:

- *Client-side verbs.* These verbs perform some kind of action on the client side.
- *Server-side verbs.* These verbs perform some kind of action on the server side.
- *Both.* These verbs perform actions on both the client and server side.

You can create a client-side verb by creating a new instance of the WebPartVerb class. The first argument that needs to be passed to the WebPartVerb constructor for a client-side verb is the verb's id. This needs to be unique. The second argument refers to the client-click event handler. This typically refers to a piece of JavaScript that needs to be executed once an end user clicks on a web part menu verb. The following code fragment shows how to create a client-side verb:

```
WebPartVerb objFirst = new WebPartVerb("FirstVerbId", ➥
"javascript:alert('Hello from verb!');");
objFirst.Text = "first verb text";
objFirst.Description = "first verb description";
objFirst.ImageUrl = "_layouts/images/loisandclark/favicon.gif";
```

If you want to create a server-side verb, you need to instantiate a new WebPartVerb class, pass it a unique verb id, and specify a server-side event handler to be executed once an end user clicks on the verb. The next code fragment shows how to create a server-side verb:

```
WebPartVerb objSecond = new WebPartVerb("SecondVerbId",
new WebPartEventHandler(SecondVerbHandler));
objSecond.Text = "second verb text";
objSecond.Description = "second verb description";
```

The final web part menu verb type, the kind that performs both client-side and server-side actions, is created by passing a unique verb id, a server-side event handler, and a client-side event handler.

You can add custom web part verbs by overriding the Verbs property of a web part and adding custom verbs to it. Listing 1-7 shows how to add custom verbs to the web part menu and define an event handler that handles a server-side verb click event:

Listing 1-7. *Adding Custom Verbs to a Web Part Menu*

```
using System;
using System.Runtime.InteropServices;
using System.Web.UI;
using System.Web.UI.WebControls;
using System.Web.UI.WebControls.WebParts;
using System.Xml.Serialization;
using Microsoft.SharePoint;
using Microsoft.SharePoint.WebControls;
using Microsoft.SharePoint.WebPartPages;
using Microsoft.SharePoint.Administration;
using Microsoft.SharePoint.Utilities;
using System.Net;
using System.Net.Mail;

namespace LoisAndClark.AspNetExample
{
  [Guid("288802c4-4dfe-45b6-bb28-49dda89ec225")]
  public class NormalPart : System.Web.UI.WebControls.WebParts.WebPart
  {
    public override WebPartVerbCollection Verbs
    {
      get
      {
        WebPartVerb objFirst = new WebPartVerb("FirstVerbId", ➥
        "javascript:alert('Hello from verb!');");
        objFirst.Text = "first verb text";
        objFirst.Description = "first verb description";
        objFirst.ImageUrl = "_layouts/images/loisandclark/favicon.gif";

        WebPartVerb objSecond = new WebPartVerb("SecondVerbId", ➥
        new WebPartEventHandler(SecondVerbHandler));
        objSecond.Text = "second verb text";
        objSecond.Description = "second verb description";

        WebPartVerb[] objVerbs = new WebPartVerb[] {objFirst, objSecond};
        WebPartVerbCollection objVerbCollection = ➥
        new WebPartVerbCollection(base.Verbs, objVerbs);

        return objVerbCollection;
      }
    }

    protected void SecondVerbHandler(object sender, WebPartEventArgs args)
    {
      //Do something...
    }
  }
}
```

This code adds two web part verbs to the web part menu: a client-side verb and a server-side verb. Both verbs are shown in Figure 1-11.

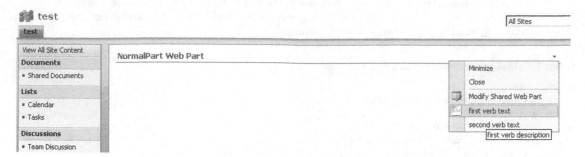

Figure 1-11. *A web part menu containing two custom verbs*

Figure 1-12 shows what happens when you click on the client-side verb. Some JavaScript will be executed that displays an alert box.

Figure 1-12. *The client-side event handler for the client-side verb in action*

In this section, you have seen that adding verbs to a web part menu enhances the user interface experience and is quite easy to accomplish.

Creating Editor Parts

If you have sufficient permissions, you are allowed to configure web parts. When you start configuring web parts via the user interface, a web part tool pane opens. Any configuration information stored in the pane is persisted in the SharePoint content database. In the section "Configuring Web Parts," earlier in this chapter, you learned how to create properties that can be configured using the web part tool pane. Figure 1-13 shows an example of a web part tool pane.

Out of the box, SharePoint offers different editors for different types of data. For instance, a string property is represented by the text box editor, while a Boolean property is represented by check boxes. In this section, you will learn how to create custom editor parts, which will be shown in the web part tool pane when you are configuring a web part.

All editor parts inherit from the EditorPart base class, so that is the first step you need to take when creating a custom editor part. Editor parts look a lot like normal web parts. For instance, if you want to add child controls to an editor part, you need to override its CreateChildControls() method. The following code fragment adds a text area consisting of five lines to an editor part:

```
protected override void CreateChildControls()
{
  _txtNormalBox = new TextBox();
  _txtNormalBox.ID = "txtNormalBox";
  _txtNormalBox.Text = "[Custom editor part]";
  _txtNormalBox.TextMode = TextBoxMode.MultiLine;
  _txtNormalBox.Rows = 5;
  Controls.Add(_txtNormalBox);
}
```

You will also need to override the ApplyChanges() method of an EditorPart instance. This method is responsible for mapping values in the editor part to corresponding properties in the associated web part. The following code fragment shows how the ApplyChanges() method sets a property in an instance of the NormalPart web part called NormalValue:

```
public override bool ApplyChanges()
{
  NormalPart objNormal = (NormalPart)WebPartToEdit;
  objNormal.NormalValue = _txtNormalBox.Text;

  return true;
}
```

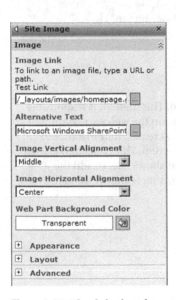

Figure 1-13. *The default web part tool pane*

■Note This code performs a downcast, which is considered a bad practice in object-oriented programming because it tightly couples the editor part and the web part. It would have been better to define an interface that is implemented by every web part that can be used in conjunction with the editor part.

The final piece of an editor part that must be implemented is the SyncChanges() method. This method is the opposite of the ApplyChanges() method; it retrieves property values from a web part and stores them in the editor part. The following code fragment shows an implementation for the

SyncChanges() method that retrieves the NormalValue property of a NormalPart web part and stores it in the text area of the web part editor tool pane:

```
public override void SyncChanges()
{
  // Make sure the text area child control is created.
  EnsureChildControls();

  NormalPart objNormal = (NormalPart) WebPartToEdit;
  _txtNormalBox.Text = objNormal.NormalValue;
}
```

So far, you have seen how to create an editor part. Before a custom editor part is shown in the web part editor tool pane, you need to implement support for this in your web part. In this example, we are creating a web part called NormalPart. First, we need to add one or more properties that are read from and written to within the editor part. The custom editor part in this section expects the presence of a NormalValue property in a web part, so that is the first thing that needs to be implemented. If you need more information on how to do this, please refer back to the section "Configuring Web Parts." The following code fragment shows how to implement the NormalValue property:

```
private string _strNormalValue = String.Empty;
[Personalizable(PersonalizationScope.Shared), WebBrowsable(false), ➥
WebDisplayName("Normal value"), WebDescription("Normal value description")]
public string NormalValue
{
  get { return _strNormalValue; }
  set { _strNormalValue = value; }
}
```

After that, you need to override the CreateEditorParts() method. This method is responsible for returning a collection of custom editor part controls that are shown in the web part editor tool pane when a web part is in edit mode. Basically, this method is used to create a new instance of one or more custom editor parts and add those to the editor part collection. This collection is used when the web part tool pane is rendered. The following code fragment shows how to add the NormalEditorPart editor part to the collection of customer editor parts that is shown when the NormalPart web part is being edited:

```
public override EditorPartCollection CreateEditorParts()
{
  NormalEditorPart objEditor = new NormalEditorPart();
  objEditor.ID = ID + "normalEditor1";
  objEditor.Title = "Normal Editor title";
  objEditor.ToolTip = "Normal Editor tooltip";
  objEditor.TabIndex = 100;
  objEditor.GroupingText = "Normal editor grouping text";

  ArrayList objEditorParts = new ArrayList();
  objEditorParts.Add(objEditor);

  EditorPartCollection objEditorPartsCollection = new
  EditorPartCollection(objEditorParts);

  return objEditorPartsCollection;
}
```

Listing 1-8 shows the complete code for a custom editor part called NormalEditorPart that is being used in a web part called NormalPart:

Listing 1-8. *Creating an Editor Part*

```
using System;
using System.Runtime.InteropServices;
using System.Web.UI;
using System.Web.UI.WebControls;
using System.Web.UI.WebControls.WebParts;
using System.Xml.Serialization;

namespace LoisAndClark.AspNetExample
{
  public class NormalEditorPart : EditorPart
  {
    TextBox _txtNormalBox;

    protected override void CreateChildControls()
    {
      _txtNormalBox = new TextBox();
      _txtNormalBox.ID = "txtNormalBox";
      _txtNormalBox.Text = "[Custom editor part]";
      _txtNormalBox.TextMode = TextBoxMode.MultiLine;
      _txtNormalBox.Rows = 5;
      Controls.Add(_txtNormalBox);
    }

    public override bool ApplyChanges()
    {
      NormalPart objNormal = (NormalPart)WebPartToEdit;
      objNormal.NormalValue = _txtNormalBox.Text;

      return true;
    }

    public override void SyncChanges()
    {
      EnsureChildControls();
      NormalPart objNormal = (NormalPart)WebPartToEdit;
      _txtNormalBox.Text = objNormal.NormalValue;
    }
  }
}
```

Listing 1-9 contains the implementation of the NormalPart web part. This web part displays the custom NormalEditorPart web part in edit mode:

Listing 1-9. *Creating a Web Part Displaying a Custom Editor Part*

```
using System;
using System.Collections;
using System.Runtime.InteropServices;
using System.Web.UI;
using System.Web.UI.WebControls;
using System.Web.UI.WebControls.WebParts;
using System.Xml.Serialization;
```

```
using Microsoft.SharePoint;
using Microsoft.SharePoint.WebControls;
using Microsoft.SharePoint.WebPartPages;
using Microsoft.SharePoint.Administration;
using Microsoft.SharePoint.Utilities;

using System.Net;
using System.Net.Mail;


namespace LoisAndClark.AspNetExample
{
  [Guid("288802c4-4dfe-45b6-bb28-49dda89ec225")]
  public class NormalPart : System.Web.UI.WebControls.WebParts.WebPart
  {
    protected override void RenderContents(HtmlTextWriter writer)
    {
      writer.Write("Normalvalue: " + NormalValue);
    }

    public override EditorPartCollection CreateEditorParts()
    {
      NormalEditorPart objEditor = new NormalEditorPart();
      objEditor.ID = ID + "normalEditor1";
      objEditor.Title = "Normal Editor title";
      objEditor.ToolTip = "Normal Editor tooltip";
      objEditor.TabIndex = 100;
      objEditor.GroupingText = "Normal editor grouping text";

      ArrayList objEditorParts = new ArrayList();
      objEditorParts.Add(objEditor);

      EditorPartCollection objEditorPartsCollection = ➥
      new EditorPartCollection(objEditorParts);

      return objEditorPartsCollection;
    }

    private string _strNormalValue = String.Empty;
    [Personalizable(PersonalizationScope.Shared), ➥
    WebBrowsable(false), ➥
    WebDisplayName("Normal value"), ➥
    WebDescription("Normal value description")]
    public string NormalValue
    {
      get { return _strNormalValue; }
      set { _strNormalValue = value; }
    }
  }
}
```

Figure 1-14 shows the end result of our efforts: the editor tool pane when the web part is in edit mode. As you can see, the custom text area that is created in our custom editor part is displayed in the tool pane.

Figure 1-14. *Adding a custom control to the web part editor tool pane*

Deploying a Web Part

If you want to deploy a web part, you can use SharePoint solution files. Basically, SharePoint solution files are cabinet files (.cab) with a different extension, namely .wsp. When you use Visual Studio 2005 extensions for Windows SharePoint Services 3.0 to create a web part, as was discussed in the section "WSS 3.0 Tools: Visual Studio 2005 Extensions," a web part solution file is created automatically for you. In this section, you will learn how to create a SharePoint solution file that allows you to deploy a web part to other SharePoint servers and/or SharePoint web applications.

Note WSP files (SharePoint solution files) can be used to deploy site definitions, site features, template files, assemblies, code access security policy files, and web parts.

To demonstrate web part deployment, we will create a new web part called MyWebPart.cs that uses the ASP.NET 2.0 Wizard control to implement a wizard. The Wizard server control enables you to build a sequence of steps that are displayed to the end user. You could use the Wizard control to either display or gather information in small steps. The Wizard control lets you define a group of views in which only one view at a time is active and is rendered to the client. Each view consists of four zones: sidebar, header, content, and navigation. The optional sidebar part contains an overview of all the steps in the wizard. The header contains the header information. The content part contains whichever control or controls you like. The navigation part consists of buttons to navigate through the steps in the wizard.

When you are constructing a step-by-step process that includes logic for every step taken, use the Wizard control to manage the entire process. The Wizard control's navigation buttons fire server-side events whenever the user clicks one of the buttons, helping to navigate to other wizard views on the same page. Navigation can be linear and nonlinear; in other words, you can jump from one view to another or navigate randomly to whichever view you like. All the controls in a wizard view are part of the page, so you can access them in code using their control IDs.

In this example, we have defined six different steps. Each step is a WizardStep control and contains a text box. The state of the text boxes in the wizard is maintained automatically. The order in which the steps are defined is completely based upon the order in which they are added to the wizard via the Add() method of the Wizard object's WizardSteps property. The WizardSteps property contains a collection of WizardSteps. Changing this order changes the order in which the end user sees them. Figure 1-15 shows the first step.

Figure 1-15. *Step 1 of the Wizard control in a web part*

The first step, the start step, always has one button called Next. The following steps will have two buttons, as seen in Figure 1-16.

Figure 1-16. *Step 2 of the Wizard control in a web part*

There are six steps in this example. The final step, step 6, has a Previous and a Finish button, as you can see in Figure 1-17.

Figure 1-17. *The final step of the Wizard control in a web part*

The MyWebPart web part creates a very simple wizard; the Wizard control itself has a lot more options that we will not cover in this chapter. The code for the web part using the Wizard control is shown in Listing 1-10:

Listing 1-10. *The Wizard Web Part*

```
using System;
using System.Runtime.InteropServices;
using System.Web.UI;
using System.Web.UI.WebControls;
using System.Web.UI.WebControls.WebParts;
using System.Xml.Serialization;
```

```
using Microsoft.SharePoint;
using Microsoft.SharePoint.WebControls;
using Microsoft.SharePoint.WebPartPages;

namespace LoisAndClark.MyWebPartLibrary
{
  [Guid("3d82fb59-c294-497d-9d47-d85c21540b06")]
  public class MyWebPart : System.Web.UI.WebControls.WebParts.WebPart
  {
    public MyWebPart()
    {
    }

    protected override void CreateChildControls()
    {
      Wizard objWizard = new Wizard();
      objWizard.HeaderText = "Wizard Header";

      for (int i = 1; i <= 6; i++)
      {
        WizardStepBase objStep = new WizardStep();
        objStep.ID = "Step" + i;
        objStep.Title = "Step " + i;
        TextBox objText = new TextBox();
        objText.ID = "Text" + i;
        objText.Text = "Value for step " + i;
        objStep.Controls.Add(objText);
        objWizard.WizardSteps.Add(objStep);
      }

      Controls.Add(objWizard);
    }
  }
}
```

Now that we have created a web part, we are ready for the next step, the creation of a Share-Point solution file. In the first part of the process, we will add a manifest file (Manifest.xml) to our web part library solution. The manifest file is used by Visual Studio 2005 and defines how to populate the cabinet file that is used to deploy the MyWebPart web part. The next procedure explains how to create a Manifest.xml file and how to add IntelliSense support to it:

1. In the MyWebPartLibrary project, choose Add ➤ New Item. This opens the Add New Item - WPLibrary dialog box.

2. In the Templates section, choose XML file.

3. In the Name text box, add the following value: **Manifest.xml**.

4. Click the Add button.

5. Click the Code window of Manifest.xml.

6. In the Properties window, click Schemas.

7. Click the ... button. This opens the XSD Schemas dialog box.

8. Click the Add button. This opens the Open XSD Schema dialog box.

9. Locate wss.xsd ([drive letter]:\Program Files\Common Files\Microsoft Shared\web server extensions\12\TEMPLATE\XML) and choose Open.

10. Click OK.

11. Add the code from Listing 1-11 to Manifest.xml:

Listing 1-11. *Creating a Manifest File*

```xml
<?xml version="1.0" encoding="utf-8" ?>
<Solution xmlns="http://schemas.microsoft.com/sharepoint/"
SolutionId="312ae869-37dc-4a74-9ecc-359fb3c1461d">
<Assemblies>
    <Assembly DeploymentTarget="WebApplication"
    Location="WPLibrary.dll">
      <SafeControls>
        <SafeControl Assembly="WPLibrary,
        Version=1.0.0.0,
        Culture=neutral,
        PublicKeyToken=9f4da00116c38ec5"
        Namespace="LoisAndClark.MyWebPartLibrary"
        TypeName="*"
        Safe="True" />
      </SafeControls>
    </Assembly>
  </Assemblies>
</Solution>
```

After adding the Manifest.xml file to the web part library project, you can go ahead and create a cabinet project to deploy the MyWebPart web part to another SharePoint server or SharePoint web application. The next procedure explains how to create a SharePoint solution file:

1. Open the WPLibrary web part library solution.

2. Choose File ➤ Add ➤ New Project. This opens the Add New Project dialog box.

3. In the Project types section, expand the Other Project Types node and choose Setup and Deployment.

4. In the Templates section, choose CAB Project.

5. In the Name text box, add the following value: **WPLibraryCab**.

6. Click OK.

7. Right-click WPLibraryCab and choose Add ➤ Project Output. This opens the Add Project Output Group dialog box.

8. In the Project drop-down list, choose WPLibrary.

9. Select Primary output and Content Files.

10. Click OK.

11. Build WPLibraryCab.

12. Locate WPLibraryCab.cab and rename it to WPLibraryCab.wsp.

13. Open a command prompt, and type the following command:

```
stsadm -o addsolution -filename wplibrary.wsp
```

■**Note** Make sure the account you are using to run this account has SharePoint farm administration rights and at least read/write access to the SharePoint content database. Otherwise, you will get the following error message: "Object reference not set to an instance of an object."

Now, the SharePoint solution is added to SharePoint. You can deploy it further using the stsadm tool, or deploy the solution via the user interface of the SharePoint 3.0 Central Administration tool. The next procedure explains how to deploy the solution using the SharePoint 3.0 Central Administration tool:

1. Open SharePoint 3.0 Central Administration.

2. Click Operations. This opens the Operations page.

3. In the Global Configuration section, choose Solution Management. This opens the Solution Management page. This is shown in Figure 1-18.

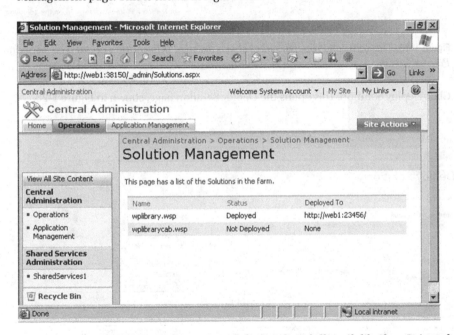

Figure 1-18. *The Solution Management page shows a list of all available SharePoint solutions.*

■**Note** The Solution Management page contains an overview of all available solutions, and indicates whether they have been deployed or not. Figure 1-18 shows two solutions: wplibrary.wsp and wplibrarycab.wsp. Wplibrary.wsp was created and deployed automatically by Visual Studio 2005 extensions for Windows SharePoint Services 3.0 (discussed in the section "WSS 3.0 Tools: Visual Studio 2005 Extensions"). The other solution, wplibrarycab.wsp, is the one created in this section. As you can see, it is not deployed yet.

4. Click the wplibrarycab.wsp link. This opens the Solution Properties page, which is shown in Figure 1-19.

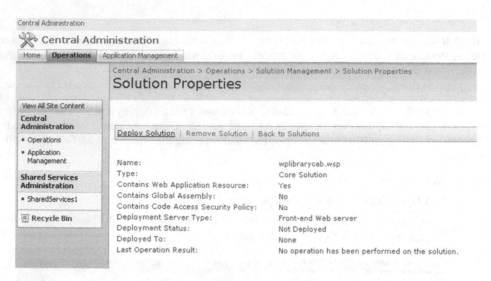

Figure 1-19. *The Solution Properties page shows detailed information about a given Share-Point solution.*

5. Click Deploy Solution. This opens the Deploy Solution page, shown in Figure 1-20.

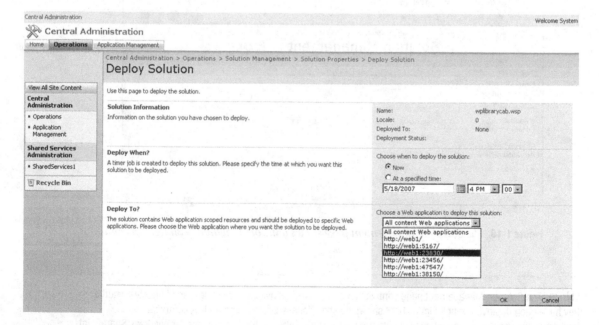

Figure 1-20. *The Deploy Solution page allows you to deploy a solution to a specific web application.*

6. In the Deploy to? section, choose a Web application to deploy this solution.

7. Click OK. This opens the Solution Management page that is shown in Figure 1-21.

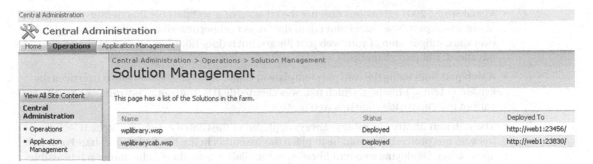

Figure 1-21. *The wplibrarycab.wsp SharePoint solution has been deployed.*

At this point, the SharePoint solution is deployed to a specific SharePoint server and a specific SharePoint web application. Before you are able to use the web parts deployed using a SharePoint solution, you need to add them to the web part gallery of the site collection:

8. Browse to the web application you have chosen in the previous step.

9. Choose Site Actions ➤ Site Settings. This opens the Site Settings page.

10. In the Galleries section, click Web Parts. This opens the Web Part Gallery page.

11. Click New. The web parts in the MyWebPartLibrary assembly should be listed; select them and click the Populate Gallery button.

You have seen how to create a SharePoint solution (.wsp) file that can be used to deploy web parts. After completing all the steps described in this section, you are ready to start using the web parts deployed via the SharePoint solution.

Enhancing Development of Web Parts with the Guidance Automation Toolkit

Since the release of Visual Studio 2005 extensions for Windows SharePoint Services 3.0 (see the earlier section "WSS 3.0 Tools: Visual Studio 2005 Extensions"), creating, deploying, and debugging ASP.NET 2.0 web parts in Visual Studio 2005 has become easy as can be. Although we imagine you will use Visual Studio 2005 extensions most of the time when doing web part development because of its ease of use, it has a major drawback: you cannot extend the functionality offered by Visual Studio 2005 extensions yourself. This means that you will have to live with the limitations of Visual Studio 2005 extensions. The following is an overview of the most common limitations that exist during web part development:

- Development using Visual Studio 2005 extensions is slow. Every time a solution is executed (by pressing F5) that contains a web part library built using Visual Studio 2005 extensions, it creates a SharePoint solution, and retracts and deletes the current version of the solution if it has been deployed before. After that, the new solution is deployed. Every web part is installed as a separate feature; during deployment, every feature that has been previously deployed is deactivated and uninstalled before it can be activated again. In the final step of a deployment, the web server is restarted using iisreset. Overall, this makes running or debugging a web part library project a time-consuming experience.

- Visual Studio 2005 extensions do not provide support for building SharePoint legacy web parts (see the section "Web Parts Overview" for detailed information about SharePoint legacy web parts).

- Visual Studio 2005 extensions obscure the creation of a .webpart file that defines metadata about a web part. The SharePoint tab of the Project properties window offers some control over the configuration of your web part library, but it does not allow you to configure advanced .webpart elements.

- A web part built using the web part template in Visual Studio 2005 extensions overrides the RenderContents() method, which removes client-side IDs from your controls. As a result, you cannot use client-side code in a web part.

- The web part library assembly is always deployed to the Global Assembly Cache (GAC). Instead, our preference would be to place this assembly in the bin folder of a SharePoint web application. Deploying web part libraries to the Global Assembly Cache makes it impossible to define custom security policies and limit the code access permissions granted to those assemblies.

- Every web part in a web part library is deployed in a separate feature. Instead, you might be interested in deploying a group of web parts as a single unit.

Visual Studio 2005 extensions makes it easy to create web parts, at the cost of having granular control over a web part library project. Whether you want to put in the time and effort to create a custom solution that is more advanced than what is offered by Visual Studio 2005 extensions is completely up to you, although we doubt that we will ever go that road ourselves.

If you want to remain in control and are interested in facilitating web part development, you can create your own web part library template. The use of the Guidance Automation Toolkit (GAT) is paramount in achieving this goal.

The GAT is an extension to Visual Studio 2005 that allows architects to automate the easy parts of development so that developers can concentrate on the other parts. The GAT can be used to create assets that are developed in-house or by third parties, such as Microsoft. In the case of building a web part, the GAT can be used to build a package you can use as a template to start making SharePoint legacy web parts in Visual Studio 2005. It can also be used to adjust Visual Studio 2005 to your specific needs for every project type. In this section, you will learn how to use the Guidance Automation Toolkit to create a template that makes creating web part libraries easier.

Guidance Automation Toolkit

In this section, we will show you how to create a web part library template using the GAT. If you want to work with the GAT, you first have to install the Guidance Automation Extensions, which can be downloaded at the Microsoft MSDN web site: http://msdn.microsoft.com/vstudio/teamsystem/workshop/gat/. Next, you should install the Guidance Automation Toolkit itself. You can find additional information about GAT at the following location: http://msdn2.microsoft.com/en-us/teamsystem/aa718950.aspx. In this book, we used the February 2007 CTP (Community Technology Preview) version of the GAT.

The GAT contains a couple of elements that work together to provide the automation functionality. The elements are recipes, actions, text template transformation templates, wizards, and Visual Studio templates, as described in the following list:

- *Recipes*: Recipes are used to automate activities that are usually performed by a developer. Most of the time, recipes automate following a series of instructions. Recipes are most suitable to automate repetitive actions.

- *Actions*: Actions are atomic units of work that are called in a defined order by recipes. The order in which actions are called is specified in the recipe definition. An action will accept input from an argument gathered by the recipe or from output received from another action that has already been run by the recipe.

- *Text template transformation templates*: Text template transformation templates (T4) are templates that contain a combination of text and *scriptlets*. Scriptlets are expressions in Visual Basic or C# that, when run, return a string that is directly inserted into the output stream of the template. The text template transformation engine is part of the GAT, and is also included in the Domain Specific Language (DSL) Toolkit, which we will discuss in Chapter 5. The templates are unfolded by this engine and the text part of a template is inserted unmodified in the template output. It is also possible to use an action to generate text from a T4 text template.

- *Wizards*: Wizards consist of a set of pages that help recipes to gather values. A recipe can have a wizard associated with it. A wizard can contain one or more steps. Steps are displayed as pages to guide the developer. Each page of the wizard will contain one or more fields. Each field is associated with a recipe argument, and includes a type converter and a user interface (UI) type editor. The type converter validates the value of a field and converts the value from a user interface representation to a type representation. The UI type editor is used to render the user interface that collects the information.

  When the wizard displays a page, it will present the developer with a number of default values. These are initial values of arguments that are either set when the recipe reference is created or obtained by the recipe framework. When a recipe has value providers for all arguments—in other words, when a wizard already has default values—the user will still have to step through the wizard, which will show these values to the developer. This gives the developer a chance to acknowledge the default values.

  It is possible that the user is not responsible for the input of a field value. Some fields may be filled in by the framework or the wizard itself. This process is known as *value propagation*. Fields that retrieve their values via value propagation will not be shown in the wizard. Value propagation is done via a combination of argument value change notifications and value providers observing the changes of other arguments (event handlers). As the user edits a field, the field value is validated and assigned to one or more corresponding arguments (parameters) that have registered their interest via value providers. After assignment, arguments are passed to a template.

  In some cases, some fields of a wizard are required. The wizard framework provided with the GAT requires the user to populate fields that correspond to required arguments. The wizard will not enable the Next or Finish buttons on a page, nor will it allow you to access later pages in the wizard from the wizard sidebar, until all fields corresponding to required arguments contain data. If an argument is not collected at all by a wizard, and the associated value provider cannot find a value, the recipe framework will not initiate actions and instead will raise an exception.

- *Visual Studio templates*: Visual Studio templates are written in XML and are used by Visual Studio to create solutions or add one or more projects or items to an existing solution. The templates are unfolded by the Visual Studio template engine. Using the GAT, you can associate Visual Studio templates with recipes. This association means that when a template is unfolded, the wizard extension calls the recipe to let it collect parameter values, also known as *arguments*. The arguments are used to execute actions that may further transform solution items created by the template. Guidance packages can be managed via the Guidance Package Manager in Visual Studio 2005. You can find the Guidance Package Manager via the Tools menu. Once a guidance package is installed and enabled for a particular solution, recipes can be executed to carry out the required tasks.

Creating the Web Part Library Template

In this section, you will learn how to create a web part library guidance package that makes creating SharePoint legacy web parts considerably easier in Visual Studio 2005. If you have not done so already, install the Guidance Automation Extensions and the Guidance Automation Toolkit.

■**Caution** Installing the Guidance Automation Toolkit can take a considerable amount of time. Do not abort the installation process.

The GAT contains a predefined solution for developing a guidance package, which we will use to create a web part library template. The next procedure discusses how to create a guidance package:

1. Start Visual Studio 2005.

2. Choose File ➤ New ➤ Project. This opens the New Project dialog window.

3. Expand the Guidance Packages node.

4. Select the Guidance Package Development node.

5. In the templates section, select the Guidance Package template.

6. In the Name text field, enter the following value: **WebPartLibrary**.

7. In the Location text field, enter the following value: C:\projects.

8. Click OK. This opens the Create New Guidance Package window.

9. In the Package Description text field, enter the following text: **Package for creating a web part library**.

10. In the Package Namespace text field, enter the following value: **LoisAndClark. WebPartLibrary**.

11. Click Finish.

The WebPartLibrary guidance package is created. A guidance package contains lots of files and folders; throughout this section, you will learn how to develop a guidance package solution that facilitates the creation of SharePoint legacy web parts.

The first step for building a web part library template is to create a new folder in the Templates ➤ Solutions ➤ Projects folder. We will call this folder WebPartLibrary. You need to add the following (empty) files to this folder: WebPart.cs, WebPartLibrary.csproj, and a WebPartLibrary.vstemplate file. Then, you need to create a subfolder called Properties and add an empty file to the Properties folder called assembly.info. Now, you are finished with the initial setup of the WebPartLibrary guidance package.

Adding a Solution Template

The WebPartLibrary.vstemplate file is a Visual Studio template that looks identical to a normal Visual Studio template except that it contains additional information used by the recipe framework. The template includes a <WizardExtension> element that specifies a class in the recipe framework that implements template extensions for the GAT. The XML in Listing 1-12 shows the content you need to add to the WebPartLibrary Visual Studio template (WebPartLibrary.vstemplate) in the Web-PartLibrary folder:

Listing 1-12. *WebPartLibrary. vstemplate*

```
<VSTemplate Version="2.0.0" Type="Project" ➡
xmlns="http://schemas.microsoft.com/developer/vstemplate/2005">
  <TemplateData>
    <Name>WebPart Library Project</Name>
    <Description>WebPart class library project </Description>
    <Icon Package="{FAE04EC1-301F-11d3-BF4B-00C04F79EFBC}" ID="4547" />
    <ProjectType>CSharp</ProjectType>
    <SortOrder>20</SortOrder>
    <CreateNewFolder>false</CreateNewFolder>
    <DefaultName>ClassLibrary</DefaultName>
    <ProvideDefaultName>true</ProvideDefaultName>
  </TemplateData>
  <TemplateContent>
    <Project File="WebPartLibrary.csproj" ReplaceParameters="true">
      <ProjectItem ReplaceParameters="true">Properties\AssemblyInfo.cs</ProjectItem>
      <ProjectItem ReplaceParameters="true">WebPart.cs</ProjectItem>
    </Project>
  </TemplateContent>
  <WizardExtension>
    <Assembly>
      Microsoft.Practices.RecipeFramework.VisualStudio, Version=1.0.60429.0, ➡
      Culture=neutral, PublicKeyToken=b03f5f7f11d50a3a
    </Assembly>
    <FullClassName>
      Microsoft.Practices.RecipeFramework.VisualStudio.Templates.UnfoldTemplate
    </FullClassName>
  </WizardExtension>
</VSTemplate>
```

This XML is called a *solution template*. Solution templates are launched via the New command on the File menu.

Adding a Project Template

The next file in the package is the WebPartLibrary.csproj file. This is a project template that contains a project description. The template creates (or unfolds) a new project in an existing solution. The project template will include references to other assemblies and will be responsible for creating any class files, the project file (.csproj), and the assembly.info file. The XML in Listing 1-13 needs to be added to the project template (WebPartLibrary.csproj) and contains code that can be used to create the web part library project:

Listing 1-13. *The Project Template*

```
<Project DefaultTargets="Build" ➡
xmlns="http://schemas.microsoft.com/developer/msbuild/2003">
  <PropertyGroup>
    <Configuration Condition=" '$(Configuration)' == '' ">Debug</Configuration>
    <Platform Condition=" '$(Platform)' == '' ">AnyCPU</Platform>
    <ProductVersion>8.0.30703</ProductVersion>
    <SchemaVersion>2.0</SchemaVersion>
    <ProjectGuid>$guid1$</ProjectGuid>
    <OutputType>Library</OutputType>
    <AppDesignerFolder>Properties</AppDesignerFolder>
    <RootNamespace>$safeprojectname$</RootNamespace>
    <AssemblyName>$safeprojectname$</AssemblyName>
  </PropertyGroup>
```

```xml
    <PropertyGroup Condition=" '$(Configuration)|$(Platform)' == 'Debug|AnyCPU' ">
      <DebugSymbols>true</DebugSymbols>
      <DebugType>full</DebugType>
      <Optimize>false</Optimize>
      <OutputPath>\inetpub\wwwroot\bin\</OutputPath>
      <DefineConstants>DEBUG;TRACE</DefineConstants>
      <ErrorReport>prompt</ErrorReport>
      <WarningLevel>4</WarningLevel>
    </PropertyGroup>
    <PropertyGroup Condition=" '$(Configuration)|$(Platform)' == 'Release|AnyCPU' ">
      <DebugType>pdbonly</DebugType>
      <Optimize>true</Optimize>
      <OutputPath>\inetpub\wwwroot\bin\</OutputPath>
      <DefineConstants>TRACE</DefineConstants>
      <ErrorReport>prompt</ErrorReport>
      <WarningLevel>4</WarningLevel>
    </PropertyGroup>
    <ItemGroup>
      <Reference Include="System"/>
      <Reference Include="System.Data"/>
      <Reference Include="System.Xml"/>
      <Reference Include="System.Web"/>
      <Reference Include="Microsoft.SharePoint"/>
    </ItemGroup>
    <ItemGroup>
      <Compile Include="WebPart.cs" />
      <Compile Include="Properties\AssemblyInfo.cs" />
    </ItemGroup>
    <Import Project="$(MSBuildBinPath)\Microsoft.CSHARP.Targets" />
</Project>
```

Defining the Final Part of the Web Part Library Guidance Package

The project template allows you to create new web part classes based on the web part template specified in WebPart.cs. Add Listing 1-14 to the WebPart.cs file:

Listing 1-14. *The Web Part Item Template*

```csharp
using System;
using System.ComponentModel;
using System.Web.UI;
using System.Web.UI.WebControls;
using System.Xml.Serialization;
using Microsoft.SharePoint;
using Microsoft.SharePoint.Utilities;
using Microsoft.SharePoint.WebPartPages;

namespace $safeprojectname$
{
  [DefaultProperty("Text"),
  ToolboxData("<{0}:$ClassName$ runat=server></{0}:$ClassName$>"),
  XmlRoot(Namespace = "$safeprojectname$")]
    public class $ClassName$ : WebPart
    {
      protected override void RenderWebPart(HtmlTextWriter output)
```

```
    {
      string htmlcode = "Hello World";
      output.Write(SPEncode.HtmlEncode(htmlcode));
    }
  }
}
```

All arguments preceded by a $ will be replaced once the project is created. Some values are entered in the wizard by the developer, and some values will have dynamic values based on other values. For example, we have decided that the default namespace of a solution will be identical to the solution name. The assembly.info file is another file that will be added to a project once a web part library project is created. It contains general information about the web part library assembly, and looks similar to WebPart.cs in that it uses arguments preceded by $. Add Listing 1-15 to assembly.info:

Listing 1-15. *Assembly.info*

```
using System.Reflection;
using System.Runtime.CompilerServices;
using System.Runtime.InteropServices;

[assembly: AssemblyTitle("$projectname$")]
[assembly: AssemblyDescription("")]
[assembly: AssemblyConfiguration("")]
[assembly: AssemblyCompany("$registeredorganization$")]
[assembly: AssemblyProduct("$projectname$")]
[assembly: AssemblyCopyright("Copyright © $registeredorganization$ $year$")]
[assembly: AssemblyTrademark("")]
[assembly: AssemblyCulture("")]
[assembly: Guid("$guid1$")]

[assembly: AssemblyVersion("1.0.0.0")]
[assembly: AssemblyFileVersion("1.0.0.0")]
```

Not only will we define a new project template, we also want to add a new item template that makes adding items that are related to the development of SharePoint legacy web parts easier. Create a new Visual Studio template in the Templates ➤ Items folder called WebPartTemplate. vstemplate (at this point, just an empty file). Then, add a new item template called WebPart.dwp. Leave the item template empty for now. This item template is responsible for creating a .dwp file. DWP files contain information about web parts. Add the XML in Listing 1-16 to the Visual Studio template (WebPartTemplate.vstemplate):

Listing 1-16. *Adding a Web Part (DWP) Item Template to the WebPartTemplate.vstemplate*

```
<VSTemplate Version="2.0.0" Type="Item" ➡
xmlns="http://schemas.microsoft.com/developer/vstemplate/2005">
  <TemplateData>
    <Name>Web Part Dwp</Name>
    <Description>Web Part Description File</Description>
    <Icon Package="{FAE04EC1-301F-11d3-BF4B-00C04F79EFBC}" ID="4515" />
    <ProjectType>CSharp</ProjectType>
    <SortOrder>10</SortOrder>
    <DefaultName>WebPart.dwp</DefaultName>
  </TemplateData>
  <TemplateContent>
    <ProjectItem ReplaceParameters="true">WebPart.dwp</ProjectItem>
  </TemplateContent>
```

```
<WizardExtension>
  <Assembly>
    Microsoft.Practices.RecipeFramework.VisualStudio, Version=1.0.60429.0, ➥
    Culture=neutral, PublicKeyToken=b03f5f7f11d50a3a
  </Assembly>
  <FullClassName>
    Microsoft.Practices.RecipeFramework.VisualStudio.Templates.UnfoldTemplate
  </FullClassName>
</WizardExtension>
<WizardData>
  <Template xmlns=http://schemas.microsoft.com/pag/gax-template ➥
  SchemaVersion="1.0" Recipe="NewItemClass"/>
</WizardData>
</VSTemplate>
```

The item template (WebPart.dwp) is used when the developer wants to add a .dwp file to the project. The item template uses a recipe called NewItemClass, which is discussed later. Add Listing 1-17 to the item template (WebPart.dwp):

Listing 1-17. *The Web Part Description Item Template*

```
<?xml version="1.0" encoding="utf-8"?>
<WebPart xmlns="http://schemas.microsoft.com/WebPart/v2">
  <Title>$TitleWebPart$</Title>
  <Description>$DescriptionWebPart$</Description>
  <Assembly>$AssemblyName$</Assembly>
  <TypeName>$Namespace$.$ClassName$</TypeName>
</WebPart>
```

All arguments preceded by a $ are replaced once the developer creates a new .dwp file. Now you have seen the solution template, the project template, the item template, and all corresponding files. The last file that needs to be changed, which we have not discussed yet, is WebPartLibrary.xml.

You can find WebPartLibrary.xml directly underneath the project node in the Solution Explorer (the root folder of the WebPartLibrary project). This file contains the XML configuration code, containing all the recipes, actions, and wizards that are relevant within this guidance package. The first part of the WebPartLibrary.xml file contains a recipe called BindingRecipe. The <Action> element contains a reference to the item template called WebPartTemplate.vstemplate. The <Arguments> element contains all arguments that are asked for in the first wizard page when you create the solution. Listing 1-18 shows the contents of WebPartLibrary.xml:

Listing 1-18. *WebPartLibrary.xml*

```
<Recipe Name="BindingRecipe">
  <Types>
    <TypeAlias Name="RefCreator" ➥
    Type="Microsoft.Practices.RecipeFramework.Library.Actions. ➥
    CreateUnboundReferenceAction, Microsoft.Practices.RecipeFramework.Library"/>
  </Types>
  <Caption>Creates unbound references to the guidance package</Caption>
  <Actions>
    <Action Name="CreateSampleUnboundItemTemplateRef" Type="RefCreator" ➥
    AssetName="Items\WebPartTemplate.vstemplate" ➥
    ReferenceType="WebPartLibrary.References.ClassLibraryReference, ➥
    WebPartLibrary" />
  </Actions>
</Recipe>
```

```
<Recipe Name="CreateSolution">
  <Caption>Collects information for the new sample solution.</Caption>
  <Arguments>
    <Argument Name="ProjectName">
      <Converter Type="Microsoft.Practices.RecipeFramework. ➥
      Library.Converters.NamespaceStringConverter, ➥
      Microsoft.Practices.RecipeFramework.Library"/>
    </Argument>
    <Argument Name="ClassName">
      <Converter Type="Microsoft.Practices.RecipeFramework. ➥
      Library.Converters.NamespaceStringConverter, ➥
      Microsoft.Practices.RecipeFramework.Library"/>
    </Argument>
  </Arguments>
  <GatheringServiceData>
    <Wizard xmlns="http://schemas.microsoft.com/pag/gax-wizards" ➥
    SchemaVersion="1.0">
      <Pages>
        <Page>
          <Title>Initial values for the new solution</Title>
          <Fields>
            <Field Label="Project Name" ValueName="ProjectName" />
            <Field Label="Class Name" ValueName="ClassName" />
          </Fields>
        </Page>
      </Pages>
    </Wizard>
  </GatheringServiceData>
</Recipe>
```

The next recipe (shown in Listing 1-19) that is important within the web part library template is called NewItemClass. This recipe contains all arguments that are collected by the wizard when you create a .dwp file. Some arguments have default values, such as assembly name and namespace.

Listing 1-19. *Recipe for the New Item Class*

```
<Recipe Name="NewItemClass" Recurrent="true">
  <xi:include href="TypeAlias.xml" xmlns:xi="http://www.w3.org/2001/XInclude" />
  <Caption>Collects information from the user</Caption>
  <Description></Description>
  <HostData>
    <Icon ID="1429"/>
    <CommandBar Name="Project" />
  </HostData>
  <Arguments>
    <Argument Name="CurrentProject" Type="EnvDTE.Project, EnvDTE, ➥
    Version=8.0.0.0, Culture=neutral, PublicKeyToken=b03f5f7f11d50a3a">
      <ValueProvider Type="Microsoft.Practices.RecipeFramework. ➥
      Library.ValueProviders.FirstSelectedProject, ➥
      Microsoft.Practices.RecipeFramework.Library" />
    </Argument>
    <Argument Name="Namespace">
      <Converter Type="Microsoft.Practices.RecipeFramework. ➥
      Library.Converters.NamespaceStringConverter, ➥
      Microsoft.Practices.RecipeFramework.Library"/>
      <ValueProvider Type="Evaluator" Expression= ➥
      "$(CurrentProject.Properties.Item('DefaultNamespace').Value)" />
    </Argument>
```

```xml
<Argument Name="AssemblyName">
  <Converter Type="Microsoft.Practices.RecipeFramework. ➥
  Library.Converters.NamespaceStringConverter, ➥
  Microsoft.Practices.RecipeFramework.Library" />
  <ValueProvider Type="Evaluator" Expression="$(CurrentProject.Name)" />
</Argument>
<Argument Name="ClassName">
  <Converter Type="Microsoft.Practices.RecipeFramework. ➥
  Library.Converters.NamespaceStringConverter, ➥
  Microsoft.Practices.RecipeFramework.Library"/>
</Argument>
<Argument Name="TitleWebPart">
  <Converter Type="Microsoft.Practices.RecipeFramework. ➥
  Library.Converters.NamespaceStringConverter, ➥
  Microsoft.Practices.RecipeFramework.Library"/>
</Argument>
<Argument Name="DescriptionWebPart">
  <Converter Type="Microsoft.Practices.RecipeFramework. ➥
  Library.Converters.NamespaceStringConverter, ➥
  Microsoft.Practices.RecipeFramework.Library"/>
</Argument>
</Arguments>
<GatheringServiceData>
  <Wizard xmlns="http://schemas.microsoft.com/pag/gax-wizards" ➥
SchemaVersion="1.0">
    <Pages>
      <Page>
        <Title>
          Collect information using editors, converters and value providers.
        </Title>
        <Fields>
          <Field ValueName="AssemblyName" Label="Assembly Name">
            <Tooltip></Tooltip>
          </Field>
          <Field ValueName="Namespace" Label="Namespace">
            <Tooltip></Tooltip>
          </Field>
          <Field ValueName="ClassName" Label="Classname Web Part">
            <Tooltip></Tooltip>
          </Field>
          <Field ValueName="TitleWebPart" Label="Title Web Part">
            <Tooltip></Tooltip>
          </Field>
          <Field ValueName="DescriptionWebPart" Label="Description Web Part">
            <Tooltip></Tooltip>
          </Field>
        </Fields>
      </Page>
    </Pages>
  </Wizard>
</GatheringServiceData>
</Recipe>
```

After customizing the code and creating your own templates, build the project and register it.
You can do this by right-clicking the WebPartLibrary project file and selecting Register Guidance

Package. This launches a recipe that is associated with the guidance package. The recipe registers the package you are developing on your computer. Registration is a form of installation that you can perform without leaving the Visual Studio development environment. It is also possible to un-register the package: this will reverse the registration.

After registering the guidance package, you can open a new instance of Visual Studio to test the functionality of the package.

Installing and Using the Web Part Library Template

In this section, we will show you how to install and use the web part library template. Download the WebPartLibrarySetup.msi file from our web site (http://www.lcbridge.nl/download). You can install the web part library template by double-clicking the Windows Installer package. Close all instances of Visual Studio .NET 2005 before installing the package. The package will install all assemblies related to the web part library template in a folder dedicated to the guidance package. The Guidance Automation Extensions do not support assemblies in the GAC and will not load assemblies located there, even if the assembly is explicitly referenced in the guidance package. Double-click the .msi file to install the package. This opens a pop-up window with a welcome text, as shown in Figure 1-22.

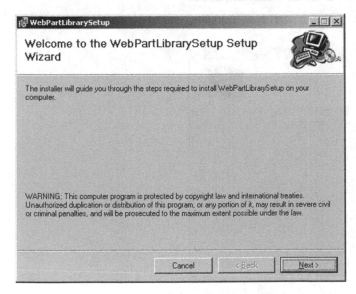

Figure 1-22. *First step of the setup of the web part library template*

Note To create the Windows Installer package, we used the Guidance Automation Toolkit Technology February 2007 CTP version, because the official GAT was not released at the time of this writing.

Next, choose the folder where you want the template to be installed and click Next. See Figure 1-23.

Click Next to start the installation, as shown in Figure 1-24.

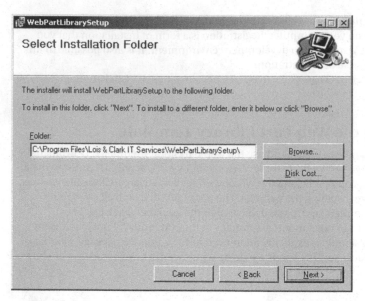

Figure 1-23. *Second step of the setup of the web part library template*

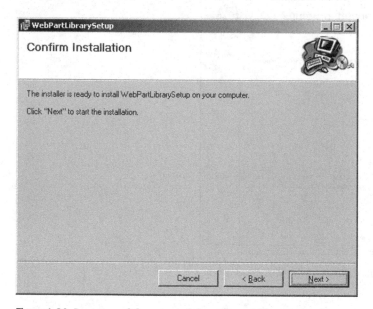

Figure 1-24. *Last step of the setup of the web part library template*

When the installation has succeeded, you will find the web part library template under Add and Remove Programs, as seen in Figure 1-25. This is where you can remove or repair the template. You cannot install two versions of the same guidance package at the same time. If you do attempt to install a guidance package with the same name as an existing guidance package, the Guidance Automation Extensions will throw an exception, informing you that you must uninstall the previous instance of the guidance package before installing the new one.

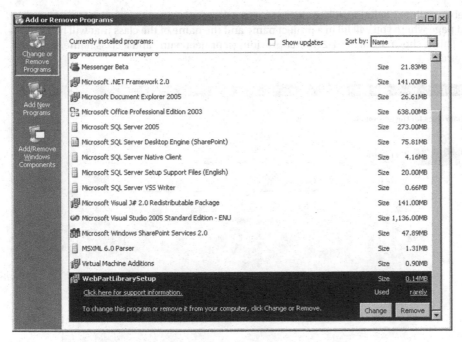

Figure 1-25. *The Add and Remove Programs window*

You will also find evidence of installing the web part library template in Visual Studio 2005. Open Visual Studio 2005 and choose File ➤ New ➤ Project. In the New Project window, you will see a new project type called Guidance Packages. Click Guidance Packages. Underneath it you will find a package called WebPartLibrary. In the right window pane, you will see a template called WebPartLibrary Solution, as shown in Figure 1-26.

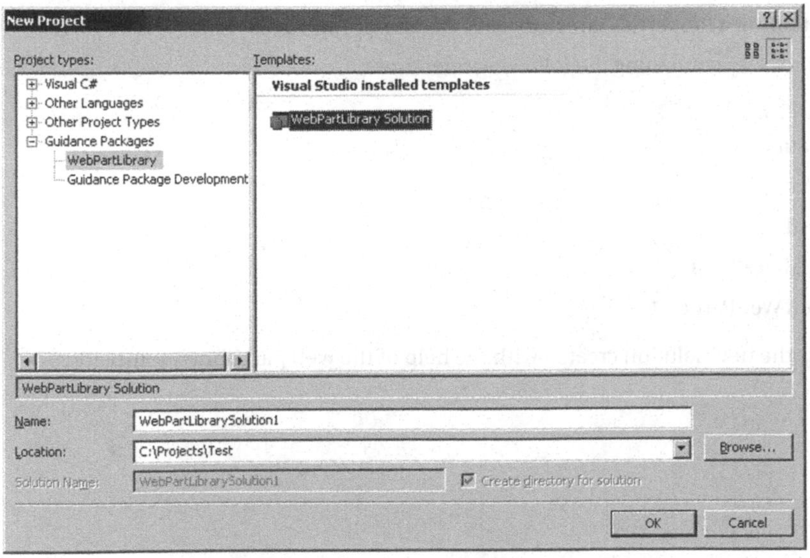

Figure 1-26. *Choose a project in Visual Studio 2005.*

Click WebPartLibrary Solution, fill in a location and a descriptive name, and click OK. This will start a wizard page where you will fill in a project name and the name of the class that will be created initially. This is shown in Figure 1-27. After providing a project name and a class name, you can finish the wizard.

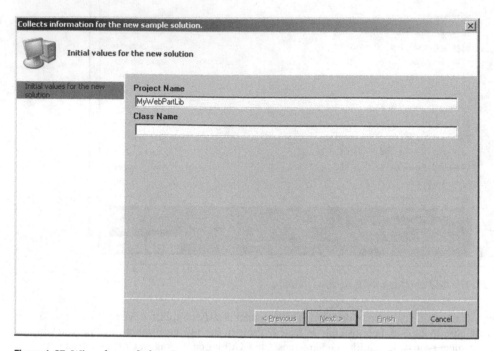

Figure 1-27. *Wizard page belonging to the project creation*

A couple of things will be created at this point:

- A solution containing a Properties directory with an assembly.info file
- A References directory containing the following references:
    - System
    - System.Data
    - System.Web
    - System.Xml
    - Microsoft.SharePoint
- A class file called WebPart.cs

Figure 1-28 shows the new solution created with the help of the web part library template.

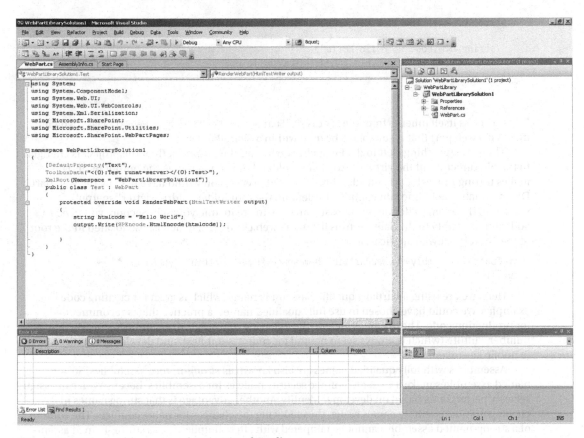

Figure 1-28. *Web part library template in Visual Studio*

The WebPart.cs class contains the code shown in Listing 1-20:

Listing 1-20. *Generated Code in a Web Part Created Using the Custom Web Part Library Template*

```
using System;
using System.ComponentModel;
using System.Web.UI;
using System.Web.UI.WebControls;
using System.Xml.Serialization;
using Microsoft.SharePoint;
using Microsoft.SharePoint.Utilities;
using Microsoft.SharePoint.WebPartPages;

namespace WebPartLibrarySolution1
{
  [DefaultProperty("Text"),
  ToolboxData("<{0}:Test runat=server></{0}:Test>"),
  XmlRoot(Namespace = "WebPartLibrarySolution1")]
  public class Test : WebPart
  {
```

```
  protected override void RenderWebPart(HtmlTextWriter output)
  {
    string htmlcode = "Hello World";
    output.Write(SPEncode.HtmlEncode(htmlcode));
  }
  }
}
```

The class itself inherits from the `Microsoft.SharePoint.WebPartPages.WebPart` class, which makes it a web part that is suitable to be used within a SharePoint site.

There are two things left to do. First, check whether the output path of the project is changed to the bin directory of the virtual server's root folder. If it is not, change the output path. This makes testing the web part considerably easier. Otherwise, you would have to copy the web part DLL manually each time you compile. By default, the root folder is [drive letter]\inetpub\ wwwroot. If the bin folder does not exist, you have to create one yourself. Second, you need to add your assembly to the SafeControls list in the web.config file, which is also located in the root of the SharePoint web application.

```
<SafeControl Assembly="MyWebPartLib" Namespace="MyWebPartLib" TypeName="*" ➡
Safe="True" />
```

Here, we are using a partially qualified assembly name, which is great for creating code examples. We could have chosen to use fully qualified names, a practice that is recommended for production code. Those names include the following information: assembly name, version number, culture (which is always set to neutral for code assemblies), and developer identity (a public key token).

Assemblies with fully qualified names are also known as *strong-named* assemblies. Strong-named assemblies make it easier to enforce security policies for assemblies, because you can assign security permissions based on developer identity. Another advantage is that strong names make creating unique assembly names easier, thus reducing the chances for name conflicts. The content of a strong-named assembly cannot be tampered with after compilation, as strong-named assemblies contain a hash code representing the binary content of the assembly. This hash code is unique for every assembly, and the .NET CLR makes sure the hash code matches the assembly content during load time. If someone has tampered with your assembly after compilation, the hash code will not match the content and will not be loaded. A final advantage is that version policies are only applied to strong-named assemblies, not to assemblies with partially qualified names. Strong names are mandatory for assemblies that need to be installed in the GAC. The next code fragment shows a SafeControl entry for a strong-named assembly:

```
<SafeControl Assembly="MyWebPartLib" Namespace="MyWebPartLib, ➡
Version=1.0.0.0, Culture=neutral, ➡
PublicKeyToken=71e9bce111e9429d" TypeName="*" ➡
Safe="True" />
```

If you want to register your web part on a SharePoint site via a Web Part Description File, you can create one by right-clicking your project and choosing Add New Item. Under Categories, you will find a new category called WebPartLibrary. Click this category and choose the template called Web Part Dwp. Give the .dwp file a descriptive name and click Add. Figure 1-29 shows the Add New Item window.

■**Note** SharePoint 2003 used .dwp (Dashboard web part) files to describe web parts. In ASP.NET 2.0, similar XML files with the extension .webpart are used for the same purpose. This version of the web part library template does not contain an item template that corresponds to .webpart files, although such a template is easy to add. Microsoft Office SharePoint Server 2007 supports the use of both web part description formats. If you are using a (legacy) .dwp file to import a web part, the web part needs to derive from the `Microsoft.SharePoint.WebPartPages.WebPart` class. Failing to do so results in an error message when you try to add the web part to a web part zone.

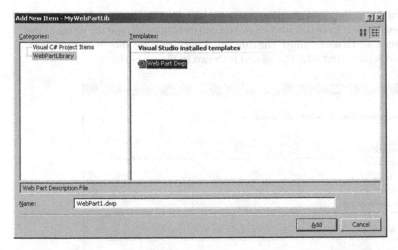

Figure 1-29. *The Add New Item window in Visual Studio 2005*

You can also create a .dwp file by right-clicking your project and then choosing Web Part Dwp, as you can see in Figure 1-30. This will open the Add New Item window as well.

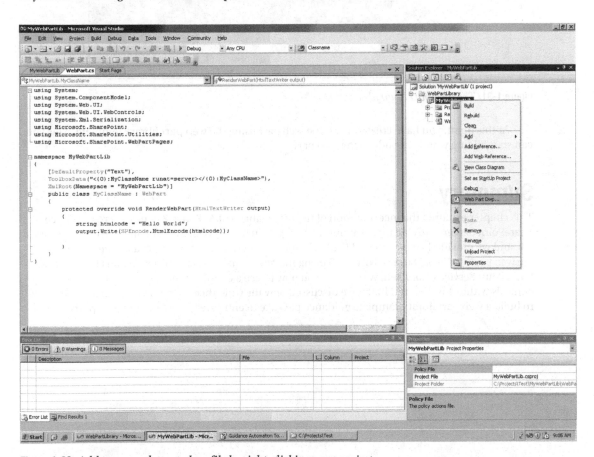

Figure 1-30. *Add a new web part .dwp file by right-clicking your project.*

This will start a wizard that collects information about the Web Part Description file. The assembly name and namespace will have default values. You will only have to type the name of the class, a title for your web part, and a description. The title and description are shown on the Share-Point site page the web part is imported into. The wizard is shown in Figure 1-31.

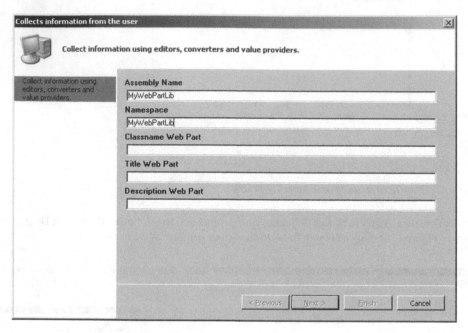

Figure 1-31. *The web part .dwp file wizard*

At this point, you have created your first web part using the web part library template. Now you can start adding your own code to the web part.

Summary

This chapter explored the incorporation of the new features of ASP.NET 2.0 into Microsoft Office SharePoint Server 2007. We talked about the integration between SharePoint and .NET Framework 2.0, and we provided an overview of the basic anatomy of web parts. Then, you learned how to create web parts in Visual Studio .NET 2005 using the new Visual Studio 2005 extensions for Windows SharePoint Services 3.0. Then, we showed you how to use a couple of the new ASP.NET 2.0 server controls within a web part. Finally, we discussed how the Guidance Automation Toolkit can be used to build a web part library template guidance package to enhance the creation of web parts.

CHAPTER 2

■ ■ ■

Creating Interactive Web Parts Using ASP.NET Ajax

Ajax and ASP.NET Ajax deliver compelling web sites that are highly responsive and offer a great user experience. You may have heard this before, and the person who told you was not lying. Ajax makes it possible to perform asynchronous communication with a server, and makes creating advanced user interfaces using JavaScript a lot easier. ASP.NET Ajax is a Microsoft implementation of Ajax.

This chapter describes what Ajax and ASP.NET Ajax are and provides an overview of the more popular ASP.NET Ajax implementations. We will also explain how to create Ajax server-side applications within the confines of a Microsoft Office SharePoint Server 2007 environment. Then we detail how to deal with the client side of Ajax within SharePoint web parts and take a look at server-side response types. From that point on, the chapter is dedicated solely to ASP.NET Ajax. We discuss several realistic examples where ASP.NET Ajax enhances the user experience within SharePoint web parts.

What Are Ajax and ASP.NET Ajax?

Ajax stands for *Asynchronous JavaScript and XML* and has been around for quite a long time. Ajax is a set of technologies that enables parts of a page to communicate directly with the server. If needed, communication can be performed asynchronously. Ajax uses a mixture of DHTML, JavaScript, and XMLHTTP to enrich the browser user interface.

Ajax-style applications really shine when you need to perform actions that take a long time to complete and you do not want to force the end user to wait. Typical examples are complex calculations, advanced form and field validation scenarios, data retrieval over slow remote connections, retrieval of huge amounts of information (for instance, scrolling a large map using Google maps or the slider functionality of Farecast.com), or data retrieval from multiple remote resources. Ajax is also great for server-polling scenarios, where you continually refresh parts of a page with the latest information, as well as in-place submission scenarios that allow users to submit information to the server without refreshing the entire page, thus providing a nice user experience. (Take a look at the feedback functionality of Amazon.com.) Ajax's rich interaction comes close to that of Windows applications.

During the last two years or so, Ajax has become quite popular. One reason is because not only do all popular browsers now support the capability to communicate directly between client and server, without requiring a complete page postback, but, because of the emergence of Ajax frameworks, interacting with those object models has become significantly easier. Another important reason why Ajax has become popular is because processor speeds of client computers are high and bandwith available to the general public has become quite decent too.

Another reason has to do with the maturity level of Ajax-style development. In its infancy, Ajax-style development included a lot of manual work. The same was true for server-side web development. ASP.NET solved many of the complexities involved in developing the server side of web applications. Now, modern Ajax frameworks such as ASP.NET Ajax solve many of the complexities of the client side of web development.

The result of Ajax-style development is a new generation of web applications that are responsive and interactive, provide advanced user interfaces, and are capable of processing data in real time.

Creating Ajax-style applications is not simple, because you have to understand the different object models each browser offers. Browser compatibility issues can be a real hassle when doing client-side development. Another disadvantage is that a significant amount of the development work is spent creating JavaScript script libraries. JavaScript is object based instead of object oriented and is type-unsafe. The JavaScript development experience does not compare to doing ASP.NET server-based development, and although there are plenty of JavaScript debugger tools around, generally, the JavaScript debugging experience is not nearly as rich as the ASP.NET debugging experience.

ASP.NET Ajax, the logical next step in the evolution of Ajax-style applications, tries to solve these problems. ASP.NET Ajax is a framework built on top of .NET 2.0 that allows developers to create Ajax-style applications combining client script libraries with the ASP.NET 2.0 server-based development framework. This makes it easy to add rich client-side behavior to ASP.NET 2.0 web applications. ASP.NET Ajax provides a set of object-oriented application programming interfaces (APIs) that make JavaScript development easier, and also offers cross-browser compatibility. ASP.NET Ajax also ships with a set of Ajax-enabled controls, the ASP.NET Control Extenders library, and offers UpdatePanels that allow you to use existing ASP.NET controls in Ajax scenarios. Finally, ASP.NET Ajax offers integrated Visual Studio 2005 development tools for client-side development, offering features such as debugging and statement completion.

The focus of ASP.NET Ajax is broader than Ajax. Ajax focuses on asynchronous communication with the server. ASP.NET Ajax is very capable of taking care of that, but goes a step further. ASP.NET Ajax tries to make client-side development easier, letting you create advanced user interfaces. The ASP.NET Ajax control toolkit (found at http://ajax.asp.net) offers a set of controls that are very easy to use and would require advanced JavaScript coding to implement yourself. At the time of this writing, the toolkit (the 2007-03-01 release) contained over 30 controls. In the section "Building an Autocompletion Web Part," you will learn how to use one of those controls. We will show a couple of screenshots to whet your appetite:

- *DragPanel*: This control is shown in Figure 2-1 and allows you to define page sections that can be dragged around the page.

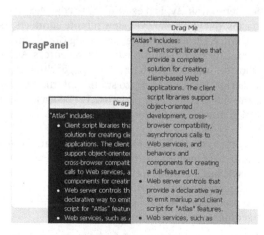

Figure 2-1. *The DragPanel control*

- *Hover Menu*: This control is shown in Figure 2-2 and lets you associate a control with a pop-up panel to display additional content.

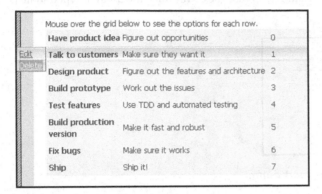

Figure 2-2. *The Hover Menu control*

- *PopupControl*: This control is shown in Figure 2-3 and can be attached to any control to open a pop-up window that displays additional content.

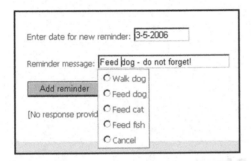

Figure 2-3. *The PopupControl*

- *Reorder List*: This control is shown in Figure 2-4 and implements a bulleted databound list with items that can be reordered interactively.

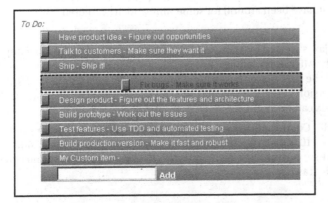

Figure 2-4. *The Reorder List control*

- *Text Box Watermark*: This control is shown in Figure 2-5 and can be attached to an ASP.NET text box control to add watermark behavior. This lets you display a default message in a text box (for example, Type First Name Here) that goes away once the user has typed some text into the text box.

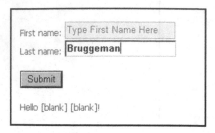

Figure 2-5. *The Text Box Watermark control*

- *Toggle Button*: This control is shown in Figure 2-6 and can be attached to the ASP.NET check box control to enable the use of custom images to show the state of the check box.

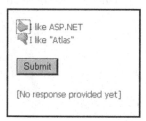

Figure 2-6. *The Toggle Button control*

Ajax Frameworks for ASP.NET

As a testament to the popularity of Ajax, if you search for it on the Internet, you will probably find a couple dozen Ajax implementations. There are Ajax frameworks written in JavaScript, C++, Java, ColdFusion, Lisp, Perl, PHP, Python, and the list goes on. Even if you limit the search to .NET frameworks, you will find more than 10 of them. The following list provides an overview of the well-known Ajax frameworks that have been around for some time and are targeted toward ASP.NET:

- *ASP.NET Ajax*: ASP.NET Ajax is created by Microsoft and as such is probably the most important Ajax framework on the Microsoft platform. ASP.NET Ajax integrates an extensive set of client script libraries with the rich, server-based development platform of ASP.NET 2.0. At the time of this writing, version 1.0 of ASP.NET Ajax was the latest official release. More information about ASP.NET Ajax can be found at http://ajax.asp.net.

- *ComfortASP.NET*: Internally, ComfortASP.NET uses a mixture of DHTML, JavaScript, and XMLHTTP, and reduces HTML traffic. The developer only implements pure server-side ASP.NET. ComfortASP.NET supports ASP.NET 1.1 and ASP.NET 2.0. More information can be found at http://www.comfortasp.de/.

- *MagicAjax.NET*: MagicAjax.NET is an open-source framework that lets you put Ajax-enabled controls on a web page within an Ajax panel. MagicAjax.NET does not require you to write any JavaScript. MagicAjax.NET supports ASP.NET 1.1 and ASP.NET 2.0. More information can be found at http://www.magicajax.net.

- *Outpost*: Outpost is a free framework that gets the HTML of page controls that have been changed and transports the changes automatically to the client in a hidden postback. Outpost supports ASP.NET 1.1 and ASP.NET 2.0. More information can be found at http://csharpedge.blogspot.com.

- *FastPage*: FastPage is a commercial framework that is easy to use, install, and configure. FastPage supports ASP.NET 1.1 and ASP.NET 2.0. More information can be found at http://fastpage.more.at.

■**Note** The web site http://www.ajaxpatterns.org is an excellent resource if you are looking for information about Ajax. The DotNet Ajax Frameworks page on this site (http://ajaxpatterns.org/DotNet_Ajax_Frameworks) contains an up-to-date list of all Ajax frameworks for ASP.NET.

As you can see, when it comes to choosing an Ajax framework for .NET, you have plenty of choices. With the ASP.NET Ajax framework being an exception, all frameworks offer support for ASP.NET 1.1 as well as ASP.NET 2.0. ASP.NET Ajax only offers support for ASP.NET 2.0. Most of the frameworks are free.

When choosing a framework, we prefer not to focus on the current features of a framework, per se. We are more interested in where the framework will be two or three years from now. We don't doubt that ASP.NET Ajax will become the primary framework for .NET developers who are doing Ajax-style development in ASP.NET 2.0 applications. As a result, in this chapter we have chosen to focus on ASP.NET Ajax and ignore the other .NET Ajax implementations.

Adding Service Virtualization to a Web Service

If you want to incorporate Ajax into your SharePoint applications, it is likely that the Ajax client side communicates with a server side implemented using web services. In this section, we will show how to create a .NET 2.0 web service in a Microsoft Office SharePoint Server 2007 environment and how to call such a web service within the context of a SharePoint site. Service virtualization is the process where you change the end point address of the web service at runtime instead of using a static address, allowing you to run the web service within the context of a SharePoint site.

In this section, we will create a test web service that we will call AskMe. Before you can use Visual Studio 2005 to create a web service, you need to do some manual work. First, using Windows Explorer, you need to create a destination folder for your web service. Then you need to create a new virtual directory in Internet Information Services Manager for this folder. The following steps describe how to create a virtual directory in Internet Information Services 6.0 for a test web service project called AskMe that is created later on:

1. Open Windows Explorer.

2. Create a folder called AskMe in [drive letter]:\inetpub\wwwroot.

3. Choose Start ➤ Run. Type **inetmgr** and click OK.

4. Expand the Local Computer node.

5. Expand the Web Sites node.

6. Expand the Default Web Site node.

7. Locate the AskMe folder, right-click it, and choose Properties.

8. On the AskMe Properties page, click Create.

9. Click OK.

Now you can use Visual Studio 2005 to create the AskMe web service project. In the following steps, you will create a web service project called AskMe and add a class to it called Mediator:

1. Open Visual Studio 2005.

2. Choose File ➤ New ➤ Web Site.

3. On the New Web Site screen, click ASP.NET Web Service.

4. Make sure Location is set to HTTP.

5. Set the URL to http://localhost/AskMe.

6. Click OK.

7. Right-click Service.asmx ➤ Delete ➤ OK.

8. Right-click the http://localhost/AskMe/ project ➤ Add New Item.

9. On the Add New Item – http://localhost/AskMe/ screen, choose the following item template: Web Service.

10. Enter the name **Mediator.asmx**.

11. Make sure the Place Code in Separate File check box is checked.

12. Click Add.

By default, a HelloWorld() method is added to Mediator.asmx. This is the method we will use to validate whether the AskMe web service project works. You can precompile the AskMe web service project if you want, but in ASP.NET 2.0 you no longer need to compile your code and put the assembly into the bin folder. The actual code for Mediator.asmx is placed in a code-behind class called Mediator.cs. The Mediator.cs class is located in the App_Code folder. If you open a browser and navigate to http://localhost/askme/mediator.asmx, you can see that the AskMe web service project works as expected.

If all you want to do is create a general web service, you are finished. If you want to create a web service that will run in a given SharePoint context (which allows you easy access to information in this context, such as the CurrentWeb object that allows access to the current SharePoint site in the context), things get a bit more complex. Web services that need to run in a given SharePoint context are stored in a virtual folder called _vti_bin. This is a virtual directory in IIS that is mapped to the [drive letter]:\Program Files\Common Files\Microsoft Shared\web server extensions\12\ISAPI folder. The name of the _vti_bin folder originates from a company called Vermeer Technologies Incorporated, which was acquired by Microsoft in the beginning of 1996. Vermeer Technologies created the original version of FrontPage. The _vti_bin folder is a special Common Gateway Interface (CGI)–like folder that contains server-side functionality that needs to be available within the entire virtual server. On a SharePoint server, the _vti_bin folder is where the default SharePoint web service files are stored.

■**Note** The influence of Vermeer Technologies on SharePoint technology does not stop with the folder name. Microsoft Office SharePoint Server 2007 uses a customized version of FrontPage Server Extensions. This is why SharePoint Designer can be used to adjust SharePoint sites. This is also why you should never install FrontPage Server Extensions on a SharePoint server.

If you reference a web service in the context of a given SharePoint site, the web service will have access to this context. For example, suppose you create the Mediator.asmx file within the AskMe web service and add it to _vti_bin. Its URL would be `http://localhost/_vti_bin/Mediator.asmx`. If you create a SharePoint site called Ajax, you can reference Mediator.asmx within the context of the SharePoint site via the following URL: `http://localhost/ajax/_vti_bin/Mediator.asmx`. We will look at this in more detail later.

Since our web service only supports a method that returns a greeting to the world, it will not help us much to test whether the web service runs successfully within a given SharePoint context. In the next step, remove the `HelloWorld()` method and replace it with a `GetCurrentSiteName()` method that returns the name of the SharePoint site in which the AskMe web service is running. In order to do that, you need to set a reference to Microsoft.SharePoint.dll, which is located in [drive letter]:\Program Files\Common Files\Microsoft Shared\web server extensions\12\ISAPI. Import the `Microsoft.SharePoint.WebControls` namespace. Add the following code to the `GetCurrentSiteName()` method:

```
return SPControl.GetContextWeb(Context).Name;
```

The resulting code looks like Listing 2-1.

Listing 2-1. *The Mediator Web Service*

```
using System;
using System.Web;
using System.Collections;
using System.Web.Services;
using System.Web.Services.Protocols;
using Microsoft.SharePoint.WebControls;

[WebService(Namespace = "http://tempuri.org/")]
[WebServiceBinding(ConformsTo = WsiProfiles.BasicProfile1_1)]
public class Mediator : System.Web.Services.WebService
{
  public Mediator ()
  {
  }

  [WebMethod]
  public string GetCurrentSiteName()
  {
    return SPControl.GetContextWeb(Context).Name;
  }
}
```

Note We have used the `[WebServiceBinding]` attribute to specify that this web service conforms to the Basic Profile 1.1 specification. This instructs Visual Studio 2005 to generate WSDL and ASMX files that adhere to this specification. More information about the Web Services Interoperability Organization (WSI) Basic Profile 1.1 can be found at the following web site: `http://www..ws-i.org`.

At this point, we have created the AskMe web service in a separate virtual folder. Now you will see how to create a web service that can be run within a SharePoint context. First, you will need to create a static discovery (.disco) file and a Web Services Description Language (.wsdl) file using the disco.exe tool. The DISCO protocol is used to discover web services located on a particular domain. A .disco file contains a list of web services and points to their WSDL files. WSDL is a language designed to describe a web service and all its methods. The following procedure explains how to create .disco and .wsdl files for the MediatorService web service:

1. Open a Visual Studio 2005 command prompt.

2. Navigate to the web service folder [drive letter]:\inetpub\wwwroot\AskMe.

3. Run the following command: `disco http://localhost/askme/mediator.asmx`.

As a result, three new files will be created in the AskMe folder: mediator.disco, mediator.wsdl, and results.discomap. Results.discomap contains references to the .wsdl and .disco files and can be used to generate web service proxy classes via the WSDL tool. In this example, we will use Visual Studio 2005 to locate the AskMe web service and create a web service proxy class. Because of this, the results.discomap file is irrelevant in this example.

The two files that are important in the example are mediator.disco and mediator.wsdl. The `Microsoft.SharePoint` namespace needs to be registered within both of the files. To do this, open the files in any text editor. In both files, locate the following line: `<?xml version="1.0" encoding="utf-8"?>`. Replace this line with the following lines of code:

```
<%@ Page Language="C#" Inherits="System.Web.UI.Page"%>
<%@ Assembly Name="Microsoft.SharePoint, Version=11.0.0.0, ➡
    Culture=neutral, PublicKeyToken=71e9bce111e9429c" %>
<%@ Import Namespace="Microsoft.SharePoint.Utilities" %>
<%@ Import Namespace="Microsoft.SharePoint" %>
<% Response.ContentType="text/xml"; %>
```

The page directives indicate that the .disco and .wsdl files are no longer XML. XML parsers will not be able to handle these directives. However, the ASP.NET engine will be able to recognize the page directives, so you need to rename both files to .aspx. Rename the mediator.disco file to Mediatordisco.aspx and save the mediator.wsdl file as Mediatorwsdl.aspx. Now you need to add support for service virtualization. This means that it needs to be possible to change the end point address of the web service at runtime. Instead of using a static address, the address of the web service depends on the context of a request. First, open Mediatordisco.aspx and locate the following line:

```
<contractRef ref="http://localhost/askme/mediator.asmx?wsdl" ➡
docRef="http://localhost/askme/mediator.asmx" ➡
xmlns="http://schemas.xmlsoap.org/disco/scl/" />
```

Replace this line with the following:

```
<contractRef ref=<% SPEncode.WriteHtmlEncodeWithQuote(Response, ➡
SPWeb.OriginalBaseUrl(Request) + "?wsdl", "'"); %> ➡
docRef=<% SPEncode.WriteHtmlEncodeWithQuote(Response, ➡
SPWeb.OriginalBaseUrl(Request), "'"); %> ➡
xmlns="http://schemas.xmlsoap.org/disco/scl/" />
```

Then locate the following line:

```
<soap address="http://localhost/askme/mediator.asmx" xmlns:q1= ➥
"http://tempuri.org/" binding="q1:MediatorSoap" ➥
xmlns="http://schemas.xmlsoap.org/disco/soap/" />
```

Replace it with the following:

```
<soap address=<% SPEncode.WriteHtmlEncodeWithQuote(Response, ➥
SPWeb.OriginalBaseUrl(Request), "'"); %> xmlns:q1= ➥
"http://tempuri.org/" binding="q1: MediatorSoap" ➥
xmlns="http://schemas.xmlsoap.org/disco/soap/" />
```

Now open Mediatorwsdl.aspx, and toward the end of the file, locate the line

```
<soap:address location="http://localhost/askme/mediator.asmx" />
```

and replace it with

```
<soap:address location=<% SPEncode.WriteHtmlEncodeWithQuote( ➥
Response, SPWeb.OriginalBaseUrl(Request), "'"); %> />
```

Find the following line:

```
<soap12:address location="http://localhost/askme/mediator.asmx" />
```

Replace that line with this:

```
<soap12:address location=<% SPEncode.WriteHtmlEncodeWithQuote( ➥
Response, SPWeb.OriginalBaseUrl(Request), "'"); %> />
```

At this point, you have successfully added service virtualization. Move the Mediatordisco.aspx and Mediatorwsdl.aspx pages to the _vti_bin folder ([drive letter]:\Program Files\Common Files\Microsoft Shared\web server extensions\12\ISAPI), because this is where all SharePoint web services are stored. By the way, if you do not move these files, you will no longer be able to compile the AskMe web service.

Because the AskMe web service is written in .NET 2.0 and uses the Microsoft.SharePoint assembly, the _vti_bin folder's web.config file needs to contain a reference to the SharePoint DLL. Add the following XML below the <system.web> element of the web.config file in the _vti_bin folder:

```
<compilation debug="false">
  <assemblies>
    <add assembly="Microsoft.SharePoint, Version=12.0.0.0, ➥
    Culture=neutral, PublicKeyToken=71e9bce111e9429c" />
  </assemblies>
</compilation>
```

The complete web.config file should resemble Listing 2-2.

Listing 2-2. *The web.config File in the _vti_bin Folder*

```
<?xml version="1.0" encoding="UTF-8" standalone="yes"?>
<configuration>
  <system.web>
    <compilation debug="false">
      <assemblies>
        <add assembly="Microsoft.SharePoint, Version=12.0.0.0, ➥
        Culture=neutral, PublicKeyToken=71E9BCE111E9429C"/>
      </assemblies>
    </compilation>
```

```
    <webServices>
      <protocols>
        <remove name="HttpGet" />
        <remove name="HttpPost" />
        <remove name="HttpPostLocalhost" />
        <add name="Documentation" />
      </protocols>
    </webServices>
    <customErrors mode="On"/>
  </system.web>
  <location path="authentication.asmx">
    <system.web>
      <authorization>
        <allow users="*"/>
      </authorization>
    </system.web>
  </location>
  <location path="wsdisco.aspx">
    <system.web>
      <authorization>
        <allow users="*"/>
      </authorization>
    </system.web>
  </location>
  <location path="wswsdl.aspx">
    <system.web>
      <authorization>
        <allow users="*"/>
      </authorization>
    </system.web>
  </location>
</configuration>
```

If you include the Mediator.asmx file in the list of default Windows SharePoint Services web services, it will be easier to reference the web service via Visual Studio 2005. You can do this by opening spdisco.aspx (also located in the _vti_bin folder) and adding the following lines within the `<discovery>` element:

```
<contractRef ref=<% SPEncode.WriteHtmlEncodeWithQuote(Response, ➡
spWeb.Url + "/_vti_bin/Mediator.asmx?wsdl", "'"); %> docRef=<% ➡
SPEncode.WriteHtmlEncodeWithQuote(Response, spWeb.Url + ➡
"/_vti_bin/Mediator.asmx", "'"); %> ➡
xmlns="http://schemas.xmlsoap.org/disco/scl/" />


<soap address=<% SPEncode.WriteHtmlEncodeWithQuote(Response, ➡
spWeb.Url + "/_vti_bin/Mediator.asmx", "'"); %> ➡
xmlns:q1="http://schemas.microsoft.com/sharepoint/soap/directory/" ➡
binding="q1:MediatorSoap" xmlns="http://schemas.xmlsoap.org/disco/soap/" />
```

If you open a browser and go to `http://localhost/_vti_bin/mediator.asmx?WSDL`, you should see a valid web service description file. Now you can add a reference to the web service from within a web part library project and access the SharePoint context from within a web part in this library. In order to complete the following steps, you must create a web part and open it in Visual Studio 2005. If you are not sure how to do this, refer to Chapter 1.

1. From within Visual Studio 2005, create a new project, right-click it, and then choose Add Web Reference.

2. Click the Web Services on the Local Machine link.

3. Locate the Mediator web service and click it.

4. Change the web reference name to MediatorService and click Add Reference.

Now you need to create an instance of the MediatorService web service and set the security credentials that are used for web service client authentication. If you do not set the security credentials correctly (by setting the Credentials property, which is shown in the next code fragment), you will get an "HTTP status 401: Unauthorized" error. You can set the correct SharePoint context via the MediatorService web service's Url property. Assign the following static value: http://localhost/ ajax/_vti_bin/mediator.asmx. This ensures the MediatorService web service is run within the context of the Ajax SharePoint site. You can also set this property dynamically by using the Url property of the current SharePoint site. The following code fragment can be added to any client such as an ASP.NET page or a web part and uses the latter approach:

```
string strValue = String.Empty;
SPWeb objSite = SPControl.GetContextWeb(Context);
strValue = objSite.Url + "/_vti_bin/mediator.asmx";
MediatorService.Mediator objMediator = new MediatorService.Mediator();
objMediator.Credentials = CredentialCache.DefaultCredentials;
objMediator.Url = strValue;
strValue = objMediator.GetCurrentSiteName();
```

Figure 2-7 shows that the web service returns the SharePoint site name from the current context.

Ajax client
Mediator.asmx says the current SharePoint site is: Ajax

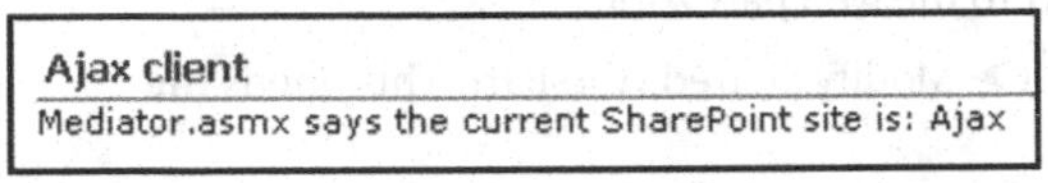

Figure 2-7. *The web service returns the SharePoint site name from the current context.*

As you have seen, creating web services in a Microsoft Office SharePoint Server 2007 environment is easy enough. However, adding service virtualization to such a web service is a bit complex because of the manual steps you have to take. The following is an overview of the steps that we have taken and described in this section to add service virtualization to a web service:

1. Create a web service.

2. In the web service, add a reference to the SharePoint assembly.

3. Use disco.exe to create .disco and .wsdl files.

4. Rename the .disco file and make it an ASP.NET page. Add support for service virtualization to the ASP.NET page.

5. Rename the .wsdl file and make it an ASP.NET page.

6. Add support for service virtualization to the ASP.NET page.

7. Copy both ASP.NET pages to the _vti_bin folder and add, if not yet present, a reference to the SharePoint assembly.

8. Add the web service to the list of default SharePoint web services.

9. Add a reference to the web service within a Visual Studio 2005 project and set the correct security credentials.

JavaScript in Web Parts

Web services are an important part of Ajax-style development. We have already taken an in-depth look at creating web services on a Microsoft Office SharePoint Server 2007 server and adding service virtualization to them. The other important part of Ajax is JavaScript. In this section, we will look in detail at JavaScript development within Microsoft Office SharePoint Server 2007 web parts. A working understanding of the concepts in this section is essential for understanding the rest of this chapter.

The Content Editor Web Part

The easiest way to add JavaScript to a SharePoint page is probably via the Content Editor web part. This method is suitable for simple and ad hoc uses of JavaScript, or to add some nice visual tricks to a SharePoint page. If you want to see an example of the latter, around Christmas time, check out the Snow web part at http://mindsharpblogs.com/todd/archive/2005/12/20/906.aspx. The Content Editor web part can be used to add formatted text, tables, hyperlinks, and images to a web part page. You can also add JavaScript by typing it straight into the Content Editor Web Part Text Entry window, as shown in the next example:

1. Go to a SharePoint page and select Site Actions ➤ Edit Page. This opens the SharePoint page in Edit Mode.

2. Choose a web part zone that is going to hold the Content Editor web part and click the Add a Web Part link. This opens the Add Web Parts — Web Page Dialog window.

3. Locate the Miscellaneous section, select the Content Editor Web Part check box, and click Add. This adds the Content Editor web part to the web part zone.

4. In the Content Editor web part, choose Edit ➤ Modify Shared Web Part. This opens the Content Editor Web Part tool pane.

5. Click the Source Editor... button. This opens the Text Entry — Web Page Dialog window.

6. Type the following JavaScript code in the Text Entry — Web Page Dialog window:

```
<script>alert("hi!");</script>
```

7. Click Save.

The JavaScript code generates a dialog box containing a hello message.

Web Part Tokens

The SharePoint web part framework contains several web part tokens that are used to aid client-side development when creating web parts. The tokens we like to use most are the _WPR_ and _WPQ_ tokens.

When rendered, the _WPR_ token is replaced with the path to the web part resources folder of the SharePoint site containing the web part. The web part resources folder is a predefined folder that can be found in the root of every web application folder. This folder is meant to store web part resources such as images or JavaScript libraries. If you use the _WPR_ token on a SharePoint site called Ajax, the token will be replaced with the following value: http://myserver/Ajax/_wpresources/WPLibrary/ 1.0.0.0_[guid].

■**Note** Another good place to store web part resources is a web resource file. The creation of web resource files is discussed in Chapter 1.

The _WPQ_ token is used to create names that are unique per web part. For example, if you create a JavaScript function called DoSomething(), there is always the possibility that another web part could create a JavaScript function with the same name. If you place the same web part on a page multiple times, you have guaranteed name conflicts. To prevent this type of problem, append the _WPQ_ token to a function name. A function called DoSomething_WPQ_() will be rendered to something like DoSomething[unique name]().

The following lines of code demonstrate the use of web part tokens and can be added to a web part:

```
protected override void RenderContents(HtmlTextWriter writer)
{
    string strValue = SPWebPartManager.ReplaceTokens(Context, ➥
    SPControl.GetContextWeb(Context), ➥
    this, ➥
    "WPQ: _WPQ_ ➥
    WPR: _WPR_ " ➥
    );
    writer.Write(strValue);
}
```

Figure 2-8 shows the result of two instances of the same web part on a single page containing this line of code.

MyWebPart Web Part [1]
WPQ: ctl00_m_g_2a836327_24c1_4d98_aa43_463b283ef1f0 WPR:
http://web1:23456/jfz/test/Ajax/_wpresources/WPLibrary/1.0.0.0__9f4da00116c38ec5

MyWebPart Web Part [2]
WPQ: ctl00_m_g_918dc03e_d4cd_46b4_a234_c7caed82fd72 WPR:
http://web1:23456/jfz/test/Ajax/_wpresources/WPLibrary/1.0.0.0__9f4da00116c38ec5

Figure 2-8. *The web part tokens*

■**Note** The ReplaceTokens() per-instance method of the Microsoft.SharePoint.WebPartPages.WebPart class in SharePoint 2003 used to return names that are more user friendly than the names returned by the per-type ReplaceTokens() method of the SPWebPartManager class. In the section "Client-side Connectable Web Parts and ASP.NET Ajax," later in this chapter, you will see an example of this.

The other available web part tokens are

- _LogonUser_: The _LogonUser_ token specifies the [domain\]user name for the currently logged-on user. The domain part of the user name is optional and does not appy in form-based authentication scenarios.

- _WPID_: The _WPID_ token specifies the control ID of the web part.

- _WebLocaleID_: The _WebLocaleID_ token specifies the locale id of the current web site.

- _WPSRR_: The _WPSRR_ token specifies the server relative class resource path, which can be used to prefix resource URLs for the browser to fetch.

■Note For more information about web part tokens, please refer to the Windows SharePoint Services 3.0 SDK.

Rendering JavaScript Within a Web Part

This section describes how to use JavaScript within web parts. When rendering JavaScript within a web part, you should register an event handler for the PreRender event in the web part constructor and render the JavaScript within the PreRender event handler. This ensures that the web part framework loads the JavaScript before the web part is rendered to the web part page.

The ClientScriptManager class, which is new in ASP.NET 2.0, can be used to manage client-side scripts. You can obtain an instance of the ClientScriptManager class via the ClientScript property of the Page object that is always available within a web part. Use the ClientScriptManager instance to add JavaScript to the page. You can use the IsClientScriptBlockRegistered() method of the ClientScriptManager class to add a JavaScript library (a .js file) to the page. The best place to store the JavaScript library is the web part resources folder. The following code fragment shows how to register a JavaScript library on a web page:

```
if (!Page.ClientScript.IsClientScriptIncludeRegistered ("MyKey1"))
{
  Page.ClientScript.RegisterClientScriptInclude("MyKey1", ➥
  "/wpresources/customlib.js");
}
```

As you can see, a unique key is used to check whether the JavaScript library is already added to the page. Do not use the _WPQ_ token as a key. The _WPQ_ token is used to create names that are guaranteed to be unique within a page. The key used here ensures that no duplicate registrations take place on a single page.

You can also render dynamic pieces of JavaScript code to a page. Use the ClientScriptManager class's RegisterClientScriptBlock() method to do this. The following code fragment shows an example:

```
if (!Page.ClientScript.IsClientScriptBlockRegistered("MyKey2"))
{
  Page.ClientScript.RegisterClientScriptBlock(typeof(string), "MyKey2", ➥
  "alert('test');", true);
}
```

■Note Generally, we prefer to use JavaScript libraries instead of dynamic pieces of JavaScript code. This makes it much easier to write and change the JavaScript code. But a disadvantage is that you cannot work with web part tokens in JavaScript libraries, so you need to take this into consideration when developing web parts. This development style may become a problem when you want to use the same web part multiple times on the same SharePoint page. You can see examples of these approaches in the sections "JavaScript On-Demand Loading" and "Building a Performance Counter Web Part," later in this chapter.

The complete code for a web part registering JavaScript on a page is shown in Listing 2-3.

Listing 2-3. *A Web Part That Renders JavaScript*

```
using System;
using System.Runtime.InteropServices;
using System.Web.UI;
using System.Web.UI.WebControls.WebParts;
using System.Xml.Serialization;
using Microsoft.SharePoint;
using Microsoft.SharePoint.WebControls;
using Microsoft.SharePoint.WebPartPages;

namespace LoisAndClark.Ajax
{
  [Guid("be6ec8e3-2706-4f52-bdf9-f6eb18fc65c0")]
  public class AjaxClient : System.Web.UI.WebControls.WebParts.WebPart
  {
    public AjaxClient()
    {
      PreRender += new EventHandler(AjaxClient_PreRender);
    }

    void AjaxClient_PreRender(object sender, EventArgs e)
    {
      if (!Page.ClientScript.IsClientScriptIncludeRegistered ("MyKey1"))
      {
        Page.ClientScript.RegisterClientScriptInclude("MyKey1", ➥
        "/wpresources/customlib.js");
      }

      if (!Page.ClientScript.IsClientScriptBlockRegistered("MyKey2"))
      {
        Page.ClientScript.RegisterClientScriptBlock(typeof(string), ➥
        "MyKey2", "alert('test');", true);
      }
    }

    protected override void CreateChildControls()
    {
      try
      {
        // ... do stuff...
      }
      catch (Exception err)
      {
        Controls.Add(new LiteralControl(err.Message));
      }
    }
  }
}
```

This web part registers a reference to a custom JavaScript library called customlib.js that should be placed in the wpresources virtual folder of the SharePoint web application holding the web part. The wpresources virtual folder was discussed previously in the section "Web Part Tokens." The web part also renders a dynamic piece of JavaScript that generates an alert message.

JavaScript On-Demand Loading

Ajax-style applications rely heavily on the use of JavaScript. If you add your JavaScript functions to JavaScript script libraries, the end user will have to wait until all script libraries have been loaded. This could take a while, as the complexity of the Ajax application increases, thus defeating the primary purpose of Ajax, which is namely to create a great user experience. In this section, we discuss JavaScript on-demand loading, a technique where JavaScript libraries are loaded as needed.

Note The on-demand approach is applied to the .NET Framework as well. The .NET Common Language Runtime (CLR) loads assemblies as needed (on-demand loading), and Intermediate Language (IL) within an assembly is compiled as needed (just-in-time compilation).

Alas, JavaScript on-demand loading is not done automatically for you. In its simplest form, the JavaScript on-demand approach consists of a piece of JavaScript code calling a web service. The web service does not return a normal response, but instead returns a piece of JavaScript code that is executed via the JavaScript eval() function. The following code fragment shows an example:

```
var strJsCode = CallWebService(); // web service returns "alert('hi');";
eval(strJsCode); // This line is equivalent to: alert('hi');
```

Note The eval() function is built into the JavaScript language; it evaluates a string and parses it on the fly. In SharePoint Portal Server 2001, the eval() function was the core of the web part rendering process. All server-side code in web parts (either VBScript or JavaScript) was retrieved from the web part XML and parsed by the eval() function when the web part was rendered.

The second solution for JavaScript on-demand loading is more sophisticated and more complex to implement. In this approach, a JavaScript function knows which JavaScript library it needs and loads the required library on demand, waits until the JavaScript library is loaded, and then calls a function within the newly loaded library.

In the following example, you should create a new JavaScript library called ondemand.js. Add the JavaScript library to the web part resources folder ([drive letter]:\inetpub\wwwroot\wpresources). The entire content of the ondemand.js JavaScript library looks like this:

```
function OnDemandHello()
{
  alert('on demand hi!');
}
```

We will show how to load this library on demand from another script library that we will call customlib.js. The customlib.js JavaScript library is registered on the page from within a web part via the RegisterClientScriptInclude() method, which was described earlier in the section "Rendering JavaScript Within a Web Part." Suppose the customlib.js library contains a function called CustomLibHello() that wants to call the OnDemandHello() function in the ondemand.js library. The CustomLibHello() function calls a function that adds the ondemand.js script library to the page dynamically, like so:

```
var objHeadElement = document.getElementsByTagName('head')[0];
var objScriptLibrary = document.createElement('script');
objScriptLibrary.id = 'OnDemandScript';
objScriptLibrary.type = 'text/javascript';
objScriptLibrary.src = '/wpresources/ondemand.js';
objHeadElement.appendChild(objScriptLibrary);
```

The JavaScript within the ondemand.js script library will not be loaded immediately, so you will have to check explicitly whether the function you want to call is already available. You can use the following code:

```
if (self.OnDemandHello)
{
  // OnDemandHello is available.
}
```

If the OnDemandHello() function is not available, you should use the setTimeout() function that is a part of the JavaScript language to try again later after *x* number of milliseconds. Listing 2-4 shows how to implement JavaScript on demand for the OnDemandHello() function in the customlib.js JavaScript library.

Listing 2-4. *On-demand Loading in a JavaScript Library*

```
function CustomLibHello()
{
  LoadOnDemand();
}

function LoadOnDemand()
{
  ensureUploadScriptIsLoaded();
  if (self.OnDemandHello == null )
  {
    alert('not yet loaded');
    setTimeout("LoadOnDemand();",2000);
  }
  else
  {
    alert('loaded');
    OnDemandHello();
  }
}

function ensureUploadScriptIsLoaded()
{
  if (self.OnDemandHello)
  {
    // OnDemandHello() is already loaded.
    return;
  }

  var objHeadElement = document.getElementsByTagName('head')[0];
  var objScriptLibrary = document.createElement('script');
  objScriptLibrary.id = 'OnDemandScript';
  objScriptLibrary.type = 'text/javascript';
  objScriptLibrary.src = '/wpresources/ondemand.js';
  objHeadElement.appendChild(objScriptLibrary);
}
```

The technique described in this section is used in advanced scenarios where performance is a problem because of the size of the JavaScript libraries used. Although one of the goals of ASP.NET Ajax is to abstract the use of JavaScript away, there are still situations where it cannot be avoided.

Debugging JavaScript

Although JavaScript is not a very advanced language, you can use Visual Studio 2005 and enjoy a rich debugging experience. If you want to debug JavaScript code, you need to do the following:

1. Open Internet Explorer and click Tools ➤ Internet Options ➤ Advanced. Uncheck Disable Script Debugging.

2. Close the browser and start it again.

Now you can debug JavaScript, as shown in Figure 2-9.

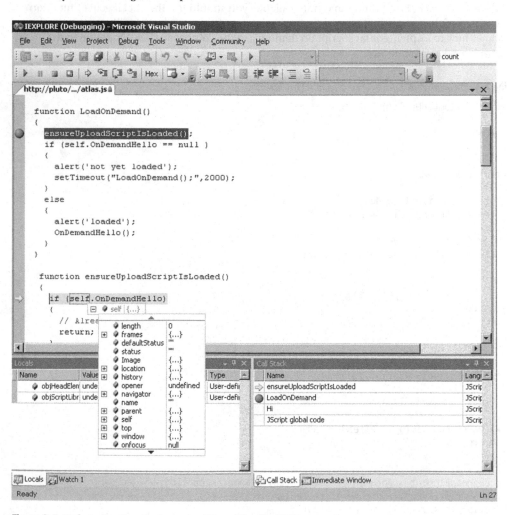

Figure 2-9. *Debugging JavaScript using Visual Studio 2005*

Visual Studio 2008, code-named Orcas, has fantastic improvements when it comes to developing solutions in JavaScript. The following is a list of the most important JavaScript support features in Orcas:

- Full JavaScript InstelliSense completion in .aspx, .htm, and .js files.

- Rich support for ASP.NET Ajax.

- The option to add IntelliSense comments that can be used to provide validation checking and type descriptors. Every JavaScript is of the type object; type descriptors allow you to define the data type that is intended, for example, an integer.

- The ability to create a release version of JavaScript code (a version without documentation, whitespace, and other non-needed content) that results in a JavaScript file that is smaller to download.

- The JavaScript debugger in Orcas allows you to debug run-time documents and switch to design-time documents.

- Type information in debug mode is far richer than it used to be.

- You can see the methods of an object in debug mode.

- You can easily navigate the JavaScript Document Object Model (DOM) visually.

- You can add visualizers to JavaScript objects.

- A proactive completion list makes suggestions while you type.

More information about the JavaScript support in Orcas can be found in the articles "JScript Debugging in Visual Web Developer Orcas" at http://blogs.msdn.com/webdevtools/archive/2007/03/09/jscript-debugging-in-visual-web-developer-orcas.aspx and "JScript IntelliSense in Visual Studio Orcas" at http://blogs.msdn.com/webdevtools/archive/2007/03/02/jscript-intellisense-in-orcas.aspx.

Remote Calls Prior to ASP.NET Ajax

In this section, we discuss how to use client-side JavaScript to communicate with web services without using ASP.NET Ajax. We will discuss techniques that have been available longer and can also be used when doing asynchronous communication with the server. This will in turn help you understand ASP.NET Ajax better.

Retrieving Data via XMLHttpRequest

Microsoft implemented the XMLHttpRequest object for the first time in Internet Explorer 5 as an ActiveX control. In Internet Explorer 7, this object has been implemented as a native script object. This is a good thing, since most companies place additional security restrictions on the use of ActiveX controls.

The purpose of the XMLHttpRequest object is to let clients retrieve and convert XML from the server and use the client-side Document Object Model to do something useful with this data. The following JavaScript code fragment calls a web service method Hi() defined within Mediator.asmx:

```
var objRequest = new ActiveXObject("Msxml2.XMLHTTP");
objRequest.open("POST", "/askme/mediator.asmx/Hi", false);
objRequest.send(null);
var strServerResponse = objRequest.responseText;
alert(strServerResponse);
```

The false option that is passed as an argument to the XMLHttpRequest object's open() method makes the call *synchronous*, meaning that the code will wait until a response comes back. The send() method completes the request. The Hi() method gives a greeting to all its clients, and its response looks like this:

```
<?xml version="1.0" encoding="utf-8" ?>
<string xmlns="http://tempuri.org/">Hi all!</string>
```

If needed, you can also pass arguments to a web service. The following code fragment shows how to pass two arguments to a web service method called Hi2():

```
var strBody = "strFirstArg=MyFirst&strSecondArg=MySecond";
var objRequest = new ActiveXObject("Msxml2.XMLHTTP");
objRequest.open("POST", "/askme/mediator.asmx/Hi2", false);
objRequest.setRequestHeader("Content-Type", ➥
"application/x-www-form-urlencoded");
objRequest.setRequestHeader("Content-Length", strBody.length);
objRequest.send(strBody);
alert(objRequest.responseText);
```

It is beneficial to the user experience to make asynchronous XMLHttpRequest calls, so that the user can continue to work on other tasks while waiting for a response. You can check if the response is ready by calling the readystate property of the XMLHttpRequest object. The readystate property always reflects the current point in the call's life cycle. Initially, upon creation, the state value is 0. After a call it is 1. When the response is back, the value of the readystate property will be 4. In the following asynchronous code example, we will use the XMLHttpRequest object's readystatechange event to define an event handler called OnResponse. The event handler will be called multiple times (once per call state) during the call life cycle. In the OnResponse event handler, we will check the readystate property to see when the response is ready, as shown in Listing 2-5.

Listing 2-5. *Calling a Web Service via the XMLHttpRequest Object*

```
objRequest = new ActiveXObject("Msxml2.XMLHTTP");
objRequest.open("POST", "/askme/mediator.asmx/Hi", true);
objRequest.onreadystatechange = OnResponse;
objRequest.send(null);

function OnResponse()
{
  if ( _objRequest.readyState != 4 )
  {
    alert('not ready yet');
    return;
  }

  // Error checking
  if ( _objRequest.status != 200 )
  {
    alert("unexpected status!");
  }

  var strResponse = _objRequest.responseText;
  alert(strResponse);
}
```

Note In this code example, we are checking for an HTTP status equal to 200, indicating that the request has succeeded. The status code indicating a valid response might be different depending on the content you are requesting. You can find an overview of HTTP status codes at http://www.w3.org/Protocols/rfc2616/ rfc2616-sec10.html.

You can use the XMLHttpRequest object's abort() method to abort a remote call, like this: _objRequest.abort();. Listing 2-6 shows a technique that aborts a remote call after five seconds have passed.

Listing 2-6. *Aborting a Web Service Call*

```
function MyRemoteCall()
{
  objRequest = new ActiveXObject("Msxml2.XMLHTTP");
  objRequest.open("POST", "/askme/mediator.asmx/Hi", true);
  objRequest.onreadystatechange = OnResponse;
  objRequest.send(null);
  setTimeout("Abort()", 5000);
}

function Abort()
{
  objRequest.abort();
  alert("abort");
}

function OnResponse()
{
  if ( _objRequest.readyState != 4 )
  {
    //alert('not ready yet');
    return;
  }

  if ( _objRequest.status != 200 )
  {
    alert("unexpected status!");
  }

  var strResponse = _objRequest.responseText;
  alert(strResponse);
}

MyRemoteCall();
```

In the previous example, you saw how to use the XMLHttpRequest object's responseText property to retrieve the response as a string. You can also retrieve the response as XML directly using the responseXML property, like so:

```
var xmlResponse = _objRequest.responseXML;
alert(xmlResponse.innerXml);
```

Note A weak point of the JavaScript language related to this topic is its inability to handle re-entrancy issues. A piece of code is said to be re-entrant if it can be called recursively and concurrently from multiple processes. This chapter does not discuss how to solve re-entrancy issues in JavaScript, although you can find general information about re-entrant code in the article "Writing Reentrant and Thread-Safe Code" at http://www.unet.univie.ac.at/aix/aixprggd/genprogc/writing_reentrant_thread_safe_code.htm.

Web Service Behavior

XMLHttpRequest is the first step in the evolution of Ajax-style application development. The XML-HttpRequest object makes communicating with web services via JavaScript possible but not easy. The next step in the evolution of building Ajax applications is the WebService behavior, which can be downloaded from the MSDN web site (http://msdn.microsoft.com/archive/default.asp?url=/archive/en-us/samples/internet/behaviors/library/webservice/default.asp). Behaviors are a way of programmatically packaging actions and associating those actions to page elements. The WebService behavior enables client-side script to invoke remote methods exposed by web services that support Simple Object Access Protocol (SOAP) and WSDL. The behavior is a simple, lightweight component that is implemented as an HTML component (HTC) file.

Note If you want to use the WebService behavior within a web part, you need to download it and preferably store it in the web part resources folder.

If you have a choice, we do not recommend using the WebService behavior, because ASP.NET Ajax is even more developer-friendly and the WebService behavior is not officially supported anymore. Having said that, Listing 2-7 shows how to use the WebService behavior. In the example, the behavior is attached to a page element, a <div> with the ID service. The useService() function of the WebService behavior ties the web service to a friendly name that can be used later to call the web service. You can call the web service asynchronously by specifying an event handler that we will call OnGetNameResult.

Listing 2-7. *Using the Web Service Behavior*

```
<html>
<body onload="InitRemoteCall();">
<div id="service" style="behavior:url(webservice.htc)"></div>

<script>
function InitRemoteCall()
{
  service.useService("http://pluto/AskMe/Mediator.asmx?WSDL","Mediator");
  var intId = service.Mediator.callService(OnGetNameResult,
  "GetCurrentSiteName");
}

function OnGetNameResult(objResult)
{
  if ( objResult.error )
  {
    alert(objResult.errorDetail.string + " " + ➥
    objResult.errorDetail.code + " " + objResult.errorDetail.raw);
  }
```

```
    else
    {
      alert(objResult.value);
    }
}
</script>
</body>
</html>
```

The previous example showed how to call the GetCurrentSiteName() web service method without passing any arguments to it. If you want to call a web service via the WebService behavior and pass multiple arguments to the web service, you can do it like this:

```
var intId = service.HelloService.callService(OnGetNameResult, ➥
"GetCurrentSiteName", "arg1", "arg2");
```

■**Note** To ensure that the useService() method works correctly, it should be placed inside a handler for the onload event, so that the first attempt to call a method in the behavior only occurs after the page has been downloaded and parsed. Web services referenced by the useServer() method need to reside on the same domain as the web server.

Web Service Message Types

At this point, you have seen how to create a web service on a Windows SharePoint Services server. You have also seen how to call web services via client-side JavaScript using the XMLHttpRequest object and the WebService behavior. This section is dedicated to discussing the types of responses that can be given by web services.

Plain Text

If a web service just needs to return simple data, a plain text response will be sufficient. If the web service returns a single value, the JavaScript code would use an XMLHttpRequest object to issue a request and store the result in a variable. Calling a web service via XMLHttpRequest was discussed in a previous section, "Retrieving Data via XMLHttpRequest." The part of the code that assigns the web service response to a JavaScript variable would look something like this:

```
var strResponse = _objRequest.responseText;
```

Plain text is suitable for simple data structures as well. Suppose a web service response contains name, city, and country information. The web service could return this information in plain text like this: MyName|MyCity|MyCountry. The advantage of this format is that it contains a minimal amount of information with very little overhead. This is only for simple data structures; if you want to pass complex data structures, you are better off using XML or JavaScript Object Notation (JSON) formats. The section "JSON Messages" later in this chapter discusses JSON in detail. The following code fragment shows an example of accepting a simple data structure in plain text format:

```
// web service response looks like this: MyName|MyCity|MyCountry
var arrResult = objRequest.responseText.split('|');
var strName = arrResult[0];
var strCity = arrResult[1];
var strCountry = arrResult[2];
```

HTML Response

Web service responses can also contain HTML. Now we are entering the domain of Web Services for Remote Portlets (WSRP). We have dedicated Chapter 6 to WSRP, so we will not discuss the ins and outs of returning HTML via a web service here.

The following line of code shows how to use an HTML response and update the contents of a page dynamically using DHTML:

```
document.getElementById('MyDisplay').innerHTML = strHtmlResponse;
```

XML Message

All web service responses are wrapped in XML (SOAP), whether the response itself is plain text, HTML, XML, or JSON. You can choose to work with XML directly in JavaScript. Let's say we have a web service with a method called Hi() that returns the following response (plain text wrapped in XML):

```
<?xml version="1.0" encoding="utf-8" ?>
<string xmlns="http://tempuri.org/">Hi</string>
```

Using the XMLHttpRequest object's responseText property returns the value Hi (in plain text). You can access the XML of the response by using the XMLHttpRequest object's responseXML property. XML can be used to transfer complex data structures and is very flexible. In addition, you can use XML schemas to define the format of an XML message in an unambiguous manner. The following code fragment shows how to work with XML using JavaScript:

```
var objXmlDom = objRequest.responseXML;
alert(objXmlDom.documentElement.firstChild);
```

JSON Messages

JSON (pronounced *Jason*) is a serialization format created in 2002 as (supposedly) a cleaner and lighter alternative to XML. It is possible to express simple as well as complex types in JSON. JSON is based on a subset of the JavaScript programming language and is very easy to parse and generate in a JavaScript programming environment. This makes JSON a well-suited, lightweight data-interchange format for browser-server communication. If you want to learn more about JSON, visit http://www.json.org/.

A JSON representation of a string is a collection of zero or more characters wrapped in double quotes. This means the JSON representation of the name William Bender looks like this: "William Bender". A JSON representation can be converted to a JavaScript (simple or complex) type using the JavaScript eval() function. You could also dynamically generate a new function that handles the conversion using the Function() function. Both approaches are shown here:

```
var strJSON = "\"William Bender\"";
var strResult = eval(strJSON);
strResult = new Function("return " + strJSON);
```

The JSON representation of a number is identical to the number itself. For example, the JSON representation of the number 7 is 7:

```
var strJSON = "7";
var intResult = eval(strJSON);
```

The JSON representation of a Boolean is either true or false. Here's an example:

```
var strJSON = "true";
var blnResult = eval(strJSON);
if ( blnResult )
{
  alert(blnResult);
}
```

An array is an ordered collection of values. The JSON representation of an array begins with a left bracket ([) and ends with a right bracket (]). Values are separated by a comma (,). The JSON representation of a number array looks like this: [1, 2, 3]. Here's an example:

```
var strJSON = "[1, 2, 3]";
var arrResult = eval(strJSON);
alert(arrResult[0]);
```

The JSON representation of a string array looks like this: ["Bob", "Sue"]. Here's an example:

```
var strJSON = "[\"Bob\", \"Sue\"]";
var arrResult = eval(strJSON);
alert(arrResult[1]);
```

Objects are unordered sets of name-value pairs. JSON representations of objects are enclosed by curly braces ({}). Each name is followed by a colon (:). Name-value pairs are separated by commas (,). Look at the following definition of a JavaScript object called Person containing Name and Age properties:

```
function Person(strName, strAge)
{
  this.Name = strName;
  this.Age = strAge;
}
```

The JSON representation of the Person object looks like this: {"Name":"Jack","Age":47}. Although you are able to use the eval() function to convert this JSON string representation to a JavaScript object containing Name and Age properties, this is more complex than converting JSON representations to simple types. Instead, we recommend you use a JSON parser to do the conversion for you.

Another argument for using a JSON parser is that the eval() function compiles and executes any JavaScript code. This makes you vulnerable to script injection attacks. A good JSON parser will offer safeguards against this sort of attack and thus will be safer.

If you want to use a JSON parser, you can download one at http://www.json.org/json.js. The parser consists of only 120 lines of code including comments and is very easy to use. Add the JSON parser to the web part resources folder ([drive letter]:\[root folder of SharePoint web application] \wpresources) and register the JavaScript library containing the JSON parser with the web part page. In an earlier section, "JavaScript in Web Parts," we explained how to register JavaScript libraries from within a web part with web part pages.

The following example shows how to convert the JSON object representation {"Name":"Jack","Age":47} to a JavaScript object using the parseJSON() function. The parseJSON() function is defined within the JSON parser library:

```
var strJSON = "{\"Name\":\"Jack\",\"Age\":47}";
var objPerson = strJSON.parseJSON();
alert(objPerson.Name + " " + objPerson.Age);
```

■**Note** It is possible to create complex object hierarchies via JSON because nested types are allowed.

It is easy to retrieve the JSON representation of a JavaScript type via the `toJSONString()` function that is defined within the JSON parser library. This is shown in the following code fragment:

```
function Person(strName, strAge)
{
  this.Name = strName;
  this.Age = strAge;
}

var objPerson = new Person("Jason", 47);
var strPerson = objPerson.toJSONString();
alert(strPerson);
```

At first look, JSON seems to be less verbose than XML. However, you should not take this for granted. We have seen complex structures where the differences between XML and JSON representations were minimal. If you care a lot about the size of data, you should consider ZIP-encoding the data before sending it to the browser. We have seen examples where the zipped XML object representation is actually smaller than the zipped JSON representation. We would advise you to experiment first if you want to claim the JSON representation is the smallest.

In our opinion, the size of a JSON message probably will not be the deciding factor when it comes to choosing a message format. A disadvantage of JSON compared to XML is that you cannot describe the structure of a JSON message the way you can describe XML messages using schemas. We also believe JSON has the disadvantage of being less readable compared to XML object representations. The big advantage of JSON is that it is a representation of JavaScript types built into the JavaScript programming language that requires very little coding and processing.

Installing ASP.NET Ajax

If you want to install ASP.NET Ajax, go to `http://ajax.asp.net`, click the Downloads link, and download ASP.NET 2.0 AJAX Extensions 1.0. After the download is complete, installation is easy; just click the ASPAJAXExtSetup.msi file and follow the setup wizard. After installation, start Visual Studio 2005. Choose File ➤ New ➤ Web Site. Under the My Templates section, you should see a new entry called the ASP.NET AJAX-Enabled Web Site template. Choose this template if you want to create a new ASP.NET Ajax–enabled web site.

You should also install the ASP.NET AJAX Control Toolkit. This toolkit offers a range of Ajax-enabled controls. Just download the toolkit and extract AjaxControlToolkit.zip somewhere on your local file system. In the section "Building an Autocompletion Web Part" later in this chapter, you will learn how to use one of the controls in the ASP.NET AJAX Control Toolkit.

Building a Performance Counter Web Part

At the time of writing, ASP.NET Ajax is not officially supported in SharePoint 2007 environments. We hear that after the release of the first service pack for Windows SharePoint Services 2007, ASP.NET Ajax will be supported. Until then, we have to jump through some hoops to add support for ASP.NET Ajax in Microsoft Office SharePoint Server 2007 environments.

Creating a Performance Counter Web Service

In the next example, we show how to build a SharePoint web part that uses ASP.NET Ajax to display server performance counters. The web part will continue updating the performance counter by polling a web service that returns performance information.

In our example, we have chosen to use the following performance counters: Processor/% Processor Time, Web Service/Total Bytes Sent, and Web Service/Bytes Received/sec. We have chosen these counters randomly—our only criterion being that the performance counter values need to change often. When implementing a performance counter web part for an enterprise, you will probably be more interested in other performance counters. For example, you could create a web part that displays the key performance counters used by the Microsoft IT staff to monitor the performance of SharePoint Products and Technologies. A detailed overview of those performance counters can be found on the following web site: http://www.microsoft.com/technet/itsolutions/msit/infowork/spsperfnote.mspx.

The following code fragment shows how to retrieve the value for the Processor Time performance counter. In order to try out the code, you need to import the System.Diagnostics namespace. As an important side note, the first call to the PerformanceCounter class's NextValue() method always returns a zero. Normally, you would create a static member containing an instance of the PerformanceCounter class, or store the instance in the ASP.NET Session object. In our implementation, we take a shortcut and call the NextValue() method twice with a two-second interval between two calls. This way we can retrieve a realistic indicator of current processor usage, instead of a zero.

```
PerformanceCounter objCounter = new PerformanceCounter();
objCounter.CategoryName = "Processor";
objCounter.CounterName = "% Processor Time";
objCounter.InstanceName = "_Total";
objCounter.MachineName = ".";  // current computer
objCounter.ReadOnly = true;

int intCurrentCpuUsage = Convert.ToInt32(objCounter.NextValue());
Thread.Sleep(2000);

return objCounter.NextValue();
```

The easiest way to retrieve performance counter names, category names, and instance names is via the Visual Studio Server Explorer. Open Visual Studio 2005 and choose View ➤ Server Explorer. Within the Server Explorer, expand Servers ➤ [server name] ➤ Performance Counters ➤ [category name] ➤ [counter name]. Then choose the instance name you are interested in.

■**Note** You can use the Extensible Performance Counter List (Exctrlst.exe) tool to enable or disable performance categories. This tool can be downloaded from the Microsoft web site (http://www.microsoft.com).

The first step to create the performance counter web part is to make a new ASP.NET Ajax–enabled virtual directory and add a web service that returns the values of various performance counters, as shown in the following steps:

1. Open Windows Explorer and navigate to [drive letter]:\inetpub\wwwroot.

2. Create a new folder and call it AskMe2.

3. Choose Start ➤ Run, and type **inetmgr**.

4. In Internet Information Services Manager, expand the [server name] (local computer) node ➤ Web Sites ➤ Default Web Site.

5. Right-click the AskMe2 folder and choose Properties.

6. In the AskMe2 Properties window, click Create.

7. Click OK.

8. Open Visual Studio 2005.

9. Choose File ➤ New ➤ Web Site.

10. Choose the ASP.NET AJAX-Enabled Web Site template. Make sure the Location type value is set to HTTP. Set the location to the following value: http://localhost/askme2.

At this point, you have created an ASP.NET Ajax web site called AskMe2. Using the following steps, add a web service to this project called PerformanceService. This service will return a couple of performance counter values. The PerformanceService web service will contain three methods: GetProcessorTime(), GetCounter2(), and GetCounter3().

1. Right-click the AskMe2 project and choose Add New Item ➤ Web Service.

2. Choose the following name: PerformanceService.asmx. Make sure the Place Code in Separate File check box is not checked.

3. Click Add.

Later on in this section, we will use ASP.NET Ajax within a web part to call this web service from the client side. To be able to support such a scenario, we need to add the [ScriptService] attribute to the web service, which indicates that the web service is intended to be used by ASP.NET Ajax. This means that requests for such web services are handled by a special ASP.NET Ajax HTTP handler. Under the hood, if this attribute is present, a JavaScript proxy is created that is able to communicate with the PerformanceTest web service. The [ScriptService] attribute is located in the System.Web.Script.Services namespace, which is a part of the System.Web.Extensions assembly. Listing 2-8 shows how to use the [ScriptService] attribute and contains the entire code for the PerformanceService web service. This code should be added in its entirety to the PerformanceService.asmx file (replacing its previous content).

Listing 2-8. *Building a PerformanceService Web Service with Support for ASP.NET Ajax*

```
<%@ WebService Language="C#" Class="LoisAndClark.PerformanceService" %>

using System;
using System.Web;
using System.Web.Services;
using System.Web.Services.Protocols;
using System.Diagnostics;
using System.Threading;
using System.Web.Script.Services;

namespace LoisAndClark
{
  [WebService(Namespace = "http://tempuri.org/")]
  [WebServiceBinding(ConformsTo = WsiProfiles.BasicProfile1_1)]
  [ScriptService]
  public class PerformanceService : System.Web.Services.WebService
  {
    [WebMethod]
    public float GetProcessorTime()
    {
      PerformanceCounter objCounter = new PerformanceCounter();
      objCounter.CategoryName = "Processor";
      objCounter.CounterName = "% Processor Time";
      objCounter.InstanceName = "_Total";
      objCounter.MachineName = ".";
      objCounter.ReadOnly = true;
```

```
        int intCurrentCpuUsage = Convert.ToInt32(objCounter.NextValue());
        Thread.Sleep(2000);

        return objCounter.NextValue();
    }

    [WebMethod]
    public float GetCounter2()
    {
        PerformanceCounter objCounter = new PerformanceCounter();
        objCounter.CategoryName = "Web Service";
        objCounter.CounterName = "Total Bytes Sent";
        objCounter.InstanceName = "_Total";
        objCounter.MachineName = ".";
        objCounter.ReadOnly = true;

        float fltPagesPerSecond = objCounter.NextValue();
        Thread.Sleep(2000);

        return objCounter.NextValue();
    }

    [WebMethod]
    public float GetCounter3()
    {
        PerformanceCounter objCounter = new PerformanceCounter();
        objCounter.CategoryName = "Web Service";
        objCounter.CounterName = "Bytes Received/sec";
        objCounter.InstanceName = "_Total";
        objCounter.MachineName = ".";
        objCounter.ReadOnly = true;

        float fltCurrentCpuUsage = objCounter.NextValue();
        Thread.Sleep(2000);

        return objCounter.NextValue();
    }
  }
}
```

In this section, we discussed how to create a web service returning information about various performance counters on a SharePoint server and showed how to implement a web part that uses Ajax to poll for this information.

Creating a Test Client

Now that you have created a web service, you'll need a test client. In the next step, you will add an .aspx page to the AskMe2 project that uses ASP.NET Ajax to call the PerformanceService web service. Click Add New Item ➤ Web Form, call the page PerformanceTest.aspx, and make sure the check box Place Code in Separate File is not checked.

There is nothing special about the page yet. You have to add some parts to it to make the page an ASP.NET Ajax–enabled client. First you need to add the ASP.NET Ajax script manager to the PerformanceTest.aspx page. You can do this manually or by opening the page in Design Mode and dragging the ScriptManager control, located in the Toolbox AJAX Extensions section, onto the page. In the following fragment, the ASP.NET Ajax script manager is used to add a reference to the PerformanceService web service:

```
<form id="form1" runat="server">
  <div>
    <asp:ScriptManager ID="ScriptManager1" runat="server">
      <Services>
        <asp:ServiceReference Path="~/PerformanceService.asmx" />
      </Services>
    </asp:ScriptManager>
  </div>
</form>
```

The ASP.NET Ajax script manager is the brains of every ASP.NET Ajax–enabled ASP.NET page. The script manager offers functionality for developers and orchestrates partial page refreshes and incremental updates, and its set of responsibilities will become even more extensive in the future. The script manager also renders all client-side registrations for the ASP.NET Ajax script library.

The next interesting bit of the PerformanceTest.aspx page is a JavaScript function called GetPerfCounter() that we will add ourselves. This JavaScript function is responsible for communicating with the PerformanceService web service from the client side.

Because the PerformanceService web service is ASP.NET Ajax–enabled, a JavaScript proxy is generated automatically that allows us to use JavaScript to talk to the web service. Every web service has a corresponding JavaScript object, every web service method a corresponding JavaScript method that is part of the JavaScript object representing the web service. A JavaScript web service method has the following format:

```
[namespace].[type name].[method name]([arguments])
```

This means that you can call the PerformanceService web service's GetProcessTime() method by calling the LoisAndClark.PerformanceService.GetProcessorTime() JavaScript method. This function is a JavaScript proxy created by the ASP.NET Ajax framework. The proxy calls the actual PerformanceService web service asynchronously. As an argument to the JavaScript proxy, you will need to pass the name of the JavaScript function (in this case OnRequestComplete()) that will handle the web service response. You can also pass the name of JavaScript function that handles failure (in this case OnRequestFailure()). If everything goes well, the web service response is passed as an argument to the OnRequestComplete() method; otherwise you need to do some error handling in the OnRequestFailure() method event handler. The following code fragment shows JavaScript code responsible for communicating with the PerformanceService web service:

```
function GetPerfCounter()
{
  LoisAndClark.PerformanceService.GetProcessorTime(➡
  OnRequestComplete, ➡
  OnRequestFailure);
}

function OnRequestComplete(strResult)
{
  var objDisplay = document.getElementById("Results");
  objDisplay.innerHTML = strResult;
}
```

```
function OnRequestFailure(error)
{
  var strStackTrace = error.get_stackTrace();
  var strMessage = error.get_message();
  var strStatusCode = error.get_statusCode();
  var strExceptionType = error.get_exceptionType();
  var strTimedout = error.get_timedOut();

  alert("Error\n" +
  "Stack Trace: " +  strStackTrace + "\n" +
  "Service Error: " + strMessage + "\n" +
  "Status Code: " + strStatusCode + "\n" +
  "Exception Type: " + strExceptionType + "\n" +
  "Timedout: " + strTimedout);
}
```

Listing 2-9 shows the complete code for PerformanceTest.aspx.

Listing 2-9. *Creating a Test Client for the Performance Counter Web Service*

```
<%@ Page Language="C#" %>
<html xmlns="http://www.w3.org/1999/xhtml" >
  <head runat="server">
    <title>PerformanceService test page</title>
  </head>
  <body>
  <form id="form1" runat="server">
  <div>

    <asp:ScriptManager ID="ScriptManager1" runat="server">
      <Services>
        <asp:ServiceReference Path="~/PerformanceService.asmx" />
      </Services>
    </asp:ScriptManager>

    <input id="GetPerformanceCounter" type="button" ➥
    value="Get Performance Counter" onclick="GetPerfCounter()" />
  </div>
  </form>

  <span id="Results"></span>

  <script type="text/javascript" language="javascript">
  <!-
  function GetPerfCounter()
  {
    LoisAndClark.PerformanceService.GetProcessorTime( ➥
    OnRequestComplete, ➥
    OnRequestFailure);
  }

  function OnRequestComplete(strResult)
  {
    var objDisplay = document.getElementById("Results");
    objDisplay.innerHTML = strResult;
  }
```

```
function OnRequestFailure(error)
{
  var strStackTrace = error.get_stackTrace();
  var strMessage = error.get_message();
  var strStatusCode = error.get_statusCode();
  var strExceptionType = error.get_exceptionType();
  var strTimedout = error.get_timedOut();

  alert("Error\n" +
  "Stack Trace: " +  strStackTrace + "\n" +
  "Service Error: " + strMessage + "\n" +
  "Status Code: " + strStatusCode + "\n" +
  "Exception Type: " + strExceptionType + "\n" +
  "Timedout: " + strTimedout);
}
//-->
</script>

</body>
</html>
```

Right-click PerformanceTest.aspx and select Set As Start Page. Press F5 to start the web application. You will see a pop-up window asking whether you would like to enable debugging. Choose Modify the Web.config to enable debugging and click OK. If you click the Get Performance Counter button, you will see how the PerformanceService web service is called via ASP.NET Ajax from the client-side application. The result is shown in Figure 2-10.

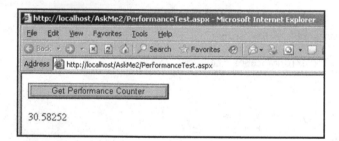

Figure 2-10. *The Get Performance Counter button*

Do not close the browser yet. Right-click PerformanceTest.aspx and select View Source. Find the <script> element containing a reference to WebResource.axd and look at it. It will look similar to the following:

```
<script src="/AskMe2/WebResource.axd?d=[encoded information] ➥
&amp;t=[encoded information] " type="text/javascript"></script>
```

The src attribute of the <script> element refers to an HTTP handler called WebResource.axd. This HTTP handler enables ASP.NET pages to load embedded resources from .NET assemblies. Examples of such embedded resources are client scripts, images, and data files. In this case, the reference to WebResource.axd will cause the server to generate the ASP.NET Ajax client library (written in JavaScript). The d argument in the URL refers to an encrypted identifier that uniquely identifies the requested web resource. The t argument is an optional time stamp for the requested assembly and is used for caching purposes.

Note Chapter 1 discusses how to create custom web resource assemblies.

If you continue looking through the HTML source of the rendered PerformanceTest.aspx page, you will find an interesting part that adds a reference to ScriptResource.axd:

```
<script src="/AskMe2/ScriptResource.axd?d=[enc info]&t=[enc info]" ➥
type="text/javascript"></script>
```

At the time of this writing, the ScriptResource.axd file is not well documented, but one of its jobs is to reduce the size of script files. Other tasks for the ScriptResource.axd file seem to include determining the culture of the user, for localization settings such as language, decimal digits, currency symbols, date-time format, and names of the month, as well as setting the client-side Sys.CultureInfo object accordingly (which is a part of the ASP.NET Ajax JavaScript framework).

The final interesting part of the rendered PerformanceTest.aspx page's HTML source adds a reference to the PerformanceService web service JavaScript proxy:

```
<script src="PerformanceService.asmx/js" type="text/javascript"></script>
```

The JavaScript proxy is responsible for communicating with the web service. At the same time, the proxy makes it very easy for the client side to call web services. At this point, you have created a web service that supports ASP.NET Ajax and created a test client for it. In the next section, you will learn how to Ajax-enable Microsoft Office SharePoint Server 2007 and eventually how to use ASP.NET Ajax in a web part.

ASP.NET Ajax-Enabling a Microsoft Office SharePoint Server 2007 Web Application

Now that we have identified the important parts of an ASP.NET Ajax client, you are ready to incorporate ASP.NET Ajax in a web part. To do this, we first need to copy some of the web.config file of an ASP.NET Ajax-enabled web site and add it to the web.config file of a SharePoint web application.

Note At the time of writing, ASP.NET Ajax is not supported officially in SharePoint environments. There are plans to add support for ASP.NET Ajax in Microsoft Office SharePoint Server 2007 in service pack 1.

Basically, to be able to support ASP.NET Ajax in Microsoft Office SharePoint Server 2007, you need to merge the web.config file of an ASP.NET Ajax-enabled web site with the contents of a web.config file for a SharePoint web application. This is a tedious and error-prone job, but for now, because of the lack of official support in Microsoft Office SharePoint Server 2007 for ASP.NET Ajax, you need to do it.

In the next procedure, we will discuss the steps required to ASP.NET Ajax-enable a SharePoint web application. First, we will copy configuration information to a SharePoint web.config file, register ASP.NET Ajax controls, and add a reference to the ASP.NET Ajax assembly (called System.Web.Extensions).

1. Open the web.config file of the AskMe2 ASP.NET Ajax-enabled web site (the ASP.NET Ajax web.config file).

2. Open the web.config file of the SharePoint web application (the SharePoint web.config file).

3. Locate the `<sectionGroup>` section in the ASP.NET Ajax web.config file. This section looks like Listing 2-10.

Listing 2-10. *The <SectionGroup> Section of the ASP.NET Ajax web.config File*

```
<sectionGroup name="system.web.extensions" ➥
type="System.Web.Configuration.SystemWebExtensionsSectionGroup, ➥
System.Web.Extensions, Version=1.0.61025.0, Culture=neutral, ➥
PublicKeyToken=31bf3856ad364e35">

  <sectionGroup name="scripting" ➥
  type="System.Web.Configuration.ScriptingSectionGroup, ➥
  System.Web.Extensions, ➥
  Version=1.0.61025.0, Culture=neutral, PublicKeyToken=31bf3856ad364e35">

  <section name="scriptResourceHandler" ➥
  type="System.Web.Configuration.ScriptingScriptResourceHandlerSection, ➥
  System.Web.Extensions, Version=1.0.61025.0, Culture=neutral, ➥
  PublicKeyToken=31bf3856ad364e35" requirePermission="false" ➥
  allowDefinition="MachineToApplication"/>

    <sectionGroup name="webServices" ➥
    type="System.Web.Configuration.ScriptingWebServicesSectionGroup, ➥
    System.Web.Extensions, Version=1.0.61025.0, Culture=neutral, ➥
    PublicKeyToken=31bf3856ad364e35">

    <section name="jsonSerialization" ➥
    type="System.Web.Configuration.ScriptingJsonSerializationSection, ➥
    System.Web.Extensions, Version=1.0.61025.0, Culture=neutral, ➥
    PublicKeyToken=31bf3856ad364e35" requirePermission="false" ➥
    allowDefinition="Everywhere"/>

    <section name="profileService" ➥
    type="System.Web.Configuration.ScriptingProfileServiceSection, ➥
    System.Web.Extensions, Version=1.0.61025.0, Culture=neutral, ➥
    PublicKeyToken=31bf3856ad364e35" requirePermission="false" ➥
    allowDefinition="MachineToApplication"/>

    <section name="authenticationService" ➥
    type="System.Web.Configuration.ScriptingAuthenticationServiceSection, ➥
    System.Web.Extensions, Version=1.0.61025.0, Culture=neutral, ➥
    PublicKeyToken=31bf3856ad364e35" requirePermission="false" ➥
    allowDefinition="MachineToApplication"/>

    </sectionGroup>
  </sectionGroup>
</sectionGroup>
```

4. Copy this section and add it to the <configSections> section of the SharePoint web.config file.

5. Locate the <controls> section within the <pages> section of the ASP.NET Ajax web.config file. This section looks like the following code fragment:

```
<pages>
  <controls>
    <add tagPrefix="asp" namespace="System.Web.UI" ➥
    assembly="System.Web.Extensions, Version=1.0.61025.0, ➥
    Culture=neutral, PublicKeyToken=31bf3856ad364e35"/>
  </controls>
</pages>
```

6. Copy the `<controls>` section and add it to the `<pages>` element in the SharePoint web.config file.

7. In the `<compilation>` section of the ASP.NET Ajax web.config file, locate the `<Assemblies>` section. This section looks like the following code fragment:

```
<assemblies>
  <add assembly="System.Web.Extensions, Version=1.0.61025.0, ➡
  Culture=neutral, PublicKeyToken=31bf3856ad364e35"/>
</assemblies>
```

8. Copy the reference to System.Web.Extensions.dll to the `<Assemblies>` section of the Share-Point web.config file. The following code fragment shows the reference to this assembly

```
<add assembly="System.Web.Extensions, Version=1.0.61025.0, ➡
Culture=neutral, PublicKeyToken=31bf3856ad364e35"/>
```

9. In the ASP.NET Ajax web.config file, locate the `<httpHandlers>` section, and copy the registrations in this section.

```
<add verb="*" path="*.asmx" validate="false"
type="System.Web.Script.Services.ScriptHandlerFactory, ➡
System.Web.Extensions, Version=1.0.61025.0, Culture=neutral, ➡
PublicKeyToken=31bf3856ad364e35"/>
<add verb="*" path="*_AppService.axd" validate="false"
type="System.Web.Script.Services.ScriptHandlerFactory, ➡
System.Web.Extensions, Version=1.0.61025.0, Culture=neutral, ➡
PublicKeyToken=31bf3856ad364e35"/>
<add verb="GET,HEAD" path="ScriptResource.axd"
type="System.Web.Handlers.ScriptResourceHandler, System.Web.Extensions, ➡
Version=1.0.61025.0, Culture=neutral, PublicKeyToken=31bf3856ad364e35" ➡
validate="false"/>
```

10. Add these registrations to the `<httpHandlers>` section of the SharePoint web.config file.

11. Locate the `<httpModules>` section in the ASP.NET Ajax web.config file and copy the Script-Module registration that looks like the following code fragment:

```
<add name="ScriptModule" type="System.Web.Handlers.ScriptModule, ➡
System.Web.Extensions, Version=1.0.61025.0, Culture=neutral, ➡
PublicKeyToken=31bf3856ad364e35"/>
```

12. Add this registration to the `<httpModules>` section of the SharePoint web.config file.

13. Go back to the beginning of the ASP.NET Ajax web.config file and locate the `<sectionGroup>` element named Scripting. Copy the fully qualified assembly name from the type attribute of this element. The following code fragment shows the fully qualified assembly name:

```
System.Web.Extensions, Version=1.0.61025.0, Culture=neutral, ➡
PublicKeyToken=31bf3856ad364e35
```

14. Locate the `<SafeControls>` section of the SharePoint web.config file and add a new `<SafeControl>` entry for the System.Web.Extensions assembly. This section looks like the following code fragment:

```
<SafeControl Assembly="System.Web.Extensions, Version=1.0.61025.0, ➡
Culture=neutral, PublicKeyToken=31bf3856ad364e35" ➡
Namespace="System.Web.UI" TypeName="*" Safe="True" />
```

15. Locate the `<system.web.extensions>` section in the ASP.NET Ajax web.config file. This section looks like Listing 2-11.

Listing 2-11. *The `<system.web.extensions>` Section of the ASP.NET Ajax web.config File*

```
<system.web.extensions>
<scripting>
  <webServices>
  <!-
  Uncomment this line to customize maxJsonLength and add a custom converter
  ->
  <!-
  <jsonSerialization maxJsonLength="500">
    <converters>
      <add name="ConvertMe" type="Acme.SubAcme.ConvertMeTypeConverter"/>
    </converters>
  </jsonSerialization>
  ->
  <!-
  Uncomment this line to enable the authentication service. Include
  requireSSL="true" if appropriate.
  ->
  <!-
  <authenticationService enabled="true" requireSSL = "true|false"/>
  ->
  <!-
  Uncomment these lines to enable the profile service. To allow profile
  properties to be retrieve and modified in ASP.NET AJAX applications,
  you need to add each property name to the readAccessProperties and
  writeAccessProperties attributes.
  ->
  <!-
  <profileService enabled="true" ➥
  readAccessProperties="propertyname1,propertyname2" ➥
  writeAccessProperties="propertyname1,propertyname2" />
  ->
  </webServices>
  <!-
  <scriptResourceHandler enableCompression="true" enableCaching="true" />
  ->
</scripting>
</system.web.extensions>
```

16. Add this information to the `<configuration>` section of the SharePoint web.config file.

17. In the ASP.NET Ajax web.config file, locate the `<system.webServer>` element. This section looks like Listing 2-12.

Listing 2-12. *The `<system.webServer>` Section of the ASP.NET Ajax web.config File*

```
<system.webServer>
  <validation validateIntegratedModeConfiguration="false"/>
  <modules>
    <add name="ScriptModule" preCondition="integratedMode"
    type="System.Web.Handlers.ScriptModule, System.Web.Extensions,
    Version=1.0.61025.0, Culture=neutral, PublicKeyToken=31bf3856ad364e35"/>
  </modules>
```

```
    <handlers>
      <remove name="WebServiceHandlerFactory-Integrated"/>
      <add name="ScriptHandlerFactory" verb="*" path="*.asmx" ➥
      preCondition="integratedMode" ➥
      type="System.Web.Script.Services.ScriptHandlerFactory, ➥
      System.Web.Extensions, Version=1.0.61025.0, Culture=neutral, ➥
      PublicKeyToken=31bf3856ad364e35"/>
      <add name="ScriptHandlerFactoryAppServices" verb="*" ➥
      path="*_AppService.axd" preCondition="integratedMode" ➥
      type="System.Web.Script.Services.ScriptHandlerFactory, ➥
      System.Web.Extensions, Version=1.0.61025.0, Culture=neutral, ➥
      PublicKeyToken=31bf3856ad364e35"/>
      <add name="ScriptResource" preCondition="integratedMode" ➥
      verb="GET,HEAD" path="ScriptResource.axd" ➥
      type="System.Web.Handlers.ScriptResourceHandler, ➥
      System.Web.Extensions, Version=1.0.61025.0, ➥
      Culture=neutral, PublicKeyToken=31bf3856ad364e35"/>
    </handlers>
  </system.webServer>
```

18. Add this section to the `<configuration>` element of the SharePoint web.config file, just after the `<system.web.extensions>` section.

As stated before, it is difficult to merge the ASP.NET Ajax part of a web.config file with a Share-Point web.config file manually. At this point, you have ASP.NET Ajax-enabled your SharePoint web application, meaning you can call ASP.NET Ajax-enabled web services within your SharePoint environment.

Ajax-Enabling a Web Part

In this section, you will learn how to create an Ajax-enabled web part that calls the Performance Counter web service. As the first step, create a new web part. If you are unsure how to do this, refer to Chapter 1. Create a new JavaScript library called ajax.js and place it in the web part resources folder. Specify an event handler for the PreRender event in the web part constructor and use the PreRender event handler to register the Ajax.js JavaScript library in it. The following code fragment shows how to do this:

```
public AjaxClient()
{
  PreRender += new EventHandler(PerformanceCounterWebPart_PreRender);
}

void PerformanceCounterWebPart_PreRender(object sender, EventArgs e)
{
  if (!Page.ClientScript.IsClientScriptBlockRegistered("Ajax"))
  {
    Page.ClientScript.RegisterClientScriptInclude("Ajax", ➥
    "/wpresources/ajax.js");
  }
}
```

The ASP.NET Ajax ScriptManager object takes care of managing the required client-side registrations. If you want your web part to use Ajax, you need to make sure an instance of the ScriptManager is registered on the page containing the Ajax-enabled web part. You can do this in the CreateChildControls() method. The following code fragment shows how to register a ScriptManager object that contains a reference to the Performance Counter web service:

```
string strPath = "/AskMe2/PerformanceService.asmx";
ServiceReference objReference = new ServiceReference();
objReference.Path = strPath;

ScriptManager objManager = new ScriptManager();
objManager.Services.Add(objReference);
Controls.Add(objManager);
```

Note Since only a single instance of a ScriptManager object is allowed on a single page, it is easier to add such a registration to the master page of a SharePoint site. In this section, the ScriptManager object is registered dynamically within the web part itself; in the section "Building a Company Contact Web Part Using ASP.NET Ajax and JSON" you will learn how to register a ScriptManager object within the master page of a SharePoint site.

The complete code listing for the performance counter web part looks like Listing 2-13.

Listing 2-13. *The Performance Counter Web Part*

```
    using System;
using System.Runtime.InteropServices;
using System.Web.UI;
using System.Web.UI.WebControls.WebParts;
using System.Xml.Serialization;
using Microsoft.SharePoint;
using Microsoft.SharePoint.WebControls;
using Microsoft.SharePoint.WebPartPages;
using System.Web.UI.WebControls;

namespace AjaxClient
{
  [Guid("be6ec8e3-2706-4f52-bdf9-f6eb18fc65c0")]
  public class AjaxClient : System.Web.UI.WebControls.WebParts.WebPart
  {
    public AjaxClient()
    {
      PreRender += new EventHandler(PerformanceCounterWebPart_PreRender);
    }

    void PerformanceCounterWebPart_PreRender(object sender, EventArgs e)
    {
      if (!Page.ClientScript.IsClientScriptBlockRegistered("Ajax"))
      {
        Page.ClientScript.RegisterClientScriptInclude("Ajax", ➥
        "/wpresources/ajax.js");
      }
    }

    protected override void CreateChildControls()
    {
      try
      {
        string strPath = "/AskMe2/PerformanceService.asmx";
        ServiceReference objReference = new ServiceReference();
        objReference.Path = strPath;
```

```
        ScriptManager objManager = new ScriptManager();
        objManager.Services.Add(objReference);
        Controls.Add(objManager);

        string strDisplay = "<div id=\"ProcessorTimeDisplay\"> ➥
        Display 1</div> \n";
        Controls.Add(new LiteralControl(strDisplay));

        strDisplay = "<div id=\"Counter2Display\">Display 2</div> \n";
        Controls.Add(new LiteralControl(strDisplay));

        strDisplay = "<div id=\"Counter3Display\">Display 3</div> \n";
        Controls.Add(new LiteralControl(strDisplay));
      }
      catch (Exception err)
      {
        Controls.Add(new LiteralControl(err.Message));
      }
    }
  }
}
```

The ajax.js JavaScript library calls the PerformanceService web service and defines several JavaScript handlers for the web service responses. The following line of code shows how to call PerformanceService's GetProcessorTime() method and define a JavaScript handler called OnProcessorTimeResponse that handles the web service response:

```
LoisAndClark.PerformanceService.GetProcessorTime(OnProcessorTimeResponse);
```

We have built a mechanism around the Ajax web service calls to make sure web service calls are made when the client-side application is ready. The complete code for Ajax.js looks like Listing 2-14.

Listing 2-14. *Building the Performance Counter JavaScript Library*

```
var intTimeOut = 5000;

function GetProcessorTime()
{
  LoisAndClark.PerformanceService.GetProcessorTime(OnProcessorTimeResponse);
}

function GetCounter2()
{
  LoisAndClark.PerformanceService.GetCounter2(OnCounter2Response);
}

function GetCounter3()
{
  LoisAndClark.PerformanceService.GetCounter3(OnCounter3Response);
}

function OnProcessorTimeResponse(objResult)
{
   var objDisplay = document.getElementById("ProcessorTimeDisplay");
   objDisplay.innerHTML = "Processor time: " + objResult;
   setTimeout("GetCounter3()", intTimeOut);
}
```

```
function OnCounter2Response(objResult)
{
   var objDisplay = document.getElementById("Counter2Display");
   objDisplay.innerHTML = "Counter 2: " + objResult;
   setTimeout("GetProcessorTime()", intTimeOut);
}

function OnCounter3Response(objResult)
{
   var objDisplay = document.getElementById("Counter3Display");
   objDisplay.innerHTML = "Counter 3: " + objResult;
   setTimeout("GetProcessorTime()", intTimeOut);
}

function Init()
{
  try
  {
    if ( LoisAndClark != null )
    {
      GetProcessorTime();
      GetCounter2();
      GetCounter3();
    }
  }
  catch (err)
  {
    setTimeout("Init()", 1000);
  }
}

Init();
```

The performance counter web part can be seen in action in Figure 2-11.

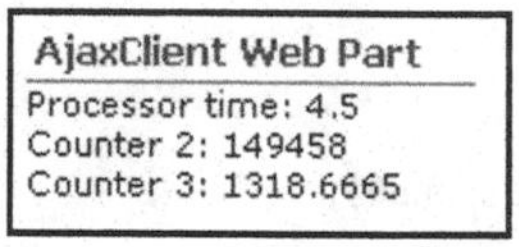

```
AjaxClient Web Part
Processor time: 4.5
Counter 2: 149458
Counter 3: 1318.6665
```

Figure 2-11. *Performance counter web part*

Building a Company Contact Web Part Using ASP.NET Ajax and JSON

In the next example, we show you how to build a company contact web part using ASP.NET Ajax and JSON. If you want to test the example, you should create a custom SharePoint list that contains a default title, company name, contact person, city, and country, and call this list ContactInfo (set the column types of all columns to a single line of text). Figure 2-12 shows the ContactInfo list.

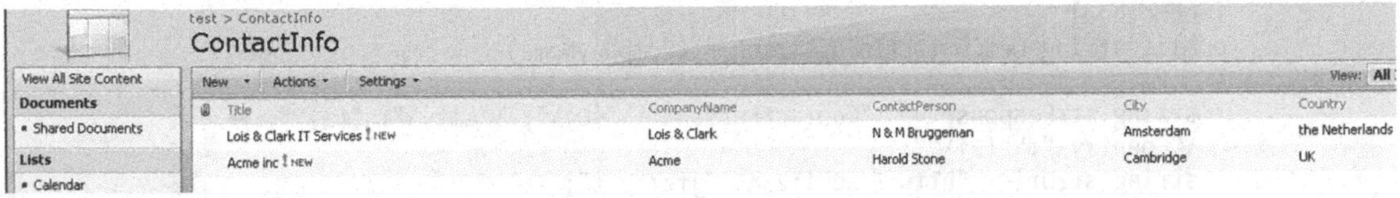

Figure 2-12. *Company contact list*

The idea behind the company contact web part is that if you type in the name of the company and click the AutoFill button, the web part will call a web service that retrieves the rest of the form information for you from the ContactInfo SharePoint list. The web service will return the data in JSON format, so the client-side application needs to be able to deal with that.

In the next step, you will create the server side of the company contact application. Add a new web service to the AskMe2 project; make sure the Place Code in Separate File check box is not checked, and name the web service ContactService.asmx. The following code will loop through every item in the ContactInfo SharePoint list.

```
SPSite objSites = new SPSite(strUrl);
SPWeb objSite = objSites.OpenWeb();
SPList objContactList = objSite.Lists["ContactInfo"];

foreach (SPListItem objItem in objContactList.Items)
{

}
```

The ContactService web service returns a JSON message containing all contact information. The ContactService web service will return a JSON message that looks like this:

```
{"ContactPerson":"[value]", "City":"[value]", "Country":"[value]"}
```

Listing 2-15 shows the complete implementation of the ContactService web service. Make sure to add a reference to the `Microsoft.SharePoint` assembly.

Listing 2-15. *The Contact Web Service*

```
<%@ WebService Language="C#" Class="LoisAndClark.CompanyContact. ➡
ContactService"%>
using System;
using System.Web;
using System.Collections;
using System.Web.Services;
using System.Web.Services.Protocols;
using Microsoft.SharePoint;

namespace LoisAndClark.CompanyContact
{
  [WebService(Namespace = "http://tempuri.org/")]
  [WebServiceBinding(ConformsTo = WsiProfiles.BasicProfile1_1)]
  [ScriptService]
  public class ContactService : System.Web.Services.WebService
  {
    public ContactService()
    {
    }
```

```
[WebMethod]
public string GetContactInfo(string strCompanyName)
{
  string strResponse = "\"ContactPerson\":\"{0}\", \"City\":\"{1}\", ➥
  \"Country\":\"{2}\"";
  string strUrl = "http://web1:23456/jfz/test";

  try
  {
    using (SPSite objSites = new SPSite(strUrl))
    {
      using ( SPWeb objSite = objSites.OpenWeb() )
      {
        SPList objContactList = objSite.Lists["ContactInfo"];
        foreach (SPListItem objItem in objContactList.Items)
        {
          string strName = objItem["CompanyName"].ToString();
          if (strName == strCompanyName)
          {
            string strContact = objItem["ContactPerson"].ToString();
            string strCity = objItem["City"].ToString();
            string strCountry = objItem["Country"].ToString();

            strResponse = "{" + String.Format(strResponse, strContact, ➥
            strCity, strCountry) + "}";
            break;
          }
        }
      }
    }

    return strResponse;
  }
  catch (Exception)
  {
    throw;
  }
}
}
```

■**Note** The GetContactInfo() method returns a JSON message. This is meant as an example. In a real enter-prise application, you should probably opt to use a third-party JSON serializer instead of writing your own.

In the section "Building a Performance Counter Web Part," you learned how to register a ScriptManager object within a web part. In this section, and the examples that will be discussed in the rest of this chapter, we will add a single registration of a ScriptManager object to the master page of a SharePoint site.

Note The preferred way of registering a `ScriptManager` object is by adding a single registration to the master page of a SharePoint site. There may be scenarios where it is not possible to add a `ScriptManager` object within a web part early enough in the page lifecycle. Although we have not encountered this situation ourselves, this issue is reported on Mike Ammerlaan's blog at `http://sharepoint.microsoft.com/blogs/mike/Lists/Posts/Post.aspx?ID=3`. Mike Ammerlaan is a program manager at Microsoft working on Windows SharePoint Services.

In the following procedure, you will learn how to use SharePoint Designer to add a single `ScriptManager` registration to the default master page of a SharePoint site.

1. Open a browser and navigate to the SharePoint site that you want to add Ajax-enabled web parts to.

2. Choose File ➤ Edit with Microsoft Office SharePoint Designer. This opens the SharePoint site in SharePoint Designer.

3. Expand the _catalogs folder.

4. Expand the masterpage gallery.

5. Double-click default.master. This opens default.master in SharePoint Designer.

6. Switch to Code view.

7. Locate the registration for the web part manager. This looks like the following code fragment:

```
<WebPartPages:SPWebPartManager id="m" runat="Server" />
```

8. Add the following registration for a ScriptManager object to this page, right after the registration for the web part manager:

```
<asp:ScriptManager ID="theScriptManager" runat="Server"/>
```

9. Save the page and close SharePoint Designer.

Now, you have successfully added a registration of a `ScriptManager` object called theScriptManager.

The web part code looks very much like the earlier example in the "Building a Performance Counter Web Part" section of this chapter. The biggest difference is that this web part locates the `ScriptManager` in the master page instead of registering a new instance of the `ScriptManager` object. The following code fragment shows how to find the `ScriptManager` object located in the master page (called theScriptManager) and how to add a reference to the Contact web service to it:

```
string strPath = "/AskMe2/ContactService.asmx";
ServiceReference objReference = new ServiceReference();
objReference.Path = strPath;

Control ctlManager = Page.Master.FindControl("theScriptManager");
ScriptManager objManager = ctlManager as ScriptManager;
objManager.Services.Add(objReference);
```

Because the web service returns a JSON response, you also need to add a reference to json.js, the JavaScript library that facilitates working with JSON. The JSON script library is discussed in further detail later in this chapter in the section "JSON Messages." You also need to register ajax.js, the custom JavaScript library that contains the logic that calls the web service and processes the response. Then you need to add the required client registrations, and add fields for company name, contact person, city, and country to the web part. If you enter a value for the company name, the example shows how to use ASP.NET Ajax to autofill the other fields. The complete code listing for the CompanyContactClient web part looks like Listing 2-16.

Listing 2-16. *The Contact Web Part*

```
using System;
using System.Runtime.InteropServices;
using System.Web.UI;
using System.Web.UI.WebControls.WebParts;
using System.Xml.Serialization;
using Microsoft.SharePoint;
using Microsoft.SharePoint.WebControls;
using Microsoft.SharePoint.WebPartPages;
using System.Web.UI.WebControls;

namespace AjaxClient
{
  [Guid("be6ec8e3-2706-4f52-bdf9-f6eb18fc65c0")]
  public class AjaxClient : System.Web.UI.WebControls.WebParts.WebPart
  {
    public AjaxClient()
    {
      PreRender += new EventHandler(PerformanceCounterWebPart_PreRender);
    }

    void PerformanceCounterWebPart_PreRender(object sender, EventArgs e)
    {
      if (!Page.ClientScript.IsClientScriptBlockRegistered("JSON"))
      {
        Page.ClientScript.RegisterClientScriptInclude("JSON", ➥
        "/wpresources/json.js");
      }

      if (!Page.ClientScript.IsClientScriptBlockRegistered("Ajax"))
      {
        Page.ClientScript.RegisterClientScriptInclude("Ajax", ➥
        "/wpresources/ajax.js");
      }
    }

    protected override void CreateChildControls()
    {
      try
      {
        string strPath = "/AskMe2/ContactService.asmx";
        ServiceReference objReference = new ServiceReference();
        objReference.Path = strPath;

        Control ctlManager = Page.Master.FindControl("theScriptManager");
        ScriptManager objManager = ctlManager as ScriptManager;
        objManager.Services.Add(objReference);

        string strCompanyName = "Name: <input id=\"CompanyName\" ➥
        type=\"text\" />";
        Controls.Add(new LiteralControl(strCompanyName));
```

```
        string strAutoFill = "<input id=\"AutoFill\" type=\"button\" ➡
        value=\"AutoFill...\" onclick=\"AutoFillRequest();\" /><br/>";
        Controls.Add(new LiteralControl(strAutoFill));

        string strContactPerson = "Contact: <input id=\"ContactPerson\" ➡
        type=\"text\" /><br/>";
        Controls.Add(new LiteralControl(strContactPerson));

        string strCity = "City: <input id=\"City\" type=\"text\" /><br/>";
        Controls.Add(new LiteralControl(strCity));

        string strCountry = "Country: <input id=\"Country\" ➡
        type=\"text\" /><br/>";
        Controls.Add(new LiteralControl(strCountry));
      }
      catch (Exception err)
      {
        Controls.Add(new LiteralControl(err.Message));
      }
    }
  }
}
```

The final part of the company contact ASP.NET Ajax solution is the content of the ajax.js JavaScript library. It contains a function called AutoFillRequest() that calls the ContactService web service. A callback function called OnAutoFillResponse() converts the web service response to a JavaScript object and uses the object to set the values of the contact person, city, and country fields. The content of the ajax.js JavaScript library looks like Listing 2-17.

Listing 2-17. *The Contact JavaScript Library*

```
function AutoFillRequest()
{
  var objCompanyName = document.getElementById("CompanyName");
  LoisAndClark.CompanyContact.ContactService.GetContactInfo( ➡
  objCompanyName.value, OnAutoFillResponse) ;
}

function OnAutoFillResponse(strResult)
{
  var objContact = strResult.parseJSON();

  var objContactPerson = document.getElementById("ContactPerson");
  objContactPerson.value = objContact.ContactPerson;

  var objCity = document.getElementById("City");
  objCity.value = objContact.City;

  var objCountry = document.getElementById("Country");
  objCountry.value = objContact.Country;
}
```

Figure 2-13 shows the company contact web part with a name typed in by the end user. In Figure 2-14, the AutoFill has filled in the rest of the fields.

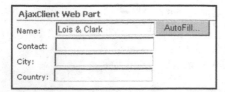

Figure 2-13. *The user types in a name in the company contact web part.*

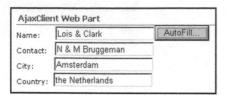

Figure 2-14. *AutoFill fills in the rest of the fields.*

In this section, you have seen how to create a web service that retrieves information from a SharePoint list and how to create a web part that uses Ajax to fetch and display this information.

Building an Autocompletion Web Part

In this section, we will discuss how to use ASP.NET Ajax controls within a web part. The example in this section uses the ASP.NET AJAX Toolkit to enhance the user interface in a powerful way. We will create an autocompletion web part using the ASP.NET Ajax AutoCompleteExtender control. We will use this control to call a web service that retrieves all SharePoint lists within a SharePoint site, starting with what is typed into a text box. Figures 2-15, 2-16, and 2-17 show how the ASP.NET Ajax AutoCompleteExtender control works.

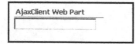

Figure 2-15. *The text box in the web part*

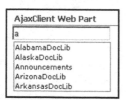

Figure 2-16. *The SharePoint lists returned by the web service*

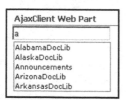

Figure 2-17. *The SharePoint lists narrowed down after more letters are typed in*

In this example, first we will create a new web service. Add another web service to the AskMe2 project you created previously and call it DocLibExtenderService.asmx. Do not place the code in a separate file. The DocLibExtenderService web service retrieves all SharePoint lists from a given SharePoint site, like this:

```
SPSite objSites = new SPSite(strUrl);
SPWeb objSite = objSites.OpenWeb();
SPListCollection objLists = objSite.Lists;

foreach (SPList objList in objLists)
{
  ...
}
```

ASP.NET Ajax autocompletion web services return string arrays containing all results starting with a given prefix. Because of this, we want to add all lists to a data structure that makes it easy to sort and filter. We have chosen to use the ADO.NET DataView to do this. The following code fragment shows how to filter and sort document libraries using a DataView.

Note In the next code example, a DataView object is used to sort the data. Alternatively, we could have used the DataTable.Select(filterExpression, sort) method.

```
DataTable dtLists = new DataTable();
dtLists.Columns.Add("ListName", typeof(string));

// code that retrieves all SharePoint lists...
// this part is shown later in this section...

foreach (SPList objList in objLists)
{
  DataRow drList = dtLists.NewRow();
  drList["ListName"] = objList.Title;
  dtLists.Rows.Add(drList);
}

// the initialization of _dvLists is shown later in this section
_dvLists = dtLists.DefaultView;
_dvLists.Sort = "listname ASC";

string strFilter = "listname LIKE 'A%'";
_dvLists.RowFilter = strFilter;
```

The ASP.NET Ajax autocompletion web service interface is very strict. Not only does it require a given signature, but the parameter names have to match exactly, otherwise the autocompletion web service will not work. Although this limits the usefulness of ASP.NET Ajax autocompletion web services, they are so powerful that it pays to work around this limitation. The ASP.NET Ajax autocompletion web service interface looks like this:

```
public string[] MyMethodName(string prefixText, int count)
```

The only variable part of this interface is the method name. You are not allowed to change the signature or parameter names. The return type needs to be some type of string array, although there is some flexibility here. In the implementation of MyMethodName(), a string array is returned, as this is one of the data types that can easily be understood by the client-side AutoComplete

extender. As another example, a generic List collection (List<string>) would work, too. The
prefixText argument contains the prefix of any match found by the autocompletion service. The
count argument limits the maximum number of results. By the way, our example autocompletion
wizard does not implement a maximum result limit and ignores the count argument. The complete
code listing for the autocompletion wizard looks like Listing 2-18.

Listing 2-18. *The Autocompletion Web Service*

```csharp
<%@ WebService Language="C#" Class="LoisAndClark.DocLibExtenderService" %>

using System;
using System.Web;
using System.Web.Services;
using System.Web.Services.Protocols;
using Microsoft.SharePoint;
using System.Collections;
using System.Data;
using System.Diagnostics;

namespace LoisAndClark
{
  [WebService(Namespace = "http://tempuri.org/")]
  [WebServiceBinding(ConformsTo = WsiProfiles.BasicProfile1_1)]
  [ScriptService]
  public class DocLibExtenderService : System.Web.Services.WebService
  {
    static DataView _dvLists = null;

    private void InitLists(string strUrl)
    {
      if (_dvLists == null)
      {
        DataTable dtLists = new DataTable();
        dtLists.Columns.Add("ListName", typeof(string));

        SPSite objSites = new SPSite(strUrl);
        SPWeb objSite = objSites.OpenWeb();
        SPListCollection objLists = objSite.Lists;

        foreach (SPList objList in objLists)
        {
          DataRow drList = dtLists.NewRow();
          drList["ListName"] = objList.Title;
          dtLists.Rows.Add(drList);
        }

        _dvLists = dtLists.DefaultView;
        _dvLists.Sort = "listname ASC";
      }
    }

    //Note: it is very important to use the correct names for the arguments!
    // The names of the arguments have to match exactly.
    [WebMethod]
    public string[] GetLists(string prefixText, int count)
    {
      string strReturn = String.Empty;
```

```
    try
    {
      string strUrl = "http://[server]/[site]/";
      InitLists(strUrl);
      string strFilter = String.Format("listname LIKE '{0}%'", prefixText);
      _dvLists.RowFilter = strFilter;

      string[] arrLists = new string[_dvLists.Count];
      for (int i = 0; i < _dvLists.Count; i++)
      {
        if ( i > count - 1 ) break;
        arrLists[i] = _dvLists[i]["ListName"].ToString();
      }

      return arrLists;
    }
    catch (Exception err)
    {
      Trace.Write(err.Message);
      throw;
    }
  }
 }
}
```

You have completed the server-side part of the autocompletion example. Incorporating the autocompletion web service into the client is made very easy, thanks to the ASP.NET Ajax AutoCompleteExtender control that can be found in AjaxControlToolkit.dll.

Using the AutoCompleteExtender control, you can tie the DocLibExtender web service to a text box called TextBox1. As the end user starts typing into the text box, ASP.NET Ajax calls the GetLists() method of the web service and shows the web service response in a <div> element called MyDisplay. The DocLibExtender web service is called as soon as the user types in a minimum number of keys in the ListsTextBox text box, which equals the value of the AutoCompleteExtender control's MinimumPrefixLength property. The maximum number of items that the client wants to retrieve equals the AutoCompleteExtender control's CompletionSetCount property, although it's up to the service whether or not to do something with this maximum. You can also specify the completion interval, which is the time it takes between service calls. The code for adding and configuring an AutoCompleteExtender control looks like this:

```
AutoCompleteExtender objAuto = new AutoCompleteExtender();
objAuto.ID = "autoComplete1";
objAuto.TargetControlID = "TextBox1";
objAuto.ServicePath = "/AskMe2/DocLibExtenderService.asmx";
objAuto.ServiceMethod = "GetLists";
objAuto.MinimumPrefixLength = 1;
objAuto.CompletionInterval = 1000;
objAuto.EnableCaching = true;
objAuto.CompletionSetCount = 12;
Controls.Add(objAuto);
```

Finally, you have to create a web part that uses the AutoCompleteExtender control. To be able to do this, you first need to set a reference to AjaxControlToolkit.dll, which can be found in [drive letter]:\[install directory]\AjaxControlToolkit\SampleWebSite\Bin.

The complete code for a web part that uses the AutoCompleteExtender control to communicate with a web service looks like Listing 2-19.

Listing 2-19. *The Autocomplete Extender Web Part*

```
using System; using System.Runtime.InteropServices;
using System.Web.UI;
using System.Web.UI.WebControls.WebParts;
using System.Xml.Serialization;
using Microsoft.SharePoint;
using Microsoft.SharePoint.WebControls;
using Microsoft.SharePoint.WebPartPages;
using System.Web.UI.WebControls;
using AjaxControlToolkit;

namespace AjaxClient
{
  [Guid("be6ec8e3-2706-4f52-bdf9-f6eb18fc65c0")]
  public class AjaxClient : System.Web.UI.WebControls.WebParts.WebPart
  {
    public AjaxClient()
    {
    }

    protected override void CreateChildControls()
    {
      try
      {
        string strPath = "/AskMe2/DocLibExtenderService.asmx";
        ServiceReference objReference = new ServiceReference();
        objReference.Path = strPath;

        Control ctlManager = Page.Master.FindControl("theScriptManager");
        ScriptManager objManager = ctlManager as ScriptManager;
        objManager.Services.Add(objReference);

        TextBox txtList = new TextBox();
        txtList.ID = "TextBox1";
        Controls.Add(txtList);

        AutoCompleteExtender objAuto = new AutoCompleteExtender();
        objAuto.ID = "autoComplete1";
        objAuto.TargetControlID = "TextBox1";
        objAuto.ServicePath = "/AskMe2/DocLibExtenderService.asmx";
        objAuto.ServiceMethod = "GetLists";
        objAuto.MinimumPrefixLength = 1;
        objAuto.CompletionInterval = 1000;
        objAuto.EnableCaching = true;
        objAuto.CompletionSetCount = 12;
        Controls.Add(objAuto);
      }
      catch (Exception err)
      {
        Controls.Add(new LiteralControl(err.Message));
      }
    }
  }
}
```

In this section, you have learned how to enhance the user interface experience by adding intelligent autocomplete behavior to a web part.

Client-Side Connectable Web Parts and ASP.NET Ajax

The SharePoint web part infrastructure allows web parts to exchange information at run time. This mechanism is called *web part connections*. Connectable web parts can communicate client-side via JavaScript, avoiding the need for a page postback when exchanging information, and server-side, requiring page postbacks whenever data is exchanged between web parts. Client-side connectable web parts and ASP.NET Ajax match each other really well. In this section, we will build two connectable web parts that offer a master-detail view. We do not provide detailed information about creating connectable web parts here. If you want to learn more about the connected web part infrastructure, refer to Chapter 5.

Note The connectable web part framework has been improved considerably in ASP.NET 2.0 compared to SharePoint 2003. However, there is no support in ASP.NET 2.0 web parts for client-side connections. This is one of the few areas where the SharePoint 2003 web part connection framework offers more capabilities than can be found in the ASP.NET 2.0 web part connection framework.

In this section, we will build two SharePoint legacy web parts that take advantage of the features offered by the SharePoint 2003 web part connection framework (which is still supported in Microsoft Office SharePoint Server 2007). We will also use the ContactService web service created previously in the section "Building a Company Contact Web Part Using ASP.NET Ajax and JSON."

The provider web part is a standard connectable web part that does not need to know anything about ASP.NET Ajax. The complete code for the provider web part looks like Listing 2-20.

Listing 2-20. *The Client-side Provider Web Part*

```
using System;
using System.ComponentModel;
using System.Web.UI;
using Microsoft.SharePoint.WebPartPages;
using System.Xml.Serialization;
using System.Web.UI.WebControls;
using System.Security;
using Microsoft.SharePoint.Utilities;
using Microsoft.SharePoint.WebPartPages.Communication;

namespace LoisAndClark.Connectable
{
  public class ProviderPart : WebPart, ICellProvider
  {
    public event CellProviderInitEventHandler CellProviderInit;
    public event CellReadyEventHandler CellReady;

    private bool _blnConnected = false;
    private string _strConnectedWebPartTitle = string.Empty;
    private string _strRegistrationErrorMsg = "An error has occurred trying ➥
    to register your connection interfaces.";
    private bool _blnRegistrationErrorOccurred = false;
    private string _strNotConnectedMsg = "NOT CONNECTED. To use this Web ➥
    Part, connect it to a client-side Cell Consumer Web Part.";
```

```
public override void EnsureInterfaces()
{
  try
  {
    RegisterInterface("MyCellProviderInterface_WPQ_",
      InterfaceTypes.ICellProvider,
      WebPart.UnlimitedConnections,
      ConnectionRunAt.Client,
      this,
      "CellProviderInterface_WPQ_",
      "Provide Cell To",
      "Provides a single value to a cell consumer Web Part.");
  }
  catch (SecurityException err)
  {
    _blnRegistrationErrorOccurred = true;
  }
}

public override ConnectionRunAt CanRunAt()
{
  return ConnectionRunAt.Client;
}

public override void PartCommunicationConnect(
  string strInterfaceName,
  WebPart objConnectedPart,
  string strConnectedInterfaceName,
  ConnectionRunAt enumRunAt)
{
  if (strInterfaceName == "MyCellProviderInterface_WPQ_")
  {
    blnConnected = true;
    _strConnectedWebPartTitle = ➡
    SPEncode.HtmlEncode(objConnectedPart.Title);
  }
}

public void CellConsumerInit(object objSender, ➡
CellConsumerInitEventArgs ➡
objCellConsumerInitEventArgs)
{
}

protected override void RenderWebPart(HtmlTextWriter output)
{
  if (_blnRegistrationErrorOccurred)
  {
    output.Write(_strRegistrationErrorMsg);
    return;
  }
```

```
if (_blnConnected)
{
  output.Write(ReplaceTokens("<P>\n"
    + "    Company name: \n"
    + "    <INPUT TYPE=\"text\" ID=\"CompanyName_WPQ_\"/>\n"
    + "    <INPUT TYPE=\"button\" ID=\"CellButton_WPQ_\" ➥
    onclick=\"CellButtonClick_WPQ_()\" VALUE=\"AutoFill\"/><br/>\n"
    + "</P>\n"

    + "<SCRIPT LANGUAGE=\"JavaScript\">\n"
    + "<!- \n"
    + "    var CellProviderInterface_WPQ_ = new Provider_WPQ_();\n"

    + "    function Provider_WPQ_()\n"
    + "    {\n"
    + "        this.PartCommunicationInit = myInit;\n"
    + "        this.PartCommunicationMain = myMain;\n"
    + "        this.CellConsumerInit = myCellConsumerInit;\n"

    + "        function myInit()\n"
    + "        {\n"
    + "            var cellProviderInitEventArgs = new Object();\n"
    + "            cellProviderInitEventArgs.FieldName = \"ProvideCell\";\n"
    + "            cellProviderInitEventArgs.FieldDisplayName = \"Provide ➥
    Cell\";\n"

    + "            WPSC.RaiseConnectionEvent ➥
    (\"MyCellProviderInterface_WPQ_ ➥
    \", \"CellProviderInit\", cellProviderInitEventArgs);\n"
    + "        }\n"

    + "        function myMain()\n"
    + "        {\n"
    + "            var cellReadyEventArgs = new Object();\n"
    + "            cellReadyEventArgs.Cell = null;\n"

    + "            WPSC.RaiseConnectionEvent ➥
    (\"MyCellProviderInterface_WPQ_ ➥
    \", \"CellReady\", cellReadyEventArgs);\n"
    + "        }\n"

    + "        function myCellConsumerInit ➥
    (sender, cellConsumerInitEventArgs)\n"
    + "        {\n"
    + "            document.all(\"ConnectedField_WPQ_\").innerText = ➥
    cellConsumerInitEventArgs.FieldDisplayName;\n"
    + "        }\n"
    + "    }\n"

    + "    function CellButtonClick_WPQ_()\n"
    + "    {\n"
    + "        var cellReadyEventArgs = new Object();\n"
    + "        cellReadyEventArgs.Cell = ➥
    document.all(\"CompanyName_WPQ_\").value;\n"
```

```
        + "        WPSC.RaiseConnectionEvent(\"MyCellProviderInterface_WPQ_\", ➥
        \"CellReady\", cellReadyEventArgs);\n"
        + "      }\n"
        + "//–>\n"
        + "</SCRIPT>\n"));
    }
    else
    {
      output.Write(_strNotConnectedMsg);
    }
  }
  }
  }
}
```

In the consumer web part, you need to add some additional client-side code. First you need to retrieve the cell value that is provided by the provider web part. Then pass this value as an argument to the JavaScript function that calls the ContactService web service. This function specifies an event handler JavaScript function that handles the ContactService response and updates the user interface. Since the response is in JSON format, you can use the parseJSON() function defined in the JSON script library (json.js) to convert the information to a JavaScript object. The JavaScript code that needs to be added to the consumer web part looks like this:

```
function myCellReady(sender, cellReadyEventArgs)
{
  if(cellReadyEventArgs.Cell != null)
  {
    AutoFillRequestWPQ1(cellReadyEventArgs.Cell);
  }
}

function AutoFillRequestWPQ1(strCompanyName)
{
  LoisAndClark.ContactService.GetContactInfo(strCompanyName, ➥
  OnAutoFillResponseWPQ1)
}

function OnAutoFillResponseWPQ1(strResult)
{
  var objContact = strResult.parseJSON();
  var objContactPerson = document.getElementById("ContactPerson");
  objContactPerson.innerHTML = objContact.ContactPerson;
  var objCity = document.getElementById("City");
  objCity.innerHTML = objContact.City;
  var objCountry = document.getElementById("Country");
  objCountry.innerHTML = objContact.Country;
}
```

The complete code for the consumer web part looks like Listing 2-21.

Listing 2-21. *The Client-side Consumer Web Part*

```
using System;
using System.ComponentModel;
using System.Web.UI;
using Microsoft.SharePoint.WebPartPages;
using System.Xml.Serialization;
using System.Web.UI.WebControls;
using System.Security;
using Microsoft.SharePoint.Utilities;
using Microsoft.SharePoint.WebPartPages.Communication;
using System.Web.UI.WebControls;

namespace LoisAndClark.Connectable
{
  public class ConsumerPart : WebPart
  {
    public event CellConsumerInitEventHandler CellConsumerInit;

    private bool _blnConnected = false;
    private string _strConnectedWebPartTitle = string.Empty;
    private string _strRegistrationErrorMsg = "An error has occurred ➡
    trying to register your connection interfaces.";
    private bool _blnRegistrationErrorOccurred = false;
    private string _strNotConnectedMsg = "NOT CONNECTED. To use this ➡
    Web Part, connect it to a client-side Cell Provider Web Part.";

    public ConsumerPart()
    {
    }

    public override void EnsureInterfaces()
    {
      try
      {
        RegisterInterface("MyCellConsumerInterface_WPQ_",
          InterfaceTypes.ICellConsumer,
          WebPart.LimitOneConnection,
          ConnectionRunAt.Client,
          this,
          "CellConsumerInterface_WPQ_",
          "Consume Cell From",
          "Consume a single value from another Web Part.");
      }
      catch (SecurityException err)
      {
        blnRegistrationErrorOccurred = true;
      }
    }

    public override ConnectionRunAt CanRunAt()
    {
      return ConnectionRunAt.Client;
    }
```

```
public override void PartCommunicationConnect(string strInterfaceName,
  WebPart objConnectedPart,
  string strConnectedInterfaceName,
  ConnectionRunAt enumRunAt)
{
  if (strInterfaceName == "MyCellConsumerInterface_WPQ_")
  {
    blnConnected = true;
    strConnectedWebPartTitle = SPEncode.HtmlEncode(objConnectedPart.Title);
  }
}

public void CellProviderInit(object objSender, ➥
CellProviderInitEventArgs objCellProviderInitEventArgs)
{
}

public void CellReady(object sender, CellReadyEventArgs cellReadyEventArgs)
{
}

protected override void CreateChildControls()
{
    string strPath = "/AskMe2/ContactService.asmx";
    ServiceReference objReference = new ServiceReference();
    objReference.Path = strPath;

    Control ctlManager = Page.Master.FindControl("theScriptManager");
    ScriptManager objMManager = ctlManager as ScriptManager;
    objManager.Services.Add(objReference);
}

protected override void RenderWebPart(HtmlTextWriter output)
{
  if (_blnRegistrationErrorOccurred)
  {
    output.Write(_strRegistrationErrorMsg);
    return;
  }

  if (_blnConnected)
  {
    output.Write(ReplaceTokens(
    "<div id=\"Result\">Result</div>"

    + "<SCRIPT LANGUAGE='JavaScript'>\n"
    + "<!- \n"
    + "function AutoFillRequest_WPQ_(strCompanyName)\n"
    + "{ \n"
    + "LoisAndClark.CompanyContact.ContactService. ➥
    GetContactInfo(strCompanyName, OnAutoFillResponse_WPQ_)\n"
    + "}\n"

    + "function OnAutoFillResponse_WPQ_(strResult)\n"
    + "{\n"
    + "var objResult = document.getElementById(\"Result\");\n"
    + "objResult.innerHTML = strResult;\n"
    + "}\n"
```

```
          + "var CellConsumerInterface_WPQ_ = new Consumer_WPQ_();\n"

          + "function Consumer_WPQ_()\n"
          + "{\n"
          + "this.PartCommunicationInit = myInit;\n"
          + "this.CellProviderInit = myCellProviderInit;\n"
          + "this.CellReady = myCellReady;\n"
          + "this.GetInitEventArgs = myGetInitEventArgs;\n"

          + "function myInit()\n"
          + "{\n"
          + "var cellConsumerInitEventArgs = new Object();\n"
          + "cellConsumerInitEventArgs.FieldName = \"ConsumerCellName\";\n"
          + "cellConsumerInitEventArgs.FieldDisplayName = \"Consume Cell\";\n"

          + "WPSC.RaiseConnectionEvent(\"MyCellConsumerInterface_WPQ_\", ➥
          \"CellConsumerInit\", cellConsumerInitEventArgs);\n"
          + "}\n"

          + "function myCellProviderInit(sender, cellProviderInitEventArgs)\n"
          + "{\n"
          + "document.all(\"ConnectedField_WPQ_\").innerText = ➥
          cellProviderInitEventArgs.FieldDisplayName;\n"
          + "}\n"

          + "function myCellReady(sender, cellReadyEventArgs)\n"
          + "{\n"
          + "if(cellReadyEventArgs.Cell != null)\n"
          + "{\n"
          + "AutoFillRequest_WPQ_(cellReadyEventArgs.Cell);\n"
          + "}\n"
          + "}\n"

          + "function myGetInitEventArgs()\n"
          + "{\n"
          + "var cellConsumerInitEventArgs = new Object();\n"
          + "cellConsumerInitEventArgs.FieldName = \"Consume Cell\";\n"
          + "cellConsumerInitEventArgs.FieldDisplayName = \"Consume Cell\";\n"

          + "return(cellConsumerInitEventArgs);\n"
          + "}\n"
          + "}\n"
          + "//->\n"
          + "</SCRIPT>\n"));
      }
      else
      {
        output.Write(_strNotConnectedMsg);
      }
    }
  }
}
```

Figure 2-18 shows a SharePoint page after importing both the consumer and provider web parts.

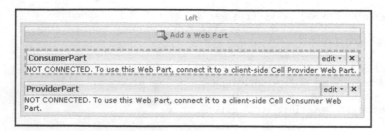

Figure 2-18. *Unconnected provider and consumer web parts*

The consumer and provider web parts are still not connected to each other. Next, you will connect the provider web part to the consumer web part. You can do so by clicking the Web Part edit menu of the ConsumerPart Web Part ➤ Connections ➤ Consume Cell From ➤ ProviderPart. This is shown in Figure 2-19.

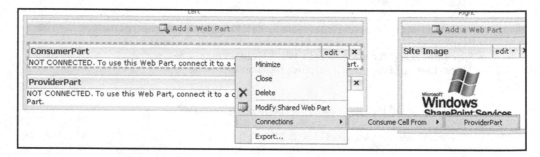

Figure 2-19. *Connected consumer and provider web parts*

After connecting the provider and consumer web parts, they should look like Figure 2-20.

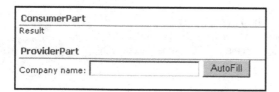

Figure 2-20. *Connected consumer and provider web parts*

If you enter a value into the company name text box and click the AutoFill button in the My Provider web part, this value will be propagated to the ConsumerPart web part. The My Client web part will use the value to call the ContactService web service via ASP.NET Ajax. The ContactService web service looks in the ContactInfo SharePoint list to see if it can find the contact information that matches the company name. Once the contact information is returned, the My Client web part updates the user interface. All of the processing is handled client-side.

To sum up, a provider part passes information to a consumer using JavaScript, thus preventing a page postback. The consumer web part uses ASP.NET Ajax to communicate with a web service on the server, using values retrieved from the provider web part. The end result is a dynamic and seamless experience for the end user, without requiring any page postback. The result is seen in Figure 2-21.

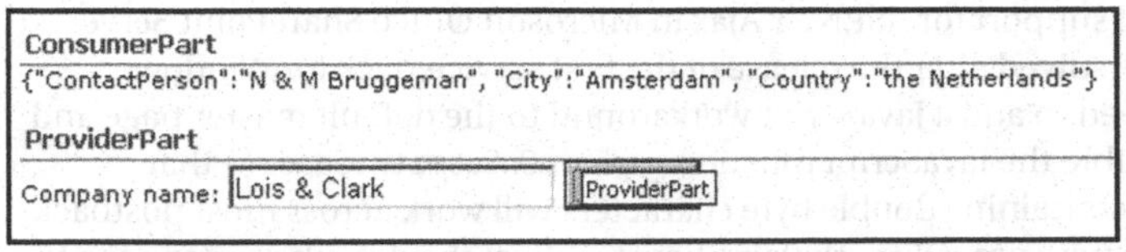

```
ConsumerPart
{"ContactPerson":"N & M Bruggeman", "City":"Amsterdam", "Country":"the Netherlands"}

ProviderPart

Company name: Lois & Clark                    ProviderPart
```

Figure 2-21. *Client-side connectable web parts and ASP.NET Ajax*

In this section, you learned how to use ASP.NET Ajax combined with scenarios using client-side connectable web parts.

Revisiting the Performance Counter Web Part

So far, you have learned how ASP.NET Ajax makes it easy to communicate in an object-based manner with web services using extensions to JavaScript, most importantly, using JavaScript proxies to interact with web services. You have also seen how to use ASP.NET controls that add Ajax capabilities to existing controls. ASP.NET Ajax consists of three parts, the final part being UpdatePanels. UpdatePanels allows you to Ajax-enable existing ASP.NET controls. In the next example of this chapter, you will see how to use UpdatePanels in web parts.

The UpdatePanel control is located in the System.Web.UI namespace and allows sections of a page to be partially rendered without a postback. All you need to do to use an UpdatePanel is to add one to a page, add some child controls to it, and define when the content of an UpdatePanel needs to be updated.

If you want to allow child control postbacks to update the content of an UpdatePanel, you need to set its ChildrenAsTriggers property to true.

The UpdateMode property of an UpdatePanel control determines when its content should be updated. By default, this property is set to Always. In this case, the content of the UpdatePanel is updated on every postback originating from anywhere on a page. If you set the UpdateMode to Conditional, the content is updated if

- The page calls UpdatePanel's Update() method.

- The postback is caused by a control that is explicitly defined as a trigger using UpdatePanel's Triggers property.

- The ChildrenAsTriggers property is set to true and one of the child controls of the UpdatePanel causes a postback.

Finally, you can add child controls to an UpdatePanel by using its ContentTemplateContainer property. The following code fragment shows how to programmatically add and configure an UpdatePanel:

```
UpdatePanel pnlHolder = new UpdatePanel();
pnlHolder.ID = "UpdatePanel1";
pnlHolder.ChildrenAsTriggers = true;
pnlHolder.UpdateMode = UpdatePanelUpdateMode.Conditional;
Controls.Add(pnlHolder);

lblDisplay = new Label();
lblDisplay.Text = "Retrieve value via Ajax";
pnlHolder.ContentTemplateContainer.Controls.Add(lblDisplay);

Button btnSubmit = new Button();
btnSubmit.Text = "Get current Processor time";
btnSubmit.Click += new EventHandler(OnSubmit);
pnlHolder.ContentTemplateContainer.Controls.Add(btnSubmit);
```

Because of the lack of official support for ASP.NET Ajax in Microsoft Office SharePoint Server 2007 (something which should be solved after the release of the first service pack for Windows SharePoint Services 2007), you need to add a JavaScript workaround to the default master page and to your web part. You need to disable the JavaScript function _spFormOnSubmitWrapper() that ensures that some types of URLs containing double byte characters will work across most postback and asynchronous scenarios. The next procedure explains how to adjust the default master page to disable the _spFormOnSubmitWrapper() function:

1. Open a SharePoint site in SharePoint Designer.

2. Open the _catalogs folder.

3. Open the masterpage gallery.

4. Open the Forms folder.

5. Double-click the default.master page.

6. Switch to Code view.

7. Add the following code to the page:

```
<script type='text/javascript'>
_spOriginalFormAction = document.forms[0].action;
_spSuppressFormOnSubmitWrapper=true;
</script>
```

Alternatively, you could add this JavaScript code to the page by registering it within a web part, like so:

```
if (Page.Form != null)
{
  string strSubmit = Page.Form.Attributes["onsubmit"];
  if (strSubmit == "return _spFormOnSubmitWrapper();")
  {
    Page.Form.Attributes["onsubmit"] = "_spFormOnSubmitWrapper();";
  }
}

ScriptManager.RegisterStartupScript(this, typeof(AjaxClient),
"UpdatePanelFixup",
"_spOriginalFormAction = document.forms[0].action; ➡
_spSuppressFormOnSubmitWrapper=true;", true);
}
```

The complete code for a web part that uses an UpdatePanel to support Ajax scenarios is shown in Listing 2-22.

Listing 2-22. *Performance Counter Web Part Using UpdatePanel Control*

```
using System;
using System.Runtime.InteropServices;
using System.Web.UI;
using System.Web.UI.WebControls.WebParts;
using System.Xml.Serialization;
using Microsoft.SharePoint;
using Microsoft.SharePoint.WebControls;
using Microsoft.SharePoint.WebPartPages;
using System.Web.UI.WebControls;
using System.Diagnostics;
using System.Threading;
using System.Text;
```

```
namespace AjaxClient
{
  [Guid("be6ec8e3-2706-4f52-bdf9-f6eb18fc65c0")]
  public class AjaxClient : System.Web.UI.WebControls.WebParts.WebPart
  {
    private Label lblDisplay;
    protected override void CreateChildControls()
    {
      base.CreateChildControls();
      EnsureUpdatePanelFixups();

      UpdatePanel pnlHolder = new UpdatePanel();
      pnlHolder.ID = "UpdatePanel1";
      pnlHolder.ChildrenAsTriggers = true;
      pnlHolder.UpdateMode = UpdatePanelUpdateMode.Conditional;
      Controls.Add(pnlHolder);

      lblDisplay = new Label();
      lblDisplay.Text = "Retrieve value via Ajax";
      pnlHolder.ContentTemplateContainer.Controls.Add(lblDisplay);

      Button btnSubmit = new Button();
      btnSubmit.Text = "Get current Processor time";
      btnSubmit.Click += new EventHandler(OnSubmit);
      pnlHolder.ContentTemplateContainer.Controls.Add(btnSubmit);
    }

    private void OnSubmit(object sender, EventArgs eventArgs)
    {
      lblDisplay.Text = "processor time: " + GetProcessorTime();
    }

    public string GetProcessorTime()
    {
      try
      {
        PerformanceCounter objCounter = new PerformanceCounter();
        objCounter.CategoryName = "Processor";
        objCounter.CounterName = "% Processor Time";
        objCounter.InstanceName = "_Total";
        objCounter.MachineName = ".";
        objCounter.ReadOnly = true;

        int intCurrentCpuUsage = Convert.ToInt32(objCounter.NextValue());
        Thread.Sleep(2000);

        return objCounter.NextValue().ToString();
      }
      catch (Exception err)
      {
        return err.Message;
      }
    }
```

```
    private void EnsureUpdatePanelFixups()
    {
      if (Page.Form != null)
      {
        string strSubmit = Page.Form.Attributes["onsubmit"];
        if (strSubmit == "return _spFormOnSubmitWrapper();")
        {
          Page.Form.Attributes["onsubmit"] = "_spFormOnSubmitWrapper();";
        }
      }

      ScriptManager.RegisterStartupScript(this, typeof(AjaxClient), ➥
      "UpdatePanelFixup", "_spOriginalFormAction = document.forms[0].action;
      _spSuppressFormOnSubmitWrapper=true;", true);
    }
  }
}
```

Figure 2-22 shows what this web part looks like in action.

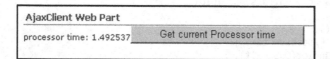

Figure 2-22. *UpdatePanel web part*

■**Note** There are a couple of web sites containing information about integrating ASP.NET Ajax and SharePoint 2007 that are worth reading. "Integrating ASP.NET Ajax with SharePoint" by Mike Ammerlaan (http:// sharepoint.microsoft.com/blogs/mike/Lists/Posts/Post.aspx?ID=3) discusses how to use UpdatePanels within web parts. The article "Use ASP.NET AJAX Framework with Windows SharePoint Services 3.0" by Laurent Cotton (http://www.bewise.fr/download/articles/article-41.doc) discusses the same topic, but contains a bit more information about the JavaScript workaround required to get the use of UpdatePanels within web parts working. The blog post "AjaxBasePart: Easy ASP.NET 2.0 AJAX Extensions 1.0 and Office SharePoint Server 2007" by Eric Schoonover (http://www.capdes.com/2007/02/ microsoft_office_sharepoint_se.html) discusses the creation of an AjaxBasePart class that makes creating ASP.NET Ajax web parts easier. Finally, CodePlex contains a project called Daniel Larson's ASP.NET AJAX Extensions Toolkit for SharePoint (http://www.codeplex.com/sharepointajax). This toolkit provides a base framework for deploying client-side Ajax controls that work against web services and XML feeds utilizing the ASP.NET Ajax framework.

In this section, you have learned how to use the ASP.NET Ajax UpdatePanel control.

Client Callbacks and the People Picker Control

There is a final topic left to discuss when it comes to implementing Ajax scenarios in SharePoint environments. Before ASP.NET Ajax was released, ASP.NET 2.0 offered another technology that lets client-side script communicate asynchronously with a server-side method. This technology is known as *client callback technology,* and although it is reasonably easy to implement, it does not offer a full-blown framework for implementing Ajax scenarios like ASP.NET Ajax does.

However, there are still powerful controls out there that use client callbacks for their implementation, such as the ASP.NET 2.0 Treeview control and the SharePoint People Picker. In this section, we will discuss how client callbacks work and then show how to build a web part that uses the People Picker to find account names and groups.

■**Note** Under the hood, client callbacks use the XmlHttpRequest object. Please refer to section "Retrieving Data via XMLHttpRequest" for more information.

The life cycle of a client callback consists of three stages:

1. A JavaScript event is fired that triggers a callback.
2. A server-side method is executed that accepts a string as a parameter and returns a string as the result.
3. A client-side JavaScript method receives the response and adjusts the user interface.

An ASP.NET page that wants to use client callbacks needs to implement the ICallbackEventHandler interface of the System.Web.UI namespace. This interface consists of two methods:

- RaiseCallbackEvent(): This method accepts data passed by client-side code.
- GetCallbackResult(): This method passes results back to a page.

An important limitation of client callbacks is that data is passed in the form of a string. If you want to transfer information that has a complex structure, you need to design some kind of system to serialize and deserialize data, or use an existing system such as JSON. You can find more information about JSON in section "JSON Messages."

Also, you need to realize that the RaiseCallbackEvent() and GetCallbackResult() methods do not have access to controls on an ASP.NET page because these methods are called out-of-band and only a part of the page life cycle is executed. The following stages still take place during a callback:

1. Init
2. Load state
3. Process postback data
4. Load
5. Callback event
6. Unload

Most modern browsers such as MSIE 5 and higher, Netscape 6 and higher, Safari 1.2 and higher, and Firefox support the use of the XmlHttpRequest object and thus allow you to use client callbacks. Use the Request.Browser.SupportsCallback property to determine whether a browser supports client callbacks. If you want to determine whether a postback is caused by a callback, use the Page.IsCallback property.

Building a People Picker Web Part

The SharePoint People Picker allows you to choose one or more account names and groups in a user-friendly way. As stated before, the People Picker is a powerful control that uses client callbacks. The people picker functionality is implemented in the PeopleEditor control, which is located in the Microsoft.SharePoint.WebControls namespace of the Microsoft.SharePoint assembly.

Figure 2-23 shows that you can type an account name into the People Picker's text box. There are two buttons on the People Picker control: Check Names and Browse.

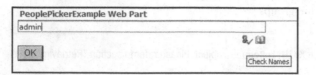

Figure 2-23. *Looking for an account name using the People Picker*

If you click the Check Names action, you start looking for the name of a user or group. This causes a client callback. As the result, a list with matching names is shown, as you can see in Figure 2-24.

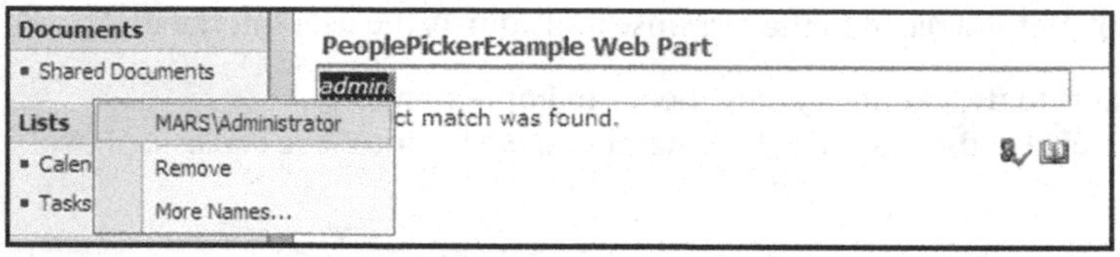

Figure 2-24. *Resolving multiple matching entries*

The end result of this search is shown in Figure 2-25.

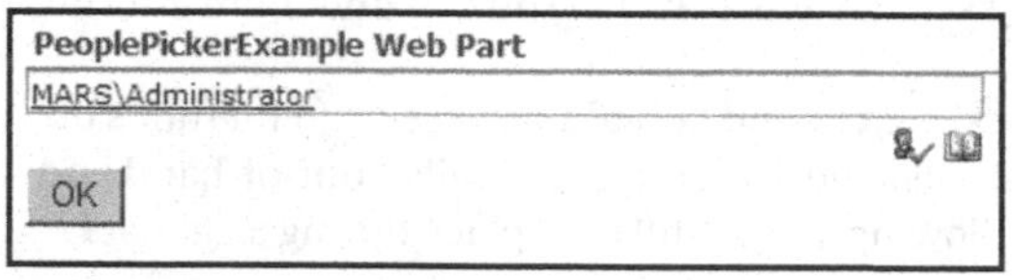

Figure 2-25. *The People Picker finds the user account.*

Alternatively, if you click on the Browse button, the Select People and Groups – Webpage Dialog window appears, which allows you to search for people and groups. This is shown in Figure 2-26.

The PeopleEditor control has a number of properties that allow you to configure it. In the next section, we will discuss the properties that we think are most important.

The `PlaceButtonsUnderEntityEditor` property determines the locations of the Names and Browse buttons. If set to `true`, the buttons are placed at the bottom-right corner of the account name text box; otherwise they are placed to the right of the text box.

The `AllowEmpty` property lets you define whether the user is required to fill in a value in the People Picker.

The `SelectionSet` property allows you to define the set of users and groups the People Picker can choose from. This set can consist of users, Active Directory distribution lists, Active Directory security groups, and SharePoint groups.

The `MultiSelect` property lets you define whether a user is allowed to specify multiple user accounts.

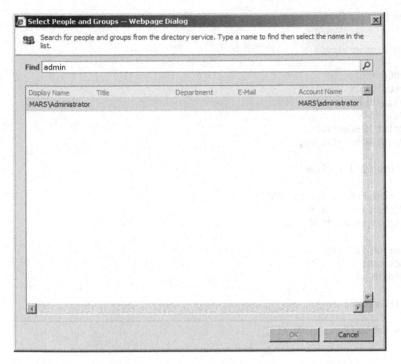

Figure 2-26. *Searching for a user account*

The following code fragment shows how to add a People Picker to a web part and how to configure it:

```
objEditor = new PeopleEditor();
objEditor.AutoPostBack = true;
objEditor.PlaceButtonsUnderEntityEditor = true;
objEditor.ID = "pplEditor";
objEditor.AllowEmpty = false;
objEditor.SelectionSet = "User,SecGroup,SPGroup";
objEditor.MultiSelect = false;
Controls.Add(objEditor);
```

You can retrieve the values selected in the People Picker by looping through the ResolvedEntities collection of the PeopleEditor object.

```
string strAccountName = String.Empty;

for (int i = 0; i < objEditor.ResolvedEntities.Count; i++)
{
  PickerEntity objEntity = (PickerEntity) objEditor.ResolvedEntities[i];
  SPUserInfo objInfo = new SPUserInfo();
  objInfo.LoginName = objEntity.Key;
  strAccountName = objInfo.LoginName;
}
```

Listing 2-23 shows the complete code for a web part that uses the People Picker.

Listing 2-23. *Web Part That Uses the People Picker*

```
using System;
using System.Runtime.InteropServices;
using System.Web.UI;
using System.Web.UI.WebControls;
using System.Web.UI.WebControls.WebParts;
using System.Xml.Serialization;
using Microsoft.SharePoint;
using Microsoft.SharePoint.WebControls;
using Microsoft.SharePoint.WebPartPages;

namespace LoisAndClark.PeoplePickerExample
{
  [Guid("93bc9836-7deb-4ce6-bc6d-91312563603b")]
  public class PeoplePickerExample : ➥
  System.Web.UI.WebControls.WebParts.WebPart
  {
    private PeopleEditor objEditor;
    private Label lblAccount;
    private Button btnPostMe;

    public PeoplePickerExample()
    {
      this.ExportMode = WebPartExportMode.All;
    }

    protected override void CreateChildControls()
    {
      lblAccount = new Label();
      lblAccount.ID = "lblAccount";
      Controls.Add(lblAccount);

      objEditor = new PeopleEditor();
      objEditor.AutoPostBack = true;
      objEditor.PlaceButtonsUnderEntityEditor = true;
      objEditor.ID = "pplEditor";
      objEditor.AllowEmpty = false;
      objEditor.SelectionSet = "User,DL,SecGroup,SPGroup";
      objEditor.MultiSelect = false;
      Controls.Add(objEditor);

      btnPostMe = new Button();
      btnPostMe.Text = " OK ";
      btnPostMe.Click += new EventHandler(btnPostMe_Click);
      Controls.Add(btnPostMe);
    }

    private string GetAccountName()
    {
      string strAccountName = String.Empty;
```

```
    for (int i = 0; i < objEditor.ResolvedEntities.Count; i++)
    {
      PickerEntity objEntity = (PickerEntity) objEditor.ResolvedEntities[i];
      SPUserInfo objInfo = new SPUserInfo();
      objInfo.LoginName = objEntity.Key;
      strAccountName = objInfo.LoginName;
    }

    return strAccountName;
  }

  private void btnPostMe_Click(object sender, EventArgs eventArgs)
  {
    string strAccountName = GetAccountName();
    lblAccount.Text = "account name: " + strAccountName;
  }
 }
}
```

This section demonstrated how to use the PeoplePicker control, a control that uses client callbacks, within a web part.

Summary

This chapter discussed Ajax and ASP.NET Ajax. We looked at some of the more popular Ajax implementations for .NET. Ajax-style applications rely heavily on communication with the server-side application. Nowadays, most of the time the server-side application will consist of web services. It can be a hassle to add service virtualization on a Microsoft Office SharePoint Server 2007 server, but you have learned how to do it. There are multiple important aspects when building the client side of Ajax-style applications. Within Ajax-style development, you can choose between various types of server responses: plain text, HTML, XML, and JSON. We showed you examples of all these message types and discussed their benefits and disadvantages.

ASP.NET Ajax is an Ajax implementation, and this chapter explained how to use it. We discussed how to install ASP.NET Ajax and how to use it within web parts. We gave detailed information about creating a performance counter web part that uses ASP.NET Ajax to provide up-to-date information about performance counters that run on the server. We also explained how to create a web part that shows company contact information that is stored in a SharePoint list. The company contact information is retrieved using ASP.NET Ajax in a JSON message format. You have seen how to use ASP.NET Ajax autocompletion in a web part and how to use ASP.NET Ajax within connectable web parts. You also learned how to use UpdatePanels within a web part. Finally, you learned what client callbacks are and how to use the People Picker in a web part.

CHAPTER 3

Enhancing Business Intelligence via SQL Server 2005 Reporting Services

Business intelligence is all about having comprehensive knowledge of all of the factors that affect your business. Business intelligence can be described as the process that transforms data into information, thus providing in-depth knowledge about customers, competitors, business partners, economic environment, or internal operations. Such knowledge helps companies gain a competitive edge, so it should come as no surprise that as of late, business intelligence has become a very popular topic.

Microsoft's Business Intelligence suite supports all facets of decision-making. It consists of such products as SQL Server Analysis Services, Office Business Scorecard Manager, and SQL Server Reporting Services. This chapter focuses on SQL Server 2005 Reporting Services—which provides web reporting on a variety of data sources, published reports, and subscriptions—in relation to Microsoft Office SharePoint Server 2007. We discuss the basics of Reporting Services and show you how to create a simple report using Business Intelligence Development Studio. Then we show you how to view a report via the Report Manager and how to use the SharePoint reporting web parts. We will also discuss how to create and deploy a report model to a SharePoint Report Center.

Introducing Reporting Services

The intent of this section is to get you acquainted and comfortable with SQL Server 2005 Reporting Services. As Reporting Services is quite a large topic, we will start with a general overview. Later in the chapter, we will cover detailed topics regarding the combination of Reporting Services and Microsoft Office SharePoint Server 2007.

Reporting Services is a middle-tier server that runs under Internet Information Services (IIS) and allows you to build a reporting environment on top of an existing web server infrastructure. With Reporting Services, it is possible to retrieve data from any available data server for any data source type that has a .NET Framework–managed data provider, OLE DB provider, or ODBC data source. The Reporting Services product consists of three main components: databases, report server, and client applications. The Reporting Services architecture is shown in Figure 3-1.

When you install Reporting Services, the following databases are created: ReportServer and ReportServerTempDB. The ReportServer database is the primary database used to store all information about reports. The ReportServerTempDB database contains cached copies of reports that are used to improve performance.

The report server is the most important component in the SQL Server Reporting Services architecture. It is responsible for responding to every client request to render a report or to perform a management request. The report server consists of two parts: a Windows service and a web service. This way the report server provides an optimized and parallel processing infrastructure for processing and rendering reports. The Windows service provides initialization, scheduling, and delivery services, as well as server maintenance. Clients can access report servers via the web service layer. It performs end-to-end processing for reports that run on demand. It also provides the primary programmatic interface for applications that integrate with a report server, for example, Report Manager, Report Builder, and SQL Server Management Studio.

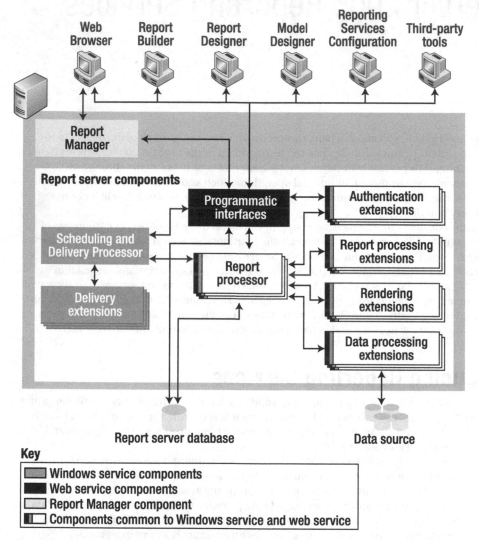

Figure 3-1. *Reporting Services architecture*

The report server can be divided into two subcomponents: report processors and extensions. Report processors support the integrity of the reporting system and cannot be modified; you can think of them as the hub of the report server. Extensions are also processors, but they perform very specific functions. Extensions will be discussed later, in the section "Reporting Services Extensions."

The following client applications are part of Reporting Services: Report Manager, Business Intelligence Development Studio, and command-line utilities. We will cover Report Manager and

Business Intelligence Development Studio in more detail later in the "Building a Report" and "Viewing a Report" sections of this chapter. First we will discuss the command-line utilities.

Reporting Services ships with three command-line utilities:

- *Rsconfig.exe*: This tool is used to configure and manage a report server connection to the report server database.

- *Rskeymgmt.exe*: This tool is an encryption key management tool. You can use it to back up, apply, create, and delete symmetric keys. You can also use this tool to attach a report server instance to a shared report server database. Encryption keys are used to encrypt credentials, connection information, and accounts.

- *Rs.exe*: This tool is a script host that you can use to perform scripted operations. Use this tool to run Microsoft Visual Basic .NET scripts that copy data between report server databases, publish reports, create items in a report server database, and more.

■**Note** If you want to learn more about the Rsconfig, Rskeymgmt, and Rs command-line tools, SQL Server 2005 Books Online (Start ➤ All Programs ➤ Microsoft SQL Server 2005 ➤ Documentation and Tutorials ➤ SQL Server Books Online) contains a complete overview of the arguments that are available for these tools and explains in detail how to use them.

Requirements for Reporting Services

In this section, we will discuss the requirements Reporting Services must meet to integrate with Microsoft Office SharePoint Server 2007. Of course, SQL Server 2005 Reporting Services must be installed on the server. When you install Reporting Services on a different server than the Microsoft Office SharePoint Server 2007 server, you must take care that the Windows SharePoint Services 3.0 object model is installed on the Reporting Services server. You can do this by installing Windows SharePoint Services 3.0 on the Reporting Services server.

■**Tip** More information about installing SQL Server 2005 Reporting Services can be found at http://technet. microsoft.com/en-us/library/ms143736.aspx.

If you want deep integration of Reporting Services and Microsoft Office SharePoint Server 2007, you have to install the SQL Server 2005 Service Pack 2.0 and the SQL Server 2005 Reporting Services Add-in for Microsoft SharePoint Technologies. The advantages of this deep integration are discussed later, in the section "SQL Server 2005 Service Pack 2.0." The Reporting Services Add-in must be installed after Service Pack 2.0, because the Reporting Services Add-in makes use of features added by the service pack. Table 3-1 shows an overview of what you must install to use Reporting Services and SharePoint.

SQL Server 2005 Service Pack 2.0

SQL Server 2005 Service Pack 2.0 was released in the first quarter of 2007. This service pack is a very important addition to SQL Server 2005 and its integration with Microsoft Office SharePoint Server 2007. Service Pack 2.0 adds new or improved features to the following components of SQL Server 2005:

- Analysis Services
- Database Engine
- Integration Services
- Replication
- Reporting Services
- Shared Tools

In this chapter, we will only pay attention to the Reporting Services features. You can download Service Pack 2.0 at the following location: http://technet.microsoft.com/en-us/sqlserver/ bb426877.aspx. Table 3-1 shows an overview of the prerequisites.

Service Pack 2.0 enables deep integration between SQL Server 2005 Reporting Services and Microsoft Office SharePoint Server 2007 (and Windows SharePoint Services 3.0). Service Pack 2.0 provides the following new features for integrating Reporting Services with SharePoint:

- With Service Pack 2.0, you can integrate a report server instance with Microsoft Office SharePoint Server 2007 or Windows SharePoint Services 3.0 via a Report Center. This way, a report can be stored, managed, and accessed via a SharePoint document library. In addition, this allows the use of standard document library features such as versioning and checking in and out.

- Service Pack 2.0 makes it possible to store reports and associated resources such as database connections in the SharePoint content database. These reports and associated resources will be automatically synchronized with the Report Server database.

- The report server contains a custom security extension that integrates with existing SharePoint permissions to control access to report server operations. Security extensions are used by the report server to take care of authenticating and authorizing users and groups. More information about Reporting Services Extensions can be found in the section "Reporting Services Extensions."

- Service Pack 2.0 comes with a new delivery extension that can be used in subscriptions to deliver reports to SharePoint libraries. Delivery extensions are used by the report server to deliver reports to various locations. More information about Reporting Services Extensions can be found in the "Reporting Services Extensions" section.

- Service Pack 2.0 updates the Reporting Services Configuration tool with a new configuration option called SharePoint integration. With this option, the report server can be configured for SharePoint integrated operations.

- Service Pack 2.0 comes with a new SOAP endpoint that can be used for managing report server content in SharePoint integrated mode.

SQL Server 2005 Reporting Services Add-in for Microsoft SharePoint Technologies

The Reporting Services Add-in must be installed after Service Pack 2.0, so you can use the Service Pack 2.0 reporting processing and management capabilities within SharePoint 2007. The Reporting Services Add-in can be downloaded from the following location: http://www.microsoft.com/ downloads/details.aspx?familyid=1E53F882-0C16-4847-B331-132274AE8C84&displaylang=en. Table 3-1 shows an overview of the prerequisites.

Table 3-1. *Installation Requirements to Enable Integration Between Reporting Services and SharePoint*

Name	Location
SQL Server 2005 Service Pack 2.0	http://technet.microsoft.com/en-us/sqlserver/bb426877.aspx
SQL Server 2005 Reporting Services Add-in for Microsoft SharePoint Technologies	http://www.microsoft.com/downloads/ familyid=1E53F882-0C16-4847-B331- 132274AE8C84&displaylang=en

The Reporting Services Add-in contains the following functionality:

- A SQL Server Reporting Services Report Viewer web part. More information about this web part can be found in the section "SQL Server Reporting Services Report Viewer Web Part."
- Web application pages that can be used to do the following:
    - Create subscriptions and schedules.
    - Manage reports and report models.
    - Manage data sources.
- Support for report server content types within SharePoint.

Mode of Deployment

SQL Server 2005 Reporting Services comes with a tool called the Reporting Services Configuration Manager. With the Reporting Services Configuration Manager, you can create a report server database and configure the connection between the report server and the report server database. You can also configure the report server database to run in Native mode or SharePoint integrated mode.

The SQL Server 2005 Service Pack 2.0 comes with two modes of deployment for report instances:

- Native mode
- SharePoint integrated mode

The default mode for a report server instance is native mode. When a report server is a standalone application that is responsible for performing activities related to reports, such as viewing and processing, it is deployed in native mode. Reporting Services provides two web parts that can be installed and used with SharePoint 2007 (both Microsoft Office SharePoint Server 2007 and Windows SharePoint Server 3.0) when the report server is in native mode. More information about these two web parts can be found in the section "Report Explorer and Report Viewer Web Parts."

■**Note** These web parts were already available before Service Pack 2.0 and were also used in SharePoint 2003.

When the ReportServer database is deployed in SharePoint integrated mode, the report server becomes part of the SharePoint web application deployment. SharePoint users can store and access reports in document libraries. The report server can be configured to interact with SharePoint integrated mode when Service pack 2.0 is installed.

When you configure a report server to run in SharePoint integrated mode, you must create a new report server database. When you connect a report server instance to a report server database running in SharePoint integrated mode, the report server's SharePointIntegrated property is automatically set to true. The report server then switches to the custom security extension and SOAP endpoint that are used when a report server is set to `SharePointIntegrated` mode. When the report server database is created with `SharePointIntegrated` mode set to true, the site hierarchy in SharePoint becomes the content hierarchy for the report server. The report server keeps track of the URLs of all reports that are stored in SharePoint. When you deploy a Report Server or Report Model project using the Business Intelligence Development Studio, you must use fully qualified URLS; relative paths are not allowed. Make sure to include file extensions in the report URL path; they are required for each item.

Note Normally, reports are stored in the report server database. Once the report server is running in SharePoint integrated mode, SharePoint acts as the content repository for all reports.

SharePoint integrated mode offers the following advantages:

- You can use document libraries to store, access, and manage reporting services reports, data sources, and report models. The section "Viewing a Report" discusses this topic.
- The SharePoint user interface can also be used to publish, view, manage, and deliver reports.
- It is possible to build Business Intelligence dashboards with Reporting Services reports.
- The workflow and collaboration features of SharePoint can be used in combination with Reporting Services reports. For instance, you could create a workflow that requires a report to be approved by somebody before it is published.

The following features are no longer supported when running a report server database in SharePoint integrated mode:

- *Report Manager*: Report Manager is a web-based report access and management tool.
- *Management Studio*: Management Studio can be used by report server administrators to manage a report server alongside other SQL Server component servers. Management Studio offers almost the same functionality as Report Manager, but has additional support for managing other server types in the same management workspace. If you try to connect to a report server running in SharePoint integration mode, you will get a pop-up window indicating that the current operation is not supported.
- *My Reports*: With the My Reports feature, users can save reports in a private folder in the report server database.
- *Linked Reports*: Linked reports are report server items that provide access points to existing reports. This acts as shortcuts to an existing report.
- *Job Management*: Job management features are features that allow you to stop a long-running report process.

Note SQL Server 2005 does not offer support for migrating existing reports built in native mode to SharePoint integrated mode. If you want to use these reports in a SharePoint environment, you must republish them in SharePoint integrated mode. In general, you should use SharePoint integrated mode if end users are planning to interact with the report server within a SharePoint environment.

Configuring Native Mode

Follow these steps to create a report server database that runs in native mode:

1. Connect to the database server that will hold the report server database. After installing Reporting Services, you can find this tool via Start ➤ All Programs ➤ SQL Server 2005 ➤ Configuration Tools ➤ Reporting Services Configuration. This opens the Report Server Installation Instance Selection window, as can be seen in Figure 3-2.

2. In the Machine Name text box, enter the name of the server running the report server. In the Instance name text box, enter the name of the SQL Server 2005 Reporting Services instance. Click Connect to connect to the Reporting Services instance.

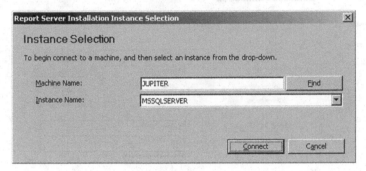

Figure 3-2. *Report Server Installation Instance Selection window*

Go to the Database Setup option in the Reporting Services Configuration Manager and follow these steps:

1. Enter a database server name.

2. Specify the name of the reporting services database. See Figure 3-3.

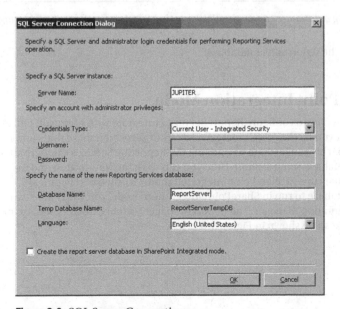

Figure 3-3. *SQL Server Connection*

3. Select the SharePoint integrated mode check box if you want to deploy the reporting database in SharePoint integrated mode. If you want to deploy the Reporting database in native mode, leave the check box unchecked. The earlier section "Mode of Deployment" discussed this topic more thoroughly.

4. Enter the credentials required to connect to the report server database, as shown in Figure 3-4.

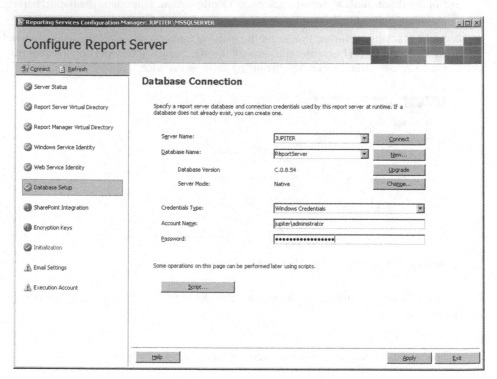

Figure 3-4. *Configuring a database connection in Reporting Services Configuration Manager*

5. Click Apply to create the report server database.

Configuring SharePoint Integration Mode

In this section, we will discuss how to configure Report Server to integrate with Microsoft Office SharePoint Server 2007. What you have to do is create a new report server database that runs in SharePoint integration mode. This can be done by opening the Reporting Services Configuration Manager and going to the Database Setup section. Here you can click the New button and make a new report server database that runs in SharePoint integrated mode, as shown in Figure 3-5.

After configuring the database to run in SharePoint integration mode, you will notice two changes in the Report Configuration Manager. The Report Manager Virtual Directory section has a gray circle and displays the message shown in Figure 3-6.

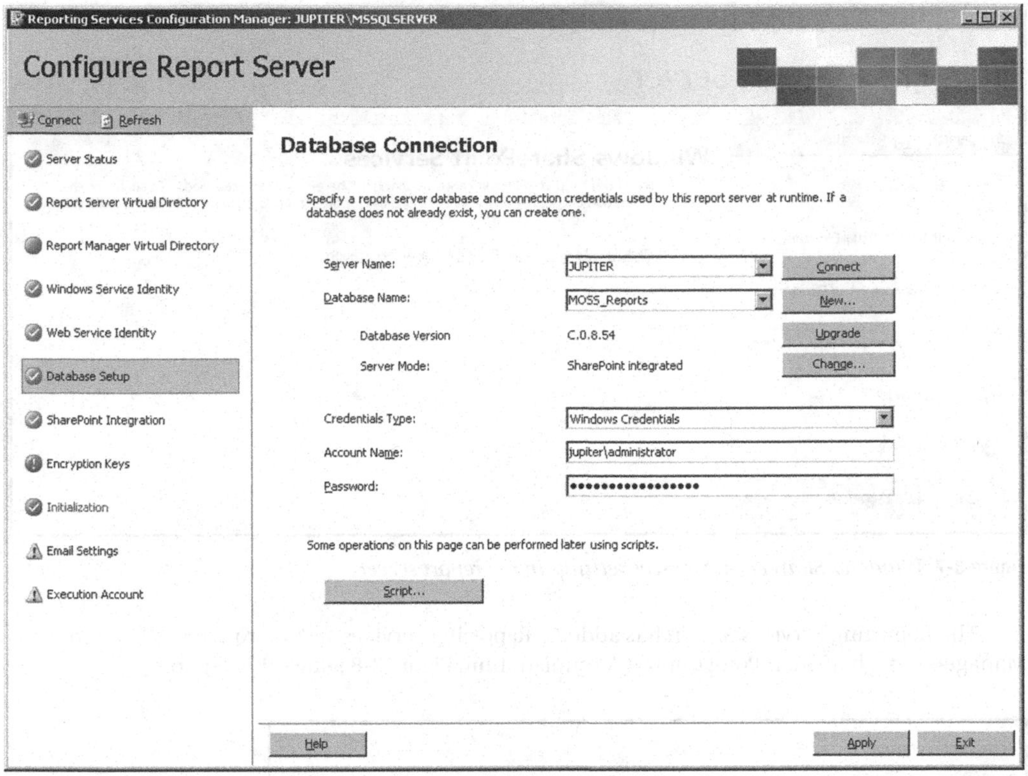

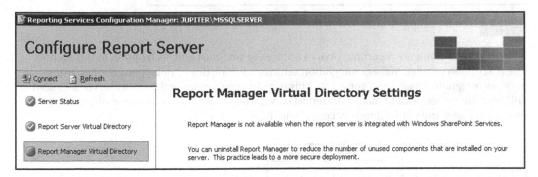

Figure 3-5. *A database connection in SharePoint integrated mode*

Figure 3-6. *Report Manager Virtual Directory Settings*

The other thing you will notice is that the SharePoint Integration option displays a green check mark and displays a message that is shown in Figure 3-7.

The next thing to do is to configure the integration with the report server in the SharePoint web application. You can do this using SharePoint Central Administration. Open SharePoint Central Administration by clicking the link in the Report Configuration window or by going to Start ➤ All Programs ➤ Microsoft Office Server ➤ SharePoint 3.0 Central Administration.

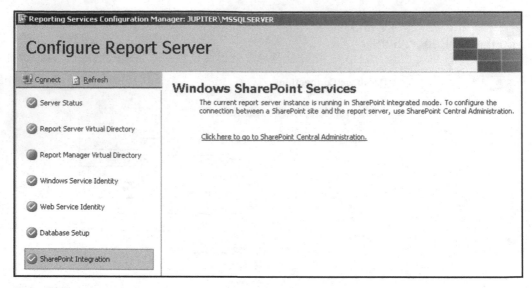

Figure 3-7. *Windows SharePoint Services settings in the report server*

The Reporting Services Add-in has added a Reporting Services section to the Application Management tab of SharePoint Central Administration. Figure 3-8 shows this section.

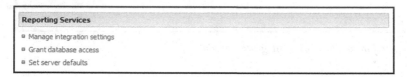

Figure 3-8. *The Reporting Services section in the Application Management tab*

In order to configure reporting services accurately, you must edit each option in this section. The first option is called Manage integration settings. Clicking this option opens the Reporting Services Integration page (see Figure 3-9). This page lets you configure the report server web service URL and the authentication mode. The report server web service URL is the name of your server plus the name of the virtual directory containing the report server.

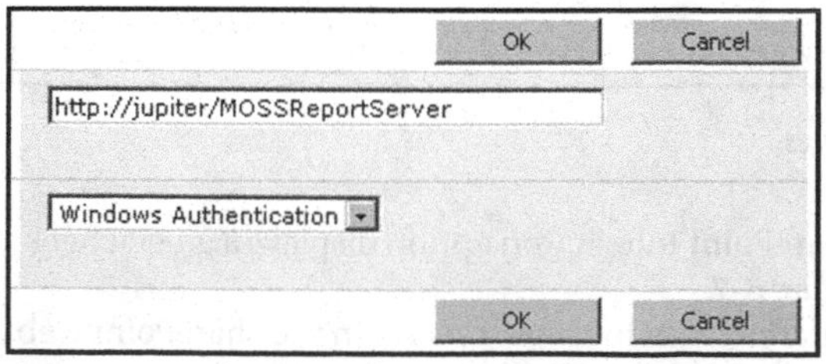

Figure 3-9. *Reporting Services Integration page*

The second option is called Grant database access. This opens a page where you can configure the server name and the instance name of the report server. Figure 3-10 shows the Grant Database Access page.

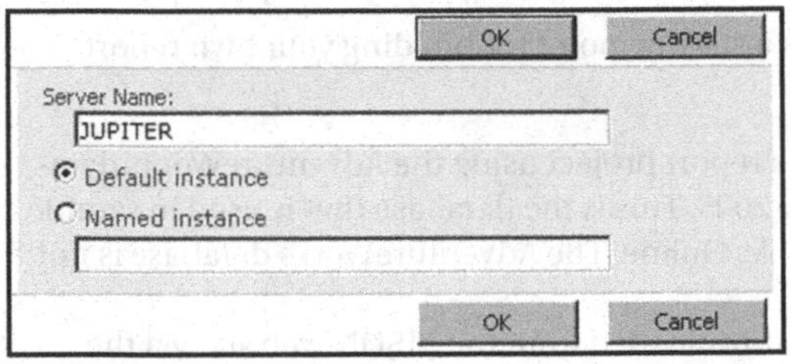

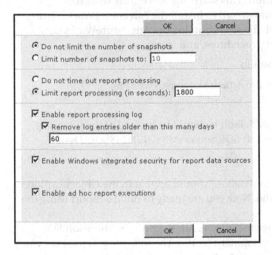

Figure 3-10. *Grant Database Access page*

With the third option, Set server defaults, you can configure how many snapshots you want to keep in the report history, set whether to use report processing timeouts, enable a report processing log, enable Windows integrated security, and enable ad hoc reporting. This is shown in Figure 3-11.

Figure 3-11. *Reporting Services ServerDefaults page*

Building a Report

It is possible to create interactive, tabular, or freeform reports that retrieve data as soon as the user opens the report. You can also create reports at scheduled time intervals. In this section, we will show you how to build a simple report. Our server configuration consists of one server with SQL Server 2005, Reporting Services, and Micosoft Office SharePoint Server 2007 installed on it.

The first thing we are going to do is build a report project using Business Intelligence Development Studio. Business Intelligence Development Studio is a Visual Studio 2005 environment with enhancements that are specific to SQL Server 2005 business intelligence solutions. When you install Reporting Services, the following project templates become available in Business Intelligence Development Studio:

- *Report Model Project*: This is used as a starting point for building your own report model. A *report model* is a simplified view of a database and is used by the Report Builder. This project type is not relevant for this chapter.

- *Report Server Project*: This is used as a starting point for building your own report.

- *Report Server Project Wizard*: This is used as a starting point for building your own report with the help of the Report Wizard.

In this section, we will describe how to create a report project using the AdventureWorks database, a sample database that ships with SQL Server 2005. This is the database that is used in sample projects and code examples in SQL Server 2005 Books Online. The AdventureWorks database is not installed by default in SQL Server 2005.

The AdventureWorks sample database can be downloaded from the MSDN web site via the Code Samples page (http://www.microsoft.com/downloads/details.aspx?FamilyId=E719ECF7-9F46-4312-AF89-6AD8702E4E6E&displaylang=en). The database is provided for three different processor types; you should download a file called AdventureWorksDB.msi for the processor type most appropriate for you.

The next steps describe how to install the AdventureWorks database.

1. Double-click the MSI file to begin installation. This starts the AdventureWorksDB – InstallShield Wizard. Follow the steps in this wizard to install the AdventureWorks database. The wizard installs the required MDF file that contains the AdventureWorks data and objects such as tables, indexes, stored procedures, and views.

2. Open Microsoft SQL Server Management Studio.

3. Right-click Databases ➤ Attach. This opens the Attach Databases window.

4. Click the Add... button.

5. Select the AdventureWorks_Data.mdf file. By default it should be located at the following location: [drive letter]:\Program Files\Microsoft SQL Server\MSSQL.1\MSSQL\Data.

6. Click OK twice.

After following these steps, the AdventureWorks database should appear in the Object Explorer window of Microsoft SQL Server Management Studio. Now you are ready to build a report using the AdventureWorks sample database.

You can open Business Intelligence Development Studio via All Programs ➤ Microsoft SQL Server 2005 ➤ SQL Server Business Intelligence Development Studio. The following steps show you how to create a report project:

1. Open Business Intelligence Development Studio and click File ➤ New ➤ Project. This opens the New Project dialog box.

2. Choose Business Intelligence Projects in the Project Types list, and choose Report Server Project Wizard in the Templates list.

3. Give the project a name and choose the location where you want to create the project. Click OK. This creates a report project.

After creating the report project, the Report Wizard will be opened. The next step is to create a report definition file.

1. Click Next on the first page of the Report Wizard; this opens the Select the Data Source page. On this page, you need to define a data source that you want to use for your report. In our example, we will make use of the AdventureWorks database.

2. Name the data source AdventureWorks.

3. Select the following type of data source: Microsoft SQL Server.

4. Specify the following connection string (replace [server] with your server name):

```
Data source=[server]; initial catalog=AdventureWorks
```

Tip http://www.connectionstrings.com is great place to find the format of connection strings for a wide range data sources.

---

5. Click Next; this opens the Design the Query page, where you can specify the query that retrieves the data for the report. You can do this manually by typing the query directly in the text box, or you can use the Query Builder. Type the following query and click Next:

```
SELECT AddressID, AddressLine1, AddressLine2, City, StateProvinceID,
PostalCode, rowguid, ModifiedDate
FROM Person.Address
```

6. On the Select the Report Type page, you can choose whether you want a tabular report or a matrix report. We'll stick to the default, the tabular one, and click Next.

7. On the Design the Table page, you can choose how to group the data in the table. In this example we select AddressLine1, Addressline2, PostalCode, and City, and click the Details button. Click Next. Figure 3-12 shows the Design the Table page.

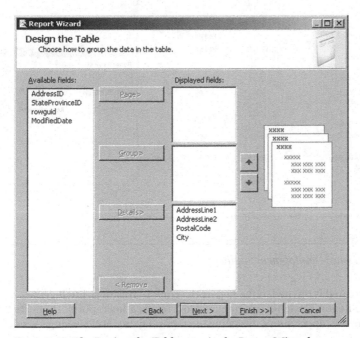

Figure 3-12. *The Design the Table page in the Report Wizard*

8. On the Choose the Table Style page, you can choose which table style you would like to use. There are six standard themes you can choose from. Click Next.

9. The Choose the Deployment Location page of the Report Wizard allows you to specify where the report is deployed. Accept the default settings and click Next.

10. The last page of the wizard offers you the chance to enter a descriptive name for the report and add a summary to it. Before you click Finish, note the check box that allows you to preview the report.

Figure 3-13 shows Business Intelligence Development Studio displaying a preview of the report that we have just created.

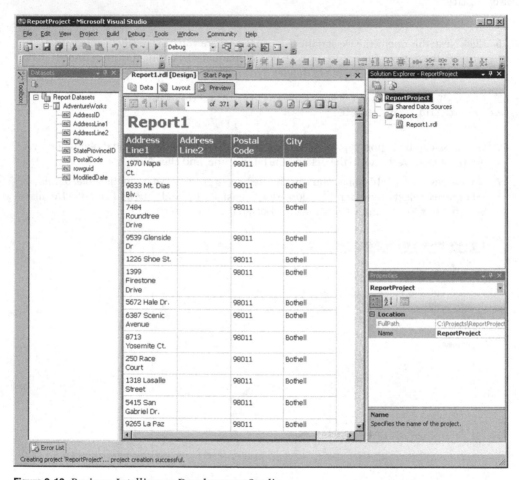

Figure 3-13. *Business Intelligence Development Studio*

The report that we created is opened in the Report Designer in Business Intelligence Development Studio. The Report Designer is a graphical tool for creating reports. There are three tabs available for building the report query, designing the report layout, and viewing a rendered version of the report:

1. On the Data tab, you generate the query that provides data to the report.

2. On the Layout tab, you arrange and format the look of the report.

3. On the Preview tab, you render the report to see what it will look like when it is saved to the report server.

Viewing a Report

There are different ways that you can run and view a report. If you want to view reports that are published to a report server, you can choose between the use of Report Manager, SharePoint web parts, or a browser. When you open a report located in the report server, it will be rendered as HTML in an HTML viewer. This HTML viewer provides page navigation and other functionality that is useful for working with a report.

You can also directly open a report server in a browser by typing the report's URL in the browser. The first part of a report URL specifies the report location; it includes the name of the web server, the name of the report server virtual directory, and the fully qualified name of the report. A *fully qualified name* includes the path to the report and concludes with the name of the report itself. The second part of a report URL specifies parameters. URL access parameters are used to configure the look and feel of a report. There are several types of parameters.

Report parameters are passed to a report. They can refer to anything you like, such as a customer ID. Report parameters can be used as variables in a report or as values for filtering report queries.

HTML viewer parameters are prefixed by rc:. These parameters indicate how to render a report. Table 3-2 provides an overview of the available HTML viewer parameters.

Table 3-2. *HTML Viewer Parameters*

Name	Description
DocMap	Shows or hides a report document map. Document maps present end users with an integrated navigation pane when a report is rendered.
DocMapID	Specifies the document map ID to scroll to in the report.
EndFind	Specifies the last page that is to be searched for the text defined in the search. This parameter is typically used in conjunction with the StartFind parameter.
FallbackPage	Specifies the page number to display if a search (FindString) or a document map selection (DocMapID) fails.
FindString	Specifies the text to search for in the report. By default, this value is empty.
GetImage	Gets a particular icon for the HTML viewer user interface.
Icon	Gets the icon for a rendering extension.
Parameters	Shows or hides the parameters area of the toolbar. You can set this parameter to true, false, or Collapsed. If the value is set to Collapsed, the parameter area will not be displayed, but can be toggled by the end user.
Section	Specifies the page number of the report page that is displayed.
StartFind	Specifies the first page that is to be searched for the text defined in the search. This parameter is typically used in conjunction with the EndFind parameter.
Stylesheet	Specifies a style sheet that is to be applied to the HTML viewer.
Toolbar	Shows or hides the toolbar. If you omit this parameter, the toolbar will be displayed.
Zoom	Sets the report zoom value to either an integer percentage or a string constant (such as Page Width and Whole Page).

Device information settings are commands that can be used to influence the report server rendering process. You do not need to provide device information settings per se, as all device information settings have default values. Table 3-3 provides an overview of the device information settings for rendering in HTML format. All device information settings commands are prefixed by rc:.

Table 3-3. *Device Information Settings Commands*

Name	Description
BookmarkID	Specifies the report section (bookmark) to jump to.
HTMLFragment	Indicates whether an HTML fragment should be created (omitting <HTML> and <BODY> tags) instead of a full HTML document.
JavaScript	Indicates whether the report supports JavaScript.
LinkTarget	Specifies the target for hyperlinks in the report.
ReplacementRoot	Specifies the path used for prefixing the value of the href attribute of the <A> tag in the report. By default, the report server provides the value for this path.
StreamRoot	Specifies the path used for prefixing the value of the src attribute of the <IMG> tag in the report. By default, the report server provides the value for this path.
StyleStream	Indicates whether styles and scripts are created as a separate stream. By default this value is false and styles and scripts are created as parts of the document.
Type	Specifies the short name of the browser type, for example, IE5, as defined in browscap.ini.

■ **Note** The browscap.ini file lists the features a browser supports. When a browser connects to a web server, it will automatically send an HTTP User Agent header. This HTTP User Agent Header is an ASCII string that will identify the browser and its version number. The BrowserType object compares the header to entries in the browscap.ini file. This way the server-side application can determine the capabilities of the client browser.

Report server command parameters are prefixed by rs:. They are targeted at the report server and are used to define the type of request being made. Table 3-4 provides an overview of the report server commands.

Table 3-4. *Report Server Commands*

Name	Description
Command	Sets the type of request being made. Supported values are GetDataSourceContents, GetResourceContents, ListChildren, and Render. GetDataSourceContents shows the properties of a given shared data source as XML. GetResourceContents renders a resource and displays it in an HTML page. ListChildren displays children of the item passed to the URL within a generic item-navigation page. Render renders the specified report.
Format	Specifies the format in which to render the report. Examples of valid values are: HTML4.0, EXCEL, CSV, PDF, and XML.
ParameterLanguage	Provides a language for the parameters passed in a URL. Culture information values consist of a language part and a region part. Valid examples of such values are en-US and nl-NL.
Snapshot	Renders a report based on a report history snapshot.

Credential parameters can be used to supply username (prefixed by dsu:) and password (prefixed by dsp:) information to the report server. The credentials are used to connect to a data source. Table 3-5 provides an overview of the credential parameters.

Table 3-5. *Credential Parameters*

Name	Description
dsu	Username that is used to access the data source
dsp	Password that is used to access the data source

To conclude this section, the following code shows an example report URL:

`http://[server]/ReportServer/Pages/ReportViewer.aspx?/Report1&rs:Command=Render.`

Figure 3-14 shows a report opened directly in the browser.

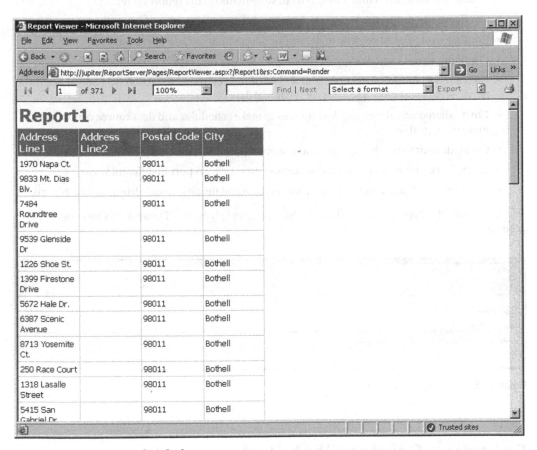

Figure 3-14. *Report opened in the browser*

Report Manager

The Report Manager installed with Reporting Services is a web-based tool to access and manage reports via Internet Explorer 6.0 and higher. You can administer a report server over an HTTP connection using Report Manager.

Report Manager's customization options are very limited; you can modify the application title on the Site Settings page and that's it. If you find that Report Manager does not meet your needs, you can develop a custom report viewer or configure SharePoint web parts to explore and view reports from within a SharePoint site.

The ability to perform a task in Report Manager depends on user role assignments. A user who is assigned to a role that has full permissions will have access to the complete set of application menus and pages available for managing a report server. A user assigned to a role that has permissions to view and run reports will only see the menus and pages that support those activities. Each user can have different role assignments for different report servers. Each user can also have different permissions for the various reports and folders that are stored on a single report server.

You can use Report Manager to perform the following tasks:

- View reports, search for reports, and subscribe to reports.

- Create and maintain a folder hierarchy to store items on the report server.

- Configure site properties.

- Configure role-based security to determine access to items and operations.

- Configure report execution properties, report history, and report parameters.

- Create report models that connect to and retrieve data from a Microsoft SQL Server Analysis Services data source or a SQL Server relational data source.

- Create shared schedules and data sources to make schedules and data source connections more manageable.

- Create data-driven subscriptions that roll out reports to a large recipient list.

- Create linked reports to reuse and repurpose an existing report in different ways.

- Use Report Builder, a report design tool to create and modify model-driven ad hoc reports.

By default, the Report Manager URL is `http://[server]/reports`. Figure 3-15 shows the Report Manager.

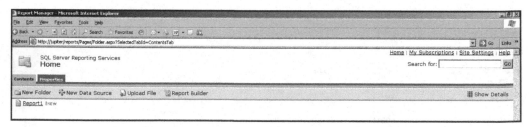

Figure 3-15. *The Report Manager*

Reporting Services Web Parts

There are a total of three web parts available for viewing Reporting Services reports. Two of the three web parts were already available in SQL Server 2000 Reporting Services Service Pack 2.0, SQL Server 2005, and SQL Server 2005 Service Pack 1.0. The following are the two legacy web parts:

- Report Explorer

- Report Viewer

These two web parts were designed for an earlier version of Microsoft Office SharePoint Server, namely SharePoint Products and Technologies 2003. They are still available for use in Service Pack 2.0, but they do not include new features or capabilities. So, if you were used to using these web parts in SharePoint Products and Technologies 2003, you can still use them in Microsoft Office SharePoint Server 2007.

The Report Explorer and Report Viewer web parts are optimized to run in a SharePoint environment, but they can also be run as stand-alone components within ASP.NET pages. The web parts cannot be customized and can only be used with reports that are built in native mode.

A report server that is deployed to run in SharePoint integrated mode cannot use these two web parts. The SQL Server 2005 Reporting Services Add-in comes with the SQL Server Reporting Services Report Viewer web part, which can be used to view reports that are built in SharePoint integrated mode. Table 3-6 shows the differences between the old web parts that were built for SharePoint 2003 and the new web parts that can be used with SharePoint integrated mode.

Table 3-6. *Differences Between SharePoint 2003 Report Web Parts and SharePoint Integrated Mode Web Parts*

SharePoint 2003 Report Web Parts	SharePoint Integrated Mode Report Web Part
The Report Explorer web part is used to display a list of reports stored on a report server. The Report Viewer web part is used to show one report. Neither web part can be customized.	The Report Viewer web part can be used to display reports. This web part can be used as a connectable web part and can be customized.
The report server is used to store, manage, and access reports.	The reports are stored, managed, and accessed via the SharePoint site.
The reports are stored in the content database.	Reports, report models, and data sources can be published and stored in SharePoint.
You must configure and maintain access on both the SharePoint site and the report server.	There is no support for data-driven subscriptions, linked reports, and Report Manager.

Report Explorer and Report Viewer Web Parts

The Report Explorer web part can be used to show available reports on a report server. This web part lets you browse the report server folder hierarchy and view reports. You can also create or edit subscriptions to a report. The subscription feature allows you to receive reports via e-mail.

The Report Viewer web part is used to view and navigate multipage reports as well as export reports to supported formats. Using web part connections, this web part can be connected to the Report Explorer web part to display the selected report within the web part page.

Installing Report Web Parts

If you want to use the reporting web parts, you must include Report Manager when installing Reporting Services. The reporting web parts that come with Reporting Services are packed into a cabinet (.cab) file. If you want to use these web parts, you will have to install them via the stsadm.exe tool. The stsadm.exe tool, a command-line tool that is a part of every SharePoint installation, offers a complete set of operations, and you can use it from the command line or within a batch file. Stsadm.exe must be run on the server itself. If you want to use the tool, you must be a member of the local administrators group on the server. You can find the stsadm.exe tool in the following folder: [drive letter]:\Program Files\Common Files\Microsoft Shared\web server extensions\12\bin\.

The CAB file that contains the reporting web parts is located in the following folder: [drive letter]:\Program Files\Microsoft SQL Server\90\Tools\Reporting Services\SharePoint. The name of this cab file is RSWebParts.cab. To install this CAB file via the command line, run the following line of code:

```
stsadm.exe -o addwppack -filename "[drive letter]:\Program ➡
Files\Microsoft SQL Server\90\Tools\Reporting ➡
Services\SharePoint\RSWebParts.cab"
```

Instead of using the operations parameter, we have used its short form, -o. After the -o parameter, you need to specify which operation needs to be performed. The name of the operation is addwppack, which adds a web part package to your server web part gallery. The filename parameter specifies the path to the cabinet file that contains the web parts and all its associated files.

If you are running SharePoint on network-load-balanced machines, you have to add the control to the <SafeControls> section of the web.config file for each additional machine. Stsadm.exe automatically adds the control to the <SafeControls> section of web.config for the SharePoint web application specified on the command line. You can find the web.config file of a SharePoint web application by following these steps:

1. Open a command prompt and type the command **inetmgr**. This opens Internet Information Services (IIS) Manager.

2. Expand the [server name] (local computer) node.

3. Expand the Web Sites node.

4. Right-click the SharePoint web application and choose Properties. This opens the [web application] Properties window.

5. Click the Home Directory tab and copy the value of the Local path text field. This value represents the path to the web.config file of the specified SharePoint web application.

The <SafeControl> element that is added to the <SafeControls> section of the web.config looks like this:

```
<SafeControl Assembly="RSWebParts, Version=8.0.242.0, Culture=neutral, ➡
PublicKeyToken= 89845dcd8080cc91" Namespace= ➡
"Microsoft.ReportingServices.SharePoint.UI.WebParts" TypeName="*" Safe="True" />
```

Using Report Web Parts

Once you have installed the reporting web parts via the stsadm.exe command-line tool, you can add them to a web part page using the SharePoint user interface. To add the web part to a SharePoint site, you must at least have web designer rights, so you are able to customize pages in the SharePoint site. After installing the reporting web parts via stsadm you do not have to add these web parts to the web part gallery for the site collection first, the addwppack operation took care of this.

The next procedure shows you how to add both reporting web parts to a SharePoint site.

1. Go to your SharePoint site and select Site Actions ➤ Edit Page.

2. Click Add a Web Part. This opens the Add Web Parts – Web Page Dialog window.

3. Scroll down to the Miscellaneous section and select the Report Explorer web part and the Report Viewer web part.

4. Click Add. This adds both web parts to the SharePoint site.

After placing both reporting web parts onto your SharePoint site, you need to configure the web parts. You can do this by clicking the web part's Web Part menu and choosing Modify Shared Web Part. This will open the Report Explorer task pane, as shown in Figure 3-16.

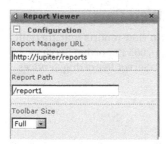

Figure 3-16. *Configuring the Report Explorer web part*

In the Report Explorer task pane, you have to configure a couple of things. First, you need to configure the Report Manager URL. This is the URL that you use to go to the Report Manager in the browser (by default, `http://[server]/reports`). The Start Path setting is optional; this can be a specific folder that is shown in the Report Manager by default. The View Mode option has two settings: Detail or List. Detail view includes metadata about the items and folders shown in the web part, such as type and subscription information. It is also possible to sort items based on metadata columns. Figure 3-17 shows the Report Explorer web part in Detail view mode. When you click a report shown in the Report Explorer web part, the report is opened in a new window.

Report Explorer				▾
Home				🖼 Report Builder
Type	Name↓	Subscription	Description	When Run
📄	Report1 !NEW			
📄	Report2 !NEW			

Figure 3-17. *The Report Explorer web part*

The Report Viewer web part can be configured by clicking the web part's Web Part menu and choosing Modify Shared Web Part. Figure 3-18 shows the Report Viewer task pane.

Figure 3-18. *Configuration of the Report Viewer web part*

In the Report Viewer task pane, you can enter the Report Manager URL. You can also specify a report path, which is optional. If you do specify a report path, you need to make sure the report path starts with a forward slash followed by the name of the report you would like to see. There are three modes for the Toolbar Size option: None, Small, and Full. The None mode will not show any kind of toolbar; the web part will only show the report. The Small mode shows the paginating part of the toolbar. The Full mode's name says it all: in this mode, the web part shows everything. Figure 3-19 shows the Report Viewer web part with the Full toolbar selected.

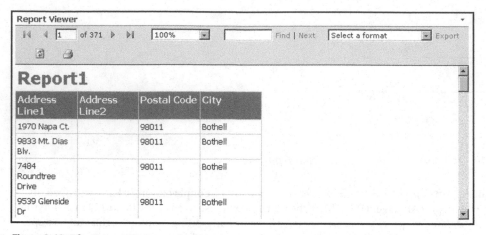

Figure 3-19. *The Report Viewer web part*

When you specify the report path for the Report Viewer web part and the start path for the Report Explorer web part, you have configured two reporting web parts that work alone. It is possible to connect the two web parts, in which case the report path and the start path properties should not be filled in. This way, once you select a report in the Report Explorer web part, it will be shown in the Report Viewer web part. Follow these steps to connect the reporting web parts:

1. Go to the Report Explorer web part, click the Web Part menu, and choose Modify Shared Web Part.

2. Again, click the Report Explorer's Web Part menu and select Connections ➤ Show Report In ➤ Report Viewer.

3. Click a report in the Report Explorer web part and notice that it opens in the Report Viewer web part.

SQL Server Reporting Services Report Viewer Web Part

The SQL Server Reporting Services Report Viewer web part can be used to view reports that are built in SharePoint integrated mode. This web part comes with the SQL Server 2005 Reporting Services Add-in. The next procedure shows you how to add and configure the SQL Server Reporting Services Report Viewer web part to a SharePoint site:

1. Browse to a SharePoint site.

2. Select Site Actions ➤ Edit Page.

3. Click Add a Web Part. This opens the Add Web Parts – Web Page Dialog window.

4. Scroll down to the Miscellaneous section and select the SQL Server Reporting Services Report Viewer web part.

5. Click Add. This adds the SQL Server Reporting Services Report Viewer web part to the SharePoint site.

The next step is to open the web part's tool pane. This can be done via the link called Click here to open the tool pane, which is shown in the web part body. Next, click the Browse button in the Report section to open the Select an Item – Web Page Dialog window. In this window, you can select a report from any library in the SharePoint site collection. If you want a report from another site collection, you can type the report URL instead. The report URL can be obtained by right-clicking the report and selecting Properties. The URL must be a fully qualified path to a report and you must replace any %20 encodings with a space when you paste the URL in the Location text box. Figure 3-20 shows the Select an Item – Web Page Dialog window.

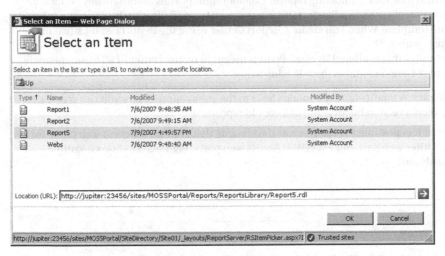

Figure 3-20. *Select an Item dialog*

You can specify a report from another site collection or SharePoint site, but the report must be located in the same web application or farm as the Report Viewer web part. Specifying the report is enough; you do not need to specify the report model or the shared data source files. The report itself contains the references to the files it needs. Figure 3-21 shows a sample report displayed in the Report Viewer web part.

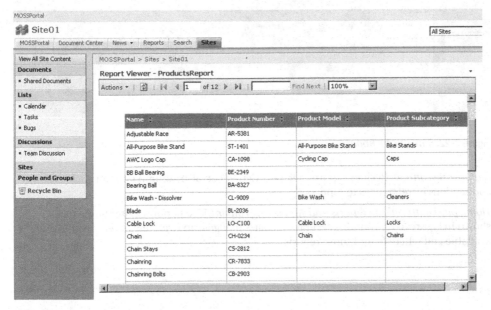

Figure 3-21. *Report Viewer web part*

Report Center

Microsoft Office SharePoint Server 2007 offers out-of-the-box functionality for generating Reporting Services reports via the Report Center. The Report Center is a SharePoint site template that can be used to create SharePoint sites for hosting reports. Collaboration portals automatically contain a Report Center. You can also create a Report Center as a separate site collection by using the existing Report Center site template. When you create a Report Center using the Report Center site template, it looks like Figure 3-22.

The Report Center that is offered by SharePoint is meant to be the center of all business intelligence data. A Report Center contains the following items:

- *Reports library*: A reports library contains links to the site's reports. Here you can create new versions, keep a version history, and archive old reports.

- *Dashboards*: It is possible to create report dashboards that contain different web parts, for example, a filter web part and Excel Web Access web parts. Figure 3-22 shows a sample report dashboard.

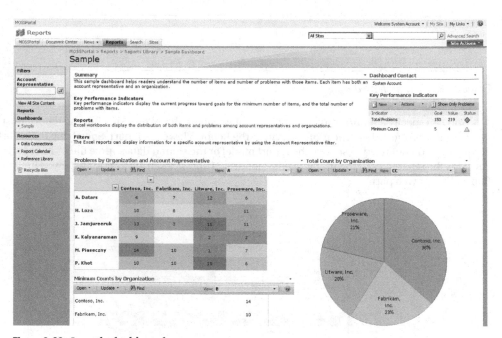

Figure 3-22. *Sample dashboard*

- *Supporting content*: Besides reports, a Report Center can also contain content such as data connections or references to reports.

- *Home page with links to reports and supporting content*: The Report Center home page, shown in Figure 3-23, contains several web parts that give an overview of reports that are available and where to find those reports.

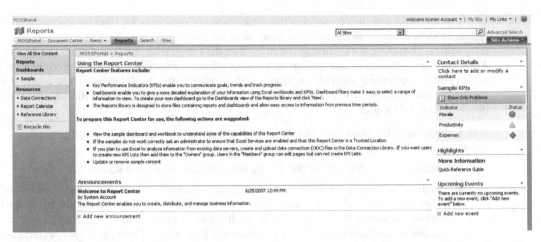

Figure 3-23. *Out-of-the-box Report Center*

Reports in SharePoint

There are two groups of people that can create reports: end users and developers. The reports that are created by end users are built using report models that have been predefined by developers. The reports that are created by developers are created using the Business Intelligence Development Studio.

Creating a report using the Business Intelligence Development Studio was already discussed in the section "Building a Report." In the following sections, we will discuss the creation of a report model, how to use a report model in SharePoint, and how to manage reports in a Report Center.

Building a Report Model

To create a report model and use it in SharePoint, you must follow these steps:

1. Create a Report Model project.

2. Create a data source.

3. Create a data source view.

4. Create a report model using Business Intelligence Development Studio.

5. Publish the report model to a SharePoint Report Center.

In this section, we will cover all these steps. Let's start with creating a Report Model project. We are going to use Business Intelligence Development Studio to create a Report Model project. The following procedure shows you how to do this:

1. Open Business Intelligence Development Studio by selecting Start ➤ All Programs ➤ Microsoft SQL Server 2005 ➤ SQL Server Business Intelligence Development Studio.

2. Select the File menu ➤ New ➤ Project. This opens the New Project dialog box.

3. Select the Business Intelligence Projects project type. From the Templates section, select the Report Model Project template. Name the project **AdventureReportModel** and click OK.

A report model project consists of three components: data sources, data source views, and report models. A report model requires a data source view, while a data source view requires a data source. Therefore, we are first going to create a data source for the report model using the AdventureWorks database. The AdventureWorks database is a sample database that ships with SQL Server 2005. More information about installing the AdventureWorks database can be found in the earlier section "Building a Report." The next procedure shows you how to add the AdventureWorks database as a data source.

1. Right-click the Data Sources folder in the Solution Explorer and select Add New Data Source. This opens the Data Source Wizard.

2. The first screen that is displayed by the wizard is the Welcoming screen. Click Next.

3. When defining a data source you have two options: create a data source based on a new connection or based on an existing connection. In this example, we are going to create a data source based on a new connection. Click the New button to start creating a new connection in the Data Source Wizard, as shown in Figure 3-24. This opens the Connection Manager dialog box.

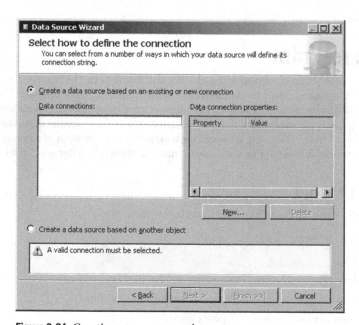

Figure 3-24. *Creating a new connection*

4. In the Connection Manager dialog, you have to specify the provider, server name, and database you are going to use. In this example, we are selecting the SqlClient Data Provider. The name of our database server is Jupiter and we are using the AdventureWorks database. The Connection Manager dialog window is shown in Figure 3-25. Click OK when you are ready.

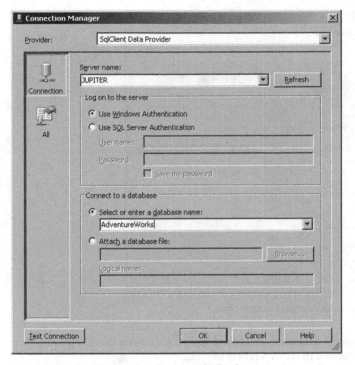

Figure 3-25. *The Connection Manager dialog box*

5. The next screen of the wizard shows an overview of the connection you have created. Click Finish.

6. The last screen of the wizard shows an overview of the selected connection string and gives you an opportunity to provide a name for the data source that you are about to create. We will leave the name as is (Adventure Works).

For a report model project, you have to create data source views based on relational data sources. The basis of the data source view consists of a list of tables that can be joined. Follow these steps to create a data source view:

1. Right-click the Data Source Views folder in the Solution Explorer and select Add New Data Source View. This opens the Data Source View Wizard.

2. The first screen is the Welcome screen. Click Next.

3. Select the data source we have just created (called Adventure Works) and click Next.

4. The Select Tables and Views screen shows all available tables you can choose from. In this example, we will select the following tables: Product, ProductSubcategory, ProductCategory, ProductReview, ProductModel, ProductModelIllustration, and ProductModelProductDescription. This is shown in Figure 3-26. Click Next.

5. The final screen of the Data Source View Wizard shows an overview of the tables you have selected and an opportunity to give the Data Source View a name. In this example we will give it the name **Adventure Works**. Click Finish.

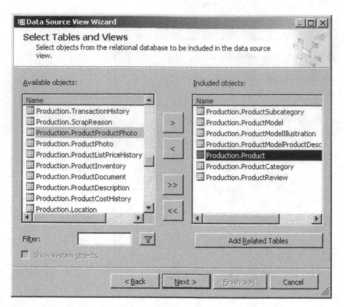

Figure 3-26. *Selected tables in data source view*

Now we are ready to create a report model based upon the data source view we just created. The next procedure explains how to create a report model.

1. Right-click the Report Models folder in the Solution Explorer and select Add New Report Model. This opens the Report Model Wizard.

2. The first screen of the wizard is the Welcome screen. Click Next.

3. The Select Data Source View screen lets you select a data source view for the report model you are about to create. This page also offers the option to create a new data source view if you have not done that already. Select the Adventure Works data source view we created and click Next.

4. On the next screen of the wizard, you can select the report model generation rules. The generation rules are divided in two passes. Table 3-7 shows the rules for the two passes of generating the report model. By default, two of the first pass rules are not selected, namely Create Entities for Non-empty Tables and Create Attributes for Non-empty Columns. Selecting these rules means that entities and attributes are created only for tables that already contain data.

■**Note** Report model entities are conceptually equivalent to tables in relational databases; report model attributes are equivalent to fields or columns within tables.

Table 3-7. *Report Model Generation Rules*

Rule Name	Description
First Pass Rules	
Create entities for all tables	Choose this rule if you want to create an entity for each table automatically.
Create entities for non-empty tables	Choose this rule if you want to create an entity for each table that contains data.
Create count aggregates	Choose this rule if you want to create an aggregate field containing the number of unique instances in an entity.
Create attributes	Choose this rule if you want to create an attribute for each column in a table automatically.
Create attributes for non-empty columns	Choose this rule if you want to create an attribute for each column that contains data.
Create attributes for auto-increment columns	Choose this rule if you want to create an attribute for an auto-increment column.
Create date variations	Choose this rule if you want to create variations for date display.
Create numeric aggregates	Choose this rule if you want to aggregate numeric fields.
Create date aggregates	Choose this rule if you want to aggregate date fields.
Create roles	Choose this rule if you want to create roles for a relationship between entities
Second Pass Rules	
Lookup entities	This rule creates lookup entities from entities containing only one field.
Small lists	This rule creates drop-down lists from entities that contain fewer than 100 values.
Large lists	This rule creates lists from entities that contain more than 500 values.
Very large lists	This rule creates a filter in a list from entities that contain more than 5,000 values.
Set identifying attributes	This rule creates identifying attributes for fields that are unique.
Set default detail attributes	This rule creates default detail attributes for fields that are displayed by default.
Role name only	This rule automatically creates the contextual name property of the Role attribute.
Numeric/date formatting	This rule adds sorting capabilities for numeric and date fields.
Integer/decimal formatting	This rule creates formatting rules for integers and decimals.
Float formatting	This rule creates formatting rules for float fields.
Date formatting	This rule creates formatting rules for date time fields.
Discourage formatting	This rule prevents grouping on fields that are unique.
Dropdown value selection	This rule creates the Value Selection property for drop-down lists that contain fewer than 200 values.

5. In this example, we will keep the default selections and click Next; see Figure 3-27.

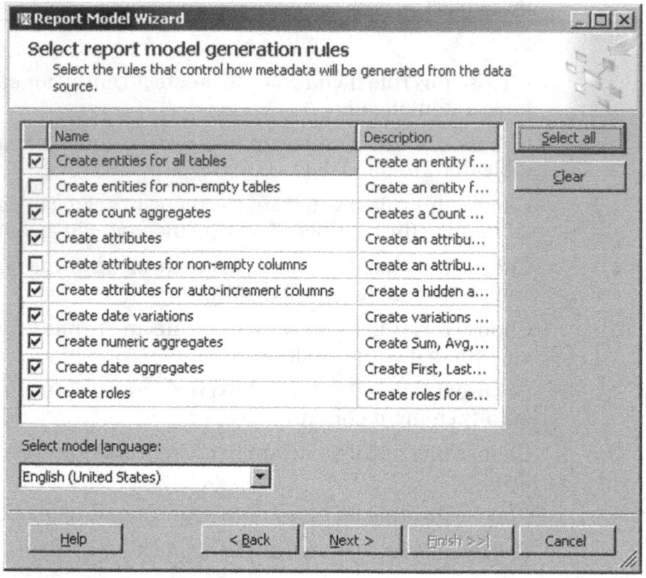

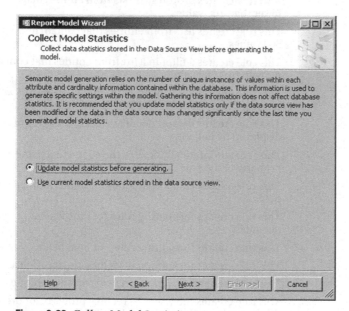

Figure 3-27. *Report Model generation rules*

6. The Collect Model Statistics page of the wizard lets you update the statistics before generating the report. This is important if there is a chance that the data has changed since the last time the report model was generated. See Figure 3-28.

Figure 3-28. *Collect Model Statistics*

7. On the Completing the Wizard screen, you can give the report model a custom name. In this example, we will use the default name: **Adventure Works**. The last thing to do is click Run to start generating the report model.

8. After generating the report model, you will see the Completing the Wizard screen again, displaying an overview of the status of the rules. Again, you will have the opportunity to give the report model a custom name and click Finish, as shown in Figure 3-29.

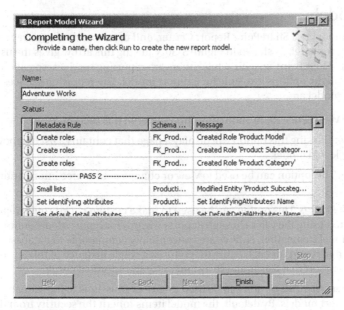

Figure 3-29. *Completing the Wizard screen*

The report model is generated and we are going to deploy the model to a SharePoint Report Center. The next procedure shows you how to do this.

1. Right-click the project in the Solution Explorer and select Project Properties.

2. Select the General Configuration property and enter the following values:

   - TargetDataSourceFolder is the URL of the SharePoint library for shared data sources. In this example that will be `http://jupiter:23456/sites/MOSSPortal/Reports/Data Connections`.

   - TargetModelFolder is the URL of the SharePoint library for report models. In this example that will be `http://jupiter:23456/sites/MOSSPortal/Reports/ReportsLibrary`.

   - TargetServerURL is the URL of the SharePoint site to which the project is deployed. In this example that will be `http://jupiter:23456/sites/MOSSPortal`.

■**Note** You need to have sufficient (read and write) permissions to the specified libraries and SharePoint site; otherwise you will receive a `Microsoft.ReportingService.RsProxy.AccessDeniedException` when you try to deploy the report model project.

---

3. Click OK.

4. Right-click the project and click Deploy. The Report model will be deployed to the Report Center you have specified.

At this moment the Report Center will contain one report model called Adventure Works and one data source, also called Adventure Works. The next section will discuss how to use the report model.

Using a Report Model

After publishing the report model to a SharePoint Report Center, end users can manage a report via the arrow next to the report model, as shown in Figure 3-30. Clicking this arrow gives the user a couple of options; some are SharePoint-specific while others are reporting services–specific. Figure 3-30 shows the list of all the options available for a report model. The reporting services specific options for a report model are

- *Load in Report Build*: We will talk more about this option later in this section.

- *View Dependent Items*: Clicking this option will display a page that contains a list of reports that depend on the selected model.

- *Manage Data Sources*: This option can be used to view or change data source information for a report or model.

- *Manage Clickthrough Reports*: This option can be used to make custom clickthrough reports (reports that are created using the ClickThrough Reports wizard) for report model entities in the selected report model (remember, entities are conceptually comparable to database tables). There can be one report for each entity that returns a single instance of this entity. There can also be one report that lists multiple instances for the specified entity.

- *Manage Model Item Security*: This option can be used to give permissions to individual model items in the report models. By default, the model items inherit the security from the report model.

- *Regenerate Report Model*: This option can be used to regenerate a report model.

End users are able to create reports using of the Report Builder. The Report Builder is a click-once design application that can be used to create and publish reports. If you use the Report Builder to build reports, you do not need a full development environment such as Visual Studio or Business Intelligence Development Studio. The first time an end user starts the Report Builder, it will be automatically downloaded from the SharePoint server and installed as a component on the end user's machine.

The Report Builder can be started from a Report Center by clicking on the arrow next to the report model and selecting Load in Report Builder from the drop-down list.

End users can use the Report Builder to create and publish reports to a SharePoint site based on the selected report model. The Report Builder consists of three areas: design, report data, and report layout. The report layout area is not opened by default when you start the Report Builder via SharePoint. This is because you have already selected a data source by clicking Load in Report Builder.

Note There are three available report templates: table, matrix, and chart. The templates all consist of prede-fined areas, such as title, total column, and filter column.

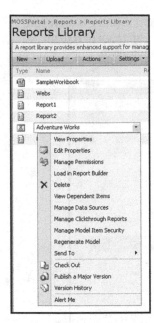

Figure 3-30. *Load in Report Builder action*

We are going to use the table template for this report, and we will start by dropping the following columns in the design area (also is called *drag-and-drop column fields*): Name, Product Number, Product Category, Product Mode. The Report Builder now looks like Figure 3-31.

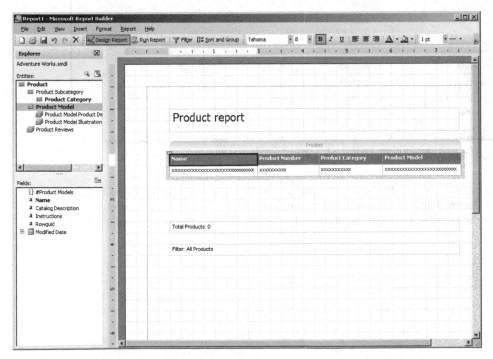

Figure 3-31. *Report Builder design area*

When these fields are added to the design area, we can click Run Report to preview the report, as shown in Figure 3-32. Each field in the report contains an interactive sorting icon next to the name of the column. If you click the sorting icon, the report will be generated again.

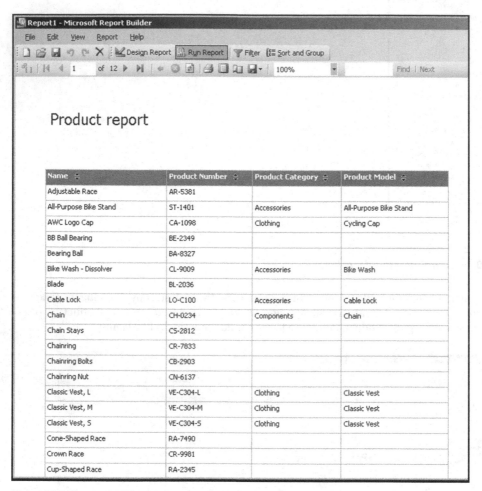

Figure 3-32. *Report Builder preview mode*

It is possible to save the generated report in SharePoint. You can do this by clicking the Save icon or selecting File ➤ Save. This opens a Save As Report window with the location already set to the report library that stores the report model. Figure 3-33 shows the Save As Report window.

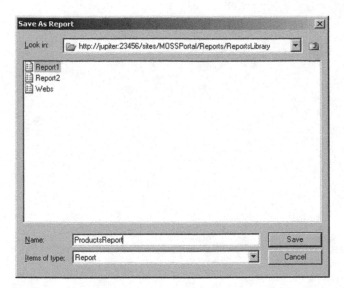

Figure 3-33. *Save As Report window*

When we return to our Report Center, we will notice, maybe after a refresh of the page, that our report is present. Clicking the arrow next to the report shows a couple of options. Some of these options are SharePoint-specific, while others are Reporting Services–specific. Figure 3-34 shows the list of the options available for a report in a report library. The Reporting Services–specific options for a report are

- *Edit in Report Builder*: This option starts Report Builder so you can change the definition of the report.

- *Manage Subscriptions*: This option can be used to manage the subscriptions for the specified report.

- *Manage Data Sources*: This option can be used to view or change data source information for a report or model.

- *Manage Parameters*: This option can be used to manage the parameters that are used in the report.

- *Manage Processing Options*: This option can be used to specify how and when report processing occurs, as well as set snapshot options and timeouts.

- *View Report History*: This option can be used to manage the history of the report.

Tip For more information about building reports using the Report Builder, you can look at the SQL Server 2005 Books Online from Microsoft. You can find the SQL Server 2005 Books Online at http://technet.microsoft.com/ en-us/sqlserver/bb428874.aspx.

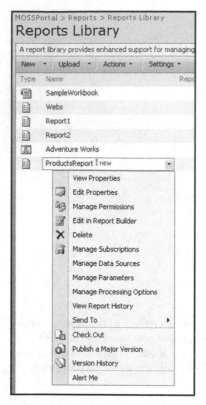

Figure 3-34. *Options available for a report*

Reporting Services Extensions

SQL Server 2005 Reporting Services is designed with extensibility in mind. A managed code
Application Programming Interface (API) is available so that you can easily develop, install, and
manage extensions consumed by many Reporting Services components. Reporting Services can
be extended in various ways:

- *Data processing extensions*: Data processing extensions make it possible to consume custom
  data and include this data into reports using the report server and Report Designer.

- *Delivery extensions*: Delivery extensions make it possible to extend the range of mechanisms
  that can be used to send report notifications to end users and to extend the subscription
  management pages of Report Manager to support subscriptions of custom delivery extension types.

- *Security extensions*: Security extensions are used by report server for authenticating and
  authorizing users and groups to the server. The default security mechanism that is used by
  report server is Windows authentication. You can create custom security models using security extensions; for example, you could create a security model based on forms-based
  authentication. A single Reporting Services installation only allows you to use one security
  extension at a time.

- *Rendering extensions:* Rendering extensions are responsible for transforming data and layout information into a specific format. By default, Reporting Services includes six rendering extensions: HTML, Excel, CSV, Image, PDF, and XML. Using the Rendering API, you can create support for other formats as well.

- *Report processing extensions:* Report processing extensions are responsible for processing report items. Using the processing API, you can create support for the processing of custom report items. By default, report server is able to process tables, charts, matrices, lists, text boxes, and images.

Every report server installation requires the presence of one or more security extensions, one or more data processing extensions, and one or more rendering extensions. Delivery and custom report processing extensions are optional and only need to be present if you want to support report distribution or custom controls.

The Reporting Services Extension Library contains all the types that make up Reporting Services. This library can be used to access Reporting Services and to extend Reporting Services components. Table 3-8 shows the namespaces that are available within the Reporting Services Extension Library.

Table 3-8. *Namespaces Reporting Services Extension Library*

Name	Description
Microsoft.ReportingServices.DataProcessing	All types located in this namespace allow you to build custom components that extend Reporting Services' data processing capabilities.
Microsoft.ReportingServices.Interfaces	All types located in this namespace allow you to create and send custom notifications via your own delivery extensions. This namespace also contains all types related to Reporting Services security extensions.
Microsoft.ReportingServices.ReportRendering	All types located in this namespace allow you to extend Reporting Services' default rendering capabilities. Custom rendering extensions can be built using the types in this namespace in conjunction with the types that can be found in the Microsoft.ReportingServices.Interfaces namespace.

Data Processing Extension Example

Data processing extensions allow you to connect to a data source and retrieve data. For example, the data processing extension for SQL Server, which is included with Reporting Services, can be used to connect to a SQL Server database and retrieve data from this database. The data processing extensions that are included with Reporting Services use a common set of interfaces that indicate the kind of functionality that needs to be implemented by each data processing extension.

If you want to add a custom data processing extension, you need to implement the complete set, or in some scenarios a *subset*, of the interfaces described in the Reporting Services data processing API, as shown in Figure 3-35.

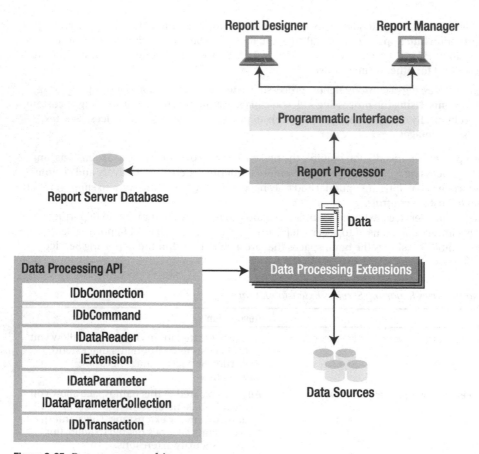

Figure 3-35. *Report server architecture*

The first thing that happens when a report server processes data via data extensions is it creates an ADO.NET connection object. The report server makes sure the correct connection string and current client credentials are included. The command text of the report is used to create a command object. In the process, the data processing extension may include code that parses the command text and creates any parameters for the command. Once the command object and any parameters are processed, a data reader is generated that returns a result set and enables the report server to associate the report data with the report layout. Figure 3-36 shows this process.

In the example described in this section, we will create a new data processing extension that will be used to create a report based on data retrieved from a SharePoint list.

■**Note** The advantage of using SharePoint lists to store data is that the user interface required to manage the information in such a list is available automatically. Having said that, storing large amounts of application data in a SharePoint list is not something we would recommend. In such cases, we think you are better off storing data in a suitable repository, such as a database.

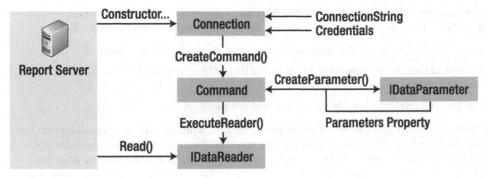

Figure 3-36. *Data processing via data extensions*

We will use a SharePoint list that contains a summary of bugs. Such lists can become rather long and it might not be so easy for a project manager to get a clear picture of the current bug status. To solve this, we are going to build a SharePoint data processing extension that creates a report based on the data in the SharePoint Bugs list. The report will show bug status as well as the developers responsible for solving the bugs.

Windows SharePoint Services 3.0 offers a web service interface that contains 21 different web services. This web service interface makes it possible for a remote report server to interact with SharePoint. We will use the Lists web service for creating the data processing extension. This web service can be used to work with lists and list data.

As far as we know, the first person to write about creating a custom data processing extension for SharePoint lists was Teun Duynstee. The example discussed in this section was based on the code found on his blog at http://www.teuntostring.net.

Developing a Custom Data Extension

The first thing you need to do to create a custom data processing extension is create a new Visual C# class library. The next steps will show you how to do this:

1. Go to Start ➤ All Programs ➤ Microsoft Visual Studio 2005 ➤ Microsoft Visual Studio 2005. This opens the Visual Studio development environment.

2. Go to File ➤ New ➤ Project. This opens the New Project dialog box.

3. Select Visual C# in the Project Types list and select Class Library in the Templates list. Enter the following name for the project: **SharePointListExtension**.

The next thing to do is to add a reference to the Microsoft.ReportingServices.Interfaces assembly, which can be found at the following location: [drive letter]:\Program Files\Microsoft SQL Server\ MSSQL.2\Reporting Services\ReportServer\bin. Follow these steps to add this reference:

1. Right-click References in the Solution Explorer and choose Add Reference.

2. In the Add Reference dialog box, click the Browse tab and browse to the following location: [drive letter]:\Program Files\Microsoft SQL Server\MSSQL.2\Reporting Services\ ReportServer\bin.

3. Click the Microsoft.ReportingServices.Interfaces.dll file and click OK.

We are going to add another reference, but this time it will be a web reference. We will refer to the Windows SharePoint Services Lists web service. Follow these steps to add the web reference:

1. Right-click References in the Solution Explorer and choose Add Web Reference.

2. In the Add Web Reference dialog box, type the URL http://[server]/ _vti_bin/Lists.asmx and click the Go button.

3. Call the web reference **WssLists** and click Add Reference.

The first class we are going to create is a connection class, which we will simply call Connection. The Connection class implements the IDbConnection and IDbConnectionExtension interfaces. This class is responsible for managing the connection to a SharePoint list and is the starting point for users of the data processing extension.

The IDbConnection interface supports the IExtension interface, which means that implementing the IDbConnection interface in a connection class implicitly means supporting the IExtension interface as well. We will discuss the IExtension interface a little bit later; first, we will take a closer look at the IDbConnection interface.

Our class will contain two constructors. The first constructor does nothing and accepts no parameters. The second constructor accepts a String parameter containing the connection string to the SharePoint list and sets the ConnectionString property, which is a part of the IDbConnection interface. The next code fragment shows the second constructor.

```
public Connection(string strConnection)
{
  ConnectionString = strConnection;
}
```

If you want to support the IDbConnection interface, you have to implement the following four methods:

- BeginTransaction(): This method begins a database transaction. In our connection class, this method is not supported and will always throw a NotSupportedException error.

```
public IDbTransaction BeginTransaction()
{
  throw new NotSupportedException();
}
```

- CreateCommand(): This method creates and returns a Command object associated with the connection. We will discuss the Command class later on.

```
public IDbCommand CreateCommand()
{
  return new Command(this);
}
```

- Close(): This method is intended to close the connection to a database. In our example it is a simple method, because we do not have a real database connection that needs to be opened and closed. Here the method just indicates that the current connection state is closed:

```
public void Close()
{
  _objConnState = System.Data.ConnectionState.Closed;
}
```

- Open(): This method is intended to open a database connection using the settings specified in the ConnectionString property of the provider-specific Connection object. What is true for the Close() method is also true for the Open() method; as we do not have a real database connection, the method just indicates that the current connection state is open:

```
public void Open()
{
  _objConnState = System.Data.ConnectionState.Open;
}
```

We also have to implement the following two properties from the IDbConnection interface:

- ConnectionString: This property gets or sets the string used to open a database. The format of the connection string expected by the SharePoint list connection class is a name/value pair that looks like this: data source=http://[server]. The "set" part of the ConnectionString property knows how to add the name/value pair to a HybridDictionary collection called _objConn:

```
public string ConnectionString
{
  get { return _strConn; }
  set
  {
    _strConn = value;
    _objConn.Add(_strConn.Substring(0,
    _strConn.IndexOf("=")).ToLower(),➥
    _strConn.Substring(_strConn.IndexOf("=") + 1));
  }
}
```

- ConnectionTimeout: This property returns the maximum time to wait while trying to establish a connection. If the timeout period has expired, the attempt is terminated and an error is generated. In this example, this property is not supported and will therefore always return 0 (zero).

```
public int ConnectionTimeout
{
  get { return 0; }
  set { }
}
```

The IExtension interface enables a class to implement the localized name of the extension (a friendly name, such as SharePointListExtension) that will be displayed in the user interface and to process extension-specific configuration information stored in the Reporting Services configuration file. The LocalizedName property and the SetConfiguration() method of the IExtension interface are implemented in the Connection class.

We have also implemented the IDbConnectionExtension interface to extend our Connection class to include support for credentials in Reporting Services. The following four properties are implemented:

- IntegratedSecurity: This property indicates whether the connection should use integrated security rather than supply a username and password. This property enables the integrated security check box and the username and password text boxes in the Data Source dialog in the Report Designer. This way credentials can be stored and retrieved by the Report Designer for data sources that support authentication. The credentials are stored securely and are used when rendering reports in preview mode.

- UserName: This property gets or sets the user name that is used when connecting to the database.

- Impersonate: This property sets the user name that is impersonated while queries are executed. This property is ignored by the report server if impersonation is not supported by the data provider.

- Password: This property gets or sets the password to use when connecting to the database.

The complete code for the Connection class looks like Listing 3-1.

Listing 3-1. *Creating a Connection Manager Class That Interacts with a SharePoint List*

```
using System;
using d = System.Data;
using System.Collections.Specialized;
using System.Security.Permissions;
using System.Security.Principal;
using Microsoft.ReportingServices.DataProcessing;
using Microsoft.ReportingServices.Interfaces;

namespace LoisandClark.SharePointListExtension
{
  public class Connection : IDbConnection, IDbConnectionExtension
  {
    private string _strConn;
    private string _strLocName = "MOSS";
    private string _strImpersonate;
    private string _strUsername;
    private string _strPassword;
    private bool _blnSecurity;
    private HybridDictionary _objConn = new HybridDictionary();
    private d.ConnectionState _objConnState = d.ConnectionState.Closed;

    public Connection()
    { }

    public Connection(string strConnection)
    {
      ConnectionString = strConnection;
    }

    public string ConnectionString
    {
      get { return _strConn; }
      set
      {
        _strConn = value;
        _objConn.Add(_strConn.Substring(0, _strConn.IndexOf("=")).ToLower(), ➥
        _strConn.Substring(_strConn.IndexOf("=") + 1));
      }
    }

    public IDbTransaction BeginTransaction()
    {
      throw new NotSupportedException();
    }
```

```
public void Open()
{
  _objConnState = d.ConnectionState.Open;
}

public void Close()
{
  _objConnState = d.ConnectionState.Closed;
}

public IDbCommand CreateCommand()
{
  return new Command(this);
}

public string LocalizedName
{
  get { return _strLocName; }
  set { _strLocName = value; }
}

public void SetConfiguration(string configuration)
{ }

public void Dispose()
{ }

public int ConnectionTimeout
{
  get { return 0; }
  set { }
}

public string strDataSourcePath
{
  get
  {
    if (_objConn.Contains("data source"))
    {
      string strUrl = (string)_objConn["data source"];
      if (!strUrl.EndsWith("/"))
      {
        strUrl = strUrl + "/";
      }
      return strUrl;
    }
    return "";
  }
}

public d.ConnectionState State
{
  get { return _objConnState; }
}
```

```
      public bool IntegratedSecurity
      {
        get { return _blnSecurity; }
        set { _blnSecurity = value; }
      }

      public string UserName
      {
        get { return _strUsername; }
        set { _strUsername = value; }
      }

      public string Password
      {
        get { return _strPassword; }
        set { _strPassword = value; }
      }

      public string Impersonate
      {
        set { _strImpersonate = value; }
      }

  }
}
```

The next class you need to create is a Command class. A Command class formulates a request and passes it on to the data source. Command requests can take many different syntactical forms, including text and XML. If results are returned, a Command object always returns results as a DataReader object. To create a Command class, you will have to implement the IDbCommand interface. The IDbCommand interface contains the following three methods:

- Cancel(): This method attempts to cancel the execution of an object implementing the IDbCommand interface. Our Command class will not support this operation; it will throw a NotSupportedException.

- CreateParameter(): This method creates a new instance of an object implementing the IDataParameter interface. In this example, we will not use parameters; the operation will return null instead.

- ExecuteReader(): This method executes a command request (the contents of the CommandText property) against the Connection object and builds a response object that supports the IDataReader interface. The DataReader class implementing this interface is discussed in detail later in this section. The ExecuteReader() method is overloaded and includes an implementation that takes a CommandBehavior enumeration as an argument. The default ExecuteReader() method accepts no parameters and calls the overload passing CommandBehavior.SingleResult as its single argument. The overloaded method calls a custom GetDataTableFromWSS() method. This method does not belong to any of the interfaces that are a part of the Data Processing API; it is just used for clarity (we'll get back to this method in a moment). ExecuteReader() methods for data processing extensions need to support schema-only requests. Schema-only requests are specified using the CommandBehavior.SchemaOnly command behavior enumeration value. A response to such requests contains type and name information about fields or columns but does not include actual data.

```
public IDataReader ExecuteReader()
{
  return ExecuteReader(CommandBehavior.SingleResult);
}

public IDataReader ExecuteReader(CommandBehavior behavior)
{
  d.DataTable objDataTable = GetDataTableFromWSS((behavior == ➡
CommandBehavior.SchemaOnly));
  return new DataReader(this._objConn, objDataTable);
}
```

The `IDbCommand` interface contains the following five properties:

- `CommandText`: This property gets or sets the text command to run against the data source. We will use this property to specify which SharePoint list we want to use. Therefore, instead of using a SQL query, we will use the name of a SharePoint list:

```
public string CommandText
{
  get { return _strText; }
  set { _strText = value; }
}
```

- `CommandTimeout`: This property gets or sets the maximum wait time before terminating the attempt to execute a command and generating an error. We have specified the wait time for our solution to be 60 seconds:

```
public int CommandTimeout
{
  get { return 60 * 1000; }
  set { }
}
```

- `CommandType`: This property indicates or specifies how the `CommandText` property should be interpreted, for example, as text:

```
public CommandType CommandType
{
  get { return _objCmdType; }
  set
  {
    if (value != CommandType.Text)
    {
      throw new NotSupportedException();
    }
    _objCmdType = value;
  }
}
```

- `Parameters`: This property gets the `IDataParameterCollection`. In this example, we will do nothing with parameters, so this property will return an empty collection.

- `Transaction`: This property gets or sets the transaction context in which the `Command` object of a SQL Server Reporting Services data provider executes. In this example we will not support transactions. The `Transaction` property returns `null`.

We promised to pay some attention to the GetDataTableFromWSS() method that gets called by the ExecuteReader() method of the Command class. This method is the core of the code for our custom data extension. We will discuss parts of the method and show the entire method in the complete code listing of the Command class.

The first part of the GetDataTableFromWSS() method sets up a proxy object that is able to call the SharePoint web service, as shown in the following code fragment. The PreAuthenticate property can be used to indicate that credentials need to send on the very first request.

```
WssLists.Lists objLists = new WssLists.Lists();
objLists.Url = _objConn.strDataSourcePath + "_vti_bin/Lists.asmx";
objLists.Credentials = GetCredential(_objConn);
objLists.PreAuthenticate = true;
objLists.Timeout = this.CommandTimeout;
```

The next part of the code calls the GetListCollection() method. This method returns an XmlNode containing the entire list collection node. The method looks for the Name attribute because it contains a GUID (Globally Unique Identifier) that identifies SharePoint lists. We are going to use this GUID when calling the web service later, as shown in this code fragment:

```
XmlNode ListCollectionNode = objLists.GetListCollection();
XmlElement xmlElem = (XmlElement)ListCollectionNode. ➥
SelectSingleNode(String.Format("wss:List[@Title='{0}']", ➥
this.CommandText), NameSpaceManager);
if (xmlElem == null)
{
  throw new ArgumentException(String.Format(" ➥
  List {0} does not exist in site {1}", this.CommandText, ➥
  _objConn.strDataSourcePath));
}

string strTechListName = xmlElem.GetAttribute("Name");
XmlNode xmlNode = objLists.GetList(strTechListName);
```

For each column in the SharePoint list, we will add a new column to our DataTable with an identical name.

■**Tip** Alternatively, if there are lots of columns in a SharePoint list, you can create a datatable based on this list and call the Clear() method to obtain a DataTable object that contains the right set of columns. This approach is not demonstrated in this section.

In SharePoint, each column has two names—one called Name and another called DisplayName. Upon column creation, these two names are always the same. Later, the DisplayName can be changed by end users. The SharePoint user interface displays the DisplayName of the column. Having taken this into account, it is better to use the DisplayName of the column as the ColumnName in our DataTable. The Name of the SharePoint column is added to a hybrid dictionary. This way we can always look up which Name belongs to a given ColumnName, as shown in this code fragment:

```
StringBuilder objStringBuilder = new StringBuilder();
HybridDictionary objDictionary = new HybridDictionary();
d.DataTable objResult = new d.DataTable("list");
foreach (XmlElement xmlField in xmlNode.SelectNodes(" ➥
wss:Fields/wss:Field", NameSpaceManager))
{
  string strName = xmlField.GetAttribute("Name");
  string strDisplayName = xmlField.GetAttribute("DisplayName");
```

```
    if (objResult.Columns.Contains(strDisplayName))
    {
      strDisplayName = strDisplayName + " (" + strName + ")";
    }
    objResult.Columns.Add(strDisplayName, TypeFromField(xmlField));
    objStringBuilder.AppendFormat("<FieldRef Name=\"{0}\"/>", strName);
    objDictionary.Add(strDisplayName, strName);
}

if (blnSchema)
{
  return objResult;
}

XmlElement fields = xmlNode.OwnerDocument.CreateElement("ViewFields");
fields.InnerXml = objStringBuilder.ToString();
```

In the following code fragment, we will load the data into the DataTable using the SharePoint web service's GetListsItems() method. The regular expression ^\\d+;# that is used in the next code fragment means that we are looking for one or more digits between zero and nine, followed by a ";" character, and a "#" character.

```
XmlNode ItemsNode = objLists.GetListItems(strTechListName, "", null, ➡
fields, "1000000", null, null);
System.Text.RegularExpressions.Regex CheckLookup = ➡
new System.Text.RegularExpressions.Regex("^\\d+;#");

foreach (XmlElement Item in ItemsNode.SelectNodes(" ➡
rs:data/z:row", NameSpaceManager))
{
  d.DataRow newRow = objResult.NewRow();
  foreach (d.DataColumn col in objResult.Columns)
  {
    if (Item.HasAttribute("ows_" + (string) objDictionary[col.ColumnName]))
    {
      string val = Item.GetAttribute("ows_" + ➡
      (string)objDictionary[col.ColumnName]);
      if (CheckLookup.IsMatch((string)val))
      {
        string valString = val as String;
        val = valString.Substring(valString.IndexOf("#") + 1);
      }
      newRow[col] = val;
    }
  }
  objResult.Rows.Add(newRow);
}
return objResult;
}
```

■**Note** The complete code listing for the Command class can be downloaded from our web site at http://www.lcbridge.nl/download/.

The next class to discuss is the DataReader class. If you want to create a DataReader class, you have to implement the IDataReader interface. The DataReader implementation must provide two basic capabilities: forward-only access over the result sets obtained by executing a command, and access to the column types, names, and values within each row. You can use the Read() method of the DataReader object to obtain a row from the results of the query.

The complete code for the DataReader class looks like Listing 3-2.

Listing 3-2. *Creating a DataReader Class for Access to the Result Sets and Columns*

```
using System;
using System.Collections;
using d = System.Data;
using System.Diagnostics;
using System.Globalization;
using System.IO;
using System.Security;
using System.Security.Permissions;
using System.Security.Principal;
using Microsoft.ReportingServices.DataProcessing;

namespace LoisandClark.SharePointListExtension
{
  public class DataReader : IDataReader
  {
    private Connection _objConn = null;
    private d.DataTable _objDataTable;
    private DataParameterCollection _objDataParameters = null;
    IEnumerator enumTable = null;

    public DataReader()
    { }

    public DataReader(Connection objConn, d.DataTable objDataTable)
    {
      _objConn = objConn;
      _objDataTable = objDataTable;
    }

    public DataReader(Connection objConn, d.DataTable objDataTable, ➥
      DataParameterCollection objParameters) ➥
      : this(objConn, objDataTable)
    {
      _objDataParameters = objParameters;
    }

    public bool Read()
    {
      if (enumTable == null)
      {
        enumTable = _objDataTable.Rows.GetEnumerator();
      }
      return enumTable.MoveNext();
    }
```

```
protected d.DataRow CurrentRow
{
  get { return (d.DataRow)enumTable.Current; }
}

public int FieldCount
{
  get { return _objDataTable.Columns.Count; }
}

public string GetName(int i)
{
  return _objDataTable.Columns[i].ColumnName;
}

public Type GetFieldType(int i)
{
  return _objDataTable.Columns[i].DataType;
}

public Object GetValue(int i)
{
  return CurrentRow[i];
}

public int GetOrdinal(string strName)
{
  foreach (d.DataColumn objColumn in _objDataTable.Columns)
  {
    if (objColumn.ColumnName == strName)
    {
      return objColumn.Ordinal;
    }
  }
  throw new IndexOutOfRangeException(" ➡
  There is no field with the name " + strName);
}

public void Dispose()
{
  _objDataTable.Dispose();
}
  }
}
```

The DataParametercollection class inherits fron ArrayList and implements the
IDataParameterCollection interface. The IDataParameterCollection interface contains
the Add() method; with this method you can populate the IDataParameterCollection class.
Listing 3-3 shows the DataParameterCollection class.

Listing 3-3. *Creating a Class That Inherits from ArrayList and Implements the IDataParameterCollection Interfaces*

```
using System;
using System.Collections;
using System.Globalization;
using Microsoft.ReportingServices.DataProcessing;

namespace LoisandClark.SharePointListExtension
{
  public class DataParameterCollection : ArrayList, IDataParameterCollection
  {
    public object this[string index]
    {
      get { return this[IndexOf(index)]; }
      set { this[IndexOf(index)] = value; }
    }

    public override int Add(object value)
    {
      return Add((IDataParameter)value);
    }

    int IDataParameterCollection.Add(IDataParameter parameter)
    {
      if (parameter.ParameterName != null)
      {
        return base.Add(parameter);
      }
      else
      {
        throw new ArgumentException("parameter must be named");
      }
    }
  }
}
```

Deploying a Custom Data Extension

Deploying a custom data extension is simple. You need to make sure the custom data extension is accessible to the report server and the Report Designer. You can do this by copying the extension to the appropriate directories and adding entries to the appropriate Reporting Services configuration files.

1. Copy your assembly to the bin directory of the report server where you want to use your custom extension. The default location is [drive letter]:\Program Files\Microsoft SQL Server\ MSSQL.2\Reporting Services\ReportServer\bin.

2. Copy your assembly to the Report Designer directory. The default location is [drive letter]: \Program Files\Microsoft Visual Studio 8\Common7\IDE\PrivateAssemblies.

3. The name of the report server configuration file is RSReportServer.config and it is located at [drive letter]:\Program Files\Microsoft SQL Server\MSSQL.2\Reporting Services\ ReportServer. Open the RSReportServer.config file in a text editor. Go to the <Data> section and add the following entry:

```
<Extension Name="MOSS" ➡
Type="LoisandClark.SharePointListExtension.Connection, ➡
LoisandClark.SharePointListExtension"/>
```

4. The name of the Report Designer configuration file is RSReportDesigner.config and it is located at [drive letter]:\Program Files\Microsoft Visual Studio 8\Common7\IDE\ PrivateAssemblies. Open the RSReportDesigner.config file in a text editor. Go to the <Data> section and add the following entry:

```
<Extension Name="MOSS" ➡
Type="LoisandClark.SharePointListExtension.Connection, ➡
LoisandClark.SharePointListExtension"/>
```

The value of the Name attribute is the unique name of the data processing extension. The value of the Type attribute is a comma-separated list that includes an entry for the fully qualified namespace of the Connection class including the class name itself, followed by the name of your assembly (do not include the extension .dll). By default, data processing extensions are visible. To hide an extension from user interfaces such as Report Manager, add a Visible attribute to the <Extension> element and set it to false.

The last thing you need to do is to add a code group for your custom assembly. Follow the next steps to add a code group for the report server and the Report Designer:

1. For the report server, you will have to add a code group to the rssrvpolicy.config file located in [drive letter]:\Program Files\Microsoft SQL Server\MSSQL.2\Reporting Services\ ReportServer. The following code is a valid code group for our custom data extension:

```
<CodeGroup
  class="UnionCodeGroup"
  version="1"
  PermissionSetName="FullTrust"
  Name="LCExtensionCodeGroup"
  Description="Code group for my data processing extension">
  <IMembershipCondition
    class="UrlMembershipCondition"
    version="1"
    Url="C:\Program Files\Microsoft SQL Server\MSSQL.2\Reporting
    Services\ReportServer\bin\LoisandClark.SharePointListExtension.dll"
  />
</CodeGroup>
```

■**Note** A *permission* allows code to perform a specific operation. A *permission set* is a collection of permissions. .NET provides seven predefined permission sets; one of them is called FullTrust. The FullTrust permission set is the most liberal of all and allows code to perform all operations. A code group specifies which permission set applies to a .NET assembly based on origin-based evidence (.NET examines where the assembly is coming from) or content-based evidence (.NET looks at the actual content of an assembly). The .NET Common Language Runtime (CLR) evaluates which code groups apply to a given assembly, and based on this information the CLR determines which permissions are granted to an assembly. The code group in the code fragment described in step one of the procedure associates the assembly SharePointListExtension.dll with the FullTrust permission set.

---

2. For the Report Designer, you can add a code group to the rspreviewpolicy.config file located in [drive letter]:\Program Files\Microsoft Visual Studio 8\Common7\IDE\ PrivateAssemblies:

```
<CodeGroup
  class="UnionCodeGroup"
  version="1"
  PermissionSetName="FullTrust"
  Name="LCExtensionCodeGroup"
  Description="Code group for my data processing extension">
  <IMembershipCondition
    class="UrlMembershipCondition"
    version="1"
    Url="C:\Program Files\Microsoft Visual Studio 8\Common7\IDE\ ➥
    PrivateAssemblies\LoisandClark.SharePointListExtension.dll"
  />
</CodeGroup>
```

Using the Custom Data Extension

Now that you have created a custom data extension, you are probably interested in learning how you can use it. Let's create a report that is based on a custom Issue Tracking SharePoint list and call this list Issues. This list contains the issues (bugs) our testers have discovered and assigned to developers. Figure 3-37 shows our sample Issues list.

Issue ID	Title	Assigned To	Issue Status	Priority
1	Error in FireFox browser ! NEW	JUPITER\pauld	Active	(2) Normal
2	Slow performance ! NEW	JUPITER\hilbertd	Active	(2) Normal
3	Broken link ! NEW	JUPITER\alfredog	Active	(2) Normal
4	Failed to open data source ! NEW	JUPITER\gwenn	Active	(1) High
5	Navigation failure ! NEW	JUPITER\alfredog	Active	(1) High
6	Small spelling mistake ! NEW	JUPITER\pauld	Active	(3) Low

Figure 3-37. *Bugs SharePoint list*

We are going to use our new SharePoint list data extension to create a report via Reporting Services. The next procedure shows you how to do this:

1. Open SQL Server Business Intelligence Development Studio by clicking Start ➤ All Programs ➤ Microsoft SQL Server 2005 and choose SQL Server Business Intelligence Development Studio.

2. Click File ➤ New Project and choose Business Intelligence Projects in the Project types list. In the Templates list, choose Report Server Project Wizard, give your project a descriptive name, and click OK. We will call our report project **IssuesReportProject**. Figure 3-38 shows the New Project dialog window.

3. Once you have clicked OK, a report project will be created and the Report Wizard will be started. The first page is a Welcome page. Click Next.

4. On the Select the Data Source page, you have to select the data source you are going to use. In the Type drop-down list, choose our custom SharePoint data extension and specify the connection string. Figure 3-39 shows the Select the Data Source page from the Report Wizard.

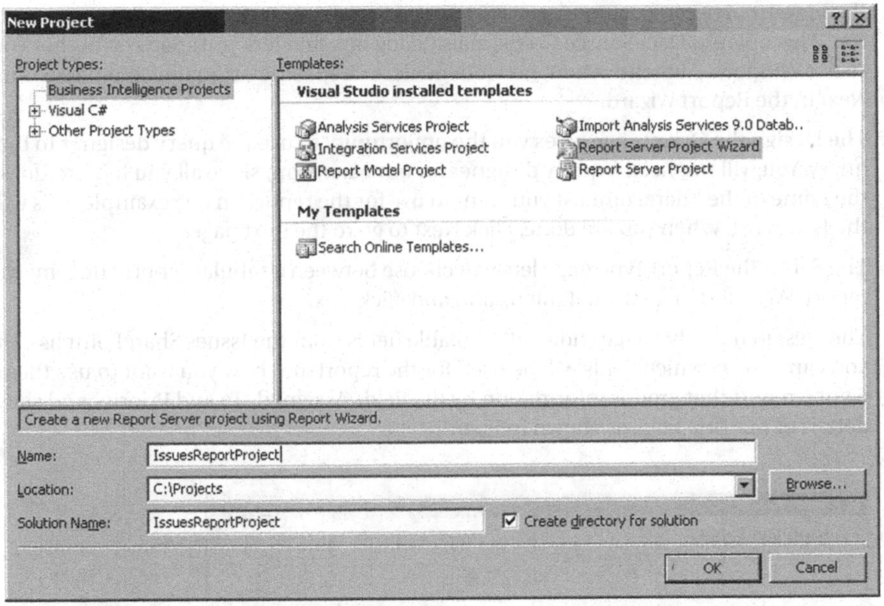

Figure 3-38. *New Project dialog window*

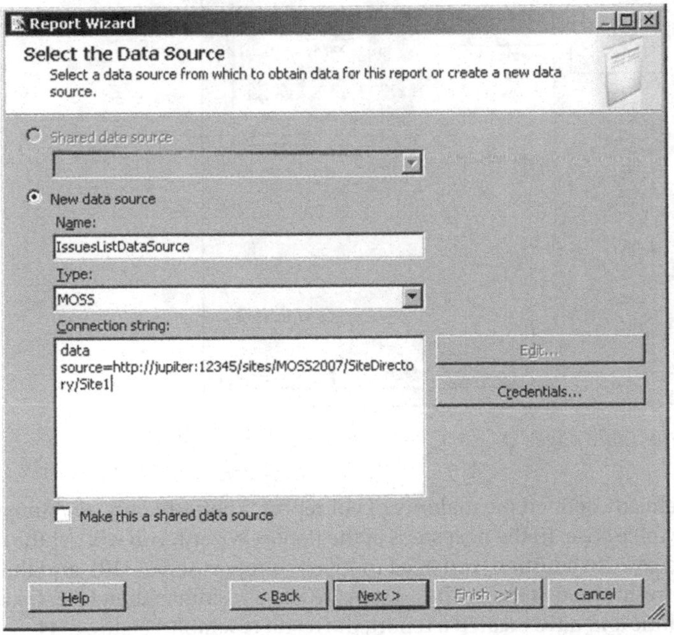

Figure 3-39. *Select the Data Source page in the Report Wizard.*

5. If you want to use a specific username and password, you have to click the Credentials button. This opens a Data Source Credentials dialog box that lets you specify whether you want to use Windows Authentication, no credentials, or a specific username and password. Click Next in the Report Wizard.

6. The Design the Query page gives you the opportunity to use the query designer to build a query. You will not need a query designer for our extension, since all you have to do is add the name of the SharePoint list you want to use for the report. In our example, this will be the Issues list. When you are done, click Next to go to the next page.

7. The Select the Report Type page lets you choose between a tabular report and a matrix report. We will stick to the default option and click Next.

8. The Design the Table page shows all available fields from the Issues SharePoint list. Here you can choose which fields will be used for the report and how you want to use them. We want a report that groups information by the fields Assigned_To and Priority and shows the details of the Title field, as shown in Figure 3-40.

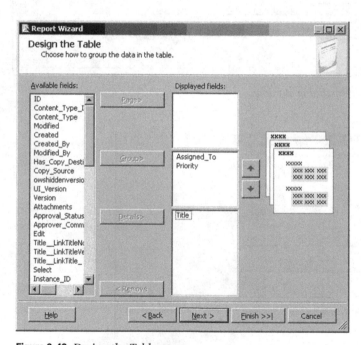

Figure 3-40. *Design the Table page*

At this point, we have already defined the majority of our report. There are only two things left to do: the table layout and the table style. In the next steps of the Report Wizard, you will get the chance to choose a table layout and style. In addition, you need to specify a report server URL and the name you would like to give your freshly made report. These steps are all very simple; therefore, we will not show them. When you are done and have created a report, the result resembles Figure 3-41.

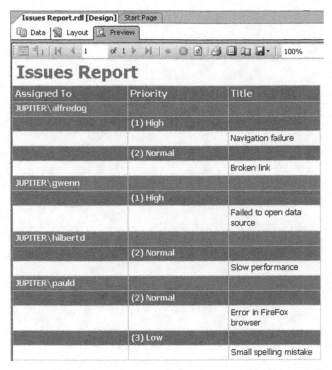

Figure 3-41. *Issues report made with the SharePoint list data extension*

Summary

In this chapter, you learned about SQL Server 2005 Reporting Services. We discussed the different report server deployment modes and how to configure those modes. You learned how to create a report using the Business Intelligence Development Studio, and how to use Report Manager. We looked at the three SharePoint Reporting web parts that are available, and how and when you should use them. You learned how to create a report model and how to use this report model in a SharePoint Report Center. Finally, we looked in detail at the architecture of reporting extensions, taking a closer look at creating custom data extensions and delivering extensions.

CHAPTER 4

■ ■ ■

Building Human-Oriented Workflows Using Windows Workflow Foundation

Every day, information workers follow work processes to get their jobs done. Some of those work processes will be quite formal, others very informal. Some of those processes will involve one or more people within the same organization; still others will involve multiple people working for different companies. These work processes have one thing in common: they are all examples of human-oriented workflows. A subset of this wide range of workflows falls in the solution domain of SharePoint 2007. SharePoint 2007 allows information workers and developers to create and use document-centric workflows.

Basics of Windows Workflow Foundation

SharePoint 2007 incorporates an infrastructure that supports the use of existing document-centric workflows as well as the creation of new document-centric workflows by either developers or information workers.

Windows Workflow Foundation (WF) forms the basis of the SharePoint 2007 workflow functionality. Windows Workflow Foundation is a part of the Microsoft .NET Framework 3.0.

Note The Microsoft .NET Framework 3.0 was formerly known as WinFX. It adds four new technologies to the .NET Framework 2.0: Windows Workflow Foundation, Windows Communication Foundation (WCF, formerly known as Indigo), Windows Presentation Foundation (WPF, formerly known as Avalon), and Windows Cardspace (WCF, formerly known as InfoCard).

Windows Workflow Foundation is not a stand-alone application; instead, it has a run-time workflow engine that can execute short-term as well as persistable workflows. The Windows Workflow Foundation run time provides additional services that are important for executing workflows such as tracking, notifications, and transactions.

Any application or service can leverage WF workflow services by hosting WF in its process. SharePoint 2007 acts as a host for WF and adds a couple of custom implementations for workflow services as well.

SharePoint 2007 offers two different tools for working with and creating workflows: SharePoint Designer 2007 and Visual Studio 2005 Designer. Both will be discussed in this chapter.

SharePoint Designer 2007 is a great tool for creating ad hoc workflows. It places the tools to create workflows well within the grasp of normal information workers. Visual Studio 2005 Designer, on the other hand, allows developers to create advanced, enterprise-level workflows. Table 4-1 provides a comparison of SharePoint Designer 2007 and Visual Studio 2005 Designer.

Table 4-1. *Comparison Between SharePoint Designer 2007 and Visual Studio 2005 Designer*

Feature	SharePoint Designer 2007	Visual Studio Designer 2005
Requires you to write code	No	Yes
Supports sequential workflows	Yes	Yes
Supports state machine workflows	No	Yes
Supports the use of custom forms within the workflow	Yes	Yes
Workflows can be started manually	Yes	Yes
Workflows can be started by an event	Yes	Yes
Workflows can associated with a list	Yes. Workflows created using SharePoint Designer 2007 can only be bound to a single list. You cannot alter this association after deployment.	Yes
Workflows can be associated with a content type	No	Yes
Workflows can be associated with a site	No	Yes
Supports the use of ASP.NET forms	Yes	Yes
Supports the use of other form technologies, such as InfoPath	No	Yes
Workflow deployment happens automatically	Yes	No, but you can use a Web Part Solution Package (.wsp) to deploy a workflow.
Step-by-step debugging is available	No	Yes

Note Actually, you can associate a workflow created in SharePoint Designer with more than one list. The auto-generated code contains hard-coded GUIDs representing a list. If you change those GUIDs, it is possible to associate a workflow with another list.

In the following sections, we will delve deeper into the concepts related to Windows Workflow Foundation.

Activities

We will begin by looking at the basic structure of a workflow. A workflow represents a business process that consists of a set of transactions which form a model to describe a real-world problem. Business transactions form the elementary building blocks of a business process. A business transaction involves two parties:

- The initiator is responsible for starting a business transaction by issuing some sort of request.

- The executor is responsible for performing some kind of action based on a request.

Conceptually, the life cycle of a business transaction consists of three phases:

1. *Order phase*: This phase starts when the initiator makes a request for some kind of action to be performed. This phase ends with a promise by the executor to perform that action.

2. *Execution phase*: In this phase, the executor performs the requested action. The action succeeds or fails. Either way, a result is reached, thus ending this phase of the business transaction life cycle.

3. *Result phase*: In this phase, the executor communicates which result was reached, which is either accepted or rejected by the initiator.

In Windows Workflow Foundation, the abstract concept of business transactions (a concept that has meaning in the external world) is translated to activities (a concept that has meaning in the software world). Activities are the building blocks of a workflow; every single step within a workflow requires an activity. Windows Workflow Foundation utilizes three different kinds of activities:

- *Simple activity*: A simple activity represents a simple action in its most basic form. An example of such a simple activity is the DelayActivity.

- *Composite activity*: A composite activity is an activity that aggregates one or more child activities within a single activity. An example of such a composite activity is the IfElse activity.

- *Rule activity*: A rule activity (also called a *data-driven activity*) drives the flow of a workflow. An example of this type of activity is the EventDriven activity.

Out of the box, the Windows Workflow Foundation framework contains a set of activities that provide functionality for the creation of workflows that contain control flow, conditions, event handling, and state management, and are able to communicate with other applications and services. Table 4-2 shows the activities that are included out of the box in Windows Workflow Foundation and that can be used in a SharePoint workflow.

Table 4-2. *Out of the Box Activities That Can Be Used in a SharePoint Workflow*

Name	Description
CodeActivity	This activity lets you add custom logic to a workflow in the form of code written using VB.NET or C#.
ConditionedActivityGroup	This activity lets you aggregate one or more child activities that are executed conditionally. The child activities can be executed based on some kind of condition that applies to the ConditionedActivityGroup activity itself, or based on a condition that only applies to the child.
DelayActivity	This activity lets you incorporate delays into workflows that are based on time-out intervals.
EventHandlingScopeActivity	This activity aggregates child activities and decides whether event handling is supported when those child activities are executed.
HandleExternalEventActivity	This activity is able to communicate with a local service by handling an event that is raised the service and is often used in conjunction with the CallExternalMethod activity.
IfElseActivity	This activity supports the ability to add decisioning mechanisms to a workflow. Such activities test for a condition and perform activities that are a part of the first branch of the IfElseActivity that matches the condition.
InvokeWebServiceActivity	This activity allows you to add web service communication within a workflow.

Continued

Table 4-2. *Continued*

Name	Description
ParallelActivity	This activity can be used to add parallel processing power (multithreading) to your workflows. This activity allows you to add two or more child Sequence activities that are executed concurrently.
ReplicatorActivity	This activity lets you create single child activities.
SequenceActivity	This activity lets you link multiple activities together that are to be executed sequentially.
SetStateActivity	This activity lets you specify a transition to a new state if you are creating a workflow that contains multiple states.
StateActivity	This activity lets you represent each separate state in a state machine type of workflow.
StateFinalizationActivity	This activity aggregates child activities that are executed whenever a StateActivity activity is finished executing.
StateInitializationActivity	This activity aggregates child activities that are executed upon entering a StateActivity activity.
SuspendActivity	This activity lets you temporarily suspend the operation of a workflow. You might want to do this if there is some kind of event or error condition that requires special attention.
TerminateActivity	This activity allows you to end workflow execution immediately. You might want to do this if an irrecoverable error condition occurs.
ThrowActivity	This activity is part of a larger exception-management framework that allows you to implement an error-handling mechanism in your workflows. This activity allows you to throw exceptions to signal unexpected conditions in your workflow.
WhileActivity	This activity adds conditional logic that enable workflows to loop until a given condition is met.

■**Note** Please note that the toolbox contains other activities that are available in normal WF workflows. They are not discussed in this section because they cannot be used in workflows in a SharePoint environment.

If you design a workflow, you can choose to make use of one of the activities belonging to this default set or you can create your own activities. Developers are free to create their own custom activity libraries and use them in other workflows. You can also use code activities to add custom code to a workflow. Code activities allow you to add basic behavior to a workflow; if you want complex behavior, such as the ability to create a composite activity that is able to contain other activities, you should create your own custom activity.

Activities can be sequential, in which case the order of workflow actions is specified at design time. Alternatively, activities can be event-driven. In such scenarios, the order of workflow actions is determined at run time in response to external events. Each activity contains the following logic/data:

- Metadata responsible for describing design time properties of the activity.

- Instance data describing the activity run-time state.

- Activity behavior in the form of programmed execution logic.

- Validation logic that can be used to validate activity metadata. This is optional.

Figure 4-1 shows a basic workflow that consists of several activities and uses custom activity libraries.

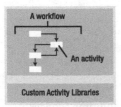

Figure 4-1. *Workflow with activities*

Components

Windows Workflow Foundation provides services as well as a framework and consists of the following components (see Figure 4-2):

- *Base activity library:* This library contains all activities that are available out of the box. Activities are essential building blocks for creating custom workflows and are discussed in the previous section, "Activities."
- *Runtime engine:* The workflow runtime engine is able to interpret and execute workflows created using Windows Workflow Foundation. The runtime engine is also responsible for keeping track of workflow state.
- *Runtime services:* The WF workflow runtime engine can be hosted by different host applications, including SharePoint. This is a very flexible system, which is made possible via the workflow runtime services. The workflow runtime services are also responsible for handling any communication between the host application and the workflow.

Figure 4-2. *Windows Workflow Foundation*

Windows Workflow Foundation ships with a couple important tools that facilitate workflow creation: a visual designer and a debugger. Both of them are integrated into Visual Studio 2005 and are discussed later in this chapter, in the sections "Visual Studio 2005 Designer" and "Debugging a Workflow."

The workflow runtime engine is hosted in-process within a host application (never as a stand-alone process) and is responsible for creating and maintaining running workflow instances. For each application domain (in .NET, the fundamental process that executes code), there can be only one workflow runtime engine. A workflow runtime engine is able to run multiple workflow instances concurrently. The runtime engine needs to be hosted by a host process, such as a console application, Windows form-based application, ASP.NET web site, or a web service. Because a workflow is hosted in-process, it can easily and efficiently communicate with its host application.

The workflow runtime engine utilizes many WF services when a workflow instance runs. The following services are included in the runtime engine:

- Execution
- Tracking
- State management
- Scheduler
- Rules

Besides the runtime engine itself, WF contains multiple runtime services. Runtime services are pluggable, so applications can provide these services in unique ways within their execution environment. Table 4-3 shows an overview of the runtime services that are provided out of the box with Windows Workflow Foundation.

Table 4-3. *Runtime Services*

Name	Description
Persistence	The persistence service is responsible for saving and loading state data to and from a persistent data store, such as an SQL Server database. Some workflows, called *persistent workflows*, need to be able to survive system reboots or run for a long period of time. Building such workflows is easier with the Windows Workflow Foundation runtime services persistence service.
Communication	The communication service is responsible for handling the communication between a workflow and other applications, services, or workflows.
Timer	The timer service handles activities within workflows that are time-related. DelayActivity, discussed previously in the section "Activities," is an excellent example of such an activity.
Tracking	The tracking service facilitates tracking and monitoring the execution flow of workflows. The tracking service also enables you to persist this information to a data store, such as a log file or an SQL Server database.
Transaction	The transaction service facilitates the incorporation of transactions within custom workflows.
Threading	The threading service facilitates the inclusion of multithreaded operations within custom workflows.

Workflow Styles

Windows Workflow Foundation supports two styles of workflow: sequential and state machine. Before you start creating a workflow project, it is important to figure out what style of workflow you want to use.

The *sequential* workflow style is used for repetitive operations such as designing a set of activities that must always be performed in the same order. The workflow follows the sequence until the last activity is completed, and the workflow always remains in control of what happens next. Such workflows are not necessarily entirely deterministic; you can use branching logic such as IfElseActivity activities or ParallelActivity activities and let the exact sequence of events vary. For example, imagine you are creating a workflow that describes the process of installing software. This is a typical scenario where you always follow the steps one by one and in the same order. Therefore, you can represent this process using a sequential workflow. Figure 4-3 shows an example sequential workflow.

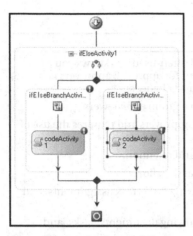

Figure 4-3. *Sequential workflow*

The *state machine* workflow style is used when you want to model your workflow as a state machine. State machine workflows are made up of different states, one being the starting state, which is the state that is entered once the workflow process begins. Each state can receive a certain set of events. Based on these events, the workflow can transition from one state to another state. In state machine workflows, the end user is always in control. That is why this type of workflow is also known as a *human-oriented workflow*. It is not required to define a final state, but if you do happen to have a final state in a workflow and the transition is made to that state, the workflow will end.

An example of a state machine workflow is an online shop where one state of the workflow process describes the situation where the customer can submit an order and wait for approval of the credit card data. Another state in the workflow process describes the situation where the customer, for the time being, is satisfied with selecting a couple of products and wants to place the order at a later time. Therefore, each customer finds himself in one of the states in the workflow process and goes to another state depending on his choices. Figure 4-4 shows a state machine workflow.

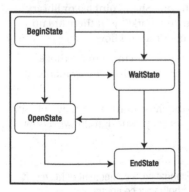

Figure 4-4. *State machine workflow*

Although you certainly can, you do not have to rush out and start creating your own workflows immediately, because, out of the box, SharePoint 2007 ships with a set of default workflows. Table 4-4 provides an alphabetical overview of the default workflows.

Table 4-4. *Overview of Default Workflows in SharePoint 2007*

Workflow Name	Description
Approval	This is probably the most basic and often-used workflows you can imagine. You can submit a document for approval; approvers can accept or reject a document or request changes.
Collect Feedback	Gathers feedback information from a group of reviewers.
Collect Signatures	Collects signatures from a group of approvers and requires the use of Microsoft Office clients.
Disposition Approval	Centered on document expiration and retention.
Group Approval	An advanced version of the Approval workflow.
Issue Tracking	Dedicated to an issue process involving tasks, task assignments, and task completion.
Translation Management	Facilitates a translation process involving documents, tasks, and translators.
Three-state	Tracks the status of an item through three states.

Creating Basic Workflows with SharePoint Designer 2007

With SharePoint Designer, it is possible to design workflows with no-code application logic. By making use of SharePoint Designer's Workflow Designer, you can create rules consisting of conditions and actions that are available out of the box in SharePoint Designer.

Designing a Workflow

Before you design the workflow, you need to make any necessary changes or customizations to your site, list, or library—for example:

- A SharePoint Designer workflow is always attached to exactly one SharePoint list or library. Your site must have at least one list or library before you create a workflow. If there are no lists in your site, you are prompted to create one when you create a workflow.

- If you want your workflow to use any custom columns or settings, you must make those changes before you create the workflow so that those columns and settings are available to you in the Workflow Designer.

- If you want your workflow to use any list or library features that are not turned on by default, such as Content Approval, you must turn on these features before you design the workflow.

■Note The workflow feature is built on the Microsoft Windows Workflow Foundation, a component of Microsoft Windows. The same version of the Workflow Foundation must be installed on both your computer and the server. The first time you create a workflow, you may be prompted to install the Workflow Foundation.

Rules: Conditions and Actions

With SharePoint Designer, you create rules to add conditional logic to the workflow. A rule in a workflow consists of conditions and actions. A rule sets up a condition, and when this condition is true an associating action will be performed. For instance, you can create a rule with a condition that checks whether a title of a document contains the word *test*, and if it does, an e-mail will be sent to the owner of the document.

Multiple conditions can be added together via And and Or clauses. You can also add more conditional branches to a workflow. With multiple branches, you will get scenarios like the following: if condition A is true then run action A; otherwise when condition A is false, run action B. When more than one conditional branch in your workflow is present, you will see a green diamond shape beside that conditional branch. Figure 4-5 shows a Workflow Designer wizard page with two conditional branches. The first branch has two conditions, an And clause, and two actions that will run in sequence.

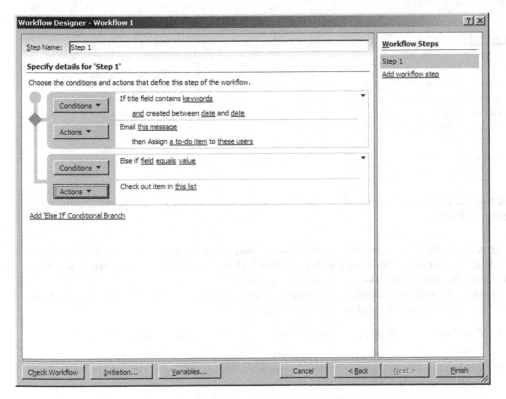

Figure 4-5. *The Workflow Designer wizard with conditions and actions in SharePoint Designer*

■**Note** It is not necessary for a conditional branch to contain a condition. A conditional branch, however, must always consist of one or more actions.

There are a lot of conditions available out of the box in SharePoint Designer. Some examples include

- The title field of a list or library contains specified keywords

- The item was created in a specific time span

- The item's file size is in a specific range of kilobytes

There are also conditions available that you can customize just the way you want. For example, you can create a custom condition that checks the value of a field with a custom value, or you can compare a field in the specified list with a value in another list. Conditions are created visually and you cannot add code fragments to these conditions.

The conditions that are available in the Conditions drop-down list depend on whether the workflow will be attached to a SharePoint list or library. You specify this list or library on the first page of the Workflow Designer wizard. Figure 4-6 shows the conditions available for a Shared Document document library.

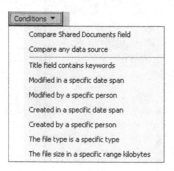

Figure 4-6. *The Workflow Designer wizard with the conditions available for the Shared Documents document library*

An action is the most basic unit of the workflow. SharePoint Designer contains several out of the box actions. If that is not enough, with Visual Studio 2005 Designer, you can create actions and deploy them to SharePoint Designer where they can be used.

There are 23 actions available in SharePoint Designer. You can use them via the Actions drop-down list. The actions are divided into the following categories:

- *All Actions*: This category contains an overview of all 23 actions available in SharePoint Designer.

- *Core Actions*: This category contains 13 core actions such as "Log to History List" and "Set Workflow Variable."

- *List Actions*: This category contains 7 list-specific actions such as "Create List Item."

- *Task Actions*: This category contains 3 task-specific actions such as "Assign a To-do item."

Figure 4-7 shows an overview of the Workflow Actions window.

Multiple actions can be associated with a condition. It is possible to run the actions in sequence, which means that first action 1 runs and then action 2 will take place, or in parallel, which means action 1 and action 2 will be performed at the same time.

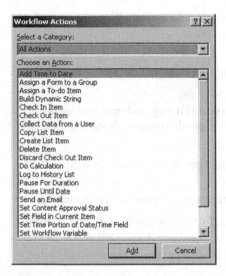

Figure 4-7. *The Workflow Actions window showing the All Actions category*

■**Note** When you specify that actions run in parallel, you will not have the guarantee that they will be performed simultaneously. The exact order of running cannot be specified; it may vary each time the workflow runs.

Creating an Example Workflow

In this section, we will create a simple example workflow using SharePoint Designer. We are going to create a workflow for an imaginary company's Human Resources department. They have placed an advertisement for a new C# developer and they expect a lot of letters and resumes. The CTO wants to read these letters and approve or decline them. If a letter is approved, the candidate will be invited for an interview. In this example, we are going to create the first part of the process: namely, a document (the letter from the candidate) will be uploaded to a document library called LettersCandidates. This document library will contain two columns: Assigned to and Status. The custom column Assigned to will contain three values: CTO, CEO, and CFO. When a document is uploaded to the document library and assigned to the CTO, the CTO will receive a new task in his Tasks list asking whether he approves or declines the document. The second custom column, Status, contains the following values: prospect, 1st interview, 2nd interview, declined, and hired.

Follow these steps to create a new document library called LettersCandidates and a new column:

1. Open a SharePoint site where you want to create a new document library.

2. Click the View All Site Content link on the left of the SharePoint site. This opens the All Site Content page.

3. Click Create. This opens the Create page.

4. Click Document Library in the Libraries section.

5. Name the document library **LettersCandidates** and click Create.

6. Select Settings in the LettersCandidates document library and click Create Column.

7. Name the column **Status**, check the Choice radio button, and enter the values: **prospect, 1st interview, 2nd interview, declined**, and **hired**. Click OK.

8. Click Create Column.

9. Name the column **Assigned to**, check the Choice radio button, and enter the values: **CTO, CEO**, and **CFO**. Click OK.

After setting up the LettersCandidates document library and adding a column, you are ready to open the SharePoint site in SharePoint Designer. The next thing to do is to start designing the example workflow. Follow these steps to create the workflow.

1. Open the SharePoint site containing the LettersCandidates document library in SharePoint Designer.

2. In the File menu, click New and select Workflow. This opens the Workflow Designer wizard.

3. In the Give a name to this workflow text box, specify the following name: **Candidates Notification WF**.

4. In the What SharePoint list should this workflow be attached to drop-down list, select the LettersCandidates document library.

5. In the Select workflow start options for items in LettersCandidates section, do the following. Uncheck the Allow this workflow to be manually started from an item check box. Check the Automatically start this workflow when an item is created check box and uncheck the Automatically start this workflow when an item is changed check box. This way the workflow will run each time an item is created. Figure 4-8 shows the first page of the Workflow Designer wizard.

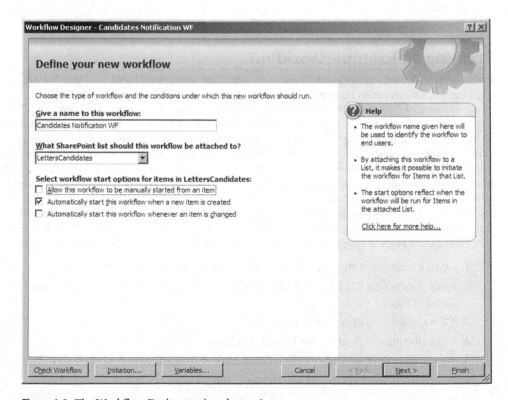

Figure 4-8. *The Workflow Designer wizard page 1*

6. Click Next.

7. In the Step Name text box, specify the following name: **AssignTaskStep**.

8. Click the Conditions drop-down list and select Compare LettersCandidates Field. The condition if field equals value is inserted, where field and value are the parameters that must be filled in.

9. Click the field parameter and select the Assigned to column. The field parameter shows a drop-down list filled with the specified document library's metadata.

10. Click the value parameter and select the CTO value. The value parameter shows a drop-down list filled with the values from the specified column. Figure 4-9 shows the value parameter's drop-down list.

Figure 4-9. *The value parameter's drop-down list in page 2 of the Workflow Designer*

11. Click the Actions drop-down list and select Collect data from a user (output to variable:collect1). The action Collect data from this user is inserted, where data and this user are parameters that must be filled in. The parameter variable:collect1 will be where we save the data that is collected from the user.

12. Click data. This opens the Custom Task wizard. Click Next.

13. In the Name text box, specify the following name: **ApprovalCTO**. Click Next.

14. Click the Add button to define a custom task field that the user can fill out. This opens the Add Field dialog box.

15. In the Field name text box, specify the following name: **DecisionCTO**. In the Information type drop-down list, choose choice (menu to choose from). Click Next.

16. In the Choices list, enter the following two choices: **Approve**, **Decline**.

17. Uncheck the Allow fill-in choices check box. Click Finish twice.

18. Click this user. This opens the Select Users dialog box. Select a user from the list of users, click Add, and click OK. Figure 4-10 shows the AssignTaskStep workflow step.

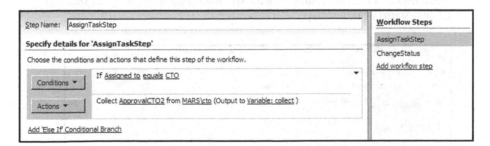

Figure 4-10. *The AssignTaskStep workflow step*

19. Click Add workflow step. This adds a new workflow step to the workflow.

20. In the Step Name text box, specify the following name: **ChangeStatus**.

21. Click the Conditions drop-down list and select Compare any data source. The condition `if value equals value` is inserted, where `value` and `value` are the parameters that must be filled in.

22. Click the display data binding icon next to the first value parameter. This opens the Define Workflow Lookup window. The Source drop-down list shows the SharePoint site's available lists. The Field drop-down list shows all fields available in the specified list. In the Source drop-down list, select Tasks. In the Field drop-down list, select DecisionCTO. In the Value drop-down list, select Approve, as shown in Figure 4-11.

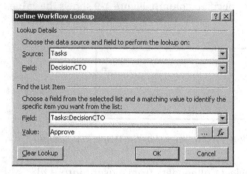

Figure 4-11. *The Define Workflow Lookup window*

23. Click OK.

24. Click the Actions drop-down list and select Set Field in Current Item. The action `Set field to value` is inserted, where `field` and `value` are parameters that must be filled in. Click the `field` parameter and select the Status value. The `field` parameter shows a drop-down list filled with the specified document library's metadata.

■**Note** It is not possible to create custom activities with SharePoint Designer. However, it is possible to make use of custom activities created using Visual Studio 2005 in SharePoint Designer. More information about creating custom activities and using them in SharePoint Designer can be found in the section "Creating and Using a Custom Activity."

---

25. Click the `value` parameter and select 1st interview. The `value` parameter shows a drop-down list filled with the values from the specified column. Figure 4-12 shows you the ChangeStatus workflow step.

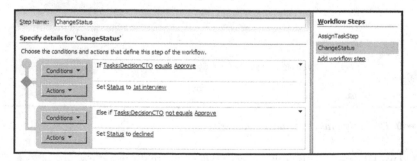

Figure 4-12. *The ChangeStatus workflow step*

26. Click the Check Workflow button to check whether your workflow contains any errors.

Tip If there is an error in your workflow, asterisks appear before and after the parameters that were not configured correctly. In addition, in the Workflow Steps section, an error symbol appears next to each step that contains an error.

---

27. Click Finish. The workflow is validated and associated with the document library.

The next set of figures walks you through the example workflow in a SharePoint site. Figure 4-13 shows you a letter from Candidate A in the LettersCandidates document library. The Candidates Notification Workflow is in progress.

LettersCandidates				▾
Type Name	Assigned to	Candidates Notification WF		Status
📄 CandidateA ! NEW	CTO	In Progress		prospect
⊞ Add new document				

Figure 4-13. *The LettersCandidates document library*

The workflow will assign a task to the CTO. This task will also be send as an e-mail to the CTO. The task can be edited and the CTO can approve or decline the document. This is shown in Figure 4-14.

Title:	ApprovalCTO2
DecisionCTO *:	Approve ▾
Related list item:	CandidateA
Save Draft Complete Task Cancel	

Figure 4-14. *The LettersCandidates document library*

After the CTO has approved or declined the document, the status of the document will change. See Figure 4-15.

LettersCandidates				▾
Type Name	Assigned to	Candidates Notification WF		Status
📄 CandidateA ! NEW	CTO	Completed		1st interview
⊞ Add new document				

Figure 4-15. *The LettersCandidates document library*

Creating Advanced Workflow Solutions with Visual Studio

The team responsible for creating Windows Workflow Foundation has also created a Visual Studio add-in called Visual Studio 2005 Designer that makes it easy to create custom workflows. Visual Studio 2005 Designer can also be used to include custom code in a workflow, or to include custom forms that are used by the workflow to communicate with the workflow users. It is also possible to create custom activities that can be used in other workflows or in SharePoint Designer.

Getting to Know Visual Studio 2005 Designer

Before even thinking about starting to create workflows, you first have to make sure your development environment is ready for the job. You have to install the following components:

- *Visual Studio 2005 extensions for .NET Framework 3.0 (Windows Workflow Foundation)*: You can download the Visual Studio 2005 extensions for .NET Framework 3.0 here: http://www.microsoft.com/downloads/details.aspx?familyid=5D61409E-1FA3-48CF-8023-E8F38E709BA6&displaylang=en.

- *Windows SharePoint Services 3.0: Software Development Kit*: You can download the Windows SharePoint Services 3.0 SDK here: http://www.microsoft.com/downloads/details.aspx?FamilyId=05E0DD12-8394-402B-8936-A07FE8AFAFFD&displaylang=en.

■**Note** Support for Workflow Services in Visual Studio 2008 (the next version of Visual Studio 2005) and .NET 3.5 has been improved. The most important new feature is the integration between Workflow Services and Windows Communication Foundation. In .NET 3.5, it is easy to invoke WCF services within WF workflows. Another interesting feature is the ability to expose a WF workflow as a WCF service.

Make sure you install the following components of the Visual Studio 2005 extensions for .NET Framework 3.0:

- Visual Studio 2005 Designer for Windows Workflow Foundation (also known as the Visual Studio 2005 Workflow Designer)

- Windows Workflow Foundation Debugger

■**Note** Visual Studio 2005 extensions for .NET Framework 3.0 requires the final version either of Windows Workflow Foundation Runtime Components, Microsoft Windows Vista, or the .NET Framework 3.0 Runtime Components. The .NET Framework 3.0 Runtime Components can be downloaded here: http://www.microsoft.com/downloads/details.aspx?displaylang=en&FamilyID=10CC340B-F857-4A14-83F5-25634C3BF043.

The Windows SharePoint Services 3.0 SDK is very helpful if you are developing solutions based on Windows SharePoint Services. The WSS 3.0 SDK contains conceptual overviews, programming tasks, and references. The WSS 3.0 SDK also includes the Workflow Developer Starter Kit for Windows SharePoint Services 3.0.

The Workflow Developer Starter Kit for Windows SharePoint Services 3.0 contains the following items:

- Visual Studio Project Templates
    - Sequential Workflow Library
    - State Machine Workflow Library
- Sample Custom Workflow
    - Simple Collect Feedback using ASPX forms

Visual Studio 2005 Designer can be used to create two types of workflows: state machine workflows and sequential workflows. A state machine workflow is a workflow that contains a number of different states where one state always acts as the starting point. Each state in such a workflow receives events, which lead to the transition to the next state. A sequential workflow is a workflow that contains a fixed sequence of steps that always must be followed in the same order.

After installing the WSS 3.0 SDK and the Visual Studio 2005 extensions for .NET Framework 3.0, two new project types appear in the Project types list of the Visual Studio 2005 New Project dialog box. Figure 4-16 shows the Workflow project types.

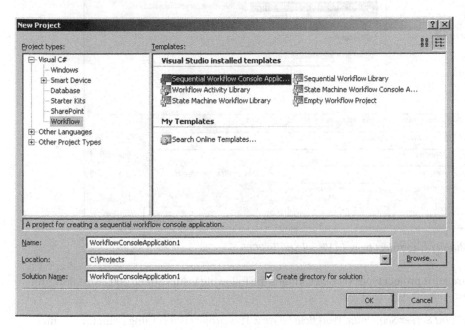

Figure 4-16. *Workflow project types in Visual Studio 2005*

The Workflow project types section contains the following Visual Studio 2005 project templates:

- *Sequential Workflow Console Application*: This project is a starting point for creating sequential workflows hosted by a console host application.

- *Workflow Activity Library*: This project is a starting point for creating your own activities that can be reused later as building blocks in a workflow.

- *State Machine Workflow Library*: This project is a starting point for creating your own state machine workflow in the form of a library (.dll).

- *Sequential Workflow Library*: This project is a starting point for creating your own sequential workflows in the form of a library (.dll).

- *State Machine Workflow Console Application*: This project is a starting point for creating state machine workflows hosted by a console host application.

- *Empty Workflow Project*: This project is an unconfigured workflow project that can include multiple workflows and/or activities.

The Workflow project types let you create generic workflow projects, but whenever you want to create a specific SharePoint workflow, you are better off if you choose one of the SharePoint workflow project types. Figure 4-17 shows the SharePoint project types.

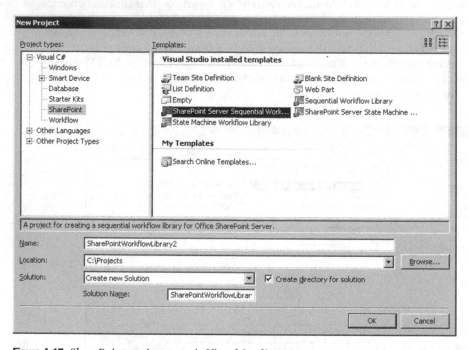

Figure 4-17. *SharePoint project types in Visual Studio 2005*

The SharePoint project types section contains the following Visual Studio 2005 workflow project templates:

- *SharePoint Server Sequential Workflow Library*: This project is a starting point for creating your own sequential workflows for Office SharePoint Server in the form of a library (.dll).

- *Sequential Workflow Library*: This project is a starting point for creating your own sequential workflows for Windows SharePoint Services in the form of a library (.dll).

- *SharePoint Server State Machine Workflow Library*: This project is a starting point for creating your own state machine workflows for Office SharePoint Server in the form of a library (.dll).

- *State Machine Workflow Library*: This project is a starting point for creating your own state machine workflows for Windows SharePoint Services in the form of a library (.dll).

Visual Studio 2005 Designer for Windows Workflow Foundation contains a visual designer that you can use to create a workflow. You can drag and drop activities from the toolbox onto the design surface, where you can configure them.

Note You are now looking at a domain-specific language (DSL) at work. A DSL is a concept closely related to software factories. If you want to find out more about software factories and DSLs, refer to Chapter 5.

The Visual Studio 2005 Designer for Windows Workflow Foundation should be familiar to experienced Visual Studio users. In addition to the design surface, there are other windows available, such as the toolbox window that contains graphical representations of activities, the properties window that lets you configure activity properties, the Solution Explorer window, and the standard Visual Studio debug windows.

Creating an Example Workflow

Once you are happy with the setup of your development environment, you are ready to move to the design phase. You could make a sketch on paper or design a model using Office Visio, or do whatever works for you, as long as you have a clear concept about what you want to accomplish in the workflow. As soon as you have reached that point, you are ready to move to the development phase.

Tip When you create a workflow for Microsoft Office SharePoint Server or Windows SharePoint Services, it is best to develop on a machine hosting a SharePoint server itself. This way it becomes much easier to deploy and debug the workflow.

The following procedure describes the steps you have to follow to develop SharePoint workflows or workflow activities with Visual Studio 2005 Designer.

- Create a workflow or workflow activity.
- Create and publish custom forms.
- Create a feature definition file and a workflow definition file. These files contain information about the workflow assembly and are used to bind the custom forms to the workflow.
- Make sure the workflow assembly is compiled as a strongly named assembly.

Note A strong-named assembly is an assembly that has a fully qualified name. Fully qualified names contain the following information: assembly name, version number, culture, and a public key token that can be used to uniquely identify the developer of the assembly.

- Deploy the workflow.
- Debug the workflow if necessary.

In this section we will discuss how to create a Microsoft Office SharePoint Server workflow with Visual Studio 2005 Designer. The other steps (deploying and debugging) will be discussed later in the sections "Deploying a Workflow" and "Debugging a Workflow." To develop a custom workflow for Microsoft Office SharePoint Server, you start by creating a SharePoint workflow project in Visual Studio 2005 Designer.

The example workflow we are going to create will be a sequential workflow for Microsoft Office SharePoint Server that can be associated with a list or library. When a document is uploaded into the document library or changed in the document library, a task will be created for a specified person.

This task contains predefined instructions and comments. When the user opens the task, she will get a custom-designed InfoPath form with instructions to complete the task. We are going to create two custom InfoPath forms, one for associating the workflow to the list or library and specifying the name of the user who will get the task, and another for completing the custom task form (and the workflow).

Creating an Initiation Form

The first thing we are going to do is to create an initiation form, which will double as an association form. More information about forms can be found in the section "Using Forms to Capture and Automate Your Processes." The initiation form will be shown when a SharePoint item is associated with a workflow. We are going to create the initiation form using InfoPath 2007.

Tip It is also possible to create custom ASP.NET forms to interact with the user in your workflow. This allows developers to choose the development model they are most comfortable with. InfoPath forms are easier to create and more powerful. When creating a workflow for Windows SharePoint services 3.0, you do not have this option: you can only use ASP.NET forms. Custom forms will be displayed to the user during some stage in the workflow. You can find more information about forms in the section "Using Forms to Capture and Automate Your Processes."

The following procedure shows how to create an initiation form.

1. Open InfoPath by clicking All Programs ➤ Microsoft Office ➤ Microsoft InfoPath 2007. This opens the Getting Started window.

2. Click Design a Form Template in the Design a Form section. This opens the Design a Form dialog box.

3. Select Form Template in the Design a new section.

4. Select Blank in the Based on area.

5. Make sure the Enable browser-compatible features only check box is checked.

6. Click OK.

Now that we have created an empty InfoPath form, we are going to design this form and add three text boxes to it. The first text box contains the name of the person to whom the task is assigned, the second text box allows the user to enter instructions, and the last text box allows the user to specify additional comments. The form will also contain a Submit button. The following procedure shows how to design such a form in InfoPath.

1. In the Design Tasks pane, click Layout.

2. Drag a Table with Title onto the form. Enter the following title: **MOSSworkflow initiation form**.

3. Drag a Custom Table with two columns and four rows onto the form.

4. In the Design Tasks tool pane, click Controls.

5. In the left column of the first row, type the following: **Assign Task to:**.

6. Drag a Textbox control onto the form in the right column of the first row. Right-click the Textbox and select Text Box Properties. In the Field Name text box, enter the following value: **assignee**. Click OK.

7. In the left column of the second row, type the following: **Instructions:**.

8. Drag a Textbox control onto the form in the right column of the second row. Right-click the Textbox and select Text Box Properties. In the Field Name text box, enter the following value: **instructions**. Click OK.

9. In the left column of the third row, type the following: **Comments:**.

10. Drag a Textbox control onto the form in the right column of the third row. Right-click the Textbox and select Text Box Properties. In the Field Name text box, enter the following value: **comments**. Click OK.

11. Drag a Button control onto the form in the right column of the fourth row. Right-click the Button and select Button Properties. In the Label text box, enter the following value: **submit**. Click OK. Figure 4-18 shows the way the InfoPath form should look.

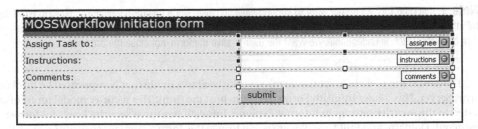

Figure 4-18. *Custom workflow initiation form*

Next, we are going to give the form fields collection (all the text boxes on the form) a unique name. We do this because we want to extract the XML schema (.xsd) file for this form and use this schema as the basis for the class we are going to use in the OnWorkflowActivation activity. The root element of the schema file will have the same name as the form fields collection. The class that will be generated from the schema file will have the same name as the schema file root element. Therefore, when you specify a unique name for the form fields collection, you will get a class with a unique name. This is especially important when you are programming a workflow that deserializes multiple forms. Follow these steps to configure the InfoPath form.

1. Go to the Design Tasks pane and click Data Source.

2. Double-click the myFields fields collection. This opens the Field or Group Properties dialog window.

3. Enter the following value in the Name text box: **InitForm**.

4. Click OK.

We are going to add two rules to the InfoPath form's Submit button. The first rule submits the form information to Microsoft Office SharePoint Server 2007; the other rule closes the form when the user clicks the Submit button. Follow these steps to add these two rules to the Submit button.

1. Right-click the Button control and select Button Properties. This opens the Button Properties dialog window.

2. On the General tab, click the Rules button. This opens the Rules dialog window.

3. Click the Add button. This opens the Rule dialog window.

4. Click the Add Action button. This opens the Action dialog window.

5. Select Submit using a data connection from the Action drop-down list. Click the Add button. This opens the Data Connection Wizard dialog window.

6. Select Create a new connection and select the Submit data radio button. Click Next.

7. Select To the hosting environment and click Next.

8. Click Finish.

9. Click OK twice.

10. In the Rules dialog window, click Add to add another rule. This opens the Rule dialog window.

11. Click the Add Action button. This opens the Action dialog window.

12. Select Close the form from the Action drop-down list. You will get a message stating the following: Prompting the user to save on close is not supported.

Note In this scenario, we do not want to support save on close, since this form will be rendered to HTML by InfoPath Forms Server 2007. As a result, the form is shown in the browser. Closing the form equates to closing the entire browser, which is undesirable. We want the user to save the form, not close the browser.

The next thing to do is to set the form's security level to a mode that is supported by InfoPath Forms Server. This allows InfoPath Forms Server to host the form. The security model for InfoPath is related to the security settings in Internet Explorer. InfoPath has three security levels for forms: Restricted, Domain, and Full Trust. We are going to give this form a Domain security level, so the form can access content that is stored in the form itself.

Tip More information about InfoPath and MOSS 2007 can be found in Chapter 8.

The next procedure shows you how to change the security level of a form.

1. Select Tools from the menu and click Forms options. This opens the Forms Options dialog window.

2. Select the Security and Trust category from the Category section.

3. Uncheck the Automatically determine security level check box and select Domain. Click OK.

The next procedure shows how to publish the initiation form. By publishing the initiation form to the workflow project's Feature files directory, you allow the initiation form to be deployed as part of the workflow feature.

1. In the File menu, click Publish. This opens the Save As dialog window.

2. Enter the following value in the FileName text box: **InitiationForm**. Then, click Save.

3. Select To a network location and click Next.

4. Click the Browse button to browse to where you keep your Visual Studio project and go to the Deployment Files\Feature Files directory to publish the form. Then, click OK.

5. Enter the following value in the Form template name text box: **InitiationForm**. Click Next.

6. Make sure the alternate access path text box is empty and click Next. This way, the initiation form can only be accessed within the workflow process (as opposed to accessing the form directly from within a browser).

7. Click Publish and then click Close.

To get the data from the submitted form into the workflow, we have to generate a class using xsd.exe. The Microsoft .NET Framework 2.0 command-line tool xsd.exe lets you generate a new class file based on the myschema.xsd form schema. The xsd.exe tool is located by default in the following location: [drive letter]:\Program Files\Microsoft Visual Studio 8\SDK\v2.0\Bin. Follow these steps to generate a new class file that is based on the form schema file.

1. Select Save as Source Files in the File menu. Browse to the location where you want to save the InfoPath source files and click OK.

Note An InfoPath template consists of a collection of form source files, including the schema file. By default, the form schema file is named myschema.xsd. You can find more information about InfoPath in Chapter 8.

---

2. Go to Start ➤ All Programs ➤ Microsoft Visual Studio 2005 ➤ Visual Studio Tools ➤ Visual Studio 2005 Command Prompt. This opens a Visual Studio 2005 Command Prompt window.

3. From the command prompt, navigate to the location of the myschema.xsd file and enter the following line of code.

```
xsd myschema.xsd /c
```

4. This generates a new class file based on the form schema called myschema.cs. Rename the schema.cs file to InitForm.cs.

5. Add the InitForm.cs class file to the workflow project.

Listing 4-1 shows the content of the InitForm.cs file. As you will notice, the name of the class is identical to the name of the form fields collection in the InfoPath form.

Listing 4-1. *Generated Code Class from myschema.xsd*

```
using System.Xml.Serialization;

[System.CodeDom.Compiler.GeneratedCodeAttribute("xsd", "2.0.50727.42")]
[System.SerializableAttribute()]
[System.Diagnostics.DebuggerStepThroughAttribute()]
[System.ComponentModel.DesignerCategoryAttribute("code")]
[System.Xml.Serialization.XmlTypeAttribute(AnonymousType=true)]
[System.Xml.Serialization.XmlRootAttribute( ➥
Namespace="http://schemas.microsoft.com/office/ ➥
infopath/2003/myXSD/2007-05-25T12:13:02", IsNullable=false)]
public partial class InitForm
{
  private string assigneeField;
  private string instructionsField;
  private string commentsField;
  private System.Xml.XmlAttribute[] anyAttrField;

  public string assignee
  {
    get { return this.assigneeField; }
    set { this.assigneeField = value;}
  }
}
```

```
public string instructions
{
  get { return this.instructionsField; }
  set { this.instructionsField = value; }
}

public string comments
{
  get { return this.commentsField; }
  set { this.commentsField = value; }
}

[System.Xml.Serialization.XmlAnyAttributeAttribute()]
public System.Xml.XmlAttribute[] AnyAttr
{
  get { return this.anyAttrField; }
  set { this.anyAttrField = value; }
}
}
```

Creating a Custom Task Form

The second form we are going to create is the task form. This form enables users of the workflow to interact with the task that is assigned to them. More information about forms can be found in the section "Using Forms to Capture and Automate Your Processes." Again, as we did in the "Creating an Initiation Form" section, we are going to create the new form using InfoPath 2007. The next procedure shows how to create a workflow task form in InfoPath 2007.

1. Open InfoPath by clicking All Programs ➤ Microsoft Office ➤ Microsoft InfoPath 2007. This opens the Getting Started window.

2. Click Design a Form Template in the Design a Form section. This opens the Design a Form dialog box.

3. Select Form Template in the Design a new section.

4. Select Blank in the Based on area.

5. Make sure the Enable browser-compatible features only check box is checked.

6. Click OK.

We are going to place one text box, one check box, and one button on the task form. The text box displays instructions to a user. This text box will be prepopulated with data from the initiation form. The check box is used to indicate that the workflow task is completed; the OK button closes the task form. The next procedure shows how to design the task form in InfoPath.

1. In the Design Tasks pane, click Layout.

2. Drag a Table with Title onto the form. Enter the following title: **MOSSworkflow edit task form**.

3. Drag a Custom Table with two columns and three rows onto the form.

4. In the Design Tasks tool pane, click Controls.

5. In the left column of the first row, type the following: **Instructions:**.

6. Drag a Textbox control onto the form in the right column of the first row. Right-click the Textbox and select Text Box Properties. In the Field Name text box, enter the following value: **instructions**. Click OK.

7. In the left column of the second row, type the following: **Task completed**.

8. Drag a Check Box control onto the form in the right column of the second row. Right-click the check box and select Check Box Properties. In the Field Name text box, enter the value **isFinished**, and select True/False from the Data type drop-down list. Click OK.

9. Drag a Button control onto the form in the right column of the third row. Right-click the Button and select Button Properties. In the Label text box, enter the following value: **OK**. Click OK. Figure 4-19 shows what the InfoPath form should look like.

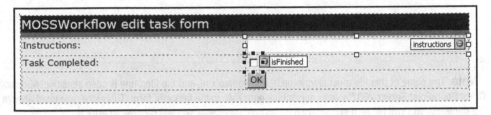

Figure 4-19. *Custom workflow edit task form*

We are going to add two rules to the Submit button of the task InfoPath form: one rule to submit the form information to Microsoft Office SharePoint Server 2007, and another rule to close the form when the user clicks the Submit button. Follow these steps to add two rules to the Submit button:

1. Right-click the Button control and select Button Properties. This opens the Button Properties dialog window.

2. On the General tab, click the Rules button. This opens the Rules dialog window.

3. Click the Add button. This opens the Rule dialog window.

4. Click the Add Action button. This opens the Action dialog window.

5. Select Submit using a data connection from the Action drop-down list. Click the Add button. This opens the Data Connection Wizard dialog window.

6. Select Create a new connection and select the Submit data radio button. Click Next.

7. Select To the hosting environment and click Next.

8. Click Finish.

9. Click OK twice.

10. In the Rules dialog window, click Add to add another rule. This opens the Rule dialog window.

11. Click the Add Action button. This opens the Action dialog window.

12. Select Close the form from the Action drop-down list. You will get a message stating the following: Prompting the user to save on close is not supported. This is precisely the way we want it, because we are going to use InfoPath Forms Services. Click OK four times.

The workflow task form is used to display data from the initiation form. In this example, we show the instructions for the task assignee that were added in the initiation form. You have to add the workflow task schema to the workflow edit task form as a secondary data source to allow Microsoft Office SharePoint Server 2007 to prepopulate the task form's Instructions field. The Item-Metadata.xml file represents the task schema. In the file, each task property that you want to use as data in your form must be defined. You can define a task property by adding an attribute with prefix ows_ and the name of the task property. In this example, that will be ows_instructions. The value of the attribute must be set to an empty string, like this: ows_instructions="". The next procedure shows you how to create the ItemMetadata.xml file.

1. Open the text editor of your choice, for example, Notepad.

2. Create a file with the following name: **ItemMetadata.xml**.

3. Add the following line of XML to the file.

```
<z:row xmlns:z="#RowsetSchema"
  ows_instructions=""
/>
```

4. Save the ItemMetadata.xml file.

Note The name of this file must always be ItemMetadata.xml, and the filename is case sensitive. Microsoft Office SharePoint Server 2007 always sends task data XML to the task edit form. Therefore, you must always add the ItemMetadata.xml file as a secondary data source. Otherwise, you will receive an error.

The following procedure shows you how to add the ItemMetadata.xml file to the task edit form as a secondary data source.

1. In the Design Tasks pane, click Data Source.

2. Click Manage Data Connection in the section Actions. This opens the Data Connections dialog box.

3. Click Add. This opens the Data Connection Wizard.

4. Select Create a new connection to and select Receive data. Click Next.

5. Select XML document and click Next.

6. Browse to the location where you have saved the ItemMetadata.xml file, select the file, and click Next.

7. Select the Include the data as a resource file in the form template or template part radio button and click Next.

8. In the Enter a name for this data connection text box, enter the following name: **ItemMetadata**.

9. Make sure the Automatically retrieve data when form is opened check box is checked. Click Finish and then click Close.

If the ItemMetadata.xml file is included as a resource file in the form, like we just did, we no longer need this file anymore. So you do not have to include the ItemMetadata.xml file in the workflow solution. The next thing to do is to bind the instructions Textbox control to the instructions attribute in the workflow schema that we have added as a data source. The following procedure shows you how to do this.

1. Right-click the instructions text box and select Text Box Properties. This opens the Text Box Properties dialog box.

2. Select the Data tab. In the Default value section, next to the Value text box, click the formula button. This opens the Insert Formula dialog box.

3. Click the Insert a Field or Group button. This opens the Select a Field or Group dialog box.

4. Select the ItemMetadata (secondary) data source from the Data Source drop-down list.

5. Select the ows_instructions attribute and click OK. Figure 4-20 shows the Text Box Properties dialog box.

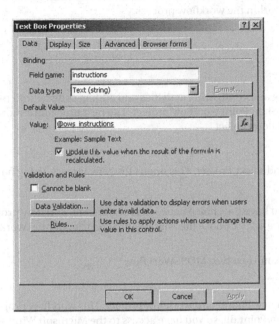

Figure 4-20. *Databinding the instructions text box to the* instructions *attribute*

6. Click OK two more times.

At this time, the instructions text box is bound to the instructions workflow task property. When the task edit form is loaded by Microsoft Office SharePoint Server 2007, this form will display the task instructions in the text box.

The next thing we need to do is set the security level of the form so it can be hosted by InfoPath Forms Server and publish the task edit form. The next procedure shows you how to do this.

1. Select Tools from the menu and click Forms options. This opens the Forms Options dialog window.

2. Select the Security and Trust category from the Category section.

3. Uncheck the Automatically determine security level check box and select Domain. Click OK.

Note When the Automatically determine security level option is checked, InfoPath will automatically select the appropriate security level for the functionality of the form. This way, the minimum level of trust that is needed for the form is enabled.

---

4. On the File menu, click Publish. This opens the Save As dialog window.

5. Enter the value **EditTaskForm** in the FileName text box and click Save.

6. Select To a network location and click Next.

7. Click the Browse button to browse to the place where you keep you Visual Studio project, go to the Deployment Files\Feature Files directory to publish the form, and click OK.

8. Enter **EditTaskForm** in the Form template name text box and click Next.

9. Make sure the alternate access path text box is empty and click Next. This way, the task edit form can only be accessed from within the workflow process.

10. Click Publish and click Close.

Developing the Workflow

Developing a workflow consists of adding and configuring activities and adding code behind these activities. The first step is creating a new SharePoint workflow project. The next procedure shows you how to create a new SharePoint workflow project.

1. Open Visual Studio 2005.

2. Click the File menu, click New, and select Project. This opens the New Project dialog box.

3. Select the SharePoint project type.

4. In the New Project dialog box, you have the choice between four different workflow project templates, as can be seen in Figure 4-25. Choose the SharePoint Server Sequential Workflow Library project type.

5. Type the following name in the Name text box: **MOSSWorkflow**.

6. Click OK.

Visual Studio 2005 Designer opens a new SharePoint workflow project. This workflow project contains a reference to the Microsoft.SharePoint.dll, so you have access to the Microsoft Windows SharePoint Services 3.0 object model in your code. It also contains a reference to the Microsoft.SharePoint.WorkflowActions.dll to enable access to predefined Microsoft Office SharePoint Server activities.

Table 4-5 shows an overview of the Microsoft Office SharePoint Server–specific activities that are added to the Toolbox pane. These activities are specially designed for use within Visual Studio 2005 Designer.

■**Note** Some of the activities mentioned in Table 4-5 (all activities starting with On*) implement the IEventActivity interface, which provides methods and properties for event-driven activities that allow consumers to subscribe to events. Such activities are important when building SharePoint workflows. Human-oriented workflows such as the ones you will be building in SharePoint typically run for an extended period of time, during which end users cannot proceed with the execution of the workflow until another end user has completed a task. To be able to build such workflows, you need to rely on activities that can support asynchronous tasks.

Table 4-5. *Microsoft Office SharePoint Server Activities*

Activity Name	Description
CompleteTask	Some activities add tasks to a SharePoint Tasks list once the workflow is started. The Approval workflow that is available out of the box is an example of such a workflow. The CompleteTask activity marks a task as completed.
CreateTask	The CreateTask activity adds a task to the SharePoint Tasks list, along with specific task properties.
CreateTaskWithContentType	The CreateTaskWithContentType activity adds a task of a specific content type to the SharePoint Tasks list.
DelayFor	The DelayFor activity delays the workflow for a specified duration.
DelayUntil	The DelayUntil delays the workflow until the specified date.
DeleteTask	The DeleteTask activity deletes a task from the SharePoint Tasks list.
EnableWorkflowModification	The EnableWorkflowModification activity enables a workflow modification form so that it can be used within the workflow.
InitializeWorkflow	The InitializeWorkflow activity initializes a new instance of the workflow.
LogToHistoryListActivity	The LogToHistoryListActivity activity logs audit information in the workflow's History List.
OnTaskChanged	The OnTaskChanged activity responds to the ITaskService.OnTaskChanged event that is raised by Microsoft Office SharePoint Server 2007 when a task associated with the workflow is edited. This activity implements the interface IEventActivity and allows you to perform asynchronous tasks.
OnTaskCreated	The OnTaskCreated activity responds to the ITaskService.OnTaskCreated event that is raised by Microsoft Office SharePoint Server 2007 when a task that is associated to the workflow is created. This activity implements the interface IEventActivity and allows you to perform asynchronous tasks.
OnTaskDeleted	The OnTaskDeleted activity responds to the ITaskService.OnTaskDeleted event that is raised by Microsoft Office SharePoint Server 2007 when a task that is associated with the workflow is deleted. This activity implements the interface IEventActivity and allows you to perform asynchronous tasks.
OnWorkflowActivated	This activity responds to the ISharePointService.OnWorkflowActivated event that is raised by Microsoft Office SharePoint Server 2007 when a workflow instance is initiated for a SharePoint item. The OnWorkflowActivated activity must always be the first activity in a Microsoft Office SharePoint Server 2007 workflow and will be ignored in the workflow if it is not the first activity. This activity takes care of the initialization of the correlation between the workflow id and the correlation token. This activity implements the interface IEventActivity and allows you to perform asynchronous tasks.

Continued

Table 4-5. *Continued*

Activity Name	Description
OnWorkflowItemChanged	The OnWorkflowItemChanged activity responds to the event that is raised by Microsoft Office SharePoint Server 2007 when an item in the list is changed. This activity implements the interface IEventActivity and allows you to perform asynchronous tasks.
OnWorkflowItemDeleted	The OnWorkflowItemDeleted activity responds to the event that is raised by Microsoft Office SharePoint Server 2007 when an item in the list is deleted. This activity implements the interface IEventActivity and allows you to perform asynchronous tasks.
OnWorkflowModified	The OnWorkflowModified activity responds to the event that is raised by Microsoft Office SharePoint Server 2007 when a user submits a modification form. This activity implements the interface IEventActivity and allows you to perform asynchronous tasks.
RollbackTask	The RollbackTask activity rolls back a task that was previously modified.
SendEmail	The SendEmail activity creates and sends an e-mail message to specified users.
SetState	The SetState activity sets the status of the workflow, as shown in the status column of the list the workflow operates on.
SharePointSequentialWorkflowActivity	The SharePointSequentialWorkflowActivity enables execution of multiple activities in a given event.
UpdateAllTasks	The UpdateAllTasks activity updates all tasks in the SharePoint Tasks list.
UpdateTask	The UpdateTask activity updates a task in the SharePoint Tasks list.

Figure 4-21 shows the MOSSWorkflow project in Visual Studio 2005 Designer. You will notice that there are a number of files that are created by default:

- *Feature.xml*: The feature definition file feature.xml contains information necessary to deploy the workflow. You can learn more about the feature.xml file in the section "Deploying a Workflow."

- *Workflow.xml*: The workflow definition file workflow.xml contains information about the workflow that SharePoint requires to instantiate and run the workflow. More about the workflow.xml file can be found in the section "Deploying a Workflow."

- *Manifest.xml*: The manifest file is used by Visual Studio 2005 and defines how to populate the cabinet file that is used to deploy the workflow project. Please refer to Chapter 1.

- *Wsp_structure.ddf*: This file specifies the structure of the .wsp solution cab file.

- *Workflow1.cs*: This class file contains the actual workflow code and components.

- *PostBuildActions.bat*: This batch file is used to deploy the workflow. If you want to learn more about deploying a workflow, please refer to the section "Deploying a Workflow."

Figure 4-21. *A SharePoint Server Sequential Workflow Library project in Visual Studio 2005 Designer*

The workflow you are creating for Microsoft Office SharePoint Server 2007 will have access to the complete context of SharePoint. In other words, your workflow can write to lists and libraries, change properties, and create, edit, and delete items. Your workflow can do everything that the user account running the workflow is authorized to do.

We are going to add the following activities to the design view of the workflow1.cs file: Create-Task, While, OnTaskChanged, and CompleteTask. The next procedure shows how to add activities to a workflow.

1. Double-click the workflow.cs file to open it in design view. By doing this, you are opening the so-called Workflow Designer.

2. As discussed in Table 4-5, every workflow starts with an OnWorkflowActivated activity. By default, each workflow contains the OnWorkflowActivated activity.

3. Double-click the workflow1.cs file in the Solution Explorer. This opens the design window.

4. Drag and drop a CreateTask activity right below the OnWorkflowActivated activity.

5. Drag and drop a While activity below the CreateTask activity.

6. Drag and drop an OnTaskChanged activity in the While activity.

7. Drag and drop a CompleteTask activity below the While activity. The workflow design view should now look like Figure 4-22.

You will notice that each activity has a red exclamation mark in its right corner, which means that the configuration of that activity is incomplete. These exclamation marks indicate that workflow configuration is not complete yet, and the workflow is not ready for use.

To finish off the workflow configuration, we start with the OnWorkflowActivated activity. Right-click OnWorkflowActivated and select Generate Handlers to create an event handler for the Invoked event. We are going to use this event to set up initial variable values. Figure 4-23 shows the Properties task pane of the OnWorkflowActivated activity.

Correlation tokens allow you to identify workflows and workflow tasks in a unique way and map them to the WF host executing the workflows. The workflow engine distills the correlation token from an incoming request to determine which workflow instance the request is meant for and then delivers the request to that instance.

The next thing we are going to do is to set the properties of the other activities one by one. Let us start with the CreateTask activity. After the workflow is started, we want it to create a task for a user; this will take place in the CreateTask activity. The next procedure shows you how to create and bind variables to the properties of the CreateTask activity.

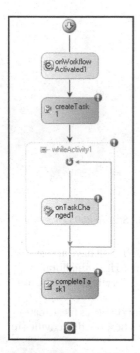

Figure 4-22. *The workflow activities*

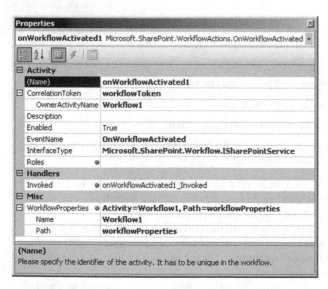

Figure 4-23. *The OnWorkflowActivated activity properties*

1. Right-click the CreateTask activity and select Properties. This opens the Properties task pane.

2. Enter the value **taskToken** for the CorrelationToken property and hit the Enter key.

3. Select the following value for OwnerActivityName: Workflow1. Workflow1 is the name of the workflow class that we are using. By adding the name of the workflow class to the OwnerActivityName property, we will ensure that the lifetime of the workflow is correctly managed.

4. Click the default value of the TaskId property and click the button with the ellipsis. This opens the Bind 'TaskId' to an activity's property dialog box.

5. Select the Bind to a new member tab.

6. Enter the following value in the New member name text box: **taskID**.

7. Select the Create Field radio button and click OK. The taskID variable contains a unique id for the task. The following simple member variable is added automatically to the code:

```
public Guid taskID = default(System.Guid);
```

8. Click the default value of the TaskProperties property and click the button with the ellipsis. This opens the Bind 'TaskProperties' to an activity's property dialog box.

9. Select the Bind to a new member tab.

10. Enter the following value in the New member name text box: **taskProperties**.

11. Select the Create Field radio button and click OK. The taskProperties variable contains information about the task. The following simple member variable is added automatically to the code:

```
public SPWorkflowTaskProperties TaskProperties = ➥
new Microsoft.SharePoint.Workflow.SPWorkflowTaskProperties();
```

The last thing you need to do with the CreateTask activity is create an event that fires when the CreateTask activity executes. You can create this event by right-clicking the CreateTask activity in the design view and selecting Generate Handlers. Figure 4-24 shows the CreateTask activity's Properties task pane.

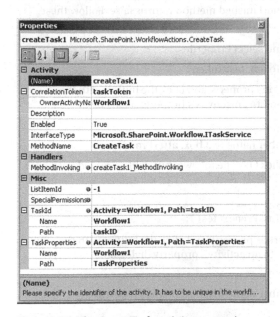

Figure 4-24. *The CreateTask activity properties*

After the workflow is assigned to a user, the workflow engine waits until the user has completed the workflow. The While activity is a loop that contains an OnTaskChanged activity. The responsibility of the While activity is to check whether the task has been changed to complete before moving on to the CompleteTask activity. The OnTaskChanged activity checks whether the task has been changed. Follow these steps to create and bind variables to the properties of the While activity.

1. Right-click the While activity and select Properties. This opens the Properties task pane.

2. Select the following value for the Condition property: **CodeCondition**.

3. Expand the Condition field, and enter the value **notFinished** for the extra field, and press Enter. This creates an event handler where you can check whether the CodeCondition of the While activity is met. Figure 4-25 shows the Properties task pane of the While activity.

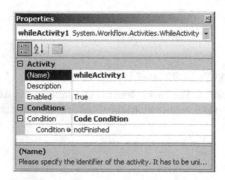

Figure 4-25. *The While activity properties*

The next activity that we will configure is OnTaskChanged. This activity is located within the While activity. That means that the While loop runs and checks the code condition until the condition is met. In this example, that will be until the notFinished method returns false. Follow these steps to set the properties of the OnTaskChanged activity.

1. Right-click the OnTaskChanged activity and select Properties.

2. Select the following value for CorrelationToken: **taskToken**.

3. Click the default value of the AfterProperties property and click the button with the ellipsis. This opens the Bind 'AfterProperties' to an activity's property dialog box.

4. Select the Bind to a new member tab.

5. Enter the following value in the New member name text box: **afterProperties**.

6. Select the Create Field radio button and click OK. The following variable is added automatically to the code:

```
public SPWorkflowTaskProperties afterProperties = ➡
new Microsoft.SharePoint.Workflow.SPWorkflowTaskProperties();
```

7. Click the default value of the BeforeProperties property and click the button with the ellipsis. This opens the Bind 'BeforeProperties' to an activity's property dialog box.

8. Select the Bind to a new member tab.

9. Enter the following value in the New member name text box: **beforeProperties**.

10. Select the Create Field radio button and click OK. The following variable is added automatically to the code:

```
public SPWorkflowTaskProperties beforeProperties = ➡
new Microsoft.SharePoint.Workflow.SPWorkflowTaskProperties();
```

Note You can use the Create Field or Create Property radio buttons. The functionality provided by both controls is comparable. Seen from an object-oriented programming perspective, it is often preferable to create a property that provides better encapsulation.

11. Click the default value of the TaskId property and click the button with the ellipsis. This opens the Bind 'TaskId' to an activity's property dialog box.

12. Select the Bind to an existing member tab.

13. Select taskID and click OK.

14. Right-click the OnTaskChanged activity in the design view and select Generate Handlers to create an event handler for the Invoked event.

Figure 4-26 shows the Properties task pane of the OnTaskChanged activity.

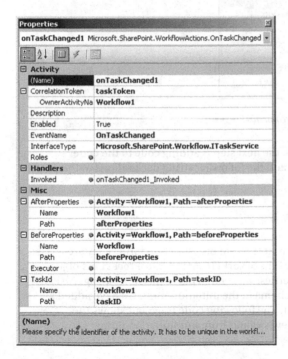

Figure 4-26. *The OnTaskChanged activity properties*

The last activity that needs to be configured is CompleteTask. The CompleteTask activity lets you initiate further steps in the process or take actions in other systems. The following procedure shows you which properties of the CompleteTask activity must be set.

1. Right-click the CompleteTask activity and select Properties.

2. Select the following value for the CorrelationToken: taskToken.

3. Click the default value of the TaskId property and click the button with the ellipsis. This opens the Bind 'TaskId' to an activity's property dialog box.

4. Select the Bind to an existing member tab.

5. Select taskID and click OK. Figure 4-27 shows the Properties task pane for the CompleteTask activity.

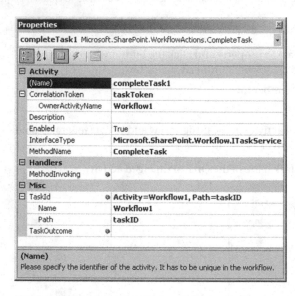

Figure 4-27. *The CompleteTask activity properties*

After adding and configuring the activities, the next step is adding code to the code view of the workflow1.cs class. We are going to add the following string declarations to the workflow1.cs class:

```
private String assignee = default(String);
private String instructions = default(String);
private String comments = default(String);
```

We will retrieve the values of these three variables from our initiation form. They are passed to the workflow as an XML string represented by the SPWorkflowActivationProperties object's InitiationData property. To access these properties, we need to parse this XML string. We can do this by using the generated class from the schema of the initiation form. We have added a class called InitForm.cs to our workflow project. The following code fragment shows the WorkflowActivated1_Invoked method that retrieves values from our initiation form:

```
private void onWorkflowActivated1_Invoked(object sender, ExternalDataEventArgs e)
{
  workflowId = workflowProperties.WorkflowId;

  XmlSerializer serializer = new XmlSerializer(typeof(InitForm));
  XmlTextReader reader = new XmlTextReader(
    new System.IO.StringReader(workflowProperties.InitiationData));
  InitForm initform = (InitForm)serializer.Deserialize(reader);

  assignee = initform.assignee;
  instructions = initform.instructions;
  comments = initform.comments;
}
```

The createTask1_MethodInvoking() method runs whenever a new task is created. We will add a unique task id (called taskID) to the task along with some other properties such as Title, Description, comments, and instructions. The Comments and instructions are custom properties that are passed to the workflow as key-value pairs via the SPWorkflowTaskProperties object's ExtendedProperties property. The createTask1_MethodInvoking() method looks like this:

```
private void createTask1_MethodInvoking(object sender, EventArgs e)
{
  taskID = Guid.NewGuid();
  TaskProperties.Title = "MOSS Workflow Task";
  TaskProperties.AssignedTo = assignee;
  TaskProperties.Description = instructions;
  TaskProperties.ExtendedProperties["comments"] = comments;
  TaskProperties.ExtendedProperties["instructions"] = instructions;
}
```

The last thing we have to do is to make sure is that the While loop stops when the task is completed. Therefore, we add a private boolean variable called IsFinished to the code.

```
private bool isFinished;
```

In the CodeCondition property of the While loop, we have specified that the notFinished() method is called. One of the arguments of the notFinished() method is ConditionalEventArgs. ConditionalEventArgs has a property called Result. If the Result property is set to false, the While loop ends. If the Result property is set to true, the While loop continues. Once the task has been finished, the isFinished variable contains the value true. The notFinished() method looks like this:

```
private void notFinished(object sender, ConditionalEventArgs e)
{
  e.Result = !isFinished;
}
```

The last bit of coding we have to do is set the isFinished variable to true when the isFinished value of the afterProperties.ExtendedProperties object is true. The onTaskChanged1_Invoked() method looks like this:

```
private void onTaskChanged1_Invoked(object sender, ExternalDataEventArgs e)
{
  isFinished = bool.Parse(afterProperties.ExtendedProperties["isFinished"]. ➥
  ToString());
}
```

Listing 4-2 shows the complete code for the workflow1.cs class.

Listing 4-2. *Complete Code for the workflow1.cs Class*

```
using System;
using System.ComponentModel;
using System.ComponentModel.Design;
using System.Collections;
using System.Drawing;
using System.Workflow.ComponentModel.Compiler;
using System.Workflow.ComponentModel.Serialization;
using System.Workflow.ComponentModel;
using System.Workflow.ComponentModel.Design;
using System.Workflow.Runtime;
using System.Workflow.Activities;
using System.Workflow.Activities.Rules;
using System.Xml.Serialization;
using System.Xml;
using Microsoft.SharePoint;
using Microsoft.SharePoint.Workflow;
using Microsoft.SharePoint.WorkflowActions;
using Microsoft.Office.Workflow.Utility;

namespace MOSSWorkflow
{
  public sealed partial class Workflow1 : SharePointSequentialWorkflowActivity
  {
    public Workflow1()
    {
      InitializeComponent();
    }

    public Guid workflowId = default(System.Guid);
    public Microsoft.SharePoint.Workflow.SPWorkflowActivationProperties ➡
    workflowProperties = ➡
    new Microsoft.SharePoint.Workflow.SPWorkflowActivationProperties();
    public SPWorkflowTaskProperties afterProperties = ➡
    new Microsoft.SharePoint.Workflow.SPWorkflowTaskProperties();
    public SPWorkflowTaskProperties beforeProperties = ➡
    new Microsoft.SharePoint.Workflow.SPWorkflowTaskProperties();

    private String assignee = default(String);
    private String instructions = default(String);
    private String comments = default(String);

    private void onWorkflowActivated1_Invoked(object sender, ExternalDataEventArgs e)
    {
      workflowId = workflowProperties.WorkflowId;
      XmlSerializer serializer = new XmlSerializer(typeof(InitForm));
      XmlTextReader reader = new XmlTextReader(new ➡
      System.IO.StringReader(workflowProperties.InitiationData));
      InitForm initform = (InitForm)serializer.Deserialize(reader);
      assignee = initform.assignee;
      instructions = initform.instructions;
      comments = initform.comments;
    }
```

```
public Guid taskID = default(System.Guid);
public SPWorkflowTaskProperties TaskProperties = ➥
new Microsoft.SharePoint.Workflow.SPWorkflowTaskProperties();

private void onTaskChanged1_Invoked(object sender, ExternalDataEventArgs e)
{
  isFinished = bool.Parse(afterProperties.ExtendedProperties["isFinished"]. ➥
  ToString());
}

private bool isFinished;
private void notFinished(object sender, ConditionalEventArgs e)
{
  e.Result = !isFinished;
}

private void createTask1_MethodInvoking(object sender, EventArgs e)
{
  taskID = Guid.NewGuid();
  TaskProperties.Title = "MOSS Workflow Task";
  TaskProperties.AssignedTo = assignee;
  TaskProperties.Description = instructions;
  TaskProperties.ExtendedProperties["comments"] = comments;
  TaskProperties.ExtendedProperties["instructions"] = instructions;
  }
 }
}
```

■**Tip** If you want more information about building workflows for SharePoint environments, you should check out the book *Workflow in the 2007 Microsoft Office System* by David Mann (Apress, 2007).

Deploying a Workflow

In this section, we will discuss the process of deploying your workflow so that it can be used within Microsoft Office SharePoint Server 2007. A custom workflow can be deployed to SharePoint as a feature. In order to do so, you must create the following files: feature.xml and workflow.xml. However, the first thing you need to do is place the workflow assembly inside the Global Assembly Cache (GAC), which means that the workflow assembly needs to be strong named.

■**Note** Strong naming is discussed in more detail in Chapter 1.

We are going to deploy the example workflow we made in the earlier section "Creating a Workflow." Follow these steps to sign your assembly:

1. Right-click the MOSSWorkflow project and select Properties.

2. Select the Signing tab and check the Sign the assembly check box.

3. Select <New> from the Choose a strong name key file drop-down list. This opens the Create Strong Name Key dialog box.

4. Specify a name in the Key file name text box and uncheck the Protect my key file with a password check box.

5. Click OK.

6. Rebuild the workflow project.

To install the assembly in the Global Assembly Cache, you can use the gacutil tool. This tool allows you to view and manipulate the contents of the GAC. The following command installs an assembly in the Global Assembly Cache.

```
gacutil /i [assembly.dll]
```

■**Tip** You can find more information about the gacutil tool at the following URL: `http://msdn.microsoft.com/library/default.asp?url=/library/en-us/cptools/html/cpgrfGlobalAssemblyCacheUtilityGacutilexe.asp`. Alternatively, you can install an assembly in the GAC by dragging and dropping it to the [drive letter] :\Windows\Assembly folder.

Creating a feature.xml File

In the next step, you have to create a feature definition file called feature.xml. This file contains all the information necessary to deploy the workflow. Follow this procedure to create a feature definition file.

1. Open the Feature.xml file in Visual Studio 2005.

2. Right-click in the Feature.xml file and select Insert Snippet ➤ SharePoint Server Workflow ➤ Feature.xml Code.

■**Note** If the code snippets are not loaded in Visual Studio 2005, you can add them yourself. Go to Tools ➤ Code Snippets Manager. Select XML in The Language drop-down list. Click Add, browse to [drive letter]:\\Program Files\ Microsoft Visual Studio 8\Xml\1033\Snippets\SharePoint Server Workflow, and click Open. Click OK. Now you will have the SharePoint Server Workflow snippet available in Visual Studio 2005.

The Id attribute of the `<Feature>` element contains a global unique identifier (GUID). You have to create your own guid. You can do this by using the guidgen.exe tool (which should be available after installing Visual Studio 2005 and C++), or you can create one yourself by calling the Guid.NewGuid() method in a C# application and copying the string result to the feature file. The Scope attribute contains the scope of the workflow assembly; in this example the scope is set to Site, which refers to a site collection–level scope. The other scopes that are available are Farm, WebApplication, and Web (which refers to a site level scope). The `<ElementManifest>` element specifies the relative path to the workflow definition file. Each workflow feature must have a workflow definition file. Listing 4-3 shows what the feature.xml file will look like.

Listing 4-3. *Content of the feature.xml File*

```
<Feature  Id="C3287B4A-2688-4cc6-C34F-92EF5B787BCE"
  Title="MOSSWorkflow"
  Description="Description of the workflow"
  Version="12.0.0.0"
  Scope="Site"
  ReceiverAssembly="Microsoft.Office.Workflow.Feature, Version=12.0.0.0, ➥
  Culture=neutral, PublicKeyToken=71e9bce111e9429c"
  ReceiverClass="Microsoft.Office.Workflow.Feature.WorkflowFeatureReceiver"
  xmlns="http://schemas.microsoft.com/sharepoint/">
  <ElementManifests>
    <ElementManifest Location="workflow.xml" />
  </ElementManifests>
  <Properties>
    <Property Key="GloballyAvailable" Value="true" />
    <Property Key="RegisterForms" Value="*.xsn" />
  </Properties>
</Feature>
```

Creating a workflow.xml File

The workflow definition file workflow.xml contains information that SharePoint requires to instantiate and run the workflow. Follow these steps to create a workflow definition file.

1. Open the Workflow.xml file in Visual Studio 2005.

2. Right-click in the Workflow.xml file and select Insert Snippet ➤ SharePoint Server Workflow ➤ Workflow.xml Code.

The Name attribute of the <Workflow> element contains the name of the workflow. The Id attribute must be a different guid than the one specified in the feature.xml file. The PublicKeyToken attribute contains the public key token of the workflow assembly. The <TaskListContentTypeId> element specifies the content type id of the content type assigned to the workflow task list (this is optional).

■**Note** By default, the content type of the workflow task is the Task base content type. The content type id of the Task base content type is 0x0108.

The <StatusPageUrl> element contains the URL of a custom workflow status page. If this URL is not specified, Microsoft Office SharePoint Server 2007 uses the default status page that is located at _layouts/WrkStat.aspx.

The <Instantiation_FormURN> and <Association_FormURN> elements contain the ids of the initiation form. You can get the id of the initiation form by opening the form in InfoPath in design mode. Select File ➤ Properties and copy the value from the ID text box. The <Task0_FormURN> element contains the id of the task edit form. Listing 4-4 shows what the workflow.xml file will look like.

Listing 4-4. *Content of the workflow.xml File*

```
<Elements xmlns="http://schemas.microsoft.com/sharepoint/">
  <Workflow
    Name="MOSSWorkflow"
    Description="Description of the workflow"
    Id="D250636F-0A26-4019-8425-A5232D592C10"
    CodeBesideClass="MOSSWorkflow.Workflow1"
    CodeBesideAssembly="MOSSWorkflow, Version=1.0.0.0, ➥
    Culture=neutral, PublicKeyToken=bebe1ea49fdec076"
    TaskListContentTypeId="0x01080100C9C9515DE4E24001905074F980F93160"
    AssociationUrl="_layouts/CstWrkflIP.aspx"
    InstantiationUrl="_layouts/IniWrkflIP.aspx"
    ModificationUrl="_layouts/ModWrkflIP.aspx"
    StatusUrl="_layouts/WrkStat.aspx">
    <Categories/>
    <MetaData>
      <Association_FormURN>
        urn:schemas-microsoft-com:office:infopath:InitiationForm: ➥
        -myXSD-2007-05-25T12-13-02
      </Association_FormURN>
      <Instantiation_FormURN>
        urn:schemas-microsoft-com:office:infopath:InitiationForm: ➥
        -myXSD-2007-05-25T12-13-02
      </Instantiation_FormURN>
      <Task0_FormURN>
        urn:schemas-microsoft-com:office:infopath:EditTaskForm: ➥
        -myXSD-2007-05-25T17-06-24
      </Task0_FormURN>
    </MetaData>
  </Workflow>
</Elements>
```

Deploying the Workflow

After creating these two XML files, you have to create a directory in the following location:
[drive letter]:\Program Files\Common Files\Microsoft Shared\web server extensions\12\
TEMPLATE\FEATURES. Specify a unique and recognizable name for this directory. Copy the
feature.xml and workflow.xml files and the InfoPath forms in this directory.

The last thing to do to deploy your workflow is install and activate the workflow via the Share-
Point Administrators tool stsadmin.exe. The stsadmin tool can be found in the following location:
[drive letter]:\Program Files\Common Files\Microsoft Shared\web server extensions\12\BIN\.
The following command will install the workflow.

```
STSADM.EXE -o installfeature -name MOSSWorkflow –force
```

To activate the workflow feature use the following command:

```
STSADM.EXE -o activatefeature -filename MOSSWorkflow\feature.xml -url ➥
http://myserver
```

Note If this does not work, open a command prompt, type **iisreset**, and try again.

Via SharePoint Central Administration, you can check whether the InfoPath forms are correctly uploaded. Open SharePoint Central Administration ➤ Application Management ➤ Manage form templates. In the Manage Form Template page, you will find the two InfoPath forms with Status set to Ready and WorkflowEnabled set to Yes, as shown in Figure 4-28.

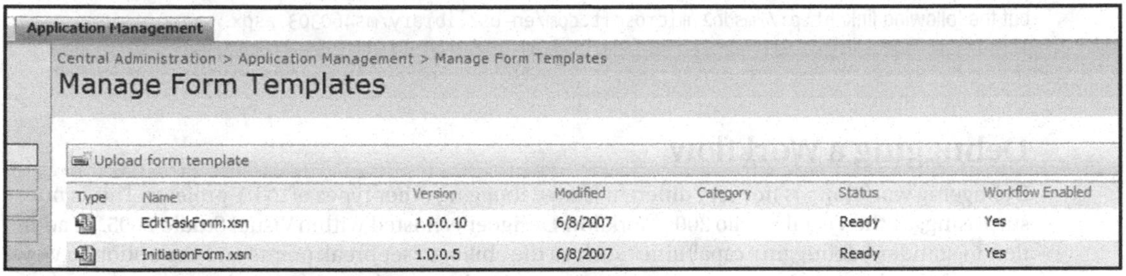

Figure 4-28. *InfoPath forms with WorkflowEnabled set to Yes*

At this point, you are ready to use the workflow in the SharePoint site. For instance, you can link the workflow to a document library, which is shown in Figure 4-29.

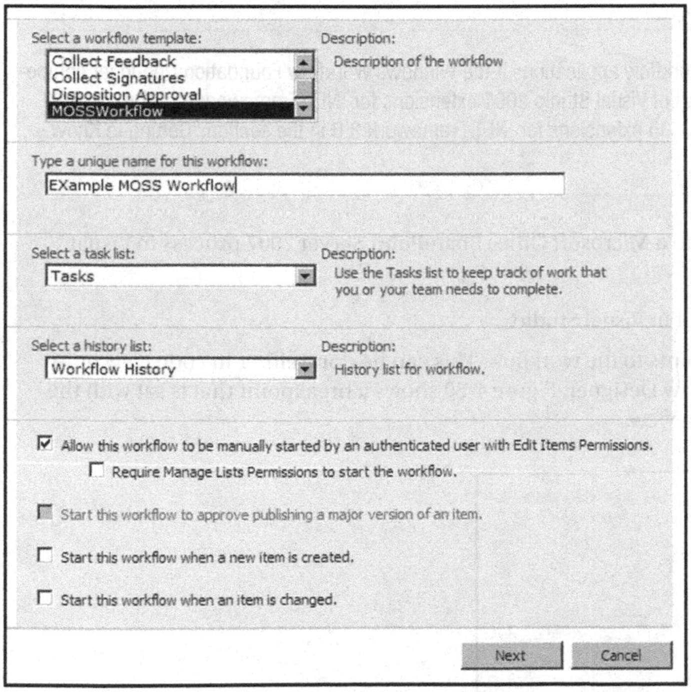

Figure 4-29. *Adding a custom workflow to a document library in SharePoint*

Note If you build the workflow solution in release mode in Visual Studio 2005 Designer, the postbuildactions.bat batch file creates and deploys a .wsp solution file that can be used for deployment on a production server. The manifest.xml and wsp_structure.ddf files are filled with the following information from the workflow project: the feature directory name, the name of the feature.xml file, the name of the workflow.xml file, and the name and relative path of the compiled workflow assembly. For more information about the deployment of a .wsp solution file, check out the following link: http://msdn2.microsoft.com/en-us/library/ms460303.aspx.

Debugging a Workflow

Debugging workflows is not very different from debugging other types of .NET projects. This is not surprising, as the Visual Studio 2005 Workflow Designer is hosted within Visual Studio 2005. In addition to standard debugging capabilities such as the ability to set break points and the option to view call stack windows, it also supports a range of visual indicators that provide information about the debugging process. It is possible to step in, step out, and step over steps in a workflow.

Two types of debugging are not supported in Visual Studio 2005 Workflow Designer:

- Just-in-time debugging of run-time exceptions in the hosting process
- Just-in-time debugging by selecting a process in the Task Manager

Note It is only possible to debug workflow applications if the Windows Workflow Foundation Debugger component is installed. This component is part of Visual Studio 2005 extensions for .NET Framework 3.0. You can find more information about Visual Studio 2005 extensions for .NET Framework 3.0 in the section "Getting to Know Visual Studio 2005 Designer."

Follow these steps to attach to a Microsoft Office SharePoint Server 2007 process in Visual Studio 2005 Designer.

1. Open the workflow project in Visual Studio.

2. Add one or more breakpoints to the workflow. This can be done either in code view or in design view in the Workflow Designer. Figure 4-30 shows a breakpoint that is set with the Workflow Designer design view.

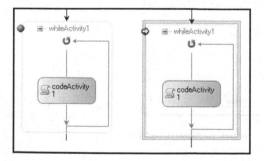

Figure 4-30. *Setting and hitting a breakpoint in the design view of the Workflow Designer*

3. Right-click the project and select Properties.

4. Select the Debug tab.

5. In the Start Action section, enter the SharePoint site URL in the Start browser with URL text box.

6. Hit F5.

7. Start your workflow in Microsoft Office SharePoint Server 2007 by selecting the action menu of an item that is stored in the Shared Documents document library. Then, choose the Workflows option and click Example Microsoft Office SharePoint Server 2007 Workflow.

Using Forms to Capture and Automate Your Processes

It is possible to make a workflow more dynamic and flexible by adding forms to it. This way, you can gather information from users at specific points in the workflow process. One important thing to know about Windows SharePoint Services workflows is that they are form-agnostic. This means that you can create forms with any technology you want as long as the forms are capable of doing the following:

- Invoking the Windows SharePoint Services 3.0 object model

- Generating the data necessary to send to the Windows SharePoint Services object model

- Receiving and parsing the required data from the Windows SharePoint Services object model

Information passed to the form is formatted as a string; this is also true for data that the form must pass back to the Windows SharePoint Services object model when the user submits the form. This string characteristically contains XML, although any data format can be used, as long as the data is a string. A common example of a form type used within SharePoint workflows is custom forms created using ASPX that use XML as the data format of choice.

There are three types of forms available in a workflow:

- Association and initiation forms

- Modification forms

- Custom task forms

Association and initiation forms are forms that are displayed before the workflow starts. This way the user can set parameters and other information for the workflow in advance.

Association forms are used to take care of how the workflow applies to a specific list, library, or content type. These forms are displayed to the person who decides to associate a workflow to a list, library, or content type. When a workflow is associated with a document library, the Add new workflow page will be displayed first. On the Add new workflow page, you can set specific settings that are common to every workflow, such as the type of workflow and which Tasks list you want to use. The next page is the association page. This page is specifically designed for this specific workflow. It will collect customized association information to create the association with the list, library, or content type.

Initiation forms are optional forms that deal with a workflow as it is associated with a specific SharePoint item. The initiation form uses the data from the association form to prepopulate initial values. Sometimes the association and initiation forms are the same form. This way you can enable users to overwrite the initial values set by the administrator.

Modification forms enable the user to make modifications while the workflow is running. With a modification form, a user can make modifications at any moment, for example, to assign a task to another user.

Custom task forms are custom forms that are specified for the tasks in a workflow. A custom task form is based on the workflow task type. Each workflow task type in SharePoint has a content type assigned with it. This content type determines whether the custom task form is specified for a certain workflow task type.

Creating and Using a Custom Activity

To get familiar with every aspect of Windows Workflow Foundation, we are also going to create a simple custom activity. We will create an activity that shows a string in a message box. Follow these steps to create a custom activity:

1. Click File ➤ New ➤ Project. The New Project dialog window will open.

2. Choose to create a Workflow Activity Library and give it the following name: **TestActivity**. Click OK.

An activity is a class that ultimately inherits from the System.Workflow.ComponentModel. Activity base class. You can create an activity based on other existing activities by inheriting from a built-in activity, a custom activity, or an activity created by a third-party vendor. If you want to build an activity that is completely new, you need to inherit from the Activity base class directly.

In this section, we are going to create a new activity that is a direct child of the base Activity class. By default, the activity class that is created when you create a Workflow Activity Library project inherits from the SequenceActivity class. To change this, go to the code view of Activity1.cs and change the base class of Activity1 to Activity.

After the Workflow Activity Library project is compiled, the new activity becomes available automatically on the toolbox, so users can drag and drop your activity onto the design view of a workflow. It is useful for an activity to have *dependency properties*, which bind their values to relevant data, including other properties in other activities that use this custom activity. Follow these steps to insert a dependency property.

1. Go to the code view of the Activity1.cs class.

2. Right-click in the class and choose Insert Snippet.

3. Choose Workflow and press Tab.

4. Choose DependencyProperty – Property and press Tab (see Figure 4-31).

Figure 4-31. *Inserting the DependencyProperty – Property code snippet*

The following code fragment shows the result of inserting this code snippet:

```
public static DependencyProperty MyPropertyProperty = ➥
    System.Workflow.ComponentModel.DependencyProperty.Register("MyProperty", ➥
    typeof(string), typeof(Activity1));

[Description("This is the description which appears in the Property Browser")]
[Category("This is the category which will be displayed in the Property Browser")]
[Browsable(true)]
[DesignerSerializationVisibility(DesignerSerializationVisibility.Visible)]
public string MyProperty
{
  get
  {
    return ((string)(base.GetValue(Activity1.MyPropertyProperty)));
  }
  set
  {
    base.SetValue(Activity1.MyPropertyProperty, value);
  }
}
```

This code creates a static instance of the DependencyProperty type and defines a property (this time a member type, not a static type) that uses the DependencyProperty static instance as a key for retrieving the run-time value of the MyProperty property.

You need to give the static member the following name: MessageProperty. The name of the actual property (the member type) will be Message. You also need to change the [Description] and [Category] attributes of the property. The values of these attributes are displayed in the Property Browser. Use the Tab key to tab through the code snippet and customize the code so it looks like the following:

```
public static DependencyProperty MessageProperty = ➥
    System.Workflow.ComponentModel.DependencyProperty.Register("Message", ➥
    typeof(string), typeof(MyTestActivity));

[Description("This is the description which appears in the Property Browser")]
[Category("This is the category which will be displayed in the Property Browser")]
[Browsable(true)]
[DesignerSerializationVisibility(DesignerSerializationVisibility.Visible)]
public string Message
{
  get
  {
    return ((string)(base.GetValue(MyTestActivity.MessageProperty)));
  }
  set
  {
    base.SetValue(MyTestActivity.MessageProperty, value);
  }
}
```

Finally, you need to add an Execute() method. This method is a mediator that manages the core tasks of the workflow. The code in this method makes use of the System.Windows.Forms namespace.

```
protected override ActivityExecutionStatus Execute ➥
    (ActivityExecutionContext executionContext)
{
  MessageBox.Show(Message);
  return ActivityExecutionStatus.Closed;
}
```

You can find the new custom activity on the Toolbox of the workflow solution used to develop the new activity (see Figure 4-32).

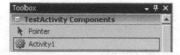

Figure 4-32. *Custom Activity1 in Toolbox*

If you want to reuse this activity in another workflow project in Visual Studio 2005 Designer, follow these steps:

1. Right-click in the Toolbox area and choose Choose Items.

2. In the Choose Toolbox Items dialog window, click the Activities tab and click Browse.

3. Browse to your activity assembly and click Open.

4. Your activity is mentioned in the list of activities and you can add a check to its check box to include it on the Toolbox (see Figure 4-33).

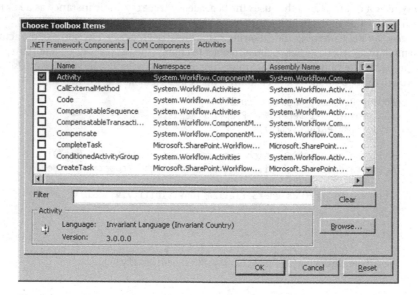

Figure 4-33. *Choose Toolbox Items dialog window*

It is not possible to create custom activities with SharePoint Designer. However, you can use custom activities created using Visual Studio 2005 in SharePoint Designer. To use a custom activity, you must make sure that the activity is added to the safe controls list in Microsoft Office SharePoint Server 2007. This way, all activities must be preapproved by a server administrator before using them. It is not possible to deploy a custom activity without the approval of a server administrator.

If you want to use a custom activity assembly in SharePoint Designer, you have to place the assembly inside the GAC, which means that the workflow assembly must be strong named. Follow the next procedure to sign your assembly:

1. Right-click the activity project in the Solution Explorer and select Properties.

2. Select the Signing tab on the left.

3. Check the Sign the assembly check box.

4. Select <New> from the Choose a strong name key file drop-down list. This opens the Create Strong Name Key dialog box.

5. Specify a name in the Key file name text box and uncheck the Protect my key file with a password check box.

6. Click OK.

7. Rebuild the activity project.

The next step is to add the activity to the action safe list in the SharePoint web application's web.config file. The web.config of file can be found via the following procedure:

1. Open Internet Information Services (IIS) Manager.

2. Expand the [server name] (local computer) node.

3. Expand the Web Sites node.

4. Right-click the SharePoint web application and choose Properties. This opens the [web application] Properties window.

5. Click the Home Directory tab and copy the value of the Local path text field.

6. Open an instance of Windows Explorer and navigate to the path found in the previous step.

7. Open the web.config file in any text editor.

Locate the `<SafeControls>` section and add a `<SafeControl>` element. This element should look like this:

```
<SafeControl Assembly="[assembly name],
  Version=1.0.0.0, Culture=neutral,
  PublicKeyToken=[public key token]"
  Namespace="[namespace name]" TypeName="*" Safe="True" />
```

The last thing to do is add an `<Action>` element, rules, and parameters to the WSS.actions file. You can find the WSS.actions file in the following location: [drive letter]:\Program Files\Common Files\Microsoft Shared\web server extensions\12\TEMPLATE\1033\Workflow. The Action element gives SharePoint Designer all the information it needs to let the action appear and function correctly. The following code fragment shows the `<Action>` element that must be added to the WSS.actions file:

```
<Action Name="TestActivity"
  ClassName="[class name]"
  Assembly="[assembly name], Version=1.0.0.0, Culture=neutral,
    PublicKeyToken=[public key token]"
  Category="Core Actions"
  AppliesTo="all">
</Action>
```

After adding a `<SafeControl>` element to the SharePoint web application's web.config file and an `<Action>` element to the WSS.actions file, the custom activity is added to the Actions list in the Workflow Designer. Figure 4-34 shows that we've added the custom activity TestActivity to the Workflow Designer in SharePoint Designer.

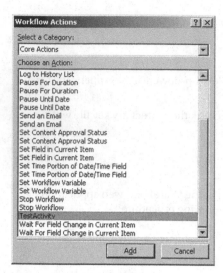

Figure 4-34. *The custom activity TestActivity in the Workflow Actions dialog window*

Summary

In this chapter, we discussed Windows Workflow Foundation. We have taken a look at the basics of Windows Workflow Foundation. Next, we discussed the two development tools available to create workflows: SharePoint Designer and Visual Studio 2005 Designer. We showed you how to create a workflow with SharePoint Designer and how to create, deploy, and debug a workflow with Visual Studio 2005 Designer. Finally, we discussed the different forms that you can use to capture and automate the workflow process.

CHAPTER 5

■ ■ ■

Building a Domain-Specific Language for Connectable Web Parts

The notion of software factories is one of the most important contemporary trends in software architecture. The main promise of software factories is the industrialization of software development, thus increasing productivity and decreasing development costs dramatically.

The ultimate goal of this chapter is to show you how to develop a part of a software factory; we will show you how to develop a domain-specific language (DSL) for creating connectable web parts. If you want to succeed in developing such a language, it is essential that you have a solid understanding of the web part connection framework. If you do not possess this knowledge already, this chapter will help you to acquire it.

Introducing Software Factories

A *software factory* is a software product line that automates parts of software development. Most discussions about software factories will probably start with a reference to the book *Software Factories: Assembling Applications with Patterns, Models, Frameworks, and Tools*, published by Wiley in 2004 (see the bibliography for more details). This book is rapidly becoming a classic, and if you want to delve deeply into the theory behind software factories, we definitely recommend it. We also advise you to take a look at the web site http://www.softwarefactories.com, which contains general information about software factories.

"Software development is an art." This is a phrase you've probably heard before. It is true: even nowadays, software development is based on the individual skills of software developers. This is sometimes referred to as *heroism*, the developers being the heroes. Developers engage in manual, labor-intensive tasks, just like other craftsmen do. Such a development style is slow and allows much room for mistakes, and the quality of software is very dependent on the skills of the individual software developers. As the art of software development matures, it must transcend to another level. We have to move toward software industrialization, which is all about assembling software products from components, automating tasks, forming product lines (the steps required to create software) and supply chains (that deliver standard components), and standardizing processes and architectures. The belief that industrialization can be accomplished for the world of software development is based on the premise that software is fundamentally like every other industry.

Although software factories help industrialize the work of software developers, we do not think this will make being a software developer boring. Software factories help automate boring tasks, thus giving developers the opportunity to spend a higher percentage of their time on the interesting bits of creating software.

A related trend is that programming languages tend to become more abstract over time. Nowadays, you can still create programs by typing code, although more and more you will have the opportunity to program by creating visual models graphically. Creating BizTalk orchestrations (Chapter 8 covers BizTalk orchestrations) and workflows created using Windows Workflow Foundation (Chapter 4 covers Windows Workflow Foundation) are excellent examples of this. This is also known as *model-driven development*, a development approach where visual modeling is used to create models to capture information in forms that can be processed easily. The goal of model-driven development does not lie in creating design documentation, but in creating models that are used to fully or partially automate its implementation. You can think of model-driven development as programming with models.

FLAWS IN UML?

The Unified Modeling Language (UML) has been successful as a language that allows developers, analysts, and architects to create models that are used for design and documentation purposes. However, UML has not been successful as a language that is used widely and effectively in creating models for model-driven development. Or to put it another way, UML has not been successful as a language to help automate software development. This is primarily caused by one of the great strengths of the language: its generality. As it turns out, automation of development requires precise languages, and UML has failed as a language that can be mapped precisely to programming languages such as C#.

Background on Domain-Specific Languages

If you are going to adopt a model-driven development approach and want to create a model that is suitable for use in a model-driven development environment, you need it to be precise and unambiguous. Because of this, a modeling language needs to be closely tied to the problem domain itself (something that does not hold true for UML). Such modeling languages are called *DSLs* or *domain-specific languages*. DSLs can be textual or graphical, although this chapter only discusses the creation of a graphical DSL. The opposite of a DSL is a *general-purpose* language. General-purpose languages are generic and can be applied to any kind of problem domain, whereas DSLs are intended to be used in a very specific problem domain.

Models created in some kind of high-level DSL need to be transformed to some other form before they are really useful. Most often, models will be transformed to either code (that can be compiled into executables) or directly into executables, but it is also possible to use a model and transform it in another lower-level DSL. Different types of model transformation exist:

- *Vertical*: Vertical transformations take some kind of higher-level model and map this model to another lower-level model. For instance, if you compile a piece of C# code into Intermediate Language (IL), a vertical transformation takes place.

- *Horizontal refactoring*: Horizontal refactoring transformations reorganize a model to improve its design but not its meaning. For instance, if you take a piece of C# code, you can use the refactoring menu items listed in the Refactor menu to improve the design, but not the meaning of code. Using these techniques is an example of horizontal refactoring.

- *Horizontal delocalizing*: Horizontal delocalizing transformations optimize a model. A typical example of this type of refactoring is the generation of binary code that is optimized to improve performance. Horizontal delocalizing transformations can also be used to specify a part or aspect of software. This is an essential part of aspect-oriented programming (AOP). For example, AOP allows you to address a part of software (let's say, security concerns), and apply this part to one or more separate software programs.

- *Oblique*: Oblique transformations combine horizontal and vertical transformations.

Typically, modeling languages are declarative, not imperative. Imperative languages focus on the *how* of software execution. Such languages describe which instructions need to be executed and do not bother to describe the desired results. Declarative languages focus on the *what* of software execution. Declarative languages describe the desired results of the execution of the software program, but do not bother to describe how these results are obtained. DSLs are used to express developer intent and are thus an example of declarative languages.

DSLs are used in model-driven development approaches, where metadata is captured in models to automate software development tasks. Model-driven development has the following features:

- Model-driven development uses DSLs that capture developer intent.
- Model-driven development allows you to create and adapt software via configuration, not coding.
- Tools that support model-driven development make it easy to generate software based on models.
- Tools that support model-driven development make it easy to create and debug models.

Components of a Software Factory

A software solution solves a problem or subproblem in a specific domain and reduces the total cost of software creation. In software factory terms, a *solution* is a production asset that makes software creation cheaper every time the solution is reused. Software factories and supply chains are used to create software that is similar and yet distinct, using the same practices, processes, tools, and materials, thus providing another level of reuse.

Software factories contain extensible tools, processes, and content, and use a software factory template based on a schema to automate (parts of) software development. A software factory schema categorizes and summarizes development artifacts that are relevant to a software factory. Examples of such artifacts are configuration files, models, and source code files.

■**Note** A software factory schema does not *contain* development artifacts; it *describes* them.

Software factory schemas also define relationships between the artifacts. Tables are very suitable for representing software factory schemas. If you represent a software factory in a table, every table cell represents a perspective or viewpoint from which you can build a certain aspect of the software. Such tables can be used to create more than one software product. A software factory schema provides a high-level overview of a software product belonging to a certain software product family, and describes the artifacts that must be developed to produce a software product in a fully or partially automated way.

The software factory schema represents the entire software development process for producing software that belongs to a certain family. Software factory schemas contain fixed and variable parts; the fixed parts remain the same for every member of the product family.

To summarize what we have discussed so far, a software factory schema describes the software factory; a software factory template contains the actual assets used to build a software product belonging to a certain software family. DSLs are assets of a software factory template and are used to capture information about some aspect (or viewpoint) of a family of software products. Multiple DSLs are needed to describe a typical business application.

Using DSL Tools

A DSL is a language designed to be useful for a specific task in a fixed problem domain, in contrast to a general-purpose language. DSLs are an important part of software factories, so it is interesting to see what you need to create a DSL. If you want to use DSLs, you will need the following tools:

- Editors for creating and maintaining specifications. For complex languages, graphical editors may be required for editing and validation.

- Language processors for producing implementations from models.

- Debugging tools to debug implementations using the DSL.

- Tools that automate other development tasks using metadata captured by models based on the language, including test generation and execution, instrumentation and measurement, configuration management, and deployment.

The first three tools can be found in the new Microsoft DSL Toolkit product, which enables users to design graphical DSLs that can be tailored to any problem domain and generate code and other artifacts from the languages. The last set of tools belongs to the realm of Visual Studio Team System and will not be discussed in this chapter. The DSL Toolkit consists of the following:

- A project wizard that supports the creation of domain models via a designer and a textual artifact generator. Domain models created with this project wizard can be tested within separate instances of Visual Studio 2005.

- A graphical designer that can be used to define and edit domain models.

- An XML format that is used for describing designer definitions. Designer definitions define the look and feel of a graphical designer hosted in Visual Studio 2005 that is used to create domain models.

- A set of code generators that is able to generate code for a DSL that is defined via a domain model definition and designer definition.

- A framework for defining templates.

Running the project wizard results in the creation of a Visual Studio DSL solution that contains two projects: DomainModel and Designer. The DomainModel project describes the DSL and allows you to visually customize and define this language. The Designer project defines the look and feel of the DSL. After creating a DSL using the DSL Toolkit, you can create a deployment package (.msi file) to distribute your DSL. We will discuss the DSL Toolkit in detail in the section "Creating the Web Part Connection Language," when we discuss the creation of the Web Part Connection Language, a domain-specific language for creating connectable web parts.

■**Note** The DSL Toolkit and the Guidance Automation Toolkit (GAT) both fall under the Software Factories Initiative umbrella at Microsoft. Basically, GAT is an extension to Visual Studio 2005 that creates rich user experiences. If you want more information about GAT, please refer to Chapter 1. Currently, integration between the two tools is limited to the shared use of the T4 templating engine (which is discussed later in this chapter in the section "Text Templates"). There are additional plans to integrate both products. For example, it will be possible to run GAT recipes from commands in a model designer that is created using the DSL Toolkit.

Web Part Connections

Now that you have more background on software factories and DSLs, we will switch to a discussion of web part connections. After that, in the next section, we will discuss how to use a DSL that aids in creating connectable web parts. In the final section of this chapter, you will learn how to create such a DSL.

Connectable web parts are able to share information and communicate with each other using predefined or custom interfaces. Connectable web parts do not have to have intimate knowledge about each other, and are thus loosely bound. This section brings you up to speed on connectable web part technology, so you will be able to follow the discussion of building a graphical DSL for web part connections later.

Microsoft Office SharePoint Server 2007 has support for the SharePoint 2003 web part connection framework as well as the ASP.NET 2.0 web part connection framework. Creating web part connections using the ASP.NET 2.0 web part connection framework is the preferred method. Because of this, it is the only method that will be discussed in detail in this chapter. If you want to learn more about the SharePoint 2003 web part connection framework, please refer to the Windows SharePoint Services 2003 SDK.

■ **Note** There are still some valid reasons for using the SharePoint 2003 web part connection framework. Create SharePoint 2003 connectable web parts if you want to create cross-page connections, connections between web parts that are outside of a web part zone, or client-side connections if you want to communicate with an existing list using the ListViewWebPart.

Background on Web Part Connections

Let's take a step back and look at the history of the connectable web part framework. The Digital Dashboard Services Component (DDSC) can be considered to be the first version of connectable web parts. The DDSC is a client-side component that was first included in SharePoint technology in 2001. It provides a standard infrastructure for services such as the following:

- *Part discovery*: A web part discovers another web part on a web part page (or a *dashboard*, as it was called in 2001).

- *Notification*: The notification system allows web parts to respond to external events that occur at the web part page or web part level.

- *Session state management*: The session state management system allows web parts to interchange information and objects within a browser session.

- *State management*: The state management system allows web part pages and web parts to maintain global state and offered access to a state persistence mechanism.

- *Item retrieval*: This allows web parts to retrieve and maintain the state of items.

Although not used as often, the DDSC is still included in Microsoft Office SharePoint Server 2007. In Microsoft Office SharePoint Server 2007, the DDSC has been renamed Web Part Services Component (WPSC), a component that plays an important role in creating client-side web part connections for web parts using the SharePoint 2003 web part connection framework. An example of such a client-side web part connection is discussed in Chapter 2.

In a nutshell, connectable web parts are web parts that can communicate with other web parts. There are two ways end users can connect web parts to each other: via the browser or using SharePoint Designer 2007. Web part connections are useful in many ways; here is an overview of the most common scenarios:

- *Master/detail*: In this scenario, a master web part provides information that allows a detail web part to show further details. For example, a web part provides an overview of all employees. If you click on the name of one of the employees, employee details are shown in another web part.

- *Parent/child*: In this scenario, a parent web part provides an overview of items of some sort; a child web part shows the children of these items. For example, a web part provides an overview of orders. If you click one of the orders, another web part shows all items belonging to this order.

- *Data entry and filtering*: In this scenario, a web part contains some kind of search or filter form. The data entered in this form is used to filter the data that is shown in another web part.

- *Alternate views*: In this scenario, a web part passes data to another web part that displays this data in some new and interesting way. For example, a web part provides an overview of order items; product A is ordered 10 times, product B 20 times. This data is passed to another web part that uses a pie chart to display this information.

- *Data enhancement*: In this scenario, a web part enhances the data shown in another web part. For example, a web part shows an overview of all employees. If you click the name of one of the employees, another web part shows a picture of this employee.

These scenarios all have in common that web parts share information and are able to communicate with each other. The intent, however, is a little bit different in every scenario.

The SharePoint 2003 Web Part Connection Framework

The SharePoint 2003 web part connection framework provides several interfaces that allow web parts to receive or pass information to other connected web parts on a web part page. The interfaces can be divided in two categories: providers and consumers. Provider web parts are able to publish data to other web parts (consumer web parts) via a web part connection. Consumer web parts are able to digest data coming from other web parts (provider web parts) via a web part connection. Every provider type is paired to a specific consumer type.

■**Note** A provider can be connected to multiple consumers. It is even possible to connect a provider to different types of consumers if an appropriate transformer is available. Transformers are discussed later in this section.

The following list provides an overview of the available interface provider/consumer pairs that are available in the SharePoint 2003 web part connections framework:

- *Cell interface provider/consumer pair*: Cell interfaces are used to pass a single value to another web part. Cell interfaces are very suitable for implementing data enhancement scenarios.

- *Row interface provider/consumer pair*: Row interfaces are used to pass a row of information to a consumer web part. Row interfaces are very suitable for implementing master/detail scenarios.

- *List interface provider/consumer pair.* List interfaces are used to pass an entire list of data (a set of rows) to a consumer web part. List interfaces are very suitable for implementing alternate-view scenarios.

- *Filter interface provider/consumer pair.* Filter interfaces are used to pass filter values to a consumer web part. Filter interfaces are very suitable for implementing data entry and filtering scenarios.

- *ParamsOut interface provider/consumer pair.* ParamsOut interfaces are used to pass a parameter list (or, if you will, a property bag containing various values) to a consumer web part.

- *ParamsIn interface provider/consumer pair.* ParamsIn interfaces are also used to pass parameters to consumer web parts. The reason why one might want to use ParamsIn interfaces lies in the fact that ParamsOut providers and consumers need to have intimate knowledge of each other (they are tightly bound). You can support scenarios to pass parameters to unknown consumers by combining a ParamsOut provider with a ParamsIn consumer. This forces an interface mismatch, which forces the SharePoint user interface to display a transformation window that allows the person connecting the web parts to choose which values need to be connected to each other. This offers more flexibility and loose coupling.

The SharePoint 2003 web part connection framework includes transformers that allow a provider and consumer web part to connect to each other, even though they implement different interfaces. The following transformers are available:

- IRowProvider to ICellConsumer

- IRowProvider to IFilterConsumer

- IRowProvider to IParametersInConsumer

- IParametersOutProvider to IParametersInConsumer

You have the option of choosing between two available clients when it comes to creating web part connections: the browser and SharePoint Designer 2007. If you are connecting web parts implementing interfaces that require the use of a transformer, you cannot always use either client. Table 5-1 shows an overview of the available clients for different transformer scenarios.

Table 5-1. *Available Clients in Different Transformer Scenarios*

Transformation	Clients
IRowProvider to ICellConsumer	Browser and SharePoint Designer 2007
IRowProvider to IFilterConsumer	Browser and SharePoint Designer 2007
IRowProvider to IParametersInConsumer	SharePoint Designer 2007
IParametersOutProvider to IParametersInConsumer	SharePoint Designer 2007

■**Note** There are some other, less-often-used ways to create web part connections. You can also create them programmatically by setting the connection ID, hard-coding the connection in the web part by setting the connection ID in the consuming web part (which is useful in testing scenarios), or by defining a web part connection within a site template.

The ASP.NET 2.0 Web Part Connection Framework

The use of the web part connection framework has been simplified considerably in ASP.NET 2.0. The connection model still consists of a provider/consumer pair. As opposed to the SharePoint 2003 web part connection framework (discussed previously in the section "The SharePoint 2003 Web Part Connection Framework"), the ASP.NET 2.0 web part connection framework makes it easy to use custom interfaces for sharing data.

Note Microsoft recommends that you create ASP.NET 2.0 web parts and connectable web parts. You should not create new web parts using the SharePoint 2003 web part connection framework, unless you are facing one of the scenarios discussed in the section "Web Part Connections."

The ASP.NET 2.0 web part connection framework allows a provider web part to implement a custom interface, and if the consumer web part understands this interface, both web parts will be able to communicate with each other over a web part connection. We will demonstrate this in the first example of this section, in which we will create a provider web part that implments an interface called IMyInterface and a client that is able to communicate with web parts implementing this interface.

Take a look at Listing 5-1, which contains an interface called IMyInterface containing a single method, GetGreeting().

Listing 5-1. *Defining a Connection Interface*

```
using System;
using System.Collections.Generic;
using System.Text;

namespace Connections
{
  public interface IMyInterface
  {
    string GetGreeting();
  }
}
```

The interface IMyInterface will be implemented by a provider web part and finally consumed by a consumer web part. This is discussed in the sections "Creating a Provider Web Part Implementing a Custom Interface" and "Creating a Consumer Web Part Consuming a Custom Interface".

Creating a Provider Web Part Implementing a Custom Interface

If you want to create provider and consumer web parts that communicate via the custom IMyInterface interface, you first need to create a provider web part that implements this interface. We will create such a provider and call it ProviderA, as can be seen in the following code fragment:

```
public class ProviderA : System.Web.UI.WebControls.WebParts.WebPart, ➥
IMyInterface
```

Next, you need to create a method that returns a control that is able to act as the provider in a web part connection. You can define a connection provider by decorating a method with the [ConnectionProvider] attribute and provide a display name for the connection. In this case, this method returns a provider supporting the IMyInterface interface. The web part connection framework will use the connection provider to retrieve an instance of IMyInterface and pass this to a connection consumer point in the consumer web part (this will be discussed later in this chapter). The next code fragment shows the connection provider retrieval method, which returns the current instance of the ProviderA class:

```
[ConnectionProvider("connection provider A")]
public IMyInterface GetProviderA()
{
  return this;
}
```

You will also need to implement the GetGreeting() method, the sole method of the IMyInterface interface. Its implementation is shown in the next code fragment:

```
public string GetGreeting()
{
  return "Hello from provider A";
}
```

After completing these steps, you have completed the essential part of a web part that can function as a connection provider communicating via a custom interface. The complete code listing for this web part is shown in Listing 5-2.

Listing 5-2. *Creating a Connection Provider Using a Custom Interface*

```
using System;
using System.Runtime.InteropServices;
using System.Web.UI;
using System.Web.UI.WebControls.WebParts;
using System.Xml.Serialization;
using Microsoft.SharePoint;
using Microsoft.SharePoint.WebControls;
using Microsoft.SharePoint.WebPartPages;

namespace Connections
{
  [Guid("8da110b0-da38-4278-8ddd-fb6989c53621")]
  public class ProviderA : System.Web.UI.WebControls.WebParts.WebPart, ➥
  IMyInterface
  {
    public ProviderA()
    {
      this.ExportMode = WebPartExportMode.All;
    }

    protected override void Render(HtmlTextWriter writer)
    {
      writer.Write("Provider web part A");
    }

    [ConnectionProvider("connection provider A")]
    public IMyInterface GetProviderA()
    {
      return this;
    }
```

```
  public string GetGreeting()
  {
    return "Hello from provider A";
  }
  }
}
```

At this point, you have successfully created a provider web part that implements a custom interface.

Creating a Consumer Web Part Consuming a Custom Interface

After building a provider that communicates via a custom interface, you will also need to build a consumer that is able to exchange data with the provider. In this example, we are creating a consumer that is called ConsumerA. First, it is convenient to define a member variable that is able to hold an instance of a provider web part. This is shown in the next code fragment:

```
private IMyInterface _objProvider;
public IMyInterface Provider
{
  get { return _objProvider; }
  set { _objProvider = value; }
}
```

Once the member variable is in place, you can define a connection consumer method, a callback point called by the web part connection framework that acts as a consumer in a web part connection. You can define a connection consumer method by decorating a method with the ConnectionConsumer attribute. This is an ideal place for setting the Provider property. The next code fragment shows how to set a reference to a connection provider:

```
[ConnectionConsumer("connection consumer A")]
public void GetProvider(IMyInterface objProvider)
{
  Provider = objProvider;
}
```

You are now ready to use the connection provider by calling its methods. The next code fragment shows an implementation of the web part Render() method that calls the GetGreeting() method of a connection provider implementing the IMyInterface interface:

```
protected override void Render(HtmlTextWriter writer)
{
  if (Provider != null)
  {
    writer.Write(Provider.GetGreeting());
  }
  else
  {
    writer.Write("no connection established");
  }
}
```

The complete code for the consumer web part that is able to communicate with the ProviderA web part created earlier in this section is shown in Listing 5-3.

Listing 5-3. *Creating a Connection Consumer for a Custom Interface*

```
using System;
using System.Runtime.InteropServices;
using System.Web.UI;
using System.Web.UI.WebControls.WebParts;
using System.Xml.Serialization;
using Microsoft.SharePoint;
using Microsoft.SharePoint.WebControls;
using Microsoft.SharePoint.WebPartPages;

namespace Connections
{
  [Guid("33ede5c2-c92a-4a32-87e6-99a14fb6b70c")]
  public class ConsumerA : System.Web.UI.WebControls.WebParts.WebPart
  {
    public ConsumerA()
    {
      this.ExportMode = WebPartExportMode.All;
    }

    protected override void Render(HtmlTextWriter writer)
    {
      if (Provider != null)
      {
        writer.Write(Provider.GetGreeting());
      }
      else
      {
        writer.Write("no connection established");
      }
    }

    [ConnectionConsumer("connection consumer A")]
    public void GetProvider(IMyInterface objProvider)
    {
      Provider = objProvider;
    }

    private IMyInterface _objProvider;
    public IMyInterface Provider
    {
      get { return _objProvider; }
      set { _objProvider = value; }
    }
  }
}
```

If you import those web parts in a SharePoint site, you will get to see a sight similar to Figure 5-1. If you are not sure how to do this, please refer back to Chapter 1. Figure 5-1 shows two provider web parts implementing the IMyInterface interface and two consumer web parts that are able to communicate with these providers. At this moment, the consumer web parts have not yet been connected to a provider.

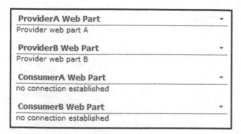

Figure 5-1. *A SharePoint page containing multiple provider and consumer web parts*

Next, you will see how to connect a provider web part to a consumer web part. If you click the drop-down arrow at the right-side of the ProviderA web part, an action menu appears. Choose the option Modify Shared Web Part, as shown in Figure 5-2.

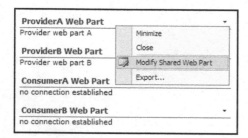

Figure 5-2. *Connecting the ProviderA web part to a consumer web part*

This opens the SharePoint page in Edit Mode. Follow these steps to connect the ProviderA provider web part to the ConsumerA consumer web part:

1. Click the Edit menu of the ProviderA web part. This opens an action menu.

2. Choose Connections ➤ Send connection provider A To ➤ ConsumerA Web Part.

3. Click OK in the ProviderA tool pane.

This connects the ProviderA web part to the ConsumerA web part. Repeat the same steps if you want to break the connection between both web parts.

■**Note** A consumer web part can only be connected to a single provider. A provider can have multiple connections to consumer web parts.

Figure 5-3 shows the user interface provided by Microsoft Office SharePoint Server 2007 when creating a web part connection.

The final figure associated to this example, Figure 5-4, shows a SharePoint page containing two provider web parts connected to two different consumer web parts.

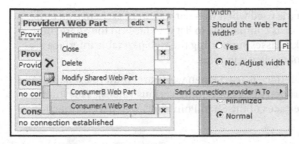

Figure 5-3. *Choosing a consumer web part*

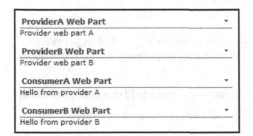

Figure 5-4. *SharePoint page containing connected web parts*

Interfaces and Transformers

As you learned in the section "The SharePoint 2003 Web Part Connection Framework," the SharePoint 2003 web part connection framework contains a set of predefined interfaces and transformers that are able to map certain predefined provider interfaces to other predefined consumer interfaces. Although this model has been simplified in the ASP.NET 2.0 web part connection framework, it still contains a set of predefined interfaces and transformers for these interfaces.

Note You should use one the predefined interfaces if they match the scenario you are trying to implement; this saves you the trouble of creating your own interface. As an added bonus, there is a set of transformers that allow you to exchange data between web parts that would have been incompatible without a transformer. Transformers are discussed later in this section.

The following is an overview of the predefined interfaces that are available in the ASP.NET 2.0 web part connections framework (all interfaces are located in the System.Web.UI.WebControls. WebParts namespace):

- IWebPartField *interface*: This interface is used when web parts want to exchange a single value. This interface is comparable to cell interfaces in the SharePoint 2003 web part connection framework. Classes supporting the web part field interface are very suitable for implementing data enhancement scenarios.

- IWebPartRow *interface*: This interface is used when web parts want to exchange a row of information. This interface is comparable to row interfaces in the SharePoint 2003 web part connection framework. Classes supporting the web part row interface are very suitable for implementing master/detail scenarios.

- IWebPartTable *interface:* This interface is used when web parts want to exchange an entire list of data (a set of rows). This interface is comparable to list interfaces in the SharePoint 2003 web part connection framework. Classes supporting the web part table interface are very suitable for implementing alternate-view scenarios.

- IWebPartParameters *interface:* This interface is used when web parts want to exchange a list of parameters (or, if you will, a property bag containing various values). This interface is comparable to the ParamsOut interfaces of the SharePoint 2003 web part connection framework.

Note We will also refer to the interfaces as the IWebPart* interfaces.

The ASP.NET 2.0 web part connection framework includes transformers that allow provider and consumer web parts to connect to each other, even though they implement different interfaces. The following ASP.NET transformers are available:

- RowToFieldTransformer: Transforms a row provider interface into a field consumer interface.

- RowToParametersTransformer: Transforms a row provider interface into a parameters consumer interface.

Building a Custom Transformer

In the previous section, you learned that the ASP.NET web part connection framework provides two transformers out of the box. In this section, you will learn how to create your own custom transformer. We will create two custom interfaces: a consumer web part that consumes the first interface, and then a provider web part that implements the second interface. We want the provider web part to provide data to the consumer web part. Normally, this fails because both web parts are incompatible. Because of this, we will create a transformer that is able to transform the data provided by the provider web part to something that is intelligible to the consumer web part. Finally, you will see how to register web part transformers in the web.config file of a SharePoint web application.

In the first step, we will create an interface called IMyFirstInterface. Later, we will create a consumer web part called FirstConsumer that is able to consume data from IMyFirstInterface provider web parts. The IMyFirstInterface interface prescribes that every class implementing it should contain a property called Name. This is shown in Listing 5-4.

Listing 5-4. *Creating the First Custom Interface*

```
using System;
using System.Collections.Generic;
using System.Text;

namespace Connections
{
  public interface IMyFirstInterface
  {
    string Name { get; set;}
  }
}
```

Then, we will create an interface called IMySecondInterface. Later, this interface will be implemented in a provider web part called SecondProvider. The IMySecondInterfaces interface prescribes that classes implementing this interface should contain a property called CurrentTitle. This is shown in Listing 5-5.

Listing 5-5. *Creating the Second Custom Interface*

```
using System;
using System.Collections.Generic;
using System.Text;

namespace Connections
{
  public interface IMySecondInterface
  {
    string CurrentTitle { get; set; }
  }
}
```

Next, we will discuss building a transformer class. Every web part connection transformer inherits from the WebPartTransformers class located in the System.Web.UI.WebControls.WebParts namespace. This class provides the basic implementation for all transformer classes that convert data between incompatible interfaces. You need to decorate this class with the [WebPartTransformer] attribute, which defines the types of connection points that the transformer supports. The first argument that needs to be passed to the transformer is the provider type (in our example, we will pass the IMySecondInterface type). Second, you need to pass the consumer type (in our example, we will pass the IMyFirstInterface type).

■**Caution** The code comment for the [WebPartTransformer] attribute states that the first argument of its constructor pertains to the consumer type, the second to the provider type. We believe in reality it is the other way around.

Finally, you will need to override the Transform() method of the WebPartTransformer class. This method is responsible for creating an object that will be used when transforming data. The complete code for the transformer is shown in Listing 5-6.

Listing 5-6. *Creating the Second Custom Interface*

```
using System;
using System.Collections.Generic;
using System.Text;
using Microsoft.SharePoint;
using System.Web.UI.WebControls.WebParts;

namespace Connections
{
  [WebPartTransformer(typeof(IMySecondInterface), typeof(IMyFirstInterface))]
  public class MyInterfaceTransformer : WebPartTransformer, IMyFirstInterface
  {
    IMyFirstInterface _objFirstObject;
    IMySecondInterface _objSecondObject;

    public override object Transform(object providerData)
    {
      _objSecondObject = (IMySecondInterface)providerData;
      return this;
    }
```

```
    public string Name
    {
      get
      {
        return _objSecondObject.CurrentTitle;
      }
      set
      {
        _objSecondObject.CurrentTitle = value;
      }
    }
  }
}
```

If you have created a web part connection transformer, you can use it by copying the assembly to the bin folder of the SharePoint web application root folder and adding a reference to it in the <transformers> section of the SharePoint web application's web.config file. This is shown in Listing 5-7.

Listing 5-7. *Creating the Second Custom Interface*

```
<transformers>
 <!-
 The other registrations for transformers are not shown in this code listing.
 They will be discussed in section "SharePoint 2007 transformers".
 ->
 <add name="MyInterfaceTransformer" ➥
 type="Connections.MyInterfaceTransformer, MyWebPartLibrary, ➥
 Version=1.0.0.0, Culture=neutral, PublicKeyToken=9f4da00116c38ec5" />
</transformers>
```

We still need to create a provider web part that implements the IMySecondInterface interface. If you need more information about this topic, please refer to the beginning of the section "The ASP.NET 2.0 Web Part Connection Framework." Listing 5-8 shows the complete code for a provider web part called SecondProvider.

Listing 5-8. *Creating a Provider Web Part Called SecondProvider*

```
using System;
using System.Runtime.InteropServices;
using System.Web.UI;
using System.Web.UI.WebControls.WebParts;
using System.Xml.Serialization;

using Microsoft.SharePoint;
using Microsoft.SharePoint.WebControls;
using Microsoft.SharePoint.WebPartPages;

namespace Connections
{
  [Guid("f4e7c5b7-5acb-4990-a7e9-511d9ec5b94e")]
  public class SecondProvider : System.Web.UI.WebControls.WebParts.WebPart, ➥
  IMySecondInterface
  {
    public SecondProvider()
```

```
    {
      this.ExportMode = WebPartExportMode.All;
    }
    protected override void Render(HtmlTextWriter writer)
    {
      writer.Write("SECOND PROVIDER");
    }

    [ConnectionProvider("connection provider")]
    public IMySecondInterface GetProvider()
    {
      return this;
    }

    private string _strTitle = "Title from second provider";
    public string CurrentTitle
    {
      get
      {
        return _strTitle;
      }
      set
      {
        _strTitle = value;
      }
    }
  }
}
```

Finally, we need to create a consumer web part that is able to consume data provided by IMyFirstInterface web parts. If you need more information about this topic, please refer to the beginning of the section "The ASP.NET 2.0 Web Part Connection Framework." Listing 5-9 shows the complete code for a consumer web part called FirstConsumer.

Listing 5-9. *Creating a Consumer Web Part Called FirstConsumer*

```
using System;
using System.Runtime.InteropServices;
using System.Web.UI;
using System.Web.UI.WebControls.WebParts;
using System.Xml.Serialization;

using Microsoft.SharePoint;
using Microsoft.SharePoint.WebControls;
using Microsoft.SharePoint.WebPartPages;

namespace Connections
{
  [Guid("07492348-a4ad-4a30-a9f5-c14bf6a3c373")]
  public class FirstConsumer : System.Web.UI.WebControls.WebParts.WebPart
  {
    public FirstConsumer()
    {
      this.ExportMode = WebPartExportMode.All;
    }
```

```
protected override void Render(HtmlTextWriter writer)
{
  if (Provider != null)
  {
    writer.Write(Provider.Name);
  }
  else
  {
    writer.Write("no connection established");
  }
}

[ConnectionConsumer("connection consumer")]
public void GetProvider(IMyFirstInterface objProvider)
{
  Provider = objProvider;
}

private IMyFirstInterface _objProvider;
public IMyFirstInterface Provider
{
  get { return _objProvider; }
  set { _objProvider = value; }
}
  }
}
```

Now, you can go ahead and place both web parts on a SharePoint page. If you have registered our custom web part connection transformer correctly, you will be able to create a connection between the SecondProvider provider web part and the FirstConsumer consumer web part.

SharePoint 2007 Transformers

In the section "Building a Custom Transformer," you have learned that you can create custom transformers and that you need to register those custom transformers in the <transformers> section of your SharePoint web application's web.config file. SharePoint provides four custom transformers:

- TransformableFilterValuesToFilterValuesTransformer: This allows filter web parts implementing the ITransformableFilterValues interface to provide data to any web part that can consume objects implementing the IFilterValues interface. This transformer always returns the first value of the first parameter of the filter web part.

- TransformableFilterValuesToParametersTransformer: This allows filter web parts implementing the ITransformableFilterValues interface to provide data to any web part that can consume objects implementing the IWebPartParameters interface.

- TransformableFilterValuesToFieldTransformer: This allows filter web parts implementing the ITransformableFilterValues interface to provide data to any web part that can consume objects implementing the IWebPartField interface.

- TransformableFilterValuesToEntityInstanceTransformer: This allows filter web parts implementing the ITransformableFilterValues interface to provide data to any web part that can consume objects implementing the IEntityInstanceProvider interface. An example of such a web part is the BusinessDataDetailsWebPart.

■**Note** If you add a web part to a SharePoint page, you will notice a Filters section in the Add Web Parts — Web Page dialog box. This section contains a range of filter web parts, such as the Business Data Catalog Filter, Choice Filter, and Date Filter. These web parts are all examples of filter web parts and are generally used to filter the contents of other web parts, such as the Links, Announcements, and Site Image web parts. Some of the available filter web parts still use the SharePoint 2003 web part connection framework; others implement the ITransformableFilterValues interface.

Building a Field Provider and Consumer

Field providers and consumers exchange single values in a web part connection. This section discusses how to build a field provider and field consumer web part. We will start by creating a web part called FieldProvider that implements the IWebPartField interface (discussed in the section "The ASP.NET 2.0 Web Part Connection Framework").

Also, you need to include a connection provider method that returns a provider that supports the IWebPartField interface. Creating a connection provider method is also discussed in section "The ASP.NET 2.0 Web Part Connection Framework." The next code fragment shows the implementation of the connection provider method for the FieldProvider web part:

```
[ConnectionProvider("My field provider")]
public IWebPartField GetFieldProvider()
{
  return this;
}
```

Also, you need to create a member variable that holds the value that will be provided to consumer web parts. In this example, we have created a property called ColumnA that contains the value default value for column a, a value that is shared by all end users. Please note that we could also have decided to allow every user to specify a unique value, in which case we would have used Personalitzation.User. The member variable is shown in the following code fragment:

```
private string _strColumnA = "default value for column a";
[
Personalizable(PersonalizationScope.Shared)
, WebBrowsable(true)
, WebDisplayName("Column A")
, WebDescription("Value for column A")
]
public string ColumnA
{
  get { return _strColumnA; }
  set { _strColumnA = value; }
}
```

Every provider web part must also provide a schema for the data that is returned by the provider. You can implement such a schema by creating a property called Schema that returns a collection of properties. In this example, we are building a field provider that returns the value of a property called ColumnA. You can use the static GetProperties() method of the TypeDescriptor class (located in the System.ComponentModel namespace) to define the schema. This is shown in the following code fragment:

```
public System.ComponentModel.PropertyDescriptor Schema
{
  get
  {
    return TypeDescriptor.GetProperties(this)["ColumnA"];
  }
}
```

Finally, if you are creating a field provider web part, you will need to implement a method called GetFieldValue(). This method will contain a reference to the field consumer web part after a connection is made. This allows the provider to communicate with the consumer. The next code fragment shows the implementation for the GetFieldValue() method:

```
public void GetFieldValue(FieldCallback callback)
{
  callback.Invoke(ColumnA);
}
```

The complete code for the field provider web part is shown in Listing 5-10.

Listing 5-10. *Creating a Field Provider Web Part*

```
using System;
using System.Runtime.InteropServices;
using System.Web.UI;
using System.Web.UI.WebControls.WebParts;
using System.Xml.Serialization;
using Microsoft.SharePoint;
using Microsoft.SharePoint.WebControls;
using Microsoft.SharePoint.WebPartPages;
using System.ComponentModel;

namespace Connections
{
  [Guid("6203652c-9d3f-4c43-8b5e-0ca00b98e4bd")]
  public class FieldProvider : ➥
  System.Web.UI.WebControls.WebParts.WebPart, IWebPartField
  {
    public FieldProvider()
    {
      this.ExportMode = WebPartExportMode.All;
    }

    protected override void Render(HtmlTextWriter writer)
    {
      writer.Write("Provider FieldProvider");
    }

    [ConnectionProvider("My field provider")]
    public IWebPartField GetFieldProvider()
    {
      return this;
    }

    public void GetFieldValue(FieldCallback callback)
    {
      callback.Invoke(ColumnA);
    }
```

```
      public System.ComponentModel.PropertyDescriptor Schema
      {
        get
        {
          return TypeDescriptor.GetProperties(this)["ColumnA"];
        }
      }

      private string _strColumnA = "default value for column a";
      [
        Personalizable(PersonalizationScope.Shared)
        , WebBrowsable(true)
        , WebDisplayName("Column A")
        , WebDescription("Value for column A")
      ]
      public string ColumnA
      {
        get { return _strColumnA; }
        set { _strColumnA = value; }
      }
    }
}
```

After creating the field provider web part, you are ready to create a field consumer web part. It is convenient to create a member variable that can store the field value provided by the provider web part. In this example, we will create a Value property that does this, which is shown in the next code fragment:

```
private string _strValue = "default consumer value";
public string Value
{
  get { return _strValue; }
  set { _strValue = value; }
}
```

You will also need to create a method that retrieves the field value from the provider and stores it somewhere. In this case, we have created a method called GetField() that stores the field value provided by the provider web part in the Value property. This is shown in the next code fragment:

```
public void GetField(object objField)
{
  if ( objField != null ) Value = objField.ToString();
}
```

Finally, you need to create a connection consumer web part that can obtain a reference to the provider web part and pass our GetField() method as a callback method to the provider web part. This is shown in the next code fragment:

```
[ConnectionConsumer("my field consumer")]
public void GetProvider(IWebPartField objProvider)
{
  FieldCallback objCallback = new FieldCallback(GetField);
  objProvider.GetFieldValue(objCallback);
}
```

The entire code for the field consumer web part is shown in Listing 5-11.

Listing 5-11. *Creating a Field Consumer Web Part*

```
using System;
using System.Runtime.InteropServices;
using System.Web.UI;
using System.Web.UI.WebControls.WebParts;
using System.Xml.Serialization;
using Microsoft.SharePoint;
using Microsoft.SharePoint.WebControls;
using Microsoft.SharePoint.WebPartPages;

namespace Connections
{
  [Guid("969e5c8f-0682-43f5-a17f-fcdd57c65f8a")]
  public class FieldConsumer : System.Web.UI.WebControls.WebParts.WebPart
  {
    public FieldConsumer()
    {
      this.ExportMode = WebPartExportMode.All;
    }

    protected override void Render(HtmlTextWriter writer)
    {
      writer.Write(Value);
    }

    [ConnectionConsumer("my field consumer")]
    public void GetProvider(IWebPartField objProvider)
    {
      FieldCallback objCallback = new FieldCallback(GetField);
      objProvider.GetFieldValue(objCallback);
    }

    public void GetField(object objField)
    {
      if ( objField != null ) Value = objField.ToString();
    }

    private string _strValue = "default consumer value";
    public string Value
    {
      get { return _strValue; }
      set { _strValue = value; }
    }
  }
}
```

If you import both web parts into a SharePoint page and connect them together (if you are not sure how to do this, please refer back to the section "The ASP.NET 2.0 Web Part Connection Framework"), you will see that the FieldConsumer web part retrieves its display value from the FieldProvider web part. This is shown in Figure 5-5.

In this section, you have seen how to use the IWebPartField interface. You can use this interface if you want to create a web part connection that allows web parts to share a single value. This way, you do not have to create your own custom interface when you want to share a single value and have the additional benefit of the RowToFieldTransformer, which allows row provider web part to provide data to field consumer web parts.

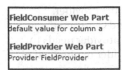

Figure 5-5. *SharePoint page containing connected web parts*

Building a Row Provider and Consumer

Row providers and consumers exchange a row of information via a web part connection. This section discusses how to build a row provider and row consumer web part. We will start by creating a web part called RowProvider that implements the IWebPartRow interface (discussed in the section "The ASP.NET 2.0 Web Part Connection Framework").

In the constructor of the RowProvider web part (which implements the IWebPartRow interface, as shown in Listing 5-12), we will create a single row of information consisting of two columns; which we will call ColumnA and ColumnB. Those columns will contain the values row provider column A value and row provider column B value. We will use a DataTable object to create this single row of information (which will be added later to the constructor of the provider web part, as is shown in Listing 5-12).

Listing 5-12. *RowProvider Constructor*

```
private DataTable _dtData;

public RowProvider()
{
  this.ExportMode = WebPartExportMode.All;

  _dtData = new DataTable();
  DataColumn objColumnA = new DataColumn();
  objColumnA.DataType = typeof(string);
  objColumnA.ColumnName = "ColumnA";
  _dtData.Columns.Add(objColumnA);

  DataColumn objColumnB = new DataColumn();
  objColumnB.DataType = typeof(string);
  objColumnB.ColumnName = "ColumnB";
  _dtData.Columns.Add(objColumnB);

  DataRow objRow = _dtData.NewRow();
  objRow["ColumnA"] = "row provider column A value";
  objRow["ColumnB"] = "row provider column B value";
  _dtData.Rows.Add(objRow);
}
```

As you might remember from the previous provider web part scenarios, you'll need to provide a connection provider method that returns an instance of an IWebPartRow provider. This is shown in the next code fragment:

```
[ConnectionProvider("my row provider")]
public IWebPartRow GetRowProvider()
{
  return this;
}
```

After that, you need to provide a schema for the data that is returned by the provider. This is a concept you should recognize from the "Building a Field Provider and Consumer" section. The difference between field providers and row providers is that a field provider needs to describe a single property (a `PropertyDescriptor` object), whereas a row provider might need to describe multiple properties. You can do this by returning a collection of property descriptions (a `PropertyDescriptorCollection` object). This is shown in the next code fragment:

```
public System.ComponentModel.PropertyDescriptorCollection Schema
{
  get
  {
    return TypeDescriptor.GetProperties(_dtData.DefaultView[0]);
  }
}
```

Finally, if you are creating a row provider web part, you will need to implement a method called `GetRowData()`. This method will contain an object reference (the callback parameter) to the row consumer web part after a connection is made. This allows the provider to communicate with the consumer. The next code fragment shows the implementation for the `GetRowData()` method:

```
public void GetRowData(RowCallback callback)
{
  DataRowCollection coll = _dtData.Rows;
  DataRowView view = _dtData.DefaultView[0];
  callback.Invoke(_dtData.Rows);
}
```

All the code for the row provider web part is shown in Listing 5-13.

Listing 5-13. *Creating a Row Provider Web Part*

```
using System;
using System.Runtime.InteropServices;
using System.Web.UI;
using System.Web.UI.WebControls.WebParts;
using System.Xml.Serialization;
using Microsoft.SharePoint;
using Microsoft.SharePoint.WebControls;
using Microsoft.SharePoint.WebPartPages;
using System.ComponentModel;
using System.Data;
using System.Globalization;
using System.Collections;
using System.Web;
using Microsoft.SharePoint.Security;
using System.Security.Permissions;

namespace Connections
{
  [Guid("371f6f56-e0f8-4df2-bc1c-bab9fbd9b092")]
  public class RowProvider : ➡
  System.Web.UI.WebControls.WebParts.WebPart, IWebPartRow
  {
    private DataTable _dtData;
```

```
public RowProvider()
{
  this.ExportMode = WebPartExportMode.All;

  _dtData = new DataTable();
  _dtData.Locale = CultureInfo.InvariantCulture;

  DataColumn objColumnA = new DataColumn();
  objColumnA.DataType = typeof(string);
  objColumnA.ColumnName = "ColumnA";
  _dtData.Columns.Add(objColumnA);

  DataColumn objColumnB = new DataColumn();
  objColumnB.DataType = typeof(string);
  objColumnB.ColumnName = "ColumnB";
  _dtData.Columns.Add(objColumnB);

  DataRow objRow = _dtData.NewRow();
  objRow["ColumnA"] = "row provider column A value";
  objRow["ColumnB"] = "row provider column B value";
  _dtData.Rows.Add(objRow);
}

protected override void Render(HtmlTextWriter writer)
{
  writer.Write("Provider RowProvider");
}

[ConnectionProvider("my row provider")]
public IWebPartRow GetRowProvider()
{
  return this;
}

public void GetRowData(RowCallback callback)
{
  DataRowCollection coll = _dtData.Rows;
  DataRowView view = _dtData.DefaultView[0];
  callback.Invoke(_dtData.Rows);
}

public System.ComponentModel.PropertyDescriptorCollection Schema
{
  get
  {
    return TypeDescriptor.GetProperties(_dtData.DefaultView[0]);
  }
}
}
}
```

Now that we have created a row provider web part, we will continue by building a row consumer web part. First, we will add a member variable to the consumer web part that is able to hold the values provided by the row provider web part. The data type of such a variable needs to be compatible with the ICollection interface. In this example, we will create a property called Data to hold the values provided by the row provider web part. This is shown in the following code fragment:

```
private ICollection _collData;
public ICollection Data
{
  get { return _collData; }
  set { _collData = value; }
}
```

You can access this property to display the values retrieved from the provider web part. The next code fragment shows how to display the values of the first two columns of the row in the Data property that is ultimately provided by the row provider web part:

Caution The implementation of the Render() method in this example has intimate knowledge about the provider. It assumes that the Data property contains data rows.

```
protected override void Render(HtmlTextWriter writer)
{
  if (Data != null)
  {
    foreach (DataRow objRow in Data)
    {
      writer.Write("column " + objRow.Table.Columns[0] + ": " + objRow[0]);
      writer.WriteBreak();

      writer.Write("column " + objRow.Table.Columns[1] + ": " + objRow[1]);
      writer.WriteBreak();
    }
  }
  else
  {
    writer.Write("Not connected");
  }
}
```

We have created a method called GetProvider() that is called by the web part connection framework, which passes an object reference to the row provider web part. This method passes a callback method (GetRow()) to the provider web part. In turn, the provider web part calls the callback method (GetRow()) and passes data to it. The GetRow() method stores the row of data that is passed to it. The following code fragment shows the implementation for the GetProvider() method:

```
[ConnectionConsumer("my row consumer")]
public void GetProvider(IWebPartRow objProvider)
{
  RowCallback objCallback = new RowCallback(GetRow);
  objProvider.GetRowData(objCallback);
}
```

Finally, the GetRow() method assigns the row of data to the Data property, as shown in the next code fragment:

```
public void GetRow(object objRow)
{
  if (objRow != null) Data = (ICollection) objRow;
}
```

The complete code for the row consumer web part is shown in Listing 5-14.

Listing 5-14. *Creating a Row Consumer Web Part*

```
using System;
using System.Runtime.InteropServices;
using System.Web.UI;
using System.Web.UI.WebControls.WebParts;
using System.Xml.Serialization;
using Microsoft.SharePoint;
using Microsoft.SharePoint.WebControls;
using Microsoft.SharePoint.WebPartPages;
using System.Collections;
using System.Data;

namespace Connections
{
  [Guid("7335c370-4451-40a3-a013-aeae97824235")]
  public class RowConsumer : System.Web.UI.WebControls.WebParts.WebPart
  {
    public RowConsumer()
    {
      this.ExportMode = WebPartExportMode.All;
    }

    protected override void Render(HtmlTextWriter writer)
    {
      if (Data != null)
      {
        foreach (DataRow objRow in Data)
        {
          writer.Write("column " + objRow.Table.Columns[0] + ": " + objRow[0]);
          writer.WriteBreak();

          writer.Write("column " + objRow.Table.Columns[1] + ": " + objRow[1]);
          writer.WriteBreak();
        }
      }
      else
      {
        writer.Write("Not connected");
      }
    }

    [ConnectionConsumer("my row consumer")]
    public void GetProvider(IWebPartRow objProvider)
    {
      RowCallback objCallback = new RowCallback(GetRow);
      objProvider.GetRowData(objCallback);
    }

    public void GetRow(object objRow)
    {
      if (objRow != null) Data = (ICollection) objRow;
    }
```

```
    private ICollection _collData;
    public ICollection Data
    {
      get { return _collData; }
      set { _collData = value; }
    }
  }
}
```

If you import both web parts to a SharePoint page and connect them together (if you are not sure how to do this, please refer back to the section "The ASP.NET 2.0 Web Part Connection Framework"), you will see that the RowConsumer web part retrieves its display value from the RowProvider web part. This is shown in Figure 5-6.

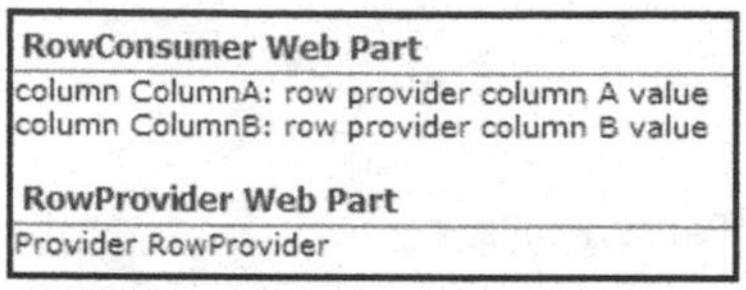

RowConsumer Web Part
column ColumnA: row provider column A value
column ColumnB: row provider column B value
RowProvider Web Part
Provider RowProvider

Figure 5-6. *Two web parts sharing a row connection*

CONNECTION TRANSFORMERS

There seems to be a flaw in the documentation of Windows SharePoint Services v3 SDK. You should be able to use the RowToFieldTransformer and RowToParametersTransformer transformers to connect row providers to field consumers and parameter consumers.

Also, you should be able to provide only a single row of data in a row provider web part, whereas the DataTable object used in the GetRowData() method allows you to specify multiple rows. So far, whenever we transform a row provider into another type of connectable web part, the transformer wizard starts correctly but it ends in an error message stating that a DataRowCollection cannot be transformed into a DataRowView. We have not been able to solve this problem yet, so make sure to check whether the Windows SharePoint Services v3 SDK has been updated in this regard.

The only working examples of row provider web parts that can be used in transformation scenarios are web parts that are based on the DataFormWebPart web part located in the Microsoft.SharePoint.WebPartPages. DataFormWebPart namespace of the Microsoft.SharePoint assembly. This web part uses the undocumented and internal SPPropertyDescriptor type, which means it can only be used by other types located in the same assembly (such as the DataFormWebPart type).

In this section, you have seen how to use the IWebPartRow interface. You can use this interface if you want to create a web part connection that allows web parts to share a row of data. This way, you do not have to create your own custom interface in scenarios where you want to share a row of data.

Building a Table Provider and Consumer

Table providers and consumers exchange a list of information. This section discusses how to build a table provider and consumer web part. We will start by creating a web part called TableProvider that implements the IWebPartTable interface (discussed in the section "The ASP.NET 2.0 Web Part Connection Framework").

In the constructor of the TableProvider web part, we will create two rows of information consisting of two columns, ColumnA and ColumnB. We will use a `DataTable` object to create this single row of information, as shown in the following code fragment:

```
public TableProvider()
{
  _dtData = new DataTable();

  DataColumn objColumnA = new DataColumn();
  objColumnA.DataType = typeof(string);
  objColumnA.ColumnName = "ColumnA";
  _dtData.Columns.Add(objColumnA);

  DataColumn objColumnB = new DataColumn();
  objColumnB.DataType = typeof(string);
  objColumnB.ColumnName = "ColumnB";
  _dtData.Columns.Add(objColumnB);

  DataRow objRow1 = _dtData.NewRow();
  objRow1["ColumnA"] = "table provider column A value row 1";
  objRow1["ColumnB"] = "table provider column B value row 1";
  _dtData.Rows.Add(objRow1);

  DataRow objRow2 = _dtData.NewRow();
  objRow2["ColumnA"] = "table provider column A value row 2";
  objRow2["ColumnB"] = "table provider column B value row 2";
  _dtData.Rows.Add(objRow2);
}
```

You also need to provide a connection provider method that returns an instance of an IWebPartTable provider. This is shown in the next code fragment:

```
[ConnectionProvider("my table provider")]
public IWebPartTable GetTableProvider()
{
  return this;
}
```

After that, you need to provide a schema for the data that is returned by the provider. The next code fragment is identical to the one described in the section "Building a Row Provider and Consumer":

```
public System.ComponentModel.PropertyDescriptorCollection Schema
{
  get
  {
    return TypeDescriptor.GetProperties(_dtData.DefaultView[0]);
  }
}
```

Then, you need to implement a method called `GetTableData()` that contains an object reference (the callback parameter) to the table consumer web part after a connection is made. This allows the provider to communicate with the consumer. The next code fragment shows the implementation for the `GetTableData()` method.

```
public void GetTableData(TableCallback callback)
{
  callback.Invoke(_dtData.Rows);
}
```

The complete code for the table provider web part can be found in Listing 5-15.

Listing 5-15. *Creating a Table Provider Web Part*

```
using System;
using System.Runtime.InteropServices;
using System.Web.UI;
using System.Web.UI.WebControls.WebParts;
using System.Xml.Serialization;
using Microsoft.SharePoint;
using Microsoft.SharePoint.WebControls;
using Microsoft.SharePoint.WebPartPages;
using System.ComponentModel;
using System.Data;

namespace Connections
{
  [Guid("64fd1be8-d803-4fb6-893a-3799a278168c")]
  public class TableProvider : ➥
  System.Web.UI.WebControls.WebParts.WebPart, IWebPartTable
  {
    private DataTable _dtData;

    public TableProvider()
    {
      this.ExportMode = WebPartExportMode.All;

      _dtData = new DataTable();

      DataColumn objColumnA = new DataColumn();
      objColumnA.DataType = typeof(string);
      objColumnA.ColumnName = "ColumnA";
      _dtData.Columns.Add(objColumnA);

      DataColumn objColumnB = new DataColumn();
      objColumnB.DataType = typeof(string);
      objColumnB.ColumnName = "ColumnB";
      _dtData.Columns.Add(objColumnB);

      DataRow objRow1 = _dtData.NewRow();
      objRow1["ColumnA"] = "table provider column A value row 1";
      objRow1["ColumnB"] = "table provider column B value row 1";
      _dtData.Rows.Add(objRow1);

      DataRow objRow2 = _dtData.NewRow();
      objRow2["ColumnA"] = "table provider column A value row 2";
      objRow2["ColumnB"] = "table provider column B value row 2";
      _dtData.Rows.Add(objRow2);
    }

    protected override void Render(HtmlTextWriter writer)
    {
      writer.Write("Provider TableProvider");
    }
```

```
[ConnectionProvider("my table provider")]
public IWebPartTable GetTableProvider()
{
  return this;
}

public void GetTableData(TableCallback callback)
{
  callback.Invoke(_dtData.Rows);
}

public System.ComponentModel.PropertyDescriptorCollection Schema
{
  get
  {
    return TypeDescriptor.GetProperties(_dtData.DefaultView[0]);
  }
}
}
}
```

The next step consists of creating a table consumer web part. Like before, we will add a member variable to the consumer web part that can hold a list of data. You can only pass data that supports the ICollection interface (located within the System.Collections namespace). The member variable is shown in the next code fragment:

```
private ICollection _collData;
public ICollection Data
{
  get { return _collData; }
  set { _collData = value; }
}
```

You also need to implement a method that can obtain a reference to the table provider web part. This method, which we will call GetProvider(), calls the GetTableData() method of the table provider web part and passes a callback method called GetTable() to the provider. The following code fragment shows the implementation for the GetProvider() method:

```
[ConnectionConsumer("my table consumer")]
public void GetProvider(IWebPartTable objProvider)
{
  TableCallback objCallback = new TableCallback(GetTable);
  objProvider.GetTableData(objCallback);
}
```

The GetTable() method is used as a callback method in the GetProvider() method. This method assigns the table of data to the Data property. The implementation for the GetTable() method is shown in the next code fragment:

```
public void GetTable(ICollection objTable)
{
  if (objTable != null) Data = (ICollection) objTable;
}
```

The complete code for the table consumer web part is shown in Listing 5-16.

Listing 5-16. *Creating a Table Consumer Web Part*

```csharp
using System;
using System.Runtime.InteropServices;
using System.Web.UI;
using System.Web.UI.WebControls.WebParts;
using System.Xml.Serialization;
using Microsoft.SharePoint;
using Microsoft.SharePoint.WebControls;
using Microsoft.SharePoint.WebPartPages;
using System.Collections;
using System.Data;

namespace Connections
{
  [Guid("50476016-46b0-4746-bcb8-ae0e70682675")]
  public class TableConsumer : System.Web.UI.WebControls.WebParts.WebPart
  {
    public TableConsumer()
    {
      this.ExportMode = WebPartExportMode.All;
    }

    protected override void Render(HtmlTextWriter writer)
    {
      if (Data != null)
      {
        foreach (DataRow objRow in Data)
        {
          writer.Write("column " + objRow.Table.Columns[0] + ": " + objRow[0]);
          writer.WriteBreak();

          writer.Write("column " + objRow.Table.Columns[1] + ": " + objRow[1]);
          writer.WriteBreak();
        }
      }
      else
      {
        writer.Write("Not connected");
      }
    }

    [ConnectionConsumer("my table consumer")]
    public void GetProvider(IWebPartTable objProvider)
    {
      TableCallback objCallback = new TableCallback(GetTable);
      objProvider.GetTableData(objCallback);
    }

    public void GetTable(ICollection objTable)
    {
      if (objTable != null) Data = (ICollection) objTable;
    }
```

```
    private ICollection _collData;
    public ICollection Data
    {
      get { return _collData; }
      set { _collData = value; }
    }
  }
}
```

If you import both web parts to a SharePoint page and connect them together (as discussed in the section "The ASP.NET 2.0 Web Part Connection Framework"), you will see that the TableConsumer web part retrieves its display value from the TableProvider web part. This is shown in Figure 5-7.

```
┌─────────────────────────────────────────────────────┐
│ TableConsumer Web Part                                │
├─────────────────────────────────────────────────────┤
│ column ColumnA: table provider column A value row 1   │
│ column ColumnB: table provider column B value row 1   │
│ column ColumnA: table provider column A value row 2   │
│ column ColumnB: table provider column B value row 2   │
│                                                       │
│ TableProvider Web Part                                │
├─────────────────────────────────────────────────────┤
│ Provider TableProvider                                │
└─────────────────────────────────────────────────────┘
```

Figure 5-7. *Two web parts sharing a table connection*

In this section, you have seen how to use the IWebPartTable interface. You can use this interface to create a web part connection that allows web parts to share a collection of data. This way, you do not have to create your own custom interface when you want to share rows of data.

Building a Parameters Provider and Consumer

Parameter providers and consumers exchange a set of one or more parameters via a web part connection. This section discusses how to build a parameter provider and consumer web part.

As in the other scenarios described in this section, first you need to implement one of the interfaces for connectable web parts. This time, you need to implement the IWebPartParameters interface (discussed in the section "The ASP.NET 2.0 Web Part Connection Framework"). As the name for our parameter provider web part, we will use ParametersProvider.

In this example, the parameters provider passes two parameters to a consumer: two variables named ColumnA and ColumnB of the data type string.

Tip In the examples in this chapter, we are using the property names ColumnA and ColumnB. They are used for educational purposes only; you are free to use other names and other data types.

The provider web part class contains two properties that contain the values that will be passed as parameters to parameter consumer web parts. The implementation of those parameters is shown in the following code fragment:

```
private string _strColumnA = "ParametersProvider column A value";
public string ColumnA
{
  get { return _strColumnA; }
  set { _strColumnA = value; }
}

private string _strColumnB = "ParametersProvider column B value";
public string ColumnB
{
  get { return _strColumnB; }
  set { _strColumnB = value; }
}
```

The implementation of the connection provider method returns an instance of an IWebPartParameters provider. The implementation looks like this:

```
[ConnectionProvider("my parameters provider")]
public IWebPartParameters GetParametersProvider()
{
  return this;
}
```

As you are probably getting used to from the other examples implementing IWebPart* interfaces, you need to provide a schema for the data returned by the provider. You do this by implementing a Schema property that loops through all the properties in the ParametersProvider web part and adds them to a collection of property descriptors. The implementation for the Schema property is shown in the next code fragment:

```
public System.ComponentModel.PropertyDescriptorCollection Schema
{
  get
  {
    PropertyDescriptorCollection objProperties;
    PropertyDescriptor[] arrProperties = ➥
    new PropertyDescriptor[Parameters.Count];
    TypeDescriptor.GetProperties(this);

    objProperties = TypeDescriptor.GetProperties(this);
    int intParameterCount = 0;
    foreach (PropertyDescriptor objProperty in Parameters)
    {
      if (Parameters[objProperty.Name] != null )
      {
        intParameterCount++;
        arrProperties[intParameterCount] = objProperty;
      }
    }

    objProperties = new PropertyDescriptorCollection(arrProperties);
    return objProperties;
  }
}
```

A parameters consumer web part must tell the provider which parameters it wishes to retrieve. To that end, the consumer will pass a collection of property descriptors to the provider.

The provider needs to keep track of the parameters a consumer is interested in. To be able to do this, we add a property called Parameters to the provider. The implementation of the property holding the list of property descriptors that the consumer is interested in is shown in the next code fragment:

```
private PropertyDescriptorCollection _objParameters;
public PropertyDescriptorCollection Parameters
{
  get { return _objParameters; }
  set { _objParameters = value; }
}
```

A parameters provider web part always needs to implement a SetConsumerSchema() method that allows a consumer to express its interest in a set of parameters provided by the provider. The implementation of this method is shown in the next code fragment:

```
public void SetConsumerSchema(➥
System.ComponentModel.PropertyDescriptorCollection schema)
{
  Parameters = schema;
}
```

Every parameters provider web part needs to implement a method called GetParametersData(). This method will contain a reference to the parameters consumer web part after a connection is made. This allows the provider to communicate with the consumer. The GetParametersData() method needs to check the Parameters property to determine that the set of parameters it returns to the consumer is indeed of interest to the consumer. If a parameter needs to be returned to the client, it is added to a state bag object. The next code fragment shows the implementation for the GetParametersData() method.

```
public void GetParametersData(ParametersCallback callback)
{
  StateBag objParameters = new StateBag();

  foreach (PropertyDescriptor objProperty in Parameters)
  {
    switch (objProperty.Name)
    {
      case "ColumnA":
        objParameters.Add("ColumnA", ColumnA);
        break;
      case "ColumnB":
        objParameters.Add("ColumnB", ColumnB);
        break;
      default:
        throw new Exception("ParametersProvider: Unknown parameter name");
    }
  }

  callback.Invoke(objParameters);
}
```

This concludes the implementation for the parameters provider web part. The complete code can be found in Listing 5-17.

Listing 5-17. *Creating a Parameters Provider Web Part*

```csharp
using System;
using System.Runtime.InteropServices;
using System.Web.UI;
using System.Web.UI.WebControls.WebParts;
using System.Xml.Serialization;
using Microsoft.SharePoint;
using Microsoft.SharePoint.WebControls;
using Microsoft.SharePoint.WebPartPages;
using System.ComponentModel;

namespace Connections
{
  [Guid("bf4ec57c-e919-4d5d-903e-10f5373ba406")]
  public class ParametersProvider : ➥
System.Web.UI.WebControls.WebParts.WebPart, IWebPartParameters
  {
    public ParametersProvider()
    {
      this.ExportMode = WebPartExportMode.All;
    }

    protected override void Render(HtmlTextWriter writer)
    {
      writer.Write("Provider ParametersProvider");
    }

    [ConnectionProvider("my parameters provider")]
    public IWebPartParameters GetParametersProvider()
    {
      return this;
    }

    public void GetParametersData(ParametersCallback callback)
    {
      StateBag objParameters = new StateBag();

      foreach (PropertyDescriptor objProperty in Parameters)
      {
        switch (objProperty.Name)
        {
          case "ColumnA":
            objParameters.Add("ColumnA", ColumnA);
            break;
          case "ColumnB":
            objParameters.Add("ColumnB", ColumnB);
            break;
          default:
            throw new Exception("ParametersProvider: Unknown parameter name");
        }
      }

      callback.Invoke(objParameters);
    }
```

```
public System.ComponentModel.PropertyDescriptorCollection Schema
{
  get
  {
    PropertyDescriptorCollection objProperties;
    PropertyDescriptor[] arrProperties = ➥
    new PropertyDescriptor[Parameters.Count];
    TypeDescriptor.GetProperties(this);

    objProperties = TypeDescriptor.GetProperties(this);
    int intParameterCount = 0;
    foreach (PropertyDescriptor objProperty in Parameters)
    {
      if (Parameters[objProperty.Name] != null )
      {
        intParameterCount++;
        arrProperties[intParameterCount] = objProperty;
      }
    }

    objProperties = new PropertyDescriptorCollection(arrProperties);
    return objProperties;
  }
}

public void SetConsumerSchema(➥
System.ComponentModel.PropertyDescriptorCollection schema)
{
  Parameters = schema;
}

private PropertyDescriptorCollection _objParameters;
public PropertyDescriptorCollection Parameters
{
  get { return _objParameters; }
  set { _objParameters = value; }
}

private string _strColumnA = "ParametersProvider column A value";
public string ColumnA
{
  get { return _strColumnA; }
  set { _strColumnA = value; }
}

private string _strColumnB = "ParametersProvider column B value";
public string ColumnB
{
  get { return _strColumnB; }
  set { _strColumnB = value; }
}
  }
}
```

Now that we have finished creating a parameters provider web part, you are ready to start creating a parameters consumer web part. This is discussed in the remainder of this section.

Let's suppose the parameters consumer web part is interested in both parameters provided by the parameters provider web part: ColumnA and ColumnB. In that case, the consumer web part needs to implement two parameters that can hold the values of those parameters. The next code fragment shows the implementation of two properties to hold the values provided by the parameters provider web part:

```
private string _strColumnA = "parameters consumer default value column A";
public string ColumnA
{
  get { return _strColumnA; }
  set { _strColumnA = value; }
}

private string _strColumnB = "parameters consumer default value column B";
public string ColumnB
{
  get { return _strColumnB; }
  set { _strColumnB = value; }
}
```

Next, the consumer needs to define a connection consumer method that lets the provider know which parameters it is interested in. You can express the desire to receive both parameters (ColumnA and ColumnB) by calling the provider SetConsumerSchema() method and passing an array of property descriptors containing descriptions of both columns. Finally, you will need to pass a callback method (GetParameters()) to the provider; this method is responsible for retrieving the parameter values from the provider. The implementation of the connection consumer method is shown in the next code fragment:

```
[ConnectionConsumer("my parameters consumer")]
public void GetProvider(IWebPartParameters objProvider)
{
  PropertyDescriptor[] objProperties =
  {
    TypeDescriptor.GetProperties(this)["ColumnA"],
    TypeDescriptor.GetProperties(this)["ColumnB"]
  };

  PropertyDescriptorCollection objSchema = ➥
  new PropertyDescriptorCollection(objProperties);
  objProvider.SetConsumerSchema(objSchema);

  ParametersCallback objCallback = new ParametersCallback(GetParameters);
  objProvider.GetParametersData(objCallback);
}
```

After all else is in place, you need to implement the GetParameters() method and retrieve the values provided by the parameters provider web part. The implementation of the GetParameters() method is shown in the next code fragment:

```csharp
public void GetParameters(IDictionary objParameters)
{
  foreach (DictionaryEntry objEntry in objParameters)
  {
    StateItem objStateItem;
    switch (objEntry.Key.ToString())
    {
      case "ColumnA":
        objStateItem = (StateItem) objEntry.Value;
        ColumnA = objStateItem.Value.ToString();
        break;
      case "ColumnB":
        objStateItem = (StateItem) objEntry.Value;
        ColumnB = objStateItem.Value.ToString();
        break;
      default:
        throw new Exception("unknown parameter");
    }
  }
}
```

The complete code for the parameters consumer web part can be found in Listing 5-18.

Listing 5-18. *Creating a Parameters Consumer Web Part*

```csharp
using System;
using System.Runtime.InteropServices;
using System.Web.UI;
using System.Web.UI.WebControls.WebParts;
using System.Xml.Serialization;
using Microsoft.SharePoint;
using Microsoft.SharePoint.WebControls;
using Microsoft.SharePoint.WebPartPages;
using System.Collections;
using System.ComponentModel;

namespace Connections
{
  [Guid("87f37650-ac8c-4ad2-9ff1-328ebf6fe4a5")]
  public class ParametersConsumer : ➥
  System.Web.UI.WebControls.WebParts.WebPart
  {
    public ParametersConsumer()
    {
      this.ExportMode = WebPartExportMode.All;
    }

    protected override void Render(HtmlTextWriter writer)
    {
      writer.Write("ColumnA: " + ColumnA);
      writer.WriteBreak();

      writer.Write("ColumnB: " + ColumnB);
      writer.WriteBreak();
    }
```

```
[ConnectionConsumer("my parameters consumer")]
public void GetProvider(IWebPartParameters objProvider)
{
  PropertyDescriptor[] objProperties =
  {
    TypeDescriptor.GetProperties(this)["ColumnA"],
    TypeDescriptor.GetProperties(this)["ColumnB"]
  };
  PropertyDescriptorCollection objSchema = ➥
  new PropertyDescriptorCollection(objProperties);
  objProvider.SetConsumerSchema(objSchema);

  ParametersCallback objCallback = new ParametersCallback(GetParameters);
  objProvider.GetParametersData(objCallback);
}

public void GetParameters(IDictionary objParameters)
{
  foreach (DictionaryEntry objEntry in objParameters)
  {
    StateItem objStateItem;
    switch (objEntry.Key.ToString())
    {
      case "ColumnA":
        objStateItem = (StateItem) objEntry.Value;
        ColumnA = objStateItem.Value.ToString();
        break;
      case "ColumnB":
        objStateItem = (StateItem) objEntry.Value;
        ColumnB = objStateItem.Value.ToString();
        break;
      default:
        throw new Exception("unknown parameter");
    }
  }
}

private string _strColumnA = "parameters consumer default value column A";
public string ColumnA
{
  get { return _strColumnA; }
  set { _strColumnA = value; }
}

private string _strColumnB = "parameters consumer default value column B";
public string ColumnB
{
  get { return _strColumnB; }
  set { _strColumnB = value; }
}
  }
}
```

If you import both web parts to a SharePoint page and connect them together (as discussed in the section "The ASP.NET 2.0 Web Part Connection Framework"), you will see that the ParametersConsumer web part retrieves its display value from the ParametersProvider web part. This is shown in Figure 5-8.

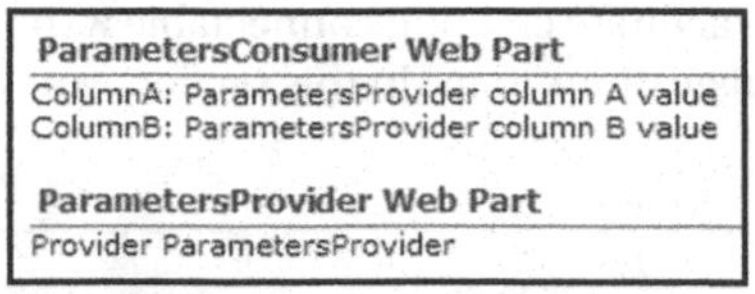

```
ParametersConsumer Web Part
ColumnA: ParametersProvider column A value
ColumnB: ParametersProvider column B value

ParametersProvider Web Part
Provider ParametersProvider
```

Figure 5-8. *Two web parts sharing a parameters connection*

As you may have noticed, the IWebPartParameters interface resembles the IWebPartRow interface quite a bit. However, there is an interesting difference. A row provider web part uses its Schema property to dictate which columns are offered to the consumer, and it is up to the consumer to decide what is does with this information.

In a scenario where the IWebPartParameters interface is used, this works quite differently. Here, the parameter consumer web part calls the parameters provider's SetConsumerSchema() method in the connection consumer point to let the provider know which parameters it will accept. The parameters provider will typically use this information to determine which parameters it provides to the consumer. This is done via the parameters provider's Schema property. This mechanism allows the consumer to express its needs, and the provider can then act on that. Therefore, the communication is a bit more advanced compared to web parts communicating via the IWebPartRow interface.

In this section, you have seen how to use the IWebPartParameters interface. You can use this interface if you want to create a web part connection that allows web parts to share a set of parameters. This way, you do not have to create your own custom interface when you want to provide parameters to other web parts and have the additional benefit of the RowToParametersTransformer that allows row provider web parts to provide data to field consumer web parts.

A Domain-Specific Language: Using WPCL 2007

A domain-specific language is a language that is closely tied to a problem domain, as opposed to general-purpose languages such as UML. DSLs can be textual or graphical and are intended to make solving a very specific problem easier than a general-purpose language ever could. DSLs are typically high-level and often need to be transformed into some other form before they are really useful. A common example is some kind of model that can be transformed into code, which in turn can be compiled into an executable.

WPCL 2007 stands for the Web Part Connection Language 2007, a DSL that integrates with Visual Studio 2005 and can be used to create ASP.NET 2.0–connectable web parts. The WPCL language

- Allows you to create a diagram that can be used to define web parts and web part connections.

- Performs basic checks to ensure the validity of a model.

- Allows you to transform a WPCL diagram into C# code that can be copied and pasted into a web part library project.

We have used the DSL tools to create a domain-specific language that makes creating connectable web parts that can be used in a SharePoint 2007 environment (or, for that matter, every other ASP.NET 2.0 web site supporting web parts) easier, and we will call this domain-specific language the WPCL.

■**Note** The WPCL is not a standard or language created by a large vendor such as Microsoft. It is a tool we have created for ourselves to facilitate the creation of connectable web parts, and you are welcome to use it as well.

If you like the idea of having a domain-specific language to facilitate creating connectable web parts, you are welcome to download the WPCL, use it, or send suggestions to us. In this section, you will learn how to install and use the WPCL 2007.

Tip If you need more information about creating connectable ASP.NET 2.0 web parts, please refer to MSDN (at http://msdn2.microsoft.com/en-us/library/system.web.ui.webcontrols.webparts(VS.80).aspx). You can also refer to the section "The ASP.NET Web Part Connection Framework" earlier in this chapter.

Installing WPCL 2007

If you want to install WPCL 2007, you need to have installed the latest release of Visual Studio 2005 SDK Version 4.0 or later. At the time of writing, this is the February 2007 version (VsSDKFebruary2007.exe). Newer versions of the SDK are released regularly; check the web site http://msdn.microsoft.com/vstudio/DSLTools/ or go to the Visual Studio 2005 Extensibility Center (http://msdn.microsoft.com/vstudio/extend/) and download the latest release of Visual Studio 2005 SDK Version 4.0.

After installing Visual Studio 2005 SDK Version 4.0, you can download the WPCL 2007 at http://www.lcbridge.nl/download. The download consists of a zip file called WPCL2007.zip. The zip file consists of several files:

- *DSLToolsRedist.msi*: This file contains the DSL Tools redistributable package containing all components required to run a DSL in a standard installation of Visual Studio 2005.

- *Readme.htm*: Contains information about the installation files and the location where you can download new versions of the WPCL.

- *settings.ini*: A configuration file used by setup.exe.

- *WebPartConnectionLanguage.msi*: Contains all components for the WPCL DSL.

- *setup.exe*: Primary installation file.

If you are missing a part of the DSL tools, setup.exe first runs DSLToolsRedist.msi to try to fix this. Do not depend on this; you really need to make sure you have installed the Visual Studio 2005 SDK Version 4.0 first. After that, the WPCL itself is installed on the client computer. If you need more information about the WPCL or want to check whether updates are available, please refer to our web site at http://www.lcbridge.nl/download.

Double-click setup.exe to install the Web Part Connection Language. This opens the WebPartConnectionLanguage Setup wizard. Follow the instructions and complete the wizard.

Note The current version (version 0.1) of the WPCL 2007 only supports C#.

Creating a New WPCL 2007 Application

If you start up Visual Studio 2005 after installing the WPCL, you will see that a new type of project appears in the New Project dialog, the WPCL 2007 Application. This is shown in Figure 5-9.

If you create a new project based on this template, you will notice that it contains two default files: test.wpcl and WebPartsTemplate.tt. This is shown in Figure 5-10.

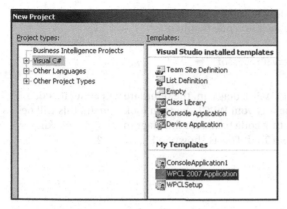

Figure 5-9. *The WPCL 2007 Application project template*

Figure 5-10. *The default contents of a WPCL 2007 project*

The Test.wpcl file is used to create WPCL diagrams; WebPartsTemplate.tt is a text template that can be used to create C# code based on a WPCL diagram. If you want to use the WPCL, you need to add new WPCL diagrams to the project. Just right-click the project name and choose Add ➤ New Item. Under the Visual C# Project Items node, you will find a new entry for a WebPartConnection-Language project item, as can be seen in Figure 5-11. We will discuss the creation of WPCL diagrams extensively in the rest of the chapter.

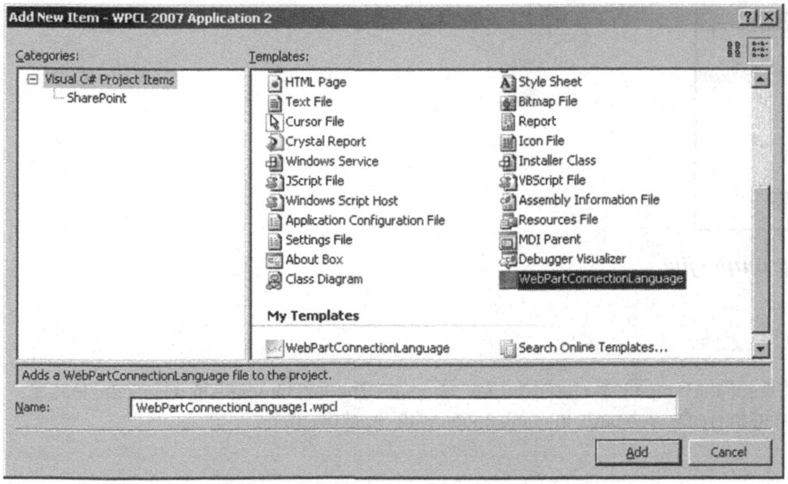

Figure 5-11. *WPCL project item*

Near the top of the WebPartsTemplate.tt file, you will find a processor directive that refers to a WPCL model called Test.wpcl. This is shown in the next code fragment:

```
<#@ WebPartConnectionLanguage ➥
processor="WebPartConnectionLanguageDirectiveProcessor" ➥
requires="fileName='Test.wpcl'" #>
```

If you let the text template refer to another WPCL diagram, the template will generate code based on that model. If you are happy with the way your WPCL diagram looks (again, this will be discussed in detail later), you can start generating code based on the diagram by right-clicking WebPartsTemplate.tt and choosing Run Custom Tool. This is shown in Figure 5-12.

Figure 5-12. *Start code generation based on a WPCL model*

As a result of this, a new output file is created. In this case, a C# class (.cs) file. This is shown in Figure 5-13.

Figure 5-13. *Text template output file*

■**Note** The tt extension in WebPartsTemplate.tt stands for *text template*. The text template in this example is a web part template that is used to create web parts in combination with .wpcl diagrams.

Elements of the WPCL

If you open a WPCL diagram (.wpcl file), the WPCL adds two new sections to the Visual Studio 2005 toolbox: WPCL General and WPCL Interfaces. Figure 5-14 shows both of these sections. The WPCL language contains several language elements that are divided over both sections.

Figure 5-14. *The WPCL toolbox*

■**Note** Figure 5-14 displays all language elements of the WPCL. The WPCL language elements can be used to create WPCL diagrams.

You can use the language elements in the toolbox to create WPCL diagrams by dragging and dropping them to the designer canvas. In this section, we will discuss every language element of the WPCL.

Let's start with the designer canvas itself. The canvas represents a WPCL model. If you click on it, the Properties window shows all properties that we have defined at the uppermost level of the language. The current version only has support for a single property, called Namespace. This is the default namespace that is used for web parts (and optionally, interfaces) that are created during code generation (when a WPCL model is transformed to C# code).

In this post, we will create several code examples using the WPCL, and we want a default namespace called LoisAndClark.TestConnections to be used within all of those samples. Figure 5-15 shows how to use the Properties window to define a default namespace within a WPCL model.

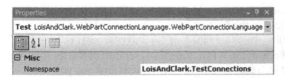

Figure 5-15. *The WPCL model*

■**Note** Although the validation rules of version 0.1 of the WPCL do not check for the presence of a namespace value, you should make sure you enter a value here.

Now, you can drop language elements to the canvas and build a WPCL model. The first language element that we'll discuss is the WebPart element. The WebPart element represents an ASP.NET 2.0 web part and looks like Figure 5-16 when it is dragged to the designer canvas of a WPCL model. WebPart elements allow you to define a web part name. In this example, this name is set to WebPart1. This name will be used as the class name of the web part during code generation.

Figure 5-16. *The WebPart element*

Web parts can have connections to each other, although there are some restrictions, such as the fact that a web part consumer is only allowed to have a single provider.

Note A limited set of validation rules is added to the WPCL to indicate flaws in the design of a WPCL diagram. The validation of a WPCL diagram can be started by right-clicking the designer canvas of the diagram and choosing Validate All.

The Connection element of the WPCL enables you to define a connection between two web parts. The direction in which the relationship is drawn determines which web part acts as the provider and which acts as the consumer. Connection elements allow you to define a label, which is only used for clarity's sake. You can use labels to annotate a WPCL diagram; this information is discarded during code generation.

Figure 5-17 shows a web part connection between two web parts called WebPart1 and WebPart2. In this case, WebPart1 acts as the provider, WebPart2 as the consumer. The connection is annotated with a default comment, Connection1, which is only used in the WPCL model and is discarded once the code generation process starts.

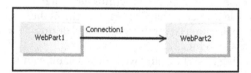

Figure 5-17. *The Connection element*

Connected web parts need some kind of interface that let them communicate with each other. You can either use one of the predefined interfaces in the System.Web.UI.WebControls.WebParts namespace (either the IWebPartField, IWebPartRow, IWebPartTable, or IWebPartParameters interface), or you can define your own custom interface. In the WPCL Interfaces section of the toolbox, you will find four representations of predefined web part connection interfaces and one you can use if you want to build a custom interface. The WPCL interface elements are shown in Figure 5-18. All elements have a Name property. In the case of the four predefined interfaces, this property is only used to annotate a WPCL diagram should you feel the need to. In the case of a custom interface, the name you specify will actually be used to generate a custom interface during code generation.

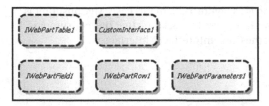

Figure 5-18. *Interface elements*

Web parts can be associated with interfaces. To be precise, a web part provider always needs to be associated with an interface. In the WPCL, a web part consumer can optionally be associated with an interface, indicating that it is compatible with a given interface. For instance, a web part consumer associated with the IWebPartField interface indicates that it supports providers implementing this interface.

The Implements element of the WPCL is used to associate web parts to interfaces, as can be seen in Figure 5-19. The Implements element has a property called Label that can be used to annotate diagrams. This information is discarded during the code transformation process.

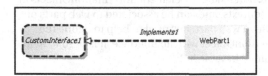

Figure 5-19. *Web part implements interface*

Figure 5-20 shows a web part provider called MyProvider that implements a custom interface called CustomInterface1. The MyProvider web part provides data to a web part consumer called MyConsumer, which does not have an explicit relationship with any interface. In such a case, the WPCL assumes it is compatible with the interface implemented by its web part provider, in this case CustomInterface1.

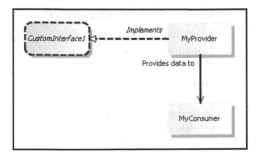

Figure 5-20. *Web part consumer implicitly associated to an interface*

■**Note** You can define the structure of an interface with the help of InformationObjects (discussed later in this section). You can see an example of this in the section "Creating a Connection Using a Custom Interface."

Figure 5-21 expresses the same meaning as previous Figure 5-20. In this case, MyConsumer is explicitly associated with the CustomInterface1 interface, thereby declaring that this consumer is compatible with web part providers implementing the CustomInterface1 interface.

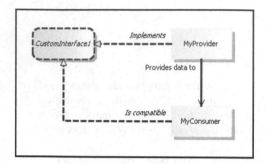

Figure 5-21. *Web part consumer explicitly associated to an interface*

The final important part of the WPCL is the InformationObject element. InformationObjects in a WPCL diagram mean different things in different contexts, and can be associated to web parts or interfaces. If you associate an InformationObject with a web part, it is used to help to define the structure of the web part. If you associate an InformationObject with an interface, it is used to help to define the structure of the interface. This is explained in Table 5-2.

Table 5-2. *The Meaning of InformationObjects*

Associated With	Context	Meaning
Provider web part	IWebPartField	Describes field used in connection
Consumer web part	IWebPartField	Describes member variable that is used to contain provider field
Provider web part	IWebPartRow	Refers to column in row of data
Consumer web part	IWebPartRow	Refers to column in row of data
Provider web part	IWebPartTable	Refers to column in table of data
Consumer web part	IWebPartTable	Refers to column in table of data
Provider web part	IWebPartParameters	Describes parameter used in connection
Consumer web part	IWebPartParameters	Describes member variable that is used to contain provider parameter
Interface	CustomInterface	Describes interface method used to provide data to consumer

Figure 5-22 shows what an InformationObject looks like once it is dragged to a WPCL diagram.

Figure 5-22. *The InformationObject element*

The InformationObject element contains several properties that allow you to describe a field, column, parameter, member, or method:

- *Data Type*: Describes the data type of a field, column, parameter, or member, or describes the return type of a method.

- *Default Value*: Describes the default value of a field, column, parameter, member, or method.

- *Name*: Describes the name of a field, column, parameter, or member, or method.

The Properties window can be used to set these properties, as seen in Figure 5-23.

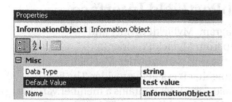

Figure 5-23. *Setting the properties of an InformationObject*

■**Note** Version 0.1 of the WPCL does not check whether you enter valid values for the InformationObject properties, so you should ensure that you enter values here. Failing to do so results in the generation of code that does not compile. We advise you to specify correct values, but even if you have not done so, you still will be able to correct the situation by changing the result code itself.

If you want to associate a web part with an information object, you can use the MapToInformation element of the WPCL. This is shown in Figure 5-24. The MapToInformation element contains a Label property that is used to annotate a diagram; this information is discarded during code generation.

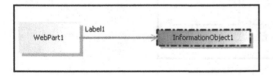

Figure 5-24. *Associating a web part with an information object*

You can use the MapCustomInterfaceToInformationObject element of the WPCL to associate an interface with an information object. This is shown in Figure 5-25. The MapCustomInterfaceToInformationObject element contains a Label property that is used to annotate a diagram; this information is discarded during code generation.

Information objects can only be associated with custom interfaces, not with the IWebPartField, IWebPartRow, IWebPartTable, and IWebPartParameters interfaces. This is because those interfaces have been predefined. For a custom interface, you will have to define exactly what it looks like.

■**Note** The section "Creating a Connection Using a Custom Interface" shows an example of defining a custom interface.

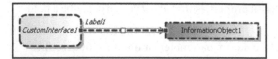

Figure 5-25. *Associating an interface with an information object*

In this section, you have learned about all the existing elements in the WPCL. In the following sections, you will learn how to use those elements to build connectable web parts.

Creating a Connection Using the IWebPartField Interface

In this example, we have added two web parts to a WPCL diagram: MyFieldProvider and MyFieldConsumer. We have drawn a Connection relationship from MyFieldProvider to MyFieldConsumer, thereby designating MyFieldProvider as the web part provider. MyFieldProvider implements the predefined IWebPartField interface, indicating that it is a field provider. The field provided by MyFieldProvider is called ProviderValueA. MyFieldConsumer contains a member variable ConsumerValue that can be used to contain the value provided by MyFieldProvider. This is shown in Figure 5-26.

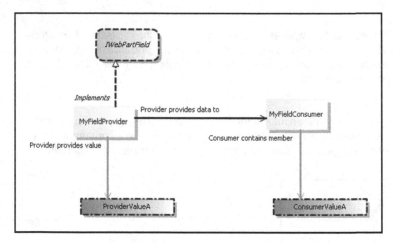

Figure 5-26. *Creating an IWebPartField connection*

■**Caution** The current version of the WPCL does not support web parts implementing multiple interfaces.

You can generate code based on this model by right-clicking WebPartsTemplate.tt (discussed in the section "Creating a New WPCL 2007 Application"). The generated code can be retrieved (when you unfold WebPartsTemplate.tt) from the file called WebPartTemplate.cs. You can then copy this code into a web part library project. If you add both web parts to the same web part page, you can connect the MyFieldProvider provider web part and the MyFieldConsumer consumer web part to each other, as can be seen in Figure 5-27.

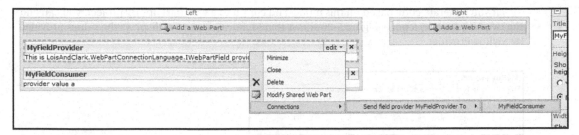

Figure 5-27. *Connecting MyFieldProvider to MyFieldConsumer*

After the web part connection has been made, the web part consumer displays the value provided by the web part provider. This is shown in Figure 5-28.

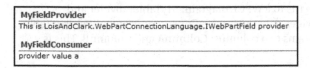

Figure 5-28. *The result of an IWebPartField connection*

Creating a Connection Using the IWebPartRow Interface

In this example, we have added two web parts to a WPCL diagram: MyRowProvider and MyRowConsumer. MyRowProvider acts as a row web part provider that provides a row consisting of two columns: ColumnA and ColumnB. This is shown in Figure 5-29.

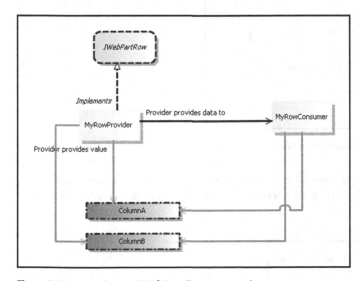

Figure 5-29. *Creating an IWebPartRow connection*

If you generate code based on this model and copy it to a web part library project, you can add the two web parts to a page. Figure 5-30 shows that MyRowConsumers displays the values provided by MyRowProvider.

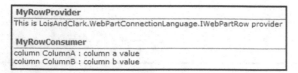

MyRowProvider
This is LoisAndClark.WebPartConnectionLanguage.IWebPartRow provider

MyRowConsumer
column ColumnA : column a value
column ColumnB : column b value

Figure 5-30. *An IWebPartRow connection*

Creating a Connection Using the IWebPartTable Interface

In this example, we have added two web parts to a WPCL diagram: MyTableProvider and MyTableConsumer. MyTableProvider provides data to MyTableConsumer over an IWebPartTable interface. It provides a data table that contains two columns: ColumnA and ColumnB. This is shown in Figure 5-31.

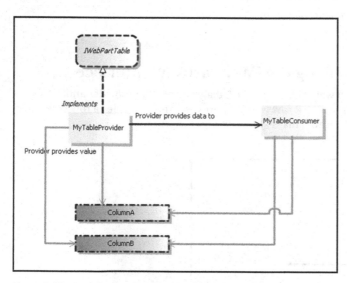

Figure 5-31. *Creating an IWebPartTable connection*

If you generate code based on this model and copy it to a web part library, you can add both web parts to a page. Figure 5-32 shows that the MyTableConsumer web part displays data provided by the MyTableProvider web part.

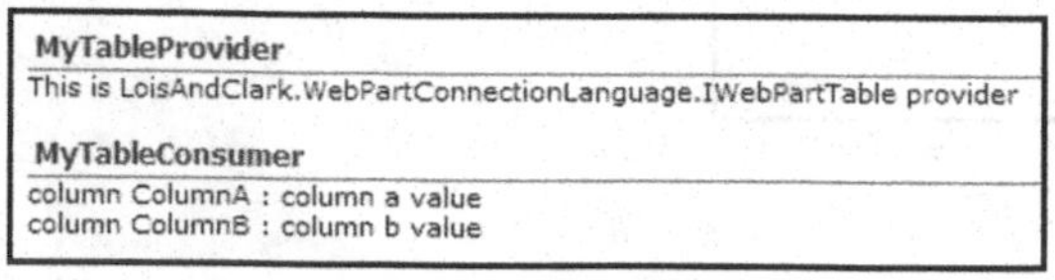

MyTableProvider
This is LoisAndClark.WebPartConnectionLanguage.IWebPartTable provider

MyTableConsumer
column ColumnA : column a value
column ColumnB : column b value

Figure 5-32. *IWebPartTable connection*

Creating a Connection Using the IWebPartParameters Interface

In this example, we have added two web parts to a WPCL diagram: MyParametersProvider and
MyParametersConsumer. The MyParametersProvider implements the IWebPartParameter interface
and provides two parameters to a consumer: ParameterA and ParameterB. This is shown in Figure 5-33.

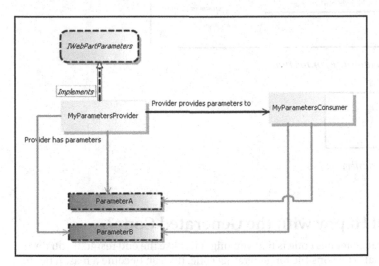

Figure 5-33. *Creating an IWebPartParameters connection*

Once you have generated the code for this model, added it to a web part library, and eventually
added both web parts to a page and connected them to each other, the ParametersConsumer web
part displays the parameters provided by the ParametersProvider web part. The end result is shown
in Figure 5-34.

ParametersProvider Web Part
Provider ParametersProvider

ParametersConsumer Web Part
ColumnA: ParametersProvider column A value
ColumnB: ParametersProvider column B value

Figure 5-34. *IWebPartParameters connection*

Creating a Connection Using a Custom Interface

In this example, we have added two web parts to a WPCL diagram: MyCustomInterfaceProvider and
MyCustomInterfaceConsumer. The MyCustomInterfaceProvider web part implements a custom
interface called IMyCustomInterface that contains a single method called GetCustomMethod(). This
is shown in Figure 5-35.

If you generate the code for this model and add this code to a web part library, you can add
both web parts to a page. Figure 5-36 shows that the MyCustomInterfaceConsumer web part displays the value provided by the MyCustomInterfaceProvider web part.

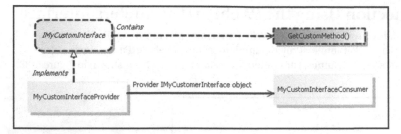

Figure 5-35. *Creating a custom interface connection*

| MyCustomInterfaceProvider |
| custom interface provider MyCustomInterfaceProvider |
| **MyCustomInterfaceConsumer** |
| custom method default value |

Figure 5-36. *Custom interface connection*

What If You Are Not Happy with the Generated Code?

The problem with any tool that generates code is that you might not like the end result. If you don't have access to the code templates responsible for generating code, this can become a reason not to use the tool.

Note Lack of access to the code templates is one of the downsides of the 1.0 version of VseWSS (Visual Studio Extensions for Windows SharePoint Services). Please refer to Chapter 1 for more information about VseWSS.

If you don't like the end result of the code generation template, there are a couple things you can do. First of all, you can e-mail suggestions to info@lcbridge.nl. If we like the ideas, we will include them in the WPCL or enhance the language so that you can specify a code style that influences the way the generated code looks. You can also change WebPartsTemplate.tt or create a new text template altogether. Finally, if you are not interested in changing the code template, you can change the end result, the code itself.

To Sum Up

The WPCL 2007 is intended to make creating connectable web parts significantly easier. It does this by providing a visual language that lets you create diagrams that can be used to create code. This code can be copied and pasted into web part library projects. Once the web part library project is compiled, the connectable web parts can be added to SharePoint 2007 pages (or any ASP.NET 2.0 page that supports web parts, provided you do not need to use any parts of the SharePoint framework).

Creating the Web Part Connection Language

In this section, we will use the Visual Studio 2005 DSL Toolkit to create a new graphical DSL for creating connectable web parts. We will call this DSL the Web Part Connection Language (WPCL) 2007.

This section explains in detail how to create the WPCL. If you want to see why you would want to use or create the Web Part Connection Language, feel free to skip ahead to the section "Using the Web Part Connection Language."

If you are creating a DSL for Visual Studio 2005, you will need to take a standard series of steps. First, you need to download and install the Visual Studio 2005 SDK Version 4.0, which contains the Domain Specific Language Tools Version 1.0. The DSL Toolkit enables you to create a graphical DSL. Then, you need to use the DSL Toolkit to create a domain model that describes how the graphical DSL works and how it should be shown within Visual Studio 2005. A standard domain model captures basic validation rules; for example, concept A has a relationship with concept B, but not with concept C. Most of the time, after creating a standard domain model, you will need to add advanced validation rules. After that, you need to create a set of text templates that is responsible for generating code based on a given model of your custom DSL. Most DSL solution development life cycles will conclude with the deployment of the DSL. To this end, you need to create a DSL setup project. You do not need to do this if you are just creating a DSL to use yourself.

We will start with a discussion of the DSL Toolkit, explain how to create a domain model, add advanced validation rules, and create a text template that can generate code for connectable web parts based on a WPCL model. We will create another text template that is able to generate code for web part description (.webpart) files, which can be used to import connectable web parts to SharePoint web sites. We will also create a setup project for our custom DSL. Finally, we will show how to use the Web Part Connection Language.

Installing the DSL Toolkit for Visual Studio 2005

In the section "A Domain-Specific Language: Using WPCL 2007," you learned that you need to install the latest version of the DSL Toolkit for Visual Studio 2005 to take advantage of the WPCL. If you have not done so already, install Visual Studio 2005 SDK Version 4.0.

Creating a Domain Model

The purpose of the WPCL 2007 is to let developers create connectable web parts in a graphical manner. The WPCL 2007 will allow you to drag shapes representing web parts to a designer canvas, connect them to other web parts, and have them implement certain interfaces required for connectable web parts in Microsoft Office SharePoint Server 2007, such as the IWebPartField interface (for clarity's sake, we will call those interfaces *IConnectable interfaces*). The WPCL 2007 will validate web part connections for you and is able to generate code based on WPCL 2007 models. The WPCL 2007 will speed up the development of connectable web parts and reduce the chances of making mistakes. If you want detailed information about the WPCL in action, please refer back to the section "A Domain-Specific Language: Using WPCL 2007."

■**Note** In WPCL 2007, we will only support ASP.NET 2.0–connectable web parts. In the previous version of this book, called *Pro SharePoint 2003 Development Techniques*, you can find a detailed description of the first version of WPCL, a language that is dedicated to supporting SharePoint 2003 connectable web parts.

Choosing a Domain-Specific Language Template

In this section, we will show how to create the domain model for the WPCL, thus laying the basis for our custom DSL. During the next procedure, you will create a new DSL Designer project used to create DSLs:

1. Start Visual Studio 2005.

2. Choose File ➤ New ➤ Project.

3. In the New Project window, in the Project Types pane, choose Other Project Types ➤ Extensibility.

4. In the Templates pane, under Visual Studio Installed Templates, choose the Domain-Specific Language Designer template.

5. Type the following name: WebPartConnectionLanguage.

6. Type the following location: C:\Projects. At this point, the New Project window should look like Figure 5-37.

7. Click OK. This opens the DSL Designer Wizard.

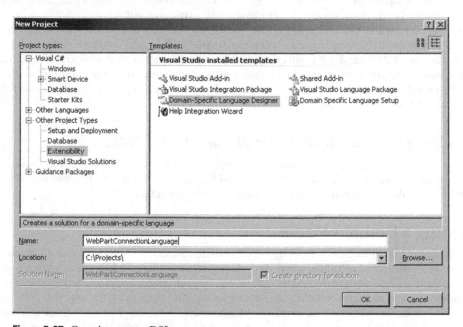

Figure 5-37. *Creating a new DSL*

The first screen of the DSL Designer Wizard lets you choose between several solution templates for DSLs. Solution templates are the starting points for defining custom DSLs. (Figure 5-42 shows the templates that are available out of the box.) The following list contains a description of each of the solution templates:

- *Class diagrams*: Choose this solution template if you want to create UML-like class diagrams. This template includes graphical symbols for classes, interfaces, several types of associations, and generalization and implementation relations. Look at Figure 5-38 to see a DSL that is built using this template.

- *Component models*: Choose this solution template if you want to create basic UML-like component diagrams. This template can be used to create a DSL that uses ports to connect components to other components. Look at Figure 5-39 to see a DSL that is built using this template.

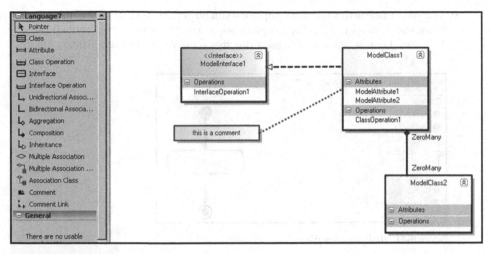

Figure 5-38. *Class diagram template*

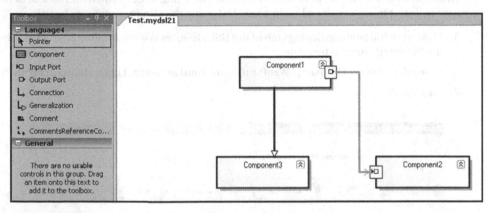

Figure 5-39. *Component model template*

- *MinimalLanguage:* Choose this solution template if the DSL you want to create is very different from any of the other solution templates. This template creates a basic language consisting of only a box and a line. The other languages already clearly define elements and rules used within a DSL; the MinimalLanguage template does not. This makes the MinimalLanguage template an ideal starting point for creating a brand new language. Look at Figure 5-40 to see a DSL that is built using this template. Shortly, we will start building a new DSL based on the MinimalLanguage template.

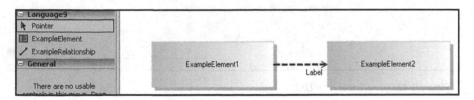

Figure 5-40. *MinimalLanguage template*

- *Task flow*: Choose this solution template if you want to create a language that deals in work-flows, states, or sequences. The template helps to create DSLs that resemble UML activity diagrams. Look at Figure 5-41 to see a DSL that is built using this template.

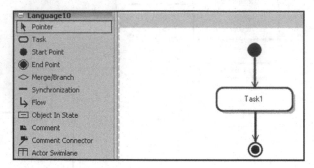

Figure 5-41. *Task flow template*

Since our own DSL, the WPCL, does not look like class diagrams, component models, or task flows, we will start from scratch and build a new DSL using the MinimalLanguage template:

1. Make sure the Solution Settings tab of the DSL Designer Wizard window is selected. Choose the MinimalLanguage template.

2. Type the following DSL name: **WebPartConnectionLanguage**. This is shown in Figure 5-42.

3. Click Next.

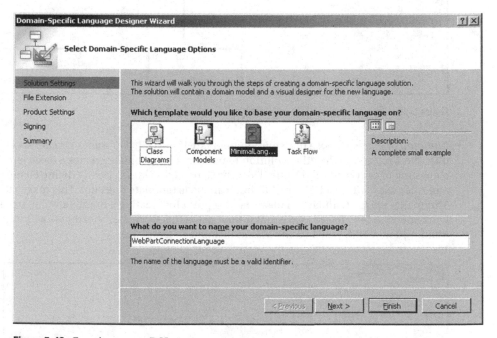

Figure 5-42. *Creating a new DSL*

Configuring the DSL Solution

Once our DSL is created, a new item template is added to Visual Studio 2005 that is associated to our language. Since we are planning to call our DSL the Web Part Connection Language, we will use the following extension: .wpcl. The following procedure explains how to create a new DSL that can generate an item template for creating WPCL models:

1. On the File Extension tab, type the following extension: **wpcl**.

2. If other tools and applications are registered to handle this extension, check the Unregister Domain-Specific Language Tools That Currently Handle This Extension check box. By default, there should be no other registrations.

3. Choose an icon to use for .wpcl model files, or leave the default setting (Default Template Icon). We have chosen to use our own company icon; the window shows a preview of it in Figure 5-43.

4. Click Next.

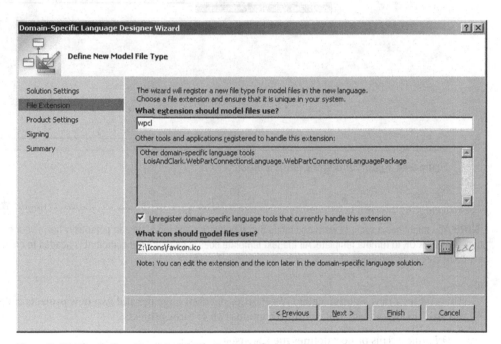

Figure 5-43. *The Define New Model File Type window*

In the next step, you need to define a few general product settings: the name of the DSL, the name of the company creating the language, and the default namespace of classes created within the DSL:

1. On the Product Settings tab, type the following product name: **WebPartConnectionLanguage**.

2. Type a company name. We have chosen the name of our own company, Lois and Clark IT Services.

3. Type the following root namespace: **LoisAndClark.WebPartConnectionLanguage**. This is shown in Figure 5-44.

4. At this point, we have not reached the end of the wizard yet, but we are satisfied with the settings we have configured so far. So let's skip the strong naming and summary windows and click Finish.

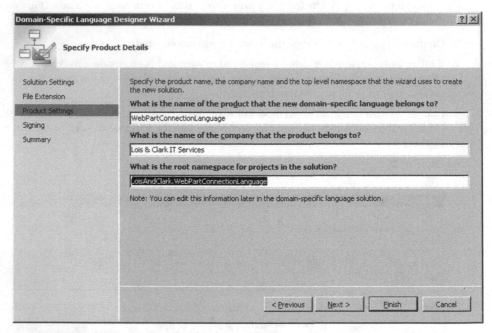

Figure 5-44. *Specify Product Details window*

Note You might see a security warning stating that running this text template can potentially harm your computer. Just click OK to run the template. All the text template does is generate the code that is needed to create a new domain-specific language.

This creates a new solution called WebPartConnectionLanguage and two new projects called Dsl and DslPackage. A basic DSL solution contains two or three projects:

- *Dsl project:* This project defines the DSL itself.

- *DslPackage project:* This project determines how the DSL Toolkit couples to Visual Studio 2005 (it determines the look and feel of the DSL).

- *Setup project:* Although not created by default, most DSL solutions will also contain a setup project. DSL Setup projects are used to deploy DSL solutions.

The Dsl and DslPackage projects contain text templates that are used to generate code. This code is required to run the DSL. As soon as the new solution is created, automatically all text templates are used to generate the required code for the MinimalLanguage template. Wait until the transformation of all text templates is finished, and then make sure that DslDefinition.dsl of the Dsl project is selected. DslDefinition.dsl contains the definition of the domain model, which defines the entities and relationships that exist in any given DSL. The default domain model for our WebPartConnectionLanguage language is shown in Figure 5-45.

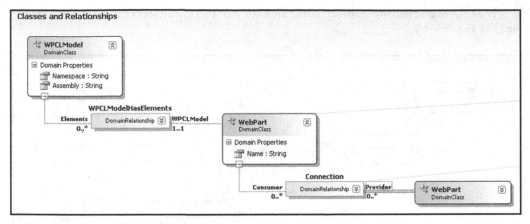

Figure 5-45. *Default domain model*

Adding Support for Web Parts

Figure 5-45 shows the MinimalLanguage template domain model. The domain model starts with the definition of the ExampleModel root domain class, which can be found at the upper-left corner of Figure 5-45. Root domain classes are the starting point of every DSL. The ExampleModel root domain class has a relationship with the ExampleElement domain class, called the ModelHasElements relationship. This relationship expresses that our WPCL consists of multiple ExampleElement instances that have a Name property. Since the ExampleModel root domain class has no other relationships, our language cannot contain other kinds of domain classes. The ExampleRelationship relationship expresses that ExampleElement instances can be related to each other. This set of rules constitutes the WPCL so far, which determines the kind of diagrams that can be created with it. Up to this point, the WPCL is not yet very useful. Figure 5-40 shows a small program created via the MinimalLanguage.

We will use this domain model and enhance it step-by-step to build our WPCL. First, you will adjust the MinimalLanguage domain model to accommodate the most basic of needs of the WPCL. You will adjust the current model so that our language consists of web parts that can be related to each other via server-side connections:

1. On the Classes and Relationships swimming lane (located on the left of the canvas, as can be seen in Figure 5-45), click the ExampleModel domain class, go to the Properties window, and change the value of the Name property to WPCLModel.

2. Right-click the DomainProperties section of the WPCLModel domain class ➤ Add New DomainProperty.

3. Set the name of the new property to the following value: **Namespace**. This property will be used as the default namespace of web parts that are generated using a WPCL model.

4. Click the ExampleElement domain class, go to the Properties window, and change the value of the Name property from ExampleElement to WebPart.

5. Click the WebReferencesTargets relationship, go to the Properties window, and change the value of the Name property from WebReferencesTargets to Connection.

6. Click the right side of the Connection relationship, go to the Properties window, and change the value of the Name property from Target to Consumers.

7. Click the left side of the ServerSideConnection relationship, go to the Properties window, and change the value of the Name property from Source to Providers.

The Classes and Relationships section of the basic Web Part Connection Language DSL should look like Figure 5-46.

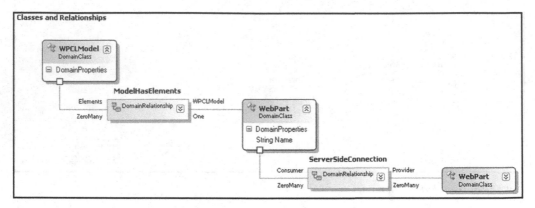

Figure 5-46. *The Classes and Relationships section*

Creating the Look and Feel for Web Parts in the WPCL 2007

You have defined a logical model of the Web Part Connection Language DSL to indicate that our WPCLModel consists of WebPart domain classes representing web parts.

The WPCL is a graphical language that allows you to create visual models that describe sets of connectable web parts and their relationships. Although we've created the logical part of the domain model that describes web parts, we have yet to translate this logic to a user interface that can be shown in Visual Studio 2005. Next, we will define what a web part shape will look like in the WPCL when displayed in Visual Studio 2005 in a WPCL model.

Although not strictly necessary, for consistency reasons we will rename the connector that binds web parts to other web parts to ConnectionConnector, because the names of the other connectors are structured in the same format.

1. Go to the right swimming lane called Diagram Elements and click the ExampleShape GeometryShape. Go to the Properties window and change the value of the Name property from ExampleShape to WebPartShape.

2. Change the InitialHeight property from 0.75 to 0.5.

3. Change the InitialWidth property from 2 to 1.

4. Change the FillColor property to Linen.

5. Click the ExampleConnector connector, go to the Properties window, and change the value of the Name property from ExampleConnector to ConnectionConnector.

The Diagram Elements section of your base WPCL DSL should look like Figure 5-47.

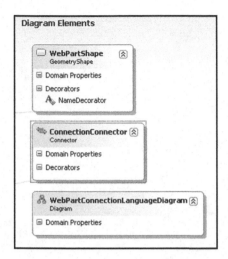

Figure 5-47. *Select domain model diagram elements*

Changing the WPCL Toolbox

If you look back at Figure 5-38, you will see that the toolbox related to class diagram items contains entries for class diagram elements such as Class, Attribute, Class Operation, and Interface. If you compare this to Figure 5-40, you will notice that the toolbox in Figure 5-40 only contains the following elements: ExampleElement and ExampleRelationship. In the next step, we will adjust the toolbox for our WPCL so that it contains elements representing web parts and web part connections. This reflects the entities defined in our logical domain model so far:

1. Click the DSL Explorer tab. This hides the Solution Explorer window.

2. Expand Editor ➤ Toolbox Tabs ➤ WebPartConnectionLanguage tab.

3. Change the Name property from WebPartConnectionLanguage to WPCL General.

4. Expand Tools.

5. Click ExampleElement. ExampleElement is an ElementTool. Change the value of the Name property from ExampleElement to WebPart.

6. Ensure that the WebPart tool is the first in the list. If it's not, right-click WebPart and choose Move Up.

7. Click ExampleRelationship. ExampleRelationship is a ConnectionBuilderTool. Change the value of the Name property from ExampleRelationship to Connection.

The toolbox definition should look like Figure 5-48.

Figure 5-48. *Changing the toolbox via the DSL Explorer*

Creating the Look and Feel for Existing Relationships

At this point, you have decided that web parts are allowed to have connections to each other in your project. Since the WPCL is a graphical language, you will also need to define what such a relationship will look like when you start to create programs written in the WPCL. First, we will create a new icon that will be used to represent a connection in our WPCL toolbox:

1. Open the Solution Explorer and go to the Resources folder of the Dsl project. Copy ExampleConnectorToolBitmap.bmp (the one that currently represents a connection), and rename the copy **ConnectionConnectorToolBitmap.bmp**.

2. If you click on this bitmap, a simple Colors toolbox appears that helps you customize the images, should you feel the need to. The images will appear later on the toolbox of our WPCL. In this case, we will leave the connection toolbox image as it is. This can be seen in Figure 5-49.

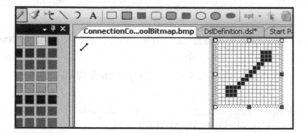

Figure 5-49. *Connection toolbox image*

Next, you will change the look and feel of the connection shape that will be used within the WPCL. Basically, what we will do in this section is make sure connections are black. Furthermore, you will add a Label property to all relationships, which allows developers using the WPCL to annotate them. You will also define that the default names of relationships will be shown at the upper-left corner:

1. Double-click DslDefinition.dsl and switch to the DSL Explorer.

2. Expand the Connection Builders node.

3. Ensure that there is a connection builder called ConnectionBuilder. This builder represents the Connection Domain Relationship.

4. In the DSL Explorer, expand the Connectors node and select ConnectionConnector.

5. Change the value of the DashStyle property to Solid.

6. In the Diagram Elements section of DslDefinition.dsl, right-click the Decorators section of the ConnectionConnector diagram element and choose Add new Text decorator.

7. Call this decorator **Label**.

8. Switch back to the DSL Explorer, expand Connectors ➤ ConnectionConnector ➤ Decorators and select Label.

9. Set the value of the DefaultText property to Connection.

10. Set the Position property to SourceTop.

■**Note** Connector maps are used to relate logical relationships to connector shapes. You can find connector maps in the DSL Explorer by expanding the Diagram node ➤ Connector Maps. If you do this, you should find a connection map called ConnectionConnector. A connection map has a property called Relationship, which refers to an existing type of relationship, in this case the Connection relationship. It has a Connector property, which refers to an existing connector, in this case ConnectionConnector.

Making a Domain Property Editable in a WPCL Diagram

You may have noticed that domain property objects have a property Is UI Read Only, which is by default set to false. For certain domain properties, it is desirable that they be shown in visual domain elements in a WPCL diagram, and can be edited there. Setting the Is UI Read Only property to false is not enough to accomplish this. In the next procedure, you will learn how to make a domain property editable in a WPCL diagram:

1. Open DslDefinition.dsl.

2. Select the IWebPartField domain class.

3. Select View ➤ Other Windows ➤ DSL Details. This opens the DSL Details – Delete Behavior of Domain Class IWebPartField window.

4. Click the Mapping Details icon. This opens the DSL Details – Share Mapping < - - > IWebPartField window.

5. Select the Decorator Maps tab.

6. In the Decorators section, check the Name check box.

7. In the Display property drop-down list, select Name.

8. Repeat the previous six steps for the following domain classes: IWebPartRow, IWebPartTable, IWebPartParameters, and CustomInterface.

You can also create editable properties for connection connectors. In the following procedure, you will see how you can do this for the ConnectionConnector and the ImplementsConnector.

1. Open ConnectionConnector in the Diagram Elements swimming lane in the DSL Details window.

2. Click the Mapping Details icon. This opens the DSL Details – Connector Mapping ConnectionConnector < - - > Connection window.

3. Select the Decorator Maps tab.

4. In the Decorators section, check the Label check box.

5. In the Display property drop-down list, select Label.

6. Repeat the same steps for ImplementsConnector.

Testing the First Version of the WPCL

Creating a domain model for the very first time is a somewhat abstract activity. It is helpful to build the DSL solution to see what you have accomplished thus far. If you switch to the Solution Explorer and click the Transform All Templates on the Solution Explorer toolbar (shown in Figure 5-50), all text templates in the DSL solution are transformed. The text templates are responsible for creating the code required for creating our WPCL.

Figure 5-50. *Transform All Templates*

After the transformation is complete, you can build the DSL solution. If you press F5 to start debugging the solution, a new instance of Visual Studio 2005 is started. The new instance of Visual Studio 2005 is a so-called *experimental build*, which means that the new instance uses its own registry hive called the *experimental hive*. This safeguards the original Visual Studio 2005 instance from any changes caused by the experimental instance. You can start Visual Studio 2005 using the experimental registry hive by running the following command from the Visual Studio 2005 command prompt:

```
[drive letter]:\Program Files\Microsoft Visual Studio 8 ➡
\Common7\IDE\devenv /RootSuffix Exp
```

The experimental hive is created upon installation of the Visual Studio 2005 SDK; installation creates a clone of the existing Visual Studio registry hive and makes a new copy in the experimental hive.

The new instance of Visual Studio 2005 shows what the WPCL looks like thus far. If it is not selected by default, double-click the file test.wpcl. This is a WPCL item that allows you to work with the WPCL. Figure 5-51 shows a sample diagram made using the base version of the WPCL you have created at this point.

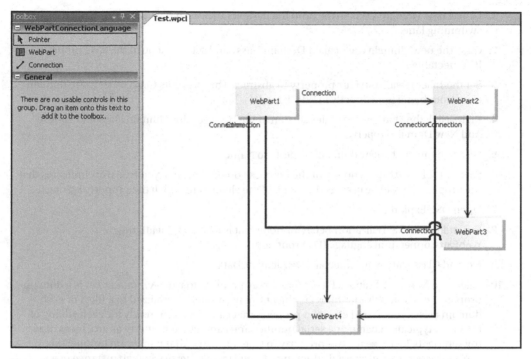

Figure 5-51. *Basic version of WPCL*

Adding IConnectable Interfaces

When building a graphical language that helps to create connectable web parts, there is no doubt that web parts and types of web part connections are key parts of such a language. However, so far, a crucial element of a language for creating connectable web parts is missing: connectable interfaces, such as IWebPartField and IWebPartRow. In the next part, we will add connectable interfaces to the WPCL.

First of all, the domain model needs to reflect the fact that not can only web parts be added to the WPCLModel root domain class, but interfaces as well. As we do not want to add a relationship between the WPCLModel root domain class and every type of connectable interface (five in total, please refer to the section "Interfaces and Transformers" for additional information), we will create a new domain class called IConnectable (a name we invented ourselves; don't try to find this one in the SharePoint documentation). You will add a relationship between the WPCLModel domain class and the IConnectable domain class called ModelHasInterfaces. The ModelHasInterfaces relationship expresses the fact that a WPCLModel can contain interfaces. In our domain model, we will make sure that every connectable interface, such as IWebPartField, inherits from IConnectable. This way, the ModelHasInterfaces relationship applies to every child of IConnectable.

You will also add a new relationship between the WebPart domain class and the IConnectable domain class, called Implements. The Implements relationship expresses the fact that a web part can implement one or more connectable interfaces.

The next procedure adds the possibility to use IConnectable classes within WPCL models:

1. Drag a new Domain Class shape onto the designer canvas in the Classes and Relationships swimming lane.

2. Click the new domain class called DomainClass1 and set the value of the Name property to IConnectable.

3. Set the InheritanceModifier property to abstract. This prevents the IConnectable domain class from being used directly in WPCL models.

4. Right-click the DomainProperties section of the IConnectable domain class and choose Add New DomainProperty.

5. Set the name of the new domain property to **Name**.

6. Set the IsElementName property of the new Name domain property to true (this indicates that the property should be used as the name of the element to which the property belongs).

7. Open DSL Explorer.

8. Expand the Xml Serialization Behavior node that is located beneath the WebPartConnectionLanguage (Dsl) root node.

9. Expand Class Data ➤ IConnectable ➤ Element Data.

10. Select the Name node and set its IsMonikerKey property to true. A *moniker key* is a domain property that uniquely identifies an object when a model is serialized to a file. For each domain class, you should choose a property that can be set differently for each sibling of the class, typically a name or a serial number. You can mark a property as an ElementName (by setting its Is Element Name property to true) to ensure that names are unique; this causes the designer to give a distinct initial value to a property when an instance of a domain class is created. Although not required, often a property that is marked as being a moniker key is also marked as being an element name.

11. In the Toolbox, click Embedding Relationship, then click the WPCLModel domain class and drag the embedding relationship all the way down to the IConnectable domain class.

12. Select the new domain relationship shape called WPCLModelHasIConnectable and set its Name property to ModelHasInterfaces.

13. Select the right side of the Implements relationship and set the Name property to Interfaces.

14. Drag a new Domain Class shape to the designer canvas and set the Name property to IWebPartField.

15. In the Toolbox, click Inheritance.

16. Click the IWebPartField domain class and drag the mouse to the IConnectable domain class. This creates an inheritance relationship where the IConnectable domain class is the parent of the IWebPartField domain class.

17. Repeat the previous three steps for the following domain classes: IWebPartRow, IWebPartTable, IWebPartParameters, and CustomInterface.

18. In the Toolbox, click Reference Relationship.

19. Click the WebPart domain class and drag the mouse to the IConnectable domain class. This creates a new reference relation between web parts and IConnectable interfaces.

20. Click the new reference relation (called WebPartReferencesIConnectable) and choose the following value for the Name property: **Implements**.

21. Right-click the Implements domain class and add a new domain property called Label.

22. Click the right side of the Implements relationship and change the Name property to IConnectableInterfaces.

Figure 5-52 shows a part of the WPCL definition. As you can see, the IConnectable domain class has several children, such as the IWebPartField domain class. The ModelHasInterfaces relationship that expresses that a WPCLModel can contain multiple interface domain classes is shown in Figure 5-52 as well.

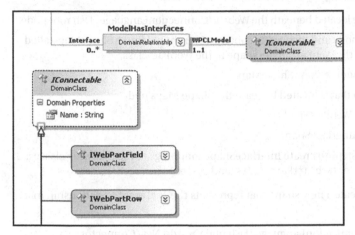

Figure 5-52. *Interfaces of Web Part Connection Language DSL*

Adding Visual Representations for Interface Items

Now that you have created IConnectable interface domain classes for the WPCL, you will need to add interface items to the toolbox as well, thus enabling developers using the WPCL to add interfaces to a WPCL diagram. In this section, you will create a new interface shape, create a new shape that is used to model the Implements relationship, create a new icon that is used in the toolbox to represent the Implements relationship, and create a new toolbox tab that hosts the new toolbox interface elements.

In the following steps, you will add a new interface shape that represents the Implements relationship:

1. Drag a new Geometry Shape to the Diagram Elements swimming lane of the designer canvas.

2. Select the new geometry shape called GeometryShape1, and set the value of the Name property to the following value: **InterfaceShape**.

3. Set the FillColor property of the InterfaceShape shape to Bisque.

4. Set the Geometry property to RoundedRectangle.

5. Set the InitialHeight property to 0.5.

6. Set the InitialWidth property to 1.

7. Set the OutlineDashStyle to Dash.

8. Switch to the DSL Explorer and expand the Shapes node that is located beneath the WebPartConnectionLanguage (Dsl) root node.

9. Right-click the InterfaceShape shape ➤ Add New TextDecorator.

10. Set the Name property to the following value: **NameDecorator**.

11. Set the `FontStyle` property to Italic.

12. Set the `Position` property to Center.

Next, you will map the newly created interface shape to the `IConnectable` domain classes. This tells Visual Studio 2005 how to display interfaces in a WPCL model:

1. Expand the Diagram node located beneath the WebPartConnectionLanguage (Dsl) root node.

2. Expand the Shape Maps node and inspect its contents. You should find a ShapeMap called WebPartShape that maps the WebPartShape shape to the WebPart class.

3. Right-click the Diagram node ➤ New ShapeMap.

4. Select the new ShapeMap that is located beneath the Shape Maps node.

5. Set the `Class` property to IWebPartField.

6. Set the `Shape` property to InterfaceShape.

7. Repeat the previous four steps to create InterfaceShape mappings to the following classes: `IWebPartRow`, `IWebPartTable`, `IWebPartParameters`, and `CustomInterface`.

Next, follow these steps to create a new shape that represents the `Implements` relationship in a WPCL model:

1. Right-click the WebPartConnectionLanguage (Dsl) node ➤ Add New Connector.

2. Expand the Connectors node and select the new connector (Connector1).

3. Set the `Name` property to the following value: **ImplementsConnector**.

4. Set the `DashStyle` to Dash.

5. Set the `TargetEndStyle` property to the following value: **HollowArrow**.

6. Right-click the ImplementsConnector node ➤ Add New TextDecorator.

7. Expand the Decorators node and select the new decorator (TextDecorator1).

8. Set the `Name` property of the text decorator to Label.

9. Set the `FontStyle` property to Italic.

10. Right-click the Diagram node beneath the WebPartConnectionLanguage (Dsl) root node ➤ Add New ConnectorMap. This opens the Pick ConnectorMap relationship and connector dialog box.

11. In the Relationship drop-down list, choose Implements.

12. In the Connector drop-down list, choose ImplementsConnector.

Now you will create a toolbox tab for the WPCL toolbox. You will add icons that represent the IConnectable interfaces to this new tab:

1. Expand the Editor node located beneath the WebPartConnectionLanguage (Dsl).

2. Right-click the Expand the Editor node and choose Add New Toolbox Tab.

3. Select the new toolbox tab and change the value of the `TabText` property from WebPartConnectionLanguage2 to WPCL Interfaces.

4. Right-click the Interfaces Toolbox tab ➤ Add New Element Tool.

5. Select the new Element tool (ElementTool1) that is located under the Tools node.

6. Set the `Name` property to IWebPartField.

7. Set the Class property to IWebPartField.

8. Set the ToolboxIcon property to Resources\ExampleShapeToolBitmap.bmp.

9. Repeat the previous six steps for the following classes: IWebPartRow, IWebPartTable, IWebPartParameters, and CustomInterface.

To complete the WPCL toolbox, you will create and add a new icon that represents the Implements relationship:

1. Click Solution Explorer and expand the Resources folder of the Dsl project.

2. Copy ExampleConnectorToolBitmap.bmp and rename the new image ImplementsConnectorToolBitmap.bmp. We have adjusted the image a little bit so that it looks like Figure 5-53.

Figure 5-53. *ImplementsConnectorToolBitmap.bmp*

3. Double-click DslDefinition.dsl.

4. Open DSL Explorer.

5. Expand Editor ➤ Toolbox Tabs ➤ WPCL General.

6. Right-click the WPCL General node ➤ Add New Connection Tool.

7. Select the new connection tool (ConnectionTool1) and set the Name property to Implements.

8. Set the Connection Builder property to ImplementsBuilder.

9. Set the ToolboxIcon property to Resources\ImplementsConnectorToolBitmap.bmp.

Making the Interface Shapes Visible on the Canvas

In earlier versions of the DSL Toolbox, this was not sufficient to make the new shapes (such as the IWebPartField shape) visible on the designer canvas of a WPCL diagram. In such cases, you needed to use the DSL Details window to specify an explicit parent element for every (new) interface domain class. Luckily, you do not have to do this anymore. Nevertheless, it might be interesting to inspect this setting in the Mapping Details of a domain shape. You will need to use this window anyway to ensure that a property in a WPCL diagram is editable, which will be discussed shortly. Opening the DSL Details window is discussed in the next procedure:

1. Click View ➤ Other Windows ➤ DSL Details. This opens the DSL Details Window.

2. On the designer canvas that allows you to create WPCL models, select the IWebPartField domain class.

3. On the DSL Details window, click the Mapping Details tab.

4. On the General Tab, note that the Parent Element path is set to ModelHasInterfaces.WPCLModel/!WPCLModel (see Figure 5-54).

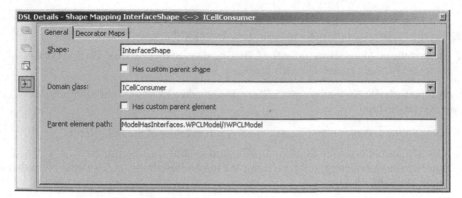

Figure 5-54. *The DSL Details window*

If you want to make sure a property in a WPCL model is editable, you need use the DSL Details window to make this happen. Follow these steps to make a property editable within a WPCL model:

1. Choose a Geometry shape that contains a property that you want to edit within a WPCL diagram.

2. Open DSL Details window (View ➤ Other Windows ➤ DSL Details).

3. Click the Mapping Details button.

4. In the Decorators list, click the Labels check box.

5. In the Display property drop-down list, choose Name.

So far, we have discussed everything you needed to do to create the WPCL. Because of space constraints, we will not discuss adding the InformationObject to the WPCL. InformationObjects are discussed in detail in the section "A Domain-Specific Language: Using WPCL 2007." The next procedure discusses a high-level overview of what you need to do to introduce InformationObjects to the WPCL (everything you need to know to follow this procedure has already been discussed in this chapter):

1. Add a domain class called InformationObject.

2. Add three domain properties to this class called Name, DataType, and DefaultValue.

3. Add reference relationship between web parts and information objects.

4. Add a visual representation for InformationObject items.

5. Add a visual representation for relationships between web parts and information objects.

6. Map domain class to shape.

7. Map connection to shape.

8. Add a relationship connector called MapInterfaceToInformationConnector.

Generating the WPCL

If you transform all text templates and run the solution, you can try out the WPCL in a new instance of Visual Studio 2005. Figure 5-55 shows the toolbox available for WPCL diagrams.

Figure 5-55. *The WPCL toolbox*

Figure 5-56 shows a model that has been created using the WPCL.

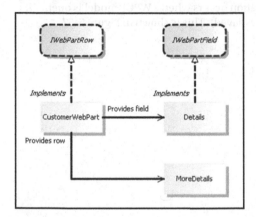

Figure 5-56. *A WPCL diagram*

Validation

The domain model created in the section "Creating a Domain Model" contains basic validation rules. For example, an IWebPartField web part provider is not allowed to provide data to an IWebPartTable consumer web part. The ability to check for semantic correctness in a domain model will only take you so far. Since the WPCL is governed by a number of additional and advanced validation rules (discussed in the rest of this section), we will need to provide another method of validation.

This is done by adding validation rules in the form of methods of partial classes. The name of a partial class corresponds to the name of the domain model class that you want to validate. The validation framework applies each validation rule to each object in the WPCL model that corresponds to the given domain class or its subclasses. This allows users of our DSL to run validation on WPCL models.

Validation Events

Validation rules can be applied to any domain class in a DSL, including the root model and relationships. You can enable validation for the following events:

- Menu: If you enable this option, users can validate a model by right-clicking anywhere in the model.
- Save: If you enable this option, users validate a model every time they save it to a file.
- Open: If you enable this option, users validate a model every time they open it from a file.
- Custom: If you enable this option, you invoke validation from your custom code.

Before you start adding custom validation rules, you should enable validation rules for the Menu, Save, and Open events. You can do this by selecting the DSL Explorer, expanding the Editor node, which is located under the WebPartConnectionLanguage (Dsl) root node, and selecting the Validation (Validation) node. Set the following properties to true: UsesMenu (validation occurs when the validate menu option is selected), UsesOpen (validation occurs when a WPCL model is opened), and UsesSave (validation occurs when a WPCL model is saved). This is shown in Figure 5-57.

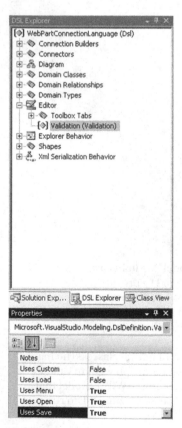

Figure 5-57. *Enabling Validation events*

Building a Validation Rule That Always Fails

In this section, you will build a set of validation rules that apply to web parts. To enable this, you will add a new partial class to the Dsl project that has a name that is identical to the WebPart domain class. This partial class will contain a validation method that responds to the following validation events: Open, Save, and Menu. In the first version of this validation method, validation will never succeed. Instead, the LogError() method of the ValidationContext object is called. This method receives three arguments: an error description, an error code, and the current domain object causing the error.

1. Right-click the Dsl project ➤ Add ➤ New Item. This opens the Add New Item – Dsl window.

2. Select the following template: Class.

3. Specify the following name: **WebPartValidation.cs**.

4. Click Add.

5. Double-click WebPartValidation.cs and add the following code:

```
using System;
using System.Collections.Generic;
using System.Text;
using System.Collections.ObjectModel;
using Microsoft.VisualStudio.Modeling.Validation;

namespace LoisAndClark.WebPartConnectionLanguage
{
  [ValidationState(ValidationState.Enabled)]
  partial class WebPart
  {
    [ValidationMethod(ValidationCategories.Open | ➡
    ValidationCategories.Save | ➡
    ValidationCategories.Menu)]
    public void ValidateConnections(ValidationContext objContext)
    {
      string strMessage = "My error description";
      objContext.LogError(strMessage, "myerrorcode", this);
    }
  }
}
```

Calling the LogError() method of a ValidationContext object results in the failure of the validation process. You can specify an error code and description that will be displayed by Visual Studio 2005 in the user interface.

Establishing the Web Part Validation Rules

Now that you have established a validation rule that fails all the time, you are ready to add real validation rules. The first set of validation rules that you will add to the WPCL is that each provider is able to communicate with a corresponding consumer of the same type. Table 5-3 shows the basic set of rules of valid web part connections. Please refer back to the section "Web Part Connections" if you need detailed information about this subject.

Table 5-3. *Basic Set of Web Part Connection Validation Rules*

Provider Interface	Consumer
IWebPartField	Field consumer
IWebPartRow	Row consumer
IWebPartTable	Table consumer
IWebPartParameters	Parameter consumer
Custom interface	Custom interface consumer

The second set of validation rules that needs to be added to the WPCL specifies the remaining compatible interfaces. Those interfaces are compatible because the web part connection framework provides transformers that are able to transform the information provided by a web part provider to something that is understandable to a web part consumer. Table 5-4 provides an overview of the available web part transformers. You can refer back to the section "Web Part Connections" if you need detailed information about this subject.

Table 5-4. *Web Part Transformers*

Provider Interface	Consumer
IWebPartRow	Field consumer
IWebPartRow	Parameter consumer

There are other validation rules that we could have implemented, such as a validation rule that prohibits circular references in web part connections. However, we have chosen to include the validation rules discussed earlier in this section and stop there. We have kept the set of validation rules simple but useful. Having said that, it is easy to extend the set of validation rules if you want to.

Implementing Web Part Validation Rules

In pseudocode, the validation process for the WPCL web part domain class looks like this:

1. Determine web parts that act as a provider to this web part.
2. Determine web parts that act as a consumer to this web part.
3. If this web part is neither a provider nor a consumer, it is valid.
4. A consumer can only have a single provider.
5. Determine interfaces implemented by consumer.
6. Every provider must implement an interface (it does not matter which one).

■Note You can associate a consumer web part with a specific interface—for instance, the IWebPartField interface—if you want to define explicitly that a web part can communicate with certain types of web part providers. You don't have to do this; the WPCL automatically assumes that a consumer web part that is not associated with a specific interface is always compatible with a provider. For documentation purposes, you might want to create an explicit association with an interface in a consumer web part if you think that is more clear.

---

7. Stop the validation process if this web part does not implement any interface. In this case, the web part is always compatible with a provider.

8. If this web part has a provider, let's determine if it's compatible with this web part.

We do not have the space for a thorough discussion of the validation rules, although the complete code can be downloaded from our web site at http://www.lcbridge.nl/download/wpcl2007/validation.txt. To give you a taste of how validating a DSL model works, we have included a couple of short code fragments.

The following code fragment shows how to retrieve the web part providers of the current object (also a web part) that is being validated:

```
LinkedElementCollection<WebPart> objProviders = Connection.GetProvider(this);
```

> **Note** The objects in the WPCL object model that are available are based on the language elements that you created throughout the section "Creating the Web Part Connection Language." You can call the WPCL object model within a text template; this will be discussed in detail in the section "Text Templates."

The following code fragment shows how to retrieve the web part consumers of the current web part being validated:

```
LinkedElementCollection<WebPart> objConsumers = Connection.GetConsumer(this);
```

The following code fragment shows how to retrieve the interfaces implemented by the current web part being validated:

```
List<string> objInterfaces = new List<string>();
foreach (IConnectable objInterface in IConnectableInterface)
{
  objInterfaces.Add(objInterface.GetType().ToString());
}
```

The following code fragment shows how to use the current ValidationContext object that is passed to the current web part being validated:

```
objContext.LogError(strErrorMessage, "ERROR", this);
```

> **Tip** If you want to debug the validation code, just use the Visual Studio 2005 editor like you are used to. Press F5 to debug the solution, which opens another instance of Visual Studio 2005. Break mode will be entered once the first breakpoint in the validation code is reached. Previously we specified that validation logic is run every time we open, save, or validate a WPCL model, so each of these events can trigger the start of a debug session.

Text Templates

So far we have created a domain model and validation logic encompassing the rules related to creating web part connections. At this point, the WPCL can be used to validate the design of and relationships between web part connections. Since we also want to generate code for connectable web parts, we will take the WPCL one step further in this section; we will use text templates to generate code.

Note The code generation techniques demonstrated in this chapter do not include advanced topics such as code regeneration or integration with source versioning systems. If you want to learn more about code generation, we advise you to read the book *Code Generation in Microsoft.NET* by Kathleen Dollard.

Text templates contain text blocks that are used to generate text artifacts, such as a C# source code (.cs) file or an HTML file. A text template generates text artifacts based on information supplied by at least one input source, typically a model.

In this section, we will create a text template that generates code for connectable web parts based on one input source only: a WPCL model. Text templates are files containing a mixture of text blocks and control logic. The control logic is typically used to manipulate the data held within a model. The data generated by the control logic combined with the data in the text blocks are used to produce an output file. A text template looks very similar to a classic ASP page, as you can seen in the next code fragment. This template counts the number of elements present in a WPCL model:

```
<#@ template ➡
inherits=" ➡
Microsoft.VisualStudio.TextTemplating.VSHost.ModelingTextTransformation" ➡
debug="true"#>
<#@ output extension=".txt" #>
<#@ WebPartConnectionLanguage ➡
processor="WebPartConnectionLanguageDirectiveProcessor" ➡
requires="fileName='Test.wpcl'" #>
The number of elements in my WPCL model:
<#= WPCLModel.Elements.Count #>
```

Templates are transformed via the Text Template Transformation Toolkit, which is included in the DSL Toolkit. The Text Template Transformation Toolkit consists of the following components:

- *Text Template Transformation Engine*: This engine is responsible for processing text templates given to it.

- *Hosts*: A host is the interface between the engine and the user environment. Out of the box, you can use the Visual Studio host or a command-line host.

- *Directive processors*: Directive processors handle directives in text templates. Directives are typically used to provide data from an input source (for example, from a model) to a text template. When using the DSL Toolkit, a directive processor is generated for each DSL, so that text templates can access the models in that language as input sources. The following code is an example of a directive processor that uses a WPCL model as input source:

```
<#@ WebPartConnectionLanguage ➡
processor="WebPartConnectionLanguageDirectiveProcessor" ➡
requires="fileName='Test.wpcl'" #>
```

Note The current version of the Text Template Transformation Engine is also called the T4 Text Templating Engine. The T4 engine is used by the DSL Toolkit, but it is also used in the GAT. Chapter 1 discusses the GAT in detail.

Text Template Syntax

A text template can contain a number of block types that can appear in any order:

- Directive
- Text
- Statement
- Expression
- ClassFeature

Directive block types provide instructions to the Text Template Transformation Engine. The syntax for a directive block type looks like this:

```
<#@ DirectiveName [ParameterName = "ParameterValue"]#>
```

There are three types of directives:

- Built-in directives
- Custom directives
- Generated directives

There are five built-in directive block types:

assembly: This directive is equivalent to using the Add Reference feature in Visual Studio 2005. This directive identifies an assembly that is to be referenced, so you can use types that are defined within the referenced assembly. The following code shows an example of an assembly directive:

```
<@ assembly name="MyReferencedLibrary.DLL" #>
```

import: This directive is equivalent to the C# using statement. It enables you to refer to types in the text template without providing a fully qualified name. The following code shows an example of an import directive:

```
<#@ import namespace="LoisAndClark.WebPartConnectionLanguage" #>
```

template: This directive allows you to specify general information about the generated transformation class, a temporary class that is compiled and executed to produce generated text. Examples of such information are code language, class inheritance, and the ability to debug. The template directive allows the use of a number of optional parameters:

- language: This parameter identifies which language is used for code inside statement and expression blocks. By default, this parameter is set to C#.
- inherits: This parameter specifies which class should be used as the base class for the generated transformation class. The base class must be derived from the ModelingTextTransformation class located in the Microsoft.VisualStudio. TextTemplating.VSHost namespace.
- culture: This parameter is used when converting expression blocks to text.
- debug: This parameter determines whether debugging is enabled in the generated transformation class. By default, debugging is set to true.
- hostspecific: This parameter is only used in combination with custom hosts. If this parameter is set to true, you are able to access a property called Host within the text template. The Host property allows you to reference the object hosting the engine.

The following code shows a valid example of a `template` directive:

```
<#@ template ➥
inherits=" ➥
Microsoft.VisualStudio.TextTemplating.VSHost.ModelingTextTransformation" ➥
debug="true"#>
```

output: This directive specifies the extension of the generated text output file. The following code example shows an output directive that specifies a .cs extension for the generated text output file:

```
<#@ output extension=".txt" #>
```

include: This directive is equivalent to the `include` statement in classic ASP. The `include` directive processes text from a specified file and includes it literally in the text template currently being processed. The following code shows an example of the `include` directive:

```
<#@ include file="c:\test.txt" #>
```

Besides the existing built-in directives, there are two other types of directives: custom and generated. Custom directives allow you to create directives that are specific to your custom tools. A typical use of custom directives is to load external data for use within a text template. Generated directives allow you to access models for use within a text template. The following code shows an example of a generated directive:

```
<#@ WebPartConnectionLanguage ➥
processor="WebPartConnectionLanguageDirectiveProcessor" ➥
requires="fileName='Test.wpcl'" #>
```

The next block type we will discuss is the text block type. A *text block* is nonprogrammatic text in a text template that is written directly and literally to the output file of the text transformation. The following code shows an example of a text block:

```
The number of elements in my WPCL model:
```

Statement blocks are used to control the flow of processing in the text template. Code statements are delineated using opening (`<#`) and closing (`#>`) text template tags and must be written in the language specified in the language parameter of the `template` directive. The following code shows an example statement block:

```
<#
  for ( int i = 0; i < 10; i++ )
  {
    WriteLine("Hello");
  }
#>
```

Expression blocks are used to add strings to the generated text output. Expression blocks are delineated by opening (`<#=`) and closing (`#>`) text template tags. The following code shows an example expression block:

```
<#= WPCLModel.Elements.Count #>
```

The final block type is the ClassFeature block type. ClassFeature blocks are used to add helper functions to avoid repeating common code. ClassFeature blocks are delineated using opening (`<#=+`) and closing (`#>`) text template tags. The following code shows an example ClassFeature block. The ClassFeature block contains a method that returns the current date and time:

```
<#@ template ➡
inherits=" ➡
Microsoft.VisualStudio.TextTemplating.VSHost.ModelingTextTransformation" ➡
debug="true"#>
<#@ output extension=".txt" #>
<#@ WebPartConnectionLanguage ➡
processor="WebPartConnectionLanguageDirectiveProcessor" ➡
requires="fileName='Test.wpcl'" #>

Current date and time: <#= GetDateAndTime() #>

<#+
  private string GetDateAndTime()
  {
    return DateTime.Now.ToString();
  }
#>
```

Running this text template results in the creation of a text file called WebPartDescriptions.txt containing the following text:

```
Current date and time: 7/10/2006 11:48:46 AM
```

You can run text templates by adding a new file to a Visual Studio 2005 project; for example, test.tt. Associate the template file with the text template generator tool by clicking test.tt and specifying the following value for the Custom Tool property: **TextTemplatingFileGenerator**. Now, if you right-click test.tt ➤ Run Custom Tool, the text template is executed. Below the text template file (test.tt), you will find a new file with an extension identical to the one specified in the output directive.

Debugging Text Templates

A text template consists of a mixture of text blocks and control logic used to combine the text blocks with the data held within a model to produce an output file. If you want to debug text templates, first you need to set the debug parameter of the template directive to true. It helps to import the System.Diagnostics namespace using the import directive, as this makes adding breakpoints easier. Then you can add a Debugger.Break() statement in the text template where you want to insert a breakpoint. The Debugger class is located in the System.Diagnostics namespace. The following code shows a valid text template containing a breakpoint:

```
<#@ template ➡
inherits=" ➡
Microsoft.VisualStudio.TextTemplating.VSHost.ModelingTextTransformation" ➡
debug="true"#>
<#@ output extension=".cs" #>
<#@ WebPartConnectionLanguage ➡
processor="WebPartConnectionLanguageDirectiveProcessor" ➡
requires="fileName='Test.wpcl'" #>
<#@ import namespace="System.Diagnostics" #>

<# Debugger.Break(); #>
The number of elements in my WPCL model:
<#= WPCLModel.Elements.Count #>
```

As soon as you run the text template, the break statement will execute and you will either be prompted for a debugging session or be taken to the applicable line of code.

Generating Connectable Web Part Code

Unfortunately, we do not have the space for a detailed discussion of the text template that can be used to generate C# code based on WPCL diagrams. The complete code for the text template is included in the WPCL itself, which can be downloaded at http://www.lcbridge.nl/vision/2007/wpcl.htm.

Deploying the Web Part Connection Language

After creating a DSL, you will need to deploy it as well. You can deploy DSL solutions by creating a special Windows Installer package (.msi). In this section, we discuss how to create such a package. If you want more detailed information about this topic, you can refer to the documentation in the Visual Studio 2005 SDK.

■**Tip** If you want to learn more about DSL deployment, check out the book *Domain-Specific Development with Visual Studio DSL Tools.*

The first step of deploying a DSL consists of creating a DSL Setup project. The next procedure explains how to do this:

1. Open the WebPartConnectionLanguage solution.

2. Right-click the solution and choose Add ➤ New Project. This opens the Add New Project dialog.

3. In the Project types section, expand Other Project Types and click the Extensibility node.

4. In the Templates section, select the Domain Specific Language Setup template.

5. In the Name text box, enter the following value: **WPCLSetup**.

6. Click OK.

Deploying this solution results in the addition of a WPCL project item that allows you to create WPCL diagrams. Since we want to create a dedicated WPCL project type based on the Debugging solution discussed throughout this chapter—which also includes the text template that can be used to generate code based on a WPCL diagram—we have not finished yet. In the next step, we will export the Debugging project template and include it in our deployment solution.

1. Start Visual Studio 2005. This time, do not open the WebPartConnectionLanguage solution yet; instead open the Debugging solution that was created earlier by the WebPartConnectionLanguage. By default, this is located in the [path to WebPartConnectionLanguage]\Debugging subfolder.

2. Choose File ➤ Export Template. This opens the Export Template Wizard.

3. On the Choose Template Type page, ensure that the Project template option is selected.

4. In the From which project would you like to create a template drop-down list, choose Debugging.

5. Click Next. This opens the Select Template Options page.

6. Change the Template name to WPCL 2007 Application.

7. Enter the following description: **Project template for the Web Part Connection Language**.

8. Click Finish.

9. Close Visual Studio 2005.

Check that Windows Explorer opens and shows a zip file that contains the WPCL project template created by the wizard (called WPCL2007.zip). In the next procedure, you will add the project template to the deployment solution:

1. Open the WebPartConnectionLanguage in Visual Studio 2005.

2. Add WPCL 2007 Application.zip to the project WPCLSetup by right-clicking the project and choosing Add ➤ Existing Item. This opens the Add Existing Item – WPCLSetup dialog.

3. Select WPCL2007.zip and click Add.

4. Double-click InstallerDefinition.dslsetup, located in the root folder of the WPCLDeploy project.

5. Locate the <vsItemTemplates> section in the InstallerDefinition.dslsetup file; directly below it, add the new <vsProjectTemplates> section shown in the following code fragment:

```
<!- -
  Omitted rest of XML of dslsetup file
  - - >
</vsItemTemplates>
<vsProjectTemplates>
  <vsProjectTemplate localeId="1033" targetDirectories="CSharp" ➥
  templatePath="WPCL 2007 Application.zip" />
</vsProjectTemplates>
```

6. Click Transform All Templates on the Solution Explorer toolbar.

7. Right-click the Deploy project ➤ Build.

Now if you click Show All Files on the Project menu, you will see two important files in the bin\Debug folder: DSLToolsRedist.msi and WebPartConnectionLanguage.msi. WebPartConnection-Language.msi contains your DSL, and DSLToolsRedist.msi contains the necessary run-time components of the toolkit for DSLs. Copy the entire contents of the bin\Debug folder and paste it to the c:\deployment folder of the computer where you want to deploy the WPCL. Create this folder if it does not exist. The destination computer must have the Visual Studio 2005 SDK installed on it. After that, double-click setup.exe and follow the steps presented in the wizard.

Now you have installed the WPCL successfully, and you can start to use it in Visual Studio 2005. If you need more information about using the WPCL, please refer to the section "A Domain-Specific Language: Using WPCL 2007."

■**Tip** If you want to uninstall the WPCL, open Control Panel and double-click Add or Remove Programs. In the list of installed programs, choose WebPartConnectionLanguage, click Remove, and click OK to confirm.

Summary

This chapter showed you how to create a DSL for creating connectable web parts. We have called this language the WPCL. The chapter started with a discussion of software factories, DSLs, and model-driven development. Because our DSL is tied to a very specific problem domain—the creation of connectable web parts—it is essential that you have a good working knowledge of the SharePoint web part connection framework. If you did not have this knowledge, this chapter provided a good overview of this framework. After that, the chapter discussed how to create, deploy, and use the WPCL using the Microsoft DSL Tool.

CHAPTER 6

■■■

Reusing Presentation Layers via Web Services for Remote Portlets

The primary goal of a portal is to stimulate collaboration and enhance efficiency by offering access to people as well as to a collection of content and application services. Gaining personalized access to information, applications, processes, and people is achieved via a single interface: the portal interface.

When building a portal, you need to determine what information your organization needs and where this information comes from. Typically, portals obtain information from local or remote data sources such as databases, transaction systems, syndicated content providers, or remote web sites. Portals render and aggregate this information into *portal pages*.

A portal page is a composite of information. Portals typically incorporate the ability to add individual components to a portal page. Such components are often referred to as *portlets*, although in SharePoint terminology we will call such components *web parts* instead.

The *Web Services for Remote Portlets (WSRP)* protocol is a web services protocol for aggregating content and interactive web applications from remote sources. In this chapter, we will discuss what WSRP is and how it can be of help in portal implementations. After that, we will look deeper into the WSRP specification. In addition, we explain how to configure a generic WSRP consumer web part in SharePoint and how to build WSRP producers.

Getting to Know WSRP

In this chapter, you will learn about WSRP and why it is important for portal products. Then, in the section "WSRP Benefits and Drawbacks," we will really delve into the theoretical side of WSRP. If you are casually interested in WSRP, you might want to glance over this section, although it helps to understand how the Microsoft Office SharePoint Server 2007 WSRP consumer web part works. Later on, in the section "Configuring a WSRP Consumer for Microsoft Office SharePoint Server 2007," we will discuss how to use WSRP in a SharePoint environment.

WSRP is an OASIS (Organization for the Advancement of Structured Information Standards) standard that simplifies the integration of remote content and applications into other applications, most notably portals. Version 1.0 of WSRP was approved in August 2003. The current version of WSRP is version 1.1; version 2.0 is in the making and will probably be approved sometime in 2007. Check the OASIS web site (http://www.oasis-open.org) if you want an update on the status of WSRP version 2.0.

WSRP defines presentation-oriented, interactive web services with a common, well-defined interface and protocol for processing user interactions and for providing presentation fragments. The presentation fragments are suited for mediation and aggregation by portals. WSRP also defines conventions for publishing, finding, and binding such services. WSRP is built on standards such as XML, SOAP, and WSDL. It would not be a serious misrepresentation to describe WSRP as a protocol that defines how to send and receive HTML via SOAP, as this is what WSRP currently is used for most often.

A specification closely related to WSRP is *Web Services for Interactive Applications (WSIA).* If you are looking for information about WSRP, you'll frequently come across references to WSIA, so we might as well prepare you for this. Both specifications are standards for presentation-oriented, interactive web services. WSRP and WSIA let you create web services that include presentation and multipage, multistep user interaction. WSRP defines interfaces to include portal-specific features; WSIA focuses on the framework for creating interactive web services.

Another specification that is mentioned a lot in discussions about WSRP is Sun Microsystems's Java Portlet specification, formerly and better known as the JSR168 specification. Where WSRP is primarily intended as a communication protocol that allows the reuse of a portlet's (or web part's) user interface within another portal, JSR 168 is a Java specification that lets Java-based portlets work within other JSR 168–compliant portal products (such as Vignette Application Portal, IBM WebSphere Portal, and BEA WebLogic Portal). With WSRP, you can share a centrally hosted portlet; with JSR 168, you can send the portlet code itself and use the portlet in another portal product.

WSIA and JSR 168 fall outside the scope of this chapter and are not discussed anymore, but at least you will be able to discern those specifications from WSRP.

The implementation of the WSRP standard requires the presence of WSRP *producers* and WSRP *consumers.* A WSRP producer contains portlets. In general, the WSRP producer implements WSRP-defined web services. To be more specific, there are two kinds of WSRP producers: complex and simple producers. A *complex producer* requires explicit consumer registration, offers more advanced features such as URL rewriting, and has support for a management interface. *Simple producers* lack these features, but do offer support for portal and portlet description, basic portlet and consumer management, and portlet markup.

A WSRP consumer communicates with presentation-oriented web services (WSRP producers). The consumer gathers and aggregates the content and displays it to the end user. Portals are a typical example of WSRP consumers. Consumers route requests from users to the appropriate WSRP producer, which in turn processes the request and sends results back to the consumer. Sometimes a consumer communicates with multiple producers and aggregates the results to send the result back to the end user. Such communication is completely opaque; the end user will never know what communication actually takes place to fulfill a user request.

Approaches for User Interface Reuse

The WSRP specification helps us reuse remote content and/or applications in a portal, but there are alternatives available that do something similar. This section discusses the remote reuse options that are available today:

- *Image*: The image approach is an easy way to reuse a part of the user interface. All you need to do is add an <IMG> tag to a web page and specify the image URL, like so: `<img src="[url]" />`. While image channels are easy to define, they are very limited. This reuse approach can only be used to display the image in the current browser.

- *Inline frame*: The inline frame approach allows you to include a web page into your own web pages. This is very easy to implement: you only need to include an <IFRAME> tag in your web page and provide the URL of the other web page you want to include, like so: `<iframe src="[url]" />`. The problem with this approach is that other web pages might not be well suited for inline framing. The look and feel of your own portal can be broken if a remote web page incorporates its own navigation system or has a distinct appearance that clashes with the style of your own portal. Quite often, remote web pages use JavaScript to prevent inline framing altogether, and some browsers might not even support inline framing at all.

- *Embedded client-side applications*: In this approach, you will build small client-side applications that will be incorporated into portal pages. At the moment, ActiveX controls, Java applets, and Flash applications are the most popular examples of embedded client-side applications. You can also use Ajax to create client-side applications (see Chapter 2), and in the near future, Microsoft's Silverlight will be added to this list. Embedded client-side applications contain the logic for obtaining content or application services. The user interfaces of such applications tend to be feature-rich and easy to replicate across pages and portals. Embedded client-side applications place restrictive demands on clients and are difficult to develop, depending on the diversity of environments where the embedded applications will be hosted.

- *RSS*: RSS stands for Really Simple Syndication. The RSS approach allows you to import content that blends in far better compared to inline-framed remote web pages. RSS content is rendered from RSS files that contain XML describing content, and from the actual content itself. The RSS specification does not support navigation mechanisms, and suppresses control over the look and feel of RSS content. The use of RSS can easily lead to links to external reference points, and thus the undesirable side effect of luring the end user away from your portal.

- *Web proxy/screen scraping*: The web proxy or screen scraping approach tries to convert well-formed HTML from remote web pages into XML and render that XML in your portal. This approach allows you to reuse remote web pages that were not even intended for reuse. This approach lets you leverage the existing HTML knowledge within an organization and gives you complete control over layout and behavior.

  There are also disadvantages to this approach. Creating implementations like this tends to be cumbersome and fragile. Cumbersome because you are consuming remote web pages that were not intended for reuse in this way and that do not have a well-defined communication interface. Consuming such remote web pages is a process of trial and error. Such implementations are fragile, because the author of a remote page typically does not know that you are reusing content and certainly cannot be held responsible for breaking your application, so whenever the content author decides to change or move the page, it probably will break your application.

  Finally, you run the risk of facing legal issues when you reuse content without the explicit consent of the content author. In situations where a third party knows that you are consuming content or application services and takes responsibility for delivering those services, the web proxy/screen scraping approach is the wrong one. In this case, you should choose an approach that allows parties to agree upon a well-defined interface.

- *Traditional web service*: In this approach, a portlet consumes XML and transforms the XML to portal content. For example, the portlet might use XSLT to do the transformation. Nowadays, portlets primarily use web services as the means to obtain XML from remote locations. The use of web services that return XML gives you complete control over layout and behavior as well as well-defined communication interfaces. As a drawback, you need to build logic into the portlets that consume web services so that they are able to do something useful with the XML they obtain. To alleviate this drawback, there are products that make consuming web services and creating a user interface very easy, such as SharePoint Designer or the Business Data Catalog technology that is part of Microsoft Office SharePoint Server 2007.

- *Proprietary remoting*: In this approach, you use a proprietary remoting protocol to obtain content or application services. In a Microsoft environment, you can use .NET remoting or DCOM to perform remote communication. Custom channels offer complete control over layout and behavior as well as well-defined communication interfaces. Portlets that use custom remoting (on the server side) to obtain data are relatively difficult to develop and result in solutions with limited interoperability.

- *WSRP*: WSRP allows a complete interactive channel to be incorporated in other applications (for example, a portal). The maintenance of this interactive channel is managed in a single location. It is easy to add interactive content or application services to a portal using WSRP. WSRP is ideal for offloading work to a server separate from the portal server. But one drawback is that the WSRP specification has not matured yet. Also, it is important to realize that WSRP is not a replacement for traditional web services; WSRP is an addition to them.

Common WSRP Architectures

In this section, we will discuss common usage scenarios for WSRP. Figure 6-1 shows a common pattern for portlets. In this pattern, the actual content is delivered via remote web services. Figure 6-1 represents a SharePoint environment where two portlets (Web Parts 1 and 2) are imported into a web part page on a SharePoint portal. The portlets consume remote web services and are responsible for implementing the presentation layer.

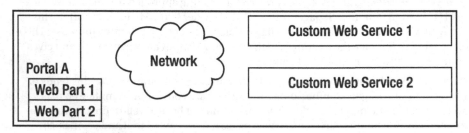

Figure 6-1. *Basic web part architecture*

In this approach, the portlets have to be installed on the portal server, or, in a server farm, on every front end of the portal server. Every portlet that uses our custom web services will need to redevelop the presentation layer. In terms of time and cost, this is not optimal.

Figure 6-2 shows how you can solve these problems while making use of WSRP. In this scenario, the business logic is wrapped in the web services Custom Web Service 1 and 2. This part of the solution is identical to the previous approach. The difference is that we will add two web services containing the presentation logic. Those web services are WSRP producers. The portlets (Web Parts 1 and 2) that contained the presentation layer are replaced with generic portlets that are able to consume WSRP services.

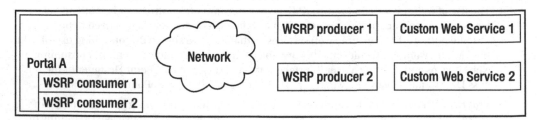

Figure 6-2. *Basic WSRP architecture*

WSRP interfaces are well-defined. All web services that implement the WSRP standard can be plugged into a WSRP-compliant portal. WSRP-compliant portals contain some kind of generic WSRP consumer portlet that is able to communicate with WSRP services. But a portal can do more when it comes to WSRP. If the portal contains a WSRP producer as well, the portal can publish any portlet it contains via a WSRP service. This will be completely opaque to the portlet developer. These WSRP services can then be consumed by other WSRP-compliant portals.

A typical WSRP architecture looks like Figure 6-3. (It looks different in SharePoint environments, but we will get to that later.) You can see that Portal A is a WSRP producer. Some of these WSRP services are consumed by Portal B, a WSRP-compliant portal that contains a generic WSRP consumer portlet to do so. The portal contains a number of portlets that are made available to other applications via Portal B's WSRP producer. WSRP consumers, such as Portal C, are able to consume Portal B's portlets via Portal B WSRP services. Portal C uses its own set of generic WSRP consumer portlets to consume those services. User agents such as browsers consume the markup returned by Portal B.

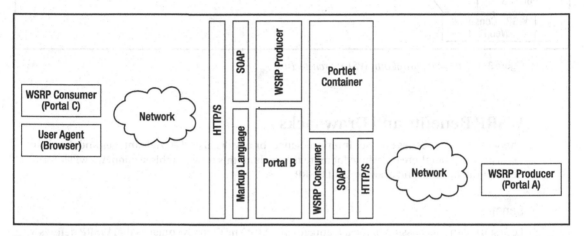

Figure 6-3. *A typical WSRP architecture*

It is important to keep this typical architecture in mind. Realizing that WSRP is created for reusing portlets at the presentation level in other portals is essential to understanding the entire specification.

When it comes to WSRP, Microsoft has a different vision compared to portal vendors implementing WSRP producers in their portal products. In the Microsoft view, a SharePoint portal consolidates all information on a big centralized server. In this view, there is no need to share the user interface of web parts via WSRP services with other portals. Instead, if you need access to content or application services, you should go to the central SharePoint portal. Do not expect a WSRP producer to be included in SharePoint technology anytime soon. However, Microsoft Office SharePoint Server 2007 does contain a WSRP consumer that is able to reuse a user interface from other applications (such as other portals).

This is not to say that WSRP cannot play a role in SharePoint portals. WSRP consumers can be of great help when consolidating content and applications in a central location. This results in an architecture as shown in Figure 6-4. Here you see a traditional web service that contains the business layer. The WSRP web service encapsulates the presentation layer. WSRP consumer web parts in various portals are able to consume these services.

■Note Since other portal products, such as IBM WebSphere, support WSRP producers, you can also use the SharePoint WSRP Consumer web part to consume services from such providers.

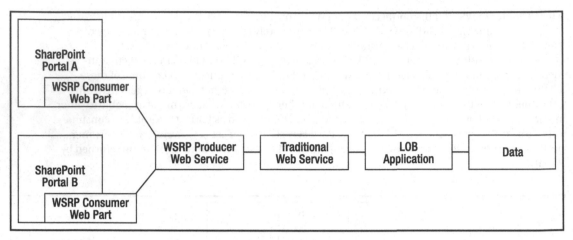

Figure 6-4. *A typical SharePoint WSRP architecture*

WSRP Benefits and Drawbacks

The section "Approaches for User Interface Reuse" briefly discussed the advantages and disadvantages of WSRP, but there is a whole lot more to say about this topic. In this section, we will look in detail at the benefits and drawbacks of WSRP.

Benefits

Let's start with a discussion of the advantages of WSRP. The first advantage is that WSRP defines a standard for remote content and application service reuse at the presentation level. Without WSRP, most scenarios for remote content and application service reuse involve custom coding. Because WSRP interfaces are common and well-defined, all web services that implement the WSRP standard can be consumed by WSRP consumers. In a portal, all you need is access to a generic WSRP consumer portlet. Using such a portlet, even nontechnical users are able to incorporate WSRP services into a portal in a plug-and-play fashion.

Another advantage of WSRP is that it allows applications to reuse presentation layers, thus saving investment in good user interfaces. Although in principle every kind of application can be a WSRP consumer, the specification is created for use in portals, as portals are applications that aggregate and reuse information.

The next advantage is related to reusing portal content itself. If you are using a portal that includes a WSRP producer (such as Vignette Application Portal, IBM WebSphere Portal, and BEA WebLogic Portal, but not Microsoft Office SharePoint Server 2007), you can integrate the user interface of your portlets into other portals. Again, this does not require any coding on your part. WSRP allows you to integrate content and application services into other applications in a fast and easy way while keeping costs low.

If you are consuming a content service, you need to determine whether the content producer or the content consumer is responsible for the look and feel of the content. An advantage of WSRP in the former scenario is that it enables content producers to maintain complete control over layout and behavior of their content. This reduces the distribution-of-updates problem frequently faced in other solutions.

WSRP is advantageous in server farm scenarios. WSRP allows content and application services to be hosted in the environment most sensible for their execution (regardless of location or platform), while remaining easy to access by WSRP consumers. This makes WSRP an attractive candidate in distributed computing and load-balancing scenarios. This results in flexible, interoperable and scalable architectures that decouple portal aggregation from portlet execution. A result of this flexibility is that it is easy to switch to new WSRP producers.

WSRP is a standard that can be used in all sorts of environments and scenarios, because it is agnostic to what and how it communicates. As a protocol, WSRP is agnostic to the markup type being communicated between WSRP producers and consumers. WSRP is also agnostic to the protocol that is used for communication. Having said that, a typical WSRP solution uses HTML as the markup type and HTTP as the communication protocol, which fits well into the security infrastructure of most companies. WSRP can be used in all sorts of environments because it builds on standards such as XML, SOAP, and WSDL, and is supported by large players in the industry (for example, BEA, IBM, Microsoft, Oracle, and Sun).

WSRP decouples deployment and delivery of applications. WSRP consumers get to use the latest version of remote content or application services, independent of where portlets are physically deployed. Portals are able to consume WSRP services without deploying any additional code on the portal server at all, resulting in zero installation effort on the portal. This way, portal developers and administrators get to focus on building and managing a portal; other developer groups can focus on building WSRP-compliant portlets.

WSRP services deliver data and presentation logic. Traditional web services are data-oriented; they contain business logic but lack presentation logic. As a result, every client needs to implement its own piece of presentation logic. Providing presentation logic via a WSRP service makes it easy to dynamically integrate business applications. This way, consumers get the complete package. This is not to say that WSRP services replace traditional web services; instead, WSRP services complement traditional web services.

Drawbacks

We have looked at the benefits of WSRP, but there are drawbacks as well. In this section, we will look into them. The goal of WSRP is rather ambitious: is it indeed possible to build highly interactive applications that can be exposed to different portal products and offer a unified and secure experience completely opaquely to the end user?

The first problem is that application service providers do not have a great incentive to build WSRP producers. For example, if you sell an ERP application that holds mission-critical data, you might ask yourself why you'd want to expose your services to other portals. This does not sound like a sure way to make money. Until now, major vendors have shown that they do not have any problems creating WSRP consumers for their products, but the effort put into creating WSRP producers for their own application services is considerably less. Having said this, this doesn't stop you from creating your own WSRP producers that can be used freely in, let's say, an intranet environment.

The next disadvantage is that although interactive, WSRP offers a limited experience compared to full-blown portlets. A normal portlet utilizes programming models such as JavaScript, DOM, and embedded client-side applications. In generic WSRP portlets, you have less control over the user interface, using JavaScript is more problematic, and some types of interactivity are hard to achieve. For example, Ajax-style development is considerably more complex in WSRP scenarios. In WSRP 1.0 and WSRP 1.1, you are allowed to include JavaScript within a markup fragment, but you cannot include JavaScript outside the <body> of the aggregated page. A WSRP portlet cannot use external style sheets provided by a WSRP consumer. You can, however, create a common look-and-feel across portlets on an aggregated page, as is discussed in the section "CSS Style Definitions." Locally running portlets will usually be faster than calling remote WSRP services. Local portlets typically have access to information about the portal server, portal site, and portal pages hosting the portlet, and to other portlets as well. In the future, new versions of the WSRP specification will solve at least some of these problems.

Another disadvantage the additional security issues in WSRP scenarios. Because WSRP consumers have little or no control over the contents of markup fragments sent by WSRP producers, unknown code (for example, client-side JavaScript) can be embedded in WSRP responses, which makes WSRP consumers vulnerable to script injection attacks. This means you need to have a considerable amount of trust in the WSRP producers you are using. The creators of the WSRP specification think this will not be a big concern for WSRP consumers because of inherent client-side JavaScript limitations. Optionally, WSRP responses can contain binary data as well, but it is up to the consumer to decide how to interpret and use this binary data.

■**Note** In addition to being subject to script injection issues, a WSRP service is exposed to the same security issues as other web services. The WSRP specification will leverage existing and forthcoming web service standards such as WS-Security. Currently, a typical WSRP solution that needs to be secure uses HTTPS and the combination of client and server certificates.

Another problem with the WSRP specification is the question about its usefulness compared to a (in some scenarios) competing and hugely successful technology: RSS. RSS can be used for basic content syndication. RSS is simple and very popular. Although WSRP provides a richer content delivery mechanism, RSS is already used in lots of content syndication scenarios, thus limiting the role WSRP can play in those scenarios.

It can be hard to work with WSRP because the WSRP specification is quite complex, although this problem is alleviated by several commercial vendors building WSRP frameworks and tools. For .NET, the only vendor we know of that is offering a WSRP framework is a company called NetUnity (http://www.netunitysoftware.com).

Another disadvantage of WSRP is related to speed and performance. WSRP introduces additional latency because user interaction needs to pass through the WSRP consumer to the remote WSRP provider. The WSRP protocol typically uses SOAP over HTTP, which brings a considerable amount of overhead. WSRP consumers send two kinds of data to WSRP consumers: form parameters and uploaded data. For HTTP POST requests, this data is sent as multipart requests to the WSRP consumer, which transports the data within a SOAP envelope to the WSRP producer. This takes up additional memory and processing power on the servers hosting WSRP consumers and WSRP producers. WSRP solutions are not optimized for speed and performance.

WSRP can be used to aggregate content from multiple sources. Although WSRP offers mechanisms to standardize the look of this content, those mechanisms are superficial, resulting in a user experience that may not always be optimal. If a WSRP consumer aggregates markup fragments from various producers, you have no guarantee that every WSRP producer will follow the same style and naming conventions. For example, Form A might contain a Submit button; a comparable Form B might contain a Proceed button. As another example, date formats might be represented in different ways in different forms. For yet another example, field and form validation requirements may differ between forms. WSRP addresses only part of this problem by specifying a standard set of CSS styles that can be defined by WSRP consumers. Although this enhances consistency, user experience usability issues remain.

A danger of using WSRP producers in a portal is that they invite you to promote portlets at the presentation level only, as this level of reuse is available automatically after creating a portlet. This results in applications that are not really built with reuse in mind, or that reuse at the wrong level. If you refer back to Figure 6-3, you will see that WSRP promotes reuse at the presentation level. If you are building applications that need to be reused, it can be a mistake to offer reuse only at the user interface level. Always consider whether it makes sense to offer a traditional web service encapsulating business logic as well. Refer back to Figure 6-4 to see a diagram depicting this kind of architecture.

Finally, there are some drawbacks to the maturity of web service standards. The WSRP specification itself does not currently include eventing, security, and caching. Instead, WSRP builds on other web service standards to provide these features. Those standards have not yet matured, which can also be said for WSRP itself.

Delving Deeper into the WSRP Specification

In most situations, developers implementing an architecture involving WSRP will have little or nothing to do with the WSRP specification itself, as this will be abstracted away by a portal or framework. This holds true for the examples discussed later in the chapter, where we will show how to use a WSRP consumer in SharePoint and build a WSRP producer using a WSRP .NET framework. Nevertheless, it is helpful to gain a better understanding of the underlying WSRP technology. In this section, we will take a closer look at the WSRP specification and discuss the most important aspects of the specification.

■Note This section describes how the interfaces that make up the WSRP specification are described in SOAP. Typically, you will not have to construct SOAP messages yourself; this will be handled by WSRP producers and consumers.

Interfaces

The WSRP specification defines four communication interfaces:

- Service Description
- Registration
- Markup
- Portlet Management

A WSRP producer may be discovered through discovery mechanisms such as UDDI (Universal Description, Discovery and Integration) and WSIL (Web Services Inspection Language). Listing 6-1 shows an example WSRP service WSDL file that specifies the locations of services responsible for implementing the four WSRP interfaces:

Listing 6-1. *Describing a WSRP Service in WSDL*

```
<?xml version="1.0" encoding="UTF-8"?>
<wsdl:definitions targetNamespace="urn:oasis:names:tc:wsrp:v1:wsdl" ➥
  xmlns:bind="urn:oasis:names:tc:wsrp:v1:bind" ➥
  xmlns=http://schemas.xmlsoap.org/wsdl/ ➥
  xmlns:wsdl=http://schemas.xmlsoap.org/wsdl/ ➥
  xmlns:soap="http://schemas.xmlsoap.org/wsdl/soap/">

  <import namespace="urn:oasis:names:tc:wsrp:v1:bind" ➥
    location="wsrp_v1_bindings.wsdl"/>

  <wsdl:service name="WSRPService">
    <wsdl:port binding="bind:WSRP_v1_Markup_Binding_SOAP" name="WSRPBaseService">
      <soap:address location="http://my.service:8080/WSRPService"/>
    </wsdl:port>
    <wsdl:port binding="bind:WSRP_v1_ServiceDescription_Binding_SOAP" ➥
      name="WSRPServiceDescriptionService">
      <soap:address location="http://my.service:8080/WSRPService"/>
    </wsdl:port>
    <wsdl:port binding="bind:WSRP_v1_Registration_Binding_SOAP" ➥
      name="WSRPRegistrationService">
      <soap:address location="http://my.service:8080/WSRPService"/>
    </wsdl:port>
```

```
    <wsdl:port binding="bind:WSRP_v1_PortletManagement_Binding_SOAP" ➡
      name="WSRPPortletManagementService">
      <soap:address location="http://my.service:8080/WSRPService"/>
    </wsdl:port>
  </wsdl:service>
</wsdl:definitions>
```

The Service Description interface is required and provides the means for a consumer to ascertain the capabilities of a WSRP producer and the portlets it has to offer. The Service Description interface defines only a single method called getServiceDescription(). This method is responsible for providing information about the capabilities of a producer in a context-sensitive manner. For example, a consumer may be required to register itself first before it is allowed to discover the full capabilities of a producer.

The following code fragment shows an example of a web service call to the getServiceDescription() method of the Service Description interface:

```
POST /wsrp/wsrp4j/WSRPServiceDescriptionService HTTP/1.0
Content-Type: text/xml; charset=utf-8
Accept: application/soap+xml, application/dime, multipart/related, text/*
User-Agent: Mozilla/4.0 (compatible; MSIE 6.0; ➡
MS Web Services Client Protocol 1.1.4322.2300)
Host: localhost
Cache-Control: no-cache
Pragma: no-cache
SOAPAction: "urn:oasis:names:tc:wsrp:v1:getServiceDescription"
Content-Length: 499

<?xml version="1.0" encoding="UTF-8"?>
<soapenv:Envelope xmlns:soapenv="http://schemas.xmlsoap.org/soap/envelope/" ➡
  xmlns:xsd="http://www.w3.org/2001/XMLSchema" ➡
  xmlns:xsi="http://www.w3.org/2001/XMLSchema-instance">
  <soapenv:Body>
    <getServiceDescription xmlns="urn:oasis:names:tc:wsrp:v1:types">
      <registrationContext>
        <registrationHandle>22.34.152.220_2039571409459_4</registrationHandle>
      </registrationContext>
    </getServiceDescription>
  </soapenv:Body>
</soapenv:Envelope>
```

The Registration interface is used to register or deregister a WSRP consumer with a WSRP producer. This interface defines the following methods: register(), modifyRegistration(), and deregister(). The register() method is used to establish a relationship between a consumer and a producer. It returns a handle that is used in all subsequent invocations the consumer makes. Consumers and producers are free to end this relationship at any time. If the consumer ends the relationship, it must call the deregister() method. A producer indicates it wants to end the relationship by informing the consumer via an error message. The modifyRegistration() method is used by the consumer to modify a relationship.

The following code fragment shows an example of a web service call to the register() method of the Registration interface:

```
<soap:Envelope xmlns:soap="http://schemas.xmlsoap.org/soap/envelope/" ➡
  xmlns:xsi="http://www.w3.org/2001/XMLSchema-instance" ➡
  xmlns:xsd="http://www.w3.org/2001/XMLSchema">
  <soap:Body>
    <register xmlns="urn:oasis:names:tc:wsrp:v1:types">
      <consumerName>wsrpConsumer</consumerName>
      <consumerAgent>wsrpConsumer.1.1</consumerAgent>
      <methodGetSupported>false</methodGetSupported>
    </register>
  </soap:Body>
</soap:Envelope>
```

The Markup interface is required and contains operations to request the generation of
markup and the processing of interactions with that markup. This interface defines the following
methods: getMarkup(), performBlockingInteraction(), initCookie(), and releaseSessions().
The getMarkup() method requests the markup for rendering the current state of a portlet. The
performBlockingInteraction() method is used for synchronization purposes. A portlet will
receive only one invocation of this method per client interaction, and will persist some sort of
state change within the portlet. The consumer has to wait for the response before invoking the
getMarkup() method on the portlets it is aggregating. This allows the WSRP producer to share state
between portlets. The initCookie() method is used in scenarios where the WSRP consumer assists
in managing state via cookies and allows the consumer to supply cookies. The releaseSessions()
method enables the consumer to inform the producer that it will no longer be using session information. The following code fragment shows an example response from a WSRP producer after a
call to the Markup interface's getMarkup()method:

```
<soapenv:Envelope xmlns:soapenv="http://schemas.xmlsoap.org/soap/envelope/">
  <soapenv:Body>
    <urn:getMarkupResponse xmlns:urn="urn:oasis:names:tc:wsrp:v1:types">
      <urn:markupContext>
        <urn:mimeType>text/html; charset=UTF-8</urn:mimeType>
        <urn:markupString>
          <![CDATA[<form name="searchForm" ➡
          action="http://localhost:7001/consumer/test.portal?_nfpb=true ➡
          &_windowLabel=search_1_1&_pageLabel=test_page_2&wsrp- ➡
          urlType=blockingAction&wsrp-url= ➡
          &wsrp-requiresRewrite=&wsrp-navigationalState=&wsrp-interactionState= ➡
          _action%3D%252FSearch%252Fsearch&wsrp-mode=&wsrp-windowState=" ➡
          method="post">
          <table>
          <tr valign="top">
          <td>First Name:</td>
          <td> ➡
            <input type="text" name="search_1{actionForm.firstName}" value=""> ~
          </td>
          </tr>
          <tr valign="top">
          <td>Last Name:</td>
          <td><input type="text" name="search_1{actionForm.lastName}" value=""></td>
          </tr>
          </table>
          <br/>
          <input type="submit" value="search">
          </form>]]>
        </urn:markupString>
```

```
          <urn:locale>en-US</urn:locale>
          <urn:requiresUrlRewriting>false</urn:requiresUrlRewriting>
        </urn:markupContext>
        <urn:sessionContext>
          <urn:sessionID>
            B9Ml78JJyZNrMbzKnPxfyXZj511LL420BfKZGmLssNGO2DbSJm3y!-1979539005
          </urn:sessionID>
          <urn:expires>3600</urn:expires>
        </urn:sessionContext>
      </urn:getMarkupResponse>
    </soapenv:Body>
</soapenv:Envelope>
```

The Portlet Management interface is used to manage portlets. It can be used for operations such as cloning portlets, destroying portlets, and retrieving portlet definitions. This interface defines the following methods: getPortletDescription(), clonePortlet(), destroyPortlets(), setPortletProperties(), getPortletProperties(), and getPortletPropertyDescription(). The getPortletDescription() method allows the producer to provide information about the portlets it offers in a context-sensitive manner. The clonePortlet() method allows the creation of a new portlet from an existing portlet. The initial state of a cloned portlet will need to be identical to the original portlet. Basically, this is a copy-by-value action that can be used to copy a producer-offered portlet, resulting in a consumer-configured portlet. You can also use the clonePortlet() method to copy previously cloned consumer-configured portlets. Consumer-configured portlets can be discarded by calling the destroyPortlets() method. Portlet properties are specific to a portlet. The setPortletProperties() method allows the consumer to set portlet properties. The getPortletProperties() method exhibits the opposite behavior: it is used to retrieve portlet meta-data. The getPortletPropertyDescription() method is used for discovering portlet properties and information such as type and description about those properties. This information can be used when generating a user interface for editing the portlet's configuration.

The following code fragment shows an example of a web service call to the clonePortlet() method of the Portlet Management interface:

```
<soap:Envelope xmlns:soap="http://schemas.xmlsoap.org/soap/envelope/" ➡
  xmlns:xsi="http://www.w3.org/2001/XMLSchema-instance" ➡
  xmlns:xsd="http://www.w3.org/2001/XMLSchema">
  <soap:Body>
    <clonePortlet xmlns="urn:oasis:names:tc:wsrp:v1:types">
      <registrationContext>
        <registrationHandle>AAAUU111yy777...</registrationHandle>
      </registrationContext>
      <portletContext>
        <portletHandle>portlet_1</portletHandle>
      </portletContext>
      <userContext>
        <userContextKey>wsrpConsumer</userContextKey>
      </userContext>
    </clonePortlet>
  </soap:Body>
</soap:Envelope>
```

State

Sometimes you need to keep track of the session state of a WSRP portlet. If you find yourself in such a situation, you can choose between multiple WSRP portlet state types:

- URL state
  - Navigational state
  - Interaction state
- Session state
- Persistent state

The URL state type can be divided in two subtypes: portlet navigational state and portlet interaction state. Portlets that use navigational state let WSRP consumers take care of keeping track of most of the state. The only part of the portlet state that gets pushed to the consumer is navigational state. Portlet navigational state identifies the current view of the portlet. Examples of the use of navigational state include support for page refreshes and bookmarks.

Portlets that use interaction state let WSRP consumers take care of keeping track of the state, but also push interaction state to the consumer. Portlet interaction state identifies what action should be taken by a portlet.

In session state scenarios, a WSRP producer establishes a session and returns some sort of handle (a session ID), which is returned by the consumer on all subsequent invocations of a portlet instance. Session state is transient, can expire, and can be stored on the consumer or producer side. Session state is user- and portlet-specific.

In persistent state scenarios, the state is kept in some type of permanent data store, typically a database, and held for the entire lifetime of a portlet. The WSRP producer is responsible for keeping track of persistent state. Persistent state is typically used to store portlet configuration.

Portlet Mode

A portlet should render different content and perform different activities based on its state and the operation requested by the end user. The WSRP specification defines a set of modes that reflects common functionality for portal-to-portlet interactions. WSRP defines the following modes:

- `wsrp:view`
- `wsrp:edit`
- `wsrp:help`
- `wsrp:preview`
- Custom mode

The `wsrp:view` mode will render portlet markup reflecting the current state of a portlet. This mode will include one or more screens that the end user can view, navigate, or even interact with. In `wsrp:edit` mode, a portlet should provide content and logic that lets the user customize the behavior of a portlet. The `wsrp:help` mode provides context-sensitive help. If a portlet is in `wsrp:preview` mode, the portlet should render a preview of the standard content shown in `wsrp:view` mode. Finally, consumers can declare additional custom modes.

Window State

Window state is an indicator of the amount of page space that will be assigned to the content generated by a portlet. It is up to the consumer to decide how much information will be rendered eventually. WSRP defines the following window states:

- `wsrp:normal`
- `wsrp:minimized`
- `wsrp:maximized`

- wsrp:solo
- Custom mode

In the wsrp:normal window state, the portlet is likely sharing the aggregated page with other portlets. Therefore, the size of its rendered output should be restricted. The wsrp:minimized window state indicates the portlet should not render visible markup. The portlet is free to include nonvisible data such as JavaScript or hidden forms. A portlet in the wsrp:maximized window state is likely to be the only portlet being rendered on the aggregated page, or the portlet is assigned more space compared to other portlets on the aggregated page. In this case, a portlet can generate richer content if it wants to. The wsrp:solo window state is comparable to the wsrp:maximized window state. It indicates that the portlet is the only portlet being rendered on the aggregated page, so the portlet is free to generate richer content. Finally, consumers are allowed to declare additional custom window states.

Markup URLs

Portlets return markup, typically in the form of HTML markup. Often, a portlet creates URLs that reference the portlet itself. When an end user clicks on a link or submits a form, eventually this should result in a new invocation to the portlet. Portlet URLs embedded in a markup fragment often cannot or should not be direct links. For example, you always have the guarantee that the end user has access to the WSRP consumer. However, the WSRP producer may be shielded from the end user. As another example, the WSRP consumer might want to perform additional operations such as enriching the end-user request with context information. In such scenarios, WSRP consumers will need to intercept end-user requests and reroute them to the WSRP producer.

To facilitate interception mechanisms, URLs need to be encoded. The encoding of URLs is also known as *URL rewriting*. There are two styles when it comes to URL rewriting:

- Consumer URL rewriting
- Producer URL writing

Consumer URL Rewriting

The consumer URL rewriting style renders the URL in markup with delimiters that are replaced by the WSRP consumer with real URLs. The disadvantage of this approach is that the consumer will become more complex and take up more processing time (this does not affect the producer). The following URL is an example of a consumer URL that is marked with delimiters and fit for consumer URL rewriting:

```
wsrp_rewrite?wsrp-urlType=render&wsrp-mode=help&wsrp-windowState=solo/wsrp_rewrite
```

Consumer portlet URLs start with the token wsrp_rewrite, appended by a "?" (question mark). The end of such a URL is another token, wsrp_rewrite, preceded by a "/" (forward slash). The content of a consumer portlet URL consists of name/value pairs separated by "&" (ampersand) characters. The names of those pairs consist of a series of well-known portlet URL parameters, which specify what the consumer needs to do. Currently, the WSRP specification defines the following portlet URL parameters:

- wsrp-urlType
- wsrp-url
- wsrp-requiresRewrite
- wsrp-navigationalState

- wsrp-interactionState

- wsrp-mode

- wsrp-windowState

- wsrp-fragmentID

- wsrp-secureURL

The wsrp-urlType portlet URL parameter must be specified first. This parameter can be set to the following values: blockingAction, render, and resource. If the wsrp-urlType parameter is set to blockingAction, the performBlockingInteraction() method is called on the portlet generating the markup. The performBlockingInteraction() method was described previously in the section "Interfaces." If the wsrp-urlType parameter is set to render, the getMarkup() method is called. Finally, if the wsrp-urlType parameter is set to resource, the WSRP consumer will try to retrieve some sort of resource, possibly in a cached manner, and return it to the end user.

The wsrp-url parameter provides the actual URL to a resource. The URL needs to be absolute and URL-escaped (for example, use & instead of &). The wsrp-requiresRewrite parameter is a Boolean parameter that tells the WSRP consumer whether it needs to parse a URL for consumer URL rewriting. The wsrp-navigationalState parameter defines the navigational state of a portlet, as determined by the WSRP consumer and send to the WSRP producer. The wsrp-interactionState parameter contains the interaction state provided by the consumer. The wsrp-mode parameter requests a change of portlet mode. Valid values are wsrp:view, wsrp:edit, wsrp:help, wsrp:preview, or a custom mode. Portlet modes were discussed in detail in the earlier section "Portlet Mode." The wsrp-windowState requests a change of window state. Valid values are wsrp:normal, wsrp:minimized, wsrp:maximized, wsrp:solo, or a custom mode. Window states were discussed in detail in the earlier section "Window State." The wsrp-fragmentID parameter specifies a portion of a URL that navigates to a place within a document. The wsrp-secureURL parameter is a Boolean parameter indicating whether a URL needs to be accessed in a secure manner. Setting this parameter to true means that both the communication between the end user and WSRP consumer and the communication between WSRP consumer and WSRP producer need to be secure.

Producer URL Writing

In the producer URL writing style, URL templates are provided by the WSRP consumer and known tokens within those templates are replaced by the WSRP producer. In this approach, the consumer passes context information to the producer. The URL template format is completely up to the WSRP consumer, as the consumer is the only party that knows what the final URL should look like. A disadvantage of this approach is that the dynamic nature of the resulting markup makes it harder to cache. The following URL is an example of a producer URL fit for producer URL writing:

```
http://www.theConsumerPortal.com/site/{wsrp-urlType}?mode= ➥
{wsrp-mode}&amp;navigationalState={wsrp-navigationalState}&amp;
```

A producer URL contains zero or more replacement tokens that are enclosed in curly braces ("{" and "}"). Any content outside the curly braces will not be modified by the WSRP producer. As an example, in the previous producer URL, the WSRP producer might replace the token {wsrp-urlType} with the value render. The list of defined parameters that can be used as replacement tokens in producer URLs is a superset of the set of consumer URL parameters. All parameters from wsrp-urlType to wsrp-secureURL are supported in producer URLs. There are also four new parameters that cannot be used in consumer URLs. These parameters help to establish the correct communication context, which helps to identify the portlet, current user, current instance of the portlet, and the current session state. The parameters are

- wsrp-portletHandle
- wsrp-userContextKey
- wsrp-portletInstanceKey
- wsrp-sessionID

The wsrp-portletHandle parameter identifies the portlet, wsrp-userContextKey identifies the current user, wsrp-portletInstanceKey identifies the current instance of the portlet, and wsrp-sessionID identifies a handle to the current session state. If the consumer includes these parameters, the producer must include these values in the producer-written URL, which helps the consumer to keep track of and establish the current context.

The producer will replace those tokens with actual handles to a portlet, user, portlet instance, and session ID. The values are provided by the consumer itself originally.

Although the exact template format of a producer URL is up to the consumer, the WSRP specification does define various templates that determine the minimal number of URL parameters that must be included in a producer URL. The WSRP specification supplies the following templates:

- blockingActionTemplate
- secureBlockingActionTemplate
- renderTemplate
- secureRenderTemplate
- resourceTemplate
- secureResourceTemplate
- defaultTemplate
- secureDefaultTemplate

The blockingActionTemplate template results in a performBlockingInteraction() method call. When this template is used, a consumer must include the following replacement tokens: wsrp-navigationalState, wsrp-interactionState, wsrp-mode, and wsrp-windowState. The secureBlockingActionTemplate template is identical to the blockingActionTemplate template, but uses secure communication (SSL connections).

The renderTemplate template results in a getMarkup() method call. When this template is used, a consumer must include the following replacement tokens: wsrp-navigationalState, wsrp-mode, and wsrp-windowState. The secureRenderTemplate template is identical to the renderTemplate template, but uses secure communication.

The resourceTemplate template fetches a resource. When this template is used, a consumer must include the replacement tokens wsrp-url and wsrp-requiresRewrite. The secureResourceTemplate template is identical to the resourceTemplate template, but uses secure communication.

The defaultTemplate template is the default template, a generic template that is used whenever a specialized template was not provided by the consumer. When this template is used, a consumer must include the following replacement tokens: wsrp-navigationalState, wsrp-interactionState, wsrp-mode, and wsrp-windowState. The secureDefaultTemplate template is identical to the defaultTemplate template, but uses secure communication.

The following code example shows typical uses of the render, blocking action, and resource producer URL templates within HTML markup:

```
<a href="[render template]">...</a>
<form action="[blocking action template]">...</form>
<img src="[resource template]" />
```

CSS Style Definitions

One of the biggest strengths of the WSRP specification is the ability to create a common look-and-feel across portlets on an aggregated page. This is done by using a common Cascading Style Sheets (CSS) style sheet for all portlets and defining a set of standard styles. Portlets must use these CSS style definitions to be able to participate in a uniform display. For example, to indicate that a text fragment is in the normal page font, you should use the portlet-font style definition:

```
<div class="portlet-font">A normal text</div>
```

■Note CSS Style definitions allow you to brand a portlet in accordance with the requirements of a page. More details about all available style definitions can be found in the OASIS WSRP specification (http://www.oasis-open.org).

Portlet Cloning

In the introduction to this chapter, we stated that portals help to gain personalized access to information, applications, processes, and people. To this end, portals typically contain portlet personalization and customization features. As the WSRP specification is targeted toward portlets, WSRP needs to support the ability for end users to have their own instances of portlets and set their own preferences on those instances. The mechanism that makes this possible is called *portlet cloning* and is done via methods defined in the portlet management interface.

In WSRP, there are two types of portlets:

- Producer-offered portlets
- Consumer-configured portlets

By default, portlets are producer-offered. They are not personalized or customized: producer-offered portlets are preconfigured and not modifiable by consumers. Since personalization and customization are important aspects of a portlet, WSRP allows consumers to clone producer-offered portlets, so that consumers can customize them and change their persistent state. After cloning, the portlet is called a consumer-configured portlet.

There are multiple ways to change the persistent state of a consumer-configured portlet. You can clone a portlet explicitly via the clonePortlet() method defined in the portlet management interface. This method takes the registration context, portlet context, and user context as parameters, and its response returns a new portlet context identifying the new portlet. You can also clone a portlet explicitly; in such scenarios the WSRP consumer creates a portlet clone that is used by a group of end users. This is completely opaque to the end user.

Namespace Encoding

Aggregating multiple portlets from different sources can lead to naming conflicts in portlet elements such as IDs of HTML tags, CSS styles, and JavaScript functions. To create unique names in markup, you can use namespaces. WSRP defines two forms of namespace encoding:

- Producer namespacing
- Consumer namespacing

With producer namespacing, the portlet uses a namespace prefix provided by the consumer to prefix elements in a portlet that need to be unique. The following code shows how producer namespacing is used to create a unique namespace for an HTML form called myform:

```
<form name="NS001_myform" ...>
```

If a portlet prefixes a portlet element that is intended to be unique with the wsrp_rewrite token, the WSRP consumer will locate it and generate a unique namespace. The following code shows how to use this token to create a unique namespace for an HTML form called myform:

```
<form name="wsrp_rewrite_myform" ...>
```

Markup Tag Restrictions

For efficiency reasons, WSRP consumers are not required to validate the markup fragments returned by producers. To allow consumers to safely aggregate multiple portlet markup fragments, there are restrictions placed on the set of markup tags that may be returned by portlets. Disallowed tags can break the coherence of an entire aggregated page. Examples of HTML tags that should never be returned by a portlet are <body>, <frame>, <frameset>, <head>, <html>, and <title>.

There are other tags that, according to the HTML specification, should never occur outside the <head> element of a document. However, some user-agent implementations might support otherwise. As a result of this, it is up to the portlet developer to use or refrain from using those tags. Examples of such tags are <base>, <link>, <meta>, and <style>.

What About WSRP 2.0?

Microsoft Office SharePoint Server 2007 only has support for the WSRP 1.1 specification (in our tests, it does not seem to have problems supporting WSRP 1.0 producers as well). The goal of this specification was to provide basic portlet capabilities, as discussed previously in this chapter. As time has passed, some features have been found to be missing in the current WSRP specification, the biggest problem lying in the lack of portlet interactivity features. Currently, the forthcoming WSRP 2.0 specification is still in draft. The WSRP specification is expected to be completed sometime in 2007.

Note You can find the latest information about the WSRP 2.0 specification at the OASIS web site at http://www.oasis-open.org. The public review draft version of the WSRP 2.0 specification from June 2006 can be found at http://www.oasis-open.org/committees/download.php/18617/wsrp-2.0-spec-pr-01.html. At the time of writing, the WSRP 2.0 specification has not been approved yet.

There are some major improvements in the WSRP 2.0 specification, such as

- Portlet coordination: This allows portlets to communicate in a loosely coupled manner with each other (comparable to web part connections in Microsoft Office SharePoint Server 2007, described in detail in Chapter 5).

- Support for the use of Ajax within portlets. Ajax is discussed in detail in Chapter 2.

- Easy-to-use portlet migration by way of portlet import and export capabilities. This improves portlet portability.

- Improved resource handling.

- Publishing and finding portlets will become easier.

- Leasing: This describes the scheduled destruction of portlets with the opportunity to extend the scheduled termination time.

- Support for portlet runtime IDs.

- Support for CC/PP: CC/PP stands for Composite Capability/Preference Profiles, a specification that allows you to describe device capabilities and user preferences.

- Improved security.

Other improvements, such as support for VoiceXML and complex data-type transport, are still under consideration. We will have to wait and see what the final version of the WSRP 2.0 specification will look like. One thing seems to be certain, though; it will take a considerable amount of time before support for the WSRP 2.0 specification is going to be incorporated into Microsoft Office SharePoint Server 2007.

Configuring a WSRP Consumer for Microsoft Office SharePoint Server 2007

Microsoft Office SharePoint Server 2007 ships with a WSRP consumer called the WSRP Consumer web part. This web part displays portlets that support WSRP 1.1 (in our tests, WSRP 1.0 portlets work just as well). In this section, we will show how to configure the WSRP Consumer web part and use it within Microsoft Office SharePoint Server 2007.

In this section, we do not yet want to create our own custom WSRP producer; this will be discussed later in the section "Implementing a WSRP Producer." Instead, we will use a test WSRP service built by NetUnity (http://www.netunitysoftware.com), a company that provides products and services that enable businesses to develop and deploy portal solutions based on WSRP using the Microsoft .NET platform.

Before using the WSRP consumer web part, you need to configure at least one trusted WSRP producer on the Microsoft Office SharePoint Server 2007 server.

■**Note** If you fail to configure a trusted WSRP producer for your Microsoft Office SharePoint Server 2007 server, you will see an error message when you try to configure a WSRP Consumer web part, stating the following: "No WSRP producers are configured for this site. Contact your administrator to configure trusted WSRP producers."

In this section, we define two trusted WSRP producers, both referring to the NetUnity test WSRP producer. Normally, we would only add one entry to the WSRP producer;\, the only reason we do this twice is to show you that the portal user interface allows you to choose a WSRP producer from the list that is available. The following procedure explains how to configure a trusted WSRP producer that refers to the NetUnity test WSRP producer:

1. Open the Config folder of Microsoft Office SharePoint Server 2007. By default, this folder can be found on the following location: [drive letter]:\Program Files\Microsoft Office Servers\12.0\Config.

2. In this folder, locate the file called TrustedWSRPProducers.xml.sample and rename it TrustedWSRPProducers.config.

3. Open TrustedWSRPProducers.config and replace its contents with Listing 6-2.

Listing 6-2. *Registering a WSRP Producer*

```
<Configuration>
  <Producer Name="Sample1" AllowScripts="true">
    <ServiceDescriptionURL>
    http://wsrp.netunitysoftware.com:80/WSRPTestService/WSRPTestService.asmx
    </ServiceDescriptionURL>
    <RegistrationURL>
    http://wsrp.netunitysoftware.com:80/WSRPTestService/WSRPTestService.asmx
    </RegistrationURL>
    <MarkupURL>
    http://wsrp.netunitysoftware.com:80/WSRPTestService/WSRPTestService.asmx
    </MarkupURL>
    <PortletManagementURL>
    http://wsrp.netunitysoftware.com:80/WSRPTestService/WSRPTestService.asmx
    </PortletManagementURL>
  </Producer>
  <Producer Name="Sample2" AllowScripts="true">
    <ServiceDescriptionURL>
    http://wsrp.netunitysoftware.com:80/WSRPTestService/WSRPTestService.asmx
    </ServiceDescriptionURL>
    <RegistrationURL>
    http://wsrp.netunitysoftware.com:80/WSRPTestService/WSRPTestService.asmx
    </RegistrationURL>
    <MarkupURL>
    http://wsrp.netunitysoftware.com:80/WSRPTestService/WSRPTestService.asmx
    </MarkupURL>
    <PortletManagementURL>
    http://wsrp.netunitysoftware.com:80/WSRPTestService/WSRPTestService.asmx
    </PortletManagementURL>
  </Producer>
</Configuration>
```

Note You can also specify a proxy address using the `ProxyAddress` attribute of the `<Configuration>` element. This address is used when outbound requests are made from the WSRP Consumer web part and no proxy is configured for the web application or the front-end server. You can also add an `<SsoApplication>` element that allows you to specify the name of the SSO application to be used when authenticating to the WSRP producer. Single Sign-On (SSO) is discussed in detail in Chapter 8. The TrustedWSRPProducers.xml.sample file contains examples of both the `ProxyAddress` attribute and the `<SsoApplication>` element.

At this point, you have defined trusted WSRP producers and web services corresponding to the four WSRP interfaces: Service Description, Registration, Markup, and Portlet Management. See the section "Interfaces" earlier in this chapter if you want more information about these interfaces.

Now you are ready to add a WSRP Consumer web part to a page in your portal. In order to test this, we have created a test SharePoint site called WSRPTest. In the next procedure, we will show you how to add and configure a WSRP Consumer web part:

Note If the WSRP consumer does not support secure communication, you will receive a warning that the WSRP producer does not use encryption, so it is possible that network communication might be intercepted. If that is not a problem, you can ignore the message and proceed.

1. Navigate to the WSRPTest site.

2. Click Site Actions ➤ Edit Page. This opens the default web part page in edit mode.

3. Choose any web part zone and click the Add a Web Part link. This opens the Add Web Parts —Webpage Dialog window.

4. Locate All Web Parts ➤ Business Data ➤ WSRP Consumer Web Part and check the WSRP Consumer Web Part check box.

■**Note** The WSRP Consumer web part can be found in any site created using any Microsoft Office SharePoint Server 2007 site definition.

---

5. Click Add. This adds the WSRP Consumer web part to the default web part page.

6. Click the Open the tool page link in the WSRP Consumer web part. This opens the Web Part tool pane.

7. Open the Producer drop-down list and select the Sample1 producer.

8. A new drop-down list called Portlet appears. This drop-down list displays all the portlets that are available on a given WSRP producer. Choose the NetUnity: Document Manager portlet.

9. Since the NetUnity test WSRP producer does not require authentication, you can keep the default User Identification setting that indicates that anonymous access is used.

10. Click OK.

Now, the WSRP Consumer web part tries to communicate with the portlet. In the meantime, the web part shows a message indicating that it is waiting for a response from the portlet server. What happens next depends on the portlet you are consuming. Some portlets will show you a screen that allows you to configure how you want to consume the portlet. Others, such as the Document Manager portlet, just show the result, as can be seen in Figure 6-5.

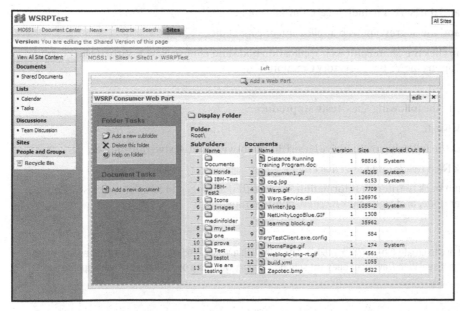

Figure 6-5. *The Document Manager portlet is consumed in a SharePoint portal.*

Implementing a WSRP Producer

In this section, we will show you how to create your own WSRP producer and consume it via the WSRP Consumer web part. On the GotDotNet web site (http://www.gotdotnet.com), you can find the WSRP web service toolkit for SharePoint Products and Technologies 2003. In the previous section, "Configuring a WSRP Consumer for Microsoft Office SharePoint Server 2007," you saw that the toolkit contains a WSRP consumer. The toolkit can also be used to create WSRP producers. As this toolkit really is no more than a proof of concept for the SharePoint development team, and the documentation is quite limited, we do not advise you to use it.

The only option for .NET developers to create WSRP producers that we know and can recommend is to use the commercial WSRP .NET framework created by NetUnity (http://www.netunitysoftware.com). This framework makes creating WSRP producers very easy. You can sign up for a limited free trial version of the framework at the NetUnity web site. The example WSRP producer created in this section is built using NetUnity software.

In this section, we are using version 2.0.0.1 of the NetUnity WSRP .NET Framework, a framework that has support for .NET 2.0. Follow the software's installation procedure and make sure you select all WSRP .NET Framework components and installation options:

- Register Framework Library in Global Assembly Cache (GAC)
- Install WSRP Producer Database Setup Utility
- Install Visual Studio 2005 Templates
- Install Documentation and Development Samples

After installing the WSRP .NET Framework, you need to create a virtual directory that is going to contain the custom WSRP producer. This is explained in the following procedure:

1. Go to the following location: [drive letter]\inetpub\wwwroot.
2. Create a new folder called **testwsrpproducer**.
3. Open a command prompt and type **inetmgr**. This opens the Internet Information Services (IIS) Manager.
4. Expand the [server name] (local computer) node.
5. Expand the SharePoint web application of your choice.
6. Right-click the SharePoint web application node and choose New ➤ Virtual Directory. This opens the Virtual Directory Creation Wizard.
7. Click Next.
8. Specify the following Alias: **testwsrpproducer**.
9. Click Next.
10. Enter the following path: **[drive letter]\inetpub\wwwroot\testwsrpproducer**.
11. Click Next twice, and then click Finish.
12. Switch back to Internet Information Services (IIS) Manager, locate the new testwsrpproducer node, and right-click it. Then, choose Properties.

Note If you try to create a new WSRP producer directly within Visual Studio 2005, you will get an error message stating the Visual Web Developer does not support creating web sites on a SharePoint web application.

---

13. Click the Create button.

14. Click OK.

Now, you have successfully created a new virtual directory that is able to hold the testwsrpproducer WSRP producer. In the next procedure, you will learn how to create your own custom WSRP producer.

1. Start Visual Studio 2005.

2. Choose File ➤ New ➤ Project ➤ Web Site. This opens the New Web Site dialog box.

3. Locate the My Templates section and choose WSRP Producer.

4. Set the Location drop-down list to HTTP.

5. In the location value text box, enter the URL of the virtual folder you created earlier. Our URL looks like this: http://localhost/testwsrpproducer.

6. Click OK. The WSRP producer is created.

You have successfully created a WSRP producer called WsrpProducer.asmx. It is easy to create a WSRP producer using the NetUnity WSRP framework; all you need to do is create a new web service that inherits from the NetUnity.WSRP.Producer class. Listing 6-3 is created using the WSRP Producer template and shows a working WSRP producer:

Listing 6-3. *Base WSRP Producer Class*

```
using System;
using System.Web;
using System.Web.Services;
using System.Web.Services.Protocols;
using NetUnity.WSRP;

[WebService(Namespace = "urn:TODO:Rename")]
[WebServiceBinding(ConformsTo = WsiProfiles.BasicProfile1_1)]
[RequiresRegistration(true)]
[SoapDocumentService(RoutingStyle=SoapServiceRoutingStyle.RequestElement)]
public class WsrpProducer : NetUnity.WSRP.Producer
{
  public WsrpProducer ()
  {
  }
}
```

This is all the code we need to create a WSRP producer that suits the purposes of the example described in this section. The [WebService] attribute can be used to specify a default namespace for the producer. The [WebServiceBinding] attribute is used to indicate that this service conforms to the WS-I Basic Profile 1.1 (you can find more information about this profile at the following location: http://www.ws-i.org/Profiles/BasicProfile-1.1-2004-08-24.html). The [RequiresRegistration] attribute indicates that this WSRP producer requires clients to be registered. By adding the [SoapDocumentService] attribute, you indicate that the web server needs to locate the correct method by looking at the HTTP Request-URI rather than the SoapAction HTTP Header.

Next, we will create two portlets. Later, the SharePoint WSRP Consumer web part will reuse the user interface of those portlets by accessing the WSRP producer.

Although our example WSRP producer contains no custom code at all, by default, a NetUnity WSRP producer is able to find all portlets in the same assembly via reflection. So, when a WSRP consumer calls the getServiceDescription() method described in the WSRP interfaces section, the metadata for all portlets in the producer assembly will be returned. You can override this behavior via the web.config file of a WSRP Producer project and restrict which portlets have their metadata returned or allow the producer to search other assemblies for portlets. In the next procedure, you will create two test portlets:

1. Right-click the App_Code folder of the TestWSRPProducer project and choose Add ➤ Add New Item.

2. In the Templates section, choose the WSRP Portlet and enter the name **TestPortlet.cs**.

3. Click Add.

4. Locate the OnRenderView() method and add the following code:

```
Response.Write("<B>Hello</B>, world!");
```

■**Note** Make sure to add portlets to the App_Code folder of the project; otherwise they will not work.

The complete code for the TestPortlet portlet looks like Listing 6-4.

Listing 6-4. *The Test WSRP Producer*

```
using System;
using System.Web.UI;
using NetUnity.WSRP;

[OfferedHandle("6406eb81-1c38-4039-94b9-19a3599dd88a")]
[Title("TestPortlet")]
[DisplayName("TestPortlet")]
[Modes(PortletMode.View, PortletMode.Edit, PortletMode.Help, ➡
PortletMode.Preview)]
[WindowStates(WindowState.Maximized, WindowState.Minimized, ➡
WindowState.Normal, WindowState.Solo)]
public class TestPortlet : NetUnity.WSRP.Portlet
{
  protected override void OnRenderView()
  {
    Response.Write("<H1>Hello World</H1>");
  }

  protected override void OnRenderEdit()
  {
    //TODO: Add code to render the edit view
  }

  protected override void OnRenderHelp()
  {
    //TODO: Add code to render portlet help text
  }

  protected override void OnRenderPreview()
  {
    //TODO: Add code to render the portlet in preview mode
  }
```

```
protected override void OnAction()
{
//TODO: Add code to handle blocking action (no rendering)
}
}
```

Now it is time to create a second portlet called AnotherPortlet.cs. The following procedure explains how:

1. Right-click the TestWSRPProducer project and choose Add ➤ Add New Item.

2. In the Templates section, choose the WSRP Portlet and enter the name **AnotherPortlet.cs**.

3. Click Open.

4. Locate the OnRenderView() method and add the following code:

```
Response.Write("<H1>Hello</H1>, from my second portlet!");
```

5. Compile the project.

At this point, you have successfully created a WSRP producer that can be consumed so that you can reuse the user interface of two test portlets. As you may have noticed, creating portlets and building HTML programmatically is very similar to creating web parts. Next, you will configure the WSRP Consumer web part so that it knows which WSRP producer to consume and which portlet to reuse.

The section "Configuring a WSRP Consumer for Microsoft Office SharePoint Server 2007" earlier in this chapter explained how to configure a trusted WSRP producer. Please refer to this section if you need more information about this topic. In the following procedure, you will learn how to add configuration information so that the WSRP consumer is able to interact with our custom WSRP producer:

1. Open the Config folder of Microsoft Office SharePoint Server 2007. By default, this folder can be found on the following location: [drive letter]:\Program Files\Microsoft Office Servers\12.0\Config.

2. In this folder, locate TrustedWSRPProducers.config.

3. Open TrustedWSRPProducers.config and add the code from Listing 6-5.

Listing 6-5. *Add the Test WSRP Producer to the SharePoint WSRP Config File*

```
<Configuration ProxyAddress="">
  <Producer Name="MyProducer" AllowScripts="true">
    <ServiceDescriptionURL>
    http://[WSRP producer URL]/testwsrpproducer/WsrpProducer.asmx
    </ServiceDescriptionURL>
    <RegistrationURL>
    http://[WSRP producer URL]/testwsrpproducer/WsrpProducer.asmx
    </RegistrationURL>
    <MarkupURL>
    http://[WSRP producer URL]/testwsrpproducer/WsrpProducer.asmx
    </MarkupURL>
    <PortletManagementURL>
    http://[WSRP producer URL]/testwsrpproducer/WsrpProducer.asmx
    </PortletManagementURL>
  </Producer>
</Configuration>
```

Note The example described in this section is very basic. If you want to create advanced WSRP producers, you should check out the samples folder called WSRPNET20Tutorial in the NetUnity Software directory.

The last step in this example is the configuration of the WSRP consumer. If you need more information on how to do this, please refer to the earlier section "Configuring a WSRP Consumer for Microsoft Office SharePoint Server 2007." If you open a browser and navigate to the SharePoint site containing the WSRP Consumer web part, you will notice the WSRP consumer lets you choose one of the available portlets. This is shown in Figure 6-6.

Figure 6-6. *Choose to consume the TestPortlet WSRP portlet.*

In this example, we chose to consume the TestPortlet WSRP portlet. This portlet displays the text "Hello World". The result is shown in Figure 6-7.

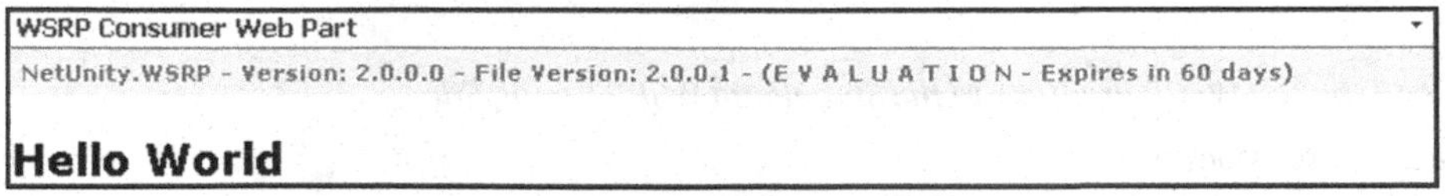

> WSRP Consumer Web Part
>
> NetUnity.WSRP - Version: 2.0.0.0 - File Version: 2.0.0.1 - (E V A L U A T I O N - Expires in 60 days)
>
> **Hello World**

Figure 6-7. *Consuming the TestPortlet WSRP portlet*

Summary

In this chapter, you learned about Web Services for Remote Portlets. You learned about other approaches for remote content and application service reuse. We looked at common architectures for solutions incorporating WSRP. Then, we discussed the advantages and disadvantages of WSRP. We looked in greater detail into the WSRP specification, taking a closer look at all the important aspects of WSRP. You also learned how to configure a generic WSRP Consumer web part for Microsoft Office SharePoint Server 2007. Finally, you saw how to create a WSRP producer using the NetUnity WSRP framework.

CHAPTER 7

■ ■ ■

Changing Code Privileges Using Impersonation, Elevation, and Delegation

Every web part is executed under a given identity. In most cases, this will be the identity of the current logged-on user. But there are times when a web part needs to be able to assume another user context in order to do its work. Normally speaking, changing identities is only a temporary situation. Assuming another user context is widely known as *impersonation*, although we prefer to use the term *impersonation* in a narrower sense. We will discern two types of user identity assumption: impersonation and elevation, which differ only in their intent. We talk about impersonation when a process does something on behalf of someone else. A well-known impersonation scenario is when a web part impersonates the identity of an end user to process a request on behalf of the user instead of using the identity of the application pool that runs the web part. A web part *elevates* when it does something that the current user is not allowed to do. In those types of scenarios, a super account is used to perform the required actions. Elevation is particularly useful for rollup-type web parts: web parts that provide overviews of some sort. You can also discern two types of impersonation based on scope. We call it *impersonation* when a server process impersonates the client security context on its local system; we call it *delegation* when the server process impersonates the client security context on a remote system. This chapter shows you all you need to know about doing impersonation, elevation, and delegation within Microsoft Office SharePoint Server 2007.

Setting Up the Development Environment

In order to test the examples discussed in this chapter, we had to set up a couple of test accounts and test web parts. If you want to try out the examples, we advise you to do the same. We have created three test user accounts, as described in Table 7-1.

Table 7-1. *Test User Accounts Used in This Chapter*

Name	Password	Group
NormalA	normala	Users
NormalB	normalb	Users
SuperB	superb	Administrators

Caution In the examples in this chapter, we often use the SuperB administrator account to demonstrate a specific technique. That does not mean that we advise you to use super accounts that are granted all the permissions
you can think of, because we do believe in granting a user account the minimal set of required permissions
needed to accomplish a task. We use these accounts for educational purposes only.

The following procedure details how to add this group of test users as local user accounts:

1. Open Windows Explorer.

2. Expand the Control Panel node.

3. Expand Administrative Tools.

4. Double-click the Computer Management node.

5. Go to Computer Management (Local) ➤ System Tools ➤ Local Users and Groups ➤ Users.

6. Right-click the Users node and choose New User.... This opens the New User dialog box.

7. Specify the following value for the User name text field: **NormalA**.

8. Specify the following value for the Password text field: **normala**.

9. Specify the following value for the Confirm password text field: **normala**.

10. Uncheck the User must change password at next logon check box.

11. Check the User cannot change password check box.

12. Check the Password never expires check box.

13. Click Create. This adds a normal user to the server.

14. Repeat the previous steps for the users NormalB and SuperB. After adding these user
    accounts, click the Close button.

15. Select the Groups node.

16. Double-click the Administrators group. This opens the Administrators Properties dialog box.

17. Click Add.... This opens the Select Users dialog window.

18. In the Enter the object names to select text area, enter the value **SuperB**, and then click the
    Check Names button.

19. Click OK. The SuperB user account is added to the local administrators group.

At this point, you have successfully added local test users to the server. In the next procedure,
you will assign SharePoint permissions to the newly created normal user accounts:

1. Open a browser and navigate to a SharePoint test site.

2. Click Site Actions ➤ Site Settings. Alternatively, if you browse to a top-level site, click Site
   Actions ➤ Site Settings ➤ Modify All Site Settings. This opens the Site Settings page.

3. In the Users and Permissions section, click the People and groups link. This opens the People and Groups: [site collection] Members page.

4. In the Groups section on the left, click the [site collection] Members link. This opens the
   People and Groups: [members group] page.

5. Click New ➤ Add Users in the list action menu. This opens the Add Users: [site] page.

6. In the Add Users section, in the Users/Groups text area, enter the following value:
   NormalA;NormalB.

7. Click the Check Names icon.

8. In the Give Permission section, under the Give Permission label, make sure the Add users to a SharePoint group radio button is selected and make sure the Add users to a SharePoint group drop-down list is set to [members group] [Contribute].

9. Click OK.

Next, we specify a Full control permission set for the remaining super test users. This is shown in the next procedure:

1. Open SharePoint 3.0 Central Administration.

2. Click Application Management. This opens the Application Management page.

3. In the Application Security section, click the Policy for Web application link. This opens the Policy for Web Application link.

4. Click Add Users. This opens the Add Users page.

5. In the Web Application section, in the Web Application drop-down list, make sure you have selected the correct SharePoint web application.

6. Click the Next button.

7. In the Choose Users section, enter the value **SuperB** in the Users text area.

8. Click the Check Names icon.

9. In the Choose Permissions section, under the Permissions label, select the Full Control - Has full control check box.

10. In the Choose System Settings section, select the Account operates as System check box. This makes sure that any changes made by the SuperB account will be recorded as made by the system instead of the actual SuperB user account.

11. Click Finish.

■**Note** Making accounts "operate as System" is a great option in impersonation, elevation, and delegation scenarios. The System account is so generic, it will be more clear to the end user that some action was executed by SharePoint itself, and not by another user. If an item in a SharePoint list is modified using an account that operates as System, the Modified By column says that an item has been changed by the System account. If you plan to create a user account and use it in such scenarios, we advise you to select this option.

Finally, we have created a new web part called SuperPart. This web part is created using the Web Part project template of Visual Studio 2005 extensions for Windows SharePoint Services 3.0, which we discussed in detail in Chapter 1. The SuperPart web part is used to demonstrate what happens when a piece of code is executed under a different identity. Complete code listings for the SuperPart web part will be provided later in the chapter.

Impersonation and Elevation Within the SharePoint Object Model

The possibilities in the Microsoft Office SharePoint Server 2007 object model for implementing impersonation and elevation scenarios have been enhanced considerably, compared to the 2003 version of the SharePoint object model.

In any .NET application, you can impersonate or elevate code privileges using the `LogonUser()` and `RevertToSelf()` Win32 API functions to access resources that are not controlled by the SharePoint API. These approaches will be discussed in detail later, in the sections "LogonUser" and "RevertToSelf and RunWithElevatedPrivileges."

In Microsoft Office SharePoint Server 2007, implementing impersonation and elevation scenarios can (and actually needs to) be done without using Win32 API functions, and has become easier as well as more reliable.

Note In SharePoint 2003, using the `LogonUser()` and `RevertToSelf()` Win32 API functions did not always work correctly when accessing resources controlled by the SharePoint API. This was a bug in the product, and the exact scenarios where these functions failed were poorly documented. This is solved with the introduction of the `SPUserToken` object and `RunWithElevatedPrivileges` method. When accessing SharePoint resources, you should always use these methods.

You can use the `SPUserToken` object to impersonate code (discussed later in the section "SPUserToken"), and you can use the `RunWithElevatedPrivileges` method to elevate code (discussed in the section "RevertToSelf and RunWithElevatedPrivileges").

LogonUser

Microsoft Office SharePoint Server 2007 offers capabilities to make requests using another user's credentials easy. These capabilities are discussed in the sections "SPUserToken" and "RevertToSelf and RunWithElevatedPrivileges." The `LogonUser()` Win32 API call is comparable to using SharePoint `SPUserToken` objects; both allow you to impersonate any given user account. The difference between the two lies in the kind of resources that you can access. Use the `LogonUser()` function to access non-SharePoint resources. `SPUserToken` objects can help you implement impersonation scenarios where you want to access resources that are controlled by the SharePoint object model.

When you pass an `SPUserToken` object to the constructor of certain objects within the SharePoint object model (such as `SPSite`), the object is instantiated within the context of the user represented by `SPUserToken`. As useful as that might be, this technique will not do you much good when you need to interact with other resources, such as accessing a file located on the server. You will still need the `LogonUser()` function for that. In this section, you will learn how to use the `LogonUser()` Win32 API call to impersonate a user account. In the next section, you will learn how to use the `SPUserToken` object.

If you want to try out the code, you should create a test SharePoint site called PrivilegesTest and make sure the user account called NormalA is added to this site and has contributor permissions. This was described in detail in the section "Setting Up the Development Environment." The current members of this site are shown in Figure 7-1.

Note User SuperB is also a member of this site, but because this account operates as a System account, it is not shown on the Members page.

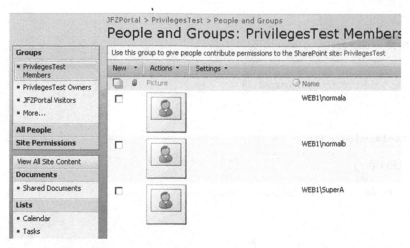

Figure 7-1. *The Manage Users page from the PrivilegesTest site*

In this section, we will use a web part called SuperPart that uses the LogonUser() function to impersonate another user account. If you try to use this web part in a SharePoint environment that runs under the default security permission set (WSS_Minimal), it fails. This is because the web part needs considerable security privileges. The easiest way to solve this is to set the trust level in the <trust> element in the web.config file of the SharePoint application's root web folder to Full, like this:

```
<trust level="Full" originUrl="" processRequestInApplicationTrust="false" />
```

This is not exactly the best security practice. If you need a reminder why setting the trust level to Full can be dangerous, try out Listing 7-1 in a web part. The code in this web part reboots the server. Make sure the trust level in the web.config file is set to Full.

Listing 7-1. *Dangers of Full Trust: Rebooting the Server Within a Web Part*

```csharp
using System;
using System.Runtime.InteropServices;
using System.Web.UI;
using System.Web.UI.WebControls.WebParts;
using System.Xml.Serialization;

using Microsoft.SharePoint;
using Microsoft.SharePoint.WebControls;
using Microsoft.SharePoint.WebPartPages;

namespace LoisAndClark.ImpersonationAndElevation
{
  [Guid("7f6654e9-6a4d-4e3b-85e3-b8f9c98cb42d")]
  public class SuperPart : System.Web.UI.WebControls.WebParts.WebPart
  {
    private const uint REBOOT = 2;

    [DllImport("user32.dll", SetLastError = true)]
    static extern bool ExitWindowsEx(uint uFlags, uint uReason);
```

```
public SuperPart()
{
    this.ExportMode = WebPartExportMode.All;
}

protected override void CreateChildControls()
{
    try
    {
        ExitWindowsEx(REBOOT, 1);
    }
    catch (Exception err)
    {
        Controls.Add(new LiteralControl(err.Message));
    }
}
}
}
```

Note This web part's constructor sets the ExportMode property to WebPartExportMode.All. This code is added automatically whenever you generate a web part using the Visual Studio 2005 extensions for Windows SharePoint Services 3.0. Although it is of no importance to the code discussed in this chapter, it might be useful to understand that this property determines which of a web part's properties can be exported. Other possible values are None and NonSensitiveData. Properties cannot be exported by default; only when they are decorated with the [Personalizable] attribute. If you set the Export mode to None, export is disabled for the web part. If you set the Export mode to NonSensitiveData, the personalization data will not be exported if the [Personalizable] attribute specifies that a property is sensitive by setting the isSensitive parameter to true.

Having noted that setting the trust level to Full is a liability in production environments, doing so is great for experimenting with code and for trying out the examples in this book. Alternatively, you can deploy assemblies to the Global Assembly Cache (GAC).

It is possible to impersonate a user account within the SharePoint object model, which is discussed in section "SPUserToken." It might also be useful to impersonate a user account to be able to access some resource on the server. For such scenarios, using the SharePoint SPUserToken object will not help you. In the next example, you will see how to use the LogonUser() Win32 API function call to access a text file on the server. We will create a text file and explicitly deny access to user NormalA. We will then impersonate the account and use the SuperB account to access the text file. The next procedure shows how to set up the test text file:

1. Create a new text file called test.txt in the c:\temp folder.

2. Add some text to this file.

3. Open Windows Explorer, right-click test.txt, and choose Properties. This opens the test.txt Properties dialog window.

4. Click the Security tab.

5. Click the Advanced button. This opens the Advanced Security Settings for test.txt window.

6. Deselect the Allow inheritable permissions from the parent to propagate to this object and all child objects check box. This opens the Security dialog window.

7. Click Copy.

8. Click OK.

9. Click the Add button. This opens the Select Users or Groups dialog window.

10. Add [domain name]\NormalA user and click OK.

11. Select the Full Control Deny check box.

Now that the test text file and its permissions are set up correctly, we are ready to create a web part that uses the user SuperB account to access the text file's contents. Reading and rendering the content of a text file in a web part can be done using the following two lines of code:

```
string strText = File.ReadAllText(@"C:\Temp\test.txt");
Controls.Add(new LiteralControl(strText + "</br>"));
```

This fails if you are logged in as user NormalA. Now, we will add code to impersonate the SuperB account. We will access the default page of the PrivilegesTest site while logged in as user NormalA, and we will read the contents of the test.txt test file.

The impersonation code makes a Win32 API call to the LogonUser() function to impersonate the SuperB user account. To do this, you will need to import two DLLs: advapi.dll and kernel32.dll. This can be done via the [DllImport] attribute, which can be found in the System.Runtime.InteropServices namespace. Add the import statements to the web part class:

```
[DllImport("advapi32.dll", SetLastError = true)]
static extern bool LogonUser(
  string principal,
  string authority,
  string password,
  LogonTypes logonType,
  LogonProviders logonProvider,
  out IntPtr token);

[DllImport("kernel32.dll", SetLastError = true)]
static extern bool CloseHandle(IntPtr handle);
```

■**Note** If you call the SetLastError() function, you can use the GetLastError() function to determine what went wrong if the call to LogonUser() fails.

Advapi32.dll contains the LogonUser() function, which attempts to log a user on to a local computer. The most important arguments that need to be passed to this function are username, domain, and password. The function returns a boolean value indicating whether the logon was successful. A handle is passed (by reference). This handle is very important because it can be used to create a new Windows identity.

You might have noticed that advapi32.dll uses the LogonTypes and LogonProviders types. These types are enumerations that can be used as arguments for the LogonUser() function. You will need to add the following code to your web part class:

```
enum LogonTypes : uint
{
  Interactive = 2,
  Network,
  Batch,
  Service,
  NetworkCleartext = 8,
  NewCredentials
}
```

```
enum LogonProviders : uint
{
  Default = 0, // default
  WinNT35,
  WinNT40, // uses NTLM
  WinNT50 // negotiates Kerberos or NTLM
}
```

The LogonTypes enumeration contains the following values:

- Interactive: This type of logon operation is used by users who log on to a machine interactively, for example, by logging on via a terminal server. This type of logon is less efficient because it caches logon information to cater to the need to perform disconnected operations.

- Batch: This type of logon operation is used by batch processes that execute operations on behalf of a user without their direct intervention. This is a high-performance logon type that does not cache logon information.

- Service: This type of logon is used by services. The account that is used must be granted the service privilege.

- NetworkCleartext: This type of logon is used by processes that access a machine from the network.

- NewCredentials: This type of logon allows a caller to clone the current security token and specify new credentials for outbound connections.

The LogonProviders enumeration contains the following values:

- efault: This option uses the standard logon provider for the system and is recommended.

- WinNT35: This option uses the Windows NT 3.5 logon provider.

- WinNT40: This option uses the Windows NT 4.0 logon provider.

- WinNT50: This option uses the Windows NT 5.0 logon provider.

Kernel32.dll contains the CloseHandle() function, which closes an open object handle. This function is used to close the handle that is the result of the LogonUser() call.

The WindowsIdentity class in the System.Security.Principal namespace represents a Windows user. It can be useful to retrieve the current Windows identity by calling the GetCurrent() method of the WindowsIdentity class, so you are able to restore the original user context later. If you call the advapi32.dll LogonUser() function, you will obtain a token that can be used to create a new Windows identity. In our example, this will be the SuperB account. If you now call the Impersonate() method of this Windows identity object, a WindowsImpersonationContext object is returned that impersonates the user represented by the WindowsIdentity object. Attempts to read the contents of the test.txt file will succeed, even if you are logged in as user NormalA, because the file is read in the security context of user SuperB.

Calling the Undo() method of the WindowsImpersonationContext object reverts the user context, and then you need to clean up the open object handle (the token) by calling the Kernel32.dll CloseHandle() function. The complete code for this web part is found in Listing 7-2.

Listing 7-2. *Using the LogonUser() Function in a Web Part*

```csharp
using System;
using System.Runtime.InteropServices;
using System.Web.UI;
using System.Web.UI.WebControls.WebParts;
using System.Xml.Serialization;
using System.Security.Principal;
using System.IO;
using Microsoft.SharePoint;
using Microsoft.SharePoint.WebControls;
using Microsoft.SharePoint.WebPartPages;

namespace LoisAndClark.ImpersonationAndElevation
{
  [Guid("47500629-54d5-4ac4-ac44-097b4ce2e3eb")]
  public class SuperPart : System.Web.UI.WebControls.WebParts.WebPart
  {
    [DllImport("advapi32.dll", SetLastError = true)]
    static extern bool LogonUser(
      string principal,
      string authority,
      string password,
      LogonTypes logonType,
      LogonProviders logonProvider,
      out IntPtr token);

    [DllImport("kernel32.dll", SetLastError = true)]
    static extern bool CloseHandle(IntPtr handle);

    enum LogonTypes : uint
    {
      Interactive = 2,
      Network,
      Batch,
      Service,
      NetworkCleartext = 8,
      NewCredentials
    }

    enum LogonProviders : uint
    {
      Default = 0, // default
      WinNT35,
      WinNT40, // uses NTLM
      WinNT50 // negotiates Kerberos or NTLM
    }

    public SuperPart()
    {
      this.ExportMode = WebPartExportMode.All;
    }
```

```
protected override void CreateChildControls()
{
  try
  {
    WindowsImpersonationContext objUserContext;
    IntPtr objToken;
    WindowsIdentity objOrgIdentity;
    WindowsIdentity objIdentity;

    bool blnReturn = LogonUser(@"SuperB", "web1", "superb", ➥
    LogonTypes.Interactive, LogonProviders.Default, out objToken);

    string strValue = String.Empty;

    if (blnReturn)
    {
      objOrgIdentity = WindowsIdentity.GetCurrent();
      objIdentity = new WindowsIdentity(objToken);
      objUserContext = objIdentity.Impersonate();

      string strText = File.ReadAllText(@"C:\Temp\test.txt");
      Controls.Add(new LiteralControl(strText + "</br>"));

      strValue += "Identity name after impersonation: " + " " ➥
      + objIdentity.Name + "<br/>";
      objUserContext.Undo();
      strValue += "Identity name when impersonation is undone: " + ➥
      objOrgIdentity.Name;

      CloseHandle(objToken);
    }
    else
    {
      strValue = "Logon failed!";
    }

    Controls.Add(new LiteralControl(strValue));
  }
  catch (Exception err)
  {
    Controls.Add(new LiteralControl(err.Message));
  }

  }
 }
}
```

The result of executing this web part is shown in Figure 7-2.

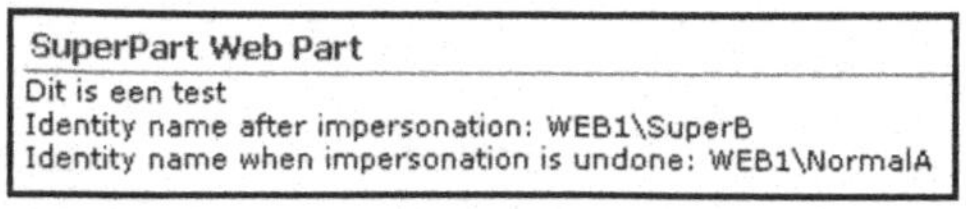

```
SuperPart Web Part
Dit is een test
Identity name after impersonation: WEB1\SuperB
Identity name when impersonation is undone: WEB1\NormalA
```

Figure 7-2. *The SuperPart web part uses the LogonUser() function to access test.txt.*

As you can see in Figure 7-2, the content of test.txt is read successfully, although we are logged in using the NormalA account, which is not allowed to read test.txt. This is because the SuperPart web part uses the LogonUser() function to impersonate the SuperB account, which has sufficient rights to read test.txt.

In this section, you have learned how to access a resource on the server using the LogonUser() Win32 API call.

SPUserToken

If you want to impersonate another user account to interact with the SharePoint object model, you can use the SPUserToken object. In Microsoft Office SharePoint Server 2007, several constructors of SPSite objects accept an SPUserToken object as one of the parameters to establish a different security context.

To demonstrate the use of the SPUserToken object, we will programmatically check out a file on behalf of a different user. We have created a test document called Test.doc and uploaded it to the Shared Documents document library (see Figure 7-3). Make sure that versioning is enabled on the Shared Documents document library. Later in this section, we will use the version history of this document to check whether the code involving the SPUserToken object has succeeded.

Note This example is chosen for educational purposes only, and is probably not something you would do in real life. Recently, we have used the SPUserToken object in combination with the PeoplePicker control (discussed in Chapter 2) to create a web part that is able to determine the roles and site access rights for any given user. That is an example of a realistic use of the SPUserToken object.

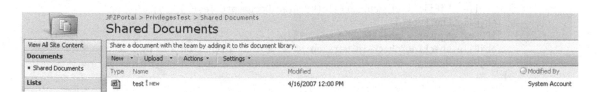

Figure 7-3. *The Shared Documents document library*

In the next example, we will programmatically check out and then check in a document. We have created a web part called SuperPart that is responsible for doing this. The code retrieves the current site collection from the current SharePoint context and gets the PrivilegesTest SharePoint site from this site collection. By default, you are not allowed to check out and check in files in SharePoint using HTTP GET requests. To get around that, our code sample allows unsafe updates on the PrivilegesTest SharePoint site. An instance of SPFile associated with the test document can be retrieved from the PrivilegesTest SPWeb instance. Finally, the code adds some information to the test document's versioning comment. The code responsible for checking out and checking in the test document looks like this (it will be added to the Load event of a web part shortly):

```
SPSite objSite = SPControl.GetContextSite(Context);
SPWeb objWeb = objSite.AllWebs["PrivilegesTest"];
objWeb.AllowUnsafeUpdates = true;
SPFile objFile = objWeb.GetFile("Shared Documents/Test.doc");
objFile.CheckOut();
SPUser objUser = objFile.CheckedOutBy;
objFile.CheckIn("check-in version: " + objFile.UIVersion + ➡
" by " + objUser.Name);
```

The complete code listing of the SuperPart web part looks like Listing 7-3.

Listing 7-3. *Checking Out a File Stored in a Document Library in a Web Part*

```
using System;
using System.Runtime.InteropServices;
using System.Web.UI;
using System.Web.UI.WebControls.WebParts;
using System.Xml.Serialization;
using Microsoft.SharePoint;
using Microsoft.SharePoint.WebControls;
using Microsoft.SharePoint.WebPartPages;

namespace LoisAndClark.ImpersonationAndElevation
{
  [Guid("47500629-54d5-4ac4-ac44-097b4ce2e3eb")]
  public class SuperPart : System.Web.UI.WebControls.WebParts.WebPart
  {
    public SuperPart()
    {
      this.ExportMode = WebPartExportMode.All;
    }

    protected override void OnLoad(EventArgs e)
    {
      SPSite objSite = SPControl.GetContextSite(Context);
      SPWeb objWeb = objSite.AllWebs["PrivilegesTest"];
      objWeb.AllowUnsafeUpdates = true;
      SPFile objFile = objWeb.GetFile("Shared Documents/Test.doc");
      objFile.CheckOut();
      SPUser objUser = objFile.CheckedOutBy;
      objFile.CheckIn("check-in version: " + objFile.UIVersion + " by " +
      objUser.Name);
    }
  }
}
```

In this example, we first navigated to a page containing the SuperPart web part while logged in as user SuperB. This caused the SuperPart web part to load and execute, which checked out and then checked in a document in a document library under the SuperB system account. Then, we logged in as user NormalA and went back to the same page, causing the creation of a new version of Test.doc under the identity of NormalA. Figure 7-4 shows the version history of the test document. The version history can be used to check our results. As you can see, the document was first updated by a system account, followed by an update by the NormalA user.

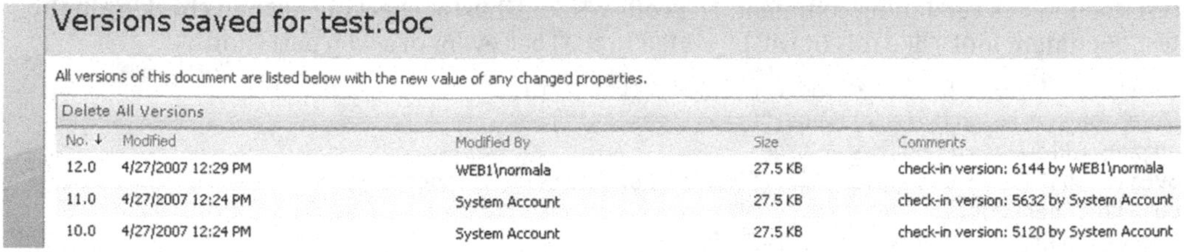

Versions saved for test.doc

All versions of this document are listed below with the new value of any changed properties.

Delete All Versions

No. ↓	Modified	Modified By	Size	Comments
12.0	4/27/2007 12:29 PM	WEB1\normala	27.5 KB	check-in version: 6144 by WEB1\normala
11.0	4/27/2007 12:24 PM	System Account	27.5 KB	check-in version: 5632 by System Account
10.0	4/27/2007 12:24 PM	System Account	27.5 KB	check-in version: 5120 by System Account

Figure 7-4. *Version history of the test document*

Now we are ready to show how to impersonate a user account using the SPUserToken object. We will access the default page of the PrivilegesTest site while logged in as SuperB, but we will check out and check in the file using the NormalB account. To make it easier to concentrate on the impersonation part of the code, copy the code concerning document modification to a new private method called CheckInAndOut() in the web part.

First, the web part needs to retrieve a valid SPUser object from the current SharePoint site representing the NormalB user account. We will use the AllUsers collection of the current SharePoint site to retrieve the NormalB user account. Then, we will need to create an instance of an SPSite object in the context of the NormalB user account. This is done by passing a valid user token representing the NormalB user account. This token is retrieved from a property called UserToken that is a member of an SPUser object. The UserToken object needs to be passed to an SPSite object's constructor in order to impersonate a given user. This is shown in the following code fragment:

```
SPUser user = web.AllUsers[@"web1\NormalB"];
SPSite objSite = new SPSite("http://web1", user.UserToken);
```

The complete code for the web part that uses the NormalB account to check out and then check in a document is shown in Listing 7-4.

Listing 7-4. *Using the SPUserToken Object in a Web Part*

```
using System;
using System.Runtime.InteropServices;
using System.Web.UI;
using System.Web.UI.WebControls.WebParts;
using System.Xml.Serialization;
using Microsoft.SharePoint;
using Microsoft.SharePoint.WebControls;
using Microsoft.SharePoint.WebPartPages;

namespace LoisAndClark.ImpersonationAndElevation
{
  [Guid("47500629-54d5-4ac4-ac44-097b4ce2e3eb")]
  public class SuperPart : System.Web.UI.WebControls.WebParts.WebPart
  {
    public SuperPart()
    {
      this.ExportMode = WebPartExportMode.All;
    }

    protected override void CreateChildControls()
    {
      try
      {
        string strValue = String.Empty;

        SPSite site = SPControl.GetContextSite(Context);
        SPWeb web = site.AllWebs["PrivilegesTest"];
        SPUser user = web.AllUsers[@"web1\NormalB"];

        CheckInAndOut(user);
      }
      catch (Exception err)
      {
        Controls.Add(new LiteralControl(err.Message));
      }
    }
```

```
private void CheckInAndOut(SPUser user)
{
  SPSite objSite = new SPSite("http://web1", ➡
  user.UserToken);
  SPWeb objWeb = objSite.AllWebs["PrivilegesTest"];

  objWeb.AllowUnsafeUpdates = true;
  SPFile objFile = objWeb.GetFile("Shared Documents/Test.doc");
  objFile.CheckOut();
  SPUser objUser = objFile.CheckedOutBy;
  objFile.CheckIn("check-in version: " + objFile.UIVersion + " by " +
  objUser.Name);

  Controls.Add(new LiteralControl(objFile.Name +
  " checked out by: " + objUser.Name));
  }
 }
}
```

The result of executing this web part is shown in Figure 7-5.

```
SuperPart Web Part
Test.doc checked out by: WEB1\normalb
```

Figure 7-5. *The SuperPart uses the SPUserToken object to impersonate the NormalB account.*

It does not matter which account you use to log in to the SharePoint site containing the SuperPart web part; the web part uses the SPUserToken object to impersonate the NormalB account and then checks out test.doc using this account. You can also use the document version history to check this.

■**Caution** As you can see, adding web parts that use this impersonation technique can have an influence on the security model of your SharePoint environment. That is why Code Access Security (CAS) and creating custom security policies are important tools for securing your environment. Basically, you should only allow web parts to impersonate user identities that you trust completely. Discussion of CAS and the creation of custom security policy files falls outside the scope of this chapter. You can find more information about this topic in the MSDN article "Microsoft Windows SharePoint Services and Code Access Security" (http://msdn2.microsoft.com/en-us/library/ms916855.aspx). The information is written for SharePoint 2003, but is still a good starting point to learn about these topics.

In this section, you have learned how to use the SharePoint SPUserToken object. We have used the SPUserToken object to add a new version to the version history of a document stored in a SharePoint list.

Encrypting Sensitive Data via DPAPI

In the previous example, user credentials were stored in the code. It is unsafe to store passwords in plain text in code. This can be avoided by saving the credentials in a configuration file and encrypting the sensitive areas using DPAPI. The *DP* part in DPAPI stands for *Data Protection*. It's an API provided by the operating system since Windows 2000. In .NET 2.0, working with DPAPI becomes significantly easier with the new ProtectedData class that is located in the System.Security.Cryptography namespace.

■**Note** Out of the box, ASP.NET 2.0 provides two encryption providers: RSA and DPAPI. In this section, we use DPAPI to encrypt sensitive data, but we could have used RSA as well. RSA is widely used in electronic commerce protocols and was created by Ron Rivest, Adi Shamir, and Leonard Adleman. The letters RSA are taken from the first letter of each surname and have no real meaning.

The ProtectedData class allows you to encrypt or decrypt data. The class's Protect() method encrypts data. The first argument of this method expects a byte array containing data. Optionally, as the second parameter, you can pass an *entropy parameter*, which is a random value designed to make deciphering more difficult. You could define a unique entropy for each application to prevent other applications from being able to decrypt your sensitive data, although the use of the entropy parameter raises the question of how to manage the entropy information securely. If you do not want to use the entropy parameter, you can pass the value null. The last parameter of the Protect() method allows you to specify the DataProtectionScope. This can be set to CurrentUser or LocalMachine mode. If you use CurrentUser, only the current user will be able to decrypt the information; in LocalMachine mode every process on the machine will be able to decrypt it. For server scenarios in which SharePoint web parts decrypt sensitive information, setting the mode to LocalMachine makes a lot of sense, because there will be no untrusted logins to the server. Client applications should always use CurrentUser mode. The following code fragment shows how to encrypt and decrypt information:

```
string strValue = "secret password";
byte[] arrSecret = Encoding.Unicode.GetBytes(strValue);
byte[] arrEntropy = {0, 1, 2};
byte[] arrEncryptedData = ProtectedData.Protect(arrSecret, arrEntropy, ➨
DataProtectionScope.LocalMachine);
byte[] orgData = ProtectedData.Unprotect(arrEncryptedData, arrEntropy, ➨
DataProtectionScope.LocalMachine);
string strSecret = Encoding.Unicode.GetString(orgData);
```

If you want to try out this code in a web part, make sure the following namespaces are imported:

```
using System.Text;
using System.Security.Cryptography;
```

In this section, you saw how to encrypt sensitive data via DPAPI.

Storing Sensitive Information in an Encrypted Way

At this point, we have shown you how to use DPAPI to encrypt and decrypt data. However, our goal is to show you how to store sensitive information in an encrypted way in a .config file, and we have not yet reached that goal.

Suppose you want to store the password for user NormalA in a .config file. You would create an <add> element under the <appSettings> configuration section, like so:

```
<appSettings>
  <add key="NormalA" value="normala" />
</appSettings>
```

You could add this manually by opening the web.config file. You could also add this information manually via a more advanced user interface by opening the web site properties of the SharePoint virtual server in Internet Information Services (IIS), clicking on the ASP.NET tab, and clicking the Edit Configuration button. You will find the Application settings under the General tab. Finally, you can also add application settings programmatically, and take care of the encryption of sensitive data at the same time. We will demonstrate the last approach.

You can use the WebConfigurationManager in the System.Web.Configuration namespace to retrieve the SharePoint web.config file. The OpenWebConfiguration() method of the WebConfigurationManager class returns a Configuration object. The Configuration object provides access to the AppSettings section in the web.config file via its AppSettings property, which returns an AppSettingsSection object. You can add application settings via the Add() method of the AppSettingsSection object. Using the ProtectSection() method of the ConfigurationSection class, you can determine whether the content of a given configuration section should be encrypted, and, if so, what data protection provider should be used. In the following code fragment, we will use the DataProtectionConfigurationProvider, which uses DPAPI.

```
string strUser = "NormalA";
string strPassword = "normala";
Configuration objConfig = ➥
WebConfigurationManager.OpenWebConfiguration(Context.Request.ApplicationPath);
AppSettingsSection objAppSettings = objConfig.AppSettings;
objAppSettings.Settings.Add(strUser, strPassword);
objAppSettings.SectionInformation.ProtectSection ➥
("DataProtectionConfigurationProvider");
objConfig.Save();
```

If you want to try out this code in a web part, you should add a reference to system.configuration.dll. You should also have write permission on the configuration file. Make sure the following namespaces are imported:

```
using System.Configuration;
using System.Web.Configuration;
```

The <AppSettings> section now looks like this:

```
<appSettings configProtectionProvider="DataProtectionConfigurationProvider">
  <EncryptedData>
    <CipherData>
      <CipherValue>AQAAANCM[…deleted stuff…]fnKLBAw==</CipherValue>
    </CipherData>
  </EncryptedData>
</appSettings>
```

As you can see, sensitive data is not stored in plain text anymore.

You don't have to do anything special to retrieve encrypted data from the SharePoint web.config file. Just do this:

```
string strSetting = WebConfigurationManager.AppSettings["NormalA"];
```

If you want to go back to a web.config file without encrypted data, use the following line of code:

```
objAppSettings.SectionInformation.UnprotectSection();
```

Note The biggest advantage of ASP.NET's built-in support for encrypting sensitive areas in the web.config file without having to change a single line of code is that you can leave sensitive areas in a development environment unprotected, and protect those areas in a production environment. This way, you'll still be able to change the web.config file easily in a development environment, and stay secure in a production environment.

Alternatively, you can use the aspnet_regiis tool to encrypt a section of the web.config file. By default, the aspnet_regiis tool can be found at the following location: [drive letter]:\WINDOWS\Microsoft.NET\Framework\v2.0.50727. The next code fragment shows how to use the tool:

```
Aspnet_regiis -pe [section name] -app [name of MOSS web application]
-prov [name of encryption provider]
```

In this code fragment, you need to pass the name of the Microsoft Office SharePoint Server 2007 web application. Then, you need to pass the name of the configuration section, for example, connectionStrings. You can choose to use DPAPI to encrypt data by specifying DataProtectionConfigurationProvider as the name of the encryption provider. If you want to use RSA instead, you should enter RSAProtectedConfigurationProvider.

You can decrypt a configuration section using the following command:

```
Aspnet_regiis -pd [section name] -app [name of MOSS virtual directory]
-prov [name of encryption provider]
```

If you prefer to pass the physical path to the Microsoft Office SharePoint Server 2007 virtual directory, you need to run the following command:

```
Aspnet_regiis -pef [section name] -app [physical path to MOSS virtual directory]
-prov [name of encryption provider]
```

This can be decrypted by issuing the following command:

```
Aspnet_regiis -pdf [section name] -app [physical path to MOSS virtual directory]
-prov [name of encryption provider]
```

The following code fragment shows a part of a <connectionStrings> section that is encrypted using RSA:

```
<connectionStrings configProtectionProvider="➥
RsaProtectedConfigurationProvider">
  <EncryptedData Type="http://www.w3.org/2001/04/xmlenc#Element" ➥
xmlns="http://www.w3.org/2001/04/xmlenc#">
    <EncryptionMethod Algorithm="http://www.w3.org/2001/04/➥
    xmlenc#tripledes-cbc" />
      <KeyInfo xmlns="http://www.w3.org/2000/09/xmldsig#">
      <EncryptedKey xmlns="http://www.w3.org/2001/04/xmlenc#">
      <EncryptionMethod Algorithm="http://www.w3.org/2001/04/xmlenc#rsa-1_5" />
      <KeyInfo xmlns="http://www.w3.org/2000/09/xmldsig#">
       <KeyName>Rsa Key</KeyName>
      </KeyInfo>
      <CipherData>
       <CipherValue>[encrypted value] </CipherValue>
      </CipherData>
     </EncryptedKey>
   </KeyInfo>
   <CipherData>
    <CipherValue>[encrypted value[</CipherValue>
   </CipherData></EncryptedData>
</connectionStrings>
```

The content of the <CipherValue> element is encrypted, thus making the contents of the <connectionStrings> configuration section unreadable to the prying eye.

■**Note** If you want to learn more about using DPAPI and RSA, go to http://msdn2.microsoft.com and look for the articles "How To: Encrypt Configuration Settings in ASP.NET 2.0 using DPAPI" and "How To: Encrypt Configuration Settings in ASP.NET 2.0 using RSA."

In this section, you learned how to add encrypted information to a web application's web.config file. ASP.NET 2.0 makes it easy to work with encrypted information in a web.config file, allowing you to access it as if it were unencrypted. This allows you to leave sensitive information unencrypted in .config files located on development machines and encrypt that information in a production environment without having to change a single line of code.

Single Sign-on

In the previous section, you saw how to encrypt sensitive data. Instead of encrypting data, you could also use SharePoint Single Sign-on (SSO) to store user credentials in the Single Sign-on database. The Single Sign-on database is also called the *credential-mapping database* and it keeps the information in a safe and encrypted way.

If you want to use the Single Sign-on service, you need to be using Microsoft Office SharePoint Server 2007, because this service is not a part of Windows SharePoint Services 3.0. You will also need to install Microsoft Office SharePoint Server 2007 in an environment using Active Directory. Furthermore, the user account that runs the Single Sign-on service needs to have an extensive set of permissions, such as membership in the local administrators group, membership in the local administrators group on the server running the configuration database, and db_owner rights for the SharePoint configuration database.

Note In Microsoft Office SharePoint Server 2007, it is possible to change the credential caching mechanism used by Single Sign-On. You can create your own or use a third-party credential caching system.

We assume you have access to a server with Microsoft Office SharePoint Server 2007 installed and Single Sign-on enabled on it. More information about enabling Single Sign-on can be found in the Microsoft Office SharePoint Server 2007 SDK, which can be downloaded from http://www.microsoft.com/downloads/details.aspx?familyid=6D94E307-67D9-41AC-B2D6-0074D6286FA9&displaylang=en, or in the book *Microsoft SharePoint Building Office 2007 Solutions in C# 2005* by Scot Hillier (Apress, 2007).

SharePoint Single Sign-on introduces a concept known as *Enterprise Application Definition*. Enterprise Application Definitions allow you to define what a set of credentials should look like for a given application. For instance, if you have a custom application that allows you to log in using a username, password, and one-time password (a password that is only valid only once and for a limited period of time), you can set up an Enterprise Application Definition that specifies that user credentials for this application consist of these three parts.

In the next example, we are going to add an Enterprise Application Definition called SuperAccount, which defines the different parts of information that form the credential information you are interested in. The next procedure explains how to create a new Enterprise Application Definition called SuperAccount:

1. Open SharePoint 3.0 Central Administration.

2. Click the Operations tab.

3. In the Security Configuration section, click Manage settings for single sign-on. This opens the Manage Settings for Single Sign-On for [server] page.

4. In the Enterprise Application Definition Settings page, click Manage settings for enterprise application definitions. This opens the Manage Enterprise Application Definitions page (shown in Figure 7-6).

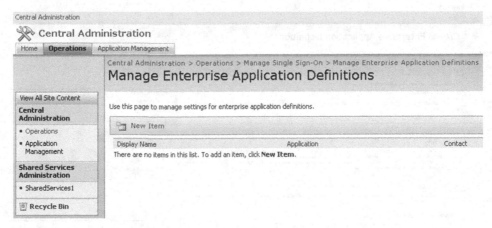

Figure 7-6. *Manage Single Sign-on page*

5. Click New Item. This opens the Create Enterprise Application Definition page.

6. Locate the Application and Contact Information section.

7. Enter the value **SuperAccount** in the Display name text box.

8. Enter the value **SuperAccount** in the Application name text box.

9. Enter **testmail@lcbridge.nl** in the Contact e-mail address text box.

10. In the Account type section, choose either Group or Group using restricted account.

Note If you want to connect to another application using a different account for every user, choose Individual as the Account type. For example, suppose a user logs in to the portal and needs information extracted from SAP within the portal. It would be a drag if users needed to type their credentials repeatedly. Choose Group or Group using restricted account to use a single account for all users. If you choose to use Group using restricted account, you indicate that you are using a single privileges account for all users, which must be used by applications that perform additional security policy enforcements when using this account. In impersonation scenarios, you should choose either Group or Restricted Group as the account type, because you generally will want to define one impersonation account for a group of users. The administrator should manage this impersonation account, not the end user.

---

11. Locate the Logon Account Information section.

12. Verify that the Field 1: Display Name text box contains the value Username.

13. Verify that the Field 2: Display Name text box contains the value Password. Ensure that the mask of this field is set to Yes. You should set the display type to mask so the password is not shown onscreen in plain text later on. Figure 7-7 shows the Create Enterprise Application Definition page.

14. Click OK.

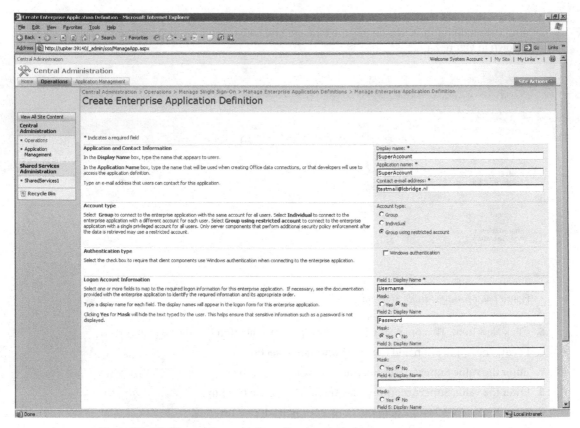

Figure 7-7. *The Create Enterprise Application Definition page*

In the next step, you need to tie the credential information template, the Enterprise Application Definition, to a group account name. The next procedure explains how to associate the SuperAccount Enterprise Application Definition with a test group account called MyApplication:

1. Click the Operations tab. This opens the Operations page.

2. In the Security Configuration section, click Manage settings for single sign-on. This opens the Manage Settings for Single Sign-On for [server name] page.

3. In the Enterprise Application Definition Settings section, click the Manage account information for enterprise application definitions link. This opens the Manage Account Information for an Enterprise Application Definition page.

4. In the Account Information section, enter the following value in the Group account name text box: **[domain name]\MyApplication**.

5. Click the Set button.

For this example, we have created a group called MyApplication. Every member of this group will be allowed to use web parts that need to elevate user privileges temporarily. This is shown in Figure 7-8.

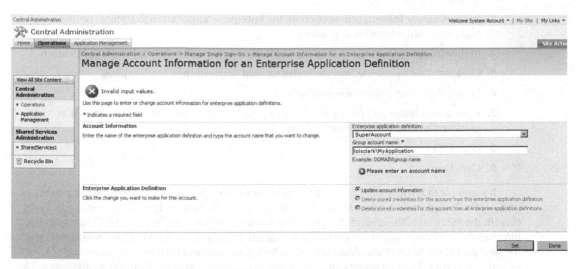

Figure 7-8. *The Manage Account Information for an Enterprise Application Definition page*

Next, you need to define the credentials of the super account that is used for impersonation. The definition for the super account credentials consists of two fields: UserName and Password. We defined these fields earlier in this section. This is shown in Figure 7-9. The next procedure explains how to define this account:

1. On the Provide [user name of the super account] Account Information page, locate the Logon Information section.

2. In the Username text field, enter the user name of the super account.

3. In the Password text field, enter the password of the super account.

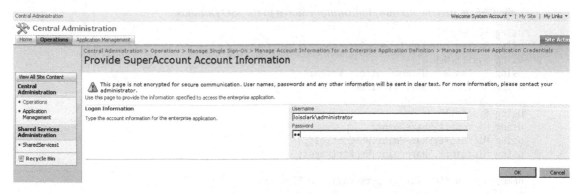

Figure 7-9. *Provide the credentials of the impersonation account*

The following procedure explains how to tie an Enterprise Application Definition to a group account name:

1. Go to Central Administration ➤ Operations ➤ Manage Single Sign-On.

2. In the Enterprise Application Definition Settings section, click Manage account information for enterprise application definitions. This opens the Manage Account Information for an Enterprise Application Definition page (shown in Figure 7-6).

3. In the Account Information section, in the Enterprise application definition drop-down list, make sure SuperAccount is selected.

4. In the Group account name section, add the following value: **[domain]\MyApplication**.

5. Click Set. This opens the Provide SuperAccount Account Information page.

6. Locate the Logon Information section.

7. Enter a user name and password. In this example, we are using the administrator account of our test domain. This is shown in Figure 7-7.

8. Click OK.

9. Click Done.

If you want to retrieve this information from the Single Sign-on service from within a web part, you will need to set a reference to Microsoft.SharePoint.SingleSignOn.dll. The Credentials class in the Microsoft.SharePoint.SingleSignOn namespace has a GetCredentials() method that retrieves the super account credentials defined earlier. Style-wise, in our view, this method is not the best part of the SharePoint object model. Although the method is called GetCredentials(), its return type is void. The first argument of the method expects an unsigned integer as argument. The documentation says this flag is reserved for internal use. Apparently you need to pass it the value 1, but the reason why is a mystery. Then you need to pass the application name, which is the name of the Enterprise Application Definition. Finally, you need to pass a string array by reference, which is filled by the GetCredentials() method with all the credential information the Single Sign-on service can find. The code looks like this:

```
string[] strCredentialData = null;
Credentials.GetCredentials(1, "SuperAccount", ref strCredentialData);
string strUserName = strCredentialData[0];
string strPassword = strCredentialData[1];
```

Listing 7-5 shows the complete code.

Listing 7-5. *Retrieving Account Information Stored in the SSO Database*

```
using System;
using System.Runtime.InteropServices;
using System.Web.UI;
using System.Web.UI.WebControls.WebParts;
using System.Xml.Serialization;
using System.Security.Principal;
using System.IO;
using Microsoft.SharePoint;
using Microsoft.SharePoint.WebControls;
using Microsoft.SharePoint.WebPartPages;

namespace LoisAndClark.ImpersonationAndElevation
{
  [Guid("47500629-54d5-4ac4-ac44-097b4ce2e3eb")]
  public class SuperPart : System.Web.UI.WebControls.WebParts.WebPart
  {

    /// <summary>
    /// Render this Web Part to the output parameter specified.
    /// </summary>
    /// <param name="output"> The HTML writer to write out to </param>
```

```
    protected override void RenderContents(HtmlTextWriter writer)
    {
      try
      {
        string[] strCredentialData = null;
        Credentials.GetCredentials(1, "SuperAccount", ref strCredentialData);
        string strUserName = strCredentialData[0];
        string strPassword = strCredentialData[1];
        writer.Write("username: " + strUserName + " password: " + strPassword);
      }
      catch (Exception err)
      {
        writer.Write("error: " + err.Message);
      }
    }
  }
}
```

It takes some time to set up Single Sign-on, but once you have that up and running, a Single Sign-on mechanism that uses a secure credential mapping database is at your disposal. Figure 7-10 shows what happens when Listing 7-5 is run.

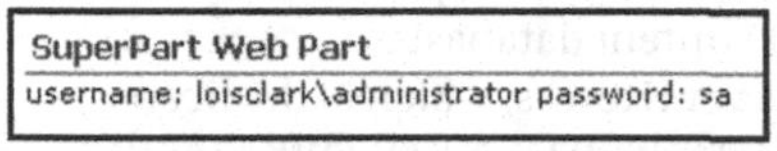

Figure 7-10. *Retrieving credentials from the credential mapping database in a web part*

■**Note** In the beginning of this section, we advised you to create a Group or Group using restricted account to create a single account that is used by a group of users, which is the way to go for impersonation and elevation scenarios. If you chose that every individual user needs to specify a different account to access another application, your code needs to catch the SingleSignOnCredsNotFoundException exception. This exception is raised whenever the credentials of a given user are not present in the credential mapping database (which is actually not a real application error) and uses the GetCredentialEntryUrl() method of the SingleSignOnLocator class to collect the correct credentials.

In this section, you have seen how to use SharePoint Single Sign-on (SSO) to store user credentials in a credential-mapping database and retrieve them again later to use in impersonation, elevation, and delegation scenarios. Single Sign-on offers the additional advantage of offering a user interface for managing the credentials in the SSO database.

RevertToSelf and RunWithElevatedPrivileges

You have seen how to store encrypted information in configuration files and how to store credentials in the Single Sign-on database. In elevation scenarios, where you want to perform actions that require more privileges than the current user has, an easier and more elegant solution is available. This solution is called *credential-less impersonation*. The first way to accomplish this is to make a call to the Win32 API RevertToSelf() function that terminates the impersonation of a client application. You can use this method if you want to access resources that are not controlled by the SharePoint API. The second way to accomplish this is to use the RunWithElevatedPrivileges()

method, which is new in Microsoft Office SharePoint Server 2007. You need to use this method if you want to access resources that are controlled by the SharePoint API.

Note In Microsoft Office SharePoint Server 2007, you should use the `RunWithElevatedPrivileges` method when implementing elevation scenarios using the SharePoint object model.

A SharePoint user context is itself an impersonated identity. SharePoint uses Internet Information Server 6 (IIS), and Internet Information Server 6 uses application pool identities as the context in which worker processes are run. If you call the `advapi32.dll` `RevertToSelf()` function or the `RunWithElevatedPrivileges` method, you will end the current user impersonation. The effect is that you will revert from a current user context (say, user account NormalA) to the original identity, which is the application pool identity.

The credentials of the application pool identity are stored safely in the Internet Information Services metabase. This trait makes the application pool identity account an ideal candidate for use in elevation scenarios. If you dump the current context and revert to the application pool's security context, it is possible to perform actions that require an extensive set of privileges while avoiding storing credentials in code.

If you have installed SharePoint (either Windows SharePoint Services 3.0 or Microsoft Office SharePoint 2007) using an existing SQL Server instance, you get to choose the application pool identity. This account becomes administrator of the SharePoint content database.

This is not the case if you install SharePoint using SQL Server Express, which is the license-free version of SQL Server. In this scenario, the predefined NT AUTHORITY\NETWORK SERVICE account is used as the security account for the application pool. By default, the Network Service account will not be a member of the SharePoint administration group, and it is not a local administrator either. The use of SQL Server Express is highly unlikely if you are using Microsoft Office SharePoint Server 2007, but it is a more feasible solution if you are using Windows SharePoint Services 3.0, which comes free with the Windows Server 2003 operating system.

In elevation scenarios, you will probably want to use some kind of super account that has at least SharePoint admin rights. You can go to the Internet Information Services (IIS) manager and change the application pool identity or, theoretically, go the SharePoint Central Administration pages and extend the permissions of the Network Service account.

Note The Network Service account is a predefined local account used by the service control manager (SCM). This account does not have a password (if you need to supply password information, it will be ignored), acts as the computer on the network, and has minimum privileges on the local computer. You should not add privileges to this predefined account, as this changes the very essence of this account.

First, we will discuss how to use the `RevertToSelf()` Win32 API call to demonstrate credential-less impersonation. If you want to use this function, you need to import Advapi32.dll into the SuperPart web part class, like so:

```
[DllImport("advapi32.dll")]
static extern bool RevertToSelf();
```

At this point, you are ready to elevate code privileges using the `RevertToSelf()` Win32 API call. It is advisable to store the current user context in a `WindowsIdentity` object so that you are able to elevate privileges temporarily. Then you can execute the code that absolutely needs to have an extensive set of privileges and go back to the original user context. This way, you limit security risks associated with user elevation.

```
WindowsIdentity objOriginalUser = WindowsIdentity.GetCurrent();
RevertToSelf();
ShowVirtualServerInfo(); // reads virtual server info
WindowsImpersonationContext objContext = objOriginalUser.Impersonate();
```

Listing 7-6 shows the complete code.

Listing 7-6. *Using the RevertToSelf() Win32 API Function*

```
using System;
using System.Runtime.InteropServices;
using System.Web.UI;
using System.Web.UI.WebControls.WebParts;
using System.Xml.Serialization;
using System.Security.Principal;
using Microsoft.SharePoint;
using Microsoft.SharePoint.WebControls;
using Microsoft.SharePoint.WebPartPages;
using Microsoft.SharePoint.Navigation;

namespace LoisAndClark.ImpersonationAndElevation
{
  [Guid("47500629-54d5-4ac4-ac44-097b4ce2e3eb")]
  public class SuperPart : System.Web.UI.WebControls.WebParts.WebPart
  {
    [DllImport("advapi32.dll", SetLastError = true)]
    static extern bool RevertToSelf();

    protected override void CreateChildControls()
    {
      try
      {
        string strValue = String.Empty;

        WindowsIdentity objOriginalUser = WindowsIdentity.GetCurrent();
        RevertToSelf();
        strValue += "application pool identity name: " + ➡
        WindowsIdentity.GetCurrent().Name + "<br/>";

        // Execute code that needs to have elevated privileges.

        WindowsImpersonationContext objContext = objOriginalUser.Impersonate();
        strValue += "original user name: " + WindowsIdentity.GetCurrent().Name;

        Controls.Add(new LiteralControl(strValue));
      }
      catch (Exception err)
      {
        Controls.Add(new LiteralControl(err.Message));
      }
    }
  }
}
```

Figure 7-11 shows what happens when this web part is executed.

```
SuperPart
application pool identity name: MARS\Administrator
original user name: MARS\NormalA
```

Figure 7-11. *Elevating code privileges using RevertToSelf()*

■**Note** If you want to implement elevation scenarios within a SharePoint web context, Microsoft recommends that you always use the `RunWithElevatedPrivileges()` method. In this section, the `RevertToSelf()` function is explained for educational purposes. You should only use this method to access resources that are not controlled by the SharePoint API.

To demonstrate the credential-less impersonation solution using the `RunWithElevatedPrivileges()` method, you can use the NormalA user account again. Our next example uses the SharePoint object model to add a node to the Quick Launch navigation bar. This is something user NormalA is not allowed to do, so this gives us a chance to show you how to elevate code privileges. The following code adds an external link to the Quick Launch navigation bar:

```
SPWeb web = SPControl.GetContextWeb(Context);
web.AllowUnsafeUpdates = true;
SPNavigationNode node = new SPNavigationNode(➥
"My Custom Node", "http://node.url", true);
web.Navigation.QuickLaunch.AddAsFirst(node);
web.Update();
```

If you open a browser, choose the Sign in as Different User option at the upper-right corner, and log in with the NormalA user account, you will see that a web part that tries to add a Quick Launch node will be denied access (the complete code for this web part will be shown later in this section). This is shown in Figure 7-12.

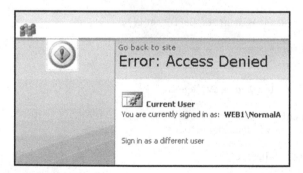

Figure 7-12. *Access is denied error in the web part*

The `RunWithElevatedPrivileges()` method can be used to execute a piece of code using elevated privileges. You can pass this method a delegate that contains the code that needs to be run. The code then runs in the context of the System Account User (SHAREPOINT\system identity). The next code fragment shows how to use an anonymous method to add a node to the Quick Launch bar:

```
SPWeb objWeb = SPControl.GetContextWeb(Context);
SPSecurity.RunWithElevatedPrivileges(delegate()
{
  using (SPSite objElevatedSite = new SPSite(objWeb.Site.ID))
  {
    using (SPWeb objElevatedWeb = objElevatedSite.OpenWeb())
    {
      // Code to add a node to the quick launch navigation bar.
    }
  }
}
);
```

Listing 7-7 shows the complete code for the SuperPart web part that uses the RunWithElevatedPrivileges() method to add a new node to the Quick Launch bar.

Listing 7-7. *Using the RunWithElevatedPrivileges Method*

```
using System;
using System.Runtime.InteropServices;
using System.Web.UI;
using System.Web.UI.WebControls.WebParts;
using System.Xml.Serialization;
using System.Security.Principal;
using Microsoft.SharePoint;
using Microsoft.SharePoint.WebControls;
using Microsoft.SharePoint.WebPartPages;
using Microsoft.SharePoint.Navigation;

namespace LoisAndClark.ImpersonationAndElevation
{
 [Guid("47500629-54d5-4ac4-ac44-097b4ce2e3eb")]
  public class SuperPart : System.Web.UI.WebControls.WebParts.WebPart
  {
    public SuperPart()
    {
      this.ExportMode = WebPartExportMode.All;
    }

    protected override void RenderContents(HtmlTextWriter writer)
    {
      string strValue = String.Empty;

      try
      {
        SPWeb objWeb = SPControl.GetContextWeb(Context);

        SPSecurity.RunWithElevatedPrivileges(delegate()
        {
          using (SPSite objElevatedSite = new SPSite(objWeb.Site.ID))
          {
```

```
            using (SPWeb objElevatedWeb = objElevatedSite.OpenWeb())
            {
                // Allow unsafe updates because you can't save changes
                // during HTTP GET requests.
                objElevatedWeb.AllowUnsafeUpdates = true;
                SPNavigationNode node = new SPNavigationNode( ➥
                "My Custom Node", "http://node.url", true);

                objElevatedWeb.Navigation.QuickLaunch.AddAsFirst(node);
                objElevatedWeb.Update();
            }
          }
        }
        );

      }
      catch (Exception err)
      {
        strValue = err.Message;
      }

      writer.Write(strValue);
    }
  }
}
```

The previous code could have been written differently using the SPSecurity.CodeToRunElevated delegate. This code is almost identical to the previous example; the difference is that this time we are using an existing method called AddQuickLaunchNode() instead of an anonymous method. Listing 7-8 shows a web part that uses the CodeToRunElevated delegate to call a named method that adds a node to the Quick Launch bar.

Listing 7-8. *Using the CodeToRunElevated Delegate to Create Elegant Code*

```
using System;
using System.Runtime.InteropServices;
using System.Web.UI;
using System.Web.UI.WebControls.WebParts;
using System.Xml.Serialization;
using System.Security.Principal;
using Microsoft.SharePoint;
using Microsoft.SharePoint.WebControls;
using Microsoft.SharePoint.WebPartPages;
using Microsoft.SharePoint.Navigation;

namespace LoisAndClark.ImpersonationAndElevation
{
  [Guid("47500629-54d5-4ac4-ac44-097b4ce2e3eb")]
  public class SuperPart : System.Web.UI.WebControls.WebParts.WebPart
  {
    public SuperPart()
    {
      this.ExportMode = WebPartExportMode.All;
    }
```

```
protected override void RenderContents(HtmlTextWriter writer)
{
  string strValue = String.Empty;

  try
  {
    SPSecurity.CodeToRunElevated objCode = new ➥
    SPSecurity.CodeToRunElevated(AddQuickLaunchNode);
    SPSecurity.RunWithElevatedPrivileges(objCode);
  }
  catch (Exception err)
  {
    strValue = err.Message;
  }

  writer.Write(strValue);
}

private void AddQuickLaunchNode()
{
  SPWeb web = SPControl.GetContextWeb(Context);
  web.AllowUnsafeUpdates = true;
  SPNavigationNode node = new SPNavigationNode( ➥
  "My Custom Node", "http://node.url", true);
  web.Navigation.QuickLaunch.AddAsFirst(node);
  web.Update();
}
}
}
```

The result of adding a node to the Quick Launch bar programmatically is shown in Figure 7-13.

Figure 7-13. *A custom node in the Quick Launch bar*

In this section, you learned how to elevate a user's privileges by switching to the context of a power user account without needing to specify a user name or password. The RevertToSelf() Win32 API is useful in elevation scenarios where you need to access resources that are not controlled by the SharePoint API; the RunWithElevatedPrivileges method is the way to go for elevation scenarios that access resources controlled by the SharePoint API. Finally, you have seen that the CodeToRunElevated delegate can be used in conjunction with the RunWithElevatedPrivileges method to create elegant code.

Delegation

Thus far, we have used impersonation and elevation techniques to access local resources. Trying to access remote resources (such as a file share) by assuming another user context is called *delegation*.

In delegation scenarios, the server process impersonates the client security context on a remote system, whereas in impersonation scenarios, the server process impersonates the client security context on its local system. In impersonation scenarios, the server cannot impersonate the client on remote systems. If you are developing web parts that access remote resources, you must take a couple of additional steps before you are able to support delegation. This section guides you through these steps.

Note In order for this to work, the delegation account needs to be in the same domain as the user account.

If you want to get delegation working, Active Directory is a requirement. You will need to set up your network to use the Kerberos authentication protocol (which requires Active Directory). You will also need to set up the computers and accounts on your network as trusted for delegation.

In the first step, you will enable Kerberos authentication on your SharePoint server. The Kerberos protocol is based on ticketing; users provide a valid user name and password to an authentication server, which hands the user a ticket that can be used on the network to request other network services.

If you want to enable Kerberos authentication on a SharePoint virtual server, you should do the following:

1. Determine the virtual server id of your SharePoint virtual server. By default, this is 1. One way to retrieve the correct virtual server id is to use the IIS Metabase Explorer, which can be downloaded from http://www.download.com. The IIS Metabase Explorer is shown in Figure 7-14.

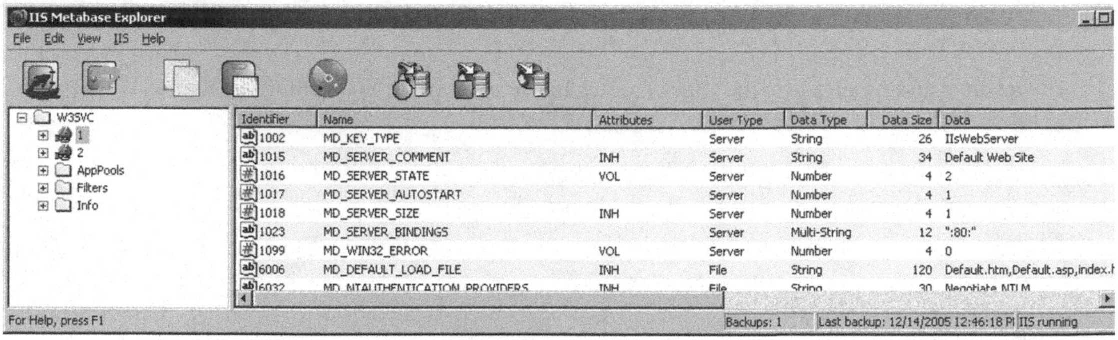

Figure 7-14. *The IIS Metabase Explorer*

2. On the SharePoint server, open a new command prompt.

3. Go the following location: [drive letter]:\inetpub\adminscripts.

4. You can use the adsutil.vbs utility (located in the adminscripts folder) to retrieve information about a given virtual server. If you want to find out which form of authentication is enabled, use the following command:

```
cscript adsutil.vbs get w3svc/1/root/NTAuthenticationProviders
```

5. The default authentication model is NTLM. This is a secure protocol that is based on encrypting user names and passwords before sending them over the network. If you have not already set the authentication provider, the previous command will return the following message: the parameter "NTAuthenticationProviders" is not set at this node.

6. To enable Kerberos authentication, issue the following command:

```
cscript adsutil.vbs set w3svc/1/root/NTAuthenticationProviders "Negotiate,NTLM"
```

7. Restart IIS by typing **iisreset** at a command prompt.

■**Tip** If you want to switch back and only allow NTLM authentication on the virtual server, issue the following command: `cscript adsutil.vbs set w3svc/1/root/NTAuthenticationProviders "NTLM"`.

In the next step, we will check that the application pool hosting the SharePoint web site is using the NT Authority\NetworkService identity. Built-in accounts such as the NetworkService account are automatically configured to work with Kerberos authentication. If you are using a domain user account, you will have to specify a service principal name (SPN) for it. There are two kinds of principal names: user principal names and service principal names. A user principal name is associated with a specific user. A service principal name is the name by which a client uniquely identifies an instance of a service and authorizes the client to use a particular service.

1. Open Internet Information Services (IIS) Manager.

2. Open the [server name] (local computer) node.

3. Open the Web Sites node.

4. Right-click your SharePoint virtual server and choose Properties.

5. Click the Home Directory tab. The Application pool drop-down list displays the application pool that hosts the SharePoint web site. Check which application pool is hosting the web site.

6. Click OK.

7. In Internet Information Services (IIS) Manager, open the Application Pools node.

8. Right-click the name of the application pool that is hosting the SharePoint web site and choose Properties.

9. Click the Identity tab.

If the security account is not one of the predefined accounts, we will use the setspn.exe tool to set a service principal name for it. The setspn.exe tool is a command-line utility that allows you to read, modify, and delete service principal names for an Active Directory property. Setspn.exe is part of the Support Tools pack, located in the Support folder on the Windows Server 2003 CD. It can also be downloaded from the following URL: http://www.microsoft.com/downloads/details.aspx?familyid=5fd831fd-ab77-46a3-9cfe-ff01d29e5c46&displaylang=en.

If you want to set a service principal name for an account, type the following command at a command prompt (the a parameter indicates that a service principal name needs to be added for this account for a given computer):

```
Setspn -a HTTP/[server] [domain name]\[user name]
```

■**Note** More information about the setspn.exe tool can be found on the Microsoft TechNet web site (http://www.microsoft.com/technet) in the article "Configuring Constrained Delegation for Kerberos (IIS 6.0)."

Next, you need to configure the SharePoint server so that it is trusted for delegation.

1. Click Start ➤ Administrative Tools ➤ Start Active Directory Users and Computers.

2. In the left pane, expand the domain node.

3. Click the Computers node.

4. In the right pane, right-click the name of the SharePoint server, and then click Properties.

5. Click the General tab.

6. Select the Trust computer for delegation check box, and click OK.

If the application pool identity is configured to use a domain account instead of a predefined account, or if you are using impersonation techniques to run the process under a domain account, you need to configure the account to be trusted for delegation before you can use Kerberos authentication.

1. If it is not open yet, click Start ➤ Administrative Tools ➤ Start Active Directory Users and Computers.

2. In the left pane, expand the domain node.

3. In the left pane, click the Users node.

4. In the right pane, right-click the name of the user account and choose Properties.

5. Click the Account tab ➤ Account Options. Select the Account is trusted for delegation check box. Then click OK.

6. Close Active Directory Users and Computers.

In this section, you have learned how to configure delegation. Delegation allows you to access remote resources within another user context. If you want to enable delegation, you need to use Active Directory and the Kerberos authentication protocol.

Impersonation in WCF

Windows Communication Foundation (WCF) is the new communication subsystem for .NET applications. It was introduced as a part of the .NET Framework 3.0, which also introduced three other major new components:

- Windows Presentation Foundation (WPF)

- Windows Workflow Foundation (WF)

- Windows CardSpace (WCS)

In this section, you will learn how to implement a WCF service that uses the application pool identity to connect to Microsoft Office SharePoint Server 2007. If you want to create a WCF service, it helps if you install either Visual Studio 2005 Extensions for .NET Framework 3.0 (WCF & WCF)—which can be found at `http://www.microsoft.com/downloads/details.aspx?familyid=F54F5537-CC86-4BF5-AE44-F5A1E805680D&displaylang=en`—or the latest version of Visual Studio 2008 (at the time of writing, this tool is still in beta). Neither tool is supported officially, but both support WCF and make creating WCF services considerably easier. The example in this section is created using Visual Studio 2008 Beta 2 Professional Edition (which can be downloaded at `http://msdn2.microsoft.com/en-us/vstudio/aa700831.aspx`).

In the example we will discuss in this section, we will create a WCF service that is hosted by Internet Information Server. Then, we will specify an application pool identity and use that in our impersonation scenario to run some code the end user is normally not allowed to execute.

In the next procedure, you will see how to create a new virtual directory for a WCF service.

1. Create a new folder at the following location: C:\Inetpub\wwwroot\TestWCFHost.

2. Open a command prompt and type **inetmgr**. This opens Internet Information Services (IIS) Manager.

3. Expand the [server name] (local computer) node.

4. Expand the Web Sites node.

5. Locate a SharePoint web site where you want to add a virtual directory for your custom WCF service, right-click it, and choose New ➤ Virtual Directory. This opens the Virtual Directory Creation Wizard.

6. Click Next.

7. Enter the following alias: **TestWCFHost**.

8. Click Next.

9. Enter the following path: **C:\Inetpub\wwwroot\TestWCFHost**.

10. Click Next.

11. Accept the default Virtual Directory Access Permissions and click Next.

12. Click Finish.

13. Right-click the newly created TestWCFHost node and choose Properties. This opens the TestWCFHost Properties window.

14. Click Create.

15. Click OK.

We will create a custom application pool for this virtual directory, specify an application pool identity under which the server will run, and associate them with each oher. This is explained in the next procedure.

1. In Internet Information Services (IIS) Manager, right-click the Application Pools node and choose New ➤ Application Pool. This opens the Add New Application Pool dialog window.

2. Specify the following Application pool ID: **WCFAppPool**.

3. Click OK.

4. Right-click the newly created WCFAppPool node and choose Properties. This opens the WCFAppPool Properties window.

5. Click the Identity tab.

6. Select the Configurable radio button.

7. Specify a user name and password.

8. Click OK.

9. Right-click the previously created TestWCFHost virtual directory (located under the Web Site node) and choose Properties. This opens the TestWCFHost Properties window.

10. In the Application pool drop-down list, choose WCFAppPool.

11. Click OK.

At this point, you have created the container that will hold the WCF service. Now, we will use Visual Studio 2008 Beta 2 to create the WCF service. This is discussed in the following procedure:

1. Start Visual Studio 2008 Beta 2 (Start ➤ All Programs ➤ Microsoft Visual Studio 2008 Beta 2 ➤ Microsoft Visual Studio 2008 Beta 2).

2. Click File ➤ New ➤ Web Site. This opens the New Web Site dialog window.

3. In the Templates section, choose WCF service.

4. Select HTTP from the Location drop-down list.

5. In the Location text box, type the URL of the virtual directory you created earlier in this section. In our case, this is http://[sharepoint web application]/TestWCFHost.

As a result, several default files are created automatically. Delete the following files: Service.svc, App_Code\Service.cs, and App_Code\IService.cs. You will notice that creating a WCF service is quite similar to creating a classic .asmx web service. The following procedure discusses creating a WCF service:

1. Right-click your project and choose Add New Item. This opens the Add New Item – [URL WCF service host] dialog window.

2. In the Templates section, choose WCF Service.

3. Enter the following name: **MyWCFService.svc**.

4. Ensure that the selected Language drop-down list is set to Visual C#.

5. Click Add.

This creates three files: MyWCFService.svc (located in the root of the project), and IMyWCFService.cs and MyWCFService.cs (both located in the App_Code folder). The MyWCFService.svc file contains of a single line of code that refers to a code-behind file. Listing 7-9 shows the file.

Listing 7-9. *The Code for MyWCFService.svc*

```
<%@ ServiceHost Language="C#" Debug="true" Service="LoisAndClark.MyWCFService" ➡
CodeBehind="~/App_Code/MyWCFService.cs" %>
```

Next, we will take a closer look at the IMyWCFService class file. In WCF, all services expose contracts that explicitly define what a service does. There are four different types of contracts:

- Service contracts that describe the operations that can be performed by the client.

- Data contracts that describe the data that is passed to and from the service.

- Fault contracts that describe errors that are raised by the service.

- Message contracts that describe how a service can interact directly with a message.

In this example, only service contracts are relevant. You can create a service contract by adding a .cs file that defines a new interface. Then, you need to decorate the interface with a [ServiceContract] attribute that exposes a normal CLR interface as a WCF contract. Every method within such an interface that needs to be exposed in the WCF contract needs to be decorated with the [OperationContract] attribute. Listing 7-10 shows the implementation for the IMyWCFService WCF service contract:

Listing 7-10. *Defining a Contract for a WCF Service*

```
using System;
using System.Collections.Generic;
using System.Runtime.Serialization;
using System.ServiceModel;
using System.Text;

namespace LoisAndClark
{
  [ServiceContract]
  public interface IMyWCFService
  {
    [OperationContract]
    string DoWork();
  }
}
```

This service contract needs to be implemented by a class. To demonstrate that impersonation has worked, we will use a piece of code that fails if the identity executing the code is not an administrator. The code retrieves the current SharePoint site and shows the collection of site groups of which the current user is a member:

```
string strValue = String.Empty;
RevertToSelf();
SPWeb objCurrentWeb = SPControl.GetContextWeb(Context);
foreach (SPRole objRole in objCurrentWeb.CurrentUser.Roles)
{
  strValue += "Role: " + objRole.Name + "<br/>";
}
```

This code fails unless you are an administrator. If we modify the code a bit so you can pass the URL of the site collection and the user name as arguments, the code looks like this:

```
public string GetUserRoles(string strUrl, string strUserName)
{
  string strResult = String.Empty;
  using (SPSite objSiteCollection = new SPSite(strUrl))
  {
    using (SPWeb objSite = objSiteCollection.OpenWeb())
    {
      SPUser objUser = objSite.Users[strUserName];
      foreach (SPRole objRole in objUser.Roles)
      {
        strResult += objRole.Name + ", ";
      }
    }
  }

  return strResult;
}
```

Listing 7-11 shows the complete code for the MyWCFService code behind file.

Listing 7-11. *Implementing a WCF Service*

```
using System;
using System.Collections.Generic;
using System.Runtime.Serialization;
using System.ServiceModel;
using System.Text;
using System.Security.Principal;
using Microsoft.SharePoint;

namespace LoisAndClark
{
  public class MyWCFService : IMyWCFService
  {
    public string DoWork()
    {
      // e.g. SHAREPOINT\system as the user name.
      return GetUserRoles("[site collection URL]", @"[user name] ");
    }

    public string GetUserRoles(string strUrl, string strUserName)
    {
      try
      {
        string strResult = String.Empty;
        using (SPSite objSite = new SPSite(strUrl))
        {
          using (SPWeb objWeb = objSite.OpenWeb())
          {
            SPUser objUser = objWeb.Users[strUserName];
            foreach (SPRole objRole in objUser.Roles)
            {
              strResult += objRole.Name + ", ";
            }
          }
        }

        return strResult;
      }
      catch (Exception err)
      {
        return err.Message;
      }
    }
  }
}
```

Before you can use the WCF service, you need to adjust the web.config file to define endpoints that can be accessed by a client. This is done by adding a new <service> element to the <services> node of the web.config file. The <service> element allows you to define the service name via the name property. You can also add an <endpoint> element that defines a service contract that is used for the WCF service (service contracts were discussed earlier in this chapter) and a binding that is used by the service. Bindings define aspects about the transport mechanism, such as the protocol or the message encoding type that are used. In this example, we will use WsHttpBinding, which uses HTTP as the transport protocol. The following code fragment shows how to define a new service endpoint that uses the IWcfImpersonator service contract and uses HTTP as the transport protocol:

```
<service name="LoisAndClark.MyWCFService">
  <endpoint
  address=""
  binding="wsHttpBinding"
  contract="LoisAndClark.IMyWCFService" />
</service>
```

You will also need to make sure that the WCF service emits metadata that is used by the client to retrieve a service description. You can do this by defining a service behavior for the service. Service behaviors affect all endpoints of a service, and you can specify which service behavior applies to a service by using the `<service>` element's `behaviorConfiguration` attribute. This is shown in the following code fragment:

```
<service
name="LoisAndClark.MyWCFService"
behaviorConfiguration="MyServiceTypeBehaviors">
```

The following service behavior needs to be added to the `<serviceBehaviors>` section of the web.config file, and specifies that any service associated to this behavior exposes metadata:

```
<behavior name="MyServiceTypeBehaviors" >
  <serviceMetadata httpGetEnabled="true" />
</behavior>
```

If you open a browser and browse to the svc file (`http://[sharepoint web application]/TestWCFService/MyWCFService.svc`), you should see a page similar to Figure 7-15.

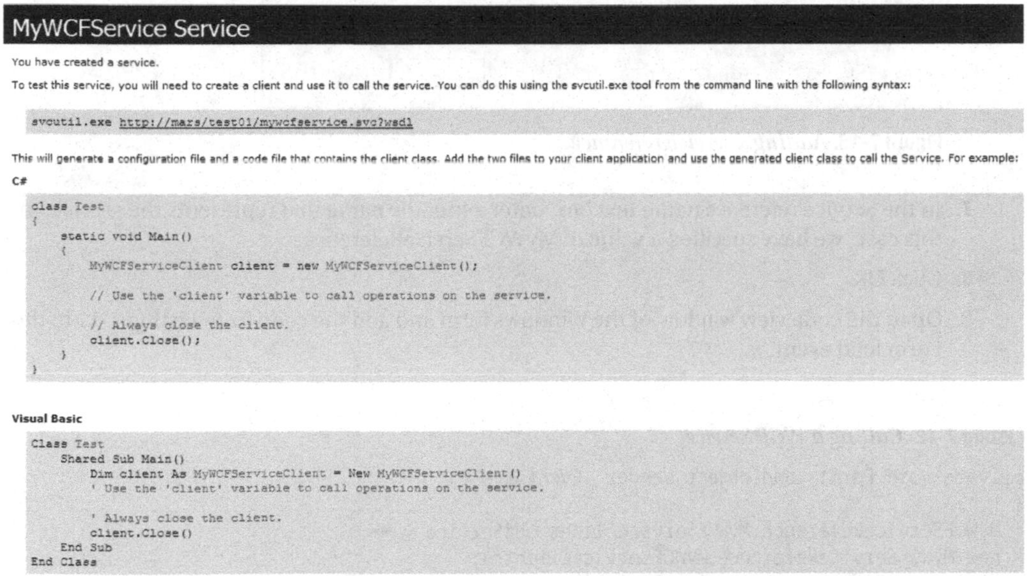

Figure 7-15. *The WCF Service description page*

The next procedure explains how to create a test client for this WCF service.

1. Right-click the solution and choose Add ➤ New Project. This opens the Add New Project dialog window.

2. In the Templates section, choose Windows Forms Application.

3. Enter the following Name: **WCFTestClient**.

4. Click OK.

5. Right-click the WCFTestClient project and choose Add Service Reference. The Add Service Reference dialog window appears.

6. In the Service URI text box, enter the URL of the MyWCFService.svc file. This is shown in Figure 7-16.

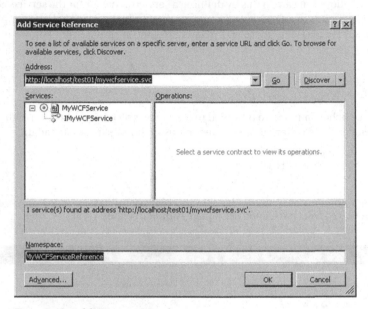

Figure 7-16. *Adding a service reference*

7. In the Service reference name text box, enter a friendly name that represents the service. In this case, we have specified a value of MyWCFServiceReference.

8. Click OK.

9. Open the code view window of the Windows form and add the code from Listing 7-12 to the Form load event:

Listing 7-12. *Calling a WCF Service*

```
private void Form1_Load(object sender, EventArgs e)
{
  MyWCFServiceReference.MyWCFServiceClient objService = ➥
  new MyWCFServiceReference.MyWCFServiceClient();
  string strResult = objService.DoWork();
  objService.Close();
}
```

You have now created a test client for your WCF service. Try it out and if everything works fine, you can add a service reference to this WCF service within web parts or SharePoint pages.

In this section, you learned how to create a WCF service that is hosted in IIS and runs under a custom application pool identity. WCF services can be used to execute code under this custom application pool identity that a normal end user would not be allowed to run.

■**Caution** In this scenario, the WCF application pool identity executes some sort of action on behalf of the end user. This is a potential security risk if everybody is allowed to communicate with the WCF service. In this case, where the WCF service is hosted by IIS, you could restrict the users that are allowed to call the WCF service (by adding IP address and domain name restrictions). There are a lot of other options when it comes to securing WCF services, but they fall outside the scope of this chapter.

Summary

You have concluded the tour on impersonation, elevation, and delegation for SharePoint 2007. You have seen how to use the LogonUser() Win32 API function to impersonate user accounts, a technique that can be used to access resources not controlled by the SharePoint API. Then, you saw how to store user credentials in a safe and encrypted way in configuration files and the Single Sign-on database. You have seen how to avoid storing credentials via credential-less impersonation. After that, you learned what delegation is and how to enable it on a SharePoint server. Finally, we discussed how to create a Windows Communication Foundation service and use that in impersonation scenarios. That concludes this chapter, and as far as we are concerned, you are ready to impersonate.

CHAPTER 8

■ ■ ■

Working with InfoPath in a MOSS 2007 Environment

When talking about Microsoft Office SharePoint Server 2007 and Office 2007, the conversation will most definitely include InfoPath 2007. This product is a rich client desktop application that is part of the Office system product suite. InfoPath 2007 can be used by teams and organizations to collect data in an efficient way. With InfoPath 2007, you can create rich and dynamic forms and publish them so users can fill them out and submit them. The fact that InfoPath forms are built using XML makes it very easy to share information in organizations. In this chapter, we discuss the basic principles of creating InfoPath forms and the connection between InfoPath 2007 and SharePoint 2007.

We will discuss site content types, which enable you to add more than one InfoPath form template to a SharePoint *form library*. Form libraries are used to store XML-based business forms, such as InfoPath forms. We will also take a look at data connection files, and see how to create and use them.

Furthermore, this chapter discusses how to access data that is stored in a SharePoint list within an InfoPath form. After that, we show you how to update and save InfoPath forms programmatically in a SharePoint form library. We will also discuss Forms Server 2007, which is a new server product that allows end users to open forms in a browser without having to install InfoPath 2007 on the client.

The final topic that is discussed in this chapter is automating business processes. If you have a need for automated collection and distribution of InfoPath forms, BizTalk Server 2006 can help you out. This chapter goes into detail about using the BizTalk Server 2006 Windows SharePoint Services adapter.

InfoPath Walkthrough

The first thing you need to find out when starting to work with InfoPath is how to design and develop an InfoPath form. The easiest way to start is by creating a form based on an existing template. You can do this by opening InfoPath and clicking Customize a Sample in the Getting Started window. InfoPath has a number of default templates that you can customize any way you want (see Figure 8-1). For this example, we will use the Expense Report template.

InfoPath runs in either design mode or published mode. Design mode lets developers set up the form structure as well as the look and feel of the form. Published mode shows how users will see the form. By default, our sample form opens in design mode, as you can see in Figure 8-2.

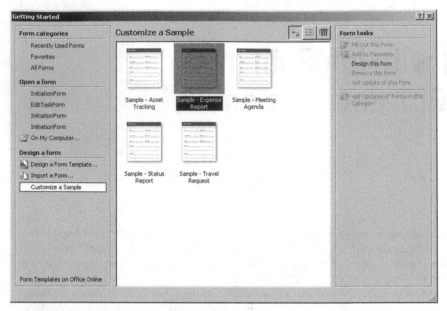

Figure 8-1. *An overview of sample forms in InfoPath*

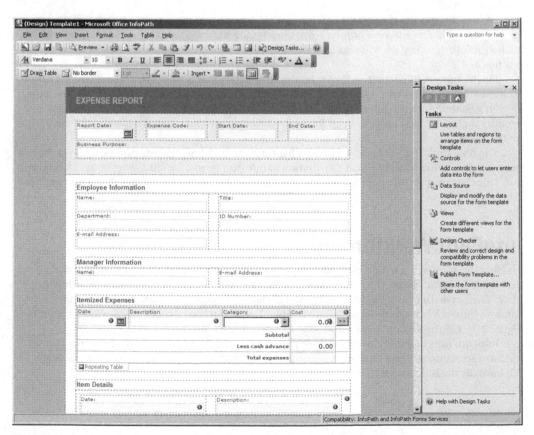

Figure 8-2. *The Expense Report sample form opened in design mode*

When you look at the Expense Report sample form, you will notice that InfoPath has taken care of the layout of the form and puts several different controls on the form. The Design Tasks task pane contains the following tasks to help you design your form:

- *Layout*: The Layout task pane is meant to create the layout of the form. With the Layout task pane, you can add tables to a form to organize the different parts of the form template. Figure 8-3 shows the Layout task pane.

Figure 8-3. *The Layout task pane*

- *Controls*: The Controls task pane will let you add controls so users can easily fill out the form. Other than standard controls (shown in Figure 8-4) you have been familiar with for years (such as text boxes and list boxes), InfoPath 2007 contains its own specific set of controls such as repeating tables, repeating sections, and choice groups. You should also note that it it is possible to create your own custom controls. The article "Creating an InfoPath Custom Control Using C# and .NET" on the InfoPath team Blog located at http://blogs.msdn.com/infopath/archive/2005/04/15/408728.aspx provides more information about this.

Figure 8-4. *The Controls task pane*

■**Note** There are a couple of controls that are not supported in browser-enabled form templates, such as the repeating recursive section, the choice group, and the horizontal repeating table. More information about browser-enabled form templates can be found in the section "Forms Services 2007."

- *Data Source*: The Data Source task pane displays the data sources that are available and bindable to the controls you have added to the form. Figure 8-5 shows the Data Source task pane. More information about data sources can be found in the section "Sharing Data Connection Files in a Data Connection Library."

Figure 8-5. *The Data Source task pane*

- *Views*: The Views task pane lets you create one or multiple views of the same InfoPath form. Views let you create a manager's view, a print view, or any other kind of view. Figure 8-6 shows the Views task pane.

Figure 8-6. *The Views task pane*

- *Design Checker*: InfoPath 2007 lets you design a form that can be opened in either InfoPath or a web browser, or both. A form is considered browser-compatible if it can be opened by a web browser. Some InfoPath features are not supported in browser-compatible forms. More information about browser-compatible forms can be found in the section "Forms Services 2007." The Design Checker task pane gives you the option to check whether there are compatibility problems. Figure 8-7 shows the Design Checker task pane.

■**Note** In the Design Checker task pane, you can also select the Verify on server check box. This allows you to view additional errors and messages detected by InfoPath Forms Services, such as the negative impact a form may have on the performance in the browser.

Figure 8-7. *The Design Checker task pane*

- *Publish Form Template:* With the Publish Form Template task, you can publish the form template to the following locations:

  - *SharePoint Server.* (This can be either Microsoft Office SharePoint Server 2007 or Windows SharePoint Services 3.0.) The form template can be published to a form library or it can be published as a site content type. If you publish a form template as a site content type, the form template can be used in multiple sites within a site collection. You can find more information about this in the section "Using Site Content Types."

  - *Forms Server 2007 server.* A browser-compatible form template can be published to a server that runs Forms Server. Users without InfoPath can still fill out the InfoPath form. You can find more information about browser-compatibility in the section "Forms Services 2007."

  - *Part of an e-mail:* A form template can be published by sending it in an e-mail using Outlook 2007. Receivers of this e-mail can open the form and fill it out.

  - *Shared network folder.* A form template can be published to a shared network folder. Users can go to the shared network folder and fill out the form.

  - *Installable file:* A form template can be published as an installable file to a shared network location. This is only possible if Visual Studio 2005 is installed on the server.

Tip Another interesting scenario is to use InfoPath 2007 to create custom Document Information Panels, in which case you need to publish the InfoPath form as a Document Information Panel template. This topic is not discussed in this chapter, but the blog post "InfoPath 2007: Customizing the default Document Information Panel" located at `http://blah.winsmarts.com/2006-12-InfoPath_2007__Customizing_the_default_ Document_Information_Panel.aspx` provides an excellent overview.

When you are finished designing the form, you can preview how it will look when it is published (see Figure 8-8) via the Preview Form button, which is located on the InfoPath toolbar.

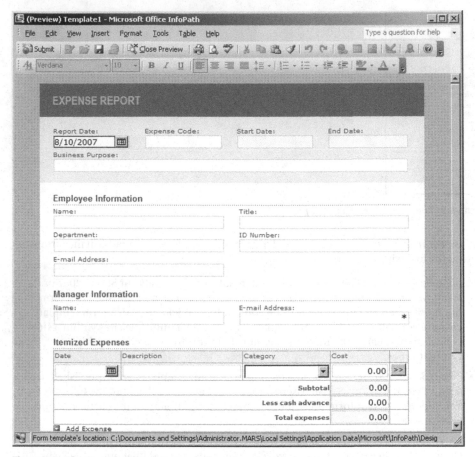

Figure 8-8. *The Expense Report sample form in preview mode*

When you are happy with the design of your form, you must first save it in order to publish the form. In this example, we are going to publish the Expense Report form to a SharePoint form library.

1. To publish a form, choose the Publish Form Template from the Design Tasks task pane. This brings up the Publishing Wizard dialog window.

2. In the first step of the Publishing Wizard, you can choose where you want to publish your form, as shown in Figure 8-9. Choose to publish the form to a SharePoint server with or without InfoPath Forms Services, and click Next.

3. In the second step of the Publishing Wizard, enter the location of the SharePoint site where you want to publish the form template. The recommended location for saving a form is the Forms Templates document library located at the root of the site collection. Click Next.

4. The next step lets you confirm that the form is browser-compatible; in this example it is. Then you can choose how you want to publish a form template. You can choose between a document library (choosing this option results in the creation of a form library), a site content template, or an administrator-approved form template. This is shown in Figure 8-10. In this example, we are going to create a document library and click Next.

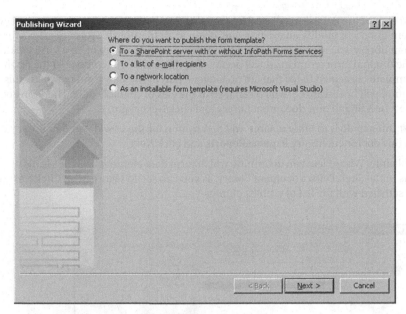

Figure 8-9. *Choose where to publish an InfoPath form.*

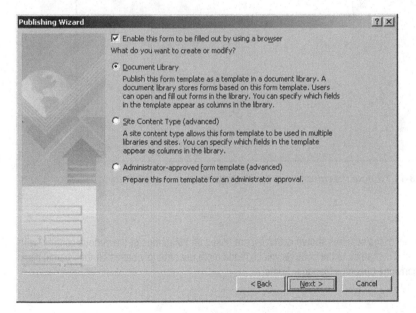

Figure 8-10. *Choose how you want to publish a form template.*

Note Make sure you are using the Enterprise edition of Microsoft Office SharePoint Server 2007 and that you have activated the "Office SharePoint Server Standard Web application features" feature for the web application.

---

5. The next step of the Publishing Wizard lets you decide whether you want to create a new document library or modify an existing one. If you want to publish a form to an existing document library, you are going to overwrite the existing one. If you open a form created using the original form template, it will do so using the new form template. If the original form template contained fields that are no longer a part of the new form template, this information will be discarded, which can lead to the loss of valuable data. Therefore, choose to create a new SharePoint document library and click Next again.

6. The next thing to do is to enter a name and description for the new document library. We will call this document library **ExpenseReports** and click Next.

7. The Publishing Wizard lets you determine which form data elements will be visible as columns in the SharePoint document library, as you can see in Figure 8-11. Click Next when you are satisfied with the list of visible columns.

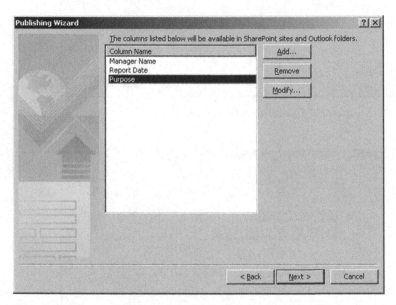

Figure 8-11. *Choose the columns in the SharePoint document library.*

Note The names of the columns shown in this list are based on the names of the various controls within the InfoPath form itself. The names of the controls will be made more user friendly based on their camel casing; for example, ManagerName becomes Manager Name.

8. To add a column, click the Add button. This opens the Select a Field or Group window. Here you can select which field you want to include in the default content type associated to the form library. Because of this, such a field will become available as a column within a SharePoint document library column. You can choose to create a new column or to add the selected field to an already existing site column group (see Figure 8-12).

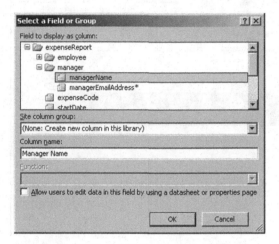

Figure 8-12. *Choose which fields you want to promote.*

9. The next step of the Publishing Wizard gives an overview of the information you entered in the previous steps. Click Finish when you are satisfied with this information.

10. The last step of the Publishing Wizard lets you know that the form was published successfully and offers the following options:

   • *Notify users via e-mail that you have published a form in a Sharepoint document library:* Selecting this option creates a new e-mail containing the form. Users receiving this e-mail can fill out the form and submit it. Figure 8-13 shows an e-mail containing the Expense Report form.

   • *Open this Document Library option:* The browser will open the document library as soon as you click the Close button.

   • *Open in Browser option:* Clicking this link will open the form in a browser using Forms Server 2007, like a user would see the form without InfoPath. Read more about Forms Server in the section "Forms Services 2007." Depending on how the form was published or what it contains, you might also need to set the form's security options.

11. In this example, we will just click the Close button and browse to the ExpenseReports form library on the SharePoint site.

Click New ➤ New Document in the ExpenseReports forms library. InfoPath opens and shows you the form in published mode. A user can fill out the form and submit it back to the form library. The form library will show all filled-out forms and the values of the promoted columns, as shown in Figure 8-14.

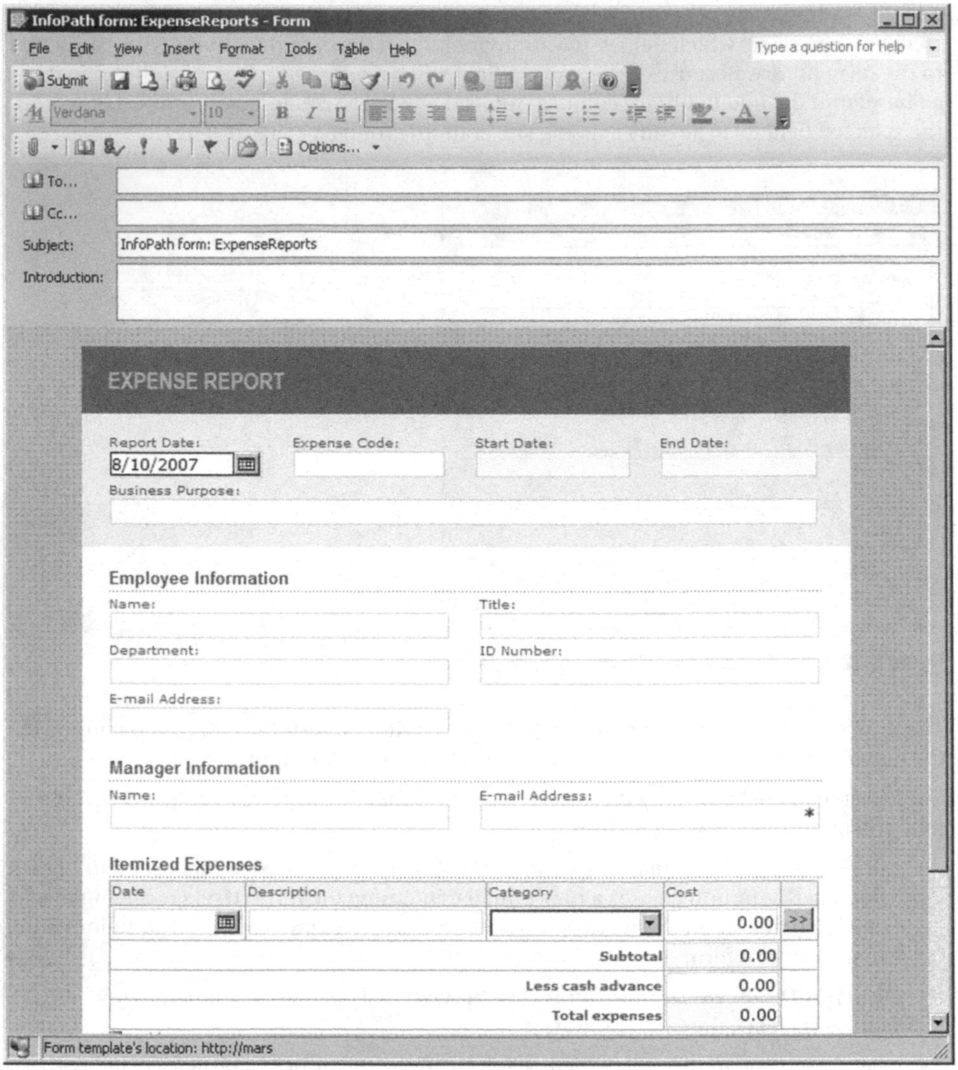

Figure 8-13. *An InfoPath form in an e-mail using Outlook 2007*

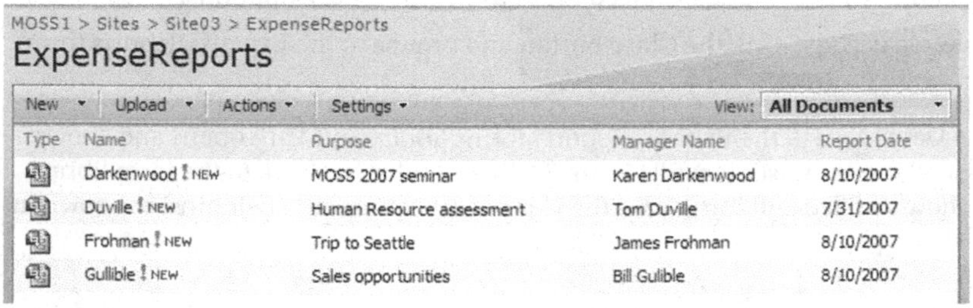

Figure 8-14. *The SharePoint form library called ExpenseReports*

Trust Levels

You can let InfoPath 2007 decide automatically what security level applies to an InfoPath form. A security level determines which features are available to the InfoPath form. InfoPath 2007 supports three separate security levels that determine what features are available to an InfoPath form:

- Full trust security level
- Domain security level
- Restricted security level

At design time, InfoPath 2007 will automatically choose the security level that provides the minimum amount of permissions that are required to execute the form successfully. You can override this behavior by choosing a different form security level manually.

You can do this by setting the security level and signing the form template with a certificate in InfoPath via Tools ➤ Form Options. This opens the Form Options window, where you can select the Security and Trust category. Figure 8-15 shows the Security and Trust category in the Form Options window. Here you can select whether you want InfoPath to automatically determine the security level or whether you want to do it manually. You can also specify a digital certificate that you want to use to sign the form template.

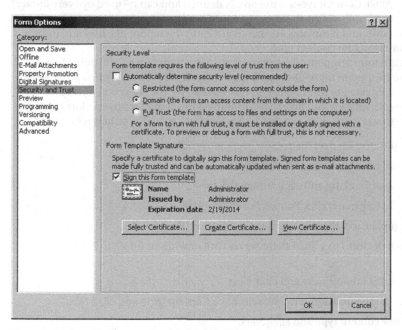

Figure 8-15. *Specify the security level in the Form Options window.*

If the developer specifies that a form must run within a certain security level, the form will only run if the client decides to grant sufficient rights to the form; otherwise the form will not open. Security levels are granted based on the location, installation type, and the (optional) presence of a digital signature.

A form is allowed to run within the full trust context when it is digitally signed with a certificate, or when the form is installed on the client via an .msi (Microsoft Installer) file. Forms running within the full trust context are allowed to access content located anywhere.

A form that runs in the domain security context is allowed to access resources that the end user is allowed to access based on the security levels specified for a zone in Internet Explorer. This means that the form is able to access data stored within the form itself or the domain of the form, and it is also allowed to access data coming from content included in the Internet Explorer Trusted sites zone, Local computer zone, and Local intranet zone.

Finally, forms running in the Restricted security level context are only allowed to access data that is stored within the form itself. If you want to find out more about the security levels of InfoPath forms, please refer to the following location: `http://office.microsoft.com/en-us/infopath/hp010967191033.aspx`.

■Note If you publish a form that runs under the Restricted security level, you can still publish it as a content type unless the form is browser-enabled. In the latter case, you will not be able to publish the form as a site content type.

Using Site Content Types

Content types are a new feature of SharePoint 2007 (Windows SharePoint Services 3.0 and Microsoft Office SharePoint Server 2007). Content types are centrally defined and can be used by every library in the site collection. Content types define the document profile of a piece of content concerning the use of columns, workflows, and templates. In SharePoint 2007, document libraries and form libraries can contain more than one content type.

Looking at an InfoPath form template, this means that a form template can be published as a site content type and can be used in more than one form library. Besides that, it is also possible to use more than one form template per form library. In this section, we will show you how to publish a form template as a site content type and how to use multiple form templates in one form library.

The next procedure shows you how to publish a form template as a site content type.

1. Open InfoPath 2007.

2. Customize a Sample on the Getting Started window.

3. Select Sample – Asset Tracking and click Design this form.

4. In the Design Tasks task pane, click Publish Form Template.

5. Save the form template locally. This opens the Publishing Wizard.

6. Choose to publish the form to a SharePoint server with or without InfoPath Forms Services and click Next.

7. Enter the name of a SharePoint site and click Next.

8. On the next page of the Publishing Wizard, select Site Content Type and click Next.

9. Select Create a new content type and click Next.

10. Specify a name for the new content type in the Name text box and click Next.

11. On the next page of the Publishing Wizard, enter a location for the form template and click Next.

12. You can add, remove, or modify a site column. Click Next when you're done.

13. Click Publish and click Close.

■**Note** The Create a new content type option is only available if you are using Microsoft Office SharePoint Server 2007 Enterprise edition and you have activated the "Office SharePoint Server Standard Web application features" feature for the web application.

We are going to repeat the previous procedure for another form template. This time we will use the Sample – Meeting Agenda form template. After publishing the Meeting Agenda sample form template, open the site content type gallery. The next procedure shows you how to do this.

1. Open the site (or site collection) where you pulished the form templates as content types in a browser.

2. If you have published the form templates to a site, click Site Actions ➤ Site Settings.

3. If you have published the form templates to a site collection, click Site Actions ➤ Site Settings ➤ Modify All Site Settings.

4. In the Galleries section, click Site content types. This opens the Site Content Type Gallery page, as shown in Figure 8-16.

MOSS1 > Sites > Site03 > Site Settings > Site Content Type Gallery
Site Content Type Gallery

Use this page to create and manage content types declared on this site and all parent sites. Content types visible on this page are available for use on this site and its subsites.

📄 Create

Site Content Type	Parent	Source
Business Intelligence		
Dashboard Page	Document	MOSS1
Indicator using data in Excel workbook	Common Indicator Columns	MOSS1
Indicator using data in SharePoint list	Common Indicator Columns	MOSS1
Indicator using data in SQL Server 2005 Analysis Services	Common Indicator Columns	MOSS1
Indicator using manually entered information	Common Indicator Columns	MOSS1
Report	Document	MOSS1
Microsoft Office InfoPath		
AssetTracking	Form	Site03
MeetingAgenda	Form	Site03

Figure 8-16. *Site Content Type Gallery*

We have published two form templates, AssetTracking and MeetingAgenda, as site content types. Now, it is time to create a form library that supports the use of content types and add these two content types. The next procedure shows you how to do this.

1. Open the site where you want to create a form library.

2. Click Site Actions ➤ Create.

3. In the Libraries section, click Form Library.

4. Specify a name for the form library and click Create.

5. Select Settings ➤ Form Library Settings.

6. In the General Settings section, click Advanced settings.

7. In the Content Types section, select Yes to allow management of content types. Click OK.

8. On the Customize page, a section called Content Types is added. This section contains one content type called Form, which is the default content type. Click Add from existing site content types. This opens the Add Content Types page.

9. Select Microsoft Office InfoPath from the Select site content types from drop-down list. This results in two available content types, namely AssetTracking and MeetingAgenda.

10. Select the two content types and click Add. This is shown in Figure 8-17.

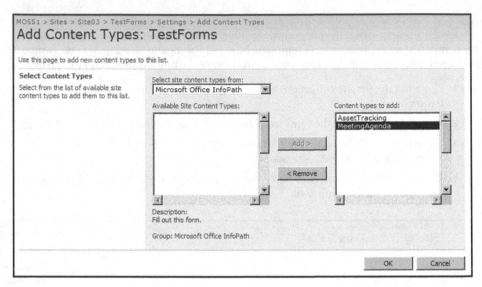

Figure 8-17. *Add Content Types page*

11. Click OK.

12. In the Content Types section, select the Form content type. This opens the List Content Type : [name content type] page.

13. In the Settings section, select Delete this content type. A pop-up window will be shown with the question: Are you sure you want to delete this list content type? Click OK.

Browse to the form library, where you have added the AssetTracking and MeetingAgenda content types. When you click New, you will notice that there are now two content types you can choose from, as shown in Figure 8-18.

Figure 8-18. *Select which form to create.*

In this section, we have shown you how to publish an InfoPath form template so that it can be used as a site content type. Site content types can be used by every library in the site collection (this can also be a document library), and it is possible to add multiple content types to one library.

Sharing Data Connection Files in a Data Connection Library

InfoPath forms can have one main data connection (primary connection) and one or more secondary data connections. A data connection can submit to or receive data from an external data source such as a web service, SharePoint list, or SQL Server database.

■**Note** InfoPath insists that you can only create a connection to a SQL Server database. It also seems to work for other types of databases, such as Oracle, although this is not supported officially. Instead, if you want to support such a scenario, you should instead create a web service that retrieves the data as XML from a third-party database.

If several form templates are using the same data connection, it is useful to create a data connection file. This connection file can be reused among different form templates so that you do not have to create a data connection for each form template.

A data connection file is an XML file with an .xml or .udc(x) extension, where udc(x) stands for Universal Data Connection.

■**Note** Data connection files follow the Universal Data Connection version 2.0 format. This is a superset of version 1.0, which is used by SharePoint Designer and Access. Udc 1.0 files use the extension .odc, which stands for Office Data Connection. Data connection files that are in the version 1.0 format cannot be used by InfoPath 2007. InfoPath is not the only technology that supports data connection files; Excel Services (a component of Microsoft Office SharePoint Server 2007, but not discussed in this book) also support the reuse of data connections.

The advantages of using data connections files are

- Data connection files can be reused; multiple forms can use the same data connection file.

- If the connection settings change, you only have to change this once in the data connection file and not in every form template that contains this data connection.

- A data connection file can include alternative authentication information that can be used when a browser-enabled form is filled out.

- It is possible for browser-enabled forms to connect to other servers in another domain when making use of data connections that use data connection files.

When you start to work with data connection files, you first need to create a SharePoint data connection library, a library where data connection files can be saved. The next procedure shows you how to create a data connection library.

1. Open a site collection in a browser.

2. Click the View All Site Content link (on the left). This opens the All Site Content page.

3. Click Create. This opens the Create page.

4. In the Libraries section, click Data Connection Library. This opens the New page.

5. Enter a name. We will enter the following name: **DataConnections**.

6. Click Create. This creates a new data connection library.

There are three ways to create data connection files. Two of those ways are easy; the other requires some work. The first, easy way, and probably the one that is used most often, is creating a data connection file via InfoPath. In InfoPath, you can covert data connections into UDC files and store them in a data connection library. You can also use Excel to create data connection files. If you want to learn more about this topic, please refer to the article "Create, edit, and manage connections to external data," located at http://office.microsoft.com/en-us/excel/HA101672271033.aspx. You can also create the UDC file manually via Notepad (or any other text editor you prefer) or via the UDC File Authoring Tool that is discussed at the end of this section. The section "Using Data from a SharePoint List" shows how to convert a data connection into a UDC file and save it in a data connection library.

Note One of the reasons why you should create a data connection file manually (or by using the UDC File Authoring Tool) instead of using InfoPath to create a data connection file is because in InfoPath, you cannot add authentication information to a data connection file. More information about authentication in data connection files can be found at the following location: http://blogs.msdn.com/infopath/archive/2006/06/14/advanced-server-side-authentication-for-data-connections-part-1.aspx.

In the remainder of this section, we will show you how to create a data connection file via a text editor and how to use the UDC File Authoring Tool. Follow these steps to create and upload a data connection file.

1. Open Notepad.

2. Copy and paste Listing 8-1 into Notepad.

Listing 8-1. *UDC File for a SharePoint List*

```
<?MicrosoftWindowsSharePointServices ➥
  ContentTypeID="0x010100B4CBD48E029A4ad8B62CB0E41868F2B0"?>
<udc:DataSource MajorVersion="2" MinorVersion="0" ➥
  xmlns:udc="http://schemas.microsoft.com/office/infopath/2006/udc">
  <udc:Name>Tasks</udc:Name>
  <udc:Description/>
  <udc:Type MajorVersion="2" MinorVersion="0" Type=""/>
    <udc:ConnectionInfo Purpose="">
      <udc:SelectCommand>
        <udc:ListId>{4008B331-501E-4E73-A147-822D01E4326C}</udc:ListId>
        <udc:WebUrl>http://[server]</udc:WebUrl>
      </udc:SelectCommand>
    </udc:ConnectionInfo>
</udc:DataSource>
```

3. Replace value of the udc:ListId element with the list id of the SharePoint list you want to use. In this example, we are going to use the Tasks list.

The data connection file starts with a processing instruction that specifies a content type id. This processing instruction associates this file with the UDC content type on a Microsoft Office SharePoint 2007 server. As a result, the Name, Title, Description, Type, and Purpose fields will be promoted into columns in the data connection library. This helps InfoPath to recognize the data connection file. The root element of the data connection file is DataSource. The DataSource element has a Major attribute to specify that the UDC version is 2.0. It also declares that the udc v2 namespace is used. The Type attribute of the Type element and the Purpose attribute of the Connection element are required. The Type attribute contains information about the type of connection that is used. The Purpose attribute contains information about the type of access of the data source. See Table 8-1 for more details. The values of the Type and Purpose attributes can be specified when we upload the UDC file into the SharePoint data connection library.

Table 8-1. *Values of the* Type *and* Purpose *Attributes*

Value	Description
Type Attribute Values of the Type Element	
SharePointList	This is a query connection to a SharePoint list.
SharePointLibrary	This is a submit connection to a SharePoint library.
Database	This is a query connection to a database.
XmlQuery	This is a query connection to an XML file.
XmlSubmit	This is an HTTP Post submit connection.
WebService	This is a query or submit connection to a web service.
Purpose Attribute Values of the Connection Element	
ReadOnly	All query connections are read-only connections.
WriteOnly	All submit connections are write-only connections.
ReadWrite	Only the WebService connection type can be ReadWrite. The XmlSubmit and XmlQuery connections must both be specified and must both reference the same WSDL.

CONVERTING A URL-ENCODED GUID

You can retrieve the GUID of a SharePoint list by browsing to the SharePoint list and clicking Settings ➤ List Settings. You can copy the URL-encoded GUID from the URL (which is the value of the list query string parameter). You can remove any URL escape codes programmatically using the JavaScript unescape() function. Copy the following line of code in the location bar of the browser and press Enter

```
javascript:unescape ➡
('%7B4008B331%2D501E%2D4E73%2DA147%2D822D01E4326C%7D');
```

The browser will display a GUID that does not contain URL encoding. In this case, the result is {4008B331-501E-4E73-A147-822D01E4326C}.

Please note that not all browsers support this little trick. Alternatively, you can create a custom HTML page that does the same job for you. This is shown in Listing 8-2.

Listing 8-2. *Converting a URL-encoded GUID*

```
<html>
  <body>
    <script language="javascript">
      document.write(➡
      unescape('%7B4008B331%2D501E%2D4E73%2DA147%2D822D01E4326C%7D'));
    </script>
  </body>
</html>
```

4. Replace the value of the udc:WebUrl element with the fully qualified URL of the SharePoint site that contains the data connection library.

5. Save the file with an .xml extension.

6. Open a browser and go to the data connection library you created earlier.

7. Click Upload ➤ Upload Document.

8. Click Browse and select the data connection file you just created.

9. Click OK.

10. On the Properties page, select the following value from the Content Type drop-down list: Universal Data Connection File.

11. Enter a name and description for the data connection file.

12. Select the following value from the UDC Purpose drop-down list: ReadOnly.

13. Select the following value from the Connection Type drop-down list: SharePoint list. This is shown in Figure 8-19. Click OK when you are ready.

14. From the action menu of the newly added data connection file, select Approve/reject and approve the data connection file.

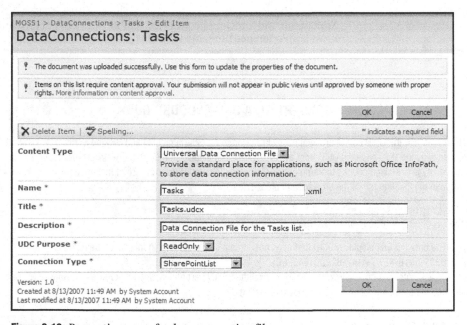

Figure 8-19. *Properties page of a data connection file*

Two members of the Microsoft InfoPath Team, Nick Dallet and Travis Rhodes, have created a UDC file authoring tool. This tool is actually an InfoPath form template and can be used to create UDC files. You can download the UDC file authoring tool from the following blog: `http://blogs. msdn.com/infopath/archive/2007/02/12/udc-file-authoring-tool.aspx`. After you have downloaded the form template, you have to republish it on your own network location; after that you can use it to create custom UDC files. Figure 8-20 shows the UDC authoring tool that is used to create a UDC file.

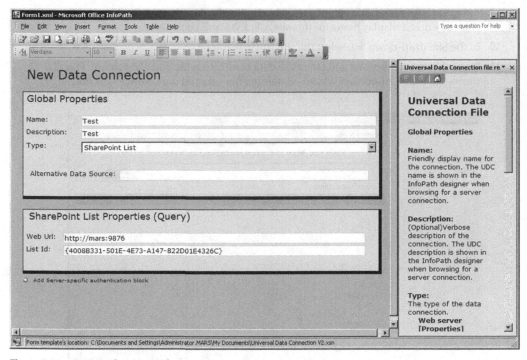

Figure 8-20. *UDC authoring tool*

Caution If you are running Windows SharePoint Services 3.0 in combination with Forms Server 2007 (described in the section "Forms Services 2007"), it is possible that the data connection files you upload to your data connection library might not be visible. For example, when you enter the URL `http://[server]/dataconnectionlib/forms`, a data connection file might not show up in the data connection library. This problem can be solved by entering the fully qualified URL (including the name of the data connection file), like this: `http://[server]/dataconnectionlib/forms/mydataconnection.udcx`. More information about this issue can be found in knowledge base article 922084: `http://support.microsoft.com/kb/922084`.

To try out the data connection file, we are going to create a very simple form template and add our data connection. For this example, we have added some dummy tasks to the Tasks list. The next procedure shows you how to create a form template that references the data connection file.

1. Open InfoPath 2007.

2. In the Getting Started window, click Design a Form Template.

3. Select Blank and click OK.

4. Click Tools ➤ Data Connections. This opens the Data Connections window.

5. Click Add. This opens the Data Connection Wizard.

6. Select Search for connections on a Microsoft Office SharePoint server and click Next.

7. Click Manage Sites. This opens the Manage Sites window.

8. Click Add. This opens the Site Details window.

9. Enter the URL of the SharePoint site that contains the data connection library. Optionally you can enter a display name for this site. Click OK and click Close.

10. In the Site drop-down list, select the site you just entered.

11. Expand data connections and select the data connection file you want to use. Figure 8-21 shows the Data Connection Wizard containing the selected data connection file.

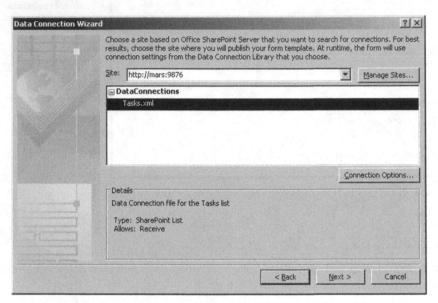

Figure 8-21. *Data Connection Wizard containing the selected data connection file*

12. Click Next.

13. The available columns for the Tasks list are shown. Select Title and click Next.

14. You can choose to store a copy of the data in the form template. If you choose to do so, the data is stored locally for use in offline mode. Choosing this option enables users to access form data if they are offline working with the form for the first time. Click Next.

15. Enter a name for the data connection. Click Finish and Close.

16. Add some text and a drop-down list to the InfoPath form and double-click the drop-down list. This opens the Drop-Down List Box Properties window.

17. In the List box entries section, select Look up values from an external data source.

18. In the Data Source drop-down list, select the data connection we just added.

19. Click the button at the right of the Entries field. This opens the Select a Field or Group window.

20. Select Title (as shown in Figure 8-22) and click OK.

21. Select the Show only entries with unique display names check box. Click OK and save the InfoPath form.

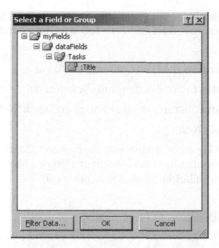

Figure 8-22. *The Select a Field or Group window*

You can test the InfoPath form by clicking File ➤ Preview Form. This opens a new instance of InfoPath with the InfoPath form in preview mode.

Using Data from a SharePoint List

Other than the option of publishing a form in a SharePoint form library, there are other ways to use SharePoint and InfoPath together. You can access data that is stored in a SharePoint list within an InfoPath form. Data stored in a SharePoint list can be accessed via the SharePoint library or list data connection, or via the SharePoint Lists web service. An advantage of using a list data connection is that it allows you to specify authentication information within the data connection itself.

■Tip If you want to use Forms Based Authentication (FBA) and create a data source that retrieves data from a SharePoint list, you cannot use the list directly. Instead, you need to access the list data via the SharePoint Lists web service.

Sometimes you want to use data listed in a SharePoint site. For example, imagine a list of users or e-mail addresses that you would like to use in an InfoPath form. We will show you how to make a drop-down list in an InfoPath form populated by the data from a SharePoint list. The SharePoint list we are going to use for this example will contain a couple of e-mail addresses. We have made a custom list called EmailAddresses and added a couple of e-mail addresses to the Title column.

We are going to work with the Expense Report form template that we saved in the ExpenseReports form library. The next procedure shows you how to edit the form template.

1. Browse to the form library. Click Settings ➤ Form Library Settings.

2. In the General Settings section, select Advanced Settings.

3. In the Document Template section, click Edit Template.

The next step is to create a secondary data connection to the EmailAddresses SharePoint list. This data connection will be used by the InfoPath form to receive data. The following procedure shows you how to do this:

1. Click Tools ➤ Data Connections ➤ Add. This opens the Data Connection Wizard.

2. Select that you want to create a new connection to Receive data and click Next.

3. Choose that you want to receive the data from a SharePoint list or library and click Next.

4. Enter the URL of your SharePoint site and click Next.

5. The Data Connection Wizard page, shown in Figure 8-23, shows all the lists and libraries that are available for providing an XML representation of the content of a list or a library of the SharePoint site you specified. Select the EmailAddresses list and click Next.

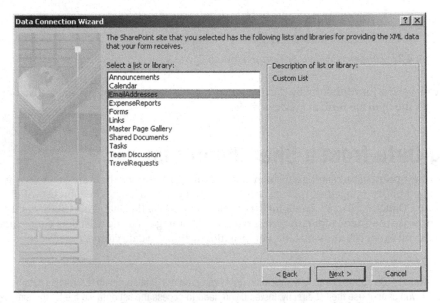

Figure 8-23. *The Data Connection Wizard page lets you choose which list to use.*

6. The next step gives you a list of all the columns that can be selected for use. Select the ID and Title columns and click Next.

7. In this step, you can choose to store a copy of the data in the form template. If you choose to do so, the data is stored locally for use in offline mode.

8. Enter a name for the data connection (we will call it **EmailAddresses**) and click Finish. This page has a check box that enables automatic data retrieval in the InfoPath form. If the content of the source SharePoint list is changed, the InfoPath form will detect this and display the latest changes in the form.

9. Click Convert. This opens the Convert Data Connection window.

10. Browse to the data connection library created earlier in this chapter (in our case http://mars:9876/DataConnections) and specify a name for the new data connection file. We will call the data connection file EmailAddresses.udcx.

11. Click OK.

12. In the Data Connection Wizard, click Close.

At this point, the EmailAddresses data connection is hooked up to the EmailAddresses SharePoint list, but not to the user interface of the form. To do this, you need to go back to the Expense Report InfoPath form template and bind the EmailAddresses data connection to the e-mail field of the manager, which is just a text box. The following procedure shows you how to do this:

1. Right-click the Manager E-mail Address text box, click Change To, and choose Drop-Down List Box.

2. Right-click the Manager E-MailAddress drop-down list box and choose Drop-Down List Box Properties. This opens the Drop-Down List Box Properties dialog window.

3. In the List Box Entries section of the Drop-Down List Box Properties dialog window, select the Look up values from an external data source option.

4. Set the Data Source to the EmailAddresses data connection, as shown in Figure 8-24.

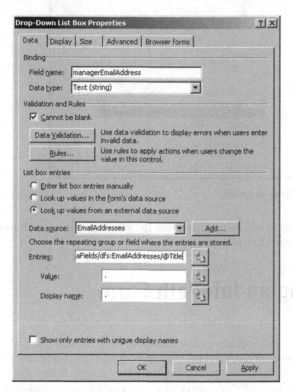

Figure 8-24. *The Drop-Down List Box Properties window*

5. Click the button at the right of the Entries field. This opens the Select a Field or Group window.

6. Select the Title field and click OK twice.

When previewing the customized form, you will see the content of the SharePoint list in a drop-down list in the InfoPath form (see Figure 8-25).

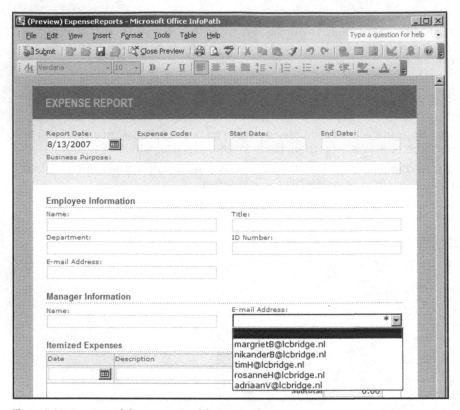

Figure 8-25. *Preview of the customized form template*

In this section, we have showed you how to use a SharePoint list as a data source and how to convert this data source into a data connection file.

Updating and Saving an InfoPath Form Programmatically

In the next example, we will show you how to update an InfoPath form programmatically and save it back to a SharePoint form library. If you want to try out the code, you should create a SharePoint site called Site03 and create a new InfoPath form without using one of the sample forms. The next procedure shows you how to create the new InfoPath form that we are going to use in this example.

1. Open InfoPath 2007.

2. In the Getting Started window, click Design a Form Template. This opens the Design a Form Template window.

3. Select a Blank Form Template and click OK.

4. In the Design Tasks task pane, click Layout. This opens the Layout task pane.

5. Drag and drop the Layout with Title layout table onto the design surface of the form.

6. Give the InfoPath form a title; in this example we will call it **Custom Form**.

7. In the Layout task pane, click Design Tasks. This opens the Design Tasks task pane.

8. In the Design Tasks task pane, click Controls. This opens the Controls task pane.

9. Drag and drop a Text Box control onto the design surface of the form. Double-click this text box. This opens the Text Box Properties window.

10. In the Field name text box, enter the following name: **Name**.

11. Add four more text boxes and give them the following Field names: **Address**, **City**, **Country**, and **Email**. Figure 8-26 shows what our form looks like in design mode.

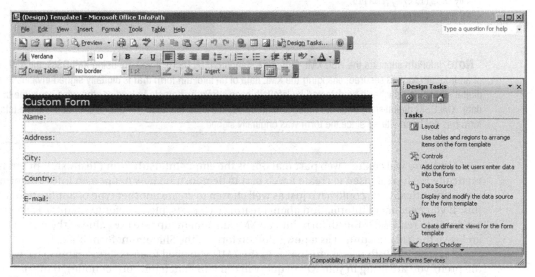

Figure 8-26. *Custom InfoPath form in design mode*

We will publish the InfoPath form to a SharePoint form library called TestFormLib. Make sure that you promote at least the Email field to the SharePoint form library. The publication of InfoPath forms was demonstrated previously in the section "InfoPath Walkthrough."

Create an empty form in this form library based on the new template and call it TestA.xml.

Open the InfoPath form (TestA.xml) in Notepad (or any other text editor) to see the XML contents. The `<mso-infoPathSolution>` InfoPath processing instruction contains attributes that describe the solution version, the version of InfoPath used to create the form, the processing instruction version, and the location and name of the InfoPath template (`href`). The `href` attribute represents the URL of the document template; this is also known as the *template pointer location*. Listing 8-3 shows the XML contents of the InfoPath form.

Listing 8-3. *XML Contents of an InfoPath Form*

```
<?xml version="1.0" encoding="UTF-8"?>
<?mso-infoPathSolution ➥
solutionVersion="1.0.0.2" ➥
productVersion="12.0.0" ➥
PIVersion="1.0.0.0" ➥
href=http://mars:9876/SiteDirectory/Site03/TestFormLib/Forms/template.xsn ➥
name="urn:schemas-microsoft-com:office:infopath:TestFormLib: ➥
-myXSD-2007-08-17T08-22-21" ?>
<?mso-application ➥
progid="InfoPath.Document" ➥
versionProgid="InfoPath.Document.2"?>
```

```
<my:myFields ➡
xmlns:my="http://schemas.microsoft.com/office/infopath/2003 ➡
/myXSD/2007-08-17T08:22:21" ➡
xml:lang="en-us">
  <my:Name></my:Name>
  <my:Address></my:Address>
  <my:City></my:City>
  <my:Country></my:Country>
  <my:Email></my:Email>
</my:myFields>
```

Note InfoPath supports the W3C XML Signature standard (XMLDSIG). If you are using XMLDSIG, the XML data of an InfoPath form is secured; changing the XML data of an InfoPath form that is digitally signed invalidates the digital signature, which will be detected by InfoPath once InfoPath attempts to load or otherwise consume the data. XMLDSIG digital signatures are most commonly used to ascertain that the XML data underlying the InfoPath form has not been altered since the form was originally signed.

Next, you will create a web part that opens the empty InfoPath form (TestA.xml) programmatically. We have chosen to create a web part to demonstrate how to open an InfoPath form programmatically; we could have just as well chosen to create another type of application to do this. If you need more information about creating web parts, please refer to Chapter 1. Then you are going to read the InfoPath form into an XML document, update the value of the e-mail field, and save the XML document as a new InfoPath form to the SharePoint form library.

Because InfoPath uses namespaces in the XML, you need to associate a namespace with the prefix you are using in your XPath query in order to match the correct nodes in the document. This namespace can be retrieved from the XML contents of the InfoPath form. This namespace is retrieved from the <myFields> element shown in Listing 8-3. You can do this by using of the XmlNamespaceManager class that is shown in Listing 8-4.

Listing 8-4. *Web Part That Uses the XmlNamespaceManager Class*

```
using System;
using System.IO;
using System.Collections.Generic;
using System.Runtime.InteropServices;
using System.Text;
using System.Web.UI;
using System.Web.UI.WebControls.WebParts;
using System.Web.UI.HtmlControls;
using System.Web.UI.WebControls;
using System.Xml;
using System.Xml.Serialization;
using Microsoft.SharePoint;
using Microsoft.SharePoint.WebControls;
using Microsoft.SharePoint.WebPartPages;

namespace LoisAndClark.TestWebPartLibrary
{
    [Guid("48b4bc88-44d5-471e-8cb6-da79a22569ff")]
    public class TestFormWebPart : System.Web.UI.WebControls.WebParts.WebPart
    {
```

```
protected override void CreateChildControls()
{
  SPWeb objSite = ➧
  new SPSite(@"http://mars:9876/SiteDirectory/Site03").OpenWeb();
  objSite.AllowUnsafeUpdates = true;
  SPFile objFile = objSite.Folders["TestFormLib"].Files["TestA.xml"];

  MemoryStream objMemoryStream = new MemoryStream(objFile.OpenBinary());
  XmlTextReader objXmlReader = new XmlTextReader(objMemoryStream);
  XmlDocument objXmlDocument = new XmlDocument();
  objXmlDocument.Load(objXmlReader);
  objXmlReader.Close();
  objMemoryStream.Close();

  XmlElement objRootElement = objXmlDocument.DocumentElement;

  XmlNamespaceManager objNamespaceManager = ➧
  new XmlNamespaceManager(objXmlDocument.NameTable);
  objNamespaceManager.AddNamespace("my", ➧
  "http://schemas.microsoft.com/office/infopath/2003 ➧
  /myXSD/2007-08-17T08:22:21");
  XmlNode objNode = ➧
  objXmlDocument.SelectSingleNode("//my:Email", objNamespaceManager);
  objNode.InnerXml = "info@lcbridge.nl";

  ASCIIEncoding encoding = new ASCIIEncoding();
  objFile = objSite.Folders["TestFormLib"].Files.Add("TestA-edited.xml", ➧
  (encoding.GetBytes(objXmlDocument.OuterXml)), true);
  }
 }
}
```

Figure 8-27 shows the programmatically created InfoPath form in a SharePoint form library.

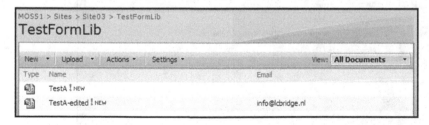

Figure 8-27. *The programmatically created InfoPath form*

Using a Submit Button

End users can save a form to a location, for example, a SharePoint form library. Alternatively, you can add a Submit button to a form that allows end users to save the form. This gives the designers of the form greater control over the saving process. For example, this allows the form designer to decide where and under which name a form is saved (so that the form adheres to naming conventions). This makes the saving process easier, which is also beneficial to the end user. Also, taking control of the submission process results in a higher level of control over the user interface.

Within an InfoPath form, you must use a secondary data connection. It is possible to submit data to more than one location by using rules.

In this example, we will show you how to submit a form to a SharePoint form library via a Submit button. We are going to create a Travel Request form. Do this by using the Travel Request sample form and publish the form to a new form library called TravelRequests. The next procedure shows you how to edit the form template.

1. Browse to the form library. Click Settings ➤ Form Library Settings.

2. In the General Settings section, select Advanced Settings.

3. In the Document Template section, click Edit Template.

The next step is to create a secondary data connection to the TravelRequests form library. This data connection will be used by the InfoPath form to submit data to a form library. The following procedure shows you how to do this:

1. Click Tools ➤ Data Connections ➤ Add. This opens the Data Connection Wizard.

2. Select that you want to create a new connection to submit data, and click Next.

3. Choose that you want to submit the data to a document library on a SharePoint site and click Next.

4. In the document library text box, enter the URL and the name of the form library. In our case, the URL looks like this: http://mars:9876/SiteDirectory/Site03/TravelRequests. You have to provide a unique file name for each form that the user submits. This file name can contain a formula, and you can use fields that are available in the form (see Figure 8-28).

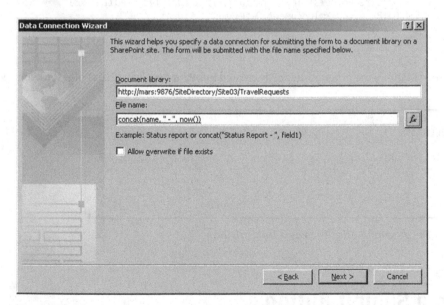

Figure 8-28. *The Data Connection Wizard page*

Use the following formula to generate a file name: concat(name, " - ", now()). The formula uses the name of the traveler (it is after all a travel request form we are making) concatenated with the current date and time. Click Next when you are ready.

5. Enter a name for the data connection. We will call the form **SubmitForm**. Click Finish.

6. Click Convert. This opens the Convert Data Connection window.

7. Browse to the data connection library created earlier in this chapter (http://mars:9876/ DataConnections) and specify a name for the new data connection file. In this example, we will call the data connection file **SubmitForm.udcx**.

8. Click OK.

9. Click Close in the Data Connection Wizard.

Now you need to configure the Submit command for the InfoPath form template. The following procedure shows you how to do this:

1. Click Tools ➤ Submit Options. This opens the Submit Options window, as you can see in Figure 8-29. Click the Allow users to submit this form radio button to enable the Submit commands and buttons.

2. Select SharePoint document library from the Send form data to a single destination drop-down list.

3. Select the SubmitForm data connection from the Choose a data connection for submit drop-down list.

4. Click the Advanced button to reveal options that let you specify what to do after the user submits the form. For example, you can choose to create a new blank form for the user. In addition, you can specify success and failure messages, which the user will see in a pop-up window after clicking the Submit button. Figure 8-29 shows the Submit Options window. Click OK when you are finished.

5. Save the form template and publish it again to the TravelRequests form library.

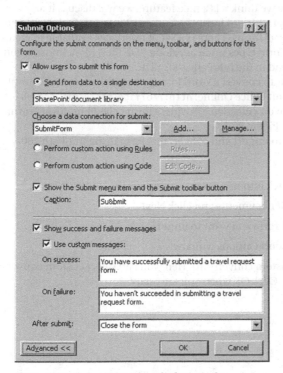

Figure 8-29. *Submit Options dialog window*

Note In the Submit Options window, you have the option to perform custom actions by using rules or code. You can use rules to submit data in the form to more than one external data source. For example, you can add a rule to submit data in the form to a web service and a database when the user clicks the Submit button.

When you go to the SharePoint form library, you will see the submitted InfoPath forms and their generated names. One of the forms in our form library is named "van Vuuren A - 2007-08-10T18_49_46" as you can see in Figure 8-30.

MOSS1 > Sites > Site03 > TravelRequests

TravelRequests

| New ▾ | Upload ▾ | Actions ▾ | Settings ▾ | | View: **All Documents** ▾ |

Type	Name	Name	Purpose	Request Date
📄	Hessels P - 2007-08-10T18_43_43 ! NEW	Hessels P	MOSS 2007 Seminar	7/29/2007
📄	Jani Chang - 2007-08-10T18_44_52 ! NEW	Jani Chang	Business Trip to Asia	8/1/2007
📄	van Vuuren A - 2007-08-10T18_49_46 ! NEW	van Vuuren A	Conference in Vancouver	8/8/2007

Figure 8-30. *SharePoint form library with submitted form*

Importing Forms

A new feature of InfoPath 2007 is the document import feature. In itself, this feature does not have anything to do with SharePoint, but since we think it is a nice feature, we will discuss it anyway. The document import feature helps users migrate Word forms (documents) into InfoPath form templates. InfoPath can convert Word and Excel forms. There is a set of interfaces available to create your own document converter for other form types, such as Adobe PDF files. More information about the available interfaces can be found in the InfoPath 2007 SDK.

In this section, we will show you how to convert a Word form to an InfoPath form. Examples of Word 2007 forms can be found at Microsoft Office Online: `http://office.microsoft.com/en-us/templates/CT101043201033.aspx`. We have downloaded a business form called Employee warning notice. In Word 2007, this form looks like Figure 8-31.

The next procedure shows you how to import and convert this form using InfoPath 2007.

1. Open InfoPath 2007.

2. In the Getting Started window, click Import a Form. This opens the Import Wizard.

3. Select InfoPath importer for Word documents and click Next.

4. Click browse and select the Word form you want to import.

5. Click Options. This opens the Import Options window.

6. Select Layout and form fields (custom conversion). Here you can select custom conversion settings, as shown in Figure 8-32. Click OK when you are ready.

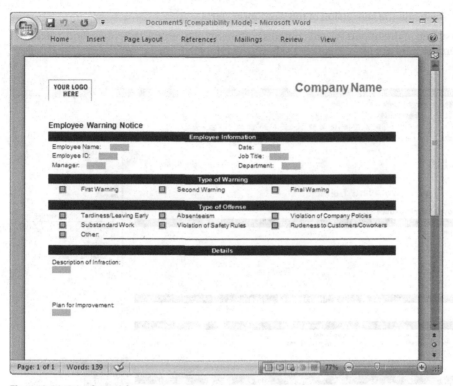

Figure 8-31. *Word 2007 form*

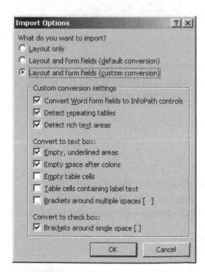

Figure 8-32. *Conversion settings*

7. Click Finish and the conversion of the Word form starts.

8. The last step of the Import Wizard contains comments concerning the conversion. Click OK to open the InfoPath form. Figure 8-33 shows the InfoPath form.

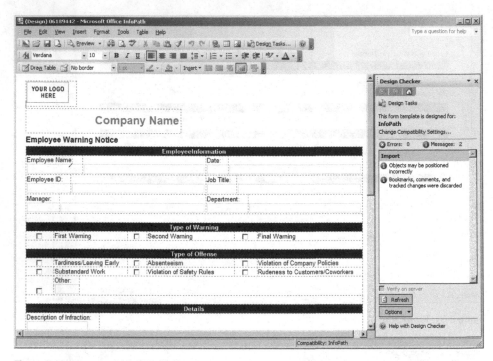

Figure 8-33. *Converted InfoPath form*

The Design Checker task pane shows warnings and errors concerning elements that were not correctly imported. Clicking an error or warning in the Design Checker task pane opens a pop-up window containing more information about this message. The Design Checker task pane can be used to check again if there are any incompatibilities.

Forms Services 2007

The biggest drawback of InfoPath 2003 was that the InfoPath client had to be installed on each client machine. In order to change this situation, InfoPath 2007 includes a new service named Forms Services 2007. By making use of Forms Services 2007, InfoPath forms will be available for end users whether they have InfoPath 2007 installed or not.

■**Note** Actually, there are two new products in the Office System product line that provide the same functionality: Forms Server 2007 and Forms Services 2007. Forms Services is a component of Microsoft Office SharePoint Server 2007 Enterprise edition. Forms Server 2007 can be purchased as a separate product that is built on top of Windows SharePoint Services 3.0. In this chapter, we will look at the Microsoft Office SharePoint Server 2007 Enterprise Edition viewpoint and discuss Forms Services 2007. However, everything you will learn about Forms Services 2007 applies to Forms Server 2007 as well.

Using Form Services, end users can fill in forms via a browser. The following list shows an overview of the browsers that are supported:

- Internet Explorer 6.x or higher
- Firefox 1.5
- Mozilla 1.7
- Netscape Navigator 7.2
- Netscape Navigator 8.1
- Safari 2.0

■**Note** If you have Microsoft Office SharePoint Server 2007 Enterprise Edition, the Forms Services 2007 component is automatically available. If you only have Windows SharePoint Services 3.0, it is possible to acquire a separate license and run Forms Server 2007 separately. By the way, you cannot use InfoPath forms within workflows when you are using Windows SharePoint Services 3.0.

An InfoPath form template consists of one package with an .xsn extension. An InfoPath client parses these files and transforms the XML files into HTML files for display. Forms Server converts the files in the package to .aspx, .css, and .jscript files to render them in a browser.

Forms Services is available as a SharePoint feature on a Microsoft Office SharePoint Server 2007 web application, which can be activated or deactivated. If you want to use it, you need to configure at least one Shared Services Provider and associate it with the web application where you want to use Forms Services. The next procedure shows how to activate the Office SharePoint Server Enterprise Web Application features feature.

1. Open SharePoint 3.0 Central Administration.
2. Click the Application Management tab.
3. In the SharePoint Web Application Management section, click Manage Web application features. This opens the Manage Web Application Features page.
4. Next to the Office SharePoint Server Enterprise Web Application features feature, click Activate.

The next thing to do is to activate the Office SharePoint Server Enterprise feature for a specified site collection. The following procedure shows how to do this:

1. Open a browser and go to your site collection.
2. Click Site Actions ➤ Site Settings ➤ Modify All Site Settings. This opens the Site Settings page.
3. In the Site Collection Administration section, click Site collection features. This opens the Site Collection Features page.
4. Next to the Office SharePoint Server Enterprise Site Collection features feature, click Activate.

Go back to the SharePoint Central Administration ➤ Application Management to configure Forms Server. Now, you will notice a new section called InfoPath Forms Services, as shown in Figure 8-34.

Figure 8-34. *InfoPath Forms Services section in SharePoint Central Administration*

Click Configure InfoPath Forms Services in the InfoPath Forms Services section to configure Forms Server. The Configure InfoPath Forms Services page gives you several configuration options, as shown in Figure 8-35. In the User Browser-enabled Form Templates section, you can configure two settings:

- *Allow users to browser-enable form template*: Deselecting this option displays the following message whenever a user uploads a browser-enabled form template to a form library: This form is browser compatible, but it cannot be browser-enabled on the selected site.

- *Render form templates that are browser-enabled by users*: Deselecting this option prohibits the form from being rendered even if the Allow users to browser-enabled form template option is selected.

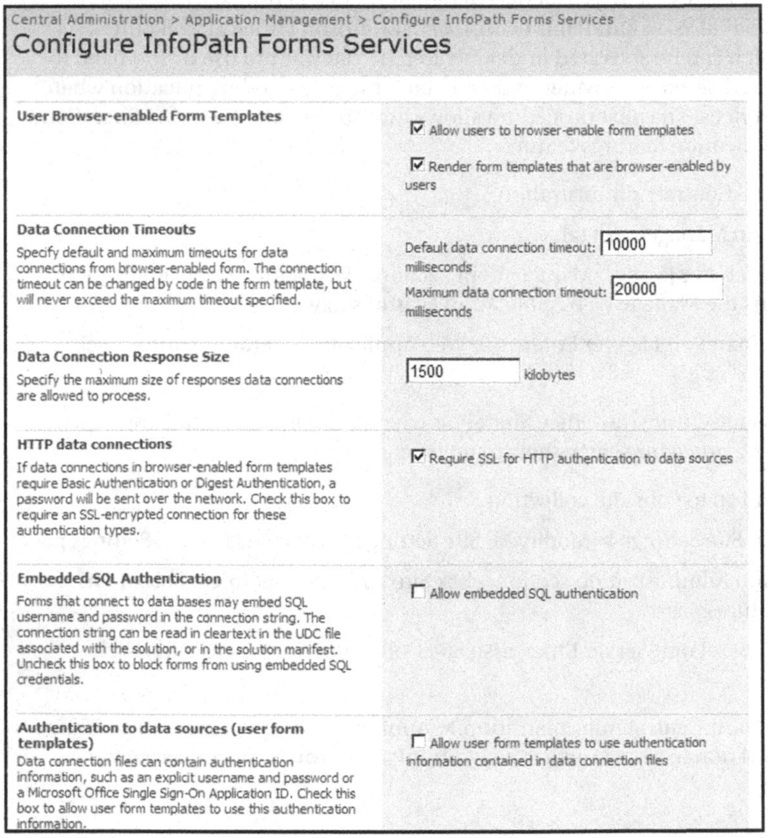

Central Administration > Application Management > Configure InfoPath Forms Services

Configure InfoPath Forms Services

User Browser-enabled Form Templates

☑ Allow users to browser-enable form templates

☑ Render form templates that are browser-enabled by users

Data Connection Timeouts

Specify default and maximum timeouts for data connections from browser-enabled form. The connection timeout can be changed by code in the form template, but will never exceed the maximum timeout specified.

Default data connection timeout: `10000` milliseconds

Maximum data connection timeout: `20000` milliseconds

Data Connection Response Size

Specify the maximum size of responses data connections are allowed to process.

`1500` kilobytes

HTTP data connections

If data connections in browser-enabled form templates require Basic Authentication or Digest Authentication, a password will be sent over the network. Check this box to require an SSL-encrypted connection for these authentication types.

☑ Require SSL for HTTP authentication to data sources

Embedded SQL Authentication

Forms that connect to data bases may embed SQL username and password in the connection string. The connection string can be read in cleartext in the UDC file associated with the solution, or in the solution manifest. Uncheck this box to block forms from using embedded SQL credentials.

☐ Allow embedded SQL authentication

Authentication to data sources (user form templates)

Data connection files can contain authentication information, such as an explicit username and password or a Microsoft Office Single Sign-On Application ID. Check this box to allow user form templates to use this authentication information.

☐ Allow user form templates to use authentication information contained in data connection files

Figure 8-35. *Configure InfoPath Forms Services*

It is possible to force forms to open in a browser even if the InfoPath client is installed on the end user's machine. The next procedure shows you how to change the form library settings.

1. Open a browser and go to a form library.

2. Click Site Settings ➤ Form Library Settings. This opens the Customize [name form library] page.

3. In the General Settings section, click Advanced settings. This opens the Form Library Advanced Settings: [name form library] page.

4. In the Browser-enabled Document section, select Display as a Web page. This is shown in Figure 8-36.

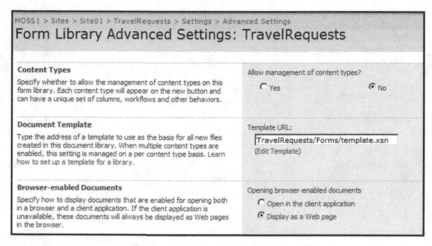

Figure 8-36. *Form Library Advanced Settings*

The end result, an InfoPath form that opened in a browser, is shown in Figure 8-37.

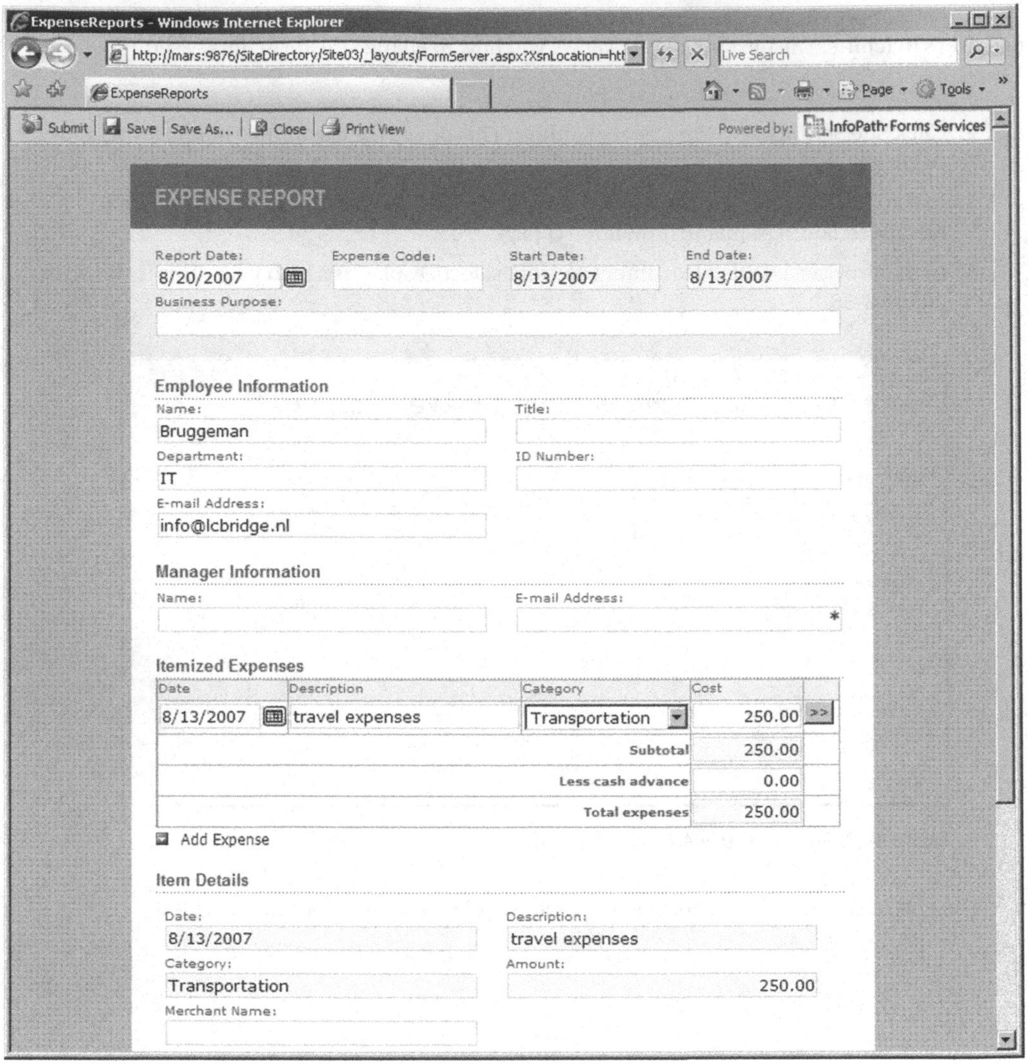

Figure 8-37. *InfoPath form opened in a browser*

Integration Between InfoPath, SharePoint, and BizTalk Server 2006

If InfoPath forms are used regularly in your company, you might need to collect or redistribute them automatically. Because InfoPath data is stored in XML, it is possible for any application to grab content from any kind of data store, generate InfoPath forms, and store those forms in a

SharePoint form library. Application-generated InfoPath forms are a great example of forms that need to be collected and redistributed to the right form libraries. The other way around is also possible; you might be interested in retrieving information from an InfoPath form and storing pieces of it in other applications.

In such application-to-application business process scenarios, you might decide that every application involved contains logic to collect or distribute InfoPath forms. This promotes code duplication and adds complexity to your IT infrastructure.

So instead, you might decide to build some kind of central messaging system responsible for all collection and redistribution of InfoPath forms. This is better, although there will come a time, sooner rather than later, when you will find it will be quite the effort to make the messaging system robust, scalable, and easy to monitor.

The final option, and probably the best way to go, is to use an existing messaging system. This is where BizTalk Server 2006 enters the picture. BizTalk Server 2006 offers integration capabilities with SharePoint 2007 (Windows SharePoint Services 3.0 and Microsoft Office SharePoint Server 2007) via the Windows SharePoint Services adapter.

In this section, we will show you how to use the Windows SharePoint Services adapter to store or retrieve InfoPath forms in and from SharePoint 2007 (this works for both Windows SharePoint Services 3.0 and Microsoft Office SharePoint Server 2007). Normally, you would use the Windows SharePoint Services adapter to transport InfoPath forms from an application to SharePoint 2007 or vice versa. You could also use the Windows SharePoint Services adapter to collect or redistribute data within SharePoint 2007. If the data you are retrieving from another application is not an InfoPath form, BizTalk Server 2006 can be used to transform the data to the required InfoPath form format, although you will have to tell BizTalk how to perform this transformation.

Note In human-oriented workflow scenarios, we do not recommend BizTalk Server 2006. The primary focus of BizTalk Server lies in facilitating process-driven workflows, where messages are exchanged between applications. Since BizTalk Server 2004, BizTalk Server contains Human Workflow Services (HWS), which is aimed at facilitating human-oriented workflows. Unfortunately, HWS has become deprecated technology. It will be supported for the next couple of years, but you have to realize no additional features have been added to the product since its release. Instead, use Windows Workflow Foundation, which is covered in Chapter 4.

Comparing Biztalk to Windows Workflow Foundation

Biztalk and Windows Workflow Foundation (WF, discussed in detail in Chapter 4) are not competitors, and Windows Workflow Foundation does not replace BizTalk. Both products complement each other. BizTalk is targeted toward application-to-application (A2A) communication, where two or more programs on one or more computers need to work together in an automated fashion; Windows Workflow Foundation is used in human-oriented workfows (workflows that need to be included as part of their applications). Table 8-2 provides a detailed comparison between both products.

You can find more information about the relation between WF and other Microsoft products such as BizTalk in MSDN article "Introducing Microsoft Windows Workflow Foundation: An Early Look", located at http://msdn2.microsoft.com/en-us/library/Aa480215.aspx#wwfi_topic3.

Table 8-2. *Comparison Between BizTalk and Windows Workflow Foundation*

BizTalk	Windows Workflow Foundation
BizTalk is targeted to toward applications.	WF is targeted toward humans.
BizTalk is a product that hosts workflows and offers numerous extension points (such as adapters).	WF is a framework that can be used to build workflows.
BizTalk workflows are hosted by BizTalk itself.	WF workflows are hosted by a client application that uses the WF framework.
BizTalk is highly scalable.	Scalability of WF workflow depends on the developer.
BizTalk supports long running transactions.	Long running transactions need to be implemented by the developer.
BizTalk supports design-time workflows.	WF supports design-time and run-time workflows.
BizTalk is primarily focused on XML. If you want create an advanced workflow, a message first needs to be transformed into XML. BizTalk provides advanced transformation capabilities.	WF does not need information in the form of XML to be able to process it.
BizTalk contains extensive tracking and management tooling.	Out of the box, WF offers rudimentary support for tracking and management.
BizTalk offers extensive cross-platform capabilities.	Out of the box, WF does not have cross-platform support.

Installing the Windows SharePoint Services Adapter

Microsoft has not yet announced official support in BizTalk Server 2006 for SharePoint 2007 technology. Nevertheless, the Windows SharePoint Services adapter still seems to work nicely for Microsoft Office SharePoint Server 2007, although you have to configure it a bit in order to get it to work. You can read more about this topic in the blog post "WSS v3 Beta 2 is out – try it with WSS adapter" (http://blogs.msdn.com/ahamza/archive/2006/06/05/WSS_v3_Beta_2_Wss_Adapter_Workaround.aspx). Adrian Hamza, a member of the BizTalk team, maintains this blog.

Unfortunately, the BizTalk 2006 Configuration Wizard does not allow you to install the Windows SharePoint Services adapter directly. If you want to use this adapter, there are three ways to do so:

- Install the Windows SharePoint Services adapter on a SharePoint 2003 server and upgrade to SharePoint 2007.

- Install the adapter web service manually by copying the web service and all related components the web service depends on from another location.

- On a SharePoint 2007 server, install Windows SharePoint Services 2.0, then install the Windows SharePoint Services adapter and remove Windows SharePoint Services 2.0 to prevent having to create the web service manually.

■**Note** The blog posts "WSS Adapter for Biztalk 2006 Usage against MOSS2007" and "BizTalk 2006 and SharePoint 2007 adapter" at http://biztalkblogs.com/fairycat/ contain more information about the manual installation of the adapter web service and its related components.

In the rest of this section, we assume you have installed the adapter web service on a SharePoint 2003 server that you are planning either to upgrade or remove. We will also assume the adapter web service still needs to be configured in order to work nicely in a SharePoint 2007 environment. The first step you need to take to configure the adapter web service is to create a new virtual directory for it. The next procedure discusses how to create a virtual directory for the Windows SharePoint Services adapter web service.

1. Open Internet Information Services (IIS) Manager.

2. Expand the [web server name] node.

3. Expand the Web Sites node.

4. Right-click the [name SharePoint web application] node and choose New ➤ Virtual Directory. This opens the Virtual Directory Creation Wizard.

5. On the Welcome to the Virtual Directory Creation Wizard, click Next.

6. On the Virtual Directory Alias page, enter the following value in the Alias text box: **BTSharePointAdapterWS**. Click Next.

7. On the Web Site Content Directory page, enter the following path: **[drive letter]:\ Program Files\Microsoft BizTalk Server 2006\Business Activity Services\ BTSharePointAdapterWS**. Click Next.

8. On the Virtual Directory Access Permissions page, accept the default settings and click Next, then click Finish.

9. Right-click the new BTSharePointAdapterWS node and choose Properties.

10. This opens the BTSSharePointAdapterWS Properties window.

11. Click the Create button.

12. Click OK.

At this point, you have successfully created a virtual directory for the Windows SharePoint Services adapter. Now, you need to adjust its web.config file so the adapter web service supports SharePoint 2007 and so you can test it.

1. Open the WSS adapter web.config file located in [drive letter]:\Program Files\ Microsoft BizTalk Server 2006\Business Activity Services\BTSharePointAdapterWS.

2. You need to define a policy that ensures that the WSS adapter uses the 2007 version of the SharePoint assembly. Paste the following code into the <configuration> section of the web.config file:

```
<runtime>
  <assemblyBinding ➡
  xmlns="urn:schemas-microsoft-com:asm.v1">
    <dependentAssembly>
      <assemblyIdentity name="Microsoft.SharePoint" ➡
      publicKeyToken="71e9bce111e9429c" />
        <bindingRedirect oldVersion="11.0.0.0" ➡
        newVersion="12.0.0.0"/>
    </dependentAssembly>
  </assemblyBinding>
</runtime>
```

3. To be able to browse to the web service page (BTSharePointAdapterWS.asmx) of the WSS adapter for testing purposes, you should comment out the <protocols> section, like so:

```
<!-
<protocols>
  <remove name="Documentation"/>
</protocols>
->
```

4. Open a command prompt and type **iisreset**.

Now, you should be able to open a browser and browse to http://[server name:port number]/ BTSharePointAdapterWS/BTSharePointAdapterWS.asmx. After installing and configuring the Windows SharePoint Services adapter, you are able to use it within your BizTalk 2006 solutions to communicate with SharePoint 2007.

Message Processing Overview

To understand how the integration between BizTalk Server 2006 and SharePoint 2007 works, you will have to take a closer look at the way BizTalk Server 2006 processes messages. Figure 8-38 shows the message-processing architecture. This figure will be explained in the rest of this section.

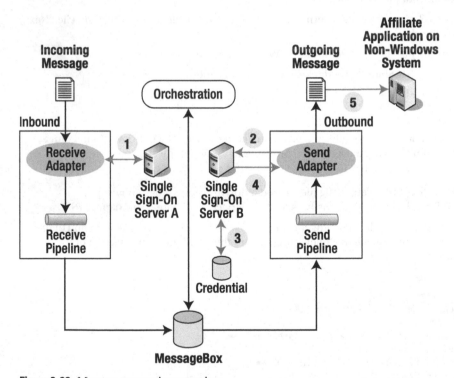

Figure 8-38. *Message processing overview*

BizTalk Server 2006 receives messages in some way via some channel. For example, a message might be delivered via FTP or e-mail. If you want to support this, you will need to create an FTP or e-mail channel that can handle such messages. Messages might be posted to a channel manually by an end user or automatically by another application. A BizTalk receive adapter picks up the message from the channel. For instance, imagine some application is posting a message to a Microsoft Message Queuing (MSMQ) queue. An MSMQ queue supports transactions and is able to store messages in a reliable way. The BizTalk MSMQ receive adapter picks up this message. The adapter passes the message to the receive pipeline. Pipelines consist of one or several components where every component in the pipeline decides whether its message-processing wants to do something with the message. For instance, the receive pipeline can validate or transform the message.

After the receive pipeline is done processing the message, the message is stored in the MessageBox, a SQL Server database. Once a message is stored in the MessageBox, it can, but does not have to, be processed by an orchestration. An *orchestration* is an XML representation of a business process and is expressed in an XML language called Business Process Execution Language for Web Services (BPEL4WS). If you want to process a message via an orchestration, the result message of the receive pipeline needs to be XML, because orchestrations are only able to work with XML. Orchestrations can be used to express complex business rules and optionally interact with the BizTalk Server Business Rule Engine (BRE) to enable people to express simple business rules in a simple manner. The BRE lets information workers adjust a subset of the total set of business rules without needing the assistance of IT personnel.

The result of any manipulation executed by an orchestration or business rule is stored in the MessageBox database. The Send pipeline picks up the message and is able to convert it to any required format. When the Send pipeline has completed its job, it passes the message to the Send adapter. The Send adapter makes sure the message arrives at some endpoint via some channel. Optionally, the Send adapter uses the Single Sign-on server to retrieve user credentials that will be used to authenticate itself at the destination point for the message. For instance, if you want to call a web service of a third-party application, the BizTalk Server SOAP send adapter makes sure the message gets there.

Windows SharePoint Services Adapter Overview

The Windows SharePoint Services adapter is an optional component of BizTalk Server 2006. It consists of two parts: a send adapter and a receive adapter. Basically, the Windows SharePoint Services receive adapter is able to pick up messages from SharePoint; the Windows SharePoint Services send adapter is able to send messages to SharePoint. To be precise, the Windows SharePoint Services adapter can do the following:

- Receive messages from Windows SharePoint Services document libraries and form libraries, optionally filtered by SharePoint views.

- Send messages to document libraries, form libraries, and SharePoint lists.

- Promote message properties.

The Windows SharePoint Services adapter architecture consists of three important components: the SharePoint adapter web service, the Windows SharePoint Services receive adapter, and the Windows SharePoint Services send adapter.

Although SharePoint offers a rich web service interface, the interface is not very friendly when it comes to managing documents. For instance, it won't let you upload a document and set its properties at the same time.

■Note If you want to upload a document and set its properties at the same time, use FrontPage RPC. An example of a client that uses FrontPage RPC is Word. More information about FrontPage RPC can be found at the following location: http://msdn2.microsoft.com/en-us/library/ms954084.aspx.

To get around this problem, the BizTalk team created its own SharePoint adapter web service called BTSharePointAdapterWS. The BTSharePointAdapterWS web service uses the SharePoint object model, and it can be used to upload and set properties of batches of files. The Windows SharePoint Services send adapter and receive adapter use this web service to communicate with SharePoint.

The Windows SharePoint Services receive adapter uses a polling mechanism to retrieve messages from SharePoint. This is less efficient when compared to an event-driven architecture, but it is also far easier to manage. At the time the BizTalk Server Windows SharePoint Services receive adapter was created, only the 2003 version of SharePoint existed. During those days, if you wanted to use the SharePoint event model instead of polling for information, all document and form libraries had to be reconfigured so they would refer to event-handling assemblies.

Note In SharePoint 2007, enabling document library events has become considerably easier through the use of SharePoint features. We will have to wait and see if the use of SharePoint features proves to be compelling enough for the BizTalk team to change the architecture of the Windows SharePoint Services adapter.

The current Windows SharePoint Services adapter architecture is very nonintrusive; SharePoint sites do not have to be aware of the fact that BizTalk Server 2006 is using them.

The Windows SharePoint Services adapter uses SharePoint versioning to provide transaction support. Whenever a receive adapter retrieves a document from SharePoint, it checks out the document before it is inserted into the BizTalk Server MessageBox database to prevent conflicts caused by duplicate insertions. The Windows SharePoint Services receive adapter performs destructive reads (the adapter removes a document after it has been read), which makes it possible to retrieve a document from a folder in a document library, process it in BizTalk Server 2006, and publish it back to the same document library folder.

Working with the Windows SharePoint Services Adapter

If you want to try out the examples in this section, you will need to have access to a computer with BizTalk Server 2006, Visual Studio 2005, InfoPath 2007, and SharePoint 2007 (either Windows SharePoint Services 3.0 or Microsoft Office SharePoint Server 2007) installed on it. The examples in this section will demonstrate how to retrieve messages from SharePoint document libraries and form libraries. We will also show how to filter messages via SharePoint views. In addition, we will discuss how to send messages to document libraries, form libraries, and SharePoint lists, and how to promote message properties.

Creating an XSD Schema

In the first part of this section, you will create an XSD schema that describes the message format. You will use a BizTalk Server project to create the schema. The BizTalk schema editor helps to create XSD schemas in a developer-friendly way. The XSD schema will be used later as the basis for an InfoPath form.

Note BizTalk schemas are no different from any other XSD. The BizTalk schema editor is just a user-friendly tool that makes creating XSD schemas easy.

Follow these steps to create a BizTalk project and an XSD schema describing the message format:

1. Start Visual Studio 2005 and choose File ➤ New ➤ Project ➤ BizTalk Projects ➤ Empty BizTalk Server Project, as shown in Figure 8-39.

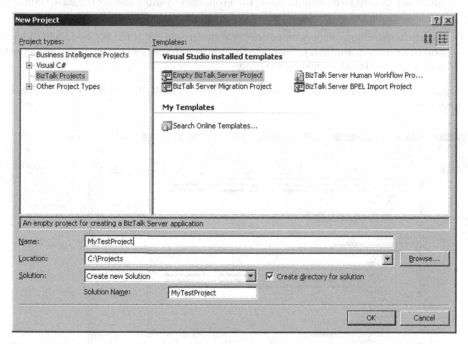

Figure 8-39. *Creating an empty BizTalk project*

2. Right-click the MyTestProject project and choose Add ➤ New Item ➤ Schema Files ➤ Schema. Enter the name **StatusReport.xsd**.

3. Rename the root element to **StatusReport** by selecting it, then right-clicking the root element and choosing Rename.

4. Right-click the StatusReport root element ➤ Insert Schema Node ➤ Child Field Element and call this item **Date**. Select the Properties window and set the Base Data Type of the Date child field element to xs:dateTime.

5. Right-click the StatusReport root element ➤ Insert Schema Node ➤ Child Field Element and call this item **Name**. Select the Properties window and set the Base Data Type of the Name child field element to xs:string.

6. Right-click the StatusReport root element ➤ Insert Schema Node ➤ Child Field Element and call this item **EmailAddress**. Select the Properties window and set the Base Data Type of the EmailAddress child field element to xs:string.

7. Right-click the StatusReport root element ➤ Insert Schema Node ➤ Child Field Element and call this item **Project**. Select the Properties window and set the Base Data Type of the Project child field element to xs:string.

8. Right-click the StatusReport root element ➤ Insert Schema Node ➤ Child Field Element, and call this item **ManagerName**. Select the Properties window and set the Base Data Type of the ManagerName child field element to xs:string.

9. Right-click the StatusReport root element ➤ Insert Schema Node ➤ Child Field Element, and call this item **BillingCode**. Select the Properties window and set the Base Data Type of the BillingCode child field element to xs:string.

10. Right-click the StatusReport root element ➤ Insert Schema Node ➤ Child Field Element, and call this item **Department**. Select the Properties window and set the Base Data Type of the Department child field element to xs:string.

11. Right-click the StatusReport root element ➤ Insert Schema Node ➤ Child Field Element, and call this item **Summary**. Select the Properties window and set the Base Data Type of the Summary child field element to xs:string.

Figure 8-40 shows the way the StatusReport.xsd schema looks in the BizTalk 2006 development environment.

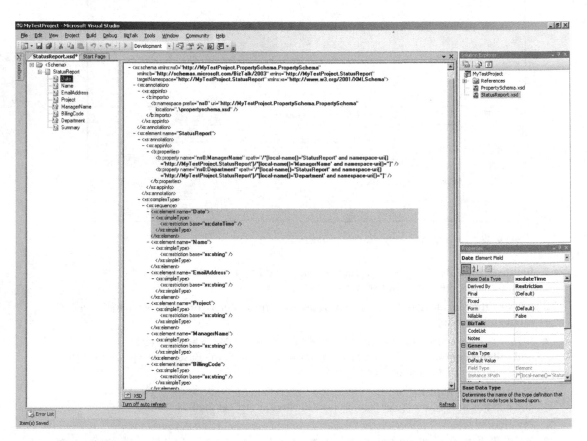

Figure 8-40. *StatusReport schema*

Creating an Orchestration

BizTalk orchestrations allow you to define a business process in a visual way in Visual Studio 2005 via the BizTalk Orchestration Designer. The BizTalk Orchestration Designer allows you to define complex workflows. In this section, you will use the BizTalk Orchestration Designer to create a simple orchestration that receives a message via a logical receive port that will be bound to a physical receive port later. The logical receive port indicates the starting point of the workflow; this is where the message enters the business process. By itself, the logical receive port does not tell you where a message is coming from. A logical receive port needs to be tied to a physical receive port that defines exactly where a message is coming from, which communication protocol is used to retrieve a message, and other metadata concerning communication. In this example, the physical receive port will be connected to a SharePoint document library so that the Windows SharePoint Services adapter knows where to retrieve messages. Normally an orchestration would process the message. However, for this example you will just pass the message to a logical send port. The logical send port defines the point where a message leaves the workflow. The logical send port needs to be associated to a physical send port that defines specifics about the location the message needs to be send to. In this example, the send port will be connected to a SharePoint document library (via a physical send port) so that the Windows SharePoint Services adapter knows where to send the messages.

1. Right-click the project MyTestProject ➤ Add ➤ New Item ➤ Orchestration Files ➤ Biztalk Orchestration, and name the orchestration **MyTestOrchestration.odx**.

2. Open the Toolbox window and drag a Receive shape to the orchestration surface in the Drop a Shape from the Toolbox Here area.

3. Drag a Send shape from the Toolbox below the Receive shape on the orchestration surface.

4. Drag a Port shape from the Toolbox to the upper left Port Surface. This starts the Port Configuration Wizard. Click Next on the welcome screen.

5. On the Port Properties window of the Port Configuration Wizard, enter the name **TestReceivePort**. Click Next.

6. On the Select a Port Type window of the Port Configuration Wizard, choose Create a New Port Type. Type the name **TestReceivePortType** as the Port Type Name. Make sure the Communication Pattern is set to One-Way. Make sure the Access Restrictions are set to Public — No Limit. Click Next.

7. On the Port Binding window of the Port Configuration Wizard, go to the Port Direction of Communication setting and select I'll Always Be Receiving Messages on This Port. For the Port Binding setting, select Specify Later. Click Next.

8. Click Finish on the Completing the Port Wizard page.

At this point, you have successfully configured a receive port. Now you are ready to configure a send port:

1. Drag a Port shape from the Toolbox to the right Port Surface. This starts a new instance of the Port Configuration Wizard. Click Next.

2. On the Port Properties window, enter the following name: **TestSendPort**. Click Next.

3. On the Select a Port Type window, select the following port type to be used for this port: Create a New Port Type. Enter the following Port Type Name: **SendPortType**. Make sure the communication pattern is set to One-Way. Set Access Restrictions to Public—No Limit.

4. On the Port Binding window, choose the following Port Direction of Communication: I'll Always Be Receiving Messages on This Port. Choose the following Port Binding: Specify Later. Click Next.

5. On the Completing the Port Wizard window, click Finish.

Now you have also configured a send port. Specify which message types can be handled by the MyTestOrchestration orchestration:

1. Go to the Orchestration View window ➤ Messages ➤ New Message.

2. Go to the Properties window and name the Identifier property **StatusReportMessage**.

3. Choose Message Type ➤ Schemas ➤ MyTestProject.StatusReport.

4. Go back to the orchestration design surface and select the Receive_1 Receive shape. Set its Activate property to True in the Properties window. Set its Message property to StatusReportMessage.

5. Select the Send_1 Send shape on the orchestration design surface. Set its Message property to StatusReportMessage.

The orchestration is almost ready. Drag a line from the TestReceivePort port shape to the Receive_1 Receive shape by keeping the left mouse button pressed. Then drag a line from the Send_1 Send shape to the TestSendPort Send port. The StatusReport orchestration should look like Figure 8-41.

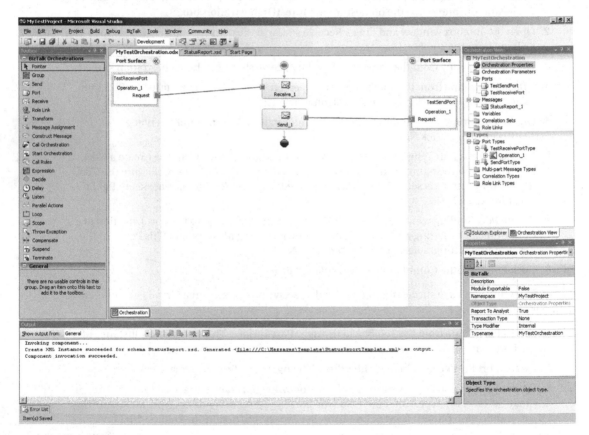

Figure 8-41. *StatusReport orchestration*

BizTalk orchestrations are compiled into .NET assemblies that are ultimately added to the Global Assembly Cache (GAC). In order to be able to do so, the MyTestProject project needs to be strong named.

Unfortunately, in BizTalk 2006 projects you do not have the ability to create strong-named key files directly via the Visual Studio 2005 user interface. In the following steps, you will strong-name the MyTestProject project:

1. Open a Visual Studio 2005 command prompt and generate a strong-named key file manually by typing **sn –k c:\MyKey.snk**.

2. Go to the Solution Explorer ➤ Properties ➤ Common Properties ➤ Assembly ➤ Assembly Key File and enter the path to the strong-name key file: **c:\MyKey.snk**.

3. Click Apply.

4. Select Configuration Properties ➤ Deployment, and set Redeploy to True. Click OK.

5. Build the MyTestProject project. After that, right-click the MyTestProject project and choose Deploy. You should see a status message indicating that the deploy succeeded.

In the test orchestration, you have defined two logical ports: a send and a receive port. In time, the logical BizTalk ports will be bound to physical BizTalk ports. We will connect the physical ports to actual locations in SharePoint sites.

Before we can bind physical ports to locations in SharePoint sites, we need to create two document libraries. First, we need to define a SharePoint document library that we will call Source. This document library will be connected to a BizTalk receive port. This document library will contain messages that will be picked up by the Windows SharePoint Services receive adapter. Second, we need to define a SharePoint document library that we will call Destination. This document library will be connected to a BizTalk send port. The Windows SharePoint Services send adapter will send all messages to this document library.

In the next step, you will create the Source and Destination document libraries and set the security settings of those libraries in such a way that the Windows SharePoint Services adapter will be able to read from and write to those document libraries. On our computer, we have used the local administrator account as our BizTalk service account. This is fine for a development server, but in a production environment, you should consider using a user account that has less privileges. You will need to add the BizTalk service account to the SharePoint Enabled Hosts group that is created during the installation of BizTalk Server 2006. Only members of the SharePoint Enabled Hosts are allowed to call the BTSharePointAdapterWS adapter Web service. This web service executes under the identity of the BizTalk service account. Because of that, you will need to make sure that the SharePoint Enabled Hosts group has contributor rights so that the adapter web service will be able to retrieve and add items from and to SharePoint lists.

After adding the BizTalk service account to the SharePoint Enabled Hosts group, the BizTalkServerApplication host instance needs to be restarted because group membership will only take place after you log off and log in again. Failing to do this will lead to "HTTP 401 — unauthorized errors" at a later stage.

Tip The Windows Event Viewer is a valuable aid when troubleshooting BizTalk solutions.

The next procedure explains how to add the BizTalk service account to the SharePoint Enabled Hosts group:

1. Go to Start ➤ Administrative Tools ➤ Computer Management.

2. Expand Local Users and Groups. Go to Groups. Locate the SharePoint Enabled Hosts group and double-click it. Click Add. Add the BizTalk service account to the group. In our example, this is the Pluto\Administrator account.

3. Open the BizTalk Server 2006 Administrator Console (Start ➤ All Programs ➤ Microsoft BizTalk Server 2006 ➤ BizTalk Server Administration).

4. In the BizTalk Server 2006 Administration Console, choose Console Root ➤ BizTalk Server 2006 Administration ➤ BizTalk Group [server name: database name] BizTalk Group [server name: database name] ➤ Platform Settings ➤ Host Instances and right-click BizTalkServer-Application ➤ Restart. Now the new security settings will be in effect.

5. Add two document libraries to a top-level SharePoint site called Test and call them Source and Destination.

6. On the Test SharePoint site, choose Site Actions ➤ Site Settings. This opens the Site Settings page for the Test SharePoint site.

7. In the section Site Collection Administration, click the Go to top level site settings link. This opens the Site Settings page for the Site Collection.

8. In the section Users and Permissions, click the People and groups link. This opens the People and Groups: [name site collection] page.

9. Click New ➤ Add Users. This opens the Add Users: [name site collection] page.

10. In the section Add Users, in the Users/Groups text area, type:[domain name]\ SharePoint Enabled Hosts group.

11. In the section Give Permission, in the Add users to a SharePoint group drop-down list, choose [name site collection] Members [Contribute].

12. Click OK.

In the following steps, you will create a physical BizTalk send port that will be connected to the Destination document library of our SharePoint site called Test:

1. Open the BizTalk Server 2006 Administration Console via Start ➤ All Programs ➤ Microsoft BizTalk Server 2006 ➤ BizTalk Server Administration.

2. Expand BizTalk Server 2006 Administration ➤ BizTalk Group [ServerName:BizTalkMgmtDb] ➤ Applications ➤ BizTalk Application 1.

3. Right-click Send Ports ➤ New ➤ Static One-Way Send Port.

4. Right-click the Send Ports node under the BizTalk Application 1 node and choose New ➤ Static One-Way Send Port. This opens the SendPort 1 — Send Port Properties screen.

5. In the SendPort1 — Send Port Properties window, type the name **WSSSendPort**.

6. In the Transport section, choose the following type: Windows SharePoint Services.

7. Choose the following Send Handler: BizTalkServerApplication.

8. Choose the following Send Pipeline: PassThruTransmit. This can be seen in the WSSSendPort — Send Port Properties window in Figure 8-42.

9. Click Configure. On the Windows SharePoint Services Transport Properties window in the General section, choose the following SharePoint Site URL: http://localhost/sites/Test.

10. In the General section, choose the following Destination Folder URL: Destination.

11. In the General section, choose the following Filename: %MessageID%.xml. This can be seen in Figure 8-43.

12. Click OK twice.

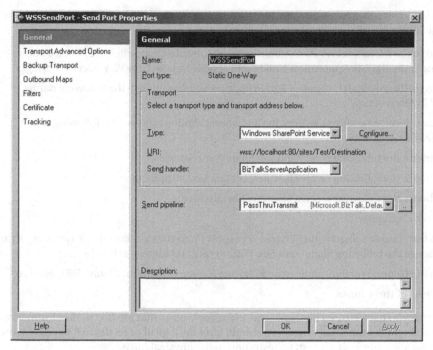

Figure 8-42. *Send Port Properties window*

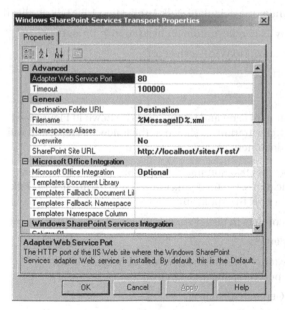

Figure 8-43. *Windows SharePoint Services Transport Properties window*

After that, you will create a physical BizTalk receive port that will be connected to the Source document library of our SharePoint site called Test:

1. Go to the BizTalk Server 2006 Administration Console. Right-click the Receive Ports node under the BizTalk Application 1 node and choose New ➤ One-Way Receive Port.

2. On the ReceivePort1 - Receive Port Properties window choose the following name: WSSReceivePort.

3. Click Receive Locations ➤ New. In the General window, choose the following name: WSSReceiveLocation.

4. Choose the following type: Windows SharePoint Services.

5. Choose the following receive handler: BizTalkServerApplication.

6. Choose the following receive pipeline: XMLReceive.

7. Click Configure.

8. In the Windows SharePoint Services Transport Properties window in the General section, choose the following SharePoint Site URL: http://localhost/sites/Test.

9. In the General section, choose the following Source Document Library URL: Source.

10. Click OK three times.

Now that you have created physical send and receive ports that are tied to the Destination and Source SharePoint document libraries, you should bind the logical ports defined in our test orchestration called MyTestProject.MyTestOrchestration to the physical ports:

1. Go to the BizTalk Server 2006 Administration Console.

2. Click the Orchestrations node under the default BizTalk Application 1 BizTalk application.

3. Right-click the MyTestProject.MyTestOrchestration orchestration ➤ Properties.

4. Click Bindings and set the Receive Port to WSSReceivePort.

5. Set the Send Port to WSSSendPort.

6. Click OK.

The result of binding the orchestration to send and receive ports is shown in Figure 8-44.

All you have to do now is start the orchestration, as shown in the following steps, and wait until new messages are placed in the Source document library.

1. Open Console Root ➤ BizTalk Server 2006 Administration ➤ BizTalk Group [Server name:BizTalkMgmtDb] ➤ Applications. On the Applications pane, right-click BizTalk Application 1 and choose Start to start the application.

2. Open the BizTalk MyTestProject project in Visual Studio 2005 and locate StatusReport.xsd.

3. Right-click StatusReport ➤ Properties.

4. Choose the following Output Instance Filename (under the General section): C:\Message\Template\StatusReportTemplate.xml. Click OK.

5. Right-click ReportStatus.xsd ➤ Generate Instance.

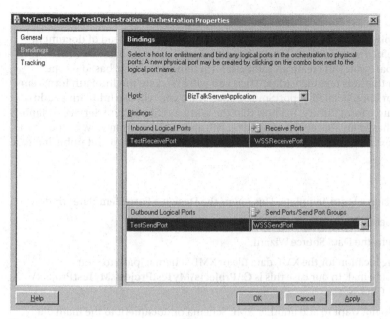

Figure 8-44. *Orchestration properties*

■Note The orchestration will start performing its task as soon as new messages arrive in the Source document library, although it will not respond to any kind of message. It looks for XML messages that adhere to our ReportStatus.xsd schema. In order to test the orchestration, you need to create an XML message that is compliant with this schema. The BizTalk Server 2006 Visual Studio 2005 add-in makes it easy to do this. It allows you to generate an XML file based on a given XSD schema.

You now have access to an XML document that adheres to the ReportStatus XSD schema. This message type can be understood by your test orchestration. If you upload this XML message to the Source document library, it will be picked up by the Windows SharePoint Services receive adapter. Then it will be processed by the MyTestOrchestration orchestration. Finally, the Windows SharePoint Services send adapter will save it in the Destination document library. Figure 8-45 shows the Destination document library after three test XML messages have been uploaded to the Source document library and have been processed by the orchestration.

Figure 8-45. *Destination document library*

Form Libraries

It is possible to bind the physical send and receive ports to form libraries instead of document libraries. This is most useful if you create an InfoPath form template and associate it with a form library. In the next part, you will create an InfoPath form template that is based on the ReportStatus.xsd schema that was created earlier. Then you will associate the InfoPath form template to a SharePoint form library called ReportSource. After that, you will use InfoPath to add test data to the ReportSource form library. To show that the Windows SharePoint Services adapter is able to filter messages based on SharePoint views, you will also add a custom view to the SharePoint form library. The next procedure explains how to create an InfoPath form and publish it to a SharePoint form library:

1. Start InfoPath 2007.

2. Choose File ➤ Design a Form Template. This opens the Design a Form Template window.

3. In the Template section, select the XML or Schema template.

4. Click OK. This opens the Data Source Wizard.

5. Enter the following location for the XML data file or XML schema: [path to your ReportStatus.xsd schema]. In our case this is **C:\Projects\MyTestProject\MyTestProject\ ReportStatus.xsd**. Click Next.

6. Specify that you do not want to add another XML Schema or document to the main data source and click Finish.

7. Drag all StatusReport elements (Date, Name, EmailAddress, Project, ManagerName, Billing-Code, Department, and Summary) to the InfoPath form. After doing some layout work, the InfoPath form might look like Figure 8-46.

Figure 8-46. *Status Report InfoPath template*

8. Publish the InfoPath template to a SharePoint form library by choosing File ➤ Publish. This starts the Publishing Wizard.

9. Choose to publish InfoPath Form to a SharePoint server with or without InfoPath Forms Services. Click Next.

10. Enter the location of the SharePoint site where you want to publish the InfoPath form. For our example, we will use a test SharePoint site located at the following location: **http://pluto/sites/test/**.

11. In this step, you can choose whether you want to create a document library, site content type, or form template. Select the Document Library radio button. Click Next.

12. In this step, you can choose whether you want to create a new document library or update the form template in an existing document library. Select the create a new Document Library radio button. Click Next.

13. Type the following name for the form library: **ReportSource**. Type the following description: ReportSource Description. Then, click Next.

14. Click Add, and add the following fields: Name, Project, ManagerName, Department. This ensures that all fields will be promoted as form library columns on the SharePoint site. You need to promote these fields because we will use those fields in later examples in this chapter. Click Finish.

15. Click Publish.

16. Select the Open this document library check box (which opens the form library you just created) and click Close.

17. Close InfoPath.

Note When the Publishing Wizard uses the term document library, it actually refers to form libraries.

Click New ➤ New Document to create some test data. We created some InfoPath forms that contain test status reports about the fictional projects A and B, as can be seen in Figure 8-47.

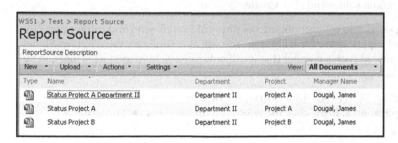

Figure 8-47. *Form library with test data*

In a later stage, you will define the Windows SharePoint Services receive adapter to pick up messages filtered by a SharePoint view. You will create a SharePoint view called ProjectView. The next procedure explains how to create this view.

1. Go to ReportSource Form Library, and select Create View from the View drop-down list. This opens the Create View: Report Source page.

2. Click Standard View.

3. Choose the following View name: ProjectView.

4. Go to the Filter section. Click the Show Items Only When the Following Is True radio button.

5. Choose the following: Show the Items When Column Value. Set its value to Project.

6. Choose the following comparison value: Is Equal To.

7. In the empty TextBox, type **Project A**.

8. Click OK.

9. Click the ProjectView option in the View drop-down list in the upper right of the page. Check that the view shows all the forms related to Project A. This can be seen in Figure 8-48.

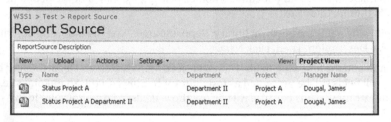

Figure 8-48. *ProjectView view*

At this point, you have created a ReportSource form library that can be used by the Windows SharePoint Services receive adapter to retrieve InfoPath forms. The InfoPath forms will be processed by your test orchestration and eventually they will be published to another form library. Next, you will create a form library called ReportDestination. The Windows SharePoint Services send adapter will use this form library as the end point to send its messages. The next procedure explains how to create the ReportDestination form library:

1. Click Site Actions ➤ Create. This opens the Create page.

2. In the Libraries section, click the Form Library link. This opens the New page.

3. Give the new form library the following name: ReportDestination.

4. Accept the other default values and click Create.

During the following steps, you will reconfigure the physical BizTalk send and receive ports to the ReportDestination and ReportSource form libraries. You will also configure the Windows Share-Point Services receive adapter in such a manner that it will only retrieve InfoPath forms that can be seen in the ProjectView SharePoint view:

1. Go back to the BizTalk Server 2006 Administration Console. Locate the Send Ports node under BizTalk Application 1. Right-click the WSSSendPort Send Port ➤ Properties ➤ Configure.

2. In the Windows SharePoint Services Transport Properties window, in the General section, change the Destination Folder URL to ReportDestination. Click OK twice.

3. Go to the Receive Ports node. Right-click WSSReceivePort Receive Port ➤ Properties ➤ Receive Locations ➤ Properties ➤ Configure.

4. In the Windows SharePoint Services Transport Properties window, in the General section, change the Source Document Library URL to ReportSource.

5. Specify the following View name: ProjectView.

6. Click OK three times.

7. Stop and start BizTalk Application 1.

After a little while, all forms related to the project Project A will disappear from the Report-Source form library. They should reappear in the ReportDestination form library. This can be seen in Figure 8-49.

Figure 8-49. *ReportDestination form library*

Note In this example, we have created a form library called ReportDestination that is not associated with a form template. Because of this, the forms published to this library open as regular XML. In this example, the forms have been renamed using GUIDs, a default action taken by BizTalk. The GUID refers to the message ID that is used internally by BizTalk. Later, in the section "Property Promotion," you will learn how to preserve the original name of a form or how to create other user friendly names.

Property Promotion

You can take InfoPath form properties and copy their values to the metadata of SharePoint libraries. This is known as *property promotion*.

You can create a ReportSource form library without associating it with an InfoPath form template. In such cases, if you let BizTalk add InfoPath forms to the form library and open them, a regular XML file opens with a schema that is compliant with the ReportStatus.xsd schema. If you have created a ReportSource form library and associated it with a template, InfoPath will be opened whenever you click the InfoPath forms in the destination document library, displaying a form that looks like the form template.

The following XML shows an example of the XML data found in our ReportDestination form library. Please notice that the namespace of this XML is http:// MyTestProject.ReportStatus.

```
<ns1:ReportStatus xmlns:ns1="http://MyTestProject.ReportStatus" ➥
xmlns:b="http://schemas.microsoft.com/BizTalk/2003" ➥
xmlns:ns0="http://MyTestProject.PropertySchema.PropertySchema">
  <Date />
  <Name>Richter, Gumball</Name>
  <EmailAddress>info@lcbridge.nl</EmailAddress>
  <Project>Project A</Project>
  <ManagerName>Vuuren van, Casey</ManagerName>
  <BillingCode />
  <Department>Department I</Department>
  <Summary />
</ns1:ReportStatus>
```

Take a look at Figure 8-50. If you look at the Windows SharePoint Services Integration section, you will see a number of columns, such as Column 01 and Column 02. Columns refer to the name of a SharePoint library property. Column values contain XPath expressions that refer to the internal structure of an XML message. The result of the XPath expression will become the value of the library property.

Figure 8-50. *Property promotion*

■**Note** You have to type in the column values yourself; the Windows SharePoint Services adapter does not provide any help.

For example, if you want to retrieve the value of the Project element, use //Project. // is a shortcut for descendant-or-self, which retrieves all nodes with the name Project located somewhere in the XML document. So if you want to promote the value of the <Project> element in the XML document to a library property called MyProperty, you would need to set Column 01 to MyProperty and set Column 01 Value to %XPATH=//Project%.

If you do not want to use the descendant-or-self shortcut, you can also use explicit XPath expressions. Since our XML contains a namespace, http://MyTestProject.ReportStatus, you will have to define the namespace alias in the General section of the Windows SharePoint Services Transport Properties.

Enter the following value for Namespace Aliases: **ns0="http://TestWindows SharePoint ServicesAdapterProject.RequestSchema"**.

This enables you to define XPath queries such as the following: %XPATH=/ns0:MyParent/MyChild/MyGrandChild%.

If you want to define multiple namespaces, you can do so by separating them with a comma. You can also use literal values in column values or combine XPath expressions and literal values. You could add the following column value: My title: %XPATH=/ns0:Request/Item/Name%'.

It is also possible to use predefined macros. For example, a %MessageID% macro is replaced at run time by a GUID. If you want, you can combine literal values with XPath expressions and macros. For example, you could define the following Filename property in the Windows SharePoint Services Transport Properties screen: MyFilename %XPATH=//Project%%MessageID%.xml.

■**Note** If you leave the `Filename` property empty on the Windows SharePoint Services Transport Properties screen, the file name on the destination end point will be identical to the file name of the source file. You can also use the %FileName% and %Extension% macros to re-create the original file name.

SharePoint List

You can send InfoPath forms to document and form libraries. It is also possible to publish message metadata to SharePoint lists. You cannot send messages themselves to a list; only promoted properties will be published to the list. It is impossible to receive messages from a SharePoint list. The following procedure explains how to create a SharePoint list and send message metadata coming from an InfoPath forms to it:

1. Go to the SharePoint Test site and choose Site Actions ➤ Create. This opens the Create page.
2. In the Custom Lists section, click the Custom List link. This opens the New page.
3. Type the following name: **DestinationList**.
4. Click Create. This opens the newly created DestinationList list.
5. Click Settings ➤ Create Column. This opens the Create Column: DestinationList page.
6. Add the following columns: **Project Name**, **Manager**, and **Department**. All columns have the same column type: Single Line of Text.
7. Click Go Back to DestinationList. The SharePoint list should look like Figure 8-51.

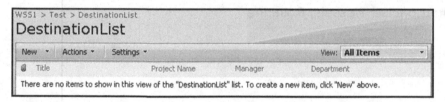

Figure 8-51. *DestinationList SharePoint list*

8. Go back to the BizTalk Server 2006 Administration Console. Go to Send Ports and double-click WSSSendPort Send Port ➤ Configure.
9. Change the SharePoint Site URL to http://pluto/sites/Test.
10. Change the Destination Folder URL to DestinationList.
11. Leave the FileName empty.
12. Copy the transport properties as seen in Figure 8-52. Click OK twice.
13. Stop and Start BizTalk Application 1.

■**Note** The `FileName` property is ignored when you are publishing messages to SharePoint lists, so it does not matter which value is entered here.

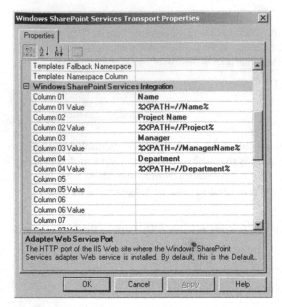

Figure 8-52. *SharePoint list transport properties*

If everything goes well, the SharePoint list DestinationList should look like Figure 8-53.

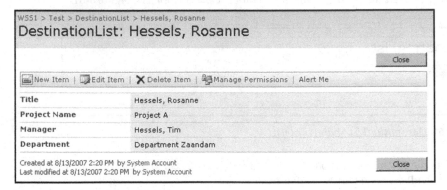

Figure 8-53. *DestinationList list item*

Moving Binary Content

All the examples related to the Windows SharePoint Services adapter you have seen so far involve InfoPath forms. We want to show that you can also use BizTalk Server 2006 to move other types of content, such as Word 97–2003–compliant documents. Orchestrations only handle XML messages, so it is impossible to implement a complex business process in an orchestration and apply that to binary content. However, it is possible to send a message via BizTalk Server 2006 without using orchestrations.

In such a scenario, messages will be processed by the receive and send ports without the intervention of any orchestration. You can define a filter on a send port that subscribes to messages that originate from a given location. In our example, we will configure the send port in such a way that it will process all messages originating from the Source document library (created earlier). We will use a Word document that is stored in a proprietary binary format to demonstrate this technique. Since a Word (*.doc) document is not XML, you need to make sure that the pipelines used by the receive and send ports are set to PassThru pipeline, not to XMLReceive pipeline.

The XML pipeline checks whether a message type is known. This means that the pipeline checks that an XSD schema is defined for the message. The XML pipeline will also check whether a message contains valid XML. The XML pipeline does not validate the message against the XSD schema itself. If the pipeline validation fails, it will lead to message suspension. So if you use the XML pipeline, all Word-compliant documents will be suspended. The PassThru pipeline does not perform any validation whatsoever, which makes it a very suitable choice for processing binary messages such as Word documents.

The following procedure explains how to configure a PassThru pipeline that processes binary messages. In this example, we will use Word 97–2003–compliant documents to demonstrate that the PassThru pipeline works:

1. Go back to the BizTalk Server 2006 Administration Console, right-click BizTalk Application 1, and choose Stop.

2. Go to Receive Locations. Double-click WSSReceiveLocation and set Receive Pipeline to PassThruReceive.

3. Click Configure. Set Source Document Library URL to Source.

4. Set the View name to Empty.

5. Click OK twice.

6. Go to Send Ports ➤ WSSSendPort ➤ Properties. Ensure the Send pipeline is set to PassThruTransmit.

7. Click Configure. Change the SharePoint site URL to http://pluto/sites/Test/.

8. Set the Destination Folder URL to Destination. Click OK.

9. Set Namespace Aliases to Empty.

10. Make sure the Windows SharePoint Services Integration section is entirely empty.

11. Click the Filters tab. Add the WSS.InListName property. Choose the == operator. Choose the following value: Source. Click OK.

12. Go to BizTalk Application 1 and choose Start. This time, click the Options button. Make sure the following four check boxes are checked: Enlist and Start All Send Ports; Enable All Receive Locations; Start All Associated Host Instances; and Resume Suspended Instances. Make sure Enlist and Start All Orchestrations is not checked. Click Start.

13. Upload a test document to the Source document library.

The result of using BizTalk Server 2006 to route a Word document from the Source document library to the Destination document library is shown in Figure 8-54.

Figure 8-54. *Destination document library*

Summary

In this chapter, you have learned how to create and publish InfoPath forms. You have learned what InfoPath trust levels are and how to publish an InfoPath form as a site content type. After that, you saw how to create a central repository holding data connections and how to consume those connections within an InfoPath form. Then, you saw how to display data coming from a SharePoint list in an InfoPath form. You also saw how to programmatically update an InfoPath form and save it in SharePoint. Next, you learned how to add a Submit button to a form that submits the form to a SharePoint library. After that, we showed you how to import a Word form into InfoPath. Then, the chapter discussed how to configure and use Forms Server 2007. Finally, we went into detail discussing how to use the combination of InfoPath, BizTalk Server 2006, and SharePoint 2007.

CHAPTER 9

Deep Traversal of SQL Full-Text Extensions

Microsoft Office SharePoint Server 2007 is an ideal repository for storing all types of content. It helps to get a grip on the unstructured information within organizations, because Microsoft Office SharePoint Server 2007 ships with a powerful search service called Microsoft Office SharePoint Server 2007 Enterprise Search. Because of this powerful search service, you can store content and find it again, solving a problem that most information workers face on a regular basis. Microsoft Office SharePoint Server 2007 Enterprise Search searches and indexes information and stores it in full-text indexes that can be retrieved later, fast and easily.

A custom Structured Query Language (SQL) was created to support full-text searching. This language is called SQL Full-Text extensions. SQL Full-Text extensions has been used for years now within a wide range of Microsoft products such as Site Server, Indexing Service, SQL Server, Exchange Server, and various SharePoint technologies. Most versions of those products support small variations in syntax, which can make the language a bit complicated to use. The different SQL Full-Text extensions dialects have been known under different exotic names such as WSS SQL, Enterprise Search SQL, and DAV:sql.

Note The WSS part of WSS SQL does not refer to Windows SharePoint Services; it refers to Web Storage System, the name of the data repository in SharePoint Portal Server 2001.

Out of the box, Microsoft Office SharePoint Server 2007 ships with a powerful set of search-related web parts. Despite this fact, you are missing out on a lot of the power that is included in the SharePoint Enterprise Search service if you only stick to using these web parts. SQL Full-Text extensions is the key to accessing this power; this chapter will focus on how to use SQL Full-Text extensions in Microsoft Office SharePoint Server 2007. In this chapter, we will look at the architecture of Enterprise Search and discuss how to programmatically use the SharePoint Search service. Finally, you will learn the ins and outs of SQL Full-Text extensions.

Search Architecture

Since this chapter talks about SQL Full-Text extensions, it makes sense to have a high level of understanding of the Microsoft Office SharePoint Server 2007 Enterprise Search architecture. Figure 9-1 shows an overview of the search architecture and its components.

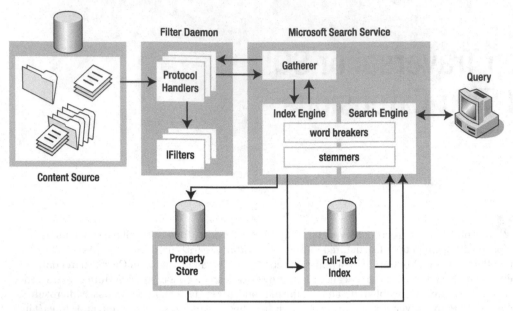

Figure 9-1. *Search architecture overview*

Let's take a look at Figure 9-1, starting from the right and working our way to the left. A query has to be written in SQL Full-Text extensions syntax and submitted to the Enterprise Search Service. The search engine runs these queries against the full-text index and property store. The full-text index contains all text content; the property store contains the properties retrieved from documents.

The index engine processes text content and properties filtered from content sources and determines what is written to the full-text index and what goes into the property store. The index engine creates an *inverse index* of content. The inverse index is a data structure with a row for each term. This row contains information about the documents in which the term appears, along with the number of occurrences and relative position of the term within each document. The inverse index allows probabilistic ranking and fast retrieval of information.

Word breakers and *stemmers* are used by both the search engine and the index engine. Word breakers determine where the word boundaries lie: they break up compound words and phrases. Stemmers generate inflected forms of a word ("run," "running," "ran").

The Gatherer manages the content-crawling process and has rules that determine what content is crawled. You can determine which content stores are crawled by configuring SharePoint Portal Server content sources. The Gatherer maintains a queue of URLs to access.

The Gatherer is responsible for accessing documents that are stored in a content source. The Gatherer defers this responsibility to the Filter Daemon. The Gatherer (via the Filter Daemon) fetches the stream of content via a protocol handler and passes it on to the appropriate filter. These filters are also called *IFilters* (because that is the name of the interface that needs to be implemented by every filter). Every document type is associated with its own IFilter. IFilters extract textual information from a specific document format. Probably the most important IFilter is the Microsoft Office filter, which can extract terms from Office formats such as Word, Excel, and PowerPoint documents. If you do not have an IFilter for a specific file type, you will not be able to search within such documents. If you want, you can create your own custom IFilters.

■Note There are several commercial vendors that specialize in building IFilters that can be used within Microsoft Office SharePoint Server 2007 environments. The IFilterShop (http://www.ifiltershop.com/) is an example of such a commercial vendor.

The Persisted Query Service or PQS (not shown explicitly in Figure 9-1) is a part of the Gatherer. The PQS is a reverse query processor that evaluates a large set of queries against a single document to determine which queries match the document. During the gathering process, the PQS determines which subscriptions match content.

As stated before, the Filter Daemon handles requests from the Gatherer. The Filter Daemon uses protocol handlers to access content sources and IFilters to filter files. Protocol handlers access data over a particular protocol or from a particular store. Examples of common protocol handlers are file protocol, HTTP, MAPI, and HTTPDAV. By default, content store types such as external web sites, SharePoint sites, Network shares, and Exchange folders are supported. It's possible to add or create custom protocol handlers.

Content sources are collections of data that must be crawled by the Enterprise Search Service. It is possible to define specific rules for crawling items within a content source. A URL identifies every item within a content source. The protocol portion determines the type of content source and thus determines which protocol handler must be used.

Working with SQL Full-Text Extensions

In this chapter, you will learn how to create a basic SQL Full-Text extensions search query and fire it at the SharePoint Search service. In this section, we will demonstrate a basic search query and use this query to demonstrate various techniques for interacting with the SharePoint Search service. In this section, you will learn how to use the SharePoint object model and the SharePoint Search web service, and finally, you will learn about a community tool that makes creating and executing SQL Full-Text extensions queries easier.

Probabilistic Ranking

The SharePoint Search engine uses probabilistic ranking to determine what item is most likely to match with whatever the end user is looking for. The SharePoint Search engine uses a complex series of algorithms to determine the ranking of indexed items. It is also possible to influence probabilistic ranking yourself; you will learn more about this throughout this chapter.

■Note In this chapter, you will see more of the algorithms that influence probabilistic ranking. If you want to learn more about the probability formula, you should read the white papers listed on the following location: http://research.microsoft.com/users/robertson/papers/trec_papers.htm.

When end users search for documents, all matching documents are assigned a rank value. Rank values are relative to the other documents matching the query. Rank values range from 0 to 1000: the higher the rank value, the more likely that a document matches the search conditions. There are a couple of factors that influence the probability calculation: for example, the number of documents in the index, the length of the document, the frequency of the query term, and the number of documents that contain the query term. The section "Rank Factors" later in this chapter takes a detailed look at these factors.

A Basic SQL Full-Text Extensions Query

The structure of a basic SQL Full-Text extensions query is not much different from a normal SQL query, so it helps if you are familiar with this. The body of an SQL Full-Text extensions query consists of several parts, as described in Table 9-1.

Table 9-1. *Basic Anatomy of an SQL Full-Text Extensions Search Query*

Name	Description
SELECT	Determines which columns are returned by the query.
FROM	Sets the search location.
WHERE	Determines which document set matches the query.
RANK BY	Influences the rank value to your liking.
ORDER BY	Specifies the sort order of the result set.

The following query is a simple query that searches a SharePoint portal and returns some information about the items located in the portal. The results that are most relevant are shown first.

```
SELECT Title, Rank, Size, Description, Write, Path
FROM portal..scope()
WHERE ORDER BY "Rank" DESC
```

If the scope part of the query confuses you, do not worry; this is explained later in the section "Scope."

Firing a Query via the SharePoint Object Model

Before we delve deeper into the syntax of SQL Full-Text extensions, we will take the simple query described in the previous section and use the SharePoint object model to fire it. To be able to follow this example, you need to create a Console Application in Visual Studio 2005 and add references to the Windows SharePoint Services, Microsoft Office Server, and Microsoft Office SharePoint Server Search components.

At this point, you have added references to all the SharePoint assemblies you need. Next, add some using directives that import .NET namespaces for types that are used a lot. This makes working with the SharePoint object model easier. Add the following code fragment to the top of the Program.cs class file:

```
using System.Data;
using Microsoft.SharePoint;
using Microsoft.Office.Server.Search.Query;
```

Listing 9-1 uses the SharePoint object model to fire a simple SQL Full-Text extensions search query (as described in the previous section). First, it uses a FullTextSqlQuery object that is able to query the SharePoint Search Service. Then, the QueryText property of the FullTextSqlQuery object is set to a SQL Full-Text extensions search query. We have also set the EnableStemming property to true. This is not really useful in this example, but later on, when we discuss stemming, it will be good to have this property enabled. After the search query is executed, you normally would do something useful with the search results. In this case, we load the result set in a flexible data container, the DataTable found in the System.Data namespace. We use the DataTable because you are probably familiar with it. Add the code from Listing 9-1 to the body of the Main() method in the Program.cs class file:

Listing 9-1. *Body of the Main() Method in the Program.cs Class*

```
string strSiteCollUrl = "http://[server]/sites/SearchPlayground";
SPSite objSite = new SPSite(strSiteCollUrl);

FullTextSqlQuery objQuery = new FullTextSqlQuery(objSite);
string strQuery = "SELECT Title, Rank, Size, Description, Write, Path ➡
FROM portal..scope() ➡
ORDER BY \"Rank\" DESC";

objQuery.QueryText = strQuery;
objQuery.ResultTypes = ResultType.RelevantResults;
objQuery.EnableStemming = true;
ResultTableCollection collResult = objQuery.Execute();

ResultTable objResult = null;
DataTable objData = new DataTable();
if (collResult.Count > 0)
{
  objResult = collResult[ResultType.RelevantResults];

  // Load query results in datatable for further processing.
  // The LoadOption parameter indicates how rows that are
  // already in the datatable are combined with incoming rows
  // with the same primary key.
  //
  // Since the DataTable is empty, the LoadOption parameter
  // does not matter in this case.
  objData.Load(objResult, LoadOption.OverwriteChanges);
}
```

If you execute this code, the SQL Full-Text extensions query is fired at the SharePoint search service and the result is loaded in an ADO.NET DataTable object. Figure 9-2 shows what the result looks like in the Visual Studio 2005 DataSet Visualizer.

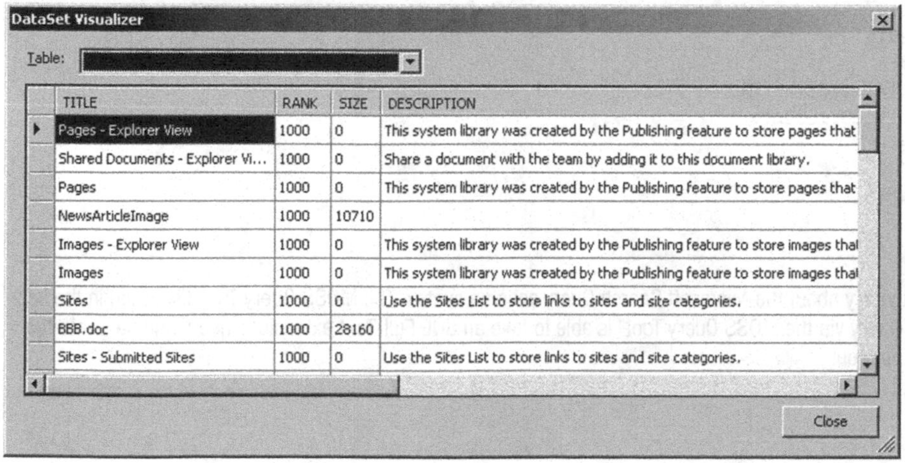

Figure 9-2. *Firing a query via the SharePoint object model*

Firing a Query via the SharePoint Web Service API

In this section, you will learn how to fire a simple query using the web service API. The next procedure explains how to create a .NET console application that uses the SharePoint web service API to fire a simple query.

1. Use the same console application described in the previous section and delete (or comment out) the code in the body of the Main() method of the Program.cs class file.

2. Right-click References and choose Add Web Reference.

3. In the URL text field, enter the following path: **http://[site name]/_vti_bin/search.asmx**.

4. In the Web reference text field, enter the following name: **SearchHost.SearchService**.

5. Click Add Reference. This adds a reference to the SharePoint Search web service.

You cannot pass SQL Full-Text extensions search queries directly to the Search web service; every query that is passed to the Search web service needs to be valid XML that adheres to the Microsoft.Search.Query schema. Listing 9-2 shows the search query described in the earlier section "A Basic SQL Full-Text Extensions Query" in XML form, adhering to the Microsoft.Search.Query schema:

Listing 9-2. *A Search Query in CAML Format*

```xml
<?xml version="1.0" encoding="utf-8" ?>
<QueryPacket xmlns="urn:Microsoft.Search.Query" Revision="1000">
  <Query domain="QDomain">
    <SupportedFormats>
      <Format>urn:Microsoft.Search.Response.Document.Document</Format>
    </SupportedFormats>
    <Context>
      <QueryText language="en-US" type="MSSQLFT">
      <![CDATA[
      SELECT Title, Rank, Size, Description, Write, Path
      FROM portal..scope()
      ORDER BY "Rank" DESC
      ]]>
      </QueryText>
    </Context>
    <Range>
      <StartAt>1</StartAt>
      <Count>100</Count>
    </Range>
  </Query>
</QueryPacket>
```

■Tip Do not worry about the Microsoft.Search.Query schema syntax. The MOSS Query Tool discussed in the section "Firing a Query via the MOSS Query Tool" is able to take an SQL Full-Text extensions query and generate the required XML for you.

At this point, you have added a reference to the SharePoint Search web service. To make programming the SharePoint Search web service easier, add the following code to the top of the Program.cs class file:

```
using System.Net;
```

The code in Listing 9-3 needs to be placed in the body of the Main() method of the Program.cs class file and uses the SharePoint Search web service to fire a simple SQL Full-Text extensions search query (as described in the section "A Basic SQL Full-Text Extensions Query"). First, a new instance of the Query web service is created. To authenticate the user correctly, the Credentials property of the Search service is set. After that, a search query is formulated that adheres to the Microsoft.Search.Query schema. Finally, the QueryEx() method is used to execute the query. The QueryEx() method returns an ADO.NET DataSet object. You can also use the Query() method, which returns a string containing XML. Listing 9-3 contains the code you need to fire an SQL Full-Text extensions query at the Search web service:

Listing 9-3. *Executing a Query via the Search Service*

```
SearchHost.SearchService.QueryService svcSearch = new ➡
SearchHost.SearchService.QueryService();
svcSearch.Credentials = CredentialCache.DefaultCredentials;
string strQuery = "<?xml version=\"1.0\" encoding=\"utf-8\" ?> ➡
<QueryPacket xmlns=\"urn:Microsoft.Search.Query\" Revision=\"1000\"> ➡
<Query domain=\"QDomain\"> ➡
<SupportedFormats> ➡
<Format>urn:Microsoft.Search.Response.Document.Document</Format> ➡
</SupportedFormats> ➡
<Context><QueryText language=\"en-US\" type=\"MSSQLFT\"> ➡
<![CDATA[ ➡
SELECT Title, Rank, Size, Description, Write, Path ➡
FROM portal..scope() ➡
ORDER BY \"Rank\" DESC ➡
]]> ➡
</QueryText> ➡
</Context> ➡
<Range> ➡
<StartAt>1</StartAt> ➡
<Count>100</Count> ➡
</Range> ➡
</Query> ➡
</QueryPacket>";
DataSet dsResult = svcSearch.QueryEx(strQuery);
```

If you execute this code, the SharePoint Search web service is called, which returns a result wrapped in an ADO.NET DataSet object. Figure 9-3 shows what the result looks like in the Visual Studio 2005 DataSet Visualizer.

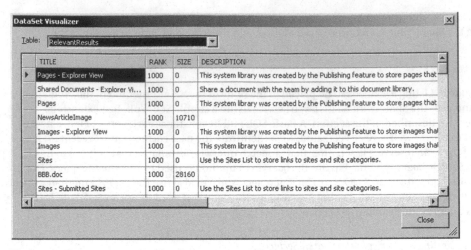

Figure 9-3. *Firing a query via the SharePoint Search web service*

Firing a Query via the MOSS Query Tool

If you have used SQL Server to some extent, you have probably used its Query Analyzer a lot. This tool allows you to create SQL Full-Text extensions queries and fire them at an SQL Server relational database. One of the first things looked for when planning to build SQL Full-Text extensions queries was a tool like the SQL Server Query Analyzer. Luckily, we found such a tool: it is called the Microsoft Office SharePoint Server 2007 query tool, a free community tool that can be downloaded from the following location: http://www.gotdotnet.com/Community/UserSamples/ Details.aspx?SampleGuid=89b3cda7-aad9-4919-8faf-34ef9b28c57b. We advise you to download and install it.

Note At the time of writing, GotDotNet is going to be phased out, although the web site promises that the User Samples will not be phased out until an alternative is available. If you cannot find the Microsoft Office SharePoint Server 2007 query tool and cannot find an alternative, send an e-mail to news@lcbridge.nl and we will send you a copy. Since we did not create this tool, we feel uncomfortable offering the tool via our web site, as this suggests we were somehow involved with the creation of the tool.

In this section, you will learn how to fire a simple query using the MOSS Query Tool. We will use the tool to fire the query described in the section "A Basic SQL Full-Text Extensions Query" of this chapter at the SharePoint Search service. The next procedure explains how to use the MOSS Query Tool.

1. Start the MOSS Query Tool.

2. In the Server Url text box, enter the name of your SharePoint site.

3. Click the Get Properties button. This retrieves the properties that are available at a given level. This is shown in Figure 9-4.

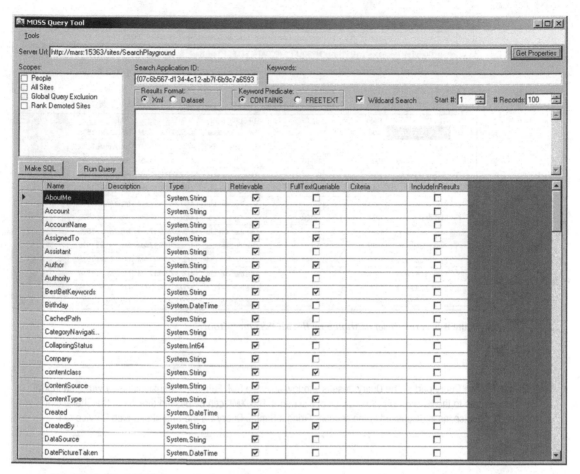

Figure 9-4. *The MOSS Query Tool*

4. Click the Make SQL button. This generates a basic search query (a query that should look quite familiar by now).

5. Locate the Results Format section and select the Dataset radio button.

Note Please make sure you have selected the Dataset radio button. If you select the Xml radio button, the tool only allows queries that include at least the following properties: Title, Rank, Size, Description, Write, and Path. If you fail to include these properties in a query, you will receive an error message indicating that your query is missing required properties.

---

6. Click the Run Query button. This executes the query and opens the Query Results #2 window. This window is shown in Figure 9-5.

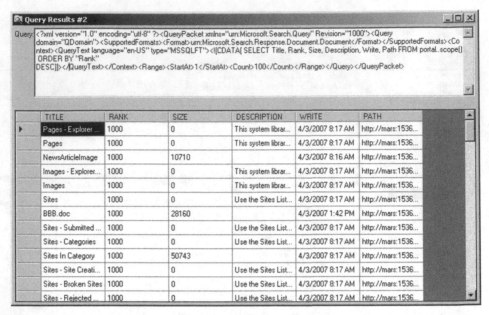

Figure 9-5. *A result set as shown by the MOSS Query Tool*

Note The Query part of the Query Results window shows a SQL Full-Text extensions query wrapped in XML that adheres to the `Microsoft.Search.Query` schema. This XML can be passed directly to the SharePoint Search Service, as is discussed in the section "Firing a Simple Query via the SharePoint Web Service API."

SQL Full-Text Extensions Syntax

This section is dedicated to the intricacies of the SQL Full-Text extensions syntax. In the section "A Basic SQL Full-Text Extensions Query" earlier in this chapter, you saw what the body of an SQL Full-Text extensions query looks like. We will assume you have a basic working knowledge of standard ANSI SQL Full-Text extensions and will discuss topics that are specific to the SQL Full-Text extensions dialect instead.

Tip The Microsoft Windows SharePoint Services 3.0 SDK contains information about SQL Full-Text extensions.

SELECT *

As you may have seen in Figure 9-4, the set of properties that is available in Microsoft Office SharePoint Server 2007 is considerable. Therefore, it would not be feasible to try a SELECT * statement. In previous versions of SQL Full-Text extensions, there were circumstances when executing a SELECT * statement was possible; in the current version, you will simply receive an error stating that your query is malformed.

Item Properties

The set of properties that can be used in the SELECT part of an SQL Full-Text extensions query is quite large; the MOSS Query Tool discussed earlier in the section "Firing a Query via the MOSS Query Tool" can be used to determine which properties are available. The following query uses a couple of the most-often-used properties. The query looks for a document with the word *Chiron* in it, which is the name of a poem by the Greek poet Bacchylides.

```
SELECT Title, Size, Rank, Created, LastModifiedTime, Path, ➥
CreatedBy, ModifiedBy, ContentType, FileExtension, FileName
FROM portal..scope()
WHERE CONTAINS (Contents, 'chiron')
```

Table 9-2 explains the meaning of the properties in the SELECT part of this query.

Table 9-2. *Common Item Properties*

Name	Description
Title	Item title.
Size	Size of file in bytes.
Rank	Value ranging from 0 to 1000 indicating how closely this item matches the search criteria.
Created	Date and time when the item was created.
LastModifiedTime	Date and time when the item was modified for the last time.
Path	Physical path to the file, including the file name.
CreatedBy	Item author.
ModifiedBy	Name of the last person who has edited the item.
ContentType	Indicates what kind of content the item is. For instance, a ContentType value of application/msword indicates the item is a Word document.
FileExtension	Suffix of item. For instance, the suffix for a Word document is doc.
FileName	The file name (including the file extension) of an item.

Scope

If you know how to use standard ANSI SQL Full-Text extensions but are unfamiliar with SQL Full-Text extensions, you probably were a bit surprised to see the FROM part of an SQL Full-Text extensions query. This part contains the scope() keyword, like this:

```
FROM portal..scope()
```

The scope allows you to define a limited range in which queries are executed. In older versions of SQL Full-Text extensions, the ability to specify search scopes was a really valuable concept. It used to indicate the name of a workspace catalog that contained the full-text index. Also, you could specify whether you wanted a deep or shallow search, indicating the search depth. In Microsoft Office SharePoint Server 2007, specifying such search scopes is no longer supported. Scope prefixes, or if you will, catalog names, are simply being ignored. The previous code fragment can be rewritten as

```
FROM scope()
```

Note We have a couple of reasons why we are still using the `portal..` prefix, even though it is meaningless nowadays. First, we do it for old time's sake. Second, the MOSS Query Tool generates the `portal..` prefix automatically, and we did not bother to remove it (we are assuming the tool does this for old time's sake as well). Third, we like its communicative value. If another developer does not have a clue what the `scope()` keyword is used for, `portal..scope()` is a hint that apparently the scope of the query is the entire portal. If you do not like any of those arguments, just omit the prefix part of the `scope()` keyword.

The fact that the ability to specify catalog names in search scopes is no longer supported does not mean that defining scopes has become useless. The syntax has just changed a bit. For instance, this query is used to search only for people:

```
SELECT Title, Rank
FROM portal..scope()
WHERE ( ("SCOPE" = 'People') )
ORDER BY "Rank" DESC
```

The following query searches for content located in SharePoint sites:

```
SELECT Title, Rank, Size, Description, Write, Path
FROM portal..scope()
WHERE ( ("SCOPE" = 'All Sites') )
ORDER BY "Rank" DESC
```

In the final example, we will search for content in *rank-demoted* sites. Rank-demoted sites are sites that are considered to contain information that is less valuable compared to normal or authoritative sites. Rank-demoted sites are discussed in more detail in the section "Rank Factors" later in this chapter. The query looks like this:

```
SELECT Title, Rank, Size, Description, Write, Path
FROM portal..scope()
WHERE ( ("SCOPE" = 'Rank Demoted Sites') )
ORDER BY "Rank" DESC
```

WHERE

WHERE clauses define filters for search results. They are simple to use and look exactly like their standard ANSI SQL counterpart. The following query looks for the word "shaida", a word taken from a poem by the American poet David Zindell:

```
SELECT Title, Rank, Size, Description, Write, Author
FROM portal..scope()
WHERE Title = 'shaida'
```

Retrieving Folders and Files

If you want to retrieve a folder, you can use the `ContentType` property to determine whether an item is a folder. The following query retrieves a list of folders:

```
SELECT Title
FROM portal..scope()
WHERE ContentType = 'Folder'
```

You can use the `FileExtension` property if you are looking for a certain type of content. The following query retrieves a list of Word documents:

```
SELECT Title, Rank, Path
FROM portal..scope()
WHERE  FileExtension = 'doc'
```

Tip If you click the Get Properties button of the Microsoft Office SharePoint Server 2007 Query Tool, you will find a list of all available columns.

Date Comparison

If you want to search for a document that was created on a given date, you might be tempted to try something like this:

```
SELECT Title, Rank, Description, Path, Created
FROM portal..scope()
WHERE Created = '4-3-2007'
```

Note The meaning of the Created property is rather tricky, and its importance rather dubious. If you upload a document to a SharePoint document library, the creation date is the date the document is added to the document library. There are certain migration tools that are able to preserve the original creation date of a document when it is migrated to a SharePoint environment, such as the Tzunami K-Wise Deployer for SharePoint Portal or Syntergy Bulk Loader. Be that as it may, we would advise you not to place to much emphasis on the meaning of the Created property.

This will not work, because the data type of the Created property is not a String; it is a DateTime. Instead, you should use the DATEADD function to use DateTime properties in comparisons. The following query shows how to search for documents that have been modified within the last 10 days:

```
SELECT Title, Rank, Description, Path, Created
FROM portal..scope()
WHERE LastModifiedTime <= DATEADD(DAY, -10, GETGMTDATE())
```

LIKE

Most filters are a bit more complex than the one described in the previous section. If you need more advanced filters, the first tool available to you in SQL Full-Text extensions is the LIKE predicate, which is also well known in standard ANSI SQL Full-Text extensions. It can be used to perform pattern-matching comparisons on a given property. The "%" (percentage) wildcard matches zero or more characters. The following query will match any document with the word "world" in the title:

```
SELECT Title
FROM portal..scope()
WHERE Title LIKE '%world%'
```

Note You cannot use the "%" wildcard within a word. A predicate such as "w%d" will not work.

You can also use the "_" (underscore) character to indicate you want to match any single character. The following query still matches any document with the word "world" in the title, and matches other words that look like "world" but do not contain the letter "r":

```
SELECT Title
FROM portal..scope()
WHERE Title LIKE '%wo_ld%'
```

Instead of allowing any character, you can also specify a narrow range. The following query accepts either "o", "u", or "i":

```
SELECT Title
FROM portal..scope()
WHERE Title LIKE '%w[oui]rld%'
```

Alternatively, you can be more liberal and accept a broader range. The following query accepts every letter in the alphabet:

```
SELECT Title
FROM portal..scope()
WHERE Title LIKE '%w[a-z]rld%'
```

Note Previous versions of SQL Full-Text extensions allowed you to use the MATCHES predicate instead of the LIKE predicate. The MATCHES predicate allowed the use of regular expressions to apply advanced pattern matching. The MATCHES predicate has been removed from the version of SQL Full-Text extensions that is used in Microsoft Office SharePoint Server 2007, and thus the availability of regular expressions within LIKE predicates is gone too.

Group Alias

The group alias predicate is simple to use and very useful. You can use the group alias predicate to provide a shorter name instead of the name of a property or a group of properties. To demonstrate the group alias predicate, we have created a document called "Carmen XL.doc," which is the title of a poem by the Roman poet Claudius Catullus. If the name Catullus is present in either the Title, BestBetKeywords, Description, or Keywords properties, the query will find the poem. The following code fragment shows how to define a group alias:

```
SELECT Title, Rank, Description, ContentType
FROM portal..scope()
WHERE
WITH
(
  "Title",
  "BestBetKeywords",
  "Description",
  "Keywords"
) AS #CustomGroup
FREETEXT (#CustomGroup, '"catullus" ')
ORDER BY "Rank" DESC
```

Tip If you want to learn more about the FREETEXT predicate, please refer to the "FREETEXT" section later in this chapter.

CONTAINS

The CONTAINS predicate can be used to search for words or phrases in text columns, for instance, in the document body. The CONTAINS predicate provides similar functionality to the FREETEXT predicate (described in the "FREETEXT" section later in this chapter), the difference being that the CONTAINS predicate is better suited for exact matches. In order to show you some examples using the CONTAINS predicate, we have created a document that contains a poem written by the American author David Zindell. All example queries in this section will search the contents of this document.

In the example query, you will learn how you can use the CONTAINS predicate to look for the presence of a complete sentence:

```
SELECT Title, Rank
FROM portal..scope()
WHERE CONTAINS('"it is shaida for a man to die too soon"')
```

* Wildcard

The following query uses the "*" (asterisk) wildcard to find a word that starts with "shai". We are looking for a document with the word "shaida" in it. The "*" wildcard can only be added at the end of the word or phrase. This is necessary to provide optimal use of the inverse index. (The inverse index was discussed in the section "Search Architecture" earlier in this chapter.) The query looks like this:

```
SELECT Title, Rank
FROM portal..scope()
WHERE CONTAINS('"shai*"')
```

ISABOUT

The ISABOUT predicate matches documents with a set of terms specified within the ISABOUT predicate and ranks the documents according to how closely each document matches the set of terms in the query.

To test the ISABOUT predicate, we have added two identical documents containing a part of the poem *Muerto de amor* by the Spanish poet Federico Lorca. In the second document, we have added two additional lines from the poem that contain the word "noche" once. The following query only finds the second document:

```
SELECT Title, Rank, Description, Path
FROM portal..scope()
WHERE CONTAINS('ISABOUT ("noche", "amor")' )
ORDER BY Title
```

You can also use the ISABOUT term to search properties. The following query shows an example:

```
SELECT Title, Rank, Description, Path
FROM portal..scope()
WHERE CONTAINS(Title, 'ISABOUT ("noche", "amor")' )
ORDER BY Title
```

FORMSOF

The CONTAINS predicate can be used in combination with the FORMSOF term, which allows you to specify word matching based on other linguistic forms of a word. You can use the FORMSOF term in two ways, using either the INFLECTIONAL or THESAURUS generation type. In this section, we will show you how to use the INFLECTIONAL generation type. (Use of the THESAURUS generation type is shown in the section "Thesaurus" later in this chapter.) The INFLECTIONAL generation type chooses alternative inflection forms for any of the matching words. This is also known as stemming, which was discussed previously in the section "Search Architecture."

The example query searches for the word "swam", but the only word that is present in the document we are looking for is "swimming". Because we're using the FORMSOF term in conjunction with the INFLECTIONAL generation type, we will find this document anyway. The following query finds documents that contain inflections of "swam":

```
SELECT Title, Rank
FROM portal..scope()
WHERE CONTAINS('FORMSOF (INFLECTIONAL, "swam") ')
```

NEAR

Another nice element of the SQL Full-Text extensions query language is the NEAR term. This lets you search for words that must be relatively close to each other, at least within 50 words. The rank value of the result will be higher the closer the words are.

We have created a document containing the names "Danlo" and "Hanuman". Danlo and Hanuman are two characters from the book *The Broken God*, which was written by David Zindell. After creating this document, we started experimenting with placing different numbers of words between Danlo and Hanuman. The following query returns documents that contain the names Danlo and Hanuman when those names are placed within at least 50 words of each other:

```
SELECT Title, Rank
FROM portal..scope()
WHERE CONTAINS('Danlo NEAR Hanuman')
```

Table 9-3 shows the result of our experiments.

Table 9-3. *Influence of the NEAR term on Probabilistic Ranking*

Rank	Words Between "Danlo" and "Hanuman"
4	0
3	5
2	10
1	30
1	49
0	50

As you can see, the rank value drops down rapidly. With only five words between the names "Danlo" and "Hanuman", the rank value is down to three, which is not very high.

Note Even the first rank value, when the words are situated right next to each other, is surprisingly low. The last time we executed this test, years ago using SharePoint Portal Server 2001, the first rank value was 24, which is significantly higher.

You can use the RANK BY clause together with the COERCION function to adjust the rank value more to your liking if you are not satisfied with the rankings found when using the NEAR term. The section "Probabilistic Ranking" earlier in this chapter showed you how to influence rank values.

FREETEXT

The FREETEXT predicate can be used to search for words or phrases in text columns, for instance, in the document body. The FREETEXT predicate provides similar functionality to the CONTAINS predicate, but the FREETEXT predicate is better suited for finding combinations of search terms.

In the next example, we will look for the presence of any of the words "shaida", "die", or "soon" in the sentence "It is shaida for a man to die too soon;". The order of the words in the query is not relevant. The following query will return our document:

```
SELECT Title, Rank, Size, Description, Write, Author
FROM portal..scope()
WHERE FREETEXT('shaida die soon')
```

Note This would not have worked if you had used the CONTAINS predicate, because the CONTAINS predicate tries to find exact matches.

LCID

If you are working in a portal environment that targets audiences of multiple nationalities, chances are that document languages become an issue when executing search queries. SQL Full-Text extensions allows you to specify the language that is used in SQL search queries. You can do this by providing a numeric locale identifier, using the LCID (locale id) keyword in the CONTAINS or FREETEXT predicate.

Note A country's LCID can be found in MSDN by searching for "LCID reference".

In the next example, we will use two different LCIDs: 1033 for the United States and 1043 for the Netherlands. The LCID influences many settings, including date format and currency format. The syntax is as follows:

```
CONTAINS | FREETEXT
( [ <column_identifier> , ] '<content_search_condition>' [, LCID ] )
```

A country's LCID can either be a decimal value or a hexadecimal value. The hexadecimal value for the United States is 0x0409.

We have created a folder called "'LCID Test" that contains one document containing the following text:

```
Io - for the Athenians
Duizendmaal
```

The first sentence is the title of a poem written by the Greek poet Bacchylides; "duizendmaal" is the Dutch word for "a thousand times." The second sentence is important in this example because it is a part of the default Dutch noise word list called noisenld.txt.

To understand this example, you need to understand that noise words are filtered twice: once during indexing and once when queries are processed. At the end of the example, we will show two queries that demonstrate how to specify the LCID that is used within the query. We will also show which effect the LCID has on the noise word list as it is applied at query time.

The locale settings of our index server are set to United States. The appropriate IFilter that processes the document during indexing reports the language to the content indexer so that the protocol handler can apply the appropriate noise word list (see the section "Search Architecture" earlier in this chapter for more information about IFilters and protocol handlers).

Since Office documents contain locale information and since our document contains US locale information, the word "duizendmaal" will be indexed because this word is not in the list of English noise words. The next query looks for the word "duizendmaal" using the United States LCID:

```
SELECT Title, Rank, Path
FROM portal..scope()
WHERE CONTAINS(Contents, 'duizendmaal', 1033)
```

If you execute this query, you will see that our document is returned, because "duizendmaal" is not a part of the English noise word list. As a result, this word is not discarded from the query. The next query looks for the word "duizendmaal" using the LCID of the Netherlands:

```
SELECT Title, Rank, Path
FROM portal..scope()
WHERE CONTAINS(Contents, 'duizendmaal ', 1043)
```

This query returns nothing, because the Dutch noise word list is applied. You will see a message stating that your query only included common words. Finally, you do not have to specify the LCID if you just want to use the default LCID use the following query:

```
SELECT Title, Rank, Path
FROM portal..scope()
WHERE CONTAINS(Contents, 'duizendmaal ')
```

Noise Words

Noise words are words that do not improve the relevancy of a matching document, and therefore are not considered useful in a search query. Words such as "and", "the", or the company name are very common and will be found in almost any document, and are therefore useless in a search query.

If you want to see which words are considered noise words, or if you want to add your own noise words to the list, you can find the default set of noise word lists at the following location: [drive letter]:\Program Files\Microsoft Office Servers\12.0\Data\Config. This folder contains noise word lists for a wide range of languages, such as English (noiseeng.txt) and Dutch (noisenld.txt). If there is not a noise word list for your language, you can add noise words to the neutral noise word file (noiseneu.txt).

Every Shared Service Provider (SSP) uses its own copy of the noise word files, taken from the default set of noise word lists ([drive letter]:\Program Files\Microsoft Office Servers\12.0\Data\Config). The set of noise word files related to an SSP can be found at the following location: [drive letter]:\Program Files\Microsoft Office Servers\12.0\Data\Applications\[application GUID]\Config. If you only have one SSP, this location is easy to find. If you have multiple SSPs, finding the correct location might be tricky. Other than trial and error, we have not found a way to link the application GUID (corresponding to the name of the gatherer application) to an SSP. The following VBScript code fragment can be used to determine the correct application GUID for an SSP, although it does not give you a handle that can be linked back to the SSP:

```
Set objGatherAdmin = WScript.CreateObject("oSearch.GatherMgr.1")

For Each objApplication in objGatherAdmin.GatherApplications
  WScript.echo " "
  WScript.echo "application name: " & objApplication.Name
Next
```

The output looks like this:

```
application name: [guid]
```

If you want to try out this code, you need to save it in a file called GetApplicationGUID.vbs. Open a command prompt and type **cscript GetApplicationGUID.vbs**. This displays a list of all available applications.

If you want to change the noise word list, you need to take a couple of steps. The following procedure explains how to add the word "test" to the English noise word list:

1. Determine which folder holds the noise word list of your choice. The list is located in [drive letter]:\Program Files\Microsoft Office Servers\12.0\Data\Applications\ [application GUID] \Config.

2. Open a noise word list file in Notepad. In this example, we will open the noise word list noiseeng.txt and add the word "test" to it.

3. Save the noise word list and close Notepad. Make sure to save the file using the ANSI encoding type.

■**Note** Saving noise word lists using the Unicode encoding type has been known to cause errors. You should also ensure that you add a carriage return after each noise word. Finally, if adding a noise word does not seem to work, you should be aware of the fact that the word breaker, which is a part of the search architecture, might break up a single noise word into separate words.

---

4. Open a command prompt and type **services.msc**. This opens the Services window.

5. Locate the search service for Microsoft Office SharePoint Server 2007 and restart it. This service is called Office SharePoint Server Search. Right-click its name and choose Restart.

6. Open SharePoint Central Administration and perform a full crawl of the content index.

■**Note** You will also find an entry for the Windows SharePoint Services 3.0 search service, called Windows SharePoint Services Search. If you have installed SQL Server including the optional Full Text search component, you will also find an entry for that search service, called Microsoft Search.

Only after a full update of the content index will any changes you have made to the noise word lists take effect. Noise words are filtered twice, the first time during the indexing phase. During indexing, any noise words found in the indexed document will not be included in the content index. The IFilter responsible for processing the document reports the document language to the protocol handler that applies the appropriate noise word list.

■Note If you want to find more information about the status of the indexing process, you can use Search Settings in SharePoint Central Administration to take a look at the available crawl logs. Alternatively, you can look in the folder [drive letter]:\Program Files\Microsoft Office Servers\12.0\Data\Applications\[application GUID]\ Projects\Search\Indexer\CiFiles to see if the content index files have been updated.

Noise words are filtered for the second time during query time. You can programmatically alter the LCID that is used within the search query; otherwise the locale of the search server is used.

If you want to check that adjusting the noise word list has had the desired effect, you can take a shortcut that does not require you to perform a full update of the content index. The following procedure explains how:

1. Start the Microsoft Office SharePoint Server 2007 Query Tool (for more information, see the earlier section "Firing a Query via the MOSS Query Tool").

2. In the Server Url text box, enter the URL of a SharePoint site collection.

3. In the Query Editor text box, enter the following query (you should adjust the keyword and LCID according to your needs):

```
select rank, author, path ,  title,  "DAV:getlastmodified"
from scope()
where freetext(*,'the',1033)
order by rank desc
```

If you have successfully added the noise word to the noise word list, the response will indicate the following: "Your query included only common words and / or characters, which were removed. No results are available. Try to add query terms."

As discussed previously in this section, the set of noise word files related to an SSP can be found at the following location: [drive letter]:\Program Files\Microsoft Office Servers\12.0\ Data\Applications\[application GUID]\Config. If you want, you can define a central location for all noise words (and thesaurus files, which are discussed in the next section). This means that you can share one set of noise words (and thesaurus files) for all SSPs you might have. You can do this by locating the following key in the registry: HKEY_LOCAL_MACHINE\SOFTWARE\Microsoft\ Office Server\12.0\Search\Setup\ContextIndexCommon LanguageResources\Override\ [Application name]\[Language]. The NoiseFile string value contains the path of the noise word file for the given language and SSP; the TsaurusFile (not a misspelling) string value contains the location of the thesaurus file.

Thesaurus

SharePoint Enterprise Search service is very good at full-text searching, but that does not help you much if you have a document containing something like the following address: 46097 Airport Road. You will find that some people try to look for "Rd.", while others for "rd" or every possible variation you can think of. Word stemming and experimenting with INFLECTIONAL forms of the FORMSOF predicate will not solve this problem for you. What you really want is to expand these abbreviations to "Road". You need the SharePoint thesaurus functionality to do this.

■Note Thesaurus files are located in the same folder as noise word list files, as described in the previous section. If you need more information about configuring thesaurus files, you can refer to the Knowledge Base article "How to customize SharePoint Server by using IFilters, noise word files, and thesaurus files" located at http://support.microsoft.com/kb/837847.

The thesaurus chooses words that have the same meaning, taken from a thesaurus dictionary. Different locales use a different thesaurus, which is stored in XML. For instance, the US LCID uses the thesaurus file tsenu.xml. You can adjust this file according to your needs. Ours looks like this:

```
<XML ID="Microsoft Search Thesaurus">
    <thesaurus xmlns="x-schema:tsSchema.xml">
        <expansion>
            <sub weight="1.0">North</sub>
            <sub weight="1.0">N.</sub>
        </expansion>
        <expansion>
            <sub weight="1.0">Rd.</sub>
            <sub weight="1.0">Road</sub>
        </expansion>
    </thesaurus>
</XML>
```

This thesaurus indicates that "Rd." can be used as a substitute for "Road". In the next example, you will learn how to use the CONTAINS predicate in combination with the FORMSOF predicate to indicate that you want to use the thesaurus. The following query looks for "Rd." and finds documents that contains "Road".

```
SELECT Title, Rank, Path
FROM portal..scope()
WHERE CONTAINS('FORMSOF(THESAURUS, "Rd.", 1033)')
```

■**Note** Make sure that you spell "Rd." correctly because it is case sensitive: "rd." will not give you any results unless you add that to the thesaurus as well.

Using the FREETEXT predicate automatically activates the thesaurus. So, the following query retrieves documents that contain the word "Road" as well.

```
SELECT Title, Rank, Path
FROM portal..scope()
WHERE FREETEXT('Rd.', 1033)
```

The thesaurus is only applied at query time; the locale of the browser is used to determine which thesaurus file is used. Server settings are created when it comes to choosing the correct thesaurus file.

■**Note** Make sure the noise word list does not contain any of the thesaurus entries.

Some Array

According to the documentation, you can use the ARRAY comparison predicate to check for values in a series of properties. In our experience, this predicate does not work anymore. We will briefly discuss how the ARRAY predicate worked in the past, in the hope that you will have more luck with the use of this predicate in the current version of SQL Full-Text extensions than we did.

The ARRAY comparison predicate can be used within a WHERE clause. WHERE clauses use the following syntax:

```
... WHERE <column> <comp_op> [ <quantifier> ] <comparison_list>
```

The ARRAY comparison predicate uses the following syntax:

```
ARRAY [ <literal> [ , <literal> ] ]
```

The ARRAY comparison predicate can be used to rewrite the following query:

```
SELECT Title, Rank, Path
FROM portal..scope()
WHERE  Title = 'zindell.doc'
OR Title = 'enigma'
OR Title = 'catullus'
```

Using the ARRAY comparison predicate, the previous query can be rewritten in a more compact way:

```
SELECT Title, Rank, Path
FROM portal..scope()
WHERE Title = SOME ARRAY ['zindell.doc', 'enigma', 'catullus']
```

The SOME keyword indicates that only one match has to be found. You could also use the ANY keyword.

Note The Microsoft Office SharePoint Server 2007 version of Enterprise Search has shown improvements when it comes to ranking rules. These are discussed in the section "Rank Factors" later in this chapter. On the other hand, some functionality has been removed from it as well. This will be discussed in more detail in the section "Removed from Enterprise Search." Although the feature is still documented, we fear the ARRAY predicate has also been removed from the current version of Enterprise Search.

RANKMETHOD

In this section, you will be introduced to a new predicate: the RANKMETHOD predicate. The RANKMETHOD predicate can be used to influence which statistical algorithm is used to rank the documents. The following statistical algorithms are available:

- JACCARD COEFFICIENT: This algorithm excludes words that do not match the search terms and calculates rank results based on the relative proportion of matching words. This is the default rank method.

- DICE COEFFICIENT: This algorithm compares matching words that are found in isolation to the frequency of multiple matching words that are found together.

- INNER PRODUCT: This algorithm uses the inner product of ranks of individual matching documents.

- MINIMUM: This algorithm calculates ranking results based on the lowest rank score from all the matching documents.

- MAXIMUM: This algorithm calculates ranking results based on the highest rank score from all the matching documents.

Note Unless you feel very strongly about any of those algorithms, we suspect you will not use this feature at all.

The next query demonstrates how to specify a ranking algorithm:

```
SELECT Title, Rank, Description, Path
FROM portal..scope()
WHERE CONTAINS
(
  Title, 'ISABOUT ("noche", "amor")
  RANKMETHOD JACCARD COEFFICIENT'
)
ORDER BY Title
```

RANK BY COERCION

The section "RANKMETHOD" showed you how to choose between ranking algorithms. This can influence the rank values of items matching a query. If you really want to influence the rank value of items, you can use the COERCION function, which can be used in conjunction with the RANK BY clause. The COERCION function comes in three flavors:

* ABSOLUTE: This assigns an absolute number to the given rank value of a matching item.

* ADD: This adds a number to or subtracts a number from the given rank value of a matching item.

* MULTIPLY: This multiplies a number with the given rank value of a matching item.

The next example demonstrates how to use the COERCION function. Again, we have borrowed a poem from the Spanish poet Federico Lorca and created two documents. The first document contains the word "amor"; the second the word "dio". In our query, we will assign an absolute rank value of 500 to the document that contains the word "amor", and we will subtract 100 from the rank value found for the document that contains the word "dio".

Note The maximum rank value is 1000. It is possible to specify a higher value via absolute coercion without getting an error message, but this does not have any effect: the maximum rank value of a matching item still remains 1000.

The query in the next example assigns a rank value of 500 to every document that contains the word "amor" in the Title property, and subtracts 100 points of the rank value of every document that contains the word "dio" in it. The query looks like this:

```
SELECT Title, Rank, Description, Path
FROM portal..scope()
WHERE CONTAINS(Title, 'amor' )
RANK BY COERCION(ABSOLUTE, 500)
OR CONTAINS( Contents, 'dio' )
RANK BY COERCION(ADD, -100)
ORDER BY Title
```

Rank Factors

Matching items that have the highest-ranking value are shown first in the search results; this is also known as probabilistic ranking. In this section, you will learn about the most important ranking values, and we will demonstrate the effects of these algorithms. To do so, we have created a folder called Ranking that contains three documents that are identical at first. Figure 9-6 shows a screenshot of this folder.

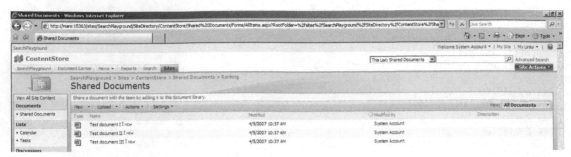

Figure 9-6. *Rank folder*

The three documents all share the same content, namely the text "Muerto de amor", which is the title of a poem by the Spanish poet Federico Lorca. In the next experiments, we execute the following query:

```
SELECT Title, Rank, Path
FROM portal..scope()
WHERE FREETEXT('muerto de amor)
ORDER BY Rank Desc
```

Note This is the query we will be using throughout this section. Whenever we refer to "the query," we are referring to this query.

Because all documents are identical, this query returns a result set of three matching documents that contain the same rank value. This is shown in Table 9-4.

Table 9-4. *Ranking of Three Identical Documents*

Document I	Document II	Document III
875	875	875

For the first experiment, we add a lot of random content to document I. The size of a document influences probabilistic ranking, which can be verified by executing the query again. The result is shown in Table 9-5.

Table 9-5. *Document Size Influences Ranking*

Document I	Document II	Document III
819	875	875

The frequency of the query term in a document influences ranking. We will demonstrate this by adding the word "Muerto" to document II five times. As you can see in Table 9-6, this improves document II's rank value.

URL surf depth influences ranking. Content that is located toward the top of a site hierarchy is considered more relevant than content that is nested deep in the site or folder hierarchy. Every "/" (forward slash) is considered to add a bit to the URL surf depth, which lowers the relevance of a document.

Table 9-6. *Term Frequency Improves Ranking*

Document I	Document II	Document III
819	884	875

To test the influence of URL surf depth, we have added identical documents to a parent site (document I), a child site (document II), and a grandchild site (document III). We have also added a child folder to the parent site and added a document (document IV) and a grandchild folder (containing document V). The structure of these test documents is as follows:

- Parent site\document I
- Parent site\child site\document II
- Parent site\child site\grandchild site\document III
- Parent site\child folder\document IV
- Parent site\child folder\grandchild folder\document V

When we fire the query again, we can see the influence of URL surf depth on relevance ranking. The result is shown in Table 9-7.

Table 9-7. *Influence of URL Surf Depth*

Document I	Document II	Document III	Document IV	Document V
875	875	873	873	871

Click distance is a variation on URL surf depth. Click distance means that Microsoft Office SharePoint Server 2007 allows you to define authoritative sites that contain information that is deemed important, as well as non-authoritative sites that contain information that is deemed less important. This influences the ranking values found for documents. In the next experiment, we will add the root site to the authoritative pages list, and add the grandchild site to the non-authoritative list. The following procedure explains how to add the root site and grandchild sites to these lists:

1. Open SharePoint 3.0 Central Administration.

2. Locate the Shared Services Administration section and click the name of the Shared Service Provider. This opens the Home page of the Shared Services Administration: [name of SSP] page.

3. Locate the Search section, and click the Search settings link. This opens the Configure Search Settings page.

4. Locate the Authoritative Pages section at the bottom of the page and click the Specify authoritative pages link. This opens the Specify Authoritative Pages page.

5. Locate the Authoritative Web Pages section and add the URL of the root site to the Most authoritative pages text area.

6. Locate the Non-authoritative Sites section and add the URL of the grandchild site to the Sites to demote text area.

7. Ensure that the Refresh now check box is selected and click OK.

After completing the procedure, the ranking values are recalculated. Once the computation has completed, execute the query again. The result is shown in Table 9-8.

Table 9-8. *Influence of Click Distance*

Document I	Document II	Document III	Document IV	Document V
881	881	871	879	877

URL SIZE LIMITS

There are limits when it comes to working with SharePoint URLs. A site name is allowed to consist of a maximum length of 128 characters. You can create multiple subsites to such a site, but the maximum URL length of such a subsite is 237 characters. This length does not include the part of the URL that is reserved for SharePoint system files and folders. For example, you can create a valid SharePoint URL of 260 characters by creating a subsite of 237 characters. Upon site creation, the system path /_layouts/newsbweb.aspx is added to the URL, which makes a total of 260 characters.

After reaching the URL site limit of 237 characters, you can still add lists and have subfolders in those lists. The maximum length of a document library is 255 characters. The maximum length of a folder name is 123 characters. The maximum length of a SharePoint URL including lists and folders is 256, excluding system files (for example, /Forms/AllItems.aspx).

The maximum length of a SharePoint URL does not include the QueryString portion (the part of the URL after the "?" [question mark] character). The maximum limit of the QueryString portion depends on browser limitations. For example, MSIE 6 supports a total of 2047 characters (almost 2K); Firefox does not really seem to have a limit.

If you want to test SharePoint URL size limits yourself, we have created a small test tool that suits our own test scenarios. We call the tool the URL Length Checker. It requires the presence of the .NET 2.0 framework and you are welcome to download it from the following location: `http://www.lcbridge.nl/UrlLengthChecker/UrlLengthChecker.zip`. The source code can downloaded from the following location: `http://www.lcbridge.nl/UrlLengthChecker/UrlLengthCheckerSource.zip`.

Another ranking algorithm looks at the relevance of a file type. Some file types are considered to be more relevant than others. For instance, according to this algorithm, a Word document is probably more relevant than a text file. In the next example, we will show that this is so. We will add two documents, a Word document (document I) and a text file (document II), and put the same content in both files. Table 9-9 shows what happens when the test query is executed.

Table 9-9. *Influence of File Type Relevancy Biasing*

Document I	Document II
875	856

The relevancy ranking of a document also depends on the language used within the document. If it is the same language used by the end user (based on the language header sent by the end user's browser), the ranking of a document is increased. If the language of the document is English, its relevancy is always increased, even if the end user uses a different language.

In our next experiment, we have created two documents. The first document (document I) contains the phrase "muerto de amor" as well as 20 English words. The second document (document II) contains the phrase "muerto de amor" as well as 20 Dutch words. Table 9-10 shows what happens to the ranking of these documents.

Table 9-10. *Influence of Automatic Language Detection*

Document I	Document II
868	867

We consider the ranking algorithms discussed so far to be the most important ones. A few others are not demonstrated in this chapter:

- *Hyperlink anchor text*: If the tooltip of a hyperlink matches the search term, this increases the relevancy of a document.

- *URL text matching*: If a portion of the document URL matches the search term, this increases the relevancy of a document.

- *Automated metadata extraction*: Certain types of documents contain special metadata that enhances the relevancy of a document. For instance, if the name of the title slide of a Power-Point presentation matches a search term, its relevancy is increased.

At this point, you have learned about different ranking algorithms used by the SharePoint Search service. You have gained some insight into the ways the search service tries to determine which documents are most relevant.

Removed from Enterprise Search

Not all parts of SQL Full-Text extensions have been improved. Some of the features of the language have been removed. In this section, we provide a small overview of those features:

- COALESCE_TABLE: Queries that include this function will not work anymore.

- *Term weighting*: Will be ignored if present in a query.

- *Field weighting*: Will be ignored if present in a query.

- UNION ALL: Will be ignored if present in a query.

- MATCHES: Queries that include this function will not work anymore.

- [prefix]..scope(): The prefix part will be ignored if present in a query.

■**Note** Of the removed features, we miss term and field weighting and the MATCHES predicate the most. We would like to have the weighting features back, because they allow you fine-grained influence over document ranking values. The MATCHES predicate is ideal for defining advanced filters using regular expressions; as such, it has been a valuable tool for information retrieval.

Common Pitfalls and Questions

This section lists common pitfalls and questions that seem to arise repeatedly when people start working with SQL Full-Text extensions. If you read the following section, you can avoid these problems.

Where Is the Document?

A common pitfall for developers is to create an SQL Full-Text extensions query that does not seem to work and find out later that the latest changes to the test document were not checked in and published. This is an easy mistake to make, and a pain to discover, because the index process only indexes the last version of a document that has been checked in. Also, make sure the content index is up to date.

ACL Support

The indexer uses a default content access account to crawl and index all content. This does not mean that every user will find all information the default content access account is allowed to see. The Security Identifier (SID) of the user making the query is evaluated against the Access Control Lists (ACLs) of the items or folders in the result sets. If a user does not have sufficient rights, items are removed from the result set before being returned to the end user.

Column Identifiers

Identifiers are used to specify the names of property names and aliases. Identifiers can contain up to 128 characters. Identifiers should only contain alphabetical characters, numbers, or underscores, and begin with a letter (regular identifier), unless they are surrounded by double quotation marks (delimited identifiers). For example, the following property name is invalid: `urn:schemas-microsoft-com:office:office#Title`. But if this property name is enclosed by double quotation marks, it is valid, like so: `"urn:schemas-microsoft-com:office:office#Title"`.

Sensitivity

Language keywords are not case sensitive. Microsoft Office SharePoint Server 2007 also supports accent-insensitive searching (by default). The following three code fragments show equivalent queries, although the casing that is used is different. The first query looks for a document with the title "test":

```
SELECT Title, Rank, Size, Description, Write, Path
FROM portal..scope()
WHERE title = 'test'
```

This query is equivalent to the following code fragment:

```
SELECT Title, Rank, Size, Description, Write, Path
FROM portal..scope()
WHERE title = 'tESt'
```

Finally, this query is equivalent to

```
select Title, Rank, Size, Description, Write, Path
from portal..scope()
where title = 'test'
```

The FREETEXT and CONTAINS predicates are case insensitive and accent insensitive. The following query looks for a document with the word "test" in its metadata:

```
SELECT Title, Rank, Size, Description, Write, Path
FROM portal..scope()
WHERE FREETEXT(DefaultProperties, 'test')
ORDER BY "Rank" DESC
```

The next query is equivalent to the previous one:

```
SELECT Title, Rank, Size, Description, Write, Path
FROM portal..scope()
WHERE FREETEXT(DefaultProperties, 'tèst')
ORDER BY "Rank" DESC
```

Noise Words as Placeholders

When using full-text predicates (CONTAINS and FREETEXT), you should remember that noise words are discarded from the search terms and are treated as placeholders that match any single word, as long as the search phrase has the same number of words as the matching phrase. This can lead to rather unexpected results.

Performance Monitor

If you want to find out more about the performance of the SharePoint Search service, you can use Performance Monitor to find extensive information about search metrics. The following performance objects are of particular interest:

- Process
- Microsoft Gatherer
- Microsoft Search

TREC

The SharePoint Search service is an impressive product that took many years of research and development time. If you are interested in this process, you can find more information at http://research.microsoft.com. A good place to start would be the home page of Stephen Robertson, head of the MS Information Retrieval and Analysis group. His home page is located at http://research.microsoft.com/users/robertson/.

We do not have to take Microsoft's word when it comes to the quality of their search product, because it is always interesting to compare this product to other search engines. The National Institute of Standards and Technology (NIST) holds an annual event during which search engines are compared to each other. This event is called the annual Text REtrieval Conference (TREC). TREC is an event in which organizations with an interest in information retrieval take part in a coordinated series of experiments using the same experimental data and queries. The results of these individual experiments are presented at a workshop where tentative comparisons may be made.

The TREC proceedings are in the Publications section of the TREC web site (http://trec.nist.gov). You can also find an overview of TREC-related whitepapers at http://research.microsoft.com/users/robertson/papers/trec_papers.htm.

Other Search Engines That Work with SharePoint

There is a wide range of other commercially available search engines or products that enhance the search experience that are able to use SharePoint as a content source. Although this list is continually growing, we have included a list of several search engines that currently have support for SharePoint. The following search engines are listed alphabetically:

- Autonomy (http://www.autonomy.com/content/News/Releases/2007/0607.en.html)
- Coveo (http://www.coveo.com/en/Products/default.aspx)
- dtSearch (http://www.dtsearch.com/WhatsNew.html)

- Endeca (http://endeca.com/byIndustry/media/intranet_km.html)
- FAST (http://gilbane.com/news/2007/07/fast_connector_for_microsoft_o.html)
- ISYS (http://search.isys-search.com/isysquery/8d62c21f-d919-4e68-90e3-4d2efddb8838/1/doc/)
- Longitude from BA-Insight (http://www.ba-insight.net/enterprise-search.html)
- Ontolica from Mondosoft (http://www.ontolica.com/)
- OpenText (http://www.opentext.com/news/pr.html?id=1653)
- Oracle (http://www.oracle.com/newsletters/information-indepth/content-management/jun-07/hot-pluggable.html)
- Recommind (http://gilbane.com/news/2007/01/recommind_updates_mindserver_p.html)
- SchemaLogic (http://www.schemalogic.com/media/pdf/Datasheet-EntSuite_for_SP.pdf)
- Vivisimo (http://vivisimo.com/html/sharepoint)
- X1 (http://www.x1.com/products/sharepoint.html)

Summary

SQL Full-Text extensions and SharePoint content databases are not replacements for standard ANSI-SQL and relational databases. However, they do offer an opportunity to get a grip on semi-structured information within organizations and offer you more ways to prevent data redundancy and weak data integrity.

In this chapter, you have seen an overview of the search architecture used by Microsoft Office SharePoint Server 2007. You have learned what probabilistic ranking is, and how to use SQL Full-Text extensions queries using the SharePoint object model, the SharePoint Search web service, and a community search tool. We have taken a detailed look at SQL Full-Text extensions syntax. Finally, we discussed some common questions and pitfalls regarding SQL Full-Text extensions.

Index

■ X

■ Z

You Need the Companion eBook

Your purchase of this book entitles you to buy the companion PDF-version eBook for only $10. Take the weightless companion with you anywhere.

We believe this Apress title will prove so indispensable that you'll want to carry it with you everywhere, which is why we are offering the companion eBook (in PDF format) for $10 to customers who purchase this book now. Convenient and fully searchable, the PDF version of any content-rich, page-heavy Apress book makes a valuable addition to your programming library. You can easily find and copy code—or perform examples by quickly toggling between instructions and the application. Even simultaneously tackling a donut, diet soda, and complex code becomes simplified with hands-free eBooks!

Once you purchase your book, getting the $10 companion eBook is simple:

❶ Visit **www.apress.com/promo/tendollars/**.

❷ Complete a basic registration form to receive a randomly generated question about this title.

❸ Answer the question correctly in 60 seconds, and you will receive a promotional code to redeem for the $10.00 eBook.

THE EXPERT'S VOICE™

2855 TELEGRAPH AVENUE | SUITE 600 | BERKELEY, CA 94705

Offer valid through 5/19/08.